SARAHA'S SPONTANEOUS SONGS

Studies in Indian and Tibetan Buddhism

This series was conceived to provide a forum for publishing outstanding new contributions to scholarship on Indian and Tibetan Buddhism and also to make accessible seminal research not widely known outside a narrow specialist audience, including translations of appropriate monographs and collections of articles from other languages. The series strives to shed light on the Indic Buddhist traditions by exposing them to historical-critical inquiry, illuminating through contextualization and analysis these traditions' unique heritage and the significance of their contribution to the world's religious and philosophical achievements.

STUDIES IN INDIAN AND TIBETAN BUDDHISM

SARAHA'S SPONTANEOUS SONGS

With the Commentaries by Advayavajra and Mokṣākaragupta

Klaus-Dieter Mathes and Péter-Dániel Szántó

Wisdom

Wisdom Publications
132 Perry Street
New York, NY 10014 USA
wisdomexperience.org

Library of Congress Cataloging-in-Publication Data
Names: Sarahapāda, active 8th century, author. | Mathes, Klaus-Dieter, author. | Szántó, Péter-Dániel, 1980– author. | Sarahapāda, active 8th century. Dohākośa. English. | Advayavajra, active approximately 11th century. Do ha mdzod kyi dka' 'grel zhes bya ba. English. | Mokṣākaragupta, active 10th century. Do ha mdzod kyi dka' 'grel zhes bya ba. English.
Title: Saraha's spontaneous songs: with the Commentaries by Advayavajra and Mokṣākaragupta / Klaus-Dieter Mathes and Péter-Dániel Szántó.
Other titles: Sa-ra-ha'i glu. English
Description: First edition. | New York: Wisdom Publications, 2024. | Series: Studies in Indian and Tibetan Buddhism | Includes bibliographical references and index.
Identifiers: LCCN 2023014316 (print) | LCCN 2023014317 (ebook) | ISBN 9781614297284 (hardcover) | ISBN 9781614297444 (ebook)
Subjects: LCSH: Mahāmudrā (Tantric rite) | Sarahapāda, active 8th century. Dohākośa. | Religious life—Buddhism—Early works to 1800.
Classification: LCC BQ7699.M34 S2713 2024 (print) | LCC BQ7699.M34 (ebook) | DDC 294.3/438—dc23/eng/20230509
LC record available at https://lccn.loc.gov/2023014316
LC ebook record available at https://lccn.loc.gov/2023014317

ISBN 978-1-61429-728-4 ebook ISBN 978-1-61429-744-4

28 27 26 25 24 5 4 3 2 1

Cover design by Gopa & Ted 2. Interior typeset by Kristin Goble.

Printed on acid-free paper that meets the guidelines for permanence and durability of the Production Guidelines for Book Longevity of the Council on Library Resources.

Printed in the United States of America.

Publisher's Acknowledgment

The publisher gratefully acknowledges the generous help of the Hershey Family Foundation in sponsoring the production of this book.

Contents

Preface

> Completely abandon thought and no-thought,
> and abide in the natural way of a small child.
> If you are firm in devotion to the teaching of the guru,
> the coemergent will spring up.
> —Saraha, *Dohākoṣa*

THERE IS NO better verse to summarize Saraha's teaching. It is the single verse that Atiśa quotes in the autocommentary on his seminal **Bodhipathapradīpa* (Eimer 1978, 183). The best way for a yogic practitioner to find liberation and realize the true nature of reality, which Saraha prefers to call "the coemergent (*sahaja*)," is to leave any conceptual assessment of reality behind, since no model of it has ever been known to withstand critical analysis. The yogin, therefore, remains in a natural way, opening up to the special instructions of a guru, whose qualities of realization can then directly enter the heart of devoted disciples. Saraha's spontaneous songs, or *dohās*, are such instructions: they represent the rare perfection of the Buddhist art of expressing the inexpressible, and they can trigger a mind-to-mind transmission that some take to have the power of directly pointing out the true nature of mind.

Saraha's spontaneous songs continue to fascinate scholar and practitioner alike, but the richness of publications and discussions of his songs should not cloud the fact that there remain fundamental, unresolved issues with the corpus. The Apabhraṃśa verses of Saraha's *Dohākoṣa* have never been critically edited on the basis of root texts that stand independent of a commentary; they are only presented as quoted in the sole surviving Sanskrit commentary written by the early Newar scholar Advayavajra. Since the publication of its first edition more than a century ago, many have noticed that a new edition of this commentary is necessary. Moreover, this is the only Indian commentary on Saraha's corpus of spontaneous songs, the *Dohākoṣapañjikā*, and it has never been translated, apart from a poor and often incomplete translation into Tibetan.

In May 2018, when Klaus-Dieter Mathes was a visiting scholar at All Souls College at Oxford University, he met Péter-Dániel Szántó, and the joint authors of this publication discovered their common interest in critically editing and translating Advayavajra's *Dohākoṣapañjikā* and comparing it with the newly discovered manuscripts of the Apabhraṃśa root texts and a Tibetan translation. This provided a solid basis for editing and translating the standard Tibetan root text and Mokṣākaragupta's commentary, which in turn allowed for the first reception history of Saraha's corpus of songs. Known as the *Dohās for the People* (a designation not known in South Asia), the standard Tibetan root text figures largely as a major Indian source for Kagyü (Bka' brgyud) mahāmudrā. We have been able to show that this Tibetan root text and Mokṣākaragupta's commentary on exactly the same corpus of spontaneous songs could hardly be direct translations from Indian originals; they often depend on the Tibetan translation of Advayavajra's *Dohākoṣapañjikā*, which is evident when the latter diverges from the Indian original.

The critical edition and analysis of all Apabhraṃśa materials have been made by Péter-Dániel Szántó alone, while Klaus-Dieter Mathes is responsible for the edition and translation of the standard Tibetan root text and Mokṣākaragupta's commentary. The main part of the work, the edition and translation of Advayavajra's commentary, represents the authors' common effort. We thank Prof. Diwakar Acharya (Oxford University) and Dr. Nirajan Kafle (Kathmandu), who assisted in editing and interpreting some parts of Advayavajra's commentary at an earlier stage of the project. Due to other duties, they could not continue to collaborate, and we are grateful for their contributions.

Special thanks also go to Michele Martin for a rigorous penultimate edit, using her meticulous eye for grammar, Tibetan language skills, and deep knowledge of the traditions discussed here.

Vienna and Budapest, February 2023

Introduction

> Having received the pith instructions of the Great Brahman [Saraha] and his spiritual sons, Master Maitrīpa[1] (986–1063)[2] composed the *Tattvadaśaka* and other works that are Pāramitā-based pith instructions, which accord with the Mantra system. Upon listening to them, Marpa said: "The essential meaning of the ultimate vehicle is to remain free from extremes while not becoming mentally engaged. I have been introduced to the Dharma of mahāmudrā." This is, among other [teachings], the textual system maintained by the great master Maitrīpa.[3]
> —Kongtrul Lodrö Thayé, *The Treasury of Knowledge*

THESE LINES MOST fittingly demonstrate the importance of Saraha's pith instructions for the Kagyü (Bka' brgyud) schools; their vivid freshness directly cuts through to the coemergent bliss of mind. Thus, Saraha has left a profound impact on various meditation traditions of Tibetan Buddhism, and modern mahāmudrā masters continue to rely on them. For the

1. The name Maitrīpa, as this Indian master is usually refered to in Tibetan sources, is derived from the vernacular Maitrīpā, which is a short form of Sanskrit Maitrīpāda ("Venerable Loving Kindness"). It is the name Maitrīpa is said to have received during his ordination from Ratnākaraśānti (ca. 970–1045). See Dpa' bo Gtsug lag phreng ba, *Chos byung mkhas pa'i dga' ston*, vol. 1, 772.21–22. In Indian texts, however, we more often find Maitrīpāda's secret tantric name, Advayavajra, which should not be confused with the Newar author of the commentary in this book. For the life of Maitrīpa, see Mathes 2021, 17–36.

2. Roerich (1949–53, 842) settled on 1007/10–1084/87, while Tatz (1994, 65) suggested ca. 1007–ca. 1085. Roberts (2014, 4 and 212n8) rightly points out, however, that the *Blue Annals* does not specify the year elements and that the life stories of Maitrīpāda's disciples require that their master already had to have passed away before Vajrapāṇi reached Nepal in 1066.

3. *Shes bya kun khyab mdzod*, vol. 3, 376.2–7: *de'ang mnga' bdag mai tri pas bram ze chen po yab sras kyi gdams ngag brnyes nas sngags dang rjes su mthun pa'i pha rol tu phyin pa'i man ngag de kho na nyid bcu pa sogs mdzad la | de rje mar pas gsan te | theg pa'i mthar thug snying po'i don | | mtha' bral yid la mi byed pa | chos phyag rgya che la ngo spros bgyis | zhes sogs nas rje mai tri chen po'i bzhed gzhung lugs | zhes gsungs |*.

most part, Saraha's pith instructions came down to us in the form of spontaneous songs (*dohā*) that allow us to partake of his realization. The most important collection of Saraha's songs is the *Dohākoṣa*, better known in Tibet as the *Dohās for the People* (*Dmangs do hā*), which found its way into the collection of *Six Works on Essential* [*Meaning*] (*Snying po skor drug*).[4] Thus it belongs to the three famous cycles of mahāmudrā works contained in the Seventh Karmapa Chödrak Gyatso's (Chos grags rgya mtsho, 1454–1506) *Indian Mahāmudrā Works* (*Phyag chen rgya gzhung*).[5]

From the time of Gampopa (Sgam po pa, 1079–1153), the Kagyü schools have distinguished a path of direct perceptions set apart from a general Mahāyāna path of inference and a Vajrayāna path of blessing. Sometimes Gampopa even criticizes ordinary Vajrayāna for descending to the level of conceptualization.[6] This immediately calls to mind one of Saraha's spontaneous songs (verse 37),[7] which the mythical siddha Śavaripa is said to have sung to empower Maitrīpāda while holding a golden vase in his hand:[8]

> When your own natural mind is completely purified,
> the [enlightened] quality of the guru enters [your] heart.
> Realizing so, [I,] Saraha, sing [this] song.
> I have not seen a single tantra, a single mantra.[9]

There is no question, however, about the general tantric context of Saraha's *Dohākoṣa*, as verse 23, for example, is on tantric feasts (*gaṇacakra*). Yet it cannot be overlooked that Saraha prefers an immediate access to the coemergent nature of mind over the more contrived approaches of formal tantric practice. This is at least what Karma Tashi Chöphel (Kar ma Bkra shis chos 'phel), a disciple of Kongtrul Lodrö Thayé (Kong sprul Blo gros mtha' yas, 1813–99), says about Saraha's *Dohākoṣa*, when he sets apart a direct path (Tib. *gseng lam*)

4. This collection already existed at the time of Bu ston Rin chen grub (1290–1364). See "Bu ston gsan yig," 115.7–116.1.

5. See Mathes 2011, 94 and 97–98.

6. Mathes 2008, 40–41.

7. In the introduction, the verse numbers are according to the recension used by Advayavajra. The standard Tibetan root text is an expanded version in comparison with this transmission. We discuss these recensions below. The reader is also invited to consult the concordance in the appendix.

8. According to Maitrīpāda's life story in the *'Bri gung bka' brgyud chos mdzod*, which further reports that Maitrīpāda harbored doubts—probably about Śavaripa's unconventional empowerment through showing a vase and singing *dohās* (for the life story, see Mathes 2015, 34–36).

9. Mathes 2014, 375.

of essence mahāmudrā from Sūtra- and Mantrayāna. While Saraha's direct approach, as Tashi Chöphel states, is only for those with sharp faculties, it can become a helpful practice for many when combined with either the sūtras or tantras.[10] As a support of his distinguishing essence mahāmudrā from Sūtra and Tantra, Tashi Chöphel refers to the *Dohākoṣa*, verses 22ab and 14ab:[11]

> There are no tantras, mantras, objects of meditation, or meditation.
> All these are causes of confusing one's mind.
> What use are butter lamps? What use are food offerings [to deities]?
> Why do we need to take up the Secret Mantra [Vehicle]?

The immediate realization of the coemergent, which Saraha cannot help but express again and again in his songs, thus seems to be independent of the sūtras and tantras, and it came to be referred to as *essence mahāmudrā*. The possibility of such an instantaneous realization has been repeatedly associated with the Chinese Chan views of Hwa shang Mo he yan, who is said to have been defeated by Kamalaśīla in the Bsam yas debate between 792 and 794.[12] It is too simple, however, to associate the subitist approach with Chinese Chan and the gradualist approach with Indian Buddhism. For example, we could identify the ascription of the subitist approach to Saraha in an early Indian source, namely the short and almost unstudied Sanskrit text *Yuktipradīpa*, "A Lamp of Reasoning."[13]

Saraha's dohās are quoted fairly often in Indic materials, which points to the

10. Mathes 2011, 102–5.

11. The verse numbering is that of the standard Tibetan root text.

12. For a good summary of the debate, see Cabezón and Dargyay 2006, 19–21.

13. The manuscript was first seen and described by Rāhula Sāṅkṛtyāyana (1937, 27–28) at Sa skya Monastery. The portions transcribed in this report are helpful in restoring some illegible portions, but there are also many misreadings. For a catalogue of the Tucci collection, see Sferra 2008, 42. For a short description of the work, see Szántó 2015b, 760. The point of the title is explained in the opening verse: the light intends to remove the darkness of those on the opposing side (Ms 1b: *vakṣye vipakṣatimirāpahayuktipradīpam*); also cf. the closing verse, in which the author states that the treatise intends to aid those who are lost on the wrong path, overcome by the darkness of false pride (Ms 3b: [...] *vimārgapatitān prati* [...] *mithyābhimānatamasā vihitāndhakārān* [...]). The author also styles his opponents children/fools (Ms 1b: *ye tāvad vadanti bālāḥ* [...]).

The text is transmitted in only one Sanskrit manuscript, which is not available for consultation. The photographs taken on behalf of Giuseppe Tucci are unfortunately of very mediocre quality, as many portions are out of focus. Moreover, it is one of the works that was never

fact that he was indeed an influential authority, but the *Yuktipradīpa* stands out, since one of Saraha's dohās is used to start a learned discussion similar to that of the Bsam yas debate. The question was whether enlightenment is sudden or gradual, a problem that has also occupied Indian tantric authors. The author of the *Yuktipradīpa*, after some careful considerations, lands on the side of the gradualists. However, in his opening statement, his debate opponent expresses his view (i.e., the so-called *pūrvapakṣa*) citing Saraha as evidence: "Surely, enlightenment is possible even if one discards actions such as meditation. How so?"[14] And here the opponent, just like Karma Tashi Chöphel, brings forth the above-quoted dohā 22ab, which teaches that all such procedures are a cause of mental confusion. Our author does not reject this approach, but he points out that this verse is taught with reference to practitioners of the fourth—that is, supreme—order and not to others, such as beginners.[15] Moreover, the author turns Saraha against his opponent by approvingly citing dohā 14ab twice and interpreting the second line as referring to those very preparations that a yogin of the supreme kind has already graduated from.

In spite of the difficulties involved in the study of this highly interesting treatise, we can gather with some certainty that at least a few authorities interpreted Saraha as a subitist and that this created some problems in exegetical circles. Unfortunately, it is at present impossible to pin down exactly when this must have taken place, because we cannot date the text with any precision, save for the fact that it must precede the twelfth century, which is the date of the manuscript itself based on paleographical grounds.[16]

In other words, Karma Tashi Chöphel's reading of a subitist position into Saraha's dohās does not necessarily reflect a Chinese influence but could also go back to an Indian tradition of interpreting Saraha. When the subit-

translated into Tibetan in spite of the text having made it to one of the country's foremost intellectual centers.

14. Ms 1b: *idam eva tāvad dhi mṛṣyate | dhyānādikriyāvyatirekeṇa buddhatvaṃ siddhaṃ bhavati na veti | nanu dhyānādikriyārahitasyāpi bodhir vidyate | katham | dheyadhāraṇamantroccāraṇa*, etc.

15. Ms 1b: *etac caturthāvasthitayoginam adhikṛtyoktam | na tv ādikarmikādikānām |* The sequence the author must have in mind is beginner yogins (*ādikarmika* or *mṛdu*), fledgling yogins (*madhya*), yogins of the highest order (*adhimātra*), and yogins of the supreme kind (*adhimātrādhimātra*).

16. The textual pool cited by the author is not very revealing. The latest authority (save for Saraha himself) figuring here is Bhadrapāda, a.k.a. Dīpaṃkarabhadra (*Maṇḍalavidhi* 413), a ninth-century disciple of Jñānapāda, a.k.a. Buddhaśrījñāna. Other authorities are what one might call "classics": Jñānapāda himself (*Samantabhadra*, a.k.a. *Caturaṅgasādhana* 161), Nāgārjuna (*Yuktiṣaṣṭikā* 31, *Mūlamadhyamakakārikā* 13.8), and Śāntideva (*Bodhicaryāvatāra* 5.109); scriptures include the *Māyājālatantra*, the *Guhyasamājatantra*, and the *Mahāvairocanābhisaṃbodhi*.

ist approach of essence mahāmudrā is combined with either a gradual Sūtra or Mantra path, Kongtrul calls it *sūtra mahāmudrā* and *mantra mahāmudrā* respectively.[17]

Just like essence mahāmudrā, sūtra mahāmudrā had become a controversial issue after Sakya Paṇḍita (1182–1251) denied its Indian origins.[18] However, Kagyü masters and other scholars, such as Gö Lotsāwa Shönu Pal ('Gos Lo tsā ba Gzhon nu dpal, 1392–1481), have pointed out that Maitrīpāda's *Tattvadaśaka* and its commentary by Sahajavajra was such an Indian source.[19] It should be noted that the combination of mahāmudrā with the "sūtras" (a Tibetan doxographical abbreviation for the Pāramitā system) does not downgrade the former to the latter but rather upgrades the Pāramitā system.[20] This upgrade is expressed by the qualifier "that accords with the Mantra system" in the definition of sūtra mahāmudrā.[21]

Further, in combination with the Mantra system, essence mahāmudrā turns into a gradual path, namely the one of creation- and completion-stage practices. A good example for this is the commentary on Saraha's songs by Karma Trinlepa (Kar ma Phrin las pa, 1456–1539), who integrated Saraha's pith instructions with a gradual mahāmudrā meditation. For Trinlepa, mahāmudrā practice starts with traditional forms of practice—such as calm abiding (*śamatha*) and the more conservative tantric techniques of breath retention—and then leads to Saraha's uncontrived states of coemergent bliss. The Tibetan commentaries on the *Dohākoṣa* tend to adopt a strategy of sanitizing controversial elements of the dohās by restricting them to the far-off state of a buddha.[22] Karma Trinlepa also relativizes Saraha's critical attitude

17. Kong sprul Blo gros mtha' yas, *Shes bya kun khyab mdzod*, vol. 3, 375–76.

18. Mathes 2016, 309–10.

19. Mathes 2019, 151–57.

20. Mathes 2019, 139.

21. Kong sprul, *Shes bya kun khyab mdzod*, vol. 3, 381.15–20: "Sūtra [mahāmudrā], or what later came to be held as mahāmudrā that combines sūtras, mantras, and ritual manuals (*kalpa*), is clearly explained in master Sahajavajra's commentary on the *Tattvadaśaka* in terms of wisdom realizing suchness, endowed with three special features: in essence it is the Pāramitā [system], it accords with the Mantra [system], and its name is *mahāmudrā*" (*...mdo lugs sam | phyis su mdo sngags rtog pa bsres pa'i phyag chen du bzhed pa 'di ni slob dpon lhan cig skyes pa'i rdo rjes mdzad pa'i de kho na nyid bcu pa'i 'grel par | ngo bo pha rol tu phyin pa | sngags dang rjes su mthun pa | ming phyag rgya chen po zhes bya ba'i khyad par gsum dang ldan pa'i de bzhin nyid rtogs pa'i ye shes su gsal bar bshad pa ltar ro* |). It should be noted that the three special features of sūtra mahāmudrā are not a direct quote from Sahajavajra's commentary but are only a condensed assessment (see Mathes 2006, 202 and n4).

22. Mathes 2019a, 274–75.

toward the crucial tantric practice of breath control by not rejecting these contrived yoga practices as such. Actually, they should lead to, or be combined with, Saraha's uncontrived and nonconceptual coemergent, which ultimately collapses everything contrived; so when this happens, a yogin should not find himself in a state of being still attached to coercive yoga practices.[23]

Essence mahāmudrā's distinction from mantra mahāmudrā was met with reservation by most tantrics of other Tibetan schools, who simply saw in Saraha's songs the expressions of advanced types of completion-stage realization well within the framework of the Mantra system. Chomden Rikpai Raldri (Bcom ldan Rig pa'i ral gri, 1227–1305) thus explains in his commentary on Saraha's above-quoted verse 37 that only those of the ultimate Way of Secret Mantra understand coemergent primordial awareness through the instruction and introduction of the guru.[24]

This brief introduction shows that the way Saraha's songs were received and commented upon is an ideal touchstone for systematically comparing the philosophies and hermeneutics of various Tibetan masters and the way they created a bridge from the sūtras to the tantras.

The Dohās

The dohās are the most distinctive literary expression of a class of tantric Buddhist masters called *siddhas*, hailed by tradition as beings of exceptional spiritual realization.[25] Essentially, these are gnomic verses; composed not just in the dohā meter proper using a kind of literary Middle Indic called Apabhraṃśa, they also purportedly convey a high degree of mystical insight and were transmitted in collections. We sometimes refer to the dohās as "songs," because we have it on good evidence that they were intoned in a variety of musical patterns (*rāga*). It should also be pointed out that the dohā genre is not confined to tantric Buddhism; in later eras, it was used to great effect by famous mystics such as Nanak and Kabir.

Among the dohās, those of the siddha Saraha take pride of place. This statement holds for the emic tradition—where at least one collection of his songs was considered so important that it became part of scripture—and also for modern scholarship, where the discovery of the dohās was seen as a literary sensation, not only in Buddhist studies but also in the wider intellectual world loosely termed the Bengal Renaissance.

23. Mathes 2019a, 282.

24. Schaeffer 2005, 139.

25. For siddhas, see Szántó 2019.

On Apabhraṃśa: The History, Linguistics, and Prosody

The language of the dohās (and the related caryāgītis) has been styled in various ways. Haraprasād Śāstrī made it unequivocal in the very title of his pioneering work that he thought of the language as Old Bengali—that is, an organic precursor of his Bengali mother tongue. This designation created quite a stir and continues to trigger debates; for example, Oriya nationalists militantly call for the language to be termed Old Oriya. Others thought of the language as some kind of vernacular.

The most cautious approach, the one we follow, is to call it simply (literary) Apabhraṃśa. Moreover, we should immediately point out that the language of Saraha's dohās (as well as of the caryāgītis and dohās by other masters) is not unitary but seems to preserve at least two registers, possibly more.

We do not think that these were vernaculars—living, spoken languages. Rather, it was a kind of literary register (or multiple registers) of Middle Indic. Just how close these linguistic registers were to the word spoken on the street is almost impossible to say. Of course, we can extrapolate from modern linguistic forms such as Bengali, which does indeed reveal some similarities. However, here we must tackle the rather serious questions: what is a language and what is a dialect? Languages, especially in India, are artificially delineated and standardized; in other words, they are political constructs (or "dialects with an army and a fleet" as the old saying attributed to Max Weinreich goes). We do not wish to go into this debate in this volume.

Apabhraṃśa passages first appear in Buddhist scriptures in a corpus later classified as the *yoginītantras*.[26] The contents and purposes of these passages vary, but most, if not all, have a strong ritual function and therefore a performative aspect.

The first of such very short songs can be found in the *Sarvabuddhasamāyogaḍākinījālaśaṃvara*, often styled—with good reason—the protoyoginītantra.[27] After this, more or less any self-respecting, lengthier

26. We are aware of similar (and perhaps earlier) developments in Śaivism (e.g., the *saṃgraha* verses of Abhinavagupta's *Tantrasāra*, but also see his *Tantroccaya* and his *Parātriṃśikāvivaraṇa*; these verses are otherwise in a rather different kind of Apabhraṃśa and are much later than the early Buddhist yoginītantra occurrences), but we will not discuss them here.

27. See Griffiths and Szántó 2015. One such passage consists of four short "songs" between 6.57 and 6.58 (Ms A 16b; Ms B 11a). The instructions say that they should be sung by four women along with offering flowers, etc. The results are said to be supernatural accomplishments, success in worship, and the ability to induce a state of possession in disciples during initiation. The lengthy chapter 9 provides further songs; here they are to be used in worship of the individual tathāgatas (Heruka, Padmanarteśvara, etc.).

yoginītantra starts transmitting Apabhraṃśa passages, for example, the *Catuṣpīṭhatantra*,[28] the *Vajrāmṛtatantra*,[29] the *Hevajratantra*, the *Vajraḍākatantra*, the *Bhagavatyāsvedāyā yathālabdhatantrarāja*,[30] the *Abhidhānottaratantra*, the *Ḍākārṇavatantra*, and the *Buddhakapālatantra*. The last of these is particularly relevant for the present discussion, because its ninth chapter incorporates a dohā that is also found in the Saraha corpus.[31] Given that the *Buddhakapālatantra* is a rather late creation, it is very likely that Saraha's collection was the direct source.

Eventually, the tantric tradition went beyond this. An important case, but one that has found little space in scholarly discourse, is that of the *Yathālabdhakhasamatantra*, a yoginītantra written entirely in Apabhraṃśa. The *mūla* itself does not seem to survive in the original, but we have a Tibetan translation[32] and a marvelous commentary on it by no less an authority than Ratnākaraśānti (ca. 970–1045),[33] from which we can reconstruct a substantial portion of the tantra. This commentary, called *Khasamāṭīkā*, has been edited but not with the greatest care.[34] Fortunately, we now have access to a near-perfect witness, Kaiser Library no. 227.

The *Khasamāṭīkā* is crucial for understanding how some learned classical authors dealt with the problematic prosody of Apabhraṃśa. For Ratnākaraśānti is pretty much the only one to tip his hand in this respect; other commentators have next to nothing to say on how they grappled with

28. See Szántó 2015a for a short overview of this tantric cycle and Szántó 2012 (1:353–54 and 362–64 passim) for discussions of the passages.

29. Sferra 2017, 436.

30. This is a completely unstudied Buddhist tantra or, better said, a cycle of three scriptures. It survives in a single, early manuscript (National Archives Kathmandu 3–359 = NGMPP reel no. A 47/16) dated 1024 CE. Overall, it seems to be a kriyātantra updated with yoginītantra material, including several Apabhraṃśa passages in the second text of the collection. The cult based on these scriptures died out.

31. See Luo 2010, 5.

32. D 441/P 80.

33. See Seton 2019.

34. Upādhyāy 1983. The editor's notes on the manuscripts he had used are misleading. His manuscript "Ka" is not NGMPP reel no. A 142/99, but A 142/11, whereas his "Kha" is not NGMPP reel no. B 25/8, but C 25/8, and not from the National Archives but the Kaiser Library, where it bears the shelf no. 227. A brief note on a short but crucial passage from this text can be found in Tucci 1954. There is also a Tibetan translation (which omits translating the passages we are going to discuss here, because the translators did not think that the metrical discussions were important to their audience): D 1424, P 2141. We thank Prof. Harunaga Isaacson for his insights regarding this work and the passage we edit and translate below.

the meter. Let us look at a telling example. After composing two verses on the basics, Ratnākaraśānti tackles the first verse as follows.[35]

Two [mnemonic] verses about [the metrical features]:

> Here, the metrical feet (*gaṇa*) are of five kinds, in two, three, four, five, and six morae [respectively]. The meter is for the most part the couplet (*dvipadī*), [of which] one quarter-verse (*pāda*) is [made up of] three or four feet.
>
> The language (*bhāṣā*) [employed] here is Apabhraṃśa, which is a distortion (*vikāra*) of Sanskrit. [The meter is] completed by rendering [a vowel] short or long [as required], by [reading it nasalized with an] *anusvāra* or by [reciting it very] quickly (*druta*) or drawn out (*vilambita*).

Couplet (*dvipadī*) is a synonym for *piece* (*khaṇḍa*) or *essence* (*vastuka*). Here, in the first couplet, the quarter verses consist of three feet. In the odd quarter-verses, the first foot contains six morae. The second [foot consists] of two morae. The others [consist] of four morae. The [enclitic] word *ca* retains the [consonant] *c*[, whereas we would usually expect merely *a*] and is out of sequence[, as we would expect it to stand after the word it precedes]. There are two *ho* syllables. One substitutes the singular genitive suffix. The second stands for the word *verily* (*khalu*) and is an indeclinable; alternatively, it is a term of address. The *o* vowels in the two *ho* syllables are to be read as shorts for the sake of the meter. To explain, in Apabhraṃśa, there is prosodical shortness of [the nor-

35. We may reconstruct the *mūla* as follows:

**pañcabuddhamaüḍassaa jassa ca tihuaṇa sāra |*
**āibuddhakaabhāvahŏ tassa hŏ khasamapaāra ||*

The translation (*chāyā*), according to Ratnākaraśānti, would be:

**pañcabuddhamakuṭāśrayasya yasya ca tri[/strī]bhuvanaṃ sāraḥ |*
**ādibuddhakṛtabhāvasya tasya ho khasamapracāraḥ ||*

Compare this with the Tibetan translation of the *mūla* (D, 106a):

gang zhig sangs rgyas lnga yi cod pan can |
sa gsum kun gyi snying po dang ldan pa |
dpal ldan dang po'i sangs rgyas ngo bo mdzad |
de ni mkha' dang mnyam par spyod ba'o ||

> mally long] *e* and *o* [vowels] due to halving (*ardhakṣaya*) as well as in the case of conjuncts [not making position (i.e., two consonants do not necessarily make the preceding vowel long)], as it is empirically observed (*yathādarśanam*).[36]

In a nutshell, these are indeed the most common problems we encounter when trying to make sense of Apabhraṃśa meter. The discretionary length of *e/o* is particularly important, which is why we employ the customary breve—that is, *ĕ/ŏ*. However, the most important point here is that even one of the most learned authors of the period admits to a somewhat unsystematic, case-by-case reading of Apabhraṃśa material.

Unfortunately, even Ratnākaraśānti is silent on *why* Apabhraṃśa is employed in the first place. We can only speculate in this respect and can probably add nothing new to the discussion.

Attributing a lower register/"distortion" of *the* language—that is, Sanskrit, as indeed Prakrits and Apabhraṃśas are seen in Indian linguistic theory—to lower classes and women is a literary convention employed in Sanskrit drama at least since the Kuṣāṇa period. The earliest such instances we have are the Central Asian fragments of Aśvaghoṣa's *Śāriputraprakaraṇa* or *Śāradvatīputraprakaraṇa*.

It is also generally thought that these registers convey meaning in a softer, more intimate way. As a consequence, they are more potent. An interesting case is mentioned by the tenth-century exegete Bhavabhaṭṭa. In his commentary to the fourth chapter of the *Vajraḍākatantra*, which contains a rain-making mantra in a non-Sanskritic register, he says:

> Now, the mantra beginning with *ghili ghili* should be understood as being in Prakrit. The same is given below in Sanskrit. [...] This is a mantra embodying the nature of all ḍākinīs. If it is recited in Prakrit (*phal pa'i skad*), it will become mastered after one recites

36. Kaiser Library no. 22, fol. 1b: *atra ślokau* |

> *iha dvitricatuṣpañcaṣaṇmātraḥ pañcadhā gaṇaḥ* |
> *prāyeṇa dvipadī vṛttaṃ pādas tricaturair gaṇaiḥ* ||
> *apabhraṃśas tu bhāṣātra vikāraḥ saṃskṛtasya sā* |
> *pūraṇaṃ hrasvadīrghatvabindudrutavilambitaiḥ* ||

dvipadī khaṇḍaṃ vastukam iti paryāyāḥ. tatra prathamāyāṃ dvipadikāyāṃ trigaṇāḥ pādāḥ. ayukpādayor ādyo gaṇaḥ ṣaṇmātraḥ. dvitīyo dvimātraḥ. śeṣāś caturmātrāḥ. caśabdo 'luptacakāro bhinnakramaḥ. hośabdau dvau. eko ṅasa (em., usa Ms) *ādeśaḥ. dvitīyaḥ khaluśabdārtham avyayaṃ saṃbodhanārthaṃ vā. hośabdayor okārasya hrasvatvaṃ pūraṇārtham. tathā hy apabhraṃśe hrasvatvam ardhakṣaya edotor yuktavarṇayoś ca yathādarśanam.*

> it one hundred thousand times. If it is recited in Sanskrit (*legs par sbyar ba'i skad*), it will become mastered after one recites it two hundred thousand times.[37]

In other words, the Prakrit mantra is mastered with half the effort in the preliminary recitation (*pūrvasevā*), and therefore it can be seen as twice as potent as its Sanskrit counterpart.

However, employing Apabhraṃśa does not mean that the author is not familiar with Sanskrit and its world, or that he is one of the people. He is simply being "folksy" in an artificial, literary way, precisely by using one of the tropes of Sanskrit literary culture.

To translate all this into our world, one might propose a thought experiment. It is probably beyond dispute that BBC English is perfectly apposite to convey serious information about the world in a clear and concise way, but it is hardly the language one would use to appeal to intimacy and emotion. Here, the vernacular of a blues song with the odd well-placed regionalism and so on is much more lucrative. But Saraha is not the unknown author of an African American spiritual (if there ever was a single author in such cases) but more like a Robert Johnson figure, a very self-conscious master of his trade made larger than life after his passing, or better yet, a Bob Dylan, who is an expert of the genre without having been part of it at a grassroots level.

These points are important to stress, because if one is not aware of them, the temptation to interpret Saraha and other siddhas as some sort of subaltern voice or even one calling out to the lower classes to instigate a revolution against the prevailing social order is indeed great (e.g., Verardi 2011, 12 passim).

On Saraha and the Dohā Collection

The multiple recensions of Saraha's dohā collection most likely show that we are not dealing with an actual, singular author but with a literary event. There can be little doubt that Saraha the person existed, but what has reached us—already from India, not just Tibet—is a version of the author made larger than life by tradition. This does not mean that the person lived in some hoary past—for instance, as early as the seventh century, as some have suggested.

37. **Vajraḍākavivṛti* (D 1415, 41b–42a): *ghi li ghi li zhes bya ba la sogs pa ni phal pa'i skad de mtshon par bya ba yin la de ni 'og nas legs par sbyar bas mtshon par bya'o* || [...] *zhes bya ba ni mkha' 'gro ma thams cad kyi rang bzhin gyi sngags so* || *de yang phal pa'i skad kyis 'bum phrag gcig bzlas pas 'grub pa legs par sbyar ba'i skad kyis 'bum phrag gnyis bzlas na 'grub par 'gyur ro* || See also Szántó 2012, 1:239.

Making a person a semi-legendary character need not take more than a generation, and indeed it can already happen during that person's lifetime. The lives and immediate afterlives of Jñānapāda[38] and Śrīmitra[39] are telling examples.

The earliest hard, yet still not entirely conclusive, evidence for the author's popularity comes from around the mid-tenth century. This is an unattributed quotation in Bhavabhaṭṭa's *Catuṣpīṭhanibandha* ad *Catuṣpīṭhatantra* 3.4.11.[40] The Catuṣpīṭha satellite literature also includes a *sādhana*, in which several of Saraha's dohās are quoted.[41]

However, this does not necessarily mean that all of Saraha's verses predate the mid-tenth century. Take, for example, verse 11c, which criticizes Buddhists engaged in elucidating the nature of the fourth empowerment. This was a debate in vogue around the first half of the eleventh century.[42]

The earliest piece of hard evidence for a Saraha dohā collection is the so-called Bagchi's Manuscript,[43] which bears the date 1101 CE in the colophon.[44] However, what this date actually means needs some elucidation. Schaeffer translates it as follows:[45]

> This *Dohākoṣa* was compiled completely, just as it was found, according to the stages of the ultimate concern, by the scholar Siri Divāarcanda in 1101, full moon of Śrāvaṇa. This book, [belonging to] Paramopāsaka Śrī Rāmavarmmaṇa, was copied just as it was by the Buddhist monk, the Elder Pathamagupta, at Śrī Nogvalaka.

We would suggest an alternate translation:

38. See Dalton and Szántó 2019.

39. See Khro phu lo tsā ba Byams pa dpal's *Paṇ grub gsum gyi rnam thar Dpag bsam 'khri shing*.

40. Szántó 2012, 1:99, 102, 411–12. The best manuscript of this commentary is Kaiser Library no. 134 (a Vikramaśīla manuscript), where the verse beginning with *jattiu païsaï* is found on fol. 39b2. The dating of Bhavabhaṭṭa is circumstantial. His localization in Bengal is somewhat more certain.

41. Szántó 2012, 1:185. At the time of writing, Szántó did not recognize these verses as Saraha's. This error is corrected in the present volume by including the fragment's quotations among the testimonia.

42. See Szántó 2020.

43. Now National Archives Kathmandu 1–1633/*vi. hindī* 3 = NGMPP reel no. A 21/13.

44. The text is as follows: *samanto jahāladdho dohākoso eso* ||*o*|| *saṅgadio paratthakāmeṇa paṇḍiasiridibāaracandreṇanti* (!) ||o|| *samvat ā tha 1 śrāvaṇaśuklapūrṇṇamyasyāṃ* (!) *śrīnogvalake paramopāsakaśrīrāmavarmaṇaḥ pustako yaṃ* | *yathā dṛṣṭaṃ tathā śākyabhikṣustha virapathamaguptena likhitavyam* (!) ||o||

45. Schaeffer 2005, 103ff.

> [Apabhraṃśa portion:] This *Dohākoṣa* "as found" is finished. It was compiled by the scholar, the glorious Divākaracandra, with the desire to benefit others. [Sanskrit portion:] [Produced in the Nepalese year] 221, bright fortnight of Śrāvaṇa, full moon. This is the book of the devoted Buddhist layman, the glorious Rāmavarman, [inhabitant] of glorious Nugal. It was copied as seen by the Buddhist monk, the elder Pathamagupta.

Perhaps the most important change here is reading the two sections of the colophon separately. The Apabhraṃśa portion is that of the compiler, Divākaracandra, while the Sanskrit passage belongs to the scribe. Thus, the compilation did not take place in 1101 CE; that year is the date of the artifact's production in Nepal. Also, Divākaracandra's motivation for his editorship is not the "stages of the ultimate concern" (Schaeffer probably understood *paratthakāmeṇa* as **paramārthakāmena*) but the benefit of others (**parārthakāmena*). As for just how much earlier Divākaracandra must have been, we have very scanty information. Isaacson tentatively suggests the second half of the eleventh century, also quoting Sakuma's estimate, which is circa 1030–1130 CE.[46] It should be stressed, however, that while this is early hard evidence for the existence of a Saraha collection, it is not the one we examine in the present work. In order to study the Divākaracandra collection, it might be reasonable to wait until a complete version emerges, as the text witnessed here is unfortunately fragmentary. Nevertheless, it is worth pointing out that at least one verse is transmitted in the Tibetan root-text version (v. 68), which is also found in the Sāṅkṛtyāyana manuscript (S, v. 77) but not in the Göttingen manuscript (the Tokyo manuscript is already finished at verse 64) or in Advayavajra's commentary.

Previous Scholarship and Our Contribution

The *fons et origo* of modern Saraha studies is Haraprasād Śāstrī's 1916 edition and study. Matters related to Saraha's *Treasury of Spontaneous Songs* (*Dohākoṣa*) were based on a single manuscript of Advayavajra's commentary found in Kathmandu during one of the Bengali scholar's visits to the valley.[47] This manuscript is now either lost or latent; we managed to trace a single folio from the original bundle, which was already detached from its origins when Śāstrī examined the text. While Śāstrī's study is pioneering and extremely

46. Isaacson 2009, 101–2.

47. Śāstrī 1959, 84–118 (first published in 1916).

valuable, the first truly scholarly study of the text, a magnificent piece even by today's standards, stemmed from the pen of Muhammad Shahidullah (1928). This monograph, written in French, is based on the aforementioned edition of the commentary, its Tibetan translation (D 2256, P 3101), and the standard Tibetan root text (D 2224, P 3068).[48] Shahidullah also gave a short grammatical overview of the difficult Apabhraṃśa language of these dohās and a helpful Apabhraṃśa–Sanskrit–Tibetan glossary, which includes all the words present in the concerned root texts. The Sanskrit commentary is used only sporadically in the annotations to his translation. This study is now also available in English translation (Ray 2007). A decade later (1938), Prabodh Chandra Bagchi came across and published more original material: a new manuscript of Advayavajra's commentary (which we re-edit here) and some stray leaves of related dohās, including some attributed to Saraha. We give a more detailed description of this witness below. This new edition was accompanied by a translation (*chāyā*) of the Apabhraṃśa lemmata (*pratīka*) into Sanskrit. Roughly two decades later, the great scholar Rāhula Sāṅkṛtyāyana (1893–1963) published his *Dohākoṣa* study in Hindi (1957). This was based on a manuscript he found near Sa skya in Tibet (see below), which was a witness of a very different recension of Saraha's verses: only the first 20 percent of this text matches the *pratīka*s of Advayavajra's *Dohākoṣapañjikā*. Curiously, Sāṅkṛtyāyana forgot about another discovery he made in the 1930s (our Ms G below). This material was the chief source for Bhayani's study and "reconstruction" of the verses (1997). While this study has many merits, not least a Sanskrit *chāyā* and an English translation, we think that Bhayani's methodology is not always right, inasmuch as he was trying to impose standard rules on the text that the author may have never observed. Moreover, the understanding of the esoteric terminology is now much better than even in the late 1990s.

Besides Shahidullah's French translation, Snellgrove 1954 was a pioneering English translation, but it is very sparsely annotated. It is somewhat difficult to ascertain what text it was based on: Shahidullah's monograph is mentioned as a source, the volume's title (Conze 1954) in which the text appeared mentions "Apabhramsa," but the introduction states that the rendering is based "largely on the Tibetan translation" and that the Apabhraṃśa text is "corrupt and obscure." Then there followed an annotated English translation by Roger Jackson (2004), again based on Shahidullah's reading of the Apabhraṃśa, and another English translation of the same material by Kurtis Schaeffer (2005), which also used Rikpai Raldri's Tibetan commentary.

48. For a description of the Tibetan texts used, see Shahidullah 1928, 4–5.

Notwithstanding these efforts, the "text" (already a tricky term) of Saraha's *Spontaneous Songs* has not yet been available in full, nor has it been stabilized to any degree of satisfaction. The discovery of two hitherto-overlooked manuscripts has helped to fill in the gaps. In fact, the present volume is the first in over six decades to bring to light new original material. These sources provided better readings in many cases, but they also created new problems. Since the *editio princeps* itself (which appeared more than a century ago), there has been a widespread scholarly consensus that a new edition of both the root text and Advayavajra's commentary on it is highly desirable. We have not only re-edited the text but also provided a full English translation replete with annotations. The language of this commentary is a very peculiar kind of Sanskrit. While there is a Tibetan translation, it is clear not only that it is based on a different recension but that the translators frequently misunderstood passages. In spite of these difficulties, the *Dohākoṣapañjikā* remains the most important document to illustrate how Saraha's words were interpreted—and sometimes misinterpreted—by tradition. As for the version in Sāṅkṛtyāyana's monograph (which was unfortunately neglected by subsequent Western studies), here we do not deal with the recension's place but provide a more precise diplomatic transcript of the manuscript, which will aid a more thorough reappraisal of this document.

While the Tibetan career of Saraha's songs has been admirably chronicled by Schaeffer, we think we have something to add to the reception history up to the formation of the standard Tibetan root text and Mokṣākaragupta's (between 1050–1202)[49] commentary, which is only available in Tibetan and now translated into English for this publication.

The critical comparison of this material allows for a first formation and reception history of Saraha's *Dohākoṣa*, a collection of spontaneous songs that gradually grew as further songs kept being inserted or added at the end. We documented this process up to the point when the collection, in the form of the standard Tibetan root text, consisted of circa 133 verses.[50] Mokṣākaragupta, who commented on the collection at this stage of development, provides an important document (D 2258, P 3103) for the *Dohākoṣa*'s reception history, as his commentary contains numerous Kālacakra explanations that are usually not found outside of specific Kālacakra texts.

As will be documented below, it is important to note that the Advayavajra

49. Nakamura 1989, 311. In verse 43 of his *Dohākoṣa* commentary, Mokṣākaragupta quotes the *Vajrāvalī*. We could not identify the verse, but if he really knew Abhayākaragupta's famous work, it would put our Mokṣākaragupta to the later end of Nakamura's time frame.

50. The precise number of Tibetan verses that lack an Indian original cannot be ascertained.

we speak of is not the famous Maitrīpāda, who also goes under this name. In his *Phyag chen rgyal ba'i gan mdzod*, Pema Karpo (Padma dkar po, 1527–96) writes:

> The [dohā] commentary of Maitrīpāda is not by the "sovereign master" (*mnga' bdag*) but similar to what we have from the [like-named] younger brother of a Nepalese venerable (*bhadanta*). He only has the same name and is not important. [However,] the commentary by Paṇḍita Mokṣākaragupta is good."[51]

As we shall see later, we have some doubt whether our Mokṣākaragupta is the famous logician and author of the *Tarkabhāṣā* from Jagaddala Monastery.

The New Manuscripts

The two aforementioned manuscripts, published here for the first time, cannot be said to have been completely unknown, since cataloguers (and those who read catalogues) were aware of them.

1. The Tokyo Manuscript

The Tokyo manuscript, that is, Tokyo University Library no. 517/old. no. 557, is part of a multiple-text manuscript (or *Sammelhandschrift*), which is incomplete in its current state of preservation. The catalogue[52] identified only two of the six works transmitted on these nineteen palm-leaf folios, and one of them was the *Dohākoṣa*. The other, called in the colophon the *Satsukhāvabodhana*, is in fact a scripture of somewhat dubious renown in the Tibetan tradition, the *Anāvilatantra*.[53] The other texts are (a) a three-folio fragment of Ratnākaraśānti's *Guṇavatī*, a commentary of the *Mahāmāyātantra*;[54] (b) a

51. *Phyag chen rgyal ba'i gan mdzod*, 29_{12-15}: *mai tri pa'i 'grel pa ni | mnga' bdag gis mdzad pa ma yin | de dang mtshan mthun pa bal po bha danta'i gcung po zhig kyang byung ba lta bus | mtshan tsam snying po mi bya pa ṇḍi ta thar pa 'byung gnas kyis 'grel pa legs so |*.

52. Matsunami 1965, 182–83. The catalogue's codicological notes are correct, so we will not insist on these here.

53. D 414/P 58. The tantra (and a discussion of its pedigree) will be published in Szántó, *forthcoming a*.

54. This fragment was not used in the 1992 *editio princeps*, but it has now been collated in an unpublished MA thesis (Damron 2014).

six-folio fragment of *Śrībhūṣaṇa's *Pañjikā*, again of the *Mahāmāyātantra*;[55] (c) a significant portion of the *Svādhiṣṭhānakramaprabheda* attributed to Āryadeva;[56] and (d) a block of five untraced, very likely scriptural, verses.[57]

We are not entirely sure of the manuscript's provenance. It was very likely purchased by Junjirō Takakusu (1866–1948) in Nepal during the "rather adventurous" 1913 Kawaguchi expedition.[58]

The *Dohākoṣa* in this witness (fols. 16b4 to 21b2) is significantly shorter than the other recensions we have been aware of. The precise number of verses cannot be ascertained because of a one-folio lacuna (folio 19 is missing), but a good estimate would be that there are only about sixty-five stanzas transmitted here. Another important feature of this witness is that it is probably the only one from India proper (i.e., not Nepal). Its right-slanting script can be seen in other manuscripts from twelfth-century Magadha. In spite of its provenance, the manuscript transmits a text that is less correct than one would reasonably expect.

Here are some noteworthy phonological traits of this version:

1. Word-initial metrically long *a* is usually spelled *ā*, which goes against the three-mora rule: *bāhmaṇehiṃ* vs. *bamhaṇehiṃ* (1a), *māṭṭī* vs. *maṭṭhī* (2a), *kājje* vs. *kajjeṃ* (2c), and so on.
2. The particle of negation is geminated: *ṇṇa* vs. *ṇa* (3d, passim), *ṇṇā* vs. *ṇā* (17c); as is the word-initial *ṇa*, as in *ṇṇagnā* vs. *ṇaggā* (7a). However, this does not seem to affect the metrical quantity of the preceding syllable.
3. Initial *jha* is occasionally geminated: *jjhāṇeṃ* (20a), *jjhāṇa* (20b), and so on.
4. There are some rather surprising degeminations: *ethu* vs. *etthu*, and so on.
5. Nasalization of word-final *e* and *i* (which seems to be optional for the scribes) is much rarer than in other witnesses.
6. Intervocalic *ma* is more common than intervocalic *ba*/*va* (i.e., the *ba-śruti*): *emaṃ* vs. *ebaṃ* (1b), *nimesī* vs. *nibesī* (5a), *khamaṇa* vs. *khabaṇa* (6c), *khamaṇāṇaṃ* vs. *khavaṇāna* (9a).
7. There are quite a few Sanskritisms in spelling: *gurudakṣiṇa* vs.

55. This text is being published in installments. See Ōmi 2009a and 2009b.

56. This significant fragment, not used in the 1990 *editio princeps*, was first identified by Tomabechi (2006, 17).

57. See also Szántó, *forthcoming a*.

58. Matsunami 1965, iii (written by N[aoshiro] Tsuji).

gurudakkhiṇa (5d), *dīpeṇa* vs. *dībeṃ* (14a), *akṣara°* vs. *akkhara°* (58a), *parameśvara* vs. *paramesara* (58c).

From a historical viewpoint, perhaps the most important verse is 45, which seems to have been rewritten in the "vulgate" version. In this reading, the verse contains the toponym *Somaṇātha* (i.e., the famous Somanātha temple on the Kathiawar peninsula in ancient Saurāṣṭra, now Gujarat), which was replaced by *Jamuṇā* (i.e., the river Yamunā) in the more common transmission. The reading with Somanātha is probably the more ancient one, because in what we see as the recast version, the meter is Mahānubhavā. As this is the only time this meter occurs in the collection, we suspect that it found its place here artificially. Could this point to at least some of the verses having western India as their origin? Given Saraha's peculiar preoccupation with criticizing the Jaina,[59] who were and are very prominent in this area, we do not find this impossible. Note also that verse 41 points to western India, as it uses the simile of a camel.

As we did not have access to this manuscript in the original, personal autopsy was impossible, but we were able to consult high-quality color images.

2. The Göttingen Manuscript

We style the second manuscript the Göttingen manuscript because we gained access to its photographs through the offices of the Niedersächsische Staats- und Universitätsbibliothek, which holds a copy of a collection of photographs taken by Rāhula Sāṅkṛtyāyana during his famous trips to Tibet.[60] The originals are in Patna and are notoriously inaccessible. The manuscript itself was found at Ngor Monastery, and its present location is unknown.

This self-standing copy (i.e., not transmitted in a multiple-text manuscript) is complete in a peculiar way. Among the ten palm-leaf folios, the last one is penned by a very different hand. It transmits some of the text from the previous folio and completes the collection, adding a colophon in Apabhraṃśa: *dohākoso amatoti* (sic!) *kidi esā siriSarahapāassa*. The second word is problematic, as we expect something like **samatto 'ti*, meaning "completed/finished" (Skt. *samāpta iti* or better yet *samāptaḥ | iti*). The rest is easy to understand, as it is modeled on Sanskrit colophons; it means "this (**eṣā*) is the work (**kṛtiḥ*) of

59. In the initial part of the work, four songs are addressed against the Jaina, three against brahmans, three against the Śaiva, and three against coreligionists.

60. For a thorough but still not quite exhaustive and precise catalogue of this collection, see Bandurski 1994. Our manuscript is described under Xc 14/16 on p. 48.

the glorious (*śrī°) venerable (*°*pādasya*) Saraha." The primary scribal hand is Old Newar, probably from the eleventh century, whereas the additional folio is in an eastern hand, or a Nepalese imitation thereof, and is clearly much later, probably from the twelfth or thirteenth century. It is not clear whether the last folio was meant to repair an incomplete copy or whether it was pillaged from another manuscript.

The Newar scribe wrote six lines per folio side, sometimes using the single string-space in lines 1–2 and 4–6, or occasionally only 6 (1b, 5ab, 6ab, 7ab, 8ab, 9ab ff.), and sometimes none (2ab, 3ab, 4a). The east Indian, or his Nepalese imitator, wrote five lines on 10a, using the string space in lines 1 and 5. The otherwise empty 1a has a librarian's scribble on it, which likely records the name of an erstwhile owner, a Newar nobleman: [*siddham*] *nārāyanabhārosa* ||, "Bhāro Nārāyaṇa's [book]." The foliation is with numerals up to 3 (with an auspicious *śrī* over no. 1) then switches to letter-numerals. The copy is clearly the work of a professional scribe. The writing not only is elegant and legible, but also records very helpful *pāda* breaks with smaller *daṇḍa*s, which sometimes slant slightly toward the left. He was also probably a Buddhist, as the scribal obeisance reads: [*siddham*] *namaḥ sarvajñāya* ||, "Homage to the omniscient [Buddha]!"

The manuscript was discovered by Sāṅkṛtyāyana at Ngor Monastery during his third expedition (1936), and the scholarly report was published in 1937 as the "second search of Sanskrit palm-leaf Mss in Tibet."[61] We come to know that the discovery of the Saraha manuscript was due not only to his legendary determination but also to sheer luck:

> The next day (14th September) we went to Shi-gar-tse. I tried my best to visit Pos-khang but it was harvest season so even after promising high rates, I was not able to get conveyance. On the 17th September I received a message from Ngor that the Steward had come and I must go at once. With great difficulty I found two ponies and one donkey for our luggage and the next day we went to Ngor. The Steward told me that he would stay only three or four days, so I must finish my work within that time. The same MS.-room was opened. Like Sa-skya, here too the Indian MSS. are mixed up with Tibetan MSS. numbering about 1,000 volumes. The Sanskrit

61. Sāṅkṛityāyana 1937, 18–19, 53–54. The codicological details are only the bare essentials: the size was 10 inches long, and 2.5 inches wide, the extent of the text sixty ślokas; one report says that the text is complete, but the other, on the very next page, already doubts this statement by adding a question mark.

> MSS., which I had separated in my last visit were put in one place. I made a little search for new MSS. in the heaps of the other MSS. and my trouble was well-rewarded when I found a complete copy of *Abhidharmakośa-bhāṣya* by Vasubandhu and a copy of Sarahapa's *Dohākośa*. For the next three days we devoted all our time in taking photographs of some of the important MSS.

The method for photographing the manuscript was simple. The leaves were pinned to a wooden board, which was then held vertically to face the camera. The two frames containing the Saraha manuscript are among the better photographs taken by the expeditions: they are only ever so slightly out of focus, which does not affect legibility.

Strangely, in narrating the same event in his Hindi autobiography, the *Merī Jīvan Yātrā*,[62] Sāṅkṛtyāyana is completely silent about the precious find that was Saraha's collection. It seems that the memory of this manuscript was clouded by other, in Sāṅkṛtyāyana's eyes more precious, finds, first and foremost philosophical works.

> On the seventeenth, the man[63] came from Ngor with an invitation, and on the eighteenth of September we arrived at Ngor once again. On the same day, the seal was broken, and I could see the library's palm-leaf manuscripts. I found a complete *Abhidharmakoṣabhāṣya* of Vasubandhu. I found two lacunose works on logic: the *Tarkarahasya* and the *Vādarahasya*. I took many photos of these books. Last year I also saw manuscripts of *Subhāṣita[ratnakoṣa]*, the *Prātimokṣa*, and the *Vādanyāya*, but I could not find them anymore. After a search, they were found in the house of the previous superintendent. From this event, one may gauge just how unguarded books are in Tibet. After staying at Ngor for four days, we returned to Shigatse.

62. Sāṅkṛtyāyana 1994, 252–53. Translation from Hindi by Szántó.

63. Employed by Kuding Rinpoche, the senior lama of Khangsar. The issue was that there was a change in the superintendent's position at Ngor, and the previous post-holder (whom Sāṅkṛtyāyana berates in no uncertain terms) never surrendered the key. It took some skilled diplomacy and a series of interventions until finally, as he subsequently says, the "seal was broken."

3. The Sa skya Manuscript

It cannot be said that Sāṅkṛtyāyana was indifferent to the charms of Saraha, since in 1957 he devoted a lengthy monograph to the dohās (and much additional material) in Hindi. Bizarrely, the Ngor manuscript was not used in this publication.[64] It seems that here we have a case of an embarrassment of riches: our best guess is that Rāhul-jī quite simply forgot about his precious and serendipitous find at Ngor. Instead, this often-overlooked masterpiece was based on yet another manuscript of Saraha's songs, one found in the vicinity of Sa skya Monastery. Sāṅkṛtyāyana himself says that the circumstances of this find were somewhat unusual:[65]

> The way in which I obtained [this manuscript of the *Dohākoṣa*] was very strange. On my second journey searching for Indian palm-leaf manuscripts, I arrived at Sa skya. There were some palm-leaf manuscripts there. Upon my inquiries, someone said that the chaplain of a local temple has a bundle of palm-leaf manuscripts in his possession. My memorable friend who has now passed away, Geshe Saṅghadharmavardhana (Gendun Chomphel),[66] went there and somehow obtained the bundle. In Tibet, palm-leaf manuscripts that came from India are thought of as extremely holy. If a drop of water that has washed a palm-leaf manuscript enters the mouth of a moribund person, his/her sins are washed away; of this they have no doubt. This is a belief similar to what we [Indians] think Ganges water does for a person on the verge of death. So it should not come as a surprise that there, too, every pious householder would wish to keep such holy things in their house. For those devotees wishing to be even more pious, the chaplain gave as holy victuals pieces he had broken off a palm-leaf manuscript, and it was for this purpose that he was in the possession of the bundle of leaves from various books. Who could say how many leaves from what variety of books have been distributed in this way? I was not going to allow this chaplain to resume custodianship of these important leaves. He did receive a small fee, so he did not object.

This witness of the text is the longest but also the most unusual one we

64. This was already noticed by Bandurski 1994, 48.

65. Sāṅkṛtyāyana 1957, 67. Translation from Hindi by Szántó. See also Szántó, *forthcoming b*.

66. I.e., Dge 'dun chos 'phel (1903–51).

know of. We have decided not to engage with it more deeply because we do not have commentaries on many of the verses. However, in order to provide solid material for further studies, we give a diplomatic transcript of this document, because many of Sāṅkṛtyāyana's readings are not accurate or have been corrected without prompting the reader. The transcript was made from the plates accompanying the edition. There are more manuscript fragments here, some of them very valuable,[67] about which Sāṅkṛtyāyana does not say anything.

The Commentator Advayavajra

Advayavajra's commentary to (a recension of) Saraha's dohās is the most valuable document we possess to gain insight into how these songs were understood in classical times, but it is also a rather problematic piece of exegesis.

First, it should be pointed out that beginning with Haraprasād Śāstrī's pioneer work, all editions and studies of Saraha's original text have so far relied on the lines quoted by Advayavajra, as no independent witnesses have been consulted. In other words, the songs were extracted from this commentary, which fortunately cites them almost in full. For this, Śāstrī used a manuscript that can no longer be located (save a folio, which eluded Śāstrī himself and which we publish here), whereas P. C. Bagchi used another manuscript of the same work, which, however, was full of gaps, as many leaves were lost during the book's preservation in Nepal.

Second, while the commentary was translated into Tibetan, there are significant differences between this Tibetan translation and the two witnesses of the version we have, which seem to be related. This created many puzzles for us. The safest position to assume is that at least two versions of the commentary were in circulation, but it is also possible that Tibetans added to and subtracted from the text according to principles that are unclear at present.

Third, the very authorship of the text is problematic. It is entirely certain that this Advayavajra is not the same Advayavajra who also went by the name Maitrīpāda (or Maitrīgupta or Maitrīpāda or just simply Maitreya) and who was active in the first half of the eleventh century. This is evident first and foremost from this author's language and style but also from doctrinal positions

67. For example, a folio containing the initial part of Dharmakīrti's *Pramāṇaviniścaya* (edited and discussed in Szántó, *forthcoming b*), a paper folio with a Sanskrit paean to Grags pa rgyal mtshan (1147–1216) written by Sugataśrī, one of the junior paṇḍitas in Śākyaśrībhadra's retinue (a reworking of this hymn is found in Tibetan translation in D 1171), dohās from other masters, etc.

he assumes, which are incompatible with what Maitrīpāda was well known to espouse.

A telltale sign of doctrinal differences is our Advayavajra's order of joys (*ānanda*) during sexual yoga. He quite clearly places coemergent joy (*sahajānanda*) in the fourth and last, culminating position, whereas Maitrīpāda was clearly the proponent of another school, which had coemergent joy in the penultimate stage. More about this will be said below.

It was in looking at the author's language that we met with the greatest difficulties. The language is Sanskrit, but it is nowhere near classical usage, nor is it grammatical Sanskrit with the license we would grant to Buddhist authors without hesitation. Instead, it is a thoroughly unique, extremely loose register of the language. Of course, it could be the case that the two manuscripts of the commentary are extremely corrupt. They no doubt are. However, this level of corruption would be a very unusual—indeed, unlikely—unique case. Instead, we must posit that it was the author himself who wrote in a nonstandard language. Curiously, we see this kind of nonstandard usage, although perhaps with different levels of extremity, in other commentators of siddha works, for example Munidatta, the exegete of the caryāgītis.[68]

Whether our Advayavajra broke grammatical standards on purpose or not, we cannot say. One cannot put it past a tantric author to have done so. We have very good evidence that tantric scriptures were thought to have been written in nonstandard registers for two reasons: one was to protect the secrecy of the teachings and the other to shatter the scholarly pride of those who cherished their Sanskrit learning. The latter also implies a very subtle point: most Brahmanical schools of thought accepted that any entity/object, for instance a cow, has always and necessarily a direct and eternal relationship with a meaning (i.e., the meaning/idea "cow") and that this meaning can be (cannot but be) expressed by means of a word, albeit the latter is no doubt conventional (*go*, *cow*, *vache*, *vacca*, *Kuh*, *tehén*, etc.). Most schools also believed that Sanskrit is the most perfect and complete language, the one that represents most clearly, precisely, and profoundly this inner relationship between external or internal objects, their meanings and their words. Buddhists debated both points with great vigor. As a product of the human mind, language is simply a superimposition on reality and is useful only for practical purposes; it does not represent/reveal any real structure of reality or its inner essence. Sanskrit is simply one language among many others.[69]

68. See Kværne 1977.

69. We thank Francesco Sferra for this description of the Brahmanical position on object and meaning.

It is also possible that the commentary we now have was not actually authored by a single person dipping his pen into ink and recording his thoughts on sheets of palm leaf, but that it is instead a loosely assembled record of his oral teachings. Let us imagine a university lecture, where the professor gives a lecture and the students then meet to compare notes before the examination. It is natural to assume that some will have noted more, some less; some will have recorded the transmitted ideas accurately and some not. It is also perfectly reasonable to imagine that the professor will have changed the lecture slightly the following year, either because of some new insights or because the audience was more advanced or asked questions that took the discourse in a different direction.

There is one peculiar aspect, which shows that the author was thinking in a vernacular and writing in Sanskrit. This feature is called the ergative construction, where transitive verbs (i.e., verbs that can assume an object) are construed with the logical subject in the instrumental case.[70] Those who know classical Tibetan will be more than familiar with this, but it should be pointed out that the native language of the Kathmandu Valley, Newar, also has this feature. Since most of our manuscripts come from this area, it is not unreasonable to assume that our author was a Newar.

In such cases, scholarship usually affixes the terms *pseudo-* or *deutero-* in front of the name, thus in our case we ought to speak of a *pseudo-* or *deutero-* Advayavajra. However, at least in some cases, this seems to suggest that either the author himself or subsequent tradition "parades" the author under the name of a more famous one so that the work might gain greater acceptance and traction. While this cannot be ruled out completely, this is not necessarily the case here: it may be simply that the two authors shared the same name. The name Advayavajra is clearly a tantric one, and as such it can be found in the lists transmitted in tantric initiation manuals. For example, Nāgabodhi, an early and influential authority in such matters, states that for those who have been determined to have an affinity with the Akṣobhya family of the maṇḍala (by the initiand's casting a flower while wearing a blindfold), the following names can be used: Hāsavajra, Vilāsavajra, Advayavajra, Lalitavajra, and so on.[71]

In spite of all the problems associated with this text, it should be stressed once again just how valuable and important it is. For this reason, it also forms

70. For example, the sentence "I am reading a book" in the ergative would sound something like "By me reading a book." This should not be confused with the passive, which would sound like "A book is read by me."

71. See Tanaka 2010, 140 (209).

the backbone of the present volume: in this part of the book, we are trying to reconstruct Saraha's songs *in the version Advayavajra had them and in the way Advayavajra understood them.* Naturally, we do not agree with him every step of the way, and indeed we find significant divergences when we examine other witnesses of the root text. These are discussed separately, where we examine the root text in its independent witnesses.

New Evidence for Advayavajra's Text

1. A New Leaf from Śāstrī's Manuscript

In this respect we cannot claim to have discovered much new material. Haraprasād Śāstrī's manuscript is still lost, hence we can access this source only through his readings printed in 1916. However, we managed to track down a leaf of this manuscript that was unknown to Śāstrī himself. We do not know through what vagary of fate this folio was separated from its bundle, but it is very clear that one leaf in a collection of strays, NGMPP A 49/18, was once part of Śāstrī's manuscript. This particular portion of the text is especially important, because it contains the commentary on Saraha's verse criticizing his fellow Buddhists.

2. Bagchi's Manuscript

As for the second manuscript, which was first discovered by Bagchi, we were able to gain access to high-quality color photographs of NAK 5–104, which was a significant improvement to the black-and-white microfilms archived as NGMPP A 932/4. When we compared these to Bagchi's edition, it became very clear that significant improvements could be made.

The manuscript is a small-format bundle (26 cm long, 5 cm wide), which was probably copied for private study and with the aim of portability. The letters are finely penned, usually in five lines per folio side. The palm-leaf folios have a single string hole slightly to the left of center. The bundle is a multiple-text manuscript that once contained at least another dohā-collection commentary by a different author.

Unfortunately, time was unforgiving to this witness, and hence there are many leaves missing. The original count of leaves was over 102 (possibly only 103); of these, only 78 are preserved. Moreover, the margins are on occasion severely damaged, causing significant loss of text, and even where the leaf itself remained intact, there are countless instances of delamination, where the writing surface peeled off, causing yet more loss and uncertain readings.

The end of the text has not been preserved, and thus the scribal colophon is missing, so we have very little information about how the manuscript was produced. The characters are what are usually called hook-topped Old Newar, a style associated with the twelfth to fourteenth centuries.

The only Apabhraṃśa text of the *Spontaneous Songs* that is from India proper (i.e., not from Nepal) and preserved at Tokyo University Library (see T above) has 65 verses. As it has gaps, we do not know the exact number of verses. Only reaching verse 77 of the standard Tibetan root text, it covers a little less than 60 percent of it. In other words, for the remaining part of the text there is no proof of existence in India or, rather, in areas of the subcontinent anywhere close to where Saraha may have lived. The Göttingen (see G above) Apabhraṃśa root text of the *Spontaneous Songs* has 112 verses. This needs to be taken with caution though, as the last original folio, which probably went missing, was replaced by a folio penned in another hand.[72] Nearly all of these verses are quoted and commented upon by Advayavajra in his commentary (in the following DKP_A). The exceptions are verses 15 and 16, which seem to be interpolations, as they explain the necessity of meditating on emptiness in union with the cultivation of compassion amid a group of verses that mock butter-lamp offerings and pilgrimage to sacred fords for bathing. Apart from verses 90 and 91, Advayavajra does not quote and comment on root verses that are not contained in G. The Tibetan translation of DKP_A (in the following DKP_{AT}) lacks the same verses 90 and 91, which read like a colophon of an earlier, shorter version of the text:

> An investigation of the psychophysical aggregates, elements, sense fields,
> sense faculties, and objects [shows that] they are [like] the water [of a mirage].
> Within these ever-newer dohā verses,
> nothing has been hidden.
>
> Hey, you paṇḍitas! I apologize.
> Nothing has been mentally fabricated here.
> Do I speak about what I received as a teaching from [my] guru
> as something to be kept completely secret?

Even though Advayavajra faithfully commented on these two verses, they must have been considered inappropriate by the compiler of the Göttingen

72. See above.

manuscript and by the Tibetan translator of the text (DKP_{AT}). This, combined with the much shorter Tokyo manuscript, points to the process of a growing collection of verses with occasional insertions or additions of single or even clusters of verses on a common topic, such as the verses 92–96 on sexual yoga that follow the colophon verses 90–91. It should be noted that the additions were not only at the end of the collection but often in between the verses. This indicates that the Tibetan translators or compilers had a sense of the collection's internal structure.

The Tibetan Reception of Saraha's Spontaneous Songs

The edition of the standard Tibetan root text and the Tibetan translations of Advayavajra's and Mokṣākaragupta's commentaries are based on the Dergé and Peking editions of the Tengyur, as they represent the two main branches of the transmission stemma. Instead of collating the other canonical recensions, we have decided to compare the two chosen canonical representatives with the Palpung edition of the Seventh Karmapa's *Indian Mahāmudrā Works* collection.

In the Kagyü tradition, Saraha's *Spontaneous Songs* consists of three cycles. Only the first cycle, the *Dohās for the People* (D 2224, P 3068), is unanimously accepted in Tibet.[73] The remaining two cycles are the *Dohās for the Queen* and the *Dohās for the King* (*Btsun mo do hā* and *Rgyal po do hā*). However, only the *Dohās for the People* can be traced back to a collection of Apabhraṃśa verses that slowly grew during its Nepalese and Tibetan reception.

As for the Tibetan translation of Advayavajra's commentary, the colophons of the Dergé and Peking Tengyur indicate that the translator was Śrī-Vairocanavajra from southern Kosala.[74] The colophon of the same text in the Palpung edition of the *Indian Mahāmudrā Works* states that Advayavajra's *Dohākoṣapañjikā* was translated by Dīpaṃkararakṣita from Kosala and the Tibetan translator-monk Ba ri—that is, Atiśa's famous translator Ba ri Lo

73. For a detailed discussion of the authenticity of the other two dohā collections in the trilogy, see Schaeffer 2005, 71ff.

74. The colophon in the Dergé (2256, *rgyud 'grel*, vol. *wi*, fol. $207a_7$) and Peking Tengyur (3101, *rgyud 'grel*, vol. *mi*, fol. $231a_{4-5}$) reads as follows: "The *Dohākoṣapañjikā*, composed by the great master Advayavajra, is completed. Translated by the great yogin from the land of Kosala in South India, Śrī-Vairocanavajra" (*do ha mdzod kyi dka' 'grel slob dpon chen po dpal gnyis su med pa'i rdo rjes mdzad pa rdzogs so | rgya gar lho phyogs yul ko sa lar sku 'khrungs pa'i rnal 'byor pa chen po śrī bai ro tsa na ba dzras bsgyur ba'o ||*). It should be noted that Southern Kośala refers to a region now in Chattisgarh and the western part of Orissa, which is not in South India. See Bosma 2018, 3.

tsā ba Rin chen grags (1040–ca. 1110).[75] The same colophon mentions that it was later corrected and finalized by Vairocanavajra.[76] The Tibetan translation of Advayavajra's commentary is unusual in that it deviates often from the Sanskrit—sometimes several sentences are not translated at all or are only summarized, and at times page-long passages in the Sanskrit have no Tibetan equivalent.[77]

The Tibetan translation of some verses in Advayavajra's commentary differs considerably from the original Apabhraṃśa *pratīka* verses. In these cases, we find a surprising accordance with the standard Tibetan root text (D 2224, P 3068, in the following DK_T), which contains all the verses from the Tibetan translation of DKP_A plus an extra 23 verses,[78] altogether 133 verses. It is difficult to say how the corpus of the 110 verses quoted in Advayavajra's commentary, or the nearly identical 112 verses of G for that matter, further grew into the 133 verses of the standard Tibetan root text. At any rate, the considerable addition of 23 verses points to a complex transmission and reception history of Saraha's *Dohākoṣa*. Since we could identify seven of these 23 extra verses in the Apabhraṃśa root witnessed by the Sa skya (S) manuscript, it can be ruled out that these extra verses are a purely Tibetan creation.

The Development of the Textual Tradition in Four Steps

Putting together the different pieces of information on the development of Saraha's songs, we can give the following, still somewhat tentative, sketch.[79] The first step is represented by the Tokyo manuscript, which, with its circa 65 verses, is the only text from India proper. The second step is marked by the two colophon verses 90–91 in Advayavajra's commentary; the group of five

75. Schaeffer 2005, 61.

76. The colophon of the commentary in the Dpal spungs edition (B $161a_{4-5}$) states: "Translated by the great yogin from the land of Kosala in South India, Mar me mdzad ra kṣi ta, and the Tibetan translator-monk Ba ri. Later it was corrected to some extent and finalized by Vairocanavajra" (*rgya gar lho phyogs kyi yul ko sa lar sku 'khrungs pa'i rnal 'byor pa chen mar me mdzad ra kṣi ta dang | bod kyi lo tsā ba dge slong ba ris bsgyur ba | slad kyi be ro tsa na ba dzras cung zad bcos te gtan la phab pa'o* ||).

77. For example, nearly the entire refutation of the Śaiva (DKP_A 78_{10}–81_4), which corresponds to more than three folios in the Newar manuscript, is not translated at all. However, it is possible that the refutation is a later interpolation in the Sanskrit text.

78. The number of the extra verses, which are not available in their Indian original, has to be taken with a grain of caution.

79. We are of course aware that the overall picture may have been more complex with series of parallel transmission mutually influencing each other, for example.

verses on sexual yoga immediately following cannot be by Saraha on account of doctrinal differences (see below). A witness for our third step is the Göttingen manuscript, which is nearly identical in sequence and number to the verses quoted in Advayavajra's commentary. At this point, the collection consists of Advayavajra's 110 verses. The fourth step is that the standard Tibetan root text has on top of these 110 verses an extra 23. With the exception of verses 62 and 85, all of these 133 verses are commented upon by Mokṣākaragupta. In nearly all cases when the Tibetan translation of Advayavajra's commentary differs from its Apabhraṃśa and Sanskrit original, both the standard Tibetan root text and Mokṣākaragupta's commentary employed the Tibetan translation of Advayavajra's text. This means that the extension of the collection from the third step onward must have happened through the medium of Tibetan language. In other words, it is possible that Mokṣākaragupta's *Dohākoṣapañjikā* (D 2258, P 3103, in the following DKP_M) never existed in its Indian original.

The collection of Saraha's songs expanded by another 258 verse lines in the *Extensive Commentary* (D 2257), translated by *Prajñāśrījñānakīrti, also known as Kor Nirūpa (1062–1102), who quotes and comments on this even further extended version of Saraha's *Dohākoṣa* with approximately 197 root text verses.[80] Schaeffer (2005, 106) opines that Kor Nirūpa knew of the standard Tibetan root text and employed it when fashioning his own Tibetan text. Kor Nirūpa traveled as a teen to Nepal after having received monastic ordination in Lhasa. In Nepal, where he was called *Prajñāśrījñānakīrti, he received teachings on the *Seven Sections of Accomplishment*, the Six Works on Essential [Meaning], and thus Saraha's *Spontaneous Songs* as well.

Our comparison of the standard Tibetan root text with the Tibetan translations of Advayavajra's (110 verse–) and Mokṣākaragupta's (133 verse–) commentaries yields a similar result, namely that in our initial part of the collection's translation and reception history, the translators of the standard Tibetan root text and Mokṣākaragupta's commentary knew and used the Tibetan translation of Advayavajra's commentary. The standard Tibetan root text suspiciously lacks a colophon in the Tengyur recensions. In its paracanonical transmissions, the Tibetan translation is once credited to the Indian scholar Vajrapāṇi and Rma ban Chos 'bar[81] and three times to Bal

80. Schaeffer (2005, 66–67) thinks that he was also the *Prajñāśrījñānakīrti that was mentioned as the translator of Advayavajra's *Mi zad pa'i gter mdzod yongs su gang ba'i glu zhes bya ba gnyug ma'i de nyid rab tu ston pa'i rgya cher bshad pa* (D 2257) and reports that some Tibetan scholars accuse *Prajñāśrījñānakīrti of being a forger of commentarial literature.

81. I.e., in the Dpal spungs block prints of the *Phyag chen rgya gzhung* collection, we read:

po Asu.[82] These attributions suggest that the collection of Saraha's songs had grown to 133 verses as it was transmitted in Tibetan in the Kathmandu Valley.

The attribution of the Tibetan translation of the standard root text to Bal po Asu raises further doubts, as Bal po Asu is said to have translated the *Dohās for the Queen* and the *Dohās for the King*, two further collections of spontaneous songs attributed to Saraha whose authenticity has even been questioned by Tibetan authorities.[83]

As for Mokṣākaragupta's commentary, even though Jayadeva and Rgya Lo tsā ba are mentioned as translators in the colophon, a corresponding Sanskrit original has not come down to us. A further important question is whether the author of this commentary was actually the Mokṣākaragupta who was a famous *pramāṇa* master from Jagaddala Monastery[84] and author of the *Tarkabhāṣā*. It is somewhat suspicious that he does not show in his *Dohākoṣa* commentary his philosophical learning, as it is not unusual to quote *pramāṇa* masters in tantric commentaries.[85] Going by its frequent Kālacakra explanations, the commentary cannot be earlier than the second half of the eleventh century, the time when the Kālacakra system became influential. Mokṣākaragupta's commentary, however, must be later still, as the colophons of Dergé, Peking, and Palpung unanimously mention Gya Tsöndrü Sengé (Rgya Brtson 'grus seng ge, 1186–1247) as translator. This, however, would fit the timeframe of Mokṣākaragupta, author of the *Tarkabhāṣā*, so he remains a possible author.

As already mentioned, our comparison of the standard Tibetan root text (DK_T) with the Tibetan translations of Advayavajra's and Mokṣākaragupta's commentaries (DKP_{AT} and DKP_M) shows that when the Tibetan translation does not exactly mirror the Apabhraṃśa verses (DK_A, i.e., the verses as transmitted by Advayavajra), DKP_M always lines up with the other Tibetan versions and goes against the Apabhraṃśa.

A good example for how DKP_{AT}, DK_T, and DKP_M diverge in the same way from the Apabhraṃśa is verse 23 as it appears as a *pratīka* in Advayavajra's *Dohākoṣapañjikā* (DK_A 23) on *gaṇacakra*. The verse is not fully quoted by Advayavajra, but going by his commentary, it is clear that he must have read a verse similar to the one in the Göttingen or Tokyo manuscripts. Line DK_A

"Taught by the Indian scholar Vajrapāṇi and translated by the translator Rma ban Chos 'bar. Corrected and finalized by the later 'Brog mi jo sras and the monk Tshul khrims rgyal ba."

82. Schaeffer 2005, 64.

83. Schaeffer 2005, 73–78.

84. Seyfort Ruegg 1981, 118.

85. See, for example, Rāmapāla's *Sekanirdeśapañjikā* (Isaacson and Sferra 2014, 265–66).

23b reads: "Summoning the assembly [of adepts][86] with plenty of alcohol (*ali*) and food (*bali*)" (G: *alibalibahala cakka pasarantem̥* |; T *alibalibahalaṃ cakka phurante*). The Tibetan for *pasarantem̥/phurante* is "satiate/fill" (*'gengs*), and probably the result of a too-literal rendering of what corresponds to forms of the Sanskrit roots *pṝ* or *sphur/sphar*. Here, a more fitting translation would have been *'gugs* ("to summon"). Tib. *'khor lo 'gengs* was thus a misinterpretation by Mokṣākaragupta, which he translated as "filling the cakras" in the sense of gradually filling them by moving the semen drop upward.

In DK$_A$ 63ab, Apa. *deva vi ppajjaï lakkha vi dīsaï appaṇu mārīi sa ki karijjaï* | ("The deity is generated and even the goal is seen. You kill yourself. What good does it you?") has been wrongly translated as: | *lha la mchod pa 'bum phrag byas gyur kyang* | | *bdag nyid 'ching 'gyur de yis ci zhig bya* | ("Although you offer the deity, one lakh has been given, you [only] bind yourself. What good does it do you?"). In his Sanskrit commentary Advayavajra explains: "When the deity is seen directly with its marks, having arisen in its [complete] form, then you kill yourself (lit. "the self dies") (*yadi tāvad devatārūpeṇotpattis tallakṣaṇaṃ sākṣād dṛśyata iti tadā ātmā mriyate* | *sā devatā kiṃ kariṣyati* |). The Tibetan translation is also misled here: "Even if you worship the statue of a deity to such an extent [that] you see [the deity itself] directly, what is the use of [such] a deity if you [thereby] bind yourself [to it]?" (*gal te re zhig lha'i gzugs su mchod cing grub pa mngon sum du mthong yang rang nyid 'ching na des lha'i dgos pa ci zhig yod de* |). Again, the standard Tibetan root text and Mokṣākaragupta's commentary (DKP$_M$ 79ab) accord with Advayavajra in Tibetan (DKP$_{AT}$).

In DK$_A$ 88c, Apa. *maï jāṇiu* (Skt. *mayā jñātam*) has been wrongly rendered into Tibetan as *gang gis ... shes pa*. In his commentary on this passage, Advayavajra has *mayā jñātam*, the correct Tibetan translation being *bdag gis shes*. The Tibetan root text and Mokṣākaragupta's quotation of DK$_T$ 109c (= DK$_A$ 88c) carry on with the incorrect *gang gis*.

In DK$_A$ 89a, Apa. *ruaṇem̥* ("by analyzing") is wrongly translated as *rang bzhin* ("nature"). Advayavajra correctly comments "by [wrongly] analyzing the coemergent (*sahajarūpeṇa*)," but the Tibetan root text (DK$_T$) and Mokṣākaragupta's quotation of DK$_T$ 111a (= DK$_A$ 89a) carry forward the mistaken translation *rang bzhin*.

In verse line DK$_A$ 92c, Saraha asks the rhetorical question "Whose expectation is not fulfilled by erotic bliss?" Advayavajra explains that beginners or yogins of lower capacities may accomplish mahāmudrā through the play of great attachment; however, the Tibetan translation of both the *pratīka* (DK$_{AT}$) and the commentary (DKP$_{AT}$) suggest the exact contrary, namely that

86. Skt.: *[gaṇa]cakra*; Tib.: "Always fill (summon?) the assembly, again and again."

one's expectations are not fulfilled. This negative assessment is then mirrored in DK$_{\text{T}}$ and DKP$_{\text{M}}$, in which it is stated that uncontaminated bliss cannot be found in the process. Mokṣākaragupta then quotes, in accordance with the Tibetan, DK$_{\text{T}}$ 112c (= DK$_{\text{A}}$ 92c), "How [can] expectations within the threefold world be fulfilled by it?" and comments, "How could the three of body, speech, and mind ever be purified [through this]?"

Read on its own, the Apabhraṃśa of lines DK$_{\text{A}}$ 93ab mean: "Either the moments belong to the bliss of the 'male adept' (*upāya*), or they belong to both (i.e., male and female adepts)" (*khaṇa uvāasuhaha ahavā ahavā veṇṇi vi soi*). But going by his commentary, Advayavajra must have understood: "The moments are [only] of bliss of the means. Or rather, this [bliss] is differentiated." The Tibetan translation in turn has: "The means is momentary, or else it is not differentiated." Both the standard Tibetan root text (DK$_{\text{T}}$ 113ab) and Mokṣākaragupta's commentary accord again with the Tibetan translation, which differs from both Saraha's intention and Advayavajra's understanding.

The Apabhraṃśa in line DK$_{\text{A}}$ 94a reads: "By calling to mind the profound" (*gambhīraï uāra hale*). The Tibetan translator must have read *uāharaṇeṃ* instead of *uāra hale*, rendering the line as: "[The teaching] is profound and vast." Again, the standard Tibetan root text (DK$_{\text{T}}$ 114a) and Mokṣākaragupta's commentary follow the misleading Tibetan translation.

In DK$_{\text{A}}$ 95d, Apa. *harei* ("steals") diverges from Tibetan *pham* ("destroys") in the Tibetan translation, the standard Tibetan root text (DK$_{\text{T}}$), and Mokṣākaragupta's commentary (DKP$_{\text{M}}$).

The context in DK$_{\text{A}}$ 96b requires taking Apa. *sukka* as semen and not the planet Venus, as the Tibetan translation wrongly suggests. In accordance with Advayavajra, who explains that the leader of the stars is the moon, a code word for semen, we must read then: "The sun of suffering sets, and the leader of stars, that is, the semen, appears" (DK$_{\text{A}}$ 96ab). DK$_{\text{T}}$ and DKP$_{\text{M}}$ both have "planet" (*gza'*), which must be Venus or some other planet but certainly not "semen."

In DK$_{\text{A}}$ 97c, Saraha says: "Get pure in supreme great bliss!" (*paramamahāsuhe sojjha*). DK$_{\text{T}}$ and DKP$_{\text{M}}$ both have "Through this supreme great bliss," which differs from the Tibetan translation of the Apabhraṃśa texts: "It is precisely this that is supreme great bliss." The point here is that DK$_{\text{T}}$ and DKP$_{\text{M}}$ were more likely developed from the Tibetan translation of the Apabhraṃśa text rather than directly translated from it.

The Tibetan translation of Apa. *kavaḍiāra* ("little bits") as *glang po skyong ba* ("elephant keeper") is noteworthy and was probably arrived at against the backdrop of DK$_{\text{A}}$ 99ab: "Seized by the huge elephant of sense objects, its trunk, he, it appears, was going to be killed." The correct translation of the remaining part of the Apabhraṃśa verse must be, however: "[But] the yogin, who is taking little bits of [the sense objects] somehow escapes from it" and not "Like an elephant keeper, the yogin escapes in the same moment." Again, DK_T and DKP_M have "elephant keeper" instead of "little bits."

In DK_A 103c, Saraha says: "Has created bondage, even without fetters" (*teṃ viṇu vandheṃ veṭhṭhi*). The other three Tibetan texts read, with slight variations: "Needs to break loose from the bondage of [such] distinctions" (*dbye bas 'ching dang bral bar bya*).

In DK_A 106d, Saraha says: "The supreme mind is of such bliss" (*ehu sokkha paru citta*). The other three Tibetan texts read: "This bliss is not other than mind / This bliss is not the supreme mind" (*bde ba 'di ni sems gzhan min*).

To sum up, these frequent deviations from the Indian material that are shared by the three Tibetan texts are a strong support for our thesis that the Tibetan translators of the standard Tibetan root text and Mokṣākaragupta's commentary knew of, and fashioned their texts after, the Tibetan translation of Advayavajra's *Dohākoṣapañjikā*.

Philosophical Analysis

False Gurus and Their Philosophical Systems

The standard Tibetan root text, as well as Mokṣākaragupta's commentary, starts with an introductory verse of warning, which is missing in Advayavajra's commentary:

> Like poisonous snakes, unworthy [gurus]
> will certainly tarnish good people
> with the stains of their faults.
> One should fear the mere sight [of them]! DK 1

It could be argued that this extra verse not only smooths out the abrupt beginning of Saraha's *Dohākoṣa* but was already there in an original Indian version, because the text would then have started with a full four-line verse instead of a slim two-line one. But Kāṇha's *Dohākoṣa* also starts by immediately coming to the point without a *maṅgala* verse, and Saraha could have been the trendsetter here. In any case, the extra verse provides an introduction that could have been responsible for Mokṣākaragupta's reading "true reality" (Tib. *de nyid*) instead of "distinction" (Apa. *bheu*, Skt. *bheda*) in verse 2, so that brahmans are refuted for not knowing true reality, instead of not knowing the proper distinction of castes. The reading "true reality" in verse 2 thus better fits the added initial verse about the tarnishing of sentient beings, for gurus are unfortunate mainly because of not knowing true reality, which they are supposed to point out to their disciples.

For Advayavajra, the first fifteen verses of the Apabhraṃśa root text are a refutation of six systems of philosophy (*ṣaḍ darśanāni*), among which the Buddhists are listed. The refutation includes Brahmanism, the followers of Śiva, the Jaina, the Buddhists, the Lokāyata, and the Sāṃkhya. Mokṣākaragupta does not recognize in Saraha's songs a refutation of systems but only a warning about the gurus in these systems who are bereft of realizing true reality and thus fake. Fake gurus among the Lokāyata and Sāṃkhya are not specified but indirectly included in his blanket warning. Mokṣākaragupta thus provides the key to understanding Saraha's critical attitude to any form of philosophy and yogic practice in a meaningful way.

Among the commentators of Saraha, Advayavajra stands out for his outspoken anti-institutional and anti-monastic attitude. For him, all Buddhist monastics, even those of the Mahāyāna orders, are reincarnations of the retinue of Māra and hell bound. Monks are accused of explaining reality in a way never heard of before based on unknown sūtras, a charge normally levied only by followers of older Buddhism against the Mahāyāna. Given their motive of gaining material wealth, they are also hell bound. Also noteworthy is the pointed critique of ascetic scholars correcting canonical texts without understanding them, a practice that dries up their mind and makes them sick. Advayavajra also criticizes some essential tantric elements like the initial practice of cultivating everything as the maṇḍala circle, which for him is indicative of not knowing the essence of Mantra-Mahāyāna. Advayavajra is less critical of other tantric features. Explaining the meaning of the fourth (i.e., the fourth empowerment)[87] is only criticized when done without having an immediate realization of the subject matter. He describes Buddhism as a system to be refuted inasmuch as its followers are too conceptual and lack compassion. However, tantric practitioners are not categorically denied the possibility of nonconceptual access to the coemergent.

In sum, Advayavajra is extremely critical of all forms of traditional Buddhism, and that includes certain forms of tantra, which had already been institutionalized by his time.[88] It thus seems that for Advayavajra the direct realization of the coemergent, the recurring topic in Saraha's collection of

87. The existence and nature of the fourth empowerment (*caturthābhiṣeka*) was one of the fiercest controversies in the tantric Buddhist intellectual world of the early eleventh century (see Szántó 2020).

88. Mathes 2019a, 268–69.

songs, is even beyond the very concept of Buddhism. Mokṣākaragupta, on the other hand, does not read into any of Saraha's verses a refutation of Buddhist or any other systems of philosophy.

The Coemergent (*Sahaja*)

All these critiques of non-Buddhist and Buddhist systems or gurus' understanding of true reality raise the question of what Saraha's own position is. In the eyes of both Advayavajra and Mokṣākaragupta, Saraha propagates an immediate access to the coemergent as the only possible means of liberation. The term *sahaja* is often translated as "inborn," "innate," or "inherent," but to avoid the impression that *sahaja* is incompatible with Madhyamaka, we have decided to render it literally as "coemergent" since it mainly refers to the coemergence or coexistence of the ultimate in the world of relative truth without the kind of ontological commitment that triggers the critique of the Mādhyamika.[89]

Still, in a tantric context, usually the ultimate is not only defined negatively as the emptiness of a non-implying negation but taken as coemergent joy, wisdom, and also great bliss. Such positive descriptions of the ultimate can already be found in Yogācāra, whose ultimate truth, or perfect nature, is taken as self-awareness or the luminous nature of mind. In the standard treatise on buddha nature, the *Ratnagotravibhāga*, the ultimate is taken to exist as buddha nature, and its inseparable qualities of purification are called "coemergent" (*sahaja*) throughout beginningless time.[90] In other words, the inseparable qualities of buddha nature coexist with the natural purity of the minds of ordinary sentient beings. As Saraha's system allows a direct access to the ultimate, the more experiential terms of Yogācāra and Tathāgatagarbha prove indispensable in describing this realization. This does not imply a reification in terms of inherent existence. In his *Pañcatathāgatamudrāvivaraṇa*, Maitrīpāda thus explains that a Madhyamaka tenet that is based on self-awareness is supreme, but he quickly informs us that awareness does not share

89. See also Guenther 1993, 22, who explains that emergence (*ja*) must be understood as the spontaneous and uncaused manifestation of the principle of complementarity (*saha*).

90. *Ratnagotravibhāgavyākhyā* ad I.127–29 (66.18–67.1): "In short, by means of this explanation of the examples [given] in the *Tathāgatagarbhasūtra*, it has been shown that all the beings are endowed with beginningless adventitious properties that are the defilements of the mind and that [at the same time] they (i.e., the beings) are endowed with the coemergent and inseparable beginningless properties of the purity of mind" (*samāsato 'anena tathāgatagarbhasūtrodāharaṇanirdeśena kṛtsnasya sattvadhātor anādicittasaṃkleśadharmāgantukatvam anādicittavyavadānadharmasahajāvinirbhāgatā ca paridīpitā* |).

any privileged status and is, like anything else, dependent origination.[91] On the sūtra path, the experience of the ultimate is characterized as luminous self-awareness, while on the tantric path the same ultimate is experienced as coemergent joy or wisdom.[92]

Saraha's Immediate Approach

Even within the tantric context, Saraha's preference for an immediate realization of the coemergent over a gradual approach stands out. This is most clear in verse DK_A 19, where Saraha questions the use of meditation in terms of whether one has realized one's coemergent blissful nature or not. In the first case, one does not need to meditate anymore, and in the second case, any meditation without access to the coemergent is fruitless. In this vein, Advayavajra even questions the very foundation of a traditional Buddhist path, such as the taking of vows. In other words, for Advayavajra, the taking of vows is equally superfluous when one is not in possession of *sahaja* experience. It should be noted that this provocative verse can hardly be explained in terms of being a secret teaching meant only for the advanced, as Saraha proclaims it loudly. Advayavajra takes this to mean "not in secret" and "openly."

Mokṣākaragupta takes a completely different turn by reading into DK_T 23 (DK_A 19) a discussion of whether the coemergent joy that is experienced during the third empowerment is already the real one, for if it were, it would not be necessary to meditate further, and if it were not present, there is nothing to meditate upon. He denies both possibilities, which means that during the third empowerment, one experiences neither the real coemergent joy nor no joy at all. This means that the third empowerment only reveals an exemplifying coemergent.[93] As interesting as this technical discussion of empowerment may be, it waters down the pungency of Saraha's ironical question about the sense of meditation. Saraha's emphasis on realizing and staying in contact with one's coemergent nature through the blessing of guru, which is his dominant topic, gets lost over a technical detail of formal tantric empowerment and practice.

91. Mathes 2015, 317–18.

92. Oral information from Thrangu Rinpoche, Kathmandu, April 2008.

93. See Nāgārjuna's *Caturmudrānvaya*, which explains in the same section Mokṣākaragupta quotes from: "All that appears as coemergent is called coemergent because it duplicates the image of the [real] coemergent. This image of the coemergent leads the adept to realize a type of wisdom that is similar to the coemergent. The coemergent is thus [only in this limited sense] the wisdom based on a consort (*prajñā*). Therefore, there is no arising of the coemergent in the wisdom based on a *prajñā* (see Mathes 2015, 120 and 392).

A further good example of Saraha's preference for relaxing into the coemergent over contrived practices such as breath control (i.e., tantric *prāṇāyāma*) are his verses DK_A 42–43. In most tantras, breath retention is a standard practice. Yet Advayavajra and Mokṣākaragupta alike brand it as painful yoga, which renders the mind fickle like a steed, and suggest that it is better to seek the stable basis of one's coemergent nature—all this in accordance with the guru's pith instructions. The fact that Saraha calls breath control ordinary yoga and also that Advayavajra addresses the yogins of breath control with the vocative "Hey, you foolish people!" indicate that Saraha did not address only advanced practitioners, who need to abandon *prāṇāyāma* after having successfully reached higher levels of the completion stage. The quotation from the *Hevajratantra* I.viii.36c hints at an advanced tantric level, but Advayavajra could have simply been quoting the *Hevajratantra* to show that "the coemergent is realized by oneself from [having accumulated] merit," without implying formal tantric practice.[94]

Saraha seems to have some reservation even toward visualizing oneself as a deity. This is clear from verse lines DK_A 63ab, where Saraha cautions us that one kills oneself when the deity has arisen in its complete form (see above). However, this warning could only be about unenlightened, worldly deities and not the Buddhist creation-stage practice.

Moreover, Saraha describes positively the *gaṇacakra* ritual in DK_A 23. One could argue that while it makes perfect sense for a tantric beginner to engage in practices of the gradual path, such as visualizing oneself as a deity or breath control, the gradual path can become an obstacle for an advanced yogin in full possession of coemergent bliss. If one does not accept such hermeneutical interpretations, namely that Saraha communicated his realization in dependence on what disciples needed in different situations on different levels of the path, the most plausible explanation would be that the *Dohākoṣa* is a loosely arranged collection of verses with heterogeneous content, possibly from different authors.

The Relation between Mind and the Coemergent

One of the most quoted verses from Saraha's *Spontaneous Songs*, verse DK_A 70, compares the relationship between cyclic existence and nirvāṇa (expressed as "calmness") to that between waves and water. Mokṣākaragupta takes cyclic existence to be the thoughts of saṃsāra and equates calmness with nirvāṇa and fundamental luminosity. Thoughts arise from luminosity like waves from

94. *Hevajratantra* I.viii.36 (91_{3-4}): *[sahajaṃ...] ātmanā jñāyate puṇyāt.*

water. "Sharing the nature of being like space" means that both of them are without arising. Here Mokṣākaragupta uses a standard Madhyamaka qualifier for emptiness, indicating that mind and the coemergent (luminosity) are identical with regard to their shared lack of an own-nature. The metaphor clearly borrows from *Laṅkāvatārasūtra* II.105:

> In the same way as there is no difference
> between waves and the ocean,
> a development (i.e., in the sense of a real distinction)[95] of the types of consciousness
> from the mind is not found.[96]

Matching cyclic existence and calmness to thoughts and fundamental luminosity also lends support to another metaphor, that of the gold nugget immersed in excrement. This is the fourth simile in the *Tathāgatagarbhasūtra* for the coemergence of buddha nature with its adventitious stains. The simile differs in that waves are always made of water, while gold does not constitute excrement. A closer look at Advayavajra's commentary on verse DK_A 100 shows that he understands the relation between cyclic existence and the coemergent in terms of being neither separate nor of a single nature. Saraha's "without a single own-nature, too" in verse DK_A 100c (Apa. *ekkasahāvem̱ vi virahia*) means that cyclic existence and nirvāṇa do not share a single own-nature and are thus beyond one and many. Instead of "without a single own-nature," the standard Tibetan root text reads: "they are without distinction in terms of having a single nature." Mokṣākaragupta glosses "in terms of having a single nature" with "not being separate in terms of object and subject" and defines the relationship between mind and the coemergent along the lines of Madhyamaka.

The way Advayavajra understands the relationship between mind and the coemergent reminds one of Yogācāra, however. In the *Saṃdhinirmocanasūtra* the corresponding categories of the conditioned realm and the ultimate are similarly defined as being free from identity and difference.[97] This relationship

95. For a discussion of *pariṇāmayati* and so on, see Schmithausen 1969, 165–66.

96. *Laṅkāvatārasūtra* 46_{15-16}: *udadheḥ ca taraṅgāṇāṃ yathā nāsti viśeṣaṇam | vijñānānāṃ tathā citteḥ*[a] *pariṇāmo na labhyate* ||

[a] According to Nanjio. The manuscripts read *citte*; we think that *vitte* is a more plausible reading.

97. The *Saṃdhinirmocanasūtra* explains four reasons each for their identity (which excludes their difference) and their difference (which excludes their identity). The four faults of difference are described as follows: If the defining characteristic of the conditioned (i.e., the relative) were different from the defining characteristic of the ultimate, (1) even seers of the truth would

is best summarized in the *Dharmadharmatāvibhāga*, in which the equality of phenomena (*dharma*) with their true nature (*dharmatā*) and their difference are both refuted.[98] Their mutual identity is ruled out on the grounds that dharmatā exists, whereas the dharmas do not exist. But, since the dharmatā is the emptiness of the duality of a perceived and perceiver (i.e., the dhar-

not be free from the defining characteristic of the conditioned. And because of not being free from them, the seers of truth would not be liberated from the bondage of characteristic signs (*Saṃdhinirmocanasūtra* III.3, 43.23–26: *gal te 'du byed kyi mtshan nyid dang | don dam pa'i mtshan nyid tha dad pa yin par gyur na ni | des na bden pa mthong ba rnams kyang 'du byed kyi mtshan ma dang ma bral bar 'gyur | 'du byed kyi mtshan ma dang bral ba'i phyir bden pa mthong ba mtshan ma'i 'ching ba las rnam par grol bar yang mi 'gyur |*); (2) the defining characteristic of the ultimate would not be the general characteristic within all defining characteristics of the conditioned (*Saṃdhinirmocanasūtra* III.4, 44.31–33: *des na 'du byed kyi mtshan nyid thams cad la don dam pa'i mtshan nyid spyi'i mtshan nyid du gyur pa ma yin par 'gyur ro*); (3) the mere selflessness or essencelessness of the conditioned would not be the defining characteristic of the ultimate (*Saṃdhinirmocanasūtra* III.5, 45.19–21: *des na 'du byed rnams kyi bdag med pa tsam dang | ngo bo nyid med pa tsam nyid don dam pa'i mtshan nyid yin par yang mi 'gyur |*; and (4) the defining characteristic of defilement and also the one of purification would be simultaneously established as different defining characteristics [for the same person] (*Saṃdhinirmocanasūtra* III.5, 45.22–23: *kun nas nyon mongs pa'i mtshan nyid dang | rnam par byang ba'i mtshan nyid kyang dus gcig tu mtshan nyid tha dad du grub par 'gyur*).

The four faults of sameness are described as follows: If the defining characteristic of the conditioned and the one of the ultimate were the same (lit. "not different"), (1) all immature ordinary beings would be also seers of the truth (*Saṃdhinirmocanasūtra* III.3, 43.15–18: *gal te 'du byed kyi mtshan nyid dang | don dam pa'i mtshan nyid tha dad pa ma yin par gyur na ni des na byis pa so so'i skye bo thams cad bden pa mthong ba yin par yang 'gyur*); (2) just as the defining characteristic of the conditioned, so would the defining characteristic of the ultimate pertain to the defining characteristic of defilements (*Saṃdhinirmocanasūtra* III.4, 44.28–30: *des na ji ltar 'du byed kyi mtshan nyid kun nas nyon mongs pa'i mtshan nyid du gtogs pa de bzhin du don dam pa'i mtshan nyid kyang kun nas nyon mongs pa'i mtshan nyid du gtogs par 'gyur ro ||*); (3) just as the defining characteristic of the ultimate is without differentiation in every defining characteristic of the conditioned, so would all of the latter lack any differentiation (*Saṃdhinirmocanasūtra* III.5, 45.12–14: *des na ji ltar don dam pa'i mtshan nyid 'du byed kyi mtshan nyid thams cad la bye brag med pa de bzhin du 'du byed kyi mtshan nyid thams cad kyang bye brag med pa dang*); and (4) the yogin would not strive for the ultimate beyond the way he sees, hears, differentiates, and perceives the conditioned (*Saṃdhinirmocanasūtra* III.5, 45.14–17: *rnal 'byor pa dag 'du byed rnams la ji ltar mthong ba dang ji ltar thos pa dang ji ltar bye brag tu phyed pa dang ji ltar rnam par shes pa las gong du don dam pa yongs su 'tshal bar yang mi 'gyur ro ||*).

For a fine translation of the entire sūtra, see Gregory Forgues, *Unraveling the Intent* (*Saṃdhinirmocana*, Toh 106), 84000: Translating the Words of the Buddha (https://read.84000.co/translation/toh106.html). Our own translation is only for reasons of consistent terminology.

98. It should be noted that the *Dharmadharmatāvibhāga* equates dharmas with saṃsāra, and dharmatā with nirvāṇa (see Mathes 1996, 70 and 117–18).

mas), it is no different from the nonexistent dharmas.[99] In his commentary on the following verse DK_{A} 101, Advayavajra refers to this freedom from identity and difference as supreme nonduality and equates it with the nature of enlightenment. Quoting Nāgārjuna's *Yuktiṣaṣṭikā*, verses 5–6,[100] Advayavajra then points out that saṃsāra and nirvāṇa do not differ inasmuch as both are merely conceptual constructs and calls this supreme nonduality, the nature of enlightenment. Still, in his commentary on DK_{A} 102, Advayavajra works out a difference between the manifold world and enlightenment: the world is subject to arising and destruction, whereas enlightenment is not.[101]

The way enlightenment is described here fits much better with the existent dharmatā in the *Dharmadharmatāvibhāga*, while the dharmas include not only saṃsāra but also Nāgārjuna's conceptually constructed nirvāṇa—notwithstanding the *Dharmadharmatāvibhāga*'s characterization of dharmatā as nirvāṇa. To sum up, it is only in view of being conceptually constructed that saṃsāra and nirvāṇa share an identity like water and waves. The relation between the mind and its coemergent nature are better compared to Advayavajra's distinction between a world, which is subject to arising and destruction, and enlightenment, which is not. Further down, in his commentary on verse DK_{A} 104, Advayavajra describes this relation in terms of adventitious stains and natural purity, or being a buddha by nature.[102]

Kālacakra Influences in Mokṣākaragupta's Commentary

Repeatedly employing the compound "reflections of emptiness" (*śūnyatābimba*; *stong nyid gzugs brnyan* or *stong gzugs*),[103] Mokṣākaragupta blends

99. Mathes 1996, 122.

100. *Yuktiṣaṣṭikākārikā* 12.1–2 and 14.12: "Those who do not see reality think in terms of *nirvāṇa* and world (i.e., *saṃsāra*). Those who do see reality do not think in terms of world and *nirvāṇa*. This duality, *nirvāṇa* and existence, does not exist. Thorough knowledge of cyclic existence—this is called *nirvāṇa*." (*nirvāṇaṃ caiva lokaṃ ca manyante 'tattvadarśinaḥ* | *naiva lokaṃ na nirvāṇaṃ manyante tattvadarśinaḥ* | | *nirvāṇaṃ ca bhavaś caiva dvayam etan na vidyate* | *parijñānaṃ bhavasyaiva nirvāṇam iti kathyate* | |)

101. See Mathes 2015a, 29.

102. If one reads *buddhaḥ* instead of Bagchi's *śuddhaḥ*. The corresponding root text has *buddha*, however, which is also supported by the Tibetan. It is interesting to note here that in a sutta from the Aṅguttara Nikāya titled *Loke*, the word *suddho* in an older or original version was replaced by *buddho*. See Rhys Davids 1933, 910–11.

103. Following the Tibetan translation, we take here Skt. *bimba* in the sense of *pratibimba*. The term *śūnyatāpratibimba* for *stong pa nyid kyi gzugs brnyan* is attested, for example, in Ratnākaraśānti's *Prajñāpāramitopadeśa*, although in the slightly different context of the third of the four Yogācāra levels of meditation, where it is synonymous with *śūnyatāpratibhāsa*. See

Saraha's songs with a crucial concept of the *Kālacakratantra*. During the initial practice of complete sense deprivation in Kālacakra's six-limbed yoga (*ṣaḍaṅgayoga*), the adept has a direct experience of so-called reflections or images that emerge from space.[104] In his commentary on verse line DK_T 92e (DK_A 74d), Mokṣākaragupta takes the reflections of emptiness (*śūnyatābimba*) or rather the reflections of the "empty" (to render the abbreviated *stong gzugs*) as purified great bliss. In a causal state—that is, when not purified—this permeates ordinary beings' self-awareness by way of constituting their mental imprints. In the commentary on the next verse (DK_T 93, DK_A 75), we are further informed that the reflections of the empty are inexpressible; then, in his explanation of verse line DK_T 95b–d (not in DK_A), Mokṣākaragupta explains that it is the reflections of the empty that are seen after fixations on head, heart, navel, secret place, and limbs have been left behind.

Moreover, the objects that are identified through contemplation are also the reflections of the empty. Verse line DK_T 95d, "Through the contemplation of the other (the nonconceptual), the winds get blocked," would mean that resting the intellect in the nonconceptual, the winds enter the central channel, and thus when dualistic appearances are severed, the reflections of the empty are seen. In his commentary on verses DK_T 100–101 (DK_A 80–81), Mokṣākaragupta adduces the *locus classicus* for the reflections of emptiness, the *Paramādibuddha* (*Sekoddeśa* 32ab). The root verses in the *Dohākoṣa* are as follows:

> Coming or going—I neither take nor abandon.
> Meeting the extraordinary woman—[105] DK_T 100
>
> The dreaming mind is based on nothing at all.
> Do not see [her] as separate from your own manifestation.[106]
> Thus you hold the Buddha in the palm of your hand.[107]
> When body, speech, and mind are not separate
> the coemergent nature shines. DK_T 101

also *Laghukālacakratantra* 5.113a (as quoted in *Vimalaprabhā*), where *bimba* is used in the sense of reflection: "[The divine mudrā is] like a reflection in the mirror." (*ādarśabimbopamā*).

104. See Orofino 1996, 129–30, and Sferra 2000, 22–23.

105. This clearly is the end of the verses in the Apabhraṃśa, as the meter changes from dohā to *pādākulaka*.

106. According to Dergé and Peking; Dpal spungs has *sems* instead of *gzugs*. The corresponding *pādākulaka* verse in the Apabhraṃśa and DKP_A reads: "When the bodhicitta is set at the forehead it shines. Do not see it as separate from your own body."

107. This line is missing in the Apabhraṃśa and DKP_A.

Mokṣākaragupta comments:

> As for "Coming or going—I neither take nor abandon," whatever the course of life is at this point, nothing should be stopped. This is as taught in the *Hevajratantra* [II.iii.42cd]: "Neither forsake sleep nor restrain the senses!" Now, to illustrate these reflections of empti[ness], [Saraha] taught "[Meeting] the extraordinary woman" and so forth. Let us say a man dreams of lying with a maiden. She would be nothing but his own mind alone appearing in such a way. Likewise, this illusory body is just one's own mind appearing in such a way. Again, the bliss of attending to the maiden in the dream is inseparable from the maiden; they are of one taste.
>
> In a like manner is one's own mind, the subjective form of bliss, the illusory body. "Do not see [her] as separate!" means perform the equality of bliss and emptiness! As taught in the *[Param]-ādibuddha*: "In the magical image, the maiden sees a form[108] not yet seen before," and in the *[Vairocanābhisam]bodhitantra[piṇḍārtha]*: "It is obtained by meditating on this rainbow-like body."[109] [In his *Pañcakrama* V.26bc,] Nāgārjuna, too, says: "This [vajra-like samādhi] is the completion stage, the illusion-like samādhi."[110] It is your own mind, that is meant by "from [your own] reflection." As for "[When] the three vajras[111] are not separate," they are the reflections of empti[ness], as it is said in the *Hevajratantra* [I.i.4b]: "The hero-being is the unity of the three existences [i.e., body, speech, and mind]."[112] Moreover, through this, bliss is taught. When the concepts on the level of body, speech, and mind are stopped, there is coemergent joy.

The repeated use of the Kālacakra-specific "reflections of emptiness" dem-

108. In *Sekoddeśa* 32ab we have "thief and so forth" instead of "form." See Orofino 1994a, 64–65. For the Sanskrit see Sferra 2006, 145: *adṛṣṭaṃ pratisenāyāṃ kumārī caurādi paśyati.*

109. Not identified, but the same two lines are quoted and attested in the *Kālacakra-garbhālaṃkārasādhana* (D 1365, fol. 192b) to be from the *Mngon par byang chub pa'i rgyud* (which is probably only short for the *piṇḍārtha*).

110. *Pañcakrama* 53_{3-4}: *vajropamasamādhis tu niṣpannakrama eva ca / māyopamasamādhiś cāpi...*

111. The root text has "body, speech, and mind" instead of "three vajras."

112. *Hevajratantra* 6_5: *sattvaṃ tribhavasyaikatā.* Ratnākaraśānti explains: "In terms of the division into body, speech, and mind, these three are the three existences (*Hevajratantra* 6_{12}: *kāyavāk-cittabhedena / traya eva bhavās tribhavam...*).

onstrates not only the influence of this late tantra on the commentary at hand but also that Mokṣākaragupta brings earlier tantras and Saraha's *Dohākoṣa* in line with Kālacakra. The reference to *Sekoddeśa* 32ab in the above quote makes it clear how Mokṣākaragupta understands this crucial term: the meditation on the reflections of emptiness is purely nonconceptual.[113] They are not imagined and compared to the magical image of something unreal seen in the divinatory mirror of a virgin. These reflections of emptiness are further compared to the manifestations of a wish-fulling jewel.[114] Related concepts are "the reflection, which is the manifold" (*viśvabimba*), or the "reflections emerging from space" (*ākāśodbhavabimba*), which stand for either an emptiness that displays supreme forms (*sarvākāravaropetā śūnyatā*) or mahāmudrā in the form of Viśvamātā (i.e., the female consort of Kālacakra) emerging from space.[115] In his commentary on verse DK_T 23 (DK_A 19), Mokṣākaragupta describes the genuinely natural bliss—which, in a typical Kālacakra context, is not yet experienced during the third empowerment—in the same way as the reflections of emptiness in the *Sekoddeśa*: "They are neither existent in the sense of not being made of atoms nor nonexistent because of appearing directly."

Commenting on Saraha in the framework of Kālacakra's *ṣaḍaṅgayoga*, Mokṣākaragupta locates the immediate access to the coemergent of the

113. In other words, these reflections of the empty are beyond the conceptually constructed duality of a perceived object and perceiving subject. See Nāropa's commentary on *Sekoddeśa* verse 27: "'In the emptiness' (*śūnye*), namely in the space, which is without perceived object and perceiving subject, one should meditate on—that is to say, make it firm through the *dhyāna* limb—that reflection, namely the reflection of the manifold [world] (i.e., the emptiness endowed with all supreme aspects), viz. the reflection that is not the object of conceptualization, that is like a dream, i.e., that is directly perceived by the yogin." (Sferra 2006, 138.3–5: *śūnya ākāśe grāhyagrāhakarahite yan nānukalpitaṃ svapnavad bimbaṃ yogipratyakṣaṃ tad bimbaṃ viśvabimbaṃ bhāvayed dhyānāṅgena sthirīkuryāt* |)

114. *Sekoddeśa*, verses 28–32b: "The meditation on this nonexistent reflection is not the [conceptual] meditation of yogins: To the mind appears neither existence nor nonexistence, because of seeing the reflections of emptiness without having imagined them. (28) Just as a virgin sees in the divinatory mirror the magical image of something unreal, so, too, the yogin sees in space past and future phenomena. (29) The object in the reflection is not something real, because she sees what is empty of real entities. Something consisting of nonexistent entities is like an illusion, a dream, or magic. (30) Yet, even though it does not exist, the manifestation of a phenomenon is observed. It is like a wish-fulfilling jewel that fulfills the hopes of limitless beings. (31) In the magical image, the virgin sees a thief and so forth not yet seen [by the officiants]." See Vienna Buddhist Translation Studies Group, under the supervision of Klaus-Dieter Mathes 2020, *Summary of Empowerment* (*Sekoddeśa*, Toh 361), 84000: Translating the Words of the Buddha (https://read.84000.co/translation/toh361.html). First translated by Orofino (1994, 612); also see Sferra 2006, 141–45.

115. Kemp 2019, 190–91.

Dohākoṣa within the strictly formal tantric system of completion-stage practice. The verses that Karma Tashi Chöphel adduces in support of sūtra mahāmudrā, such as "There are no tantras, no mantras, no objects of meditation, or meditation. All this is the cause of confusing one's mind (DK_T 26ab, DK_A 22ab),"[116] must be seen then as the description of an advanced completion stage, where mantras are not needed anymore, just as in *Hevajratantra* I.x.43–44:

> [There] is neither recitation of mantras, nor [prescribed] observances, nor fire offering,
> neither the deities of the maṇḍala nor the maṇḍala [itself].
> [The enlightened mind is] the recitation of mantras, [prescribed] observances,
> the fire offering, the retinue of the maṇḍala, and the maṇḍala [itself].[117]

A further consequence of blending the concepts of the reflections of emptiness with coemergent joy is that this elevates the reflections to the level of ultimate truth, such that they are expressive of uncontrived primordial qualities.

The Sequence of the Four Joys and Moments

Isaacson and Sferra opine that the dohā quoted by Rāmapāla in his *Sekanirdeśapañjikā* explanation of coemergent joy during the third moment could be by Saraha:

> Two [drops] have fallen, two are equal; [two drops are] falling from the Vajra, [two drops are] touching the Lotus. [The two drops that are] falling from the Vajra are Akṣobhya; [the two drops that are] touching the Lotus are Vajra[sattva]. The cause is sealed by the effect—this is the King of great bliss.[118]

This would link Saraha with the tradition of Ratnākaraśānti and Maitrīpāda, which presents the sequence of the four moments and four joys in a different way from the mainstream represented by famous scholars such as Kamalanātha,

116. Mathes 2011, 102–3.

117. Mathes 2015, 126.

118. Isaacson and Sferra 2014, 294.

Abhayākaragupta, Raviśrījñāna, and Vibhūticandra.[119] The standard sequence of the four joys are: joy (*ānanda*), supreme joy (*paramānanda*), intense joy (*viramānanda*),[120] and coemergent joy (*sahajānanda*). The first three increasingly intense joys are experienced while the drop (sometimes four drops) of bodhicitta descends the central energy channel. Preventing it from moving out of the vajra, the adept experiences coemergent joy.[121] The part of drop yoga described in the verse above corresponds to the experience of coemergent joy when two of the four descending drops are released from the vajra. The fourth joy is then *viramānanda* taken in the sense of "joy of no joy," which, according to Maitrīpāda's system, arises during the fourth moment of relaxation. A particular interpretation of the *Hevajratantra* serves as a canonical support of this reading;[122] however, Rāmapāla lends even better support to his master's system by citing a dohā verse from Saraha (which, however, is not found in our *Dohākoṣa* collections) in which the technical details for the experience of coemergent bliss place it in the third position.

Given that the correct sequence of the four joys was a subject of considerable debate in late Indian Buddhism, it is unlikely that a particular master would sometimes teach the coemergent joy in the third position and sometimes not. If the dohā on drop yoga quoted in Rāmapāla's commentary on the *Sekanirdeśa* really is by Saraha, then verse DK$_A$ 94cd quoted in Advayavajra's commentary could hardly be by Saraha. The two lines clearly support the mainstream position:

> During coemergent bliss in the fourth [moment],
> it is known by experiencing [the goal] as one's natural state. DK$_A$ 94cd

The standard Tibetan root text and Mokṣākaragupta are in support of this. Interestingly, Vibhūticandra attributes this verse in his *Amṛtakaṇikoddyotanibandha*[123] to Līlāvajra, not to Saraha. This, combined with Saraha presumably taking coemergent joy to arise in the third position, gives strong support for our theory that the verses on sexual yoga (DK$_A$ 92–96) after the

119. Kvaerne 1977, 34–35.

120. Note that in Maitrīpāda's system, *viramānanda* means the joy of no joy.

121. Mathes 2015, 312.

122. For the technical details, see Mathes 2009, 99–106.

123. Ed. 63$_{20}$: *sahajāṇanda ca catukkhaṇa ṇiasamveaṇajā[ṇa]* ||. Except for the additional *ca* the lines read exactly as in our Apabhraṃśa text (G 96cd) and Advayavajra's *pratīka* (DK$_A$ 94cd). The reading *-kkhaṇa* against *-khaṇĕ* accords with E$_B$N.

Apabhraṃśa colophon verses DK_A 90–91 in Advayavajra's commentary are an insertion or, together with the remaining verses, a later addition to an originally shorter version of Saraha's collection of songs.

Apart from these considerations, the way Advayavajra comments on the verse lines DK_A 94cd shows that he cannot be Maitrīpāda:

> In this way, during coemergent joy at the fourth moment, notwithstanding what is imagined by [other] people, you know your own awareness.

What is imagined by other people refers to those who identify the goal between supreme joy and the joy of no joy—that is, Ratnākaraśānti's and Maitrīpāda's camp. It could be argued that as a commentator Advayavajra faithfully explained the verse according to its intent and refrained from reading his understanding into it. But a further support of Advayavajra not following Maitrīpāda is found in the commentary on verse line DK_A 52c, which is about abandoning the extremes of both existence and nonexistence and also the meeting point between the two. Advayavajra comments:

> Once duality has been abandoned, the meeting point between the two (i.e., existence and nonexistence) is not obtained in the middle of supreme [joy] and [the joy] of no joy[, as taught] by those who do not understand the true middle.

This means that those who identify the goal of coemergent joy in the middle of supreme joy and the joy of no joy, namely those of Maitrīpāda's camp, do not understand the true middle. This, together with fundamental differences in style and grammar, excludes the possibility of our Advayavajra being Maitrīpāda, who also goes under this name.

In this introduction we have sketched out some of the complexities in Saraha studies: how learned Indic and Tibetan authors grappled with his spiritual inheritance, the textual and doctrinal challenges surrounding the transmission of his songs and their exegesis, and where the legacy of this fascinating figure is situated in the overall framework of late tantric Buddhism. We hope to have convinced our readers that Saraha, whether the person or the literary event, was a towering authority in the overall history of Vajrayāna and that despite at least four centuries of engagement with his legacy in South Asia proper, no less than a millennium of study in the Tibetan tradition, and over one hundred years of modern scholarship, there are still important gaps to fill. We thus hope not only to make a contribution to this effort in the following pages but also to outline further avenues for research. While Saraha himself seems to have shunned discursive thought, he would have no doubt agreed that some degree of engagement with "conventional reality" is useful.

Part 1. Advayavajra's Commentary

The Indian and Tibetan Texts of the *Dohākoṣapañjikā*

Abbreviations used in the edition

.. one *akṣara* missing

||| two or more *akṣaras* missing

ac ante correctionem

NGMPP Nepal German Manuscript Preservation Project

om. omittit/omittant

pc post correctionem

[] *in the text*: missing in N; *in footnotes*: only partially visible in N

<> inserted in the margin

Sigla

A A single folio of the *Dohākoṣapañjikā* misplaced in the *Sahajāmnāyapañjikā* (NGMPP reel no. A 49/18, exposures 82–83)

ĀM *Ālokamālā*

B Dpal spungs edition of *Indian Mahāmudrā Works* (*Phyag chen rgya gzhung*), vol. *āḥ*, fols. 121b4–161a5

BCA *Bodhicaryāvatāra*

D Dergé Tengyur, Tōh. no. 2256, *rgyud 'grel*, vol. *wi*, fols. 180b3–207a7

E_B The Sanskrit edited by Prabodh Chandra Bagchi. See Bagchi 1938, 72–148.

E_L Lindtner's (2003) edition of the *Ālokamālā*

E_{Sh} The Sanskrit edited by Haraprasād Śāstrī on the basis of his transcript made from an unknown Nepalese manuscript in 1897 or 1898 in Kathmandu (Śāstrī 1916, 4–5). The edition is from Śāstrī 1959, 84–118.

E_{ShM} Manuscript reading recorded by Śāstrī in E_{Sh}

G Ms Niedersächsische Staats- und Universitätsbibliothek Göttingen Xc 14/16. Praemittit : [$1b_1$] [*siddham*] namaḥ sarvajñāya ||

HT *Hevajratantra*

N NGMPP reel no. A 932/4, 17b3–102b5. The Nepalese manuscript of Hemraj Sharma (now at the National Archives, Kathmandu)

P Peking Tengyur, no. 3101, *rgyud 'grel*, vol. *mi*, fols. 199a7–231a5

PV *Pramāṇavārttika*

RGV *Ratnagotravibhāga Mahāyānottaratantraśāstra*

YṢ *Yuktiṣaṣṭikā*

In the following cases variant readings have not been recorded:

daṇḍa against double *daṇḍa*

internal sandhi, like *kiñcit* against *kiṃcit*

rgga against *rga*

sa against *śa* or *ṣa*

sattva against *satva*

sandhi observed / not observed

shad against double *shad*

yang against *'ang*

Sarahapādīyadohākoṣasya pañjikā

[E_B 72, E_{Sh} 84, N 17b4] <siddhaṃ>[1] namaḥ śrīvajrasattv[ā]ya |

[1] The beginning is ornamented by a *siddham* sign

| rgya gar skad du | do ha ko ṣa pa nydzi[1] kā | | bod skad du | do ha mdzod dka' 'grel | dpal rdo rje sems dpa' la phyag 'tshal lo |

[1] BD *nytsi*

namaskṛtya jagannāthān gurūn satatam ādarāt |
likhyate dohākoṣasya ([1]sarahāmnāya[1])pañji[kā] ||

[1] $E_B E_{Sh}$ *sahajāmnaya-* N *<śa[ra]>janmāya-* Nac *janmāya-*

| rtag tu gus pas bla ma ni |
| 'gro ba'i mgon la phyag 'tshal te |
| do ha mdzod kyi dka' 'grel ni |
| sa ra ha nas[1] brgyud la[2] bri |

[1] DP *pa'i* [2] BD *pa*

[N 18a] sarojavajrapādaiś ca kṛte[1] tadāgamānugā[2] |
na kiñ cāpūrvam uddiṣṭaṃ ([3]bhagavatkathitāt purā[3]) ||

[1] $E_B E_{Sh}$N *kṛtaṃ* [2] $E_B E_{Sh}$N *–gaṃ* [3] $E_B E_{ShM}$ *bhagavatā kathitaṃ purā* N *bhagavān kathitā pur[ā]* E_{Sh} *bhagavatkathitaṃ purā*

| padma rdo rje'i zhabs [P 199b] kyis ni |
| ([1]byas la lung gi rjes 'brangs nas[1]) |
| bcom ldan 'das kyis sngon gsungs las |
| sngon med cung zad brjod[2] pa med |

[1] B *lung gi rjes su 'brangs nas bya* DP *des byas lung gi rjes 'brangs nas* [2] P *med*

[ṣa]ḍda[rśaneṣu yat] tattvaṃ[1)] na jānanti tadāśritāḥ |
jātivādādim āśritya[2] brāhmaṇādir[3] nirarthakaḥ[4] ||
[1] N *yat ta<tvaṃ>nna* [2] N *āśṛtya* [3] E_{B}N *-ādi* [4] E_{B} *–kāḥ*

| bstan[1] pa drug gi [B 121b] de nyid ni[2] |
| de la brten[3] pas mi shes so |
| rigs la rtsod pa sogs brten[4] nas |
| bram ze la sogs don med yin |
[1] B *ston* [2] P *la* [3] B *bsten* [4] BD *bsten*

bhramanti ṣa[ḍgatau] bhraṣṭā mokṣāmokṣātma[1]garhitāḥ |
pratyakṣañ cānumānañ ca pramāṇadvayabāhyakāḥ ||
[1] E_{ShM} *–ātmā-*

| bdag lta thar pa las nyams shing |
| 'gro ba drug gi 'khor bar 'khor |
| mngon sum dang ni rjes dpag gi |
| tshad[1] ma gnyis kyi[2] phyir spangs shing |
[1] D *mtshan* [2] P *kyis*

san[1]mārgavirahāc caiva[2] pāpamitrasusaṅgrahāḥ[3] |
tasmād gurvārādhanaṃ yat kriyate sādhubhiḥ [sa]dā ||
[1] $E_{B}E_{Sh}$ *samyag* N *samya..* [2] E_{ShM} *ceva* [3] N *-treṣu saṅgrahāḥ* $E_{B}E_{Sh}$ *-treṣu saṅgatāḥ*

| sdig pa'i grogs po brten[1] pa yis |
| yang dag lam las nyams pa yin |
| de phyir bla ma bsten pa ni |
| legs 'dod rnams kyis rtag tu bya |
[1] BD *bsten*

tasya tuṣṭyā bhaven muktir ihaloke paratra ca |
dadāti sarvasadbhāvaṃ tathāgatoktam ādarāt || i[ti][1]
[1] E_{B} om. *iti*

| de mnyes pa las thar pa ni[1] |
| 'jig rten 'di dang pha rol 'byung |
| de bzhin gshegs gsungs bden pa kun |
| mnyes byed slob ma dag la ster |
[1] BDP *dang*

[N 18b] atra tāvat ṣaḍ darśanāny ucyante | brahma-īśvara-arhanta-bauddha-lokāyata-sāṃkhyāś ca | eteṣāṃ krama[vya]tikrameṇa granthakāra[1] āha | *vamhaṇehim* ityādi *ṇa jāṇia tullem* iti paryanta[m |] [E_{B} 73] [brā]hmaṇasya nirāsārtham ucyate | tatra

[1] E_{ShM} *–kārāra* N *-kāram*

'dir[1] re zhig bstan[2] pa ni rnam pa drug ste[3] | tshangs pa pa dang | dbang phyug pa dang | gcer bu pa dang | rgyang 'phen[4] pa dang | grangs can pa dang | sangs rgyas pa'o | | de rnams go rim[5] dang go rim[5] las bzlog pa'i ([6]sgo nas[6]) gzhung mkhan pos bstan pa ni | bram [D 181a] zes bye brag mi shes par | zhes bya ba la sogs pa nas chos dang chos min mnyam dang[7] mi[8] mnyam mi shes | | zhes bya ba'i bar ni bram ze sun dbyung ([9]bar bya[9]) ba'i phyir brjod de | bram zes bye brag mi shes par | | zhes bya ba ni[10] |

[1] B *de la* [2] B *ston* D *bsnyen* P *brten* [3] DP *ni* [4] DP *pan* [5] DP *rims* [6] B *tshul* [7] B om. [8] P om. [9] DP om. [10] B *la*

([1]bahmaṇĕhĭṃ ajāṇaṃtĕhĭṃ[1]) bheu | (1a)

[1] E_{B} *vamhaṇehi ma jāṇanta hi* E_{Sh} *vamhaṇehi na jāṇanta hi*

| bram ze[1] ni mi shes pa ste | (1a)

[1] B *zes*

brāhmaṇā na jā[na]nti bhedaṃ ([1]prabhedañ ceti[1]) | tat kathaṃ ([2]bhedaḥ kasya[2]) ([3]bheda ity āha[3]) | tatra prathamato[4] jātibhedam[5] | teṣā[ṃ vā]kyaṃ[6] yataś catur[7]varṇānām uttamo brāhmaṇavarṇaḥ | tan[8] niṣidhyate pramāṇā-gamayuktyā[9] [ca] |

[1] N *prabhedaṃ caiti* [2] E_{B}N *bhedakasya* E_{Sh} *bhedasya* [3] E_{Sh} *bhedam ucyate* E_{ShM} *bhedam ute* [4] E_{B} *–taḥ* N *-ta* [5] E_{B} *-bhedaḥ* E_{Sh} *-bhedaḥ(ṃ)* [6] N *-kya* [7] N *catu-* [8] N *taṃ* [9] E_{Sh} *pramāṇāgamābhyāṃ yuktyā*

([1]zhes gsungs te |[1]) so so'i bye brag mi shes ([2]pa'o | | de la so so'i bye brag mi shes pa de ni[2]) ji ltar yin zhe na | | dang po[3]) rigs kyi bye brag la[4] | de ([5]dag gi[5]) lung las kyang | rigs bzhi'i nang nas mchog tu gyur pa ni bram ze yin zhes smra ba de lung dang rigs pa dang ldan pas sun dbyung [B 122a] bar bya ste |

[1] DP om. [2] D *pa de* P *pa'o | | de la so so'i bye brag mi shes pa de* [3] BP *po'i* [4] B *kas* [5] B *dge ni*

tarhi [yadi] [N 19a] tāvad jātyā brāhmaṇaḥ[1] | brāhmaṇo mukham āsīd iti[2] vacanāt | tadā ([3]tasmin kāle ca[3]) ([4]brāhmaṇa ucyate[4]) | ([5]no 'nyasmāt[5]) | tat katham | iha [E_{Sh} 85] pratyakṣa([6]pramāṇato yoni[6])sambhava eveti[7] | pūrvābhāvaḥ[8]

| ta[smād e]kābhāve anekaṃ[9] paryālocita[10]vastu na syāt | teṣām api yan mukham āsīd iti mṛṣaiva[11] vaca[naṃ dhūrta]vacanād[12] iti | athavā saṃskāreṇa brāhmaṇaḥ | tad evaṃ[13] na bhavati | [(14]kathaṃ na bhavati | āha[14)] | [antya]jasyāpi saṃskāraḥ kriyate | sa kathaṃ na brāhmaṇaḥ syāt | tasmād na sidhyati jāti[ḥ] | tat kathaṃ jāt[yabhāve na][15] [N 19b] vedaḥ svayambhūḥ | āha |

[1] N *-ṇa* [2] N *āsī<d i>ti* [3] E_{B} *tasmin kāle* E_{Sh} *tasminn eva kāle* E_{ShM} *tasmin eva kāle* [4] N *brāhmaṇocya ..* [5] E_{B} *ayam eva syāt* N *.. dyam eva syāt* E_{ShM} *ṇo nyasmāt* [6] E_{B} *-pramāṇetarayoni-* E_{Sh} *-pramāṇāt yoni-* N *-pramāṇataḥ |yoni-* [7] E_{B}N *-sambhavam eveti* E_{ShM} *-sambhava ceti* [8] E_{B} *pūrvabhāvas* [9] $E_{B}E_{Sh}$N *aneka-* [10] E_{Sh} *–taṃ* [11] $E_{B}E_{Sh}$ *mṛṣeva* [12] N *racanād* [13] E_{Sh} *eva* [14] E_{Sh} *katham āha* E_{ShM} *katha āha* [15] $E_{B}E_{Sh}$ *jātyabhāvena*

khyod kyi lugs la[1] bram ze ni tshangs pa'i kha las[2] skyes so zhes zer ba'i phyir | gang gi tshe rigs kyi bram ze[3] zhes zer na | sngon gyi dus na [P 200a] de[4] bram ze yin gyi | da ltar gyi dus na de[4] bram ze ma yin par thal te | sngon gyi [(5]de ni[5)] 'das zin [(6]pa dang[6)] | da ltar[7] 'dir ni mngon sum gyi tshad mas bram ze rnams bud med kyi skye gnas las byung ba'i phyir sngon gyi bram ze de[8] ni med do | de'i phyir rigs gcig med pa bzhin du gzhan bye brag mang po'ang[9] med do | de rnams bdag[10] gi lung gis tshangs pa'i kha las skyes so zhes zer ba de'ang sgyu can gyi tshig yin pas rdzun[11] tshig go | | yang na 'dus byas [12] las[13] bram ze yin par 'dod na | de'ang[14] ma yin te | rigs ngan yang 'dus byas [(15]ni ci[15)] ma yin te | [16] yin no | | de'i phyir rigs ma grub pas rig byed rang byung ji ltar 'grub ste | mi [(17]grub bo[17)] | zhes[18] pa'o |

[1] DP *las* [2] DP *nas* [3] P *ze'i* [4] DP om. [5] P om. [6] BP *pas* [7] B *lta* [8] DP om. [9] DP *po yang* (et passim) [10] BD *dag* [11] D *brdzun* [12] B inserts *pa* [13] DP *la* [14] DP *de yang* (et passim) [15] D *ci ste* P *te* [16] D inserts *ma* [17] P *'grub* [18] P *ces*

evaï paḍhiaü e caü-veu | iti | (1b)

E_{B} evaï paḍhiaü e ccaüveu E_{Sh} evaï paḍhiaü e caüvea N e evaï paḍhiaü u ccaüveu

| gyi na rig byed bzhi dag 'don[1] | (1b)

[1] DP *'dod*

[(1]jātibhedam ajānadbhir[1)] eva[ṃ][2] pa[ṭhitāś] caturvedāḥ | ṛksāma[3]yajvatharvāś ca | [(4]etad evā[4)]ntyajānāṃ na virudhyante[5] | pāṭhādikaraṇaṃ ceti[6] | [dva]yor nāvabodhāt | atha śabdamātre cāvabodhaḥ | tadā sarveṣām api sādhāraṇatvam āyāti | [yathā vyā]ka[7]raṇamadhye vedāntasya śabdaḥ sādhyate | tad eva śabdamātraṃ lokoktilakṣaṇam[8] | na punaḥ pa[ramārthataḥ] kiñcit[9] |

[1] E_{B} *jātibhedajānadbhir* [2] E_{B} om. *evaṃ* [3] N *ṛjusāma-* [4] E_{B} *etac cā-* [5] E_{B} *virudhyate* [6] E_{B} *-dhikaraṇañ ceti* N *-dikaraṇa[ṇc]e..* [7] N *–ha-* [8] E_{B} *lokātilakṣaṇam* N *lokoktilakṣyaṇam* [9] $E_{B}E_{Sh}$ *paramārthaḥ kaścit*

zhes[1] gsungs te | rigs kyi bye brag mi shes pa rnams kyis[2] rang rang gi rig byed bzhi 'don te | snyan ngag gi rig byed dang | srid srung dang | nges brjod dang | mchod sbyin gyi rig byed do | | 'di nyid klog pa la sogs pa ni rigs ngan rnams [(3]yang dang[3)] 'gal ba med de | bram ze dang rigs ngan gnyis [4] kyang klog pa las don mi shes pa[5] 'dra ba'i phyir ro | | yang na gal te bram ze rnams kyis sgra tsam de[6] rtogs so zhe na | de ltar[7] na ni sgra tsam gyis rtogs pa ni thams cad kyi thun mong yin te | ji ltar sgra'i [B 122b] nang na rig byed kyi[8] sgra sgrub[9] pa de[10] ni sgra tsam nyid de | 'jig rten pas brjod pa'i[11] mtshan nyid yin gyi | don dam par[12)] brjod pa ni[13] cung zad [D 181b] kyang med do |

[1] P *ces* [2] P *kyi* [3] DP *dang yang* [4] P inserts *kyis* [5] DP *par* [6] DP om. [7] BD *lta* [8] BD *kyis* [9] P *grub* [10] P om. [11] D *pas* [12] D *pa* P *par ni* [13] P om.

śabdaṃ cānityarūpakaṃ[1] na nityo[2] bhavati svayambhūś ceti | katham ucyate nityam[3] iti | yathā [lokasya] [N 20a] sattā [E_B 74] nāsti anityatvād iti | tathā tad vilīnam | vedeṣu prāmāṇyaṃ nāsti | kārakābhāvān na[4] viro[dhaḥ | grāmo nā]sti kutaḥ sīmā | tat kathaṃ kārakaṃ nāsti[5] | āha | svayam eva siddha[(6]tvān na puruṣakārarū[pam asti] | tac ca na |[6)] pratyakṣe 'pi skandhānāṃ[7] vināśo 'stīti | pratītyasamutpādatvāt | pūrvābhāvāt para[sya sattā] nāsti māyāvadrūpadarśanāt | saṃyogamātram eveti | bhrāntyā sambhavāt | evaṃ sarva[saṃsāraṃ bhrā]ntimātratayā 'jānānāḥ ṣaḍgatau bhramanti | tan[8]nirodhāt sarvaṃ susthaṃ bhavatīti | anenāpi [vedaḥ kriyamā][N 20b] traṃ bhavati[9] | kāraṇābhāve kāryasyopacārataḥ[10] | alīkam eveti vistaraḥ | tasmād avi[pramāṇatve sarvaṃ] kriyate | sa cāha |

[1] E_BN *śabdañ ca nityarūpakaṃ* E_{SH} *śabdo v[ā]nityarūpako* [2] E_B *nityaṃ* [3] E_{sh} *nitya* [4] E_B *-bhāvāt* N *-bhāvād* E_{ShM} *-bhāvāna* [5] E_{ShM} *nāstiḥ* [6] $E_B E_{Sh}$ *-tvāt puruṣakārakarūpaṃ tac ca* N *-tvādṛṇ puruṣakārarū* ||| *tac ca* [7] E_{Sh} *karmmaṇā(nā)* [8] N *taṃ* [9] E_BN *tan na bhavati* E_{Sh} *na bhavati* [10] E_B *-caraṇam* E_{Sh} *-cāraṇam*

[(1]de bzhin[1)] sgra mi rtag pa'i ngo bo nyid yin pas sgra rtag pa dang rang byung du ji ltar brjod de[2] | mi brjod do | | ji ltar 'jig rten pa rnams ni yod pa ma yin te | mi rtag pa nyid yin pa'i phyir ro | de bzhin du rig byed la tshad ma med do[3] | | byas pa ni nyams pa yin gyi | rig byed la ni[4] nyams pa med do | | grong gtan med par[4] grong gi mtshams gsal bar [P 200b] yod do[1] zhes zer ba bzhin no | | ji ltar na byed pa po med pa yin zhes dris pa la | lan du rang gis[5] grub[6] pa'i ngo bo nyid yin pa'i phyir | skyes bus byas pa nyid ni ma yin no zhes zer na | de ni ma yin te | mngon sum gyis kyang phung po rnams 'jig pa yod par dmigs te | rten 'brel [7] yin pa'i phyir rgyu med pas 'bras bu med de[8] | sgyu ma lta bu'i ngo bo nyid du [9] mthong ba'i phyir ro | | rgyu dang rkyen tshogs pa tsam las [10] 'khrul pa 'byung ba'i phyir ro[11] | de ltar 'khor ba ma lus pa 'khrul pa tsam du mi shes pa rnams 'gro ba rigs[1] drug gi 'khor bar 'khor ro | | de la 'khrul pa de dag[11] 'gags[12] na ma lus pa[13] bde ba la gnas par 'gyur ro | | 'thad pa 'dis kyang rig byed ni bya ba tsam ste | rgyu med pa'i 'bras bu brtags pas 'bras bu gang las skye ste | rdzun[14] pa nyid do zhes rgyas par sbyar ro | | de'i phyir rdzun[14] pa ma lus pa byed [B 123a] par[15] ston pa ni |

[1] DP om. [2] P *do* [3] B *de* [4] DP *pas* [5] BDP *gi* [6] B *rig* [7] B inserts *tsam* [8] D *do* [9] BD insert *ma* [10] B inserts *'bras* [11] P om. [12] BD *dgag* [13] D *par* [14] DP *brdzun* [15] DP *pa*

maṭṭī*tyādinā* aggi huṇantā[1] | iti | (cf. 2ab)

[1] N *huṇantem iti* E_B *huṇantam ti* E_{Sh} *huṇanteti*

kiṃ tena agnihotreṇa ca |

ka[jjeṃ vira]hia huavaha-homeṃ[2] | iti | (2c)

[1] N$E_B E_{Sh}$ kajje [2] N *–me* E_{Sh} *virahia bbhamavaha iti*

kāryavirahitenāgnihotreṇa | ghṛtādihomaṃ nāsti | kathaṃ [paramārtha] m ajānatāñ ca ([1]phalaṃ na[1]) bhavati | tadā-antyajasyāpi tādṛśaṃ[2] bhaven niṣkevalam[3] |

[1] E_{Sh} *phalaṃ* [2] E_{Sh} *tādṛśaṃ tādṛśaṃ* [3] E_{ShM} *nikevalam*

akkhi ḍa[hāvia] kaḍueṃ dhūmeṃ[1] | iti | (2d)

[1] $E_{Sh} E_B$ *dhumeṃ* N *dhu-me*

atyantakaṭudhūmena[1] cakṣuṣi dāhaṃ karoti | yayā[2] rogapīḍā bhaviṣyati[3] | [tarhi] [N 21a][4] kathaṃ teṣāṃ tattvam | āha | parama[5]brahmam iti | tac ca nānāprakāraṃ vadanti | brahmajñānam ityādi | tatra parama[5]brahmam iti ([6]yājñaikavacanam | homena[6]) brahmatvaṃ yānti |

[1] N *–ṇa* [2] E_B *yathā* [3] N *bhaviṣya* ||| [4] N fol. 21 is missing (E_B only reports from Haraprasād Śāstrī's edition) [5] E_B *para-* [6] $E_B E_{Sh}$ *yājñikavacanahomena*

| khyim na gnas shing me la sreg |
| don med sbyin sreg[1] byed pa ni |
| du bas mig la gnod par byas[2] | (2a–c)

[1] P *b sreg* [2] BDP *bas*

| zhes bya ba gsungs te |

| sa chu ku shas dag par byed | (2d)

| ces bya ba la sogs pa smos te | | me la sreg[1] pa ni | me la bsregs[1] pas don ci yod | | ces bya ba ste | don med pa'i mar la sogs pa'i sbyin sreg gis ni mchog gi don ma shes na 'bras bu med do | gal te 'bras bu yod na rigs ngan gyis kyang de lta bu byas pas 'bras bu yod par 'gyur te | nges par de 'ba' zhig gis ni du bas mig la gnod par byas[2] te | shing rlon pa'i du bas mig gdungs pas na[3] zhing sdug bsngal bar 'gyur ro | | de lta na de kun gyi[4] de nyid gang yin zhe na | tshangs pa dang mchog gi tshangs pa yin no zhes zer te | de'ang tshangs pa'i ye shes ni rnam pa sna tshogs su smra [D 182a] ste | mchog gi tshangs pa ni mchod sbyin pa gcig [P 201a] pu'i tshig ste | sbyin sreg gi sgo nas thar[5] par[6] 'dod do[7] |

[1] P *bsreg* [2] B *bas* [3] B *na na* [4] D *gyis* [5] P *thob* [6] D *pa thob par* [7] B *pas*

tac ca svargakāmopabhogaphalaṃ [E_{B} 75] teṣām abhilaṣitañ ca | tayā śvetacchāganipātanayā narakādiduḥkham anubhavanti | sandhyā[1]bhāṣam ajānānatvāt[2] | tasmād brahma brahmahatyā vety āpādi | sarvaṃ brahmam iti vacanāt |

[1] E_{B} *sandhā-* [2] $E_{B}E_{Sh}$ *ajānānatvāt ca*

mtho ris kyi longs spyod la nye bar longs spyod pa'i[1] 'bras bu 'dod pa'o | 'dod pa des ra dkar mo bsad nas mchod sbyin byas pas | bsad pas[2] dmyal ba la sogs pa'i sdug bsngal nyams su myong ste | dgongs pas gsungs pa'i don ni mi shes pa'i phyir ro | de'i phyir kun tshangs pa'i rang bzhin yin pas tshangs pa bsad pa ste | thams cad du tshangs pa'i rang bzhin yin no | zhes [B 123b] bram ze'i lung las snang ba'i phyir ro |

[1] P *par* [2] BP *pa*

evaṃ brahmajñānam iti | tad api na sidhyati | kutaḥ |[1] yac caturthavedātharvaṇe | na ca teṣāṃ yogācāradarśanaṃ | sa na vetti[2] | vedatrayeṣu pāṭhamātram api na siddham | tadā saty avicchinnaṃ mṛṣaiva vacanam | atha tatroktaṃ sarvaṃ nāsti brahmajñānam | tadā vedatrayasya prāmāṇyaṃ nāsti tathā niṣedhāt | caturthasyātharvaṇasya sa nāsti | [E_{Sh} 86] anyonyavirodhāt | tasmād (3dhi nāgameṣu3) kathaṃ brahmajñānaṃ sidhyati | asiddham eveti |

[1] E_{B} *kuto* [2] E_{B} *veti* [3] E_{B} *hi āgameṣu* E_{Sh} *dhīnāgameṣu*

| de ltar tshangs pa'i ye shes gang yin pa de'ang[1] mi 'grub ste | bzhi pa mchod sbyin gyi rig byed ni rnal 'byor gyi spyod pa mi shes pas rig byed gsum du[2] mchod sbyin byed kyi | tshig brjod pa tsam yang bkag go | | de ltar rgyun chad pas mchod sbyin byed kyi tshig 'di ni rdzun[3] pa'o | | 'dir[4] mchod sbyin gyi nang na tshangs pa'i ye shes las gzhan thams cad med do zhes zer bas | | de ltar yin pas rig byed gsum yang tshad ma ma yin te | des na bkag pa'i phyir ro | | de ci'i phyir zhe na | rig byed gsum nas kyang bkag pa'i phyir ro | | de lta na ni (5rig

byed[5)] bzhi pa mchod sbyin byed [(6]kyi rig byed kyang[6)] la[7] med de | rig byed gsum ga[8] bkag pa'i phyir ro | | de'i phyir lung gi tshig med pas tshangs pa'i ye shes ga la 'grub [(8]ste | mi 'grub[8)] bo zhes bya ba'i don no[9] |
[1] DP *de yang* (et passim) [2] B *nas* [3] BP *brdzun* [4] DP *'di* [5] DP om. [6] BDP om. [7] D *ka* P om. [8] P om. [9] P *to*

athavā yady anubhavaṃ bhavati | tadātyantamṛṣā vacanam | kutaḥ | yadi[1] sarvaṃ śūnyam iti vastuna upalabdhir nāsti kutas tajjñānaṃ bhavati | anubhavañ ca sākāratvenopalabdhis tadājñānam eveṣyate | sarvavastuno anupala[N 22a] mbhād iti | vastu ca lokakalpitam ajñānasvabhāvam | na punaḥ paramārthaḥ syād iti paramārthaś cā[smaddarśa]ne sadguror[2] mukhāl labhyata iti |
[1] E_{B} *yat* [2] N *sadguro*

gal te tshangs pa'i ye shes nyams su myong ba yod do zhe na | shin tu'ang rdzun[1] gyi tshig ste | dngos po thams cad stong pa nyid[2] yin pas mi dmigs na de'i ye shes ji ltar yod de | med do | nyams su myong ba'ang rnam pa dang bcas par[3] dmigs pa nyid yin na | de'i tshe de nyid shes pa yin te[4] phyi rol gyi dngos po thams cad mi dmigs pa'i phyir ro | dngos po ni 'jig rten pas btags[5] pa ste | mi shes pa'i rang bzhin can[6] yin pas don dam par mi 'gyur ro | | kho bo [P 201b] cag gi lugs kyi[7] don dam pa ni bla ma'i zhal las rnyed pa yin [B 124a] no |
[1] DP *brdzun* [2] Delete *nyid*? [3] DP *pas* [4] BP *pas* [5] P *brtags* [6] P om. [7] D *kyis*

evaṃ brāhmaṇasya punar api catvāro bhedāḥ | brahmacārī vānas[pa]tya-gārhapatya-yatiś ca | tad apy asaṅgatam | kutaḥ | yataḥ bālatve nāsti niścayaḥ | rakṣaṇabhakṣaṇādibhāveṣu | tathā brahmacāritvaṃ sarvadarśanānāṃ[1] dṛḍhapratijñāyaiva[2] kriyate | ājīvaṃ yāvat | na teṣāṃ niścayaḥ | punar api vivāhādinā[3] gārhapatyam āśrayanti | tatrāpi ca na niścayaḥ | [(4]vānaspatya[4)] [N 22b]tvam āśrayanti dhyānamantrajapādikaraṇena[5] | tatra [E_{B} 76] ca na[6] niścayaḥ yadi yatitvam abhilaṣati | sarvaya[jñopa]vītādīnāṃ dhāraṇād bhakṣaṇān nāsti brāhmaṇacaṇḍālayor bhedaḥ | prastāvataś[7] caṇḍālatva[m eve]ti satyam | kuto | yataḥ brāhmaṇī coracaṇḍālādinā bhraṃśaṃ karoti | tadā brāhmaṇo vedam ālocayati | tena tasyā[8] brāhmaṇyā ghṛtayonikaraṇāc chuddhiḥ syād iti tasmāt sarvaṃ [(9]caṇḍālakarmaiveti[9)] | punar api yater api trayaḥ prabhedāḥ | daṇḍi-ityādi | evaṃ
[1] N *-darśanā<nāṃ>* [2] E_{Sh} *–pratibandhaḥ* [3] N *vihārādinā* [4] N *vālas* ||| [5] $E_{B}E_{Sh}$ *kāraṇena* [6] N om. [7] E_{Sh} *e(pra)tāvatā(to)* [8] N *tasya* [9] N *caṇḍāla* ||| *veti*

| de ltar bram ze'i bye brag[1] kyang bzhi ste | tshangs par spyod pa dang | nags la gnas pa dang | khyim du gnas [D 182b] pa dang | dka' thub pa'o | | de'ang rigs[2] pa ma yin te | de[3] ci'i phyir zhe na | byis pa'i dus su[4] bsrung ba dang bza'

ba la sogs pa mi shes pas | tshangs par spyod pa ni bstan[5] pa thams cad kyi lugs kyis[6] ji srid 'tsho'i bar du dam bcas pa brtan po nyid du[7] byas pa yin pas | 'dir byis pa rnams la ni de lta bu'i nges pa med de | yang bag ma la sogs pa byas pa'i sgo nas khyim la brten pa yin no | de la'ang nges pa med de | yang tshangs par spyod pa la sogs pa srid pas so | | nags na gnas pa[8] nyid la brten nas bsam gtan dang bzlas pa la sogs pa byed de | mi byed pa'ang srid pa'i phyir ro | | gal te bka' thub tu[9] mngon par 'dod na'ang thams cad mchod phyir thogs par 'chang[10] ba dang bza' ba gnyis kyis bram ze dang rigs ngan gnyis la[11] bye brag med do | | gnas skabs kha cig tu bram ze nyid rigs ngan nyid de | ji ltar bram ze mo rkun mo[12] dang rigs ngan gyi spyod pa byas[13] pa[14] de'i tshe bram ze rnams kyi[15] rig byed kyi lung bltas nas | bram ([16]ze mo'i[16]) mtshan ma mar dang rtswa[3] ku shas[17] bkrus[18] nas bram zes 'thungs pas bram ze dag par 'dod pa ni rigs ngan gyi bya ba [19] nyid do | yang bka' thub la ([3]bye brag[3]) gsum ste |

[1] B *brag gis* [2] P *rig* [3] DP om. [4] DP *ni* [5] DP *brtan* [6] P *kyi* [7] DP *yin par* [8] BDP *pa'ang de* [9] B *par* [10] D *'tshad* [11] DP om. [12] DP *ma* [13] P *byed* [14] DP *pas* [15] B *kyis* [16] DP *ze'i* [17] D *sha* [18] DP *bskus* [19] BP inserts *de*

daṇḍi[1] tidaṇḍī[2] bhaaveṃ[3] veseṃ
[viṇu][N 23a]ā[4] hŏiaï haṃsa-ueseṃ[5] | iti | (3ab)

[1] E_{Sh} *eka(va)daṇḍi* E_{B} *ekadaṇḍī* E_{Sh} *eva daṇḍi* [2] E_{B}N *tridaṇḍī* E_{Sh} *tridaṇḍi* [3] E_{Sh} *bhaavaṃ* [4] N *-pā* [5] N *-em*

| dbyu gu dbyu gu gsum dang legs[1] [B 124b] ldan gzugs[2] | (3a)

[1] P om. [2] DP om.

ekadaṇḍī tridaṇḍīti bhagavadveṣaṃ[1] bhavati | evaṃveṣeṇa[2] [viha]rati | punar apy etadvrataṃ tyājyaṃ karoti | anyam āśrayanti[3] | etad evāha |

[1] $E_{B}E_{Sh}$N *bhagavaveśaṃ* [2] E_{B} *veśena* N *ve* ||| [3] E_{B} *āśrayati*

viṇ[uā hŏi]aï[1] haṃsa-uveseṃ[2] | iti | (3b)

[1] E_{B} *hoiaï* E_{Sh} *vinayā hoia* [2] E_{B} *haṃsa-ueseṃ* N *haṃsaüasem*

zhes gsungs te | de ltar dbyu gu gcig pa dang | dbyu gu gsum pa dang | | legs ldan pa'i cha lugs can no | | yang des de lta bu'i dka' thub spangs nas gzhan la brten[1] pa ston pa ni | | 'dul ba pa dang ngang[2] pa'i cha lugs can dag gis[3] | zhes gsungs te |

[1] P *rten* [2] D *dad* [3] DP *gi*

yāvan na paramahaṃsaveṣaṃ[1] bhavati tāvaj jñā[naṃ na labhyate | ']sarvasaṃnyāsatvāt[2] | tad api ca na bhavati | kutaḥ | avidyāvāsanāgrahagṛhītatv[āt | pra]tyakṣaṃ dṛśyate | gārhapatyatyāgakāle sarvaṃ yat kiñcid draviṇādi

vastu sā[dhitaṃ tat sarvaṃ putra][N 23b] pautrādibhyo dattam | na[3] sarvasattveṣu sādhāraṇaṃ karoti | na[3] kevalaṃ jā[tim avaropaṇaṃ karoti madī]yakulāvi[4]naṣṭatvāt | tasmāt |
[1] E_B *-veśaṃ* N *–vesam* [2] $E_B E_{Sh}$ *sarvasanyāsatvāt* N *sarvaṃ sanyāsatvāt* [3] E_B om. [4] E_{Sh} *madīyakulākulā-*

ji srid mchog gi ngang[1] pa'i cha lugs su [P 202a] ma gyur pa de srid du ye shes mi rnyed de | bya ba kun ma[2] spangs pa'i phyir ro zhe na | de'ang ma yin te | ci'i phyir zhe na | ma rig pa'i bag chags kyis ([3]yongs su[3]) gzung[4] ba'i phyir ro | mngon sum du mthong ste | khyim thabs[3] spangs te[5] bka' thub byed pa'i dus su ([7]rang gi nor la sogs pa ji snyed[6]) yod pa de thams cad bu dang ([7]tsha bo[7]) la sogs pa la ster zhing sems can kun la mi ster bar[8] rang gi rigs brgyud[9] 'ba' zhig la chags ([10] ([11]par byed[11]) pas rang gi rigs brgyud[10]) nyams par mi 'dod do | de'i phyir
[1] D *dad* [2] P *nas* [3] DP om. [4] DP *bzung* [5] DP *nas* [6] DP *ji snyed rang gi nor la sogs pa* [7] P *tsha'o* [8] DP *te* [9] DP *rgyud* [10] D om. [11] P om.

naṣṭās te mūrkhadehino 'satkarmavādinaḥ sadā |
[na jānanty eva] sattattvaṃ[1] mohitāḥ pūrvakarmataḥ ||
[1] E_{Sh} *sattasattvaṃ*

| nyams shing rmongs pa yi ni lus |
| rtag [D 183a] tu legs ([1]min pa[1]) smra ba |
| bden pa nyid ni des[2] mi shes |
| sngon gyi las kyis[3] rmongs par byas |
[1] BP *smin la* [2] DP *de* [3] P *kyi*

([1]te ca[1]) svayaṃ naṣṭāḥ parān api nāśayanti | e[tad evāha] | micchehītyādi[2] |
[1] E_BN *tayā ca* E_{Sh} *te tayā* [2] E_{Sh} *micche ityādi*

de dag gis ni rang nyid[1] nyams shing gzhan yang nyams par byed do | de nyid bstan pa'i phyir |
[1] DP *yang*

[E_B 77] micchehiṃ jaga vāhia bhūlleṃ | iti | (3c)

| 'gro ba rnams ni 'khrul pa nyid du bkol[1] | (3c)
[1] B inserts *bas bslus*

mṛṣāvākyena samasta[1]jagan mū[rkhalokaḥ ku]mārgeṣu vāhitaḥ | idaṃ ca |
[1] E_{Sh} *samastaṃ*

zhes gsungs te | 'gro ba rnams ni rmongs pa lam[1] ngan pa la zhugs pa rnams so | | 'khrul pa ni rdzun[2] pa'i ngag gis so | | gzhan yang |
[1] B *las* [2] D *brdzun*

dhammādhamma[1] ṇa jāṇia tulleṃ | iti | (3d)
[1] E_B dharmmādharmma

| chos dang chos min mnyam dang[1] mi mnyam mi[2] shes | (3d)
[1] BD om. [2] P om.

iha dharmāḥ sarvapadārthāḥ [sattvani][N 24a]kāyādirūpāḥ karu[1]ṇāviṣayāś ca tadrahitā[2] anye 'dharmāḥ[3] | kāryādilakṣaṇāḥ[4] tābhyāṃ tulyam advayaṃ | na jā[na]nti viśiṣṭamārgam iti siddhāntaḥ saṃkṣepataḥ | ([5]vistaro 'nyatrāvaseyaḥ[5)] | na punaḥ puṇyapāpādi tulya[m i]ti |
[1] E_B *kara-* [2] E_{Sh} *tatra hitā* [3] E_{Sh} *'dharma-* [4] E_BE_{Sh}N *kāyādilakṣaṇāḥ* [5] N *vistarānyatrāvaseyaṃ*

zhes gsungs te | 'dir [B 125a] chos [1] ni dngos po'i chos thams cad de | sems can gyi rigs la sogs pa'i ngo bo snying rje'i yul du gyur pa rnams so | | gzhan de dang bral ba ni chos ma yin pa ste | bya ba ma yin ([2]pa byed ([3]pa la sogs[3)2)] pa'i mtshan nyid dang ldan pa rnams so | | mnyam pa ni de dag[4] gnyis su med pa'o | | mi shes pa ni khyad par can[5] gyi lam mi shes pa ste | mdor bdus na khyad par can gyi grub mtha' mi shes[6] zhes pa'o || rgyas par na[7] gzhan du shes par bya'o | | dge ba dang sdig pa gnyis mnyam pa ni ma yin no |
[1] B inserts *thams cad* [2] D om. [3] P om. [4] DP *dang* [5] D om. [6] B *shes pa'o* [7] BD *ni*

idānīm īśvarāśritānām ucyate | aïri-ityādi dakkhiṇa uddeseṃ iti ([1]paryantena ca[1)] | [E_{Sh} 87] [a]tra
[1] E_B *atra*

| da ni dbang phyug la brten[1] pa rnams sun dbyung ba'i dbang du byas nas | e ri'i lus la zhes ([2]bya ba[2)] la sogs pa nas ([3]bla ma'i[3)] yon [4] rnams len zhes [P 202b] bya ba'i bar gyis gsungs te | de la'ang[5] |
[1] D *brtan* [2] B om. [3] D inserts *tan* [4] B inserts *par byed pa yin* [5] P *la*

aïriĕhiṃ[1] uddhūlia[2] cchāreṃ | iti | (4a)
[1] N *-hi* [2] E_BE_{Sh} *uddūlia*

| e[1] ri[2] lus la thal bas byugs[3] | (4a)
[1] D *i* [2] B *ri'i* [3] BD *byug* P *dbyugs*

ayirīti uddhūlitaṃ[1] kṣāreṇa[2] | evaṃ bāhyabhasmanā ([3]mrakṣitam aṅgāni[3]) bhagavadvapur[4]niścayam ajñātatvāt[5] | punar api
[1] E_BE_{Sh} *uddūlitaṃ* [2] E_BN *cchāreṇa* [3] E_{Sh} *mrakṣitāṅgāni* [4] E_BN *bhagaveṣu* E_{Sh} *bhagaveśu* [5] E_B *atattvāt* E_{Sh} *ajñānāt* N *ajñātattvāt*

| zhes bya ba ni lho phyogs pa'i mu stegs pa'i slob dpon gyis thal bas lus la byugs[1] pa ni phyi rol gyi thal bas lus g.yogs pa ste | legs ldan gyi lus la nges pa ma rnyed pa'i phyir ro | de'ang |
[1] BD *byug*

sīsasu[1] vāhia e jaḍa-bhāreṃ | iti | (4b)
[1] E_B *sosasu*

| mgo la ral pa'i khur bu khur | (4b)

śirasi [N 24b] nānākeśakṛtaṃ jaṭābhāraṃ vahanti | anyac ca

zhes gsungs te | mgo la skra sna tshogs kyis byas pa'i ([1]ral pa'i[1]) khur bu khur ba'o | | gzhan yang 'jig rten pa la tshul 'chos byed cing |
[1] B om.

gharahī vaïsī[1] dīvā jālī | iti | (4c)
[1] N *va-asī*

lokasya kuhanayā [sva]sthāneṣu pradīpaṃ prajvālya sthitatvāc ca[1] |
[1] E_{Sh} om.

koṇahĩṃ[1] vaïsī ghaṇṭā cālī | iti | (4d)
[1] N *koṇahi* E_{Sh} *koṇehiṃ*

| rang gi khyim du zhugs shing mar me sbar nas 'dug pa'o |
| mtshams su 'dug nas dril bu 'khrol | (4cd)

īśānak[o]ṇam[1] āśritya ghaṇṭāṃ cālayati | punar atraiva |
[1] N *-ṇam*

zhes pa ni dbang ldan du 'dug nas dril bu dkrol ba'o |

akkhi ṇivesī āsaṇa[1] bandhī | iti | (5a)
[1] E_B *āsana*

| skyil krung bcas nas [B 125b] mig (1btsums te1) | (5a)
[1] P *btsum ste*

etac ca kuhan[āyā][1] mūlalakṣaṇam | cakṣu[2]ni[3]meṣonmeṣābhyāṃ kṛtam | āsanaṃ padmāsanaṃ[4] (5paryaṅkaṃ vā nibandhanaṃ5) kṛtvā | [tad]anu
[1] E_{Sh} *kuhaṇayā* [2] E_{B} *cakṣur* N *cakṣuṣi* [3] N om. [4] E_{B} om. [5] E_{Sh} *paryaṅkanibandhanaṃ*

zhes bya ba ni | tshul 'chos kyi rab chen po ni 'di nyid de | mig bar bar du blta zhing btsums[1] nas skyil krung bcas pa ni rdo rje'i skyil mo krung[2] ngo | | de nas
[1] D *btsum* [2] P *klung*

[E_{B} 78] kaṇṇehiṃ khusakhusāi[1] jaṇa[2] dhandhīti[3] | (5b)
[1] E_{B} *khusukhusāha* N *khusukhusāï* (metrically problematic, perhaps *khusakhusaïṃ*) [2] E_{B} *jana* [3] E_{B} *dhandhī*

| rna bar shub shub skye bo bslu ba[1] ni | (5b)
[1] P om.

evaṃ pūrvoktam ayirikasya lakṣaṇaṃ dṛṣṭvā dhandhajanā[nāṃ] [N 25a] heyopādeyam ajānatāṃ[1] ca karṇābhyāṃ khusakhusāyati | anyonyam ālocayanti | idaṃ viśiṣṭamā[rgaṃ ta]trāhaṃ lagno 'smi śṛṇuta[2] janāḥ |
[1] E_{B} *-āñ* [2] N *śṛṇu*

de [D 183b] ltar sngon du bstan pa'i e[1] ri'i slob dpon gyi[2] mtshan nyid mthong nas[3] rmongs pa'i skye bo blang bya dang dor bya mi shes pa rnams kyi[4] rna bar (5shub shub bo || phan tshun gsal ba ni5) gang la nga[6] gnas pa'i lam 'di ni khyad par can yin pas khyed cag[7] rnams nyon cig zer ba'o |
[1] D *i* [2] P *gyis* [3] B *na* [4] P *kyis* [5] BDP *phan tshun shub shub* [6] DP *dag* [7] DP om.

raṇḍī muṇḍī aṇṇa vi veseṃ | iti | (5c)

| yugs sa mo dang tso[1] reg[2] mo |
| 'di 'dra'i cha lugs gzhan 'ongs la | (5c[3])
[1] BP *tsho* [2] P *rag* [3] Counted as one *rkang pa*

raṇḍīti svāmirahitā | muṇḍīti māsikopavāsikī[1] yā | anyāḥ punar nānāveśadhāriṇyo vratinyaḥ | (2tās tasya mārge sammagnā iti2) | evaṃ (3kiṃviśiṣṭasya guror3) ity ata āha[4] | niṣkevalam tarhi |
[1] E_{Sh} *-vāsitī* [2] E_{B}N *tābhis tasya mārgamagnābhiḥ* [3] E_{B}N *kiṃviśiṣṭo 'sya gurur* E_{Sh} *-viśiṣṭasya guror* [4] E_{Sh} missing for a longer part after *āha*.

zhes pa ni[1] yugs sa mo ni khyo dang bral ba'o | | tso reg[2] mo ni zla gcig la 'khor gcig[3] za ba'o | | gzhan ni sna tshogs kyi cha lugs kyis gnas pa'i dka' thub rnams ([4]so | de rnams[4]) rang gi lam de la[5] 'jug[6] cing ngo bstod[7] pa'o | | de[8] lta bu'i bla ma[9] de[4] la khyad par ci yod ce na |
[1] B *la* [2] P *rag* [3] D *cig* [4] P om. [5] DP om. [6] B *gzhug* [7] BDP *ston* [8] B *da* [9] P *med*

> ([1]dikkhijjaï[2] iti |[1]) (5d)
> [1] E_{Sh} om. [2] N *-jaï*

([1]bimbakaṃ dṛśyate | kiṃ tat |[1])
[1] E_{Sh} om.

> ([1]guru-dakkhiṇa-uĕseṃ[2] | iti |[1]) (5d)
> [1] E_{Sh} om. [2] E_B *uddeseṃ* N *uddes-em*

> | dbang rnams bskur zhing bla ([1]ma yi[1]) |
> | yon rnams len par byed pa yin | (5d[2])
> [1] B *ma'i* [2] Counted as one *rkang pa*

([1]dakṣiṇoddeśamātreṇa[2] svārthihetunā sattvān [N 25b] kleśeṣu nipātayanti svayam ajānānatvāc[2] ca |[1])
[1] E_{Sh} om. [2] N *dakṣiṇe uddeśamātreṇa* [3] E_BN *ajānatāñ*

| zhes pa ni rang gi don du yon blang ba'i ched du dbang bskur zhing sems can rnams nyon mongs pa la sbyor bar byed pa de[1] rang nyid kyis mi shes pa'i phyir ro | | des[2] ni dbang [P 203a] phyug la brten pa rnams sun dbyung ba'o |
[1] P *ni* [2] D *de*

([1]kiñcid etad evāha[1]) | sarvam ([2]īśvaram iti cet tan[2]) na bhavati | kathaṃ na [bhava]tīty āha | pramāṇāgamayuktyā[3] ca | tarhīha saṃkṣepata ucyate | iha hi sarvaṃ nāma na kiñci[d vastv a]sti[4] | kathaṃ tat | yasmāt pṛthivyādidhātavaḥ sarve piṇḍaparamāṇavo rūpakāyāś[5] ca | paramāṇavaś ca ṣaḍbhāgabhedena[6] nopalabhyante | tadā[7] vastu na vastu | katham īśvara iṣyate 'siddhatvāc[8] ca | vyāpakābhāve vyāpyasyopalabdhir[9] nāsti |
[1] E_B *kiñci(t) caitad evāha* E_{Sh} om. [2] E_B *īśvaram iti cet* E_{Sh} *īśvaramayam iti cet tan* [3] E_{Sh} *pramāṇāgamābhyāṃ yuktyā* [4] E_{Sh} *sphurati* [5] E_{Sh} *–kāś* [6] E_{Sh} *–bhede-* [7] E_{Sh} *tadā ca* [8] E_{Sh} *siddhatvāc* [9] N *vyāpasyopalarbdhir*

athavā kartṛtvaṃ vadanti iti cet | tadoc[yate] [N 26a] tan na | ([1]kathaṃ na[1]) |

krameṇa[2] ca ([3]yugapad vā na nityenārthaḥ[3]) kriyate | [E_B 79] tasmān nāsty eva tasya bahir vastu | a[dhyātma]kalpitaṃ vā |

[1] E_BE_{Sh} *katham* [2] N *krame* [3] E_{Sh} *yugapaddhānanityo 'rthaḥ*

etad evāha | śaktaś cet kiṃ | deśakālādir apekṣyeta | tasmād yugapan na sy[ā]t | kiṃ tat sṛjet asau | apekṣataś ([1]cānyaṃ vastu[1]) na nityo nāpi śaktir bhavati | ([2]bhāvas tu[2]) nityo nāsti | kutaḥ | bhāvaś ca[3] kṣaṇikaḥ[4] sarvakālataḥ | anyac ca viṣayaviṣayibhyāṃ neṣyate |

[1] E_BN *cānyāṃ vastu* E_{Sh} *cānyavastūn* [2] E_{Sh} *bhāvavastu* [3] E_{Sh} om. [4] N *kṣaṇika*

kutaḥ | yataś[1] cakṣurbhyāṃ rūpādīn[2] dṛśyate bhrāntimātrataḥ | vicāreṇāpi[3] ghaṭapaṭādi[4] na dṛ[N 26b]śyate | tatpūrvābhāvāt | kathaṃ paramāṇvādi uktalakṣaṇatayā viṣayībhavati | tathā[5] skandhādīnā[ṃ] | la[kṣa]ṇaṃ na piṇḍaparamāṇavo[6] bāhyakam iti |

[1] N *yaś* [2] E_{Sh} *rūpādir* [3] E_BE_{Sh} *vicāreṇāpi yat* [4] E_{Sh} *-ādiṣu* [5] E_BE_{Sh}N *yathā* [6] E_{Sh} *-ṇu-*

atha yadi nīlapītādyābhāsasya[1] khyātis tad api na bhavati | pratyakṣavirodhenātmanas[2] tasya sattā nāsti | tat kathaṃ | cakṣurvijñānādiṣu grāhyagrāhakabhāvena pravṛttiḥ sati bhrāntim[3] eveti | bālajanaiḥ kalpitam idaṃ | śvetam idaṃ pītam idam ityādi[4] |

[1] E_BN *nīlapītyādyābhāsasya* E_{Sh} *nīlapītābhyāṃ bhāsasya* [2] NE_{Sh} *-virodhena nātmanas* E_B *-virodhena nātmatas* [3] E_{Sh} *bhrāntimātram* [4] E_{Sh} *iti*

punar evāha |

> adhītam[1] api nābhyastaṃ[2] gacchaty apyayanaṃ[3] punaḥ |
>
> [1] E_BN *apītam* [2] N *nabhyastaṃ* [3] E_B *ayanaṃ* E_{Sh} *adhyayanaṃ*

tasya kiṃ nāma rāhi[tye[1] dhārāvāhi][N 27a]nī vijñaptir[2] na bhavati | tadā kathaṃ[3] vismaryate |

[1] E_BE_{Sh} *yava* [2] E_B *viśaptir* [3] E_BE_{Sh} insert *na*

([1]anyac ca[1]) vaiṣamyaśaila[2]jātānām api [mahodadher] mānātyantānāṃ[3] tathā sūkṣmāṇuparimāṇānāṃ[4] ko vā kuryāt | tad akarma[5] karoti vā balaśā[6]litvād iti cet | sa evonmattavad[7] bhavati | nāśakāle śramam ātmanaḥ kathaṃ nāśa[ye]d iti |

[1] E_B *annac ca* [2] E_BE_{Sh} *-śela-* [3] E_BN *mānātyantaṃ* E_{Sh} *nāmātyantaṃ* [4] E_{Sh} *sūkṣāṇāṃ* [5] E_BE_{Sh} *akarmakaḥ* N *karmaḥ* [6] N om. *-śā-* [7] E_{Sh} *evonmatto*

athavāśaktam eva kriyate | ayaskāntopalādīnāṃ ca śastrādyākarṣaṇaṃ ([1]pra[ti na] niṣidhyate[1)] | tat punar vijñānāgame niṣiddhaḥ | kāyānusmṛtyupasthānādyasthānatvāt | kāyaṃ punaḥ [N 27b] kutsitapañjaraṃ vicārād avastu | etad āha

[1] E_B *pratiniṣidhyate* E_{Sh} *prati na sidhyati*

[E_B 80, E_{Sh} 88] asthipañjarato māṃsaṃ[1] prajñāśastreṇa mocaya[2] || BCA V.62cd

[1] E_B *nāṃsaṃ* [2] E_B *mocayet* N *moca ..*

asthīny api pṛthak kṛtvā paśya majjānam antataḥ |
kim atra sāram astīti svayam[1] eva vicāraya[2] || BCA V.63

[1] Nac *astī | stasvayam* [2] E_BN *vicāritam*

lālāmūtrapurīṣabāṣparudhirasvedāntramedovasā-
pūrṇaḥ kāyakaliḥ[1] sadā vraṇamukhaiḥ prasyandate cāśuciḥ[2] | iti | (not identified)

[1] E_{Sh} *kāyakale* [2] E_BN *cāśuci*

tasmān na vijñānasya sthānam asti | vāsanāmātram eveti | tac cāvidyāvaśāj jāyate | taiḥ[1] sarve doṣāḥ saṃbhavanti | tathā coktaṃ |

[1] E_{Sh} *te*

([1]saty ātmani[1)] parasaṃjñā sva[para][N 28a]vibhāgāt parigrahadveṣau |
anayoḥ sampratibaddhāḥ sarve doṣāḥ prajāyante | iti | PV II.219c–220b

[1] PV *ātmani sati*

tasmāt pra[sid]dhaṃ pratītyasamutpādalakṣaṇam iti | yadi vāvalambate[1] kiñcid devatātmaśarīraṃ | tan na bhavati | [ku]taḥ | yadīśvaraṃ nāstitayā rahitaṃ kim ([2]anyaṃ devatā[2)] sādhayati | ([3]tanmayam iti[3)] vacanāt | tasmān [na] bhavati |

[1] E_{Sh} *-lambayate* [2] E_B *anyaṃ devatāṃ* E_{Sh} *anyatraiva tāṃ* [3] E_{Sh} *tan na yati-*

atha yugapad anubhavaṃ sādhyate | tad api na bhavati | pūrve 'numānasya sattāsiddhā[1] |

[1] E_{Sh} *satta niṣiddhā* N *–sattā 'siddhāḥ*

[ya]di vā dhunanakampanādyāveśaṃ kurute | tadā kuhikārasatyaṃ[1] sākṣād anubhaveyuḥ | nirupalambhatvāt | ta[N 28b]d api pratyātmavedakena bhavati | etad evāha |

[1] $E_B$$E_{Sh}$N *-satya*

pratyātmavedyatā[1] tasya kīdṛśī nāma kathyatām |
pratyātmavedyaṃ[2] vadatāṃ vastutvaṃ tasya ceṣṭitam[3] ||
[1] $E_B E_{Sh}$N *pratyātmavedatā* [2] N *-vedya* [3] E_{Sh} *cepsitam*

idaṃ tad iti (¹tad vaktum¹) aśakyam[2] iti codyate |
(³svaniścayaṃ tad³)anyeṣāṃ niścayotpādanāya tu || [E_B 81]
[1] E_{Sh} *vastutvaṃ* [2] $E_B E_{Sh}$N *tad aśakyam* (hypermetrical) [3] E_{Sh} *sa niścayavad*

sādhavas tu[1] pravartante nityam avyabhicāriṇaḥ |
(²vedakasya bhaved²) vedyaṃ vedyābhāve [na] vedakaḥ ||
[1] E_{Sh} *ca* [2] E_B *vedakasya yad* (hypermetrical) E_{Sh} *vedakasya ca yad* N *vedakaṇṭhadayed*

vedyavedakayor evam abhāvaḥ[1] kin nu[2] neṣyate[3] | iti
[1] E_BN *abhāvataḥ* (hypermetrical) [2] E_{Sh} *kim u* [3] N *-ti*

tasmāt pratītyasamutpādam eveti | [ī]śvarāśritaṃ nirastam[1] ||
[1] E_{Sh} *-śritaḥ nirastaḥ* N *-śritaṃ nirastaḥ*

idānīṃ kṣapaṇakānām ucyate | tatra *dīhaṇakkha jjaï*[1] ityādi (²*tāvaṃ* [*para keva*][N 29a]*la sāhaï* iti²) paryantena | evaṃ
[1] E_B *dīhaṇakkhajaï* E_{Sh} *dīhaṇakkha* [2] E_{Sh} *tāvapara kevaka sāha iti*

da[1] ni gcer bu pa rnams yin te | sen mo ring zhing zhes bya ba la sogs pa nas | lus kyi bka' thub tsam gyis gdung[2] | | zhes bya ba'i bar (³gyis bstan³) te |
[1] D *nga* [2] DP *gdungs* [3] D *gyis ston* P *gyi ston*

dīhaṇakkha jje[1] maliṇeṃ[2] veseṃ | iti | (6a)
[1] E_BN *dīhaṇakkha jjaï* E_{Sh} *dīkṣaṇakhajje* [2] E_{Sh} *maline*

| sen mo ring zhing [1] de'i lus dri ma'i cha byad can | (6a)
[1] DP insert *ni*

arhantāśritā[1] eva[2] dehinaḥ[3] sa[rva]lokāḥ kapaṭakuhanatvena[4] bhakṣitāḥ | malinaveśadhāriṇaḥ svayaṃ tattvam ajānānāś ca punar api [sva]śarīreṣu[5] duḥkhadāyakāḥ | tam āha |
[1] E_BN *-śrita* [2] E_{Sh} *evāmī* [3] N *-na* [4] E_{Sh} *-hānālobhena* N *-hanātvena* [5] E_{Sh} *-śarīre*

ṇaggala hŏia[1] upāḍia keseṃ | iti | (6b)
[1] EBN *hoi*

nagnena prāptaṃ keśānām utpāṭanena karmaṇā na [(1]paramārthaṃ kiñcit[1)] | evam uktena kiṃ syāt |
[1] $E_{B}E_{Sh}$ *paramārthaḥ kaścit*

(missing in the Tibetan)

khavaṇĕhi jāṇa viḍaṃ[bi]a[1] veseṃ | iti | (6c)
[1] ESh *-viya*

kṣapaṇakena mārgaṃ[1] viḍambitaṃ yādṛśaṃ tādṛśaṃ na bhavati |
[1] $E_{B}E_{Sh}$N *mārga*

| zhes bya ba ni lus can [1] sgyu dang g.yo la [B 126a] brten nas rang gi 'dod pa gang yin pa de la ni thar pa'i lam med do |
[1] P inserts *dang*

kutaḥ | nityānityavyava[hāra][N 29b]tvāt tanmārgam ajānanāc[1] ca | [(2]teṣāṃ yam āśrayaṃ kurvanti taiḥ[2)] |
[1] E_{B} *ajānānāc* E_{Sh} *ajānatāñ* [2] E_{Sh} *te pāpam āśrayaṃ kurvanti te*

| de[1] ci'i phyir zhe na | dngos po gcig la rtag pa'ang ma yin | mi rtag pa'ang ma yin zhes zer [(2]ba dang |[2)] lam mi shes pa'i phyir ro | | gang dag de [3] la brten pa ni [(4]thar pa thob pa'i lam med do | | zhes so | de ci'i phyir zhe na[4)] |
[1] D om. [2] DP *zhing* [3] B inserts *rnams* [4] P om.

[E_{Sh} 89] appaṇa[1] vāhia mokkha-uveseṃ[2] | iti | (6d)
[1] E_{Sh} *appaṇu* [2] E_{Sh} *ueseṃ*

| [(1]thar pa'i[1)] ched du bdag nyid bkol | (6d)
[1] D om. P *thar pa thob pa'i*

[ā]tmanaḥ kukarmakumārgeṣu vāhitaṃ[1] mokṣoddeśena | tac ca mokṣaṃ[2] na sidhyate[3] | vakṣyamāṇatvāt |
[1] NE_{B} *vāhitvaṃ* [2] E_{B} *mokṣe* [3] E_{B} *sidhyati* E_{Sh} *dṛśyate*

| zhes[1] gsungs te |[2] bdag nyid las ngan pa dang lam ngan pas gnod par byed cing thar pa'i ched du byas kyang thar pa ni mi 'grub ste[3] | 'og nas 'chad pa'i phyir ro |
[0] P is not available from here up to B 127b1 [2] From here on P is available from the insertion starting from P210b2 [3] D *sta*

jaï ṇaggā via hoi mutti tā[1] | iti[1] | (7a)
[1] N *ityādi*

| gcer bu[1] gang zhig grol gyur na | (7a)
[1] P *bus*

yadi nagnānāṃ[1] bhavati muktis tadā
[1] E_B *magnānāṃ*

tā[1] suṇaha siālaha | iti | (7b)
[1] E_B om.

śvāna[1]śṛgālādīnāṃ kiṃ na bhavati muktiḥ | atha |
[1] $E_B E_{Sh}$ *śva-*

| zhes gsungs te | gal te gcer[1] bu tsam gyis grol ba yin na khyi dang [(2]bong bu[2)] la sogs pa'ang[3] cis mi grol te | grol bar mi[3] 'gyur ro | yang |[4]
[1] P inserts *te* [2] DP *ce sbyang* [3] DP *pa* [4] DP 7b is not recognized as root text

[E_B 82] lomupāḍaṇeṃ[1] atthi [(2][si]ddhi tā[2)] | iti | (7c)
[1] E_{Sh} *lomoppāḍane* [2] E_{Sh} *siddhia*

| spu btogs pas ni grol gyur na | (7c)

lomotpāṭitena[1] siddhir asti yadi tadā
[1] E_{Sh} *lomotpāṭaṇena*

juvaïṇiambaha[1] | iti | (7d)
[1] E_{Sh} *-ṇityambaha*

yuvatistrīṇāṃ ni[tyaro][N 30a][1]motpāṭanakarma | tāsāṃ nitambasya kiṃ na muktiḥ syāt | atha vā
[1] N fol. 30 is missing (Bagchi reports from Haraprasād Śāstrī only)

| zhes gsungs te | gal te ba[1] spu btogs pas grol ba yin na bud med gzhon nu ma rnams[2] spu ngan rtag tu btogs[3] pas bud med grol bar 'gyur ro | [4]
[1] DP om. [2] D om. [3] D *btags* [4] 7d is not recognized as root text

picchīgahaṇe diṭṭha[1] mokkha | iti | (8a)
[1] E_{Sh} *diṭhṭhi*

| mjug spu g.yobs[1] pas thar thob na | (8a)
[1] P *g.yabs*

kṣapaṇakena mayūrapicchikāgrahaṇena yadi mokṣo dṛṣṭaḥ |

tā kariha turaṅgaha | iti | (8b)

tadā hastyaśvānāṃ gūḍhapakṣareṣu (?) mayūrapicchakābharaṇamālayā mokṣo bhavati | na bhavatīti yāvat | anyac ca |

uñcheṃ[1] bhoaṇeṃ hoi jāṇa | iti | (8c)
[1] E_{Sh} *ubbheṃ*

uñchitabhojanena yadi bhavati jñānam |

tā kariha[1] turaṅgaha[2] | (8d)
[1] E_{Sh} *karia* [2] E_{B}N om.

ityādi pūrvavad eva[1] |
[1] E_{Sh} read *eva* as a part of the following stanza.

zhes gsungs pa [D 184a] ni gcer bu pa gang[1] gis rma bya'i sgro'i chun po blangs shing lag pas[2] g.yobs[3] pas grol ba yin na | rma bya dang g.yag la sogs pa[4] grol bar 'gyur ro | | langs te za bas grol gyur[5] na | zhes smos te | gal te langs te za bas grol na rta dang glang po che[6] la sogs pa[4] ci'i phyir mi grol [(6]te | grol[6)] bar thal [B 126b] lo | [7]
[1] P *gang zhig* [2] DP *pa* [3] D *g.yob* P *g.yabs* [4] B *pa'ang* [5] P *bar 'gyur* [6] DP om.
[7] *Dohākoṣa*, 8b–d not recognized as root text

Saraha bhaṇaï khavaṇāṇa mokkha mahu[1] kimpi ṇa bhāvaï | iti | (9ab)
[1] E_{B} *maha*

| de la mda' bsnun na re gcer bu pa'i |
| theg pas[1] thar pa nga[2)] mi 'dod | (9ab)
[1] DP *pa'i* [2] B *nam yang*

saroruhavajrapādenoktaṃ kṣapaṇakānāṃ yan mokṣaṃ tan mama kiñcinmātraṃ na pratibhāsate | kuta iti ced āha

| zhes pa[1] ni sa ra ha'i zhal na re | nam mkha'i gos can rnams kyi thar pa gang yin pa de ni kho bo cung zad kyang mi 'dod do zhes pa'o |
[1] P om.

tatta-rahia-kāāṇa tāva para kevala sāhaï[1] | iti | (9cd)
[1] E_{Sh} *sāha*

| de nyid dang ni bral [(1]gyur zhing[1)] |
| lus kyi dka' thub tsam gyis gdung[2] | (9cd)
[1] DP *ba yi* [2] DP *gdungs*

tattvarahitaṃ | kim anyam tāvad | ātmanā 'jānatā[1] pare 'pi lokāḥ kevalam anarthaikapāte |
[1] E_{Sh} *'jñānatā*

| zhes[1] gsungs te | de kho na nyid dang bral zhing ci'ang ma[2] shes pas 'jig rten pa gzhan yang don med pa la sbyor zhing lhung bar byed do |
[1] P *shes* [2] B *mi*

yadā teṣāṃ siddhānto yaj jīva[1]nikāyādilakṣaṇaṃ nityaṃ[2] | punar api yat teṣāṃ vacanam asti tad vanasya patīnāṃ jīvam iti | tan na bhavati | kasmān na bhavati ity āha | skandhādīnāṃ vināśo bhavati yadā tadā 'nityam[3] | evam eko jīvanikāyaḥ[4] | dvitīyaṃ[5] vanaspatayas[6] tṛṇavanakānanā[N 31a]di | [E_B 83] tṛtīyaṃ pṛthivyādi caturdhātavaś ca | evaṃ ṣaḍ jīvanikāyāḥ[7] |
[1] $E_B E_{Sh}$ *bīja-* [2] $E_B E_{Sh}$ *anityaṃ* [3] $E_B E_{Sh}$ N *'nitya* [4] E_{Sh} *jīvati kāyaḥ* [5] $E_B E_{Sh}$ *dvitīya* [6] E_{Sh} *vanasya yaḥ* | [7] E_{Sh} *-nikāyāś ca*

etat sarvaṃ na bhavati | kutaḥ | yataḥ sa[rve ja]ḍadhātavaḥ | teṣāṃ kutra[1] jīvam upalabhyate | na labhyata iti[2] yāvat | atha puruṣāyattaṃ jīvaṃ | tat pū[rva]m īśvaranirākaraṇe nirastam | etaduktena kiṃ syāt | sarvam evānityarūpaṃ syāt | kathaṃ tarhi pratītyasamutpannatvam[3] | pratītyasamutpādaṃ ca bhrāntirūpam | lokasya[4] sthiratvābhāvāt |
[1] E_{Sh} *kuto* [2] E_B *labhyate iti* N *labhyateti* [3] E_{Sh} *samutpannatvam* [4] N *lokaś ca*

ihalokaṃ vihāya svargādigamanaṃ karoti | bauddhānām api[1] tādṛśam | iha janmani[2] sattvārthaṃ kṛtv[ā][N 31b] tadā skandhapariṇāmenānyalokaṃ gatvā sattvārthaṃ niṣpādya punar api tatparityāgāt skandhādigrahaṇa[ṃ kur]vantīti | sarvakālataḥ | alāta[3]cakravat (7pūrvakaru[4]ṇāpraṇidhānāc ca | kin tu (5viśeṣam asti teṣāṃ5) māyāvat | na satyaṃ na mṛṣā ca | lokarūḍhyā[6] punar nityarūpam iti siddham | nārhantavat |7) ki[n tu] teṣāṃ nityarūpaṃ[8] mokṣaṃ | tan na bhavati | kutaḥ | yatas teṣāṃ vacanaṃ traidhātuka[9]syopari cchatrākā[raṃ] mokṣaṃ[10] tac ca ṣaḍa[11]śītisahasrayojanānāṃ pramāṇam | etad eva na siddhyati | yataḥ traidhātukasya vi[nā][N 32a]śo 'sti | chatraṃ kutra sthāne tiṣṭhati | tasmāt (12mokṣaṃ nityarūpaṃ12) na bhavati | anityam eveti syā[t | iti] saṃkṣepataḥ | vistareṇānyatrāvaseyam |

[1] E_B *bodhanām api* E_{Sh}N *baudhānām iti* | [2] E_BN *janmanā* [3] N *alā-* [4] E_B *–ra-* [5] E_B *viśeṣa ... m* N *viśaṣam asti* ||| *m* [6] E_B *lokarūpyā* [7] E_{Sh} om. [8] N *-rūpa* [9] E_BE_{Sh} *traidhātudhātuka-* [10] N *mokṣa* [11] N *ṣaḍā-* [12] E_B *mokṣanityabhūyaṃ* E_{Sh} *mokṣanityarūpaṃ*

idānīṃ śrama[1]ṇānām ucyate | tatra cellū[2] [ityādi] naü paramattha[3] ekka teṃ[4] sāhiu iti[5] paryantam[6] |

[1] N *śrava-* [2] E_BE_{Sh} *cellu* [3] E_B *-matya* E_{Sh} *-maccha* [4] E_B *tteṃ* [5] E_B om. [6] E_{Sh} *paryante*

| da ni nyan thos rnams bstan[1] te | dge tshul [P 211a[2]] zhes bya ba la sogs pa nas | (3des na don dam gcig kyang grub pa med3) | ces bya ba'i bar du'o | | de'ang[4]

[1] DP *ston* [2] Still from the inserted part [3] B *de dag don dam par ni cis mi 'grub* DP *de dag don dam pa (B par) ni gcig mi 'grub* [4] DP om.

cellū[1] bhikkhu[2] jĕ tthavira-uveseṃ[3] |
(4vandehiṃ pavvajjiu4) veseṃ[5] | iti | (10ab)

[1] E_BE_{Sh} *cellu* [2] E_{Sh} *bhikkha* [3] E_BE_{Sh} *tthaviraüeseṃ* N *tthaviraüdeseṃ* [4] E_B *vandehia pavvajjiu* E_{Sh} *vandehia yajjaï* N *vandehiṃ pa* ||| [5] E_{Sh} *ueseṃ* N *uvesem*

| dge tshul dge slong gnas brtan gzugs[1] |
| ban de [2] 'di ltar rab byung nas | (10ab)

[1] B *zhes bya ba'i* [2] B inserts *rnams ni*

[E_B 84, E_{Sh} 90] cellū[1] daśaśikṣāpadī[2] | bhikkhuḥ[3] koṭiśikṣāpadī[4] | sthaviro[5] daśava[rṣopa]pannaḥ[6] | te sarve kāṣāyadharavandyarūpamātraṃ[7] pravrajyāṃ gṛhṇanti | (8te no deśana8)bhi(9kṣaṇaśīlatvenāpy uttamāḥ9) | [N 32b] na (10tattvatas tattvam10) ājānanti[11] | śaṭhakapaṭarūpeṇa sattvān viheṭhayanti | yad uktam bhagavatā |

[1] $E_B E_{Sh}$ *cellaḥ* [2] E_{Sh} *-śiṣya[ḥ] yadā* [3] E_B *bhikṣu* E_{Sh} *bhikṣuḥ* [4] E_{Sh} *-śiṣyā yadā* [5] $E_B E_{Sh}$ *sthaviro yo* N *sthaviro yat* [6] E_{Sh} *sayanaḥ* N *-nna* [7] E_B *–vattvārūpamāraṃ* E_{Sh} *–vanto rūpamātra-* [8] E_B *tena deśana* N *te no deśena-* [9] E_B *kṣaṇaśīlatvakṣamān nācaranti* E_{Sh} *kṣaṇaśīlakṣamā[ḥ] | caranti* N *kṣuṇaśīlatvena |||* [10] E_{Sh} *tatha-tattvam* [11] E_B *jānanti* N *ajānanti*

| zhes smos te | dge tshul rnams[1] ni bslab pa'i gnas bcu pa'o | | dge slong rnams[1] ni bslab pa'i gnas nyis brgya lnga bcu (2rtsa gsum2) pa'o | | gnas brtan ni bsnyen par rdzogs nas lo bcu lon pa'o | | bande ni de rnams la gzhan dang gzhan gyis phyag 'tshal ba'i ched du rab tu byung bar khas blangs nas bsod snyoms dang bslabs pa la slob kyang mchog ni ma yin te | de nyid mi shes pa'i phyir dang | sgyu dang tshul 'chos kyi gzugs kyis sems can rnams kyi[3] dmod[4] pa'i phyir | de ltar yang[5] bcom ldan 'das kyis |

[1] DP om. [2] DP om. [3] BD *kyis* [4] DP *smod* [5] P om.

paści[me kāle] paścime samaye mayi parinirvṛte pañcakaṣāyakāle ca ye bhikṣavaḥ mama śāsane bhavi[ṣyanti] | te sarve śaṭhakapaṭaratā bhaviṣyanti | tathā gṛhārambhe[1] sati kṛṣivāṇijyādiratāḥ[2] | sa[rvapāpa]karmāṇi kariṣyanti | śāsane[3] viḍambakāḥ ye[4] pūrve mārakāyikāḥ[5] (6sarve te6) śramaṇa[rūpeṇā]vatariṣyanti | tatra madhye saṃghasthavirās te sāṃghikopabhogaṃ[7] hariṣyanti | ityādi vistaraḥ |

[1] E_{Sh} *gṛhārante* [2] E_{Sh} *kṛṣivāṇijyavratāḥ* N *kṛṣavāṇijyādiratāḥ* [3] E_{Sh} *śāsanā* [4] E_BN *yat* [5] N *-kā* [6] E_BN *tat sarve te* E_{Sh} *te sarve* [7] E_{Sh} *–bhoga[ḥ]*

nga yongs su mya ngan las 'das nas phyi ma'i tshe[1] snyigs ma lnga dang ldan pa'i [B 127a] dus su nga'i bstan pa la dge slong gang zhig 'byung ba rnams ma lus par g.yo[2] sgyu dang tshul 'chos la dga' bar 'gyur ro[3] | | de bzhin du khyim la brtson nas[4] zhing (5rmod pa5) dang 'tshong byed pa la sogs pa la dga' zhing sdig pa'i las byed pa la dga' bar 'gyur ro | | bstan pa la bzhad gad byed par 'gyur te | de rnams ni [D 184b] sngon gyi dus na bdud kyi rigs kyi lha yin zhing[6] | da[7] ltar ni dge sbyong[8] gi gzugs kyis 'ongs nas gnas pa'o[9] | | de rnams kyi nang nas gnas brtan kha cig gis[10] dge 'dun gyi longs spyod thams cad 'phrogs[11] shing rang gi dbang du byas nas longs spyod |

[1] DP *tshe phyi ma'i dus na* [2] DP om. [3] B *te* [4] DP *zhing* [5] DP *rmo ba* [6] DP *te* [7] D *de* [8] P *slong* [9] P *so* [10] B *ni* [11] D *phrogs*

ces bya ba la sogs pa rgyas par gsungs so |

[na teṣāṃ] [N 33a] bodhiḥ | tat kathaṃ | ye śrāvakayānam āśritās teṣām uktalakṣaṇena bhaṅgaḥ | bhaṅgāt punar narakaṃ yānti | a[tha śi]kṣārakṣaṇamātreṇa vinayoktalakṣaṇena[1] svargopabhogamātraṃ bhavati | na punar bodhir uttamā | [ku]taḥ | yadā sthavirāryānandaḥ parinirvṛtas tadā tena na kasyacit samarpitam | śrāvaka[2]bodhir upadeśaḥ[3] ([4]sa syāt[4]) | atha mahāyānam āśrayanti | tatrāpi niścayaṃ na bhavati | kutaḥ | yataḥ pūrvaṃ[5] mārakāyikatvāt | yadi vā susthitaṃ tad apy aniścitam | etad evāha |

[1] $E_B E_{Sh}$N *–lakṣaṇāyāḥ* [2] E_{Sh} *-ke* [3] N *upadeśaṃḥ* [4] E_{Sh} *syāt* [5] $E_B E_{Sh}$ *pūrva-*

| de'i phyir de rnams la byang chub med do | | gang nyan thos kyi theg pa la brten pa sngon du bstan pa'i mtshan nyid dang ldan pa de rnams ni gal te bslab pa zhig na dmyal bar 'gro ba'o | | yang na bslab pa ma zhig cing bsrungs pa tsam po[1] [P 211b[2]] des ni mtho ris kyi longs spyod tsam thob kyi | byang chub mchog ni med do | | gal te theg pa chen po la brten to zhe na | de la'ang nges pa med de | sngon bdud kyi ris[3] kyi lha yin pa'i phyir ro | | gal te legs par gnas pa yin na'ang de lta na'ang nges pa med do | de nyid bstan pa'i phyir |

[1] P *pos* [2] Still from the inserted part [3] BP *rigs*

koi sutanta-vakkhāṇa baïṭṭho[1] | [i][N 33b]ti | (10c)

[1] E_B *vaïṭṭī* E_{Sh} *boïṭhṭhe* N *vai* |||

| kha cig mdo sde 'chad par byed la zhugs | (10c)

kvacid bhikṣuḥ tattvavyākhyānaṃ karoti | pūrveṇāśrutatayāsau[1] punar narakādigamanaṃ karoti [dravyā]dilobhena ca |

[1] $E_B E_{Sh}$ *–tayā sa*

zhes gsungs te | dge slong kha cig rdzas ([1]la sreg[1]) pa'i dbang gis sngon ma mthong ba'i mdo sde la [B 127b] sogs pa'i de nyid 'chad pas[2] ni dmyal bar 'gro ba'o | [P 211b3[3]]

[1] DP *kyi srid* [2] DP *pa* [3] End of the misplaced portion

[E_B 85] kŏvi ([1]ciṇṭe kara sosaï[1]) diṭṭho | iti | (10d)

[1] E_{Sh} *cittem̐ kara sosaï* Npc *cittai kara sosaï* Nac *tai kara sosaï*. Unmetrical

| [P 203a3] la la bsam khral mang pos[1] bskams pa mthong | (10d)

[1] B *byas*

kvacid ([1]vai cintā[1]) sarvadharmāṇāṃ[2] kriyate[3] va[da]nti punaḥ ([4]kriyate sākṣād

dṛśyate | tenāpy ayuktaṃ kriyate | kvacit śramaṇādi |[4)] āgama[pu]stakākṣaravicintamānaḥ[5] tat śodhānaṃ[6] karoti | drakṣyan[7] tatpāṭhānavabodhād apāyagati[ṃ yā]syati | evaṃ vi[8]cintayāpi cittaśoṣaṃ[9] ca[10] karoti | te rogā babhūvuḥ |
[1] E_{B} *vai cittā* E_{Sh} *vaicitryaṃ* [2] E_{B}N *sarvadharmā* [3] E_{Sh} *karoti* [4] E_{B} om. [5] E_{Sh} *-cintena* N *-cintamāna* [6] E_{B}N *sādhanaṃ* [7] E_{Sh} *rakṣyaṃ* [8] E_{B} om. [9] N *cittaśoṣaṃñ* [10] E_{Sh} om.

zhes gsungs te | kha cig ma thos pa'i chos la blta[1] rtog mang po byed pa de'ang rigs pa ma yin no | | dge sbyong kha cig lung gi [(2]pu sti[2)] mang po bltas nas [(3]gtug byed de[3)] lung gi don mi shes pas sdig pa'i [(4]grogs por[4)] 'gro bar 'gyur ro | | de ltar bsam khral mang po byas pas[5] lus bskams te nad dang ldan par 'gyur ro |
[1] DP *lta* [2] P *po ti* [3] B *zhu gtugs byas te* D *zhu gtugs byed de* [4] DP *'gro bar* [5] D *pa las*

aṇṇata[1]hiṃ[2] [A recto begins] mahajāṇa hi[3] dhā[viu][4] | (11a)
[1] E_{Sh} missing from here up to the commentary on 16b (*nirddhandhaṃ yā-*) [2] E_{B}N *aṇṇau tahi* E_{Sh} *aṇṇau ta..* [3] A ||| *ānaha?* E_{B} *mahajāṇahiṃ* N *mahaāṇahiṃ* [4] A *dhāviuṃ* E_{B}N *dhā[vaï]*

[N 34 is missing]

| kha cig theg pa che la rgyug byed cing | (11a)

[(1]anyo bhikṣur yas tatra mahāyāne lagna tena mantramahāyānaṃ[2] yojayati | tam āha ||[1)]
[1] Missing in $E_{B}E_{Sh}$N [2] A *mantraṃ mahāyāna*

| zhes gsungs te | dge slong kha cig theg pa chen po'i don la 'jug cing | de nyid kyis[1] theg pa chen po la sbyor bar byed do |
[1] D *kyi*

[(1]maṇḍalacakkatĕ saala[2] vibhāviu iti[1)] | (11b)
[1] Missing in $E_{B}E_{Sh}$N [2] A *saṃmala* (missing in E_{B}N)

| gzhan dag dkyil 'khor 'khor lo ma lus bsgom[1] | (11b)
[1] DP *sgom*

[(1]etena mantramahāyānagarbhitam aśrutvā mahāyānamātreṇeti | etad[2] api narakādigamanaṃ karoti | anyac ca ||[1)]
[1] Missing in $E_{B}E_{Sh}$N [2] A .. *tad* (missing in E_{B}N)

| zhes gsungs te | 'dis ni theg pa chen po sngags[1] kyi nga rgyal la brten nas de'ang dmyal ba la sogs par 'gro ba'o | gzhan yang
[1] P *sngar* | *sa*

> [(1]koï vakkhāṇa[2] caüṭhṭhihi laggo iti |[1)] (11c)
> [1] Missing in $E_B E_{Sh}$N [2] A *vakkhana*

> | kha cig bzhi pa'i don 'chad pa la zhugs | (11c)

[(1]kvacid bhikṣuś caturthīha vaibhāṣika[2]sūtrāntikayogācāramadhyameṣu vyākhyānasya lagnas[3] tattvarahitatayā[4] vāgjālamātraṃ | athavā || kvacic caturthasya sahajopadeśavyākhyānasya lakṣaṇaṃ[5] tad api pustakagarbhadṛṣṭimātreṇātmanājñātvā | yadi vā jānāti tadā [(6]kiṃ vyākhyānaṃ[6)] karoti | evaṃ parasparavirodhena rau[7]ravādiṣu yānti |
[1] Missing in $E_B E_{Sh}$N [2] A *vebhāṣikra* [3] A *lagna* [4] A *rahitayā* [5] A *lakṣaṇa* [6] A *ki vyākhyāna* [7] A *ro-*; For all: missing in E_BN

[(1]zhes gsungs[1)] te | dge slong kha cig bzhi pa'i don 'chad pa ni bye brag tu[2] smra ba dang | mdo sde pa dang | rnal 'byor spyod pa pa[2] dang | dbu ma pa[1] la [(3]zhugs pa[3)] | de'ang tshig gi [D 185a] brjod pa mang po[1] tsam ste | de nyid med pa'i phyir don med do | yang na bzhi [(4]pa'i don[4)] ni lhan cig skyes pa ste | de'i man ngag 'chad pa la zhugs te | de'ang[5] [(6]pu sti[6)] la[2] bltas pa'i [P 203b] nga rgyal tsam gyis 'chad cing | rang gis[7] don ni mi shes so | | [(2]shes so[2)] zhe na'ang | de'i tshe bshad pas ci zhig bya ste | de ltar[8] na phan tshun [B 128a] 'gal ba spyod pas dmyal bar 'gro ba'o |
[1] P om. [2] BP om. [3] B *zhugs te* P *sogs pa* [4] BD *pa'i don* [5] D *de* [6] P *po ti* [7] BDP *gi* [8] B *lta*

> [(1]| koï ṇihālaṇĕ maggahi bhaggo iti |[1)] (11d)
> [1] Missing in $E_B E_{Sh}$N

> | kha cig dpyad cing bltas pas lam las nyams | (11d)

[(1]kvacid vicāra[2]pratibhāvite sati mārgasya vikṣepaṃ karoti | atyantanir[3] vikalpatvāt te 'pi karuṇārahitatayā kumārgeṣu patanti |[1)]
[1] Missing in $E_B E_{Sh}$N [2] A *vicārā-* [3] A *–ni-*

| zhes pa ni [(1]kha cig[1)] blta zhing dpyad pas rang gi 'dod [(2]pa'i sa lam[2)] las rnam par nyams te | lam ni rtog[3] dpyod[4] kyi yul las 'das pa'i phyir ro | | de'ang snying rje dang bral bas [(5]lam ngan pa[5)] rnams su lhung ngo |
[1] B om. [2] DP *pa* [3] B *brtag* [4] B *dpyad* [5] DP *mya ngan las 'das pa*

(1| la la nam mkha'i khams la rtog par byed |
| gzhan yang stong nyid (2lta bar2) ldan par byed pa de |
| phal cher mi mthun phyogs la zhugs pa yin |1)

[1] Missing in the *pañjikā* and the Apabhraṃśa root texts. Supplied from the Tibetan root text (D 2224, P 3068) [2] DP *ldan par*

(1kalpitabāhyāṅgasakte sati na[2] (?) punar api |||1)

[1] Missing in $E_B E_{Sh}$N [2] A *-śakte śati | na*

| ces gsungs te | la la dag gis[1] nam mkha'i khams la rtog cing dpyad pas rang gi 'dod pa mi 'grub ste | (2brtags pa'i2) phyi rol gyi yan lag can la mngon par zhen pa'o[3] |

[1] D *gi* [2] B *brtag pa* D *brtag pa'i* [3] DP *pas so*

(1sahaja cchaḍḍi[2] (3ṇivvāṇa jĕ3) dhāviü |1) (12a)

[1] Missing in $E_B E_{Sh}$N [2] A *cchantri* [3] A *ṇivvāṇaha*

| lhan cig skyes pa bor nas ni |
| mya ngan 'das pa gzhan la rgyug | (12a)

(1sahajāt[2] paraṃ nāsti muktiḥ nirvāṇādilakṣaṇā | tadaprajñātanāma[3]paryāyamātreṇānyaṃ nirvā1)[N 35a]ṇaṃ gamiṣyanti bhrāntāś[4] ca | tayā[5] bhrāntyā apāyagamanaṃ karoti[6] | tasmād bhrāntir nāma vikalpaḥ | [bhrānti][7]varjanād muktiḥ | evaṃ |

[1] Missing in $E_B E_{Sh}$N [2] A *sahājāt* [3] E_BN *sāpi* [4] A *bhrāṃtyā* E_BN *bhrāntyā* [5] AE_BN *tena* [6] A *ka .. ti* [7] A *tayā*

ces gsungs te | lhan cig skyes pa bor[1] nas mya ngan las 'das pa'i mtshan nyid gzhan med do | | de (2ni mi2) shes pas ming gi rnam grangs tsam gyi sgo nas 'khrul pa'i phyir gzhan gyi mya ngan las 'das pa la 'jug par 'gyur bas | de ltar 'khrul pas ngan 'gror 'gro bar 'gyur ro | | de'i phyir 'khrul pa ni rnam par rtog pa ste | de spangs pas grol ba'o | | de ltar |

[1] B *spangs* [2] DP *ma*

ṇaü paramattha ekka[1] tĕṃ sāhiu | iti | (12b)

[1] N *ekan*

| (1de dag1) don dam [2] gcig (3mi grub3) | (12b)

[1] B *des ni* [2] P inserts *pa* [3] B *kyang grub pa med* P *gcig gis mi 'grub*

tena[1] śramaṇādinā[2] yuktyā vicāryamāṇe[3]na śrāvakādiparamārtham ([4]ekaṃ na[4]) sādhitaṃ | niṣkevalaṃ[5] vratacaryādinā[6] jīvikāhetunā pravṛttir iti | tatra samudāyārtham āha |

[1] N *teṇa* [2] A *śramaṇādinādi* [3] N *–ne* [4] A *eka na* E_BN *ekaṃ* [5] A *–vala* [6] A *vrataca .. dinā*

| ces gsungs te | des ni dge sbyong[1] la sogs pa rnams kyis[2] rig pas dpyad bzhin[3] nyan thos la sogs pa'i mya ngan las 'das pa gcig kyang mi 'grub bo | | 'tsho ba'i ched du brtul zhugs dang spyod pa 'ba' zhig la zhugs pa'o | de la bsdus pa'i don ni |

[1] DP *ba* [2] B *kyi* D om. [3] DP *bzhin pa'i*

> jo jasu[1] jeṇa hŏia[2] saṃtuṭṭho[3] |
> mokkha ki labbhaï jhāṇa-[pa]viṭṭho[4] | iti | (13)
>
> [1] AE_B *joesu* [2] AE_B *hoi* [3] A *saṃṭuṭhṭho* [4] A *jjhāṇapaïṭṭho*

> | gang zhig gang la mos ([1]par gyur pa de[1]) |
> | theg pa der zhugs thar pa ([2]thob bam[2]) [B 128b] ci | (13)
>
> [1] P *pa des* [2] B *rnyed dam*

yo yena dṛṣṭena bhavati ([1]saṃtuṣṭas tasya[1]) mārgamātraṃ[2] śrāvakayānādi bhagavatā sanda[A verso]rśitaṃ[3] | [N 35b] na[4] tatra yāneṣu praviṣṭā mokṣaṃ labhanti[5] | vācyavācakalakṣaṇo [6] bhavatīti | yāvat ([7]sa[dgurvāradhanaṃ na] kriyate[7]) tāvad duṣprāpyam ity evaṃ tattvarahitatayā[8] tīrthikādinā[9] ca | ([10]samudāyam āha[10])

[1] A *satuṣṭasya* E_BN *saṃtuṣṭaṃ tasya* [2] A *-mātra* [3] A *sanda..taṃ* [4] E_BN om. [5] AE_B *labhante* [6] The *na* in E_BN must be deleted [7] E_B *sa ... kriyate* [8] E_BN *-rahitayā* [9] A *tīthikādinā* [10] AE_B *samudāyenāha*

| zhes gsungs te | gang dang gang mthong bas mos pa gang yin pa de ni nyan thos kyi theg pa'i lam tsam ste | de bcom ldan 'das kyis bstan te | theg[1] pa de la zhugs [P 204a] pa rnams kyis thar pa [2] mi 'thob ste | brjod bya rjod [D185b] byed kyi mtshan nyid can yin pa'i phyir ro | | ji srid du bla ma la bsnyen bkur ma byas pa de srid du rnyed par dka'o | zhes bya ba'i don do | de ltar phyi rol gyi[3] mu stegs pa la sogs pa de nyid dang bral ba thun mong[4] ba rnams la ston pa ni |

[1] B *thog* [2] BP insert *ni* [3] D om. [4] P *mongs*

> kin taha dīveṃ[1] kin taha ṇivĕjjeṃ[2] | ityādi | (14a)
>
> [1] A .. *veṃ* [2] A *ṇavijeṃ*

| mar mes [1] lha bshos des ci bya | (14a)
[1] B inserts *ci bya*

kiṃ darśanena kiṃ tannamaskāreṇa |

zhes gsungs te | ci zhig mthong ba dang phyag byas pas ci zhig bya zhes pa'o |

kin taha kijjaï[1] mantaha seveṃ | iti[2] | (14b)
[1] N *ki* ||| *i* [2] AE$_B$N om.

| sngags kyi bzlas brjod [1] ci zhig bya | (14b)
[1] BD insert *kyis ni*

kiṃ tena kartavyaṃ[1] mantrasevanayā | athavā | kiṃ[2] pradīpena kiṃ naivedyena[3] | [jñā]narahitatayā na kiñcit kāryam[4] asti | tathā |
[1] A *kattavya* [2] A *kiṃ te* [3] A *naidyena* [4] A *kā .. m*

zhes gsungs te | de nyid dang bral ba'i mar me dang | lha bshos dang | sngags [1]bzla ba[1] la sogs pas ci zhig[2] bya ste | dgos pa cung zad kyang[2] med do | | zhes dgongs pa'o[3] |
[1] DP *bzlas pa* [2] DP om. [3] DP *so*

| gsang sngags bsten[1] pa de ci dgos | (not counted as *pratīka* line)
[1] DB *bstan*

| zhes pa ni sngags bsten[1] pa ste | sngags kyi bzlas pas ci zhig[2] bya zhes pa'o | yang na ye shes kyi[3] de nyid dang bral ba'i mar me dang lha bshos kyis ni dgos pa cung zad kyang med do zhes pa'o | de ltar yang
[1] B *bstan* P *brten* [2] P om. [3] D *kyis*

[E$_B$ 86] kin taha[1] tittha tapovaṇa jāi[2] | iti[3] | (14c)
[1] N *kittaha* [2] A *jā* [3] N *it*

| bab stegs 'gro dang dka' thub dang |
| nags la 'gro bas ci zhig bya | (14c[1])
[1] Based on the Apabhraṃśa the two lines are counted as one *rkang pa*.

kiṃ tatra[1] [(2]tīrtha[ṃ vārāṇa][N 36a]syādi[2)] kiṃ tena [(3]tapovanagamanena[3)] |
[1] A could be *tat* [2] A *tīrtha vārānasyādi* [3] E$_B$N *tapovane gamanayā*

| zhes gsungs te | 'bab stegs ni vārāṇasī[1] la sogs pa dang | nags su 'gro ba la sogs pas ci zhig bya zhes pa'o |

[1] B *vāraṇāsī* P *vāraṇasi*

mokkha ki labbhaï[1] pāṇi-ṇahāi[2] | iti | (14d)

[1] A *labbaï* [2] A *pāṇihi nāī* E_BN *pāṇī hnāi*

| chu yis[1] khrus byas tsam gyis ni |
| thar pa rnyed par 'gyur ram ci | (14d[2])

[1] DP *la* [2] Based on the Apabhraṃśa the two lines are counted as one *rkang pa*.

anenoktena tīrthāśraye[1] pānīyasnānapavitreṇa ([2]kiṃ mokṣo[2]) labhyate | na labhyata iti yāvat[3] |

[1] A *tīrthyāśrayeṇa* E_B *–āśrayena* N *–āśra..* [2] A *ki mokṣaṃ* N *ki mokkho* [3] A *yāt*

| zhes gsungs te | 'dis ni khrus stegs[1] la [B 129a] brten nas chus[2] khrus byas pas thar pa ci la thob ste | mi thob ces pa'o |

[1] B *stegs gang* [2] DP *chu la*

cchaḍḍahu re ālīā[1] bandhā | iti[2] | (15a)

[1] A *alīā* E_BE_{Sh}N *ālīkā* [2] A om.

| ([1]kye hoḥ[1]) brdzun[2] zhing log pa de bor la | (15a)

[1] DP *kyi ho* [2] B *rdzun*

he[1] puruṣā mithyābandhanaṃ kukalyāṇamitroktaṃ tīrthādikaṃ[2] tyajatha[3] |

[1] E_B *heya-* [2] A *kukalyāṇamitroktatīrthyāditvaṃ* E_B *kalyāṇamitroktaṃ tīrthādikaṃ* N *kalyāṇamitroktaṃ tīrthyādikaṃ* [3] E_B *tyajata*

| zhes gsungs te | kye skyes bu rnams brdzun[1] pa'i 'ching ba log pa'i bshes gnyen gyis smras pa'i khrus kyi[2] stegs la sogs pa 'di thong zhes pa'o |

[1] B *rdzun* [2] DP om.

yena narakādiṃ yāsyantu[1] | lokāyatamatādinā[2] ca | nāsti dattaṃ nāsti hutaṃ[3] na santi śramaṇā ([4]nāsti brāhmaṇaḥ[4]) | nāsti [pa]ralokaḥ |

[1] E_B *yāsyatha* [2] E_B *–dīnāñ ca* N *–dināc ca* [3] A *hṛtaṃ* [4] A om. (This makes it the first half of an āryā.)

| 'jig rten rgyang 'phen[1] la sogs pa'i 'dod pas dmyal ba la sogs par 'gro ba gang yin pa 'di'ang[2] thong zhes pa'o | sbyin pa med do | | sbyin sreg med do | | dge sbyong med do | [P 204b] | bram ze med do | | 'jig rten pha rol med do |
[1] DP *phan* [2] DP *'di*

> yāvaj jīvet sukhaṃ jīvet ([1]nāsti mṛtyor[1]) agocaraḥ |
> bhasmībhūtasya dehasya punarā[ga]manaṃ[2] [ku][N 36b]taḥ[3] ||
> iti |
> [1] A *nāsti mṛtyur* $E_{B}E_{Sh}$N *tāvat mṛtyor* [2] A *-mana* [3] A *ku* ||| *ti*

ucchedadṛṣṭinā[1] ca |
[1] E_{B}N *-dṛṣṭitvāc*

> | ma shi bar du bde bar 'tsho |
> | shi nas ([1]de yi[1]) spyod yul med |
> | lus kyang thal ba bzhin song nas |
> | slar 'tsho ba lta ga la yod |
> [1] BDP *de'i*

| ces bya ba la sogs pa spang bar bya ba nyid yin te | chad par lta ba yin pa'i phyir ro |

athavā sā[ṃ]khyā[1] vadanti |
[1] A *sākhyā* E_{B} *sāṃkhyā[ḥ]*

> sāṃkhyāḥ pradhānam icchanti nityaṃ lokasya kāraṇam | BCA IX.126cd

ityādinā[1] śāśvataḥ | tena kiṃ kriyate na kalyāṇam iti cet |
[1] AE$_{B}$ *kāraṇetyādinā* N *kāra* ||| *tyādinā*

| yang [D 186a] grangs can pa rnams na re |

> | rtag tu 'gro ba rnams kyi rgyu |
> | grangs can gtso bo yin par 'dod | BCA IX.126cd

| ces bya ba la sogs pas[1] rtag[2] par khas len to[3] | | ([4]de yis dge ba ci yi phyir[4]) mi byed ce na |
[1] DP *pa* [2] P *brtag* [3] DP *no* [4] B *de ci'i phyir dge ba* D *de'i dge ba ci'i phyir*

so muṃccahu[1] jo acchahu dhandhā | iti[2] | (15b)
[1] $E_B E_{Sh}$N *muñcahu* [2] $E_B E_{Sh}$N *ityādi*

| gang gis 'ching bar [(1]byed pa[1)] thong | (15b)
[1] B *gyur pa de yang*

samudāyārthena[1] viśiṣṭacaryāṃ sūcayann āha[2] | sanmārgeṣv[3] adhimokṣaṃ kuru | yena kṛte sati [(4]svārthaṃ parārthaṃ ca karoti[4)] | ayuktamārgaṃ muñca[5] tyaja | yena dhandhatāyāṃ sthitiṃ[6] na kariṣyasi | su[7]mārgeṇa nirdhandhaṃ[8] yā[9]syasi | sahajam eveti nānyat[10] | evaṃ
[1] A ||| *na* [2] A *ā ..* [3] A *sanmāgeṣ ..* E_B *sanmārgeṣu* [4] A *svārthaṃ parārthaṃ karoti* E_BN *svārthaṃ kariṣyasi* [5] E_BN *muñcasi* [6] A om. E_BN *sthitir* [7] E_B *san-* [8] A *nirddharddhaṃ* [9] A ends; from here available in E_{Sh} [10] E_BN *nānyaḥ*

| zhes gsungs te [(1]| rigs pa ma yin pa'i lam bor cig | gang gis rang gi blo rmongs par gnas pa de thong zhig ces pa'o |[1)] | mdor bsdus na[2] khyad par can gyi lam ston te | dam pa'i lam[3] la mos par gyis dang | de la mos par byas pa gang gis rang gi don dang gzhan gyi don 'grub pa'o[4] | | [(4]de la[4)] log pa'i lam gnyis[5] dang bral nas lhan cig skyes pa de[5] [B 129b] nyid rnyed par 'gyur te | | gzhan gyis ni ma yin no |
[1] DP: this passage is two lines further down between *'grub pa'o* | and | *de la log*
[2] BD *nas* [3] P *chos* [4] DP *po* [4] D *des* [5] DP om.

tasu pariāṇeṃ aṇṇa ṇa koi | iti | (15c)

| de nyid yongs su shes na gzhan med de | (15c)

[tasya sa][N 37a]hajasya parijñāne 'nyaṃ mokṣaṃ na kiñcid asti |

| zhes bya ba ni | de nyid [1] lhan cig skyes [(2]pa ste[2)] | de yongs su shes na gzhan du[3] [4] thar pa [5] cung zad kyang med do zhes pa'o |
[1] B inserts *ni* [2] DP *pa'i ye shes te* [3] DP *yang* [4] B inserts *ni* [5] BP insert *ni*

avareṃ[1] gaṇṇeṃ[2] [(3]savva vi[3)] soi | iti[1] | (15d)
[1] E_{Sh} *avare* [2] E_{Sh} *aṇe* [3] E_{Sh} *sajjaï* [4] E_B om.

| gzhan gyis[1] rnam pa kun kyang 'di nyid[2] yin te | (15d)
[1] DP *gyi* [2] BD om.

anyair sarvair mokṣa[2][samūhaṃ ya]t parikalpitaṃ pṛthak pṛthak tat [(3]sarvaṃ sahajam eveti[3)] nānyat | kiṃ tu[4] tat sahajam[5] [(6]ajānānāś ca[6)] [bhramanti

saṃ]sāre ghaṭīyantravat | sa ca (7sadgurūpāsite7)nopalabhyate | tatra sahaje vācyavāca(8kau na la8)bhyete |
2 N *moha-* 3 N *sarvasahajeti* 4 E_B om. E_{Sh} *tat* 5 E_{Sh} *sahaja* 6 E_{Sh} *ajānanto* 7 E_BE_{Sh} *sadguruparyupaśrite-* 8 N *–nādi ..*

1zhes gsungs te1 | gzhan thams cad kyi2 thar pa'i tshogs gang yin par brtags3 pa de kun kyang lhan cig skyes pa 4 'di nyid yin pas gzhan du5 med do | | de ltar6 yin na7 lhan cig skyes pa ni8 brjod bya dang9 brjod byed9 kyi10 'brel ba'i sgo nas mi rnyed do11 |
1 P om. 2 B *kyis* 3 B *brtag* D *rtag* 4 D inserts *ni* 5 D *na* P *ni* 6 DP *lta* 7 B *na'ang* 8 DP om. 9 P om. 10 B om. 11 B *de*

[E_B 87] vācyavācaka(1sambandhān na vidyet sahajaṃ triṣu1) |
deśanāpadayogena khyāpi[taṃ2 bhagava]tā3 kvacit ||
1 E_{Sh} *-sambandhā na santi sahaje trayaḥ* E_B *-sambandhāt na vidyet sahajas triṣu* 2 E_B *sthāpitaṃ* 3 E_{Sh} *bhagavān*. The last *pāda* is unmetrical.

| brjod bya rjod byed 'brel ba ste |
| gsum gyis1 lhan cig skyes mi rnyed |
| bstan pa'i tshig gi2 sbyor ba yis3 |
| bcom ldan 'das kyis cung zad gsungs |
1 P *gyi* 2 B *gis* 3 B *yin*

[E_{Sh} 91] pustake dṛśyamāne1 ca sattvārthāya na saṃvidāt2 |
(3yad yad drakṣyati vastuś ca3) bhrāntirū[pādi]kalpanā |
1 N *dṛṣṭamāne* 2 E_{Sh} *saṃvidhāt* 3 E_{Sh} *yad drakṣyati vastusaṃjñā*

| glegs bam mthong ba tsam gyis ni1 |
| sems can rnams kyis mi rtogs phyir |
| gang dang gang gis dngos mthong ba |
| rang bzhin 'khrul zhing rtog2 pa ste |
1 DP *te* 2 DP *rtogs*

tat tad vastu na dṛśyeta abhrā[N 37b]ntaṃ guruparvayā || iti |

| [P 205a] de dang de yi1 dngos mi mthong |
| 'khrul med bla ma brgyud pas so | de'i phyir |
1 BD *yis*

tasmāt |

| de'i phyir |

sovi paḍhijjaï[1] ... | ityādi | (16a)
[1] E_{Sh} *patrija* N *paḍijjaï*

| klog pa de yin ... | (16a)

pāṭhasvādhyāyādi yat kiṃci[l][1] lokottaraṃ[2] sahajamayaṃ yāti[2] | na kevalaṃ lokottaraṃ laukikam[3] apy āha
[1] E_{Sh} *kiñcit kriyate* [2] E_B *śāstrapurāṇādi* N .. *kottaraṃ* [2] E_BN *yāti* [3] N *lokikaṃ*

zhes bya ba la sogs pa gsungs te | klog pa dang 'don pa cung zad ci byed pa thams cad 'jig rten las 'das pa'i lhan cig skyes pa'i ngo bo nyid yin no | | 'jig rten las 'das pa 'ba' zhig ni ma yin te | 'jig rten pa'i yang |

sattha[1]-purāṇeṃ[2] [vakkhāṇijjaï] | iti | (16b)
[1] E_{Sh} *gaccha* [2] E_{Sh} *purāṇe*

| bstan bcos rnying pa 'chad pa'ang de yin no | (16b)

yat kiṃcit śāstrapurāṇādivyākhyānaṃ kriyate tat sarvaṃ sahajasyaiva nānyasya | tad āha |

zhes gsungs te | gang cung [D 186b] zad bstan bcos rnying pa la sogs pa 'chad pa [1] de [2] thams cad lhan cig skyes pa nyid yin te | gzhan ni ([3]ma yin no[3]) | yang |
[1] B inserts *la sogs pa* [2] B inserts *dag* [3] B *med do*

ṇāhi sŏ diṭhṭhi jŏ tāu ṇa lakkhaï | iti | (16c)

| de lta [B 130a] bu yi lta bas[1] ni |
| mtshon par nus pa yod min te | (16c)
[1] BP *ba*

evaṃ sahaja uktakramād yāvat puruṣair[1] na la[kṣitas[2] tāva]t tena mokṣaṃ na dṛṣṭaṃ | yena kleśakṣayaṃ tatkṣaṇāt karoti | kathaṃ dṛśyetety[3] āha |
[1] E_{Sh} *puruṣe[ṇa]* [2] $E_B E_{Sh}$ *-aṃ* [3] E_{Sh}N *dṛśyatety*

| zhes [(1]gsungs te[1)] | de ltar lhan cig skyes pa[2] bstan pa'i rim pas ji srid du skyes bus[3] lam ma mtshon na de srid du thar pa mi 'thob ste | gang gis[4] de'i dus de[5] nyid du nyon mongs pa zad par byed pa'o[6] | de ji ltar rtogs she na |
[1] DP *pa ni* [2] B *par* [3] P *bu* [4] BDP *gi* [5] P om. [6] B *yin no*

ekkeṃ vara ... | ityādi | (16d)

| 'on kyang gcig tu zhes bya ba la sogs pa (16d)

[eke][N 38a]na[1] niḥkevalena varapravaragurupādāpekṣitena labhyate[2] | evaṃ spa[3]ṣṭārtham āha |
[1] $E_B E_{Sh}$ *etena* [2] E_BN *lakṣyate* [3] N *pra-*

gsungs te | 'di ni bla ma mchog gi zhabs la gus pas rnyed do | | de gsal bar bya ba'i don du |

jaï guru-vuttaü[1] hi[aa]hi[2] païsaï | iti | (17a)
[1] E_{Sh} *buttavo* [2] $E_B E_{Sh}$N *hi[a]ï*

| gal te bla mas gsungs pa ni |
| gang gi snying la bzhugs pa na[1] | (17a)
[1] DP *ni*

yad gurū[1]ktamārgaṃ hṛdayagataṃ bhavati | tadā
[1] N *guro-*

| zhes gsungs te | gal te bla mas gsungs pa'i lam snying la bzhugs shing rtogs pa de'i tshe[1] |
[1] D *phyir*

[E_B 88] ṇiccia hatthеṃ[1] ṭhāvia[2] dīsaï[3] | iti[4] | (17b)
[1] E_B *itthe* E_{Sh} *hakha-* N *hatteṃ* [2] $E_B E_{Sh}$N *ṭhavia* [3] E_{Sh}N *udīsaï*
[4] $E_B E_{Sh}$ om.

| lag pa'i mthil du bzhag pa'i gter mthong [1] [(2]'dra ba'o[2)] | (17b)
[1] DP insert *ba* [2] B *'dra*

yathā kvacit puruṣena cintāmaṇiḥ[1] prāpyate | tadā niścitaṃ taduddeśena[2] dānādi kriyate | tenehāpi sahajasvarūpe prāpte sati cintāmaṇivat sarvasattvān tanmayaṃ karoti | sarvasvaṃ[3] draviṇādi tyājyaṃ karoti | ([4]īdṛśaṃ mārgam a[4])jānanāt | granthakāraḥ sarahetyādinā[5] paridevanāṃ [karo][N 38b]ti |

[1] N *maṇiṃ* [2] E_{Sh} *taddudeśe* [3] N *sa* ||| *vā* [4] E_{Sh} *īdṛśasya mārgasyā-* [5] E_{B} *Saraha ityādinā*

| zhes gsungs te | ji ltar skyes bu kha cig gis yid bzhin gyi nor bu rnyed na | de'i tshe de'i stobs kyis nges par sbyin pa la sogs pa byed do | | de bzhin du 'dir yang lhan cig skyes pa'i ngo bo nyid thob na yid bzhin gyi nor bu ([1]lta bu[1]) sems can thams cad lhan cig skyes pa'i ngo bo nyid du byed pa dang | nor la sogs pa'i dngos po thams cad yongs su gtong bar byed do | | 'di lta bu'i lam mi shes pas gzhung mkhan po mda' bsnun na re | 'di skad smra zhes mi shes pa'i yul la yid gdung bar byed pa'o |

[1] BDP *yin pas*

[1] jaga vāhia āleṃ[2] | iti | (17c)

[1] According to the commentary the line should start with *Saraha bhaṇaï* [2] E_{Sh}N *ālem*

[P 205b] | 'gro ba rnams ni 'khrul pas bslus | (17c)

sarvaṃ[1] jagad ālena mithyayā[2] tīrthikādinā vāhitam[3] iti |

[1] E_{B} *sarva* [2] $E_{B}E_{Sh}$ om. N *mithyā* [3] N *vāhita*

| zhes pa ni 'gro ba thams cad 'khrul pa ste | mu stegs pa'i lam la sogs pas bslus pa'o |

ṇiasahā[va] ṇa[1] lakkhiu[2] bāleṃ[3] | iti | (17d)

[1] $E_{Sh}E_{B}$N *ṇaü* [2] E_{Sh} *laïu* [3] E_{Sh}N *bālem*

| gnyug ma yi yang rang [B 130b] bzhin ni |
| byis pa rnams kyis ma mtshon no | | (17d)

tair bālajātīyair nijasvarūpaṃ sahajasvabhāvam[1] idaṃ na lakṣitaṃ | na ca[2] [sad]gurava ārādhitāḥ | tadā te[3] ṣaḍgati[4]duḥkham anubhavanti | etad eva na kevalaṃ tīrthikasya śramaṇasyāpy[5] āha

[1] E_{B} *sahajasvabhāvam* [2] $E_{B}E_{Sh}$N om. [3] N om. [4] $E_{B}E_{Sh}$N *ṣaḍgatyādi* [5] E_{B} *śramaneṣu* N *śramāneṣv-*

zhes bya ba ni byis pa'i skye bo rnams kyis gnyug ma'i rang bzhin lhan cig skyes pa ma mtshon pa ni bla ma dam pa mnyes par ma byas pas so | | de'i phyir de rnams 'gro ba rigs drug gi sdug bsngal nyams su myong par 'gyur ro | skyon 'di rnams ni mu stegs pa 'ba' zhig gi ni[1] ma yin gyi | dge sbyong la'ang yod pa yin par bstan pa'i phyir | [D 187a]

[1] P om.

jhā[1]ṇa-hīṇa pavvajeṃ[2] rahiaü | iti | (18a)

[1] E_{Sh} *mā-* [2] E_{Sh} *-jje*

| bsam gtan med cing rab tu[1] byung ba'ang[2] med | (18a)

[1] P om. [2] BP om.

yadā tena śramaṇena samyagjñānahīnena [(1]pravrajyā gṛhītā[1)] vinayādilakṣaṇaṃ śikṣārakṣaṇaṃ kṛtaṃ vā teṣāṃ phalaṃ na [bhava][N 39a]ti | kuta āha |

[1] $E_B E_{Sh}$ *pravrajyāgṛhīta-*

| ces gsungs te | gang gi tshe yang dag pa'i ye shes dang bral ba'i dge sbyong des rab tu byung ba blangs te | 'dul ba las byung ba'i mtshan nyid kyi bslab pa la bslabs[1] kyang de rnams la 'bras bu med do | de ci'i phyir zhe na |

[1] DP *slob*

gharahi vasante[1] bhajjeṃ[2] sahiaü | iti[3] | (18b)

[1] E_BN *vasanteṃ* [2] E_BN *bhajje* E_{Sh} *tajje* [3] E_BN om.

| khyim na gnas shing[1] chung ma [2] dang [3] lhan[4] cig tu | (18b)

[1] DP *pa'i* [2] DP insert *dag* [3] B inserts *ni* [4] B *ldan* (hypermetrical)

yadā gṛhārambhādy āśrayaṇaṃ[1] karoti tadā vratabhaṅga[s te]na sarvaṃ[2] caryādīnāṃ[3] bhaṅgaḥ | ekapratijñābhaṅgena[4] sarveṣāṃ bhaṅgaḥ | yathā ekena puruṣeṇa viṣabhakṣaṇena sarveṣu jantuṣu[5] [E_{Sh} 92] bhayam[6] jāyate | [(7]tac ca[7)] eke mriyamāṇe[8] sarveṣāṃ na bhakṣite 'pi viṣamaraṇabhayaṃ jāyate | tadā yat kiṃcid [E_B 89] bhakṣitavyaṃ[9] tat sarvaṃ suparīkṣitena bhakṣaṇaṃ karoti | viṣatattvaṃ vābhyasyati[10] | tac cādāv[11] eva [(12]suniścitaṃ tena[12)] no cet bhaṅgaṃ[13] jāyate | evaṃ yat kiṃcid vratacaryādi gṛhyate [ta][N 39b]t sarvaṃ dṛḍhapratijñāyeti | tasya ca |

[1] $E_B E_{Sh}$ *āśramaṃ na* [2] E_B *sarvaṃ ca* E_{Sh} *sarva-* [3] E_{Sh} *–nāñ ca* [4] E_B *–gena ca* [5] N *jantu* [6] $E_B E_{Sh}$ *bhaṅgaṃ* N *bhaṅgaṃ* [7] E_{Sh} *tasminn* [8] N *-ne* [9] $E_B E_{Sh}$ *bhakṣitaṃ* N *bhakṣite* [10] N *cābhyasyante* [11] N *cāv* [12] $E_B E_{Sh}$ *suniścitatayā* N *suniścitaṃ tayā* [13] $E_B E_{Sh}$ *bhaṅgaḥ*

| zhes gsungs te | gang gi tshe khyim la sogs pa la brten par gyur pa de'i tshe

spyod lam phun sum tshogs pa nyams pas tshul khrims nyams te[1] | dam bcas pa gcig nyams pas[2] thams cad nyams par 'gyur ro | | ji ltar skyes bu gcig gis dug zos nas zhi[3] ba mthong ba las skyes bu gzhan[4] kun kyang dug la 'jigs pa [(5]skye ste[5)] | de'i tshe gang cung zad bza'[6] ba[7] legs par brtags te za bar byed pa'am | dug gi de nyid la bslab par bya'o | | de'i phyir dang po nyid nas legs par dpyad cing brtags par[8] bya'o | de ltar ma byas na[4] nyams par 'gyur ro | | de ltar gang cung zad spyod lam dang bka' thub la sogs pa[9] blangs [B 131a] pa de [10] thams cad dam bcas pa brtan po'i sgo nas bsrung bar bya'o |

[1] DP *pa dang* [2] B *na* [3] B *'chi* [4] P om. [5] B *skyes te* [6] D om. P *zas* [7] DP om. [8] B *la* [9] P *pas* [10] B inserts *dag*

jaï bhiḍi visaa[1] ramanta ṇa muccaï | iti | (18c)

[1] E_{Sh} *viṣaa*

| [(1]gang zhig 'dod[1)] pa'i yon tan rnams |
| spyod pa yis kyang ma grol na | (18c)

[1] D *yang gang zhig* | | *'dod* P *yang* | *gang zhig 'dod*

yadi sudṛḍha[1]viṣayasevāratiṃ na tyajati | tadā granthakāreṇa |

[1] E_B *ca dṛḍha-* E_{Sh} *dṛḍha-*

| zhes gsungs te | gal te legs [P 206a] [(1]par brtan pas yul bsten[1)] pa'i dga' ba mi gtong na | de'i tshe mda' bsnun na re de nyid ni

[1] B *par dpyod cing brtags pas yul bsten* D *shing brtan pas yul brten* P *shing brtan pas yul bden*

pariāṇa ki vuccaï[1] | iti | (18d)

[1] E_BN *muccaï* E_{Sh} *uccaï*

| yongs su shes pas min zhes[1] smra | (18d)

[1] BDP *shes*

tadānyaparijñānena kim uktena | kṣaṇikasukhātyāgāt yena duḥkham anubhavanti | atha viṣayasevāpañcakāmādinā na mucyante sati parijñāne | tadānyaśuṣka[1]parijñāne[2] vācye ukte kin | na [(3]mucyanta iti[3)] yāvat |

[1] E_B *–anye śuṣka-* E_{Sh} *–anyena sustha-* [2] E_{Sh} *-nena* [3] E_B *mucyate iti* E_{Sh} *mucya iti* N *mucyateti*

| zhes gsungs te | de'i tshe gzhan yongs su brjod pa la dgos pa ci yod de | skad cig ma'i bde ba ma spangs pa'i phyir gang gis sdug bsngal nyams su myong ba

nyid du byed pa'o | | yang na yul gyi bde ba 'dod pa'i yon tan lnga la de nyid shes pas longs spyod kyang grol bar mi 'gyur na de'i tshe [(1]gzhan yongs su brjod pa la[2] dgos pa ci yod de | skad cig[1)] ye shes skam po brjod [(3]pa des[3)] grol lam ste | mi grol lo zhes bya ba'i don no[4] |

[1] P om. [2] D *las* [3] DP *pas* [4] DP *to*

[ja]ï paccakkha [(1]ki jhāṇeṃ kijjaï[1)] |
aha[2] parokkha [(3]andhāra mavijjaï[3)] | iti[4] | (19ab)

[1] E_BN *kīaa* E_{Sh} *khāṇe ki kīya* [2] E_B*jaï* (em. based on G) [3] E_BN *andhāra dhīaa* E_{Sh} *muttvā rama vīaa* (em. based on G) [4] E_BN om. Metrical problem in *pāda* b

| gal te mngon sum[1] du gyur [2] na |
| bsam gtan gyis ni ci zhig bya |
| gal te lkog tu gyur na yang |
| mun pa yis ni bkol ba'o | (19ab)

[1] DP om. [2] P inserts *pa*

yadi pratyakṣaṃ tadā dhyānena[1] ki[ṃ kriya][N 40a]te | yadā idaṃ parokṣaṃ na dṛṣṭam andhakāramadhye kiṃ dṛśyate | anena kim uktaṃ syāt | sarvāṇi pravrajyā[dīni] vratāni kiṃ kriyante | andhakāramadhye ca paraloka[2]phalam adṛṣṭatvāt | anumānahetunā ca [kiṃ ta]t pratyakṣaṃ jñānam āha |

[1] E_{Sh}*jñānena* [2] N *paraloke*

zhes gsungs te | gal te [D 187b] mngon sum du gyur na de'i tshe bsam gtan gyis[1] ci bya | gal te lkog tu gyur nas[2] ma mthong na mun pa 'jal ba dang 'dra ste[3] | ci'ang mthong bar mi 'gyur ro | 'dis ci bstan zhe na | brtul zhugs la[4] rab tu byung ba la sogs pa brtul zhugs ma lus pa ci'i phyir byed de | mun pa nang 'jal ba dang 'dra bar 'jig rten pha rol [B 131b] gyi[5] 'bras bu ma mthong ba'i phyir ro | | mngon sum gyi shes pa de ji lta bu yin zhe na |

[1] P *gyi* [2] DP *pas* [3] DP *pas* [4] B *las* [5] B *pa'i*

[(1]sarahetyādi[1)] |

[1] E_B *sarahem̩ ityādi*

kaḍhḍhiaü[1] rāva ... | (19c)

[1] E_{Sh} *kaḍhiu*

| mda' bsnun ngas[1] ni [2] bos [(3]nas smra[3)] | (19c)

[1] B *nga* [2] B inserts *'di skad* [3] DP *pa yin*

guptaṃ na kṛtaṃ sarvalokeṣu mayātivyakt[e]na mahānādoccāritam | kiṃ tat |

| zhes gsungs te | gsang[1] nas smras[2] pa ni ma yin te | sems can thams cad la skad chen pos gsal por bdag gis[3] de nyid bstan pa'o | | de'ang gang yin zhe na |
[1] P *bsangs* [2] DP *bzlas* [3] P *gi*

sahaja-sahāva ṇa bhāvābhāva | iti | (19d)

| lhan cig skyes pa'i rang bzhin ni |
| dngos dang dngos med ma yin no | (19d)

atra bhāvaś cakṣurādyālokitaṃ[1] yad vastu manaḥparikalpanayā ca | ([2]tat kutaḥ[2]) | yataḥ sarvaṃ[3] sahajasvabhāvena vastuviśvam utpādi[taṃ] | [N 40b] tad evaṃbhūtaparikalpanayā mucyate | tathā coktam |
[1] E_{B} *-ādyālokena* E_{Sh} *–ādi | lokena* N *–ādyālokanaṃ* [2] $E_{B}E_{Sh}$N *tatra kutaḥ* [3] N *sarva*

| [1]zhes gsungs te[1] | 'dir dngos po ni mig la sogs pa la snang ba'i dngos po gang yin pa dang | yid kyis brtags[2] pa'i dngos po rnams so | | gang gi phyir de dag thams cad lhan cig skyes pa'i ngo bo nyid sna tshogs su skyes pa'o | | zhes de ltar rtog par byed na | de'ang grol bar mi [P 206b] 'gyur ro | de bas na so so rang gis rig par bya ba yin pas dngos po med pa ma yin no | de ltar yang |
[1] DP om. [2] D *brtag*

[E_{B} 90] nāpaneyam ataḥ[1] kiṃcit prakṣeptavyaṃ[2] na kiṃcana |
draṣṭavya[ṃ bhū]tato bhūtaṃ bhūtadarśī vimucyate || iti |
[1] E_{Sh} *yat* [2] N *prakṣeptaṃ*

| 'di las[1] bsal bya ci yang med |
| bsnan[2] par bya ba[3] cung zad med |
| yang dag nyid la yang dag blta[4] |
| yang dag mthong na[5] rnam par grol | (RGV I.154?)
[1] BDP *la* [2] DP *gzhag* [3] B *ba'ang* [4] DP *lta* [5] P *nas*

tat kathaṃ | yuktim[1] āha | ([2]idaṃ tad dvipadāḥ[2]) sukhenotpannā[ḥ] | sukham icchantaś[3] ca mātṛ[4]pitṛsaṃyogāj jāyante[5] | tatpratyātmavedyatayā nābhāvaḥ[6] | kutaḥ | tanmayatvenāvācyatvāt[7] | saiva maraṇāntikaṃ sukham iti bhāvaḥ | ata eva
[1] E_{B} *yukti* E_{Sh}N *yuktir* [2] E_{Sh} *tadā tad vipadādayaḥ* [3] N *icchantā* [4] E_{Sh} *mātā-* [5] N *jāyate* [6] E_{Sh} *na bhāvaḥ* [7] E_{B} *–tvāt ca* N *-tvāc ca*

| zhes gsungs so | de ji ltar zhe na | rig pa[1] bstan par bya ste | 'dir [2] rkang gnyis la sogs pa bde ba las skyes shing | bde ba 'dod pa'i pha dang ma'i sbyor ba las skye bar 'gyur ro | ma rtogs pa de cis lan zhe na | de'i phyir so so rang gis rig par bya ba yin pas dngos med[3] min[4] no | de ci'i phyir zhe na | de'i rang bzhin brjod [B 132a] du med pa'i phyir 'chi ba'i mtha'i[5] bde ba zhes ([6]bstan te[6]) | de nyid kyi phyir |

[1] B *par* [2] B inserts *yang* [3] D *med pa* [4] DP *ma yin* [5] B *mthar gyi* [6] P *ston to*

jallaï maraï [uva]jjaï ([1]vajjhaï |
tallaï[1]) parama-mahāsuha sijjhaï | iti | (20ab)

[1] E_{Sh} om.

| gang la brten te 'chi ba dang |
| skye dang gnas dang 'ching 'gyur ba |
| de la brten nas mchog gi ni |
| bde ba chen po mchog 'grub bo | (20ab)

yena sukhena mriyante tenaivotpadyante | [utpa][N 41a]nnāś ca tasminn eva badhyante | prākṛtasukha[1]kalpanayā ca | sa ca tenaiva samyaggurūpadeśaṃ[2] parijñāya gṛhītvā paramamahā[sukhaṃ] sidhyatīti bhāvaḥ | evaṃ *Saraha* ityādi[3] subodham | asya pratinirdeśam āha

[1] N om. *–sukha-* [2] E_B *samyakguruṃ* [3] I.e., *Saraha bhaṇaï haüṃ pukkarami pasuloa ṇa jāṇaï ki kkarami* (according to G) (= 20cd)

| zhes gsungs te | bde ba gang gis 'chi[1] bar 'gyur ba de nyid kyis skyes nas gnas shing 'ching ste | de nyid [D 188a] phal pa'i bde ba la chags pa'i phyir ro | | de nyid kyang yang dag pa'i bla ma'i[2] brgyud pas[3] blangs na[4] mchog gi bde ba chen po ([5]'grub bo[5]) zhes bya ba'i don no[6] | skad gsong[7] zhes bya ba la sogs pa ni go sla ba'o | | de so sor bshad pa ni |

[1] BDP *'ching* [2] B *ba* [3] B *pa las* [4] D *nas* [5] D om. [6] DP *to* [7] DP *gsang*

[E_{Sh} 93] jhāṇa-rahia ki kīaï jhāṇeṃ[1] |
jŏ avāa[2] tahiṃ[3] kāhi[4] vakhāṇeṃ[5] | iti | (21ab)

[1] E_{Sh} *jhāṇe* [2] E_{Sh} *avāca* [3] N *tahi* [4] E_{Sh} *kāi* [5] E_{Sh} *vakkhyānem*

| bsam gtan dag dang bral bas na |
| bsam gtan gyis ni ci zhig bya |
| rnal 'byor lung gang brjod du med |
| de la ji ltar bshad du yod | (21ab)

atra prathamaṃ tāvaj[1] jñānaṃ vācyavācaka[la]kṣaṇādirahitaṃ | tat kim idam | sahajaṃ jñānam | kalpitatayā kiṃ kriyate | heturahitatvena phalavyavasthā nāsti | yasmād[2] yad avācyaṃ tatra kiṃ vyākhyānaṃ [(3]kriyata iti[3)] yāvat | tathā coktaṃ

[1] E_B *tāvaja* E_{Sh} *bhāvaj* [2] $E_B E_{Sh}$ *tasmāt* [3] E_{Sh} *kripata iti* N *kriyateti*

| ces gsungs te | 'dir dang por re zhig sems ni brjod bya dang brjod byed kyi mtshan nyid dang bral ba'o | de gang yin zhe na | lhan cig skyes pa'i ye shes te | de ni rtog pas[1] byas pa ma yin te | rgyu dang 'bras bu dang bral ba'i phyir 'bras bu'i rnam par gzhag pa med do | de'i phyir gang brjod du med pa de la ji ltar bshad du yod ces pa'o | de ltar [P 207a] yang |

[1] P *par*

[E_B 91] iti tāvan[1] mṛṣā [sarvaṃ[2] yāvad][N 41b] yāvad vikalpyate |
tat satyaṃ tat tathābhūtaṃ tattvaṃ yan na [(3]vikalpyate || iti[3)] ||
(ĀM 40)

[1] E_{Sh} *yāvat* [2] E_{Sh} *vākyaṃ* [3] N *vikalpyateti*

| di ni re zhig rdzun[1] kun te |
| ji srid ji srid rtog[2] gyur pa |
| ji ltar gyur pa de de bzhin[3] |
| de nyid gang du[4] mi rtog pa'o | (ĀM 40)

[1] DP *brdzun* [2] BP *rtogs* [3] DP *bden* [4] B *du'ang*

kiṃ tad bhavatīti punar apy āha |

[rūpa]m asya mataṃ svacchaṃ[1] nirākāraṃ nirañjanam |
śakyaṃ ca na hi taj jñātum abuddhena[2] kathañcana || iti | (ĀM 53)

[1] E_{Sh} *śaśvat* [2] E_BN *abuddheṣu* E_{Sh} *abudhena*

| gzhan yang |

| 'di yi rang bzhin [(1]dwangs pa[1)] ste |
| rnam pa med cing rdul bral ba |
| sangs rgyas ma [B 132b] gtogs gzhan gyis ni |
| de ni rtogs par mi nus so | (ĀM 53)

[1] DP *dang ba*

buddho 'pi na ta[thā] vetti yathāyam itaro janaḥ[1] |
pratītyatāṃ[2] tu tasyaiva tāṃ jānāti sa eva hi || (ĀM 54)

[1] E_{Sh} *naraḥ* [2] $E_B E_{Sh}$ *pratītya tāṃ* N *pratītatā*

| cig[1] shos skye 'gros rtogs pa ltar |
| sangs rgyas kyis kyang mi rtogs so |
| de nyid rten cing 'brel 'byung nyid |
| de nyid sangs rgyas kho nas shes | (ĀM 54)

[1] D *gcig*

tasmād ajñānāvṛtair[1] na lakṣitaṃ tattvam | kim ajñānam etad ity āha |

[1] E_{B} *–vṛtter* E_{Sh} *vṛttena*

| zhes gsungs so | | de'i phyir mi shes pas g.yogs pa rnams kyis de nyid rtogs par mi nus zhes pa'o | | mi shes pa de gang yin zhe na |

bhava-muddeṃ[1] saala hi jaga vāhiu |
ṇiasahāva ṇa[2] keṇavi sāhiu[3] | iti | (21cd)

[1] E_{Sh} *mudde* [2] $E_{B}E_{Sh}$N *ṇaü* [3] E_{Sh} *gāhiu* N *yāhiu*

| srid pa'i phyag rgyas 'gro ba rnams |
| ma lus pa ni khol por byas |
| gnyug ma yi[1] ni rang bzhin ni[2] |
| sus kyang blangs pa yod ma yin | (21cd)

[1] P *yis* [2] B *nyid*

bhavamudrayā sakalaṃ[1] jagad[2] vāhitaṃ | bhavamudrāṅganā[3] kalmaṣahṛdayā sattvavañcakā[4] [N 42a] ca[5] | tayā jagad dāsīkṛtaṃ | yad icchati prāṇātipātādi tat sarvaṃ kāmalobhena kārayati | tayā ca kṛtam u[nma]ttavat | tasmān nija-svabhāvaṃ[6] samyaktattvaṃ na kenacit sādhitaṃ bhavati | anyac ca mantra-tantrādideśanayā dravyalobhena jagan mohitaṃ | tam āha

[1] E_{Sh}N *sakala* [2] N *jaga* [3] $E_{B}E_{Sh}$N *–āṅkenā* [4] $E_{B}E_{Sh}$ *–vañcikā* N *vañca ..* [5] E_{Sh} om. [6] E_{Sh} *–va-*

| zhes gsungs te | srid pa'i phyag rgyas 'gro ba ma lus pa rnams[1] dbang du byas pa yin te | srid pa'i phyag rgya ni yan lag can ma ste | sems sdig che ba dang rgyu dang ldan pa des 'gro ba rnams khol por byas pas | gal te 'dod na 'dod pa'i srid pas srog gcod pa la sogs pa thams cad byed pa la 'jug ste | 'dod pa'i bde ba des 'gro ba [D 188b] kun smyon pa lta bur byed pa'i phyir ro | | de'i phyir rang bzhin gnyug ma ni yang dag pa'i de nyid do | sus kyang blangs pa med pa ni sus kyang rtogs[2] pa med pa'o | gzhan yang nor la[3] sred[4] pas sngags dang rgyud la sogs pa bshad pas 'gro ba rnams rmongs par byed par 'gyur ba de[5] ni |

[1] P om. [2] D *rtog* [3] D *gyis* P *gyi* [4] DP *srid* [5] DP om.

manta ṇa tanta ṇa dhea ṇa dhāraṇa | iti | (22a)

| rgyud med sngags kyang med pa ste |
| bsam bya dang ni bsam gtan med | (22a)

etena[1] granthakāreṇa karuṇāvaśād uktaṃ mantratantreṇa rahitatayā mokṣaṃ na labhyate | taiḥ

[1] N *eteṇa*

| ces gsungs ste | | 'di ni gzhung byed pa pos snying rje'i dbang gis gsungs te | rgyud dang sngags tsam pos ni thar pa thob pa ma yin no | de dag gis ni |

savvavi re vaḍha vibbhamakāraṇa[1] | iti | (22b)

[1] E_{Sh} *karaṇām*

[B 133a] | kye hoḥ[1] rmongs pa 'di[2] kun [3] 'khrul pa'i rgyu | (22b)

[1] DP om. [2] DP *de* [3] B inserts *rang yid*

he mūḍha sarvabhaveṣu vibhavakāraṇaṃ sampattikāraṇaṃ vibhramam[1] | yena bhrāntyā duḥkham anubhava[nti] [N 42b] | tasmāt |

[1] $E_B E_{Sh}$ *vibhramaḥ*

| zhes gsungs te | kye blun po rgyud dang sngags de dag ni srid pa [P 207b] thams cad phun sum tshogs pa'i[1] 'byor pa'i rgyu'o | yang na 'khrul pa ni gang gis[2] sdug bsngal nyams su myong bar byed pa'o | | de'i phyir |

[1] B *par* [2] D *gi*

[E_B 92] asamala citta ma jhāṇeṃ[1] kharaḍaha[2] | iti | (22c)

[1] E_{Sh} jhāṇaï [2] E_{Sh} *jhāṇaï* E_B *kharaḍaï* E_{Sh} *kharataha*

| dri ma med pa'i sems la ni |
| bsam gtan gyis kyang bslad mi bya | (22c)

nirmalacittaṃ mā ajñānena asvacchīkuru | kathaṃ ([2]nirmalam ucyate[2]) | cittasaṃjñā dvividhā laukikī[3] lokottarā ca | yal laukikaṃ[4] tad vikalpalakṣaṇaṃ pūrvaṃ nirā[kṛ]tam | yal lokottaraṃ nirmalaṃ dharmakāyalakṣaṇaṃ ([5]sahajarūpaṃ vā[5]) | ata evāha |

[1] E_BN *tāvac chīkuru* E_{Sh} *gavacchīkuru* [2] $E_B E_{Sh}$ *tan nirmalam ucyate* N *nimma* ||| *cyate* [3] N *lokikī* [4] N *lokikaṃ* [5] E_B *sahajasvarūpaṃ vā* E_{Sh} *sahajasvarūpatvāt*

| zhes gsungs te | dri ma med pa'i sems mi shes pas ma[1] bslad cing ma bcings pa[2] zhes bya ba'i don no[3] | ci'i phyir dri ma med ce na | sems zhes bya ba ni gnyis te | 'jig rten dang | 'jig rten las 'das pa'o | | 'jig rten pa'i rnam par rtog pa'i mtshan nyid can ni sngon du sun phyung zin to | 'jig rten las 'das pa gang yin pa de ni lhan cig skyes pa'i ngo bo'am chos kyi sku'i mtshan nyid do | de'i phyir |

[1] D *mi* [2] P om. [3] DP *to*

suha acchanta ma appaṇu[1] jhagaḍaha | iti | (22d)

[1] E_{Sh} *-ṇū*

| bdag nyid bde gnas[1] ([2]gdung ma byed[2]) | (22d)

[1] B *ba la gnas* D *nas* [2] B *ma gdungs shig*

etena nirvikalpasukharūpaṃ sarvaṃ traidhātukaṃ[1] vyavasthitaṃ | | tadā na pṛthaktvenātmano parābhavīkuru | tadā sukhamayatvena idaṃ kuru | kiṃ tad āha

[1] E_{Sh} *–ka-*

| ces gsungs te | 'dis ni rnam par mi rtog pa'i bde ba chen po'i ngo bo nyid du khams gsum du[1] rnam par gnas pa'o | de bas na bdag nyid brlag par ma byed cig ces bsdug bsngal la[2] ma gnas zhes bya ba'i don te[3] | bde ba'i rang bzhin du gyis shig ces ba'o | de ji ltar bya zhe na |

[1] DP om. [2] P om. [3] D *to*

khā[anteṃ ityādi] [N 43a] † caü †
bhaa[1]loaha paryantam iti | (23)

[1] N *bhua*

| za zhing 'thung[1] la zhes bya ba la sogs pa nas
mnan nas 'gro ba'i bar gyis ni (23)

[1] B *'thungs*

[E_{Sh} 94] etena ca saprapañcacaryāpi sūcitā bhavati yathā[1] indrabhūtipāde[na kṛtā] | khānapānena[2] pañcakāmopabhogeṣu[3] suratakrīḍā kartavyā[4] | punar api padmabhājanādinā gṛhītvā bali[ṃ dā]syati | mahācakradevatārūpeṇa sthāsyati | etena[5] bhavyalokānāṃ jñānasiddhir mahāmudrāsiddhir bhaviṣyati | taiś ca tīrthikādīnāṃ bahubhayabhavaloko mastakeṣu pādanyāsaṃ karoti | vaineyaṃ karoti | etena mahāmudrā[6] sādhyate | tasyāḥ kim upadeśam[7] ity āha

[1] $E_B E_{Sh}$ *yadā* [2] $E_B E_{Sh}$N *khāne pāne na* [3] E_{Sh} *–bhoga-* [4] E_BN om. [5] E_{Sh} *etena ca* [6] E_SN *mahāmudrā yā* [7] $E_B E_{Sh}$ *uddeśam*

spros pa dang bcas pa'i spyod pa gcig[1] ston te | ji ltar rgyal po indra bhū[2] tis byas[3] pa lta bur[4] za ba dang | 'thung ba dang | 'dod pa'i yon tan lnga la longs [B 133b] spyod cing gnyis sprod pa'i bde ba [D 189a] gyis shig ces pa'o | [5] yang dang yang du 'khor lo 'gengs | zhes pa ni[6] | yang thod pa la sogs pa blangs la gtor ma sbyin zhing | tshogs kyi 'khor lor 'dus pa'i[7] gang zag rnams lha'i gzugs kyis gnas pa'o | | 'dis ni 'grub par 'gyur te | skal ba dang ldan pa'i 'jig rten pa rnams ye shes 'grub[8] pa ste | phyag rgya chen po'i dngos grub 'grub pa'o | rmongs pa'i 'jig rten ni mu stegs pa la sogs pa'i 'jig rten pa bsten pa ste | de'i mgo bor rdog[9] pas mnan nas 'gro ba (10ni de10) thams [P 208a] cad 'dul bar byed pa'o | | 'dis ni phyag rgya chen po 'grub pa ste | de'i gdams ngag gang yin zhe na |

[1] DP om. [2] P *bhu* [3] D *byis* [4] DP *bu* [5] B inserts *rtag tu* [6] DP *dang* [7] D *lo'i* P *lo ba'i* [8] DP *grub* [9] P *bdog* [10] D om.

> [E_B 93] jahi (1maṇa pavaṇa ṇa1) sañcaraï ravi sasi [ṇā][N 43b]ha[2] pavesa[3] |
> taï[4] vaḍha citta visāma karu saraheṃ[5] kahia uesa[6] | iti | (24)

[1] E_{Sh} *mana pavana na* [2] N *–haṃ* [3] E_{Sh} *paveśa* [4] N *tahi* [5] E_{Sh} *sarahe* [6] E_{Sh} *uveśa*

| gang du[1] rlung dang yid[2] (3mi rgyu3) |
| nyi ma zla ba (4'jug pa med4) |
| de la rmongs pa[5] sems ngal sos[6] |
| mda' bsnun gyis ni man ngag bstan | (24)

[1] B *tshe* [2] DP *sems* [3] B *ni mi rgyu shing* [4] B *mi 'jug par 'gyur ba* P *'jug med pa* [5] DP *pas* [6] B *bso bar gyis* [7] B inserts *nas song*

yatra sarvajantuṣu svarūpasvasa[ṃveda]natayā guror ādeśāt necchiteṣv[1] api cittaviśrāmaṃ kuru yatra mahattvaṃ prāpsyasi[2] | tasmin sthāne ma[na]saḥ pavanasya ca sañcāro na bhavati | tatraiva raviśaśinoḥ[3] praveśaniṣkāśau[4] na staḥ | na tu kalpanāmātrāt[5] sarve niruddhā bhavanti | yathā bālaiḥ sandhābhāṣām[6] ajānadbhir manaḥ[7]pavanādinirodhā[8]ś[raya]ḥ kalpitaḥ | (9tan na9) | katham | ihocyate | nirodho nāma niṣedhavācī | kiṃ tena ka[ṣṭacaryayā | yāvac charīraṃ vāyvādi][N 44a]vāhanaṃ bhavati | tāvad vāyunirodhena śarīraṃ nirodhyate mriyate vā | tasmāt sadgurūpadeśāt boddha[vyaṃ] | sarahetyādi subodham | kiṃ tu pavanarūpaṃ bodhicittaṃ | (10tac cāmṛtaṃ10) manaḥsukharūpaṃ[11] | evaṃ (12ravi[śa]śi rāgavirāgo 'nayoḥ12) (13kalpitasahajo jāyate13) | na bhavati[14] grāhyaḥ |[15]

[1] E_B *nesthiteṣv* E_{Sh} *necchitvete* [2] E_BN *–ti* [3] E_{Sh} *raviśaśināha paveśa iti* [4] E_B *–śo* [5] E_B *–mātraṃ tat tu* E_{Sh} *–mātraṃ* N *–mātrā tu* [6] E_BE_{Sh} *sandhābhāṣam* N *sandhyabhāṣam* [7] N *mana-* [8] N *–ām* [9] E_BE_{Sh}N *tatra* [10] E_BN *tadāmṛtaṃ* [11] E_B

manaḥ sukharūpaṃ [12] E_{Sh} *raviśaśirāgavirāgeṇa yaḥ* [13] E_B *kalpitasahajo yatra* E_{Sh} *kalpitasahajaḥ sa yatra* N *kalpitasahaja jāyatra* [14] E_{Sh} *bhavati sa* [15] E_B *grāhya*

| zhes gsungs te | gang bla ma'i man ngag gis skye 'gro thams cad kyis[1] de kho na nyid rang gis nyams su myong ba yin[2] de la sems ngal bsos[3] pa dang bdag nyid chen po 'thob[4] par 'gyur ro | de lta bu'i gnas pa de la rlung dang sems ni mi rgyu zhing | de nyid la nyi ma dang zla ba (5'byung ba dang5) 'jug pa med de | de[5] rnam par rtog pa med pa tsam po[5] ni ma yin te | dngos po thams cad 'gag[6] par 'gyur ba'o | ji ltar byis pa rnams kyis dgongs te bstan pa'i skad mi shes pas | yid dang [B 134a] rlung mnyam par 'gag pa la brten nas sdug bsngal bar 'gyur ro | de bas na 'dir 'gog pa ces bya ba ni dgag pa'i tshig ste | rlung 'gog pa dang[5] rba rlabs kyi[7] (5'gog pa la5) dgos pa ci yod ces pa'o | ji srid du lus yod par rlung rgyu ste | de srid rlung 'gags pas 'gog pa'i snyoms 'jug gam | 'chi[8] bar 'gyur ba ste | de'i phyir bla ma dam pa'i man[9] ngag las shes par bya'o | mda' bsnun zhes bya ba la[10] sogs pa ni go sla'o | 'on kyang rlung ni byang chub kyi sems so | | de nyid bdud rtsi'ang yin te | yid bde ba'i ngo bo'o | | de ltar nyi ma dang zla ba ni 'dod chags dang 'dod chags [D 189b] dang bral ba'o | de dag (11gis brtags pa'i blos ma yin par11) lhan cig skyes pa gang yin pa de blang bar bya'o |

[1] P *kyi* [2] BP om. [3] DP *sos* [4] DP *thob* [5] DP om. [6] P *'gags* [7] BD *kyis* [8] BDP *'ching* [9] BP *gdams* [10] P *ni* [11] D *gi rtag pa ma yin pa'i* P *gis brtags pa ma yin pa'i*

evam upadeśe prāpte sati |

> ekku karu ityādi
> phuḍa[1] pucchahi gurupāvā[2] | (25a and 28d)
> [1] E_{Sh} *phuta* [2] E_{Sh} *bhāva yāva* N *pāva*

itiparyantaṃ subodham |

de lta bu'i gdams ngag[1] ni thob nas |
[1] DP *pa*

> | gnyis su mi bya gcig tu'ang[1] (2mi bya ste2) | | zhes bya ba nas
> bla ma'i zhal las[3] gsal bar dris | | zhes bya ba'i bar ni go sla'o | (25a and 28d)
> [1] P *tu* [2] D *min* P *bya* [3] DP *nas*

[25b–28c are provided in DP:]

| rigs la bye brag med par ni |
| khams gsum ma[1] lus 'di thams cad [2] |
| 'dod chags chen po gcig tu 'gyur | (25b–d)
[1] P om. [2] BP insert *la*

| de ni[1] thog ma bar mtha' med |
| srid min mya ngan 'das pa min |
[P 208b] | bde ba chen po mchog 'di la |
| bdag dang gzhan du yod ma yin | (26)
[1] D *de*

| mdun dang rgyab dang phyogs bcu ru |
| gang gang mthong ba de de nyid |
| de ring da ltar 'khrul pa chad |
| da ni su la yang dri mi bya | (27)

| dbang gang du nub gyur tsam na |
| rang gi ngo bo nyams par gyur |
| grogs[1] dag de ni lhan cig skyes | (28a–c)
[1] D *gegs*

[E_B 94] kiṃ tu sarvam upadeśair[1] vyāptaṃ | tena tat[2] kuryāt sarvaṃ tanmayam iti bhāvaḥ | yadi bhrāntir asti kadācit[3] tadā punar a[pi] [N 44b] gurupādasyāntike[4] sphuṭataratvena pṛcchāṃ kuru yena nirbhrānto bhaviṣyasi | tadā tenāpi ([5]sa upadeśo[5]) dīyate | tam āha [6]
[1] N *upadeśe* [2] E_BN *yat* [3] E_{Sh} om. [4] E_BN *–kaṃ* [5] E_{Sh} *yam upadeśo* N *samupadeśo* [6] E_BE_{Sh} insert *jahi maṇa ityādi* | N *jahi maṇetyādi*

| 'on kyang thams cad bla ma'i gdams ngag gis khyab pa'o | | de'i phyir de thams cad lhan cig skyes pa'i rang bzhin du gyis shig ces pa'o | | kha cig tu gal te 'khrul pa yod na de'i tshe bla ma'i zhabs kyi gan du gsal por dri bar gyis shig dang | des 'khrul pa med par 'gyur ro | | des na de'i tshe bla ma'i bka' lung gi[1] gdams ngag bsten[2] pa'i tshul gsungs te |
[1] BD *gis* [2] P *sten*

jahi maṇa maraï pavaṇa ho kkhaa jāi | iti (29ab)

| yid ni gang shi rlung [B 134b] gar dengs | (29ab)

yatra[1] [hi] mano mriyate pavanaś[2] ca kṣayaṃ yāti | na kevalaṃ tad dvayam[3] | anyac ca |

[1] E_{Sh} *atra* [2] E_BN *–añ* [3] N *advayam*

| zhes gsungs te | gang gi phyir yid shi ba dang rlung yang zad cing dengs bar 'gyur ro | de gnyis 'ba' zhig ni ma yin te[1] | gzhan yang |

[1] B *gyi*

ehu so[1] paramamahāsu[ha] rahia kahimpi[2] ṇa jāi | (29cd)

[1] E_{Sh}N *se* [2] N *kahiṃpi*

| 'di ni bde chen mchog yin te |
| spangs nas gar yang mi 'gro'o | (29cd)

itīdaṃ vacanāt sādhitam | paramamahāsukhasaṃpattir[1] yena prāptā[2] | tenāpi[3] rahitaṃ | samyaggurūpadeśaṃ vinā[4] vācyavācak([5]ābhāvaṃ [ta ...[5]) na] [N 45a] kiñcid bhavati | kiṃ tu rahia iti[6] na sthitam | kahimpi[7] ṇa jāi na gataṃ[8] kvacit | [9] vacanagamyaṃ na bhavatīti bhāvaḥ | tathā coktaṃ

[1] E_BE_{Sh} *samāpattyā* N *saṃpa[ttyā]* [2] E_BE_{Sh}N *prāptaṃ ca* [3] E_BE_{Sh}N *tad api* [4] E_{Sh} *yadi kariṣyasi* [5] E_BE_{Sh} *–ābhāvaṃ tasya kathaṃ tattve pi* [6] E_{Sh} om. [7] N *kahipi* [8] E_{Sh} *gamanaṃ* [9] E_BE_{Sh} insert *vacanaṃ* N is not clear but has three extra *akṣaras*.

| zhes gsungs te | 'dis[1] 'di ltar ston te | mchog gi bde ba chen po gang gis [2] thob pa ([3]de'ang bral ba ste[3]) | yang dag pa'i bla ma'i gdams ngag med par[4] brjod bya dang[5] rjod byed kyi 'brel pa bstan[6] pa'i sgo nas cung zad kyang mi snyed do zhes pa'o | gar yang mi 'gro'o zhes ([7]bya ba[7]) ni gang du'ang mi 'gro ba ste | ngag gi spyod yul ma yin zhes dgongs pa'o[8] | de skad du [D 190a] yang |

[1] D om. [2] BDP insert *ma* [3] P *de nga spangs pa* [4] DP *pas* [5] B om. [6] DP *ston* [7] DP *pa* [8] D *so*

buddher agocaratayā na girāṃ ([1]pracāre dūre[1]) guroḥ[2]
prathitavastukathāvatāraḥ |
tat tu krameṇa karuṇādiguṇāvadāte śraddhāvatāṃ hṛdi padaṃ
svayam ādadhāti ||

[1] E_B *pracāroddhāre* E_{Sh} *-pracāroddhārau* N *pracāro dūre* [2] E_BE_{Sh}N *guru-*

| blo yi spyod yul ma yin ngag gi spyod yul dag las 'das |
| bla mas bstan pa'i[1] dngos po brjod cing 'jug pa dag la ring |

| de yang [(2]rim gyis[2)] snying rje dag sogs yon tan dri med pas[3] |
| dad ldan sems kyi go 'phang la ni rang nyid kyis ni 'char[4] |
[1] P *pas* [2] BDP *rigs kyi* [3] DP *pa'i* [4] B *'chad*

| zhes[1] gsungs so |
[1] B *ces*

atraiva[1]
[1] N *atreva*

saa[1]samvitti ma karahu rĕ dhandhā |
bhāvābhāva sugati re bandhā[2] | iti | (30ab)
[1] E_{Sh} *saï* [2] E_{B} *vandhā* E_{Sh} *vandha*

| kye ho[1] rang rig[2] 'di la ma [P 209a] 'khrul zhig |
| dngos po[3] dngos po med pa ni |
| bde bar 'gro ba'ang 'ching ba ste | (30ab)
[1] B *hoḥ* [2] DP *gi* [3] B *dang*

[E_{B} 95; E_{Sh} 95] svasaṃvittim anādikalpanayā sukhaṃ mā kariṣyasi | yadi kariṣyasi dhandhatāṃ yāsyasi | tasmād bhāvaṃ vā uktalakṣaṇam abhāvaṃ vāpi sugati[N 45b]r vā vikalpitaṃ | he mūḍha sarvaṃ [(1]tad bandhanaṃ bhavati[1)] | nāsti suvarṇalohanigaḍayor bhedaḥ tasmāt tyājyam eveti | tathā coktam
[1] E_{B}N *tat buddhatvaṃ na sambhavati*

| zhes gsungs te | rang rig pa ste | thog ma med pa'i dus nas brtags pa'i bde ba zhes grogs po dag rtog par ma byed cig | gal te byed na rmongs par 'gyur ro zhes pa'o | | de'i phyir dngos po ste | gong du bstan pa'i mtshan nyid dang | dngos po med pa'i mtshan nyid ni bde 'gro'i rnam par rtog pa ste | [1] kye rmongs [B 135a] pa de dag[1] thams cad 'ching ba yin no | | gser gyi sgrog dang lcags kyi sgrog gnyis[2] 'ching bar [(3]byed pa la[3)] bye brag med de | de'i phyir 'di thams cad bor bar bya'o |
[1] B inserts *des* | [2] DP *la* [3] DP om.

paramārthavikalpe 'pi nāvalīyeta[1] paṇḍitaḥ |
ko hi bhedo vikalpasya śu[bhe] vāpy aśubhe 'pi vā || (ĀM 6)
[1] N *nāvalīyet*

| de ltar [(1]dam par yang rtog[1)] ste |
| 'jug par mi 'gyur mkhas pa yin |

| dge ba dang ni mi dge yang |
| rtog pa nyid du[2] bye brag med | (ĀM 6)
[1] B *don dam par yang ni rtog pa med pa* D *dam par yang rtog pa med pa* [2] B *de*

nādhārabhedād bhedo 'sti vahner[1] dāhakatāṃ prati |
spṛśyamāno[2] dahaty eva candanair[3] jvalito 'py asau || (ĀM 7) iti
[1] $E_B E_{Sh}$N *vahni* [2] N *pṛśyamāno* [3] N *candane*

| mes ni sreg par byed pa la |
| bud shing khyad kyis[1] bye brag med |
| reg bzhin (2gtan nas sreg pa2) ste |
| tsa nda na la 'bar[3] me yang ngo | (ĀM 7)
[1] BD *kyi* [2] DP *pas na de sreg* [3] P *mar*

etena kiṃ kriyatām[1] ity āha
[1] E_{Sh} *kriyate*

'di ji ltar bya zhe na |

ṇiamaṇa muṇa[hu] rĕ ṇiuṇeṃ[1] joi |
jima jala jalahi[2] milante soi[3] | iti | (30cd)
[1] E_{Sh} *ṇiuṇe* [2] E_{Sh} *–hiṃ* [3] E_{Sh} *i*

| kye hoḥ[1] rnal 'byor gnyug ma yi |
| yid la nan tan gyis la ltos |
| ji ltar chu la chu 'dres bzhin | (30cd)
[1] DP *ho*

nipuṇaṃ mano[1] nirmalaṃ [bhāvābhā][N 46a]varahitaṃ prabhāsvaramayaṃ vā drakṣyasi[2] | he yūyaṃ[3] yoginaḥ nipuṇena yogena ca yogaṃ ca cittavṛtt[er e]kāgratā[4]lakṣaṇaṃ jñānajñeyalakṣaṇaṃ vā | sa ca yādṛśaṃ jalasya jalaṃ miśritaṃ tādṛśaṃ (5sambhavati cet5) |
[1] N *mana* [2] $E_B E_{Sh}$N *-ti* [3] N *tvayā* [4] E_B *ekāgra-* [5] E_BNpc *sa bhavati yogaṃ bhavati cet* E_{Sh} *sa bhavati cet*

| zhes gsungs te | kye hoḥ[1] rnal 'byor pa (2gnyug ma'i yid gcig tu gtod dang |2) dngos po dang dngos po med pa spangs pa[3] 'od gsal gyi ngo bo nyid la ltos shig ces pa'o | | gcig tu gtod[4] pa'i rnal 'byor ni sems kyi 'jug pa dmigs pa la sems rtse gcig pa'am | shes pa dang shes bya'i mtshan nyid do | | de'ang gang chu la

chu bzhag[5] pa bzhin du bzhag[5] ste | 'dres[6] pa de lta bur gyur na rnal 'byor du 'gyur ro |

[1] DP om. [2] DP *gcig tu sdod dang gnyug ma'i yid* [3] DP *pa'am* [4] DP *sdod* [5] P *gzhag* [6] P *'dris*

> jhāṇeṃ[1] mokkha ki cāhu rĕ[2] āleṃ[3] |
> māā[4]jāla ki lehu rĕ koleṃ | iti | (31ab)

[1] E_{Sh} *jhāṇe* [2] E_{Sh} *śahure* [3] E_{Sh} *ālĕ* [4] E_{Sh} *māyā*

> | rdzun[1] pa'i bsam gtan dag gis ni |
> | thar pa nyid ni ji ltar rnyed |
> | sgyu 'phrul gyi[2] ni drwa ba [D 190b] dag |
> | ji ltar pang du blang bar bya | (31ab)

[1] D *brdzun* [2] P *gyis*

alīkena dhyānena keśoṇḍukādyābhāsena[1] he mūḍhapuruṣa kiṃ[2] mokṣam adhigacchasi | tas[māt] [(3]tat tapo[3)] duratikramaṃ[4] | kutaḥ | māyājālaṃ samastaṃ tribhuvanaṃ | kiṃ gṛhyate svāṅgotsaṅgeṣu | na pārya[ta[5] iti] [N 46b] yāvat | kiṃ tu |

[1] E_{Sh} *keśoṇḍrakādyākāreṇa* [2] E_B *ki* [3] E_B *taṃ tayo* E_{Sh} om. N *taṃ tapo* [4] E_{Sh} *–maḥ* [5] $E_B E_{Sh}$ *-te*

| zhes gsungs te | [(1]rdzun pa'i bsam gtan ni rab rib can gyi skra shad lta bur thar pa thob par ga la 'gyur te | mi 'gyur |[1)] | de'i phyir de lta [B 135b] bu'i bka' thub des shin tu rnyed par dka'o | | [P 209b] de[2] ci'i phyir zhe na | sgyu 'phrul drwa[3] ba ni khams gsum ma lus pa'o | | ji ltar pang du blang bar bya ba ni de lta bus rtogs[4] par mi nus zhes pa'o | 'on kyang

[1] DP om. [2] DP *brdzun pa'i skra shad ni rab rib can gyi lta bur thar pa rtogs par ga la 'gyur te mi 'gyur ro |* [3] DP *dra* [4] P *rtog*

> [E_B 96] vara[1]guruvaaṇa[2] paḍijjaha[3] sacceṃ[4] |
> Saraha bhaṇaï maï kahiaü vacceṃ[5] | iti | (31cd)

[1] N *varu-* [2] E_BN *guruvaaṇeṃ* E_{Sh} *guruvaaṇe* [3] E_BN *paḍijjahu* E_{Sh} *pattijaha* [4] E_{Sh} *maye* N *savveṃ* [5] E_B *vāṃce* E_{Sh} *vācĕ* N *vācem*

> | bla ma [(1]dam pa'i gsung la yid ches gyis[1)] |
> | mda' bsnun[2] [(3]na re[3)] nga yi ngag gis bstan | (31cd)

[1] DP *mchog gis gsungs pa rnams | thams cad la ni yid ches kyis* [2] P *snun* [3] DP om.

yadi tāvat guruvacanasya [(1]satyatām asti[1)] | tadā mayā saroruhapravaraguruṇā[2] vacanena kathitam idaṃ dohakoṣādi[3] |
[1] E_B *satyatāsti* [2] $E_B E_{Sh}$ N *–guru-* [3] $E_B E_{Sh}$ *-dinā*

| zhes gsungs te | gal te re zhig bla ma'i bka'[1] bden par yid ches [(2]par byas pa[2)] de'i tshe bla ma mtsho skyes rdo rje mchog gi zhabs kyis[3] gsung gis ngas 'dir do ha ko ṣa'i[4] 'grel[5] pa byas so |
[1] P *bkas* || [2] D *pa* P om. [3] BD *kyi* [4] D *sha'i* [5] P *'brel*

paḍhameṃ jaï āāsa visuddho | iti | (32a)

| gdod nas dag pa'i[1] nam mkha[2] la | (32a)
[1] B *pa* [2] B *mkha'i rang bzhin*

evaṃ guruvacane[1] pratītikṛte sati yaḥ sarvabhāvāyāsaḥ[2] sa viśuddho bhavati | kutaḥ |
[1] $E_B E_{Sh}$ *–nasya* [2] N *sarvabhavā*

| zhes gsungs te | de ltar bla ma'i gdams ngag gis[1] yid ches par byas na srid pa thams cad kyi ngal ba[2] gang yin pa de dag[3] thams cad dag par 'gyur ro | | de[3] ci'i phyir zhe na |
[1] P *gi* [2] P *las* [3] DP om.

cāhănte cāhăntĕ diṭṭhi[1] ṇiruddho | iti | (32b)
[1] E_{Sh} *diṭhṭhi* N *diddhi*

| bltas shing bltas shing mthong ba 'gag[1] [(2]par 'gyur[2)] | (32b)
[1] D *dga'* [2] DP om.

yathā dṛṣṭyā[1] cakṣuṣā vyavalokanena nimeṣonmeṣanirodhena ca yad dūrato marīcikādipānīya[N 47a]sya[2] darśananirodho bhavati | tathaiva[3] ihāpi vicāryamāṇena[4] sarvaṃ tanmayībhavati nānyathā | kiṃ [(5]vicāryata iti[5)] | gurūpadeśāmukhī[(6]bhāvasahitaḥ[6)] prabandhataḥ | sa ca na vikalpabhāvanā jālādivat | yadi vā te[nai]va buddhatvaṃ | tadā pratītyatāṃ janayati | sa cāndhakārābhāvālokavat[7] chāyābhāvātapavat[8] viśiṣṭa[9]nirmāṇakāyo ['tra] jāyate | manonirodhena tu viśiṣṭa[10]dharmakāyasvabhāvaṃ[11] bhavati | sa ca sarvamayam iti bhāvārthaḥ | na punar [(12]mana iti[12)] | na kiṃcit syād[13] iti | tat pratītiṃ[14] janayati | pratītyasamutpādatvāc ca | evam a[jā][N 47b]natām[15] āha |
[1] $E_B E_{Sh}$ N *dṛṣṭvā* [2] E_{Sh} *marīcijālādipānīyasya* N *marīcikādipā* ... ||| *sya* [3] E_{Sh} *tathā* [4] E_B N *-nena* [5] N *vicāryateti* [6] E_B N *–bhāvasahitaḥ* E_{Sh} *–bhāvaṃ sad iti* [7] $E_B E_{Sh}$

-bhāvād ālokavat [8] E_BE_{Sh} *–bhāvād ātapavat* [9] E_BE_{Sh}N *viśiṣṭaṃ* [10] N *viśiṣṭaṃ* [11] E_BE_{Sh} *–vo* [12] Npc *maṇam iti* Nac *maṇim iti* [13] E_{Sh} *vād* [14] E_{Sh} *–tiñ ca* [15] N *-tānāṃ*

| zhes gsungs te | ji ltar thag ring ba[1] la smig rgyu la chur mthong ba yang dang yang du bltas pas mthar 'gag[2] par 'gyur ro | de bzhin du 'dir yang dpyad bzhin pas thams cad khyad par can gyi chos sku'i rang bzhin du[1] 'gyur te | gzhan du ni ma yin no | | ji ltar dpyad ce na | bla ma dam pa'i gdams ngag mngon du byas pa'i rgyun[3] gyis[4] ni de'ang rnam par rtog pa'i sgom pa ni smig rgyu'i chu bzhin no | gal te de nyid las[5] sangs rgyas 'grub ([6]par 'gyur ro[6]) zhes zer[7] na | de'i tshe sangs rgyas rten 'brel [B 136a] du 'gyur ro[8] | mun pa med pa'i snang ba bzhin no | | grib[9] ma med pa dang nyi 'od bzhin du khyad par can gyi sprul pa'i sku 'di las 'byung ngo | | yid[10] 'gog pa las ni khyad par can gyi chos kyi[11] sku'i rang bzhin du 'gyur ro | | de'ang thams cad kyi rang bzhin yin no zhes ([12]dgongs te[12]) | de'ang[13] de la yid shi zhing 'gag pa zhes ni mi bya'o | | de lta bu [14] mi [D 191a] shes pa rnams la |

[1] D om. [2] D *'gags* [3] B *rgyu mtshan* [4] D *gyi* [5] DP *kyis* [6] DP *po* [7] B om. [8] B *te* [9] B *dri* [10] D *yi dags* [11] DP om. [12] B *dgongs pa ste* [13] DP *yang* [14] B inserts *nyid*

> [E_B 97; E_{Sh} 96] eseṃ[1] jaï āāsa-vikālo |
> nia-maṇa-dosĕṃ[2] ṇa bujjhaï[3] bālo | iti | (32cd)
>
> [1] E_{Sh} *ese* [2] E_{Sh} *dose* [3] E_BE_{Sh} *vujjhaï* N *vujhaï*

> | ([1]'di lta'i[1]) mkha' la gang gi[2]) dus su 'gog |
> | gnyug ma'i yid kyi skyon [P 210a] gyis ([3]byis pa bslus[3]) | (32cd)
>
> [1] DP *'di lta bu'i nam* [2] BD *zhig* P *zhig gi ni* [3] DP *ni | | byis pa rnams kyis mgo'o*

īdṛśaṃ ya[di] āyāsānāṃ vikālo notpādakālaḥ | sarveṣāṃ saṃhārakālam iti bhāvaḥ | tadā niyamena[1] bhāvāsa[2]ktadoṣatayā na vidanti bālajātīyāḥ[3] tīrthikādyāś ca | etad āha | ([4]tenaiva saha vedāntenaiva sāṃkhyāḥ[4]) kṣapaṇakā[5] ([6]matā vipralabdhabudhayo[6]) viditāḥ | viditaparamārthadṛḍhacittaṃ prapiṇḍyaikātmadṛṣṭya[7]bhiniviṣṭāḥ | aprāptavinayakālatayā ca mahākāruṇikair apy upekṣitā bhūyaḥ saṃsāragranthim[8] e[va dṛ][N 48a] ḍhayanto 'nukampanīyā eva | karuṇāśālināṃ vipadi varttamānā iti na dveṣārhāḥ | ye tu [sau]gatanetrikāḥ te 'pi vastu[9]dhiyaḥ sāṃsārikanairvāṇika[10] pakṣāvabodhapaṭavo na svākhyā[ta]siddhāntānugabuddhibhiḥ pratāryanta[11] iti vistaraḥ | tasmāt |

[1] E_B *ṇiamaṇa* [2] N *bha.. śa* [3] E_{Sh}N *-yā* [4] E_B *teneha saha vedāntenaiva śāṃkhyāḥ* Npc *tenaiva saha vedāṃ* (tops are missing) *tenaiva śāṃkhyā* Nac *tenaiva śāṃkhyā*

[5] E_{Sh} *aṇṇakā* [6] E_{B} *matā vipralabdhā buddhayo* N *matavipralabdhābuddhayo* [7] E_{B} *–dṛṣtyā-* [8] E_{Sh} *-grantham* [9] N *casta-* [10] E_{Sh} om. *–nairvāṇika-* [11] E_{Sh} *pathyanta*

| zhes gsungs te | de lta bu'i nyon mongs pa dus su 'gog pa ni mi[1] skye ba'i dus te | thams cad kyis[2] 'jig pa'i dus zhes dgongs so | de'i tshe nges par srid[3] pa la mngon par zhen pa'i skyon gyis byis pa dang[4] mu stegs pa rnams bslus te | ma rig pa'o | | de nyid kyi phyir |

[1] DP *ma* [2] BP *kyi* [3] D *sred* [4] P om.

ahimaṇadosě[1] ṇa lakkhia[2] tatta | iti | (33a)

[1] $E_{B}E_{Sh}$ *ahimāṇadoseṃ* N *ahimaṇadūāseṃ* [2] E_{B} *lakkiu*

| nga[1] rgyal [2] skyon gyis [3] de nyid ([4]mtshon mi nus[4]) | (33a)

[1] P *rang* [2] D inserts *gyi ni* P inserts *gyis ni* [3] DP insert *ni* [4] DP *mtshon par mi nus so*

mithyājñānābhimānadoṣais tattvaṃ na vijñātam |

| zhes gsungs te | log pa'i shes pa'i nga rgyal gyis de nyid mtshon par mi nus so |

tĕna[1] dusaï[2] saala jāṇu[3] sŏ detta[4] | iti | (33b)

[1] $E_{B}E_{Sh}$ *teṇa* [2] $E_{B}E_{Sh}$N *dūsaï* [3] E_{Sh} *jāṇaï* [4] $E_{B}E_{Sh}$ *datta*

| theg pa ma lus sun 'byin zhing[1] | (33b)

[1] DP *cing*

sadoṣatayā dūṣitaṃ bhavati sakalaṃ yānaṃ mārgaś[1] ca taiḥ | daitya[2]puruṣava[d] [N 48b] anena

[1] $E_{B}E_{Sh}$ *mārgañ* [2] E_{B}N *ādaitya-*

| zhes gsungs te | de skyon dang ldan pas ma lus pa'i theg pa ([1]dang lam[1]) sun 'byin te[2] | ma rungs pa'i skyes bu bzhin no |

[1] P om. [2] P *cing*

jhāṇeṃ mohia saala vi loa | iti | (33c)

| 'jig rten ([1]ma lus[1]) ([2]rang rang[2]) theg pas rmongs | (33c)

[1] DP *pa kun* [2] P om.

sarvalokaḥ svasvayānaṃ tīrthikādīnāṃ yānam [eve]ti | idam

| zhes gsungs te | 'jig rten pa kun rang rang gi theg pa ste | mu stegs pa kun rang rang gi theg pas[1] rmongs pa'o |

[1] D *pa rnams* P *pa ste*

ṇia-sahāva ṇa[1] lakkhaï ([2]koi a[2]) | iti | (33d)

[1] $E_{B}E_{Sh}$N *ṇau* [2] E_{B} *koa* E_{Sh}N *koi*

| gnyug ma'i rang bzhin gang yin [B 136b] pa |
| de ni sus kyang ([1]rtogs pa med[1]) | (33d)

[1] DP *ma rtogs so*

nijasvabhāvaṃ sahajaṃ[1] sarvakālam avasthānāt | sa na lakṣitaṃ[2] kenacit lokenājñānāvṛteneti granthakāraḥ paridevanāṃ karoti | punaḥ |

[1] $E_{B}E_{Sh}$ *sahaja-* [2] $E_{B}E_{Sh}$ *lakṣitaḥ*

| ces gzhung byed pa'i mkhan po ha las pa'o |

[E_{B} 98] cittaha mūla ṇa[1] lakkhiaü sahajeṃ tiṇṇa[2] vitattha |
tahiṃ[3] jīvaï vilaa jāï[4] vasiaü tahi phuḍa[5] ettha[6] | iti | (34)

[1] E_{Sh} *na* [2] E_{Sh} *tinna* N *tiṇṇi* [3] E_{Sh}N *tahi tahi* [4] N *ja ..* [5] E_{B} *phuta* E_{Sh} *hata* [6] E_{Sh} *ettham?*

| yang sems kyi rtsa ba ni[1] mi[2] mtshon te |
| lhan cig skyes pa de nyid gsum |
| ([3]gang dang gang skyes gang du[3]) nub |
| ([4]de na[4]) gsal por gnas pa'o | (34)

[1] DP om. [2] D om. [3] DP *de dang der skyes de ru nub* [4] B *gang du* D *de ni*

anena sthiram upadeśaṃ dṛḍhāpayati | cittaheti[1] cintāyā | [upadeśa][N 49a] syaikam[2] | tathā mūlaṃ na lakṣitaṃ [3] guruṇāṃ vacanena sthāpitaṃ dvitīyaṃ | sahajasya svabhāvarūpaṃ lakṣake[ṇa] na[4] lakṣitaṃ | evaṃ tattvatrayaṃ lakṣyalakṣaṇalakṣakaṃ vitathaṃ atathyaṃ | yadi gṛhyate tadā sarvaṃ cittacaitanyarūpakā bhavanti | etenopadeśasya sattā na syāt | tasmin sthāne vīrapuruṣā j[ī]vantaḥ sūrā viralā[5] yoginaḥ jāyante | tasmāt he putra īdṛśeṣu sthāneṣu[4] vasitavyaṃ | tasmin sarvadharmā nilīnāḥ kāryāḥ sa paramārtha ity ucyate | tad evāha |

[1] E_B *cittaha iti* [2] E_B *-aikaṃ* N *-aikā* [3] E_BE_{Sh} insert *yad* [4] E_B om. [5] E_{Sh} *kaścid viralā*

zhes gsungs te | 'dis gdams ngag gsal por bstan[1] te | sems kyis ni gdams ngag sems pa ste gcig[2] | de bzhin du rtsa ba mi mtshon[3] pa ni bla ma'i gsung gis bstan pa'i don [4] mtshon pa[5] dang[6] gnyis | lhan cig skyes pa'i rang bzhin gyi ngo bo nyid mtshon byed kyis ma[7] mtshon pa dang | de[8] nyid rnam pa gsum gyis de ltar mtshon bya dang[(9]| mtshon byed dang |[9)] mtshon pa po gsum rdzun[10] zhing log pa ste | [11] | [D 191b] [(12]gal te bzung nas kyang de'i[12)] [P 211b3] tshe thams cad sems las byung ba'i ngo bor 'gyur te | des ni gdams ngag gi brgyud pa rgyun 'chad[13] par 'gyur ro | | de lta bu'i gnas [B 137a] la rnal 'byor pa dpa' bo 'ga' tsam grol bar 'gyur ro | | de'i phyir bu[14] 'di lta bu la gnas par bya'o | | de la chos thams cad [15] 'jig[16] par byed [(17]pa ni[17)] don dam pa zhes bya'o |

[1] DP *ston* [2] B *gcig dang* [3] DP *mngon* [4] B inserts *ma* [5] DP *byed* [6] D *de* [7] P *mi* [8] P *da* [9] D om. [10] DP *brdzun* [11] P inserts *de ltar yin na ... dmyal bar 'gro'o* (P 210a7–211b3=P 204b7); BD insert *de ltar yin na ... zhes gsungs so* (B 136b4–6, D 191a7–b2) [12] D *de'i* P om. [13] DP *chad* [14] BD om. [15] B inserts *la* [16] BDP *'jug* [17] B *pa'i*

jayati sukharāja ekaḥ kāraṇa[ra][N 49b]hitaḥ sadodito[1] jagatāṃ |
yasya ca nigadanasamaye vacanadaridro babhūva sarvajñaḥ || iti ||

[1] E_{Sh} *-te*

| de nyid bde ba rgyal[1] po gcig tu rgyal gyur cing[2] |
| 'gro ba rnams la rtag 'char rgyu rkyen bral gyur pa |
| gang zhig gi[3] ni de nyid brjod pa'i dus dag na |
| thams cad mkhyen pa dag kyang tshig gis phongs |

[1] BDP *chen* [2] B *cig* [3] BDP *gis*

| zhes gsungs so |

evaṃ |

mūlarahia[1] jo cintaï tatta[2] |
guru-uvaesem̩ etta viatta[3] | (35ab)

[1] E_B *mūlaraiia* N *mūla* ||| ia [2] E_{Sh} *tatu* [3] E_{Sh} *viatu* N *vianta*

[B:] | rtsa ba bral ba'i de nyid gang sems pa |
| bla ma'i gdams ngag gis ni de rnams yod | (35ab)

[DP:] | rtsa ba bral ba'i de nyid ni |

| gang gis sems pa bla ma yi |
| man ngag gis ni de nyid rtogs | (35ab)

yaḥ kaścid mūlarahitaṃ tattvaṃ cintayati | ([1]gurūpadeśenaitat[1]) puruṣaratnair viditaṃ tattvam iti | † [2] viditaṃ gurūpadeśam astavyasta[3]mārga([4]yāyine siddham[4]) | †
[1] N *gurūpadeśam etad* [2] E_{Sh} inserts *na* [3] E_{Sh} *vyaste pi* [4] E_{Sh} *yāyino siddham* N – *yāni si*

| ces[1] gsungs te | gang kha cig rtsa ba dang bral ba'i de nyid sems pa ni bla ma'i man ngag ste | de nyid [2] skyes bu[3] ([4]nor bu[4]) rin po ches[5] rtogs pa'o |
[1] DP *zhes* [2] B inserts *kyis* [3] B *bus* [4] DP om. [5] B *che*

[E_B 99; E_{Sh} 97] Saraha bhaṇaï vaḍha jāṇahu[1] caṃge |
cittarūa[2]-saṃsāraha bhaṅge | iti | (35cd)
[1] N *jāhu* [2] E_B *–rua*

[B:] | mda' bsnun na re rmongs pa legs par shes par gyis |
| sems kyi rang bzhin 'khor ba 'joms pa de yin no | (35cd)

[DP:] | chos rnams mda' snun gyis smras zhes par byos |
| gang zhig 'khor bar 'joms pa ni |
| sems kyi ngo bo nyid yin no | (35cd)

etena granthakāraḥ[1] spaṣṭārthaṃ vadati[2] | yaḥ kaścic cittarūpabhāvanā sā[3] saṃsārasya bhaṅga[4]hetukā bhave[t tadā-ukta][N 50a]ḥ | gurūpadeśena tattvaṃ lakṣyate[5] dṛḍhaniścayena | yaś cittarūpaḥ[6] saṃsāraś[7] cittamayo[8] vā ([9]tasya bhaṅgaḥ[9]) sambha[va]tīti[10] bhāvaḥ | tasmāt tat tattvaṃ |
[1] N *-ra* [2] N *vadanti* [3] N *sa* [4] $E_B E_{Sh}$N *bhaya-* [5] N *-ti* [6] E_{Sh} *–rūpāḥ* [7] E_{Sh} *–ra* [8] E_{Sh} *-yā* [9] E_{Sh} *tasya na* N *tasya bhaṅgo* [10] E_{Sh} *saṃsaratīti*

zhes gsungs te | 'di ni gzhung mkhan pos gsal por bstan[1] te | ([2]gang gang[2]) cig sems kyi ngo bo nyid bsgom pa ([3]de nyid[3]) 'khor ba 'jig pa'i rgyur gyur ro[4] | | bla ma dam pa'i gdams ngag gis de nyid nges pa brtan pos mtshon [P 212a] pa des sems kyi 'khor ba de 'jig[5] par 'gyur ro zhes ([6]dgongs pa'o[6]) | | de'i phyir |
[1] DP *ston* [2] BDP *gang kha kha* [3] P *des ni* [4] B *pa'o* [5] P *'jigs* [6] DP *gsungs so*

ṇiasahāva ṇa[1] kahiaü baaṇeṃ[2] | iti | (36a)
[1] $E_{Sh} E_B$N ṇaü [2] $E_B E_{Sh}$ *aṇṇeṃ* N *-em*

[B:] | gnyug ma'i rang bzhin ngag gis brjod du med | (36a)

[DP:] | gnyug ma'i rang bzhin de nyid ni |
| ngag gi brjod du yod ma yin | (36a)

nijasvabhāvaṃ svayambhūrūpaṃ[1] nānyena kathitaṃ tīrthikādinā | tadā kena
| sadguruṇety āha
[1] E_B –*svarūpaṃ*

| ces[1] gsungs te | rang bzhin nam[2] | gnyug ma ni rang byung[3] gi shes pa'i ngo
bo nyid do | | gzhan gyis[4] brjod ya ma yin pa ni mu stegs pa[5] la [D 192a] sogs pa
rnams [B 137b] kyis so | | 'o na de gang gis bstan[6] zhe na |
[1] DP *zhes* [2] DP om. [3] D *'byung* [4] P *gyi* [5] B om. [6] DP *ston*

> dīsaï guru-uvaesaha[1] ṇaaṇeṃ[2] | iti | (36b)
> [1] E_B -*ḍavaeseṃ* E_{Sh} -*uaeseṃ* N *uvaeseṃ* [2] $E_B E_{Sh}$ *na aṇṇeṃ* N
> *naaṇem*

| bla ma'i gdams ngag (1mig gis1) mthong (2bar 'gyur2) | (36b)
[1] B *gis ni* DP *mig* [2] DP om.

mayā sarahena[1] dṛṣṭaṃ[2] sadgurūpadeśena saugatāśrayeṇa[3] nānyeneti | gurū-
padeśacakṣuṣāvaga(4taṃ | paribhāṣitum4) yat tan mūko 'smi[5] iti | īdṛśaṃ
yasyāsti tasya guṇam āha
[1] N *sarahena* [2] E_{Sh} om. [3] N -*yena* [4] E_{Sh} –*tayā paricittaṃ* N *taṃ* | *paribhāvituṃ*
[5] E_BN *asminn*

| zhes gsungs te | sa ra ha bdag gis[1] bla ma sangs rgyas la bsten[2] pa'i (3bla ma'i3)
gdams ngag gis[4] rtogs[5] pa yin gyi[6] | gzhan gyis ni ma yin no | bla ma'i gdams
ngag gis nyams su myong ba'o | | de ltar 'di lta bu la yon tan ci yod ce na |
[1] B *nyid* [2] D *brten* P *brtan* [3] DP om. [4] P *gi* [5] DP *rtog* [6] D *gyis*

> ṇaü tas[u do][N 50b]sa jĕ[1] ekkavi ṭṭhāi | iti[2] | (36c)
> [1] E_B *dosao* [2] E_BN om.

| 'di la skyon ni rdul tsam med | (36c)

na tasya doṣasya ekaṃ[1] sthānam asti | yena |
[1] E_{Sh} om.

| ces gsungs te | 'di la skyon[1] gyi gnas rdul tsam yang med do | [(2]| gang gi phyir zhe na |[2)]
[1] P *sngon* [2] P om.

dhammādhamma sŏ sohia[1] khāi | iti | (36d)
[1] N *moḍ-hia*

| chos dang chos min mnyes nas zos[1] | (36d)
[1] B *zos pa yis*

gu[rū]padeśena dharmādharmaṃ pūrvoktalakṣaṇaṃ[1] śodhanīyatvāc[2] ca | śodhitaṃ bhakṣaṇaṃ karoti | asyaivopa[cā]ram āha |
[1] N *-ṇa* [2] E_B *–tvāt*

| zhes gsungs te | bla ma dam pa'i gdams ngag gis sngon du bstan pa'i chos dang chos ma yin pa dag par byas nas za zhing longs spyod par byed do | | 'di'i[1] nye bar spyod pa ni |
[1] P *de'i*

[E_B 100] ṇiamaṇa savveṃ[1] sohia javveṃ |[2] iti | (37a)
[1] E_{Sh} *save* [2] N *-em*

[B:] | gang tshe gnyug ma'i yid ni thams cad sbyangs | (37a)

[DP:] | gang gi tshe na gnyug ma'i yid |
| thams cad spyangs pa de'i tshe | (37a)

evaṃ amana[1]sarvadharmāḥ svabhāvotpannāḥ |[2] notpāditāḥ kenacit | yathā tṛṇavanagulmādayaḥ svabhāvenotpannā vilayaṃ yānti | tadvad iha [dv]ipadaś[3] catuṣpadādayaḥ svabhāvenotpannā nirmanā vilayaṃ yānti hi | [(4]na kenacid utpāditā bhavanti[4)] | [tat kathaṃ] [N 51a] dṛśyate | utpādādi mayā kṛtā ime[5] rūpādayaḥ | bhrāntyā 'jñāninām vacanam etat | tatparityāgo[6] [yasmin] kṣaṇe tasminn eva kṣaṇe sarvadharma[7]śodhanaṃ | tanmayatvāc ca bhakṣitaṃ bhavati |
[1] E_BE_{Sh} *manaḥ* [2] E_BN *–nnā* [3] E_BE_{Sh} *pada-* [4] N bottoms are missing [5] N *imaṃ* [6] E_BE_{Sh} *–parityāgāt* N *–pariyago* (? not clear) [7] N om. *–dharma-*

| zhes gsungs te | de ltar chos thams cad yid la [(1]mi byed[1)] pa ste | ngo bo nyid kyis ma skyes pas gzhan rgyu la sogs pa la ltos pa med pa'o | | gang gi tshe yid

la 'khrul pa yod pa spangs pa de'i tshe chos thams cad dag par 'gyur ba yin te | de'i rang bzhin yin pa'i phyir ro |

[1] DP *byed pa med*

guruguṇa hiyae[1] païsaï [ta]vveṃ[2] | iti | (37b)
[1] N *hiae* [2] N *-bbem*

| ([1]de'i tshe[1)] bla ma'i yon tan snying la 'jug | (37b)
[1] DP om.

guruṇā dattopadeśaguṇaṃ[1] svahṛdaye[2] praviṣṭaṃ tatra śodhana-bhakṣaṇādi[3]kāleṣu kāy[ā]di sarvaṃ dadātīti pratyayāt | na punar gurūpadeśaṃ vivadanti[4] | na ca[5] kiṃcit dadātīti[6] graharūpatvā[n] na[7] vettīti bhāvaḥ |

[1] E_{B} *–añ ca* E_{Sh} *–aś ca* [2] E_{Sh} *hṛdaye* [3] E_{B} *–bhakṣādi* [4] N *vidanti* [5] $E_{B}E_{Sh}$N om. [6] N *dadatīti* [7] N *ne*

ces pa ni | bla mas byin pa'i man ngag gi yon tan rang gi snying la zhugs shing rtogs na de la dag par byed pa dang | za ba'i dus su lus la sogs pa gtong[1] bar byed pas yid ches pa'o | | bla ma'i gdams ngag rtogs nas kyang gzhan la mi ster na | des gdams ngag ma rtogs zhes bya ste | shin tu 'dzin [B 138a] chags [P 212b] dang ldan pa'i phyir ro |

[1] B *btang*

evam[1] amaṇeṃ[2] muṇi saraheṃ gāhiu | iti | (37c)
[1] E_{B} evaṃ N *eva* [2] $E_{B}E_{Sh}$N *maṇe*

[B:] | 'di ltar yid med thub pa mda' bsnun [1] gis rtogs | (37c)
[1] B inserts *dag*

[DP:] | 'di lta bu yid med pa |
| thub pa mda' bsnun nga yis[1] rtogs | (37c)
[1] P *yi*

([1]īdṛśam amanena[1)] lakṣitam amana[2]lakṣi[taṃ] | [N 51b] athavā[3] | evam anena munir bhagavān | paramārtharūpakaṃ saroruhavajrapādenoktaṃ | dharmadhātulakṣaṇaṃ na [pu]naḥ | śaśaviṣāṇavan na kiṃcid amanam[4] | tathā coktaṃ |

[1] $E_{B}E_{Sh}$ *īdṛśaṃ manasā* N *īdṛśaṃ manena* [2] $E_{B}E_{Sh}$N *mana-* [3] E_{Sh} om. [4] $E_{B}E_{Sh}$ *amanaḥ*

| zhes gsungs te | 'di lta bur[1] yid med pas[2] mtshon pa'am | yang na [(3]de ltar[3)] yid med [(3]pa ni[3)] thub pa ste | bcom ldan 'das so | | de ni slob dpon mtsho skyes rdo rje'i zhabs yin te | des don dam pa'i ngo bo nyid de[4] chos kyi dbyings kyi mtshan nyid du[5] gsungs pa'o | | yid med ni ri bong gi rwa [D 192b] lta [(6]bur ci'ang[6)] med pa ni ma yin no |

[1] BD *bu'i* P *bu* [2] DP *par* [3] DP om. [4] D *kyi* P om. [5] DP om. [6] D *bu yang* P *bu ci yang*

sāvasthā kāpy avijñeyā mādṛśaiḥ[1] śūnyatocyate |
na punar[2] lokarūḍhyaiva[3] nāstikyārthānupātinī || (ĀM 142)

[1] E_{B}N *mādṛśāṃ* E_{Sh} *mādṛśā* [2] N *puna* [3] E_{B} *lokarūḍheva* E_{Sh} *laukikād eva* N *lokarūḍhova*

| de ltar de yi gnas skabs su ye shes[1] |
| kho bo lta bus stong par brjod [2] |
| yang na[3] 'jig rten grags pa yi |
| med pa ltar rjes 'brangs[4] pa min | (ĀM 142)

[1] B adds *ni* [2] B inserts *pa* [3] DP *ni* [4] P *'brel*

nāstitā[1]rūpam evāsyā[2] vyavahā[rārtham a]stitā[3] |
niḥsvabhāveṣu dharmeṣu kasya cāstitvanāstitā[4] || (ĀM 143)

[1] E_{Sh} *nāsti [sva]-* [2] $E_{B}E_{Sh}$N *-sya* [3] E_{L} *-ārthasaṃsthitā* [4] E_{L} *kasya vā sto 'stināstite*

| don ni med pa'i ngo bo nyid |
| tha snyad tsam du yod pa nyid |
| rang bzhin med pa'i chos rnams la |
| yod nyid med nyid ga la yod | (ĀM 143)

[E_{B} 101; E_{Sh} 98] na smartavyaṃ tvayety ukte smaraty[1] eva niṣedhitam[2] |
yathā tathaivāsacchabdāt [(3]so 'ntaraṃ[3)] pratipadyati || iti vistaraḥ | (ĀM 144)

[1] N *-tv* [2] $E_{B}E_{Sh}$ *nipeṣitam* [3] E_{B} *sottaraṃ* E_{L} *sāntaraṃ*

| khyod[1] nyid dran par mi bya bar[2] |
| bkag pa nyid de dran par byed |
| ji ltar de bzhin med sgra las |
| zhi ba dag ni sgrub par byed | (ĀM 144)

[1] P *khyed* [2] DP *ba*

athavā yadi vadanty abhyāsāt [N 52a][1] kleśāvṛtamanonirodhena[2] viśiṣṭaṃ mano buddhatvarūpaṃ jāyate | tadā katham anenoktena kiṃcit syāt | siddhaṃ paramārthaṃ mama sarveṣu tadāśritatvāc[3] ceti | tan na bhavati | kathaṃ tad ity āha |

[1] N folio no. 52 is missing [2] $E_B E_{Sh}$ *virodhena* [3] E_B *tadāśritā*

| ces [(1]gsungs pa yin no[1)] | gal te sgrib pa dang bcas pa'i yid 'gags pas khyad par can gyi yid sangs rgyas su [(2]ji ltar[2)] 'grub ce[2] na |

[1] DP *rgyas par gsungs so* [2] DP om. [2] DP *tsam*

tanta ṇa[1] manta ṇa[2] ekka vi cāhiu | iti | (37d)

[1] $E_B E_{Sh}$ om. [2] $E_B E_{Sh}$N *ṇaü*

[B:] | sngags dang rgyud rnams gcig kyang ngas ma mthong | (37d)

[DP:] | sngags rnams dang ni rgyud rnams ni |
| gcig kyang bdag gis ma mthong ngo | (37d)

tantro bahuprakāraḥ | tantroktā mantrās | teṣu siddhāntaṃ[1] nānā svaparakalpitaṃ mayā ekamātraṃ na prekṣitaṃ bhāvyabhāvakādilakṣaṇam | kutas te[2] lokānāṃ vaineyamātraṃ na punar viśiṣṭaphalaṃ tato jāyate | tathā coktam |

[1] E_B om. [2] $E_B E_{Sh}$ *taiḥ*

| zhes gsungs te | rgyud ni rnam pa mang po'o[1] | | de las gsungs [(2]pa ni[2)] sngags te | de rnams kyi grub[3] mtha' rang[4] dang gzhan gyis brtags pa'i lta ba dang | sgom pa dang | bsgom bya dang | sgom pa po la sogs pa'i mtshan nyid bdag gis gcig kyang ma mthong ngo | de[4] ci'i [B 138b] phyir zhe na | de ni 'jig rten pa 'dul ba'i phyir gsungs te | khyad par can gyi 'bras bu ni ma mthong ngo | |

[1] P *po* [2] B *pa'i* [3] P *pa'i* [4] DP om.

[(1]āḥ kim[1)] abhyāsa[2]yogena ādiśuddhā svabhāvikā |
prakṛtyaiva hi sā siddhā tathatā na vikalpajā ||

[1] $E_B E_{Sh}$ *āsthim* [2] E_B *ādhyāsa* E_{Sh} *ābhyāsa*

| rnal 'byor goms pas ci zhig bya |
| gdod[1] nas dag pa'i ngo bo nyid |
| rang bzhin gyis ni grub pa ste |
| rtog las de bzhin nyid mi skye |

[1] D *ka*

abhāvalakṣaṇā[1] bodhiḥ sarvadharmāś ca tanmayāḥ |
atas tāṃ[2] prārthayec caryā[3] nijaskandhaplavopamā[4] || iti
[1] $E_B E_{Sh}$ *-ṇād* [2] $E_B E_{Sh}$ *tat* [3] $E_B E_{Sh}$ *caryāṃ* [4] $E_B E_{Sh}$ *-pamām*

| dngos med mtshan nyid byang chub ste |
| chos rnams ma lus [P 213a] de dngos nyid |
| de phyir spyod pas bskul ba ni |
| rang gi phung po gzings bzhin no |

tasmāt |

bajjhaï kammeṇa jaṇo[1] kammavimukkeṇa hoi maṇamokkhaṃ |
iti | (38ab)
[1] $E_B E_{Sh}$N *uṇo*

| de'i phyir |

| 'gro kun rnams[1] las (2kyis 'ching 'gyur2) te |
| las las grol (3na yid kyi3) thar pa yin | (38ab)
[1] B *kun* [2] B *kyis so sor bcings gyur* D *kyis 'cings 'gyur* P *kyi 'ching 'gyur* [3] D *ba'i* P *yid* (B is supported by Apa. but violates the meter.)

yena karmaṇā jantavo vibadhyante tatparityāgādhimokṣeṇa ca bhavati manomokṣaṃ | mokṣaṃ cātmātmīyavikalparahitatayā | mithyābhāvanayā manaḥsaṃjñaiva bandhanāt tasya nirodhaḥ | evaṃ parijñāne yugapat (1manomokṣa iti1) bhāvārthaṃ cāha |
[1] E_B *-mokṣeṇeti* E_{Sh} *-manomokṣeti*

| zhes gsungs te | las gang gis skye bo rnams 'ching ba de nyid btang na yid kyi thar pa yin no | | thar pa ni bdag dang bdag gir 'dzin pa'i rnam par rtog pa dang bral ba'o | | log[1] par bsgom[2] pa'i yid kyis[3] mtshan mar 'dzin pa nyid 'ching ba yin no | | de ltar chags pa de yongs su shes pa ni yid kyi thar pa yin no zhes dgongs pa'o[4] |
[1] DP *legs* [2] D *bsgoms* [3] DP *kyi* [4] DP *so*

maṇa-mokkheṇa aṇūṇaṃ pāvijjaï parama-ṇivvāṇaṃ | iti (38cd)

| yid kyi thar pa gzhan du mi rnyed de |
| de ni mchog gi mya ngan 'das pa yin | (38cd)

manomo[N 53a]kṣeti[1] manaś ca mokṣaṃ ca | anayor anyonyaṃ[2] niścitaṃ paraspararahitaṃ paramanirvāṇalakṣaṇaṃ prāptiḥ |
[1] E_B *–kṣeṇeti* E_{Sh} *-kṣeṇa* [2] E_B *anyonyaṃ*

| zhes gsungs te | (1de ltar gang du1) yid kyi thar pa ni[2] (3yid dang thar pa de3) phan tshun [D 193a] du ma spangs pa ni nges par mchog gi mya ngan las 'das pa'i mtshan nyid do |
[1] P om. [2] DP *de* [3] D om.

[E_B 102] cittekka sa[ala]-bīaṃ bhavaṇivvāṇo[1] vi jassa viphuranti |
iti | (39ab)
[1] E_{Sh}N *-ṇā*

| sems nyid gcig pu kun gyi sa bon te |
| gang las srid dang mya ngan 'das [1] 'phro ba | (39ab)
[1] P inserts *pa rnams*

evaṃ uktanirvāṇe[1] 'prāpte[2] sati tadā (3kā cittasthitiḥ3) | cittāt sakalam avidyādibījaṃ[4] bhavanirvāṇātmakāś[5] cāśakyā visphuranti | te bhavasthāyikāś[5] ca na bhavatīti yāvat | tasmāt |
[1] E_{Sh} *–ṇa-* [2] $E_B E_{Sh}$N *prāpte* [3] E_{Sh} *citte [ba]ddhe sati* N *kaḥ cittasthi* [4] E_B *avidyābījaṃ* [5] E_{Sh}N *-kā*

| zhes gsungs te | de ltar gong du bstan pa'i mya ngan las 'das pa'i mtshan nyid ma thob na de'i tshe[1] ji ltar bsam zhe na | sems [2] las ma lus pa'i ma rig pa'i sa bon las byung ba 'khor ba [B 139a] dang mya ngan las 'das pa'i mtshan nyid dag par mi nus par snang zhing 'phro ba'o | | de dag kyang srid pa'i ngo bo nyid du rnam par gzhag par mi nus so | de'i phyir
[1] P *phyir* [2] P inserts *de*

taṃ cintāmaṇi-rūaṃ paṇamaha icchā-phalaṃ dei[1] | iti | (39cd)
[1] E_B *denti*

| 'dod pa'i 'bras bu ster bar byed pa yi |
| yid bzhin nor 'dra'i sems la phyag 'tshal lo | (39cd)

paramanirvāṇasya viśeṣaṇaṃ[1] cintāmaṇirūpaḥ | tasya praṇāmaṃ kuruta | kutaḥ | [i][N 53b]cchāphalaṃ[2] dadātīti tena[3] hetunā | icchā ca mahākaruṇā

jagadarthātmikā | tad[4]vāñchāphalaṃ yena pūr[it]am anābhogataḥ saiva gurus tasyeti[5] cintāmaṇis tathā | evaṃ |
[1] $E_B E_{Sh}$N *viśeṣaṇaṃ sa* [2] N *-phala* [3] E_B om. [4] E_BN *tāṃ* [5] E_BN *tasyaiti*

| zhes gsungs te | mchog gi mya ngan las 'das pa'i khyad par ni yid bzhin gyi nor [(1]bu lta bu'o[1)] | | de la phyag 'tshal lo | | de ci'i phyir zhe na | 'dod pa'i 'bras bu ster [(2]bar byed pa'i[2)] phyir ro | | 'dod pa ni snying rje chen pos 'gro ba'i don byed pa'i bdag nyid de | de ni lhun gyis grub pa'i 'bras bu gang gis [P 213b] ster ba'o | | de nyid ni[3] bla ma[4] yid bzhin gyi nor bu lta bu'o | de ltar yang[3] |
[1] P *bu'o* [2] DP *ba'i* [3] DP om. [4] P *ma'i*

> cittem̐ bajjhem̐ bajjhaï mukkem̐ [mu]kkei ṇatthi[1] sandeho[2] | iti | (40ab)
> [1] E_{Sh} *ṇiva* [2] E_B *-hā*

> | sems bcings[1] na ni bcings pa yin |
> | grol bas grol bar the tshom med | (40ab)
> [1] B *bcing*

cittena baddhena vikalpādinā badhyanti | punar api tatparijñānāt muktiṃ lapsyanti | evaṃ tritayaḥ[1] bandhana[2]mukti[3]muktabandheṣu[4] | tatra muktir[5] adva[6]yeneti nāsti sandehaḥ | evam aparijñānāt saṃsāre vibhramanti bālajātīyāḥ[7] | paṇḍitāḥ mucya[nte] |
[1] E_{Sh} *[aya]ntritaḥ* [2] E_B *bandha-* [3] $E_B E_{Sh}$N *–mukta-* [4] E_{Sh} *mukta muktabandha teṣu* [5] E_B *muktiḥ* N *–mukti* [6] E_{Sh} *dva-* [7] N *–yāṃ*

| ces gsungs te | sems [(1]bcings pa[1)] ni rnam par rtog pa la sogs pas bcings pa'o | | de ltar yang[2] | de dag shes pas grol ba 'thob[3] par 'gyur te | grol ba ni gnyis su med pa'i ye shes te | des grol ba la [4] the tshom med do[5] | de ltar ma shes na byis pa'i skye bo rnams [(2]'khor bar[2)] 'khyams par 'gyur ro | de'i dbang du byas nas |
[1] B *bcing ba* [2] P om. [3] DP *thob* [4] B inserts *ni* [5] B *de*

> [E_{Sh} 99] ba[jjhanti[1] je][N 54a]ṇa vi jaḍā lahu[2] parimuccanti tĕṇa[3] vi buhā[4] || iti | (40cd)
> [1] $E_B E_{Sh}$N *va[jjhati* [2] E_{Sh} om. [3] $E_B E_{Sh}$N *tena* [4] E_{Sh} *budhā* E_B *vuhā*

> | blun po gang gis 'ching 'gyur ba |
> | mkhas [(1]rnams de yis 'grol bar 'gyur[1)] | (40cd)
> [1] DP *pa de yi rnam par grol*

yenaiva pañca[1]kāmopabhogādinā mūrkhalokā ba[dhyante] | tenaiva sati parijñāne guror ādeśāt paṇḍitā laghu śīghrataḥ saṃsārād muktā bhava[nti | ta]thā coktaṃ |

[1] E_B *vañca-*

> [E_B 103] | yenaiva viṣakhaṇḍena mriyante sarvajantavaḥ |
> tenaiva viṣatattvajño viṣeṇa sphoṭayed viṣaṃ || iti (HT II.ii.46)

tathā punaḥ |

| zhes gsungs te[1] | gang gis 'dod pa'i yon tan lnga la longs spyod pas rmongs pa'i 'jig rten pa rnams 'ching bar 'gyur ba de nyid kyis | bla ma'i gdams [B 139b] ngag rtogs pa yod pa'i mkhas pa rnams myur du 'khor ba las grol bar 'gyur ro | | de ltar yang |

[1] DP om.

> baddho dhāvaï dahadihahiṃ[1] mukko ṇiccala ṭhāi[2] | iti | (41ab)

[1] N *-hi* [2] E_{Sh} *ṭhṭhāi*

> | bcings pa rnams ni phyogs bcur rgyug |
> | btang na mi g.yo brtan par gnas | (41ab)

yathā puruṣa ātmātmīya[1]vikalpanena badhyamāno daśadiśi dhāvati ṣaḍ[2]gatisaṃsāre vibhramanti[3] | tathā sa eva puru[N 54b]ṣaḥ samyagmārgāt muktaḥ | tadā ([4]niścale nānātvaparimukte[4]) sthāne sthitatvāt[5] dharmakāyātmaka[6] iti bhāvaḥ |

[1] E_BN *ātmīya-* [2] N *ṣaṭ* [3] $E_B E_{Sh}$ *vibhramati* [4] $E_B E_{Sh}$ *niścalenātmaparimukte* [5] E_{Sh} *sthitaṃ* [6] E_{Sh} *-kam*

| zhes gsungs te | ji ltar skye 'gro bdag [D 193b] dang bdag gir 'dzin pa'i rtog pas bcings pa 'gro ba drug gi 'khor bar 'khor zhing 'khyams te | skye 'gro de nyid yang dag pa'i lam gyis grol ba na | de'i tshe sna tshogs su ([1]snang ba[1]) lhag par mos pa las mi g.yo ba'i gnas la gnas pa ni chos kyi sku'i bdag nyid yin no zhes dgongs pa'o[2] |

[1] P om. [2] DP *so*

> emaï karahā pekkhu sahi vivaria[1] mahu paḍihāi || iti | (41cd)

[1] $E_B E_{Sh}$ *viharia*

> | grogs dag 'di ni rnga mo bzhin |
> | go ([1]bzlog pa ni nga yis[2] rtogs[1]) | (41cd)

[1] B *ldog par ni bdag gis 'dod* [2] P *yi*

samudāyato 'tra yathā karabha[1] [u]ṣṭraḥ mahābhāreṇa baddhas tadā vegena dhāvati | dhārayitum aśaktaḥ[2] | saiva[3] bhāratyāgād muktaḥ kṣaṇe [(4]niścala eka[4)]sthāne sthitas tathā īdṛśaṃ[5] karabham iva svakīyaṃ cittaṃ sākṣād viharati | tādṛśaṃ mama pratibhāsate vyapadeśārthokta[6]lakṣaṇād iti | idānīm asya kāryam āha

[1] E_{Sh} *karaha* [2] E_{Sh}N *aśakyaḥ* [3] E_B *sa eva* [4] E_{Sh} *niśca[la]ś caika-* [5] N *īdṛśa* [6] E_{Sh} *vyapadeśārthāḥ*

| zhes[1] gsungs te | 'dir bsdus pa'i don ni ji ltar rnga mo la khal chen po bkal na nus tshad kyis rgyug ste sus kyang gzung bar mi nus pa de nyid | khal phog pa'i dus na sa gzhi la brtan[2] pa de bzhin du | de lta bu'i rnga mo dang 'dra ba'i sems rang gi rnam pa can du [(3]sdad do[3)] | | 'di'i dgos pa ni |

[1] B *ces* [2] BD *brten* [3] BD *snang ba'o*

pavaṇarahia[1] [N 55a][2] appāṇa ma cintaha |
kaṭṭhajoëṃ[3] saggo[4] ma bandaha || iti (42ab)

[1] N *pavaṇa* ||| *a* [2] N fols. 55–62 are missing [3] E_B *kaṭhṭha joi* E_{Sh} *kaṭṭhajoiṇā* [4] E_B *ṇāsagga* E_{Sh} *sagga*

| rlung spangs rang nyid ma sems shig[1] |
| zhing gi rnal 'byor [P 214a] dag gis kyang |
| sna yi rtse mor [(2]ma gtugs shig[2)] | (42ab)

[1] BD *shing* [2] D *ma gtug cing* P *rab btug cing*

[E_B 104] pavaneti vāyuḥ | nāsikāśvāsocchvāsalakṣaṇaṃ | tadrahitatayā ātmānaṃ na drakṣyati | kutaḥ | yāvat vāyvāśritaṃ śarīraṃ tadrahitena śarīrasya kutaḥ sthānam asti | evaṃ gurūpadeśāt vāyus tanmayaṃ kṛtvā kutrātmanā[1] | na labhyante | tasmāt tyaja | kaṣṭena yogena vikalpātmakena tasyāḥ saṃgaṃ na kriyatām iti niścayaḥ | kiṃ kriyata ity āha

[1] $E_B E_{Sh}$ *kutrātmāno*

| ces[1] gsungs te | rlung ni[2] sna bug nas 'byung ba dang 'jug pa'i mtshan nyid kyi[3] rlung [(4]ste |[4)] spangs pa ni rang nyid med cing shi ba'o zhes bya'o | | [5] ci'i phyir zhe na | ji[6] srid du rlung gnas pa de srid du lus [7] gnas la | rlung med na lus [8] gang du gnas te | mi gnas so | | de ltar bla ma'i man ngag gis[9] rlung dang lus [B 140a] kyi bdag nyid du byas nas[10] de la lus dmigs te | gzhan du[11] ni lus mi dmigs so | shing gi rnal 'byor ni rnam par rtog pa'i bdag nyid kyi rnal 'byor la chags par mi[12] byed ces pa'o | | nges par ji ltar bya zhe na |

[1] P *zhes* [2] D om. [3] BP *kyis* [4] B *de* [5] B inserts *de* [6] BP om. [7] B inserts *la* [8] BP insert *la* [9] P *gi* [10] B *na* [11] DP om. [12] B *ma*

arĕ vaḍha sahaje[1] saï para rajjaha |
mā bhavagandhabandha paḍicajjaha | (42cd)
[1] E_{Sh} *-ja*

| e (1ma hoḥ rmongs rnams1) lhan cig skyes pa mchog tu son |
| srid pa'i bag chags 'ching ba spongs[2] | (42cd)
[1] DP *ma'o skye bo rmongs pa rnams* [2] B *yongs su spangs*

he mūḍhapuruṣa[1] alpāśayaṃ tyaja[2] | (3mahāśayaṃ kuruṣva3) | kiṃ tat | sahajaṃ gaveṣaya | tatpraveśe[4] mahārthatayā śaktiṃ kuru | mā bhavagandheti | bhavasya gandho (5gandharvasattvaḥ | tayā5) gatyāgatibhāvād yair bhavabandhanam alātacakravad bhavati tasmin mā tvaṃ saktiṃ kuru |
[1] E_BE_{Sh} *mūḍha puruṣa* [2] E_BE_{Sh} *tyajasi* [3] E_B *kuruṣva mahāśayaṃ* [4] E_B *tat praveśe*
[5] E_BE_{Sh} *gandharvasattvatayā*

| zhes gsungs te | kye rmongs pa'i skye bo bsam pa chung ngu thong la | bsam pa rgya chen po gyis shig | de gang yin zhe na | lhan cig skyes pa tshol zhig | de la zhugs la don chen po la lhag par mos par gyis shig pa'o | | srid pa'i bag chags ni bar ma[1] do'i skye ba'o | | (2des na2) | srid par (3'gro 'ong3) srid pa'i 'ching ba ste | | mgal me'i 'khor lo bzhin du 'gyur ba'i phyir de la chags par ma[4] byed cig[5] spongs[6] | | zhes bya ba'i don no[7] |
[1] P om. [2] P *de nas* [3] P *'gro ba dang 'ong bas* [4] D *mi* [5] D *gcig* P om. [6] B *spangs* P *spongs par* [7] DP *to*

ehu maṇa mellaha pavana turaṅga sucañcala |
sahajasahāve sa vasaï hoi niccala | iti | (43)

| 'di na yid dang rlung ni g.yo phyir[1] phyor[2] |
| shin tu mi srun[3] pa yi rta 'dra thong |
| lhan cig skyes pa'i rang bzhin rtogs gyur na[4] |
| de yis [D 194a] yid ni brtan par 'gyur ba yin | (43)
[1] DP *zhing* [2] BDP *phyar* [3] P *bsrun* [4] DP *ba*

īdṛśaṃ manaḥ pavanaṃ ca suṣṭhu cañcalam iva turaṅgo yathā 'sya nirantaratvāt | tat tyājyaṃ kuru | idaṃ grāhayiṣyasi | kiṃ tat | sahajasvabhāvasthānaṃ gurūpadeśataḥ[1] | tenāśritena sākṣān niścalaṃ bhaviṣyati | ātmanā jñāyate puṇyād[2] iti vacanāt | asya viśeṣaṇam āha |
[1] E_BE_{Sh} *–deśaḥ* [2] HT I.viii.34c

| zhes gsungs te | de lta bu'i yid dang rlung ni ([1]shin tu'ang[1]) dul[2] mi thub cing g.yo ba'i rta lta bu ste | de gtang ngo | | 'di gzung bar bya ste | gang zhe na | lhan cig skyes pa'i rang bzhin gyi gnas bla ma dam pa'i gdams ngag la brten nas mi g.yo zhing[3] brtan par 'gyur te | rang gi bsod nams dbang [P 214b] gis rtogs | | zhes bya ba la sogs pa gsungs pa'i [B 140b] phyir ro | 'di'i khyad par ni |

[1] P *zhi na yang* [2] DP om. [3] B *ba'i phyir*

javveṃ[1] maṇa attha[2]maṇa jāi taṇu tuṭṭaï bandhaṇa |
tavveṃ[1] samarasa sahaje vajjaï ṇaü sudda ṇa vamhaṇa || iti | (44)

[1] E_{Sh} *javve* [2] E_{Sh} *accha-*

| gang tshe yid ni nye bar 'gags[1] gyur na |
| ([2]de'i tshe na 'ching ba thams cad 'chad[2]) |
| gang la lhan cig skyes pa ro mnyam pa |
| de la dmangs[3] rigs dang ni bram ze med | (44)

[1] DP *nub* [2] B *de'i tshe lus kyi 'ching ba rnam par chad* [3] B *rmongs*

[E_{Sh} 100] yasmin kṣaṇe vikalpamano 'stam itaṃ bhavati tasmin sarvabandhanaṃ vinaśyati | na kevalam ātmano[1] bandhanamātraṃ viśeṣeṇa tasmin kāle samarasaḥ[2] sahaje[3] varjanaṃ sarvalokānāṃ [E_B 113][4] karoti | tayā na śūdraṃ brāhmaṇādi[5] jātiviśeṣaṃ bhavati siddhaṃ | sarve lokā ekajātinibaddhāś ca sahajam eveti bhāvaḥ | tasyaivānusaṃsām āha | nāsti sahajāt paraṃ siddhāntam iti | evaṃ

[1] E_{Sh} *-nā* [2] E_{Sh} *–sa-* [3] E_{Sh} *–jaṃ* [4] E_B: Pages 105–12 are identical with pages 115–22 [5] E_B *brājñaṇādi*

| ces gsungs te | rnam par rtog pa'i yid gang gi tshe 'gags ([1]pa de'i[1]) tshe bcings pa thams cad spong bar byed do | | bdag nyid 'ba' zhig 'ching ba med pa ni ma yin gyi[2] | de'i tshe khyad par du ([3]lhan cig skyes pa'i ro mnyam pas[4] skyes 'gro thams cad [5] 'jug par byed do | | de'i tshe dmangs[6] rigs dang bram ze'i rigs la'ang khyad par med do | | des don 'di kun[7] 'grub ste | 'jig rten pa thams cad lhan cig skyes pa'i ngo ([8]bo nyid du[8]) rigs gcig go zhes dgongs pa'o[9] | | de'i phan yon bstan[10] pa ni |[3]) lhan cig skyes pa las ma gtogs[11] pa'i grub mtha' gzhan med par bstan pa'i phyir | [11]

[1] P *pa'i* [2] D *gyis* [3] P om. [4] D *pa la* [5] BP insert *la* [6] B *rmongs* [7] D om. [8] D *bor* [9] D *so* [10] D *ston* [11] DP *rtogs* [11] P inserts *'di na chu bor rigs gcig go zhes dgongs so | | de'i phan yon ston pa ni lhan cig skyes pa las ma rtogs pa'i grub mtha' gzhan med par bstan pa'i phyir |*

etthu sĕ sura-sari jamuṇā etthu sĕ gaṅgāsāaru |
etthu paāga vaṇārasi etthu sĕ canda divāaru | iti | (45)

| 'di na [(1]ga ṅgā[1)] ya mu na [(2]yin te[2)] |
| 'di na[3] ga ṅgā rgya mstho 'phrad [(4]pa ste[4)] |
| [(5]'di na[5)] pra[6] ya gā[7] [(8]dang wā ra nā sī'o[8)] |
| 'di na[3] [(9]zla ba nyi ma gsal byed[9)] yin | (45)

[1] DP *chu bo* [2] DP om. [3] B *ni* [4] B *pa 'di* DP om. [5] B om. [6] P *pa* [7] BDP *gha* [8] D *yin te* | *'di na wā rā ṇa sī nyid* P *yin te* | | *'di na ba ra ṇa si nyid* [9] P *nyi ma zla ba*

evam asti suṣṭhu krīḍā | kuto | 'sti svaparātmanaḥ[1] sahajena avicchinnapravāhād iti | saiva yamunāgaṅgādināmā ca | na punaḥ pānīyasnānādhāratayā | kiṃ tu yamunā sarvayānatadāśrayā[2] ca | gaṅgā tatparigamanaśīlā | sāgaraś[3] ca sarvasamādhyupadeśasamudratvaṃ | prayāgaṃ ca advayatvād vārāṇasī cādvayaṃ[4] dvayanivāraṇāt | candradivākarau ca rāhugrahaṇatayā[5] upadeśāgninā sarvaṃ bhakṣayed iti | na kevalaṃ tīrthādi sahajaṃ[6] pīṭhopapīṭhādiṣu ca | tam āha

[1] E_B *svasvaparātma-* E_{Sh} *svaparātma-* [2] E_B *–yāṃ* [3] $E_B E_{Sh}$ *sāgarañ* [4] $E_B E_{Sh}$ *cādvaya-* [5] E_B *-tathā* [6] $E_B E_{Sh}$ *sahaja*

| zhes gsungs te | [(1]'di ltar[1)] lha'i chu bo 'di rnams ni [(2]rang dang gzhan[2)] gyi lhan cig skyes pa rgyun mi 'chad pa la ro gcig pa'o | | 'di[3] nyid la gaṅgā dang ya mu na la sogs pa'i ming btags pa yin gyi[4] | khrus byed pa'i rten gyi chu bo ni ma yin no | | 'on kyang ya mu na ni theg pa [5] thams cad 'di[3] la brten pa'i phyir ro | | gaṅgā ni de nyid du rtogs[6] shing 'gro ba'i ngang tshul can yin no | ga ṅgā dang rgya mtsho 'phrad [B 141a] pa ni stong pa dang snying rje ro gcig pa la 'gro ba ma lus pa 'jug pa'o | rgya mtsho ni ting nge 'dzin gyi gdams ngag thams cad kyi rgya mtsho yin pa'i phyir ro | | [(7(8]pra ya gā[8)] ni gnyis su med pa'i phyir ro[7)] | | [(9]wā ra ṇā sī'ang[9)] gnyis su med pa ste | de[10] gnyis 'gog [(11]pa'i phyir ro[11)] | zla ba dang nyi ma gza' rā [D 194b] [(12]hu las[12)] gzung ba'i dus su gdams ngag gi dus kyi me [(13]rā hu la'i[13)] ngo bo nyid kyis[14] [(15]thams cad za'o[15)] zhes pa'o | | khrus stegs la sogs [(16]pa 'ba' zhig lhan cig skyes pa [(17]yin par ma zad[17)] kyi | gnas dang nye ba'i gnas la sogs pa'ang lhan cig skyes pa'i ngo bor bstan pa'i phyir |[16)]

[1] B *ji ltar* P *'dir* [2] BD *rang bzhin* P *dang gzhan* [3] B *de* [4] D *gyis* [5] B inserts *chen po* [6] B *gtogs* [7] P om. [8] B *pra ya gha* D *bra ya gha* [9] P *ba ra ṇa se yang* [10] DP om. [11] DP *pa'o* [12] DP *hus* [13] DP *hū* [14] DP *kyi* [15] DP *bram ze'o* [16] P om. [17] D *gnas par ma byas*

kkhettu pīṭha upapīṭha ĕtthu | iti | (46a)

[(1]| zhing kun gnas dang nye ba'i gnas la[2] sogs |[1)] (46a)
[1] P om. [2] D om.

evaṃ kṣetropakṣetrādi sarvaṃ hi caturviṃśatisthānāni | na[1] bāhya-bhramaṇakāryam asti | sa ca |
[1] $E_B E_{Sh}$ *sa*

([1]| zhes ([2]bya ba[2]) gsungs te | zhing dang nye ba'i zhing la sogs[1]) [P 215a] pa[3] gnas nyi shu rtsa bzhi ni [5] lhan cig skyes pa'i ngo bo nyid yin pas phyi rol du 'khyams[6] pa la sogs pa mi bya'o |
[1] P om. [2] B om. [4] DP *pa'i* [5] DP insert *'dir* [6] D *'khyam*

maïṃ[1] bhamaï pariṭhṭhao | iti | (46b)
[1] E_{Sh} *maï*

[B:] | ngas ni 'khyams te bltas pas rtogs par gang smra ba | (46b)

[DP:] | ngas ni 'khyams shing[1] bltas shing rtogs | (46b)
[1] D *te*

mayā paribhramaṇe[1] sthāpitaḥ[2] | yoginyupadeśād bāhyādhyātmikaṃ viśvaṃ sukhamayam eveti bhāvārthaḥ | etena kim uktaṃ syāt | svaśarīraṃ sukharūpaṃ tasya dhātuḥ pīṭhādirūpatayā bāhyeṣu pravṛttiḥ | tenāha
[1] $E_B E_{Sh}$ *paribhramaṇa-* [2] $E_B E_{Sh}$ *-ta*

| zhes gsungs te | bdag gis[1] phyin[2] te bltas shing rtogs[3] pa ni rnal 'byor ma'i gdams ngag gis[4] rnam par gzhag[5] ste | phyi dang nang gis [6] bsdus pa'i sna tshogs bde ba chen po'i ([7]bdag nyid[7]) yin no zhes dgongs pa'i don no[8] | | 'dis ni 'di ston[9] te | rang gi lus ni bde ba'i[10] ngo bo de'i khams gnas la sogs pa'i rang bzhin yin pa'i phyir phyi rol du 'jug par mi bya'o | | de'i phyir |
[1] P *gi* [2] DP *phyir* [3] D *rtog* [4] DP *gi* [5] B inserts *pa* [6] P *gi* [7] DP *rang bzhin* [8] D *to* [9] B *ltar bstan* [10] B *ba'i chen po'i*

dehāsarisaa tittha maïṃ[1] suha aṇṇa[2] ṇa diṭhṭhao[3] || iti | (46cd)
[1] E_{Sh} *maï* [2] E_{Sh} *a* [3] E_B *dīṭhṭhao* E_{Sh} *dīṭhṭhatta*

| lus dang 'dra ba'i 'bab stegs gnas[1] |
[B 141b] | bde ba gzhan du[2] ma mthong ngo | (46cd)
[1] P om. [2] DP *ni*

dehā[1] śarīrasadṛśaṃ tīrthaṃ sukharūpaṃ yadi bhavati tadā sustham | yadā śarīrasadṛśaṃ tīrthaṃ mayā sukhaṃ naṣṭam iti tasmād abhinnena vihartavyaṃ yogineti | evaṃ punar ādhyātmikeṣu pīṭhādiṣu[2] ca saṃcarādināvagantavyaṃ[3] teṣu ca sukhamayena saṃcāraṃ na vāyumātreṇeti | tasmād dharmamahāsukhamayaṃ pīṭhādi siddham | ittham ādhyātmikapīṭhādidevatādhiṣṭhānavato niṣpannayogino bāhyapīṭhādibhramaṇam anarthakam | yathoktam |

[1] Skt. *dehaḥ* [2] E_B *–deṣu* [3] E_B *–tavvaṃ*

| zhes gsungs te | gang[1] gis[2] lus dang 'dra ba'i khrus stegs bde ba'i rgyur[3] mi mthong ngo | | de'i phyir rnal 'byor pas gnyis su med par gnas par bya'o | | de ltar gzhan yang nang gi bdag nyid kyi[4] gnas pa[5] la sogs pa la kun tu spyod pas[6] rtogs par bya ste | de rnams la bde ba'i rang bzhin gyis[7] kun tu spyod pa yin gyi | lus 'ba' zhig tsam ni[8] gnas pa [9] ma yin no | | de'i phyir mchog gi bde ba chen po gnas la sogs pa'i rang bzhin du grub pas | 'di ltar nang gi bdag nyid kyi gnas la sogs pa'i[10] lha rnams kyis[11] byin gyis brlabs pa'i rdzogs pa'i rnal 'byor pa phyi rol gyi yul du 'gro ba la dgos pa med do |

[1] DP *rang* [2] BDP *gi* [3] DP *rgyu* [4] B *kyis* [5] DP om. [6] BD *pa* [7] DP *gyi* [8] BD *na* [9] B inserts *ni* [10] P *pa la* [11] DP *kyi*

> [E_B 114] caturviṃśatibhedena pīṭhādy ([1]atra vyavasthitaṃ[1]) |
> atas tadbhrahmaṇenaiva[2] khedaḥ kāryo na tāttvikaiḥ ||
>
> [1] E_BE_{Sh} *atraiva saṃsthitaṃ* [2] E_BE_{Sh} *tadgrahaṇārthena* (cited without reference in the *Abhisamayamañjarī*)

> | ji ltar nyi shu rtsa bzhi'i bye brag gis |
> | gnas la sogs pa 'di la[1] gnas |
> | de'i phyir de nyid shes pa yis[2] |
> | ([3]'khyams shing[3]) ngal bar mi bya'o |
>
> [1] D *dag* [2] P *yi* [3] P *'khyam zhing*

> yadi tattvavihī([1]naḥ syād[1]) bhrāntyāveśān na kiṃcana |
> atha tattvo[2]petās te syur bhrāntyā teṣāṃ na kiṃcana || iti |
>
> [1] E_BE_{Sh} *-nasya* [2] E_BE_{Sh} *tatro-*

> | gal te de nyid bral gyur na |
> | 'khyams pas dgos pa cung zad med |

tasmād abhinnarūpam iti niścayaḥ | tam āha |

[D 195a] ([1]| zhes gsungs te |[1]) de'i phyir gnyis su med pa'i ngo bo nyid gnas yin no zhes dgongs pa'o[2] | | de nyid bstan pa ni |

[1] BDP om. [2] DP *so*

saṇḍa-puaṇi-dala-kamalagandha-kesara-varaṇālem̩ | iti | (47ab)

| 'dab ldan padma'i[1] [P 215b] sdong po[2] ge sar gyi[2] dbus |
| [(2]shin tu phra ba'i[2)] snal ma dri dang kha dog ldan | (47ab)
[1] DP *pad* [2] DP om.

dṛṣṭāntena padmasya pṛthagbhāvaṃ tyaja | sa na ca ekaikasya paryāyasya saṇḍo[1] yathā puaṇi[2] padmapatraṃ dalaṃ ca kamalaṃ ca gandhakeśaraṃ ca varam utkṛṣṭaṃ nālaṃ ca | evam |
[1] $E_B E_{Sh}$ *saṇḍa* [2] E_{Sh} *pūaṇi*

| zhes gsungs te | dpe'i sgo nas padma'i 'dab ma la sogs pa'i [(1]tha dad dang bye brag[1)] spang bar bya ste | de[2] thams cad kyang padma'i ngo bo nyid du gcig go |
[1] DP *bye brag tha dad pa* [2] DP om.

[E_{Sh} 101] chaḍḍahu [(1]vĕṇṇi ma[1)] karahu sŏsa[2] ṇa laggahu vaḍha ālem̩ || iti | (47cd)
[1] $E_B E_{Sh}$ *veṇima ṇa* [2] E_{Sh} *sosaṃ*

| de ltar bye brag [(1]thong zhig rmongs pa[1)] rnams |
| kye[2] log par 'dzin pas ma [(3]gdungs [B 142a] shig[3)] | (47cd)
[1] P *ngo bor cig rmongs* [2] DP om. [3] P *gdung zhig*

he paśupuruṣa uktapadmasya pṛthagbhāvaṃ tyaja[1] ekaikasya paryāyasya | mā[2] cittaśoṣaṃ kuru | tasmād īdṛśasyājñānavākyasya nānāśāstropacārāt sukhabāhye mā lagasi[3] | tathā |
[1] $E_B E_{Sh}$ *tyajata* [2] $E_B E_{Sh}$ om. [3] $E_B E_{Sh}$ *lagassi*

| ces gsungs te | kye rmongs pa padma'i bye brag re re'i rnam grangs kyi sgo nas padma[1] tha dad pa yin no | zhes sems gdung bar ma byed cig | 'di lta bu[2] mi shes pa'i ngag tshig[3] sna tshogs kyi[4] bstan bcos las nye bar bstan pa bde ba las phyi rol du gyur pas bsten[5] par mi bya'o | | de ltar yang |
[1] D *padma'i* [2] DP *bu'i* [3] DP om. [4] B *kyis* [5] D *bstan*

kā mantasatthem̩[1] khaa[2] jāi pucchaha kulahīṇao |
vamha viṭhṭhu [(3]teloa saala jahi[3)] ṇilīṇao | iti | (48)
[1] $E_B E_{Sh}$ *matattha* [2] E_{Sh} *khaya* [3] E_{Sh} *tahiṃ ta loa sahajahi*

| [(1]sngags kyi bstan bcos dgos med de[1)] |
| zad phyir dris na rigs med bzhin[2] |

| tshangs pa khyab 'jug 'jig rten gsum |
| ma lus gang du song[3] zhing[4] zhi | (48)

[1] DP *'dod pa'i sngags kyi bstan bcos ni* [2] DP *phyir* [3] D *son* [4] DP *nas*

kiṃ mantraśāstreṇa sahajabāhyena[1] | pṛcchāṃ kuru | tair vinā sarvamantraśāstraṃ kṣayaṃ yāti | yathā kulahīnena[2] putreṇāsāreṇa ca pitur abhāvāt sarvaṃ yat kiṃcit draviṇādi kṣayaṃ yāti sarvaṃ rājādinā gṛhyate | evaṃ tattvahīnena sarvamantraśāstraṃ dharmaṃ vā avidyā[3]gṛhītair kṣayaṃ yāti evaṃ samudayārthaḥ | sahajākāśavat tyaktvā vikalpa[4]jñānāśrayāt nāmadheyamātraṃ | na labhate tathāgato 'nyaś ca | tasmin sarvaṃ kṣayaṃ yāti | [E_B 115] evaṃ kulapañcatathāgatādi[5] sarve[6] hinā bhavanti | yasmin sthāne anye ca brahmviṣṇumaheśvarādīni tasmin sakalalokā līnā lagnā na kiṃcit tattvavido bhavanti | tasmāt sarvaśāstratattvavedinas tair vinā niṣphalā iti | tathā coktam |

[1] E_B *-ṇa* [2] E_B *kula hīnena* [3] E_{Sh} *avidyādi-* [4] E_BE_{Sh} *vikalpanāṃ* [5] E_B *–di-* [6] E_{Sh} *sarvaṃ*

| zhes [1] gsungs te | lhan cig skyes pa las phyi rol du gyur pa'i sngags kyi bstan bcos la dgos pa med de | lhan cig skyes pa med na sngags kyi bstan bcos thams cad (2zad cing nyams2) par 'gyur ro | | yid mi[3] ches[4] nas dris pa dang | rigs med pa'i bus pa'i nor mi dbang ba bzhin no | | ji ltar rigs brgyud bsrung[5] ba'i bu ma yin pa'i pha shi na nor thams cad rgyal po la sogs pas khyer ba bzhin no | de ltar de kho na nyid la[6] dman na bstan bcos ma lus pa'am[7] chos rnams ma rig pas bzung bas (2zad cing nyams2) par 'gyur ro | | bsdus pa'i don ni | lhan cig skyes pa nam mkha' lta bur byas te | spangs na rnam par rtog pa'i rnam par shes[8] pa la brten te[9] | de bzhin gshegs pa'am | gzhan gyi ming tsam yang mi 'thob pa'i phyir te[6] | bstan bcos de (10dag thams cad10) zad par 'gyur ro | de ltar yang[6] | [B 142b] (11de bzhin11) gshegs pa rigs lnga la sogs pa thams cad lhan cig [P 216a] skyes pa'i ngo bo[12] zhi bar 'gyur zhing | gzhan yang de la tshangs pa dang | khyab 'jug dang | bde byed dang | 'jig rten [13] [D 195b] (6ma lus pa6) thams cad kyang zhi bar 'gyur ro | | de med na thams cad la de nyid rig pa med cing byas pa thams cad 'bras bu[14] med ces pa'o |

[1] B inserts *bya ba* [2] DP *nyams shing zad* [3] B *ma* [4] B *chis* [5] B *srung* [6] DP om. [7] B *pa'i* [8] P *rtog* [9] D *nas* [10] D *de thams cad* P om. [11] B *bde bar* [12] BP *bor* [13] DP insert *pa* [14] BP om.

caturaśītisāhasre dharmaskandhe mahāmuneḥ |
tattvaṃ ye vai na jānanti sarve te niṣphalā iti ||

| thub pa chen po'i[1] chos phung po |
| brgyad khri bzhi stong grangs snyed[2] de[3] |

| gang gis de nyid mi shes pa |
| de dag thams cad don med yin |
[1] BDP *pos* [2] D *tshad* [3] BD *kyi*

ata āha |

| zhes gsungs pa'ang[1] | 'di nyid kyi phyir |
[1] DP *so*

are[1] putto[2] bojjhu rasarasaṇa susaṇṭhia avejja[3] |
vakkhāṇa[4] paṭhantehi jagahi[5] ṇa jāṇiu sojjha | iti | (49)
[1] E_{Sh} *yare* [2] E_{Sh} *putta* [3] E_{Sh} *arejja* [4] E_{Sh} *-kkhaṇa* [5] E_B *jagaïï*

kye hoḥ[1] |
[1] DP om.

| dngul chu'i bcud len mi shes pas[1] |
| sa bcings (2dbyer mi phyed pa yongs su spangs2) |
(3| 'chad pa dang ni 'don pa yis |3)
(4| de shes par ni nus ma yin |4) (49)
[1] DP *pa'i* [2] D *dbye ba mi phyed spong* P *dbyer mi phyed pa spongs*
[3] DP | *gro ba 'chad cing 'dod pa yis* | [4] B | *'gro bas de ni mi shes so* |

he putra tvayā rasarasāyanasādhanakāle sphuṭataraśuddhim ajānāno yathā naṣṭaḥ tathā rāgādiśuddhim ajānāno naṣṭaḥ | tvam īdṛśaṃ mā kuru | rāgād abhilaṣitadharmādiṣu krīḍā yā sā tattvarahitatayā suṣṭhu saṃgṛhītā avidyaiveti | na kevalaṃ tat tvaṃ prati | anye ca lokāḥ vyākhyānaṃ kurvanti paṭhanti[1] ca | teṣāṃ sarvaṃ niṣphalaṃ bhavati | kutaḥ | jagat saṃsārasya ajñānāt | yaḥ punar jānāti | tasyocyate |
[1] E_B *ṣaṭhanti*

| zhes gsungs te | skyes bu[1] dngul chu'i bcud len sgrub pa'i dus su de dag par byed pa'i thabs gsal por mi shes pas[2] ji ltar nyams pa de bzhin du | 'dod chags la sogs pa dag par mi shes na rang nyams par 'gro ste | khyed kyis[3] 'di lta bu ma byed cig[4] ces pa'o | | 'dod chags kyi dbang gis mngon par 'dod pa'i yul lnga la de nyid dang bral bas rol pa gang yin pa de ni shin tu'ang ma rig pas gzung ba kho na'o | | khyed 'ba' zhig ni ma yin te | skye bu gzhan dag 'chad par byed par gang 'dod pa de dag ni 'bras bu med do | | de ci'i phyir zhe na | skye 'gro 'khor

ba de nyid kyis[5] yang[4] dag par mi shes [B 143a] pa'i phyir ro | | yang de nyid[6] shes pa'i dbang du byas nas |
[1] B *bus* DP *na* [2] DP *pa* [3] B *kyi* [4] DP om. [5] P *kyi* [6] B inserts *mi*

> arĕ putta[1] tatto[2] vicittarasa kahaṇa ṇa sakkaï vatthu[3] |
> kapparahia suhaṭhāṇu varajagu uajjaï[4] tatthu[5] | iti | (50)
> [1] E_{B} *-to* E_{Sh} *–tta* [2] E_{Sh} *–tta* [3] E_{Sh} *vattha* [4] E_{Sh} *uvajjaï* [5] E_{Sh} *tattha*

> | skyes bu de nyid sna tshogs kyi[1] |
> | ro 'di rdzas su bstan mi nus |
> | bde ba'i gnas mchog rang bzhin spangs |
> | 'gro ba nye bar skye ba der | (50)
> [1] DP *kyis*

he śiṣya he[1] putra yat tattvaṃ vicintitaṃ tasya rasaṃ svānubhavakathanaṃ na śakyate | idaṃ vasturūpaṃ nīlapītādyākāraṃ tadvat | kiṃ tat | svasaṃvedyaṃ | yataḥ "tāṃ jānāti sa eva hi" || tasmāt kalparahitaṃ sukhasthānaṃ yasmāc chreṣṭajagat[2] tattvarūpam iti bhāvaḥ | evaṃ [E_{B} 116] dhyānena[3] nopalabhyate svabhāvasiddhatvād guruparijñānamātreṇopalabhyate nābhimānādinā | tad āha |
[1] $E_{B}E_{Sh}$ om. [2] E_{B} *–jaga* [3] E_{B} *dhmānena*

zhes gsungs te | skyes bu slob ma gang gis de nyid rnam par bsams pa[1] de'i ro[2] nyams su myong ba dang bcas pa brjod par mi nus te | dngos po 'di ni ser po'o zhes bstan [P 216b] par nus pa bzhin du ni ma yin no || de bstan[3] pa ni |
[1] B *la* [2] B om. [3] DP *ston*

> buddhi viṇāsaï maṇa maraï jahi tuṭṭaï[1] ahimāṇa |
> so māāmaa[2] paramakalu tahiṃ kim bajjhaï jhāṇa | iti | (51)
> [1] E_{Sh} om. [2] E_{Sh} *māyāmaya*

> [B:] | blo ni rnam par 'gags shing yid zhi ba |
> | de yi tshe na mngon pa'i nga rgyal chad |
> | de ni sgyu ma'i rang bzhin mchog gi cha pa ste |
> | de la bsam gtan 'ching ba des ci bya | (51)

> [DP:] | blo ni rnam 'gag[1] yid zhi ba |
> | gang du mngon pa'i nga rgyal chad |
> | de ni sgyu ma'i rang bzhin nyid |

| mchog gi cha rtogs de'i[2] tshe |
| bsam gtan 'ching ba des ci bya | (51)
[1] D *'gags* [2] D *pa yi*

[E_{Sh} 102] evaṃ guruṇā dattasa[1]hajāmukhīkaraṇād yat kiṃcit kalpitāṃ buddhiṃ vināśayati vismaraṇaṃ karoti | vikalpamano mriyate bāhyādivastulakṣaṇakaṃ na bhavati | tasmin sthāne abhimānatā ahaṃkāra ātmātmīyakalpanā truṭyati kṣayaṃ yāti | yasmāt sa māyāmayaparamakalārūpaṃ kaleti ṣoḍaśī[2] kaleva nārthaṃ karoti kiṃcit | tad iha hi dhyānabandhanena kiṃ kāryam asti | manaḥpa[3]rikalpitatayā nāstīti yāvat | tasya viśeṣaṇam āha |
[1] E_B *datta sa-* [2] E_B *-śo* [3] E_B *manaḥ pa-*

zhes gsungs te | de ltar bla mas lhan cig skyes pa mngon du [(1]bya ba'i[1)] tshul bstan zhing byin pa ste[2] mngon du byas na ji srid rnam par rtog [(3]pa'i blo[3)] 'gags[4] pa ni mi dran pa'o | | rnam par rtog pa'i [D 196a] yid zhi bas phyi rol la sogs pa'i dngos por mtshon zhing 'dzin par mi byed do | | de lta bu'i gnas la mngon pa'i nga rgyal dang | bdag dang bdag gir 'dzin pa'i rnam par rtog pa bcad cing zad de | de nyid sgyu ma'i rang bzhin mchog gi cha pa[5] ste | cha ni bcu drug pa'o | | de lta bu'i don gyi bya ba gang ci'ang mi byed pa'o | | de'i phyir 'dir bsam gtan gyi 'ching ba des ci bya ste | yid kyis brtags[6] pa la dgos pa ci'ang med do zhes bya ba'i don no[7] | de'i[8] khyad par bstan[9] [B 143b] pa ni |
[1] DP *byas pa'i* [2] B *de* [3] PD *pa* [4] D *'gag* [5] DP om. [6] B *rtag* [7] D *to* [8] DP *'di* [9] DP *ston*

bhavahi[1] uajjaï khaahi ṇivajjaï |
bhāva-rahia puṇu kahi uvajjaï || iti | (52ab)
[1] E_{Sh} *-hiṃ*

| srid pa la[1] skyes mkha' la zad |
| dngos po spangs nas[2] gang las skye | (52ab)
[1] BDP *las* [2] B *na*

yasmin sthāne[1] bhavabhakṣitaṃ punar apy atraiva kṣayavivarjitam | evaṃ bhāvābhāvarahitaḥ | bhūyaḥ kasminn asty[2] utpādaḥ | nopapadyata iti yāvat | etaduktena nāstikaṃ na bhavatīti | kutaḥ | yataḥ buddhādilakṣaṇaṃ sarvaṃ māyāvad bhāvābhāvam iti prasaṅgaḥ | kiṃ tarhi kalpanayogāt tat | tathoktam[3] evaṃ punaḥ |
[1] E_{Sh} *sthāna* [2] E_BE_{Sh} *apy* [3] E_BE_{Sh} *tathoktaḥ*

| zhes gsungs te | gnas gang srid pa zos pa de kho na la (1dngos po dang1) dngos po med pa'ang med do | | de ltar dngos po dang dngos po med pa[2] spangs pas yang[3] skye bar ga la 'gyur te | skye ba med ces pa'o | | de ltar smras pas chad par lta bar yang mi 'gyur te | sangs rgyas la sogs pa'i mtshan sgyu ma lta bur dngos po dang dngos po med pa'i rnam par rtog pas bzung nas brjod pa'i phyir ro | de ltar yang |

[1] P om. [2] D om. P *na* [3] B *kyang*

viṇṇa vivajjia jou[1] vajjaï |
acchaï siriguruṇāha kahijjaï | iti | (52cd)

[1] E_{Sh} *joo*

| dbye ba spangs nas gang skyes pa |
| dpal ldan bla ma mgon po yis |
| bstan pa de[1] la gnas par bya | (52cd)

[1] P *'di*

dvayavarjiteṣu dvayeṣu yogaṃ madhyamopalabdhivivarjibhiḥ paramaviramayor madhyame[1] nopalabhyate ity āśayaḥ | sarvam advayam eveti | tad api varjanāt tāṃ sthitiṃ kuru | yatra śrīguruṇā śirasā kathanaṃ kuru | atyāścaryarūpaṃ śiraścālanam eveti | tasmād anena nyāyena idaṃ viharaṇaṃ kuru |

[1] E_B *–me-*

| zhes gsungs te | dbye ba spangs pa ni gnyis su med pa'i ye shes te | gang dbus su nye bar dmigs pa'o | | spangs zhes (1bya ba1) ni mchog dang dga' bral [P 217a] gyi dbus su de nyid spangs nas nye bar mi dmigs so zhes dgongs pa'o[2] | | thams cad gnyis su med pa nyid yin pas de thams cad spangs nas dpal ldan bla mas gsungs pa spyi bos[3] blang bar bya'o | | de'i phyir rigs[4] pa 'dis gnas par bya ste |

[1] DP *pa* [2] DP *so* [3] DP *bor* [4] DP *rig*

[E_B 117] dekkhahu suṇahu parīsahu khāhu |
jigghahu[1] bhamahu baïṭhṭha uṭhṭhāhu | ityādi | (53ab)

[1] E_{Sh} *jighahu*

| mthong dang thos dang reg[1] pa dang |
| za[2] snom 'chag[3] dang gnas su gnas | (53ab)

[1] P *rig* [2] DP *zas* [3] B *'chags*

atra yat kiṃcic cakṣuṣā drakṣyasi karṇābhyāṃ śabdaṃ śṛṇavati paridhānaṃ vastrādi śarīraṃ gavacchasi ca mukhena[1] bhakṣaṇaṃ kurvanti[2] nāsayā[3]

sugandhaṃ durgandhaṃ vā jighrasi bhramaṇaṃ vā caṃkramaṇaṃ vā karoṣi āsane niṣaṇṇo 'si uttiṣṭhasi vā |
[1] $E_B E_{Sh}$ *sukhena* [2] $E_B E_{Sh}$ *kuruvanti* [3] E_B *nāśayā*

| zhes gsungs te | 'dir gang ([1]mig gis[1]) cung[2] zad mthong ba dang | rna bas sgra thos pa de dang | reg[3] pa ste | gos gyon pa dang | khar za ba dang | snar snom pa dang | gnas su gnas pa ni stan la gnas pa'o |
[1] DP om. [2] P *chung* [3] P *rig*

āla-māla-vyavahāreṃ[1] pellaha |
maṇa cchaḍḍu ekkākāra ma ca[2]llaha | ityādi | (53cd)
[1] E_{Sh} *–re* [2] E_{Sh} *cca-*

| cal col gtam[1] dang lan smra [B 144a] la |
| sems[2] ([3]rnam gcig[3]) las mi bskyod[4] | (53cd)
[1] DP *gtan* [2] P *sebs ni* [3] B *gcig gi rnam pa* [4] B *'da'*

ālamālaṃ[1] krayavikrayādi tair vyavahāreṇa kālaṃ kuruṣva | manaś caitad[2] advayayogān na calatu[3] anyamanapṛṣṭā(?)kāraṇakarttrādinā ekākārasvabhāvena paribhramaṇaṃ mā kariṣyasi | te narakādiduḥkham anubhavanti | tasmāt sad[4]gurūpadeśasmaraṇaṃ kuru | tam āha |
[1] E_B *-la* [2] $E_B E_{Sh}$ *cetad* [3] $E_B E_{Sh}$ *calaṃ tu* [4] E_B *tad-*

| zhes[1] gsungs te | cal col gyi gtam ni nyo tshong la sogs pa'i gtam mo | | sems gcig gi[2] rnam pa ni gnyis su med pa'i rnal 'byor las[3] mi 'da' ba'o | | de'i phyir bla ma dam pa'i gdams ngag dran par bstan[4] pa [D 196b] ni |
[1] DP *ces* [2] P *gis* [3] DP *pas* [4] DP *ston*

guru-uvaeseṃ[1] amiarasu dhāvahi ṇa pīaü jehi |
bahu satthattha marutthalihiṃ tisie ma[N 63a]riaü[2] tehi | iti[3] |
(54)
[1] E_{Sh} *-so* [2] N *-rivvaü* [3] E_B om.

| ([1]gang zhig[1]) bla ma'i man ngag bdud rtsi'i ro |
| gang gis tshim[2] par mi 'thung pa ([1]de ni[1]) |
| ji ltar 'gron[3] po ([1]mang po[1]) mya ngan gyi[4] |
| thang la skom pas[1] gdungs[5] te[1] shi ba bzhin | (54)
[1] DP om. [2] DP *ngoms* [3] D *'gro na* [4] D *gyis* [5] D *gdung*

gurūpa[1]deśam amṛtarasaṃ[2] mahāvegena paridhāvitatayā yaiḥ kāpuruṣ[air]

na p[ītaṃ][3] tair[4] viśvasattvārthaṃ bhagnam | yathā marusthalīṣu bahu-saṃghātaṃ[5] tṛṣitaṃ pānīyarahitatayā tatra sārthavāhakena[6] kvacit gopya[7]sthāneṣu pānīyaṃ dṛṣṭaṃ | tena kauṣīdāpāyitā[8] iti matvā[9] [E_{B} 118] [(10]svārthe 'jñātā[10)] teṣu[11] noktaṃ[12] tayā sarvaṃ saṃbādhitaṃ[13] bhavati | evaṃ paramparayā[14] sarvasattvā vināśi[15][tā bha]vanti | upadeśasya svalakṣaṇam āha |
[1] E_{B} *-ṣa-* [2] E_{Sh} *–saṃ sa* [3] E_{Sh}*pīnaṃ* [4] $E_{B}E_{Sh}$ *tena* N *.. na* [5] E_{B} *–saṃghāta* N *-sadghāta* [6] N *.. rthakena* [7] E_{Sh} *saugha-* E_{B}N *śoṣya-* [8] E_{B} *koṣadāyārpitā* E_{Sh} *koṣadāyāpitā* [9] E_{Sh} *ititvā[t]* [10] E_{B} *sārthair ajñātā* E_{Sh} *sārthair* [E_{Sh} 103] *ajñāta-* N *sārthe jñātā* [11] E_{Sh} *leṣu* [12] E_{B} *nokta-* [13] N *saṃvādhitaṃ* [14] E_{B}N *–rāyā* E_{Sh} *–rāyātarahitatayā* [15] $E_{B}E_{Sh}$N *-ṣa-*

| zhes gsungs te | bla ma dam pa'i gdams ngag gi[1] bdud rtsi'i ro mgyogs pa chen por song ste mi 'thung[2] pa de ni sna tshogs kyi[3] sems can gyi don las nyams pa yin te | ji ltar mya ngan gyi thang la tshong pa mang po skom pas gdungs pa la | tshong dpon gyis[4] phyogs gcig tu chu sbas nas yod par[5] shes pa bstan pa las | brtson 'grus dang ldan pa rnams[6] der song ste 'thung[2] pas 'tsho'o | | brtson 'grus med pa rnams ni 'chi'o[7] | gdams ngag gi[8] rang gi mtshan nyid bstan[9] pa ni |
[1] D *gis* [2] B *'thungs* [3] D *kyis* [4] P *gyi* [5] P *pas* [6] DP om. [7] DP *shi'o* [8] DP *gis* [9] DP *ston*

cittācitta vi pariharahu[1] tima acchahu jima vālu |
gu[ruva][N 63b]aṇeṃ[2] diḍhabhatti[3] karu[4] hoiaï[5] sahaja ulālu || iti[6] (55)
[1] Nac *parihara* [2] E_{Sh} *-ṇe* [3] E_{Sh} *bhakti* [4] N *laru* [5] E_{B} *hoi-jaï* E_{Sh} *haï-haï* N *hoi-haï* [6] E_{B}N om.

| bsam dang bsam [(1]min rab tu[1)] spangs nas ni |
| [(2]ji ltar[2)] bu chung tshul[3] du gnas par gyis[4] |
| bla ma'i lung la brtan[5] zhing[2] gus byas[2] na[6] |
| lhan cig skyes pa skye bar [(7]the tshom med[7)] | (55)
[1] DP *ma yin* [2] DP om. [3] DP *bzhin* [4] B *mdzod* P *gyi* [5] D *bstan* [6] D *nas* [7] DP *nges*

cintā[1] jñānajñeyādi | acintā[2] niḥsva[bhāvādi] | tābhyāṃ parihāraṃ kuryād [(3]bālam iva[3)] sthitiṃ kuru | niṣ[4]kevalaṃ gurūpadeśasya dṛḍhabhakti[ṃ ka]roṣi[5] | yena sahajasyollālanaṃ[6] bhavati | ullālanaṃ[7] ca nirantarābhyāsena tanmayaṃ yāsyati | tanmayañ ca sarvāvaraṇarahitam avācyaṃ cety āha |
[1] E_{B}N *cittā* [2] N *acittā* [3] E_{Sh} *bālasyeva* [4] N *niḥ-* [5] E_{Sh} *kuru* E_{B}N *karosi* [6] E_{B}Nac *–sahajasyollāpanaṃ* Npc *-sahajasyollāsanaṃ* E_{Sh} *sahajasya ullālanam lopo na* [7] E_{B}N *ullāpanaṃ*

| ces[1] gsungs te | bsam [P 217b] pa ni ([2]shes pa dang[2]) shes bya bsam pa'o | | bsam min ni rang bzhin med pa la sogs pa ste | de[2] gnyis spangs pa'o | | nges [B 144b] par[3] bla ma dam pa'i gdams[4] ngag la brtan por gus pa gyis la bu chung gi tshul du gnas par ([5]gyis shig[5]) dang | des lhan cig skyes pa de ji lta ba skye bar 'gyur te | de la goms pas de'i rang bzhin yang lhan cig skyes par 'gyur ro | | de'i rang bzhin yang sgrib pa thams cad dang bral zhing[6] brjod du med par[7] ston te |

[1] DP *zhes* [2] DP om. [3] DP *pa dang* [4] DP *man* [5] DP *mdzod cig* [6] DP *ba* [7] P *pa*

> akkharavaṇṇo[1]pama[2]guṇarahio[3] |
> bhaṇaï[4] ṇa jānaï ([5]e maï[5]) kahio[6] | ity (56ab)
>
> [1] E_{Sh} *–varṇo* [2] E_{Sh} *para-* N *pama-* [3] E_{Sh} *rahije* [4] $E_B E_{Sh}$ bhanaï N ||| *maï* [5] E_{Sh} *somāï* [6] E_BN *kahiao* E_{Sh} *kahije*

> | kha dog yi ge yon tan mchog |
> | dpe spangs brjod du mi nus par |
> | de ni bdag gis bstan pa yin | (56ab)

akṣaravarṇābhyāṃ sa ca nopalabhyate | athavā ([1]'kṣaram iti[1]) ([2]paramākṣaraṃ tasya ([3]varṇam idam[3]) ([4]sukhamayam agrāhyam anākhyeyam[4]) | evam upamārahitaṃ[5] vacanaparam[2)6] [parayā na jānītaṃ] [N 64a][7] sa īdṛśaḥ mayā saroruhenoktaṃ | tathā coktaṃ |

[1] $E_B E_{Sh}$ *'kṣaroti* N broken away [2] Added by a second hand in the lower margin [3] $E_B E_{Sh}$N *varṇedaṃ* [4] E_B *sukhamamā 'grāhyakhyānam* E_{Sh} *sukhamayā 'grāhyakhyānam* N *sukhamayā 'grāhyākhyāna* [5] $E_B E_{Sh}$N *–rahita* [6] N *–raṃ-* [7] N fols. 64–65 are missing

| zhes gsungs te | kha dog dang yi ge gnyis mi dmigs so | | yang na yi ge ni don dam pa'i yi ge ste | de'i[1] kha dog ni ([1]'di nyid[1]) bde ba chen po'i rang bzhin yin pas gzung bar bya ba ma yin pa nyid du brjod do | de ltar dpe med pa ni gang gcig nas gcig tu brgyud[2] pas mtshon pa'i sgo nas mi rtogs pa'o | | bdag gis mtshon ([3]pa ni[3]) sa ra has 'di skad smras pa'o | de ltar yang |

[1] DP om. [2] B *brjod* [3] P *ni bdag*

> yāvān kaścid vikalpaḥ prabhavati manasi tyājyarūpaḥ sa sarvaḥ
> yo 'sāv ānandarūpaḥ hṛdayasukhakaraḥ so 'pi saṃkalpamātraḥ |
> [E_B 119] yad vā vairāgyahetos tad api yad ubhayaṃ tad
> bhavasyāgrahetur
> nirvāṇaṃ nānyad asti kvacid api viṣaye nirvikalpātmabhāvāt || iti

| ji snyed rnam par rtog pa[1] yid las byung ba de ni thams cad yang dag par bya ste |
| bde ba'i ngo bo gang de nyid kyang snying la ([2]bde skyed[2]) de yang rnam par rtog pa tsam |
| gang yang 'dod bral rgyur gyur de yang gnyis ka[3] gang min de ni[4] srid pa'i gtso bo'i rgyu |
| rnam par mi rtog bdag nyid las ma gtogs pa'i yul la mya ngan 'das pa cung zad med |

[1] BDP *pa'i* [2] D *bde ba bskyed de* [3] P *bde bskyed* D *ga* [4] DP *yang*

tasmāt |

| ces gsungs [D 197a] so | | de ci'i phyir zhe na |

so paramesaru[1] kāsu kahijjaï |
suraa kumārī jima[2] paḍivajjaï | iti | (56cd)

[1] E_{Sh} *–suru* [2] E_{Sh} *jimahu*

| dbang phyug mchog de su la bstan |
| gzhon nus[1] bde ba snying zhugs[2] bzhin | (56cd)

[1] BDP *nu'i* [2] B *zhen*

bhrāntyā yāvat sattvanikāye[1] ([2]sthito 'pi[2]) sa paramatattvaṃ parameśvaro 'nyasiddhāntābhāvāt kasya pṛthag[3]janāvasthitasya kathayāmi hi tat | kathanamātreṇa teṣu na[4] pravṛttiḥ | kiṃ tarhi yathā[5] kumāryaḥ ([6]sakhibhya ālocayanti[6]) | ālocayanti pratyayaṃ kurvanti | prathamataḥ tvayā svāmine gatvā surata[7]sukham anubhūtam | tan mayi sākṣād vadasi niścitam etat | gatvā sā punar asya gṛhād āgatya sakhinā ca pṛcchyate[8] pūrvoktaṃ kīdṛśam iti | tā ucuḥ | tvayā sākṣāt svāminā sahānubhavakāle jñeyam iti | sukhotpādaṃ na kiṃcid sākṣāt te vaktum avācyatvāt | tam iva gurūpadeśaṃ na punaḥ kumārīsukham iti vasturūpaṃ pratipādayati | etad evāha |

[1] E_B *–yaḥ* E_{Sh} *–yaiḥ* [2] E_BE_{Sh} *sthitepi* [3] E_B *pṛthaka-* [4] E_BE_{Sh} om. [5] E_B *yayā* [6] E_BE_{Sh} *sakhībhyālocayanti* [7] E_B om. *surata-* [8] E_BE_{Sh} *pṛcchati*

[B 145a] zhes gsungs te | sems can gyi ris la ci yod ([1]pa de ni[1]) 'khrul pa ste | de la gnas su zin gyi dbang phyug dam pa de[2] ni mchog gi de nyid do | | de gzhan gyi grub mtha' la med pa'i phyir ([3]ro |[3]) su la ni so so'i skye bo'i gnas skabs su ci la brjod par bya | [P 218a] brjod pa tsam gyis mi 'jug pa'i phyir ro | | de[2] ci'i phyir zhe na | ([2]ji ltar[2]) gzhon nu ma'i bde ba skyes[4] pa ltar[2] gzhan la brjod par mi nus pa'i phyir ro | | de dang 'dra bas bla ma dam pa'i gdams ngag med par rtogs par bya bar mi nus so | | de bstan[5] pa ni |

[1] D *pa ni* P *ni* [2] DP om. [3] B om. [4] B *shes* [5] DP *ston*

> bhāvābhāvem̩[1] jo parihīṇo[2] |
> tahim̩[3] jaga saala asesa vilīṇo | iti | (57ab)
> [1] E_{Sh} *–ve* [2] $E_B E_{Sh}$ *parahīṇo* [3] E_{Sh} *tahi*

> | dngos dang dngos med gang spangs pa |
> | der ni 'gro ba ma lus thim | (57ab)

([1]yady acintyam̩[1)] paramam̩ tattvam | bhāvābhāvayoḥ karuṇā[2]śūnyatādvayatvāt rahitam[3] | tasmin jagat ([4]sakalam aśeṣam̩[4)] buddhavajradharādikalpitātmakam̩ vilīnam̩ tanmayena nirupalambhāt |

[1] $E_B E_{Sh}$ *yadi cintyam̩* [2] $E_B E_{Sh}$ *kāraṇa-* [3] $E_B E_{Sh}$ *rahitaḥ* [4] $E_B E_{Sh}$ *sakalaśeṣa*

| zhes gsungs te | gang gi tshe bsam gyis mi khyab pa ni mchog gi de nyid yin te | dngos po dang dngos po med pa dag pa'i stong pa dang snying rje dbyer mi phyed pa yin pas de dang bral[1] ba'o | | de la 'gro ba ma lus pa ni brtags[2] pa'i sangs rgyas dang rdo rje 'chang la sogs pa ste | thim pa ni de'i rang bzhin yin pas mi dmigs pa'i phyir ro |

[1] BDP *'dra* [2] D *rtag*

> ([1]javvem̩ tahim̩[1)] maṇa ṇiccala thakkaï |
> tavvem̩[2] bhavasam̩sārahi[3] mukkaï | iti | (57cd)
> [1] E_{Sh} *javyĕ hi* [2] E_{Sh} *tavya* [3] $E_B E_{Sh}$ *-ha*

> | gang tshe ([1]de ru[1)] yid ni[2] brtan ([3]gnas pa[3)] |
> | ([4]de'i tshe srid dang mya ngan 'das las grol[4)] | (57cd)
> [1] DP *der* [2] DP om. [3] DP *par gnas* [4] DP *de yi tshe na 'khor ba dang* | | *mya ngan las grol bar 'gyur*

[E_B 120; E_{Sh} 104] uktakrameṇa yadi tatra mano niścalatvena sthitam ātmātmīyādikalpanārahitatvāt | tasmin kāle bhavāt ṣaḍgatisam̩sāradoṣāt mukto bhavati | anyathā[1] kṛte sati doṣāṇy āha |

[1] $E_B E_{Sh}$ *anayā*

| zhes gsungs te | gong du bstan pa'i rim pas gal te yid brtan par gnas pa ni bdag

dang bdag gir 'dzin pa dang bral ba de'i tshe 'gro ba rigs drug gi 'khor ba'i[1] skyon las grol bar 'gyur ro | de ltar ma byas na skyon ni |

[1] P om.

jāva ṇa appahiṃ para pariāṇasi |
tāva ki dehāṇuttara pāvasi | iti | (58ab)

[B:] | gang tshe bdag gzhan [B 145b] yongs su mi shes pa |
| de'i tshe bla med lus ni gang las rnyed | (58ab)

[DP:] | gang gi tshe na bdag dang gzhan |
| ngo mi shes pa de yi tshe |
| bla med lus ni ga la rnyed | (58ab)

yāvan nātmani[1] paramotkṛṣṭaṃ tattvarūpaṃ parijānāsi tāvat kiṃ dehasya śarīrasya[2] nirmāṇakāyātmakasya vyāpakasya cānuttaraṃ tattvaṃ tadvyāpakatvāt prāpsyasi | yasmād ekānekatvam āyāti tasmād ātmagrahaviparyāsāt sarveṣāṃ tādṛśaṃ bhavati | kasmāt | anuttara-tattva[3]prasaṅgād iti | ([4]tathā coktam |[4])

[1] $E_B E_{Sh}$ *nātmānaṃ* [2] E_{Sh} *śarīra-* [3] E_{Sh} *–tva* [4] E_B om.

ces gsungs te | ji srid bdag gis[1] phul du byung ba de kho na nyid ma rtogs pa de srid du rang gi lus sprul pa'i sku'i bdag nyid dam | chos kyi skus khyab pa'i ngo bo nyid bla na med pa'i bde ba chen po de kho na nyid ci la 'thob ([2]par 'gyur | mi 'gyur ro[2]) | de ltar yang[3]

[1] P *gi* [2] DP *ste* | *mi thob par 'gyur* [3] DP om.

e maï ka[N 66a]hio[1] bhanti[2] ṇa kavvā[3] |
appahi appā vujjhasi tavvā | iti | (58cd)

[1] E_{Sh} *kahije* [2] E_{Sh} *bhati* [3] E_{Sh} *kadyā*

[B:] | nga yis bstan pa 'di la 'khrul par ma byed cig |
| rang gis rang la legs par shes par gyis | (58cd)

[DP:] | bstan pa 'di la ma 'khrul par |
| rang gis rang la legs par rtogs | (58cd)

īdṛśaṃ mayā saroruhenoktam[1] | [tasya bhrā]ntiṃ na kadācit kuru | tayā bhrāntyā cātmanātmānam tadā[2] jānāsi | idaṃ tya[ktvā nānyat] kiṃcid asti | tenāha |

[1] E_B *saroruhoktaṃ* N *śaroruha* ||| [2] E_{Sh} adds *[na]*

| zhes gsungs te | de ltar sa ra ha bdag gis bstan pa 'di la 'khrul par ma byed cig | 'di bor nas gzhan cung zad kyang med do | zhes bya ([1]ba'i don[1]) [P 218b] de nyid rang gis[2] rang la legs par rtogs par 'gyur ro |
[1] DP *ba'o* | | [2] D *rig*

ṇaü aṇu naü paramāṇu vicintao[1] |
aṇavarabhā[vahi phuraï[2]] surattao[3] | iti | (59ab)
[1] E_B *vicintaje* N *vicittao* [2] E_{Sh} *sphuraï* [3] N *surattao*

| rdul dang rdul bral ma sems shig |
| dngos por rgyun du zhen ([1]cing 'phro[1]) | (59ab)
[1] DP *med 'bro*

na aṇuparamāṇavaḥ bhāvanayā cintitāḥ[1] | anavaratam[2] [yogādibhāva]ne visphuritam[3] suratam[4] vā | yadi kriyate[5] |
[1] N *–taḥ* [2] E_BE_{Sh} *anavarata-* N *ana* ||| [3] N *visphuratam* [4] E_BE_{Sh} om. [5] N *kriyataḥ*

| zhes gsungs te | rdul dang rdul bral[1] gnyis sems kyis ma bsam[2] pa la rgyun [D 197b] mi 'chad pa'i bde ba chen po gcig tu snang ngo |
[1] D om. [2] B *bsams*

[E_B 121] bhaṇaï Saraha ([1]bhiḍi etta vimattaŏ | iti[1]) | (59c)
[1] E_B *bhanti eta vimattaje* E_{Sh} *bhanti etta vimattaje* N *bhiḍi etta* |||

| mda' bsnun ([1]gyis smras pa de tsam zhig[1]) | (59c)
[1] B *na re nan tan gyis la soms*

[etad dhi mā][N 66b]traṃ kalpanātmakaṃ jñānam | etena yogena vimatir bhavati | na samyak[tvaṃ hi mayā kathitam |]

| ces[1] gsungs te | rtog pa thams cad dang bral ba'i rnam par mi rtog pa[2] de kho na nyid yin no [3] | | de lta bu'i rnal 'byor la sems log par mi bya ste | bdag gis yang dag par bstan pa'i phyir ro |
[1] B *zhes* [2] DP *pa'i* [3] DP insert *zhes pa'o*

[arĕ] ṇikŏlī[1] bujjhaha[2] paramatthaŏ[3] | iti | (59d)
[1] E_BE_{Sh} *ṇikkoli* [2] N *bujjhasi* E_{Sh} *bujjhahu* [3] E_BE_{Sh} *-tthaje* N *-thao*

| kye [1] ma lus don dam pa[2] shes par gyis[3] | (59d)
[1] DP insert *hoḥ de'i tshe* [2] DP om. [3] B *'gyur*

are mūḍhapuruṣa[1] [nikkolī[2] nirmūlī akulī ca] | sarvabījādhārādirahitaṃ[3] tat paramārthaṃ vedasva[4] | ta[m āha] |
[1] $E_B E_{Sh}$ *mūḍha puruṣa* [2] E_B *tikkolī* [3] E_BN *-tas* [4] E_BN *vadasva*

| zhes gsungs ste | kye grogs po rmongs pa ma lus pa ni rtsa ba med pa dang rigs[1] med [B 146a] pa ste | thams cad sa bon dang | rten dang | gnas la sogs pa dang bral ba gang yin pa de nyid la don dam pa nyid[2] go bar bya'o | | de ltar yang |
[1] D *rang rig* [2] DP *zhes*

> [nirmūlaḥ[1] paracetātmā[2] nirmūlā] bhāvanātmakā[3] |
> nirmūlaṃ jñeyasat[4]tattvaṃ akulā hi tathāgatāḥ[5] || [iti] |
> [1] $E_B E_{Sh}$N *-lā* [2] $E_B E_{Sh}$ *paracetanmā* [3] E_{Sh} *nāṃśakā* [4] $E_B E_{Sh}$ *jñeyase* N *jñeyasa* [5] $E_B E_{Sh}$ *tathāgatā* N *ta* |||

> | rtsa ba med pa gzhan sems bdag |
> | bsgom pa'i bdag nyid rtsa ba med |
> | bden pa'i shes bya rtsa ba med |
> | rigs med de bzhin gshegs pa'o |

[tasmāt svarūpeṇa sphu]rate necchayā | tadāsaṅgāt suratam iti evam[1] artham |
[1] N *etam*

zhes gsungs so | de'i phyir rang gi ngo bo nyid kyis[1] snang zhing 'dod pa ni ma yin te | de la zhen pa med pas legs ([2]par shes[2]) pa'o | | de lta bu'i don ni |
[1] P *kyi* [2] D *shes* P *zhes*

> ghare[1] [([2]acchaï bāhire[2]) pucchaï |
> paï] [N 67a] dekkhaï paḍi[3]vesī pucchaï || iti | (60ab)
> [1] E_B *–reṃ* [2] E_{Sh} *accha ghare bāhire kuru* [3] E_{Sh} *paï-*

> | khyim na yod pa phyi rol ([1]dag tu[1]) 'tshol[2] |
> | khyim ([3]na mthong ba khyim mtshes dag la 'dri[3]) | (60ab)
> [1] P om. [2] DP *tshol* [3] DP *bdag khyim tshes dag la 'dri*

yathā[1] ([2]kasyāścid yoginyā[2]) svagṛhe ([3]svajanam asti[3]) bahiḥ pṛ[cchati] kutra sthitaḥ | punaḥ priyaṃ svāminaṃ paśyati samīpasthaṃ gṛhe pṛcchati | kutra sthita iti | ta[thā] svadehe tattvaṃ vyavasthitaṃ bahir anyat jñānaṃ pṛcchati | ajñāna([4]m eveti[4]) |
[1] E_{Sh} *atha* [2] $E_B E_{Sh}$N *kaścid yogīnāṃ* [3] E_{Sh} *svajanosti* [4] E_{Sh} *seseti*

zhes gsungs te | bud med kha cig rang gi khyim na skyes bu bzhag[1] nas khyim mtshes[2] la 'dri ba de bzhin du | rang gi lus la de nyid gnas pa[3] bor nas gzhan la 'dri ba de ni mi shes pa'i rang bzhin no |
[1] D *gzhan* [2] DP *tshes* [3] D *par*

punaḥ svānubhavaṃ ([1]guror ādeśāt[1]) paśyaty[2] anubhavati | [E_{Sh} 105] tadā samīpavarttī yaḥ kaścit kathaṃ tattvam iti pṛc[cha]ti | tenājñānam eveti | yad ajñānaṃ sa[3] grāhaṇīyam yataḥ sarvabhāvā saṃskṛtā[4] | tat kiṃ jñāyate | [evaṃ] [N 67b] [pu]nar dṛḍhāpayati | sarahetyādi |
[1] E_{Sh} *gurūpadeśāt* [2] N *paśyatyasyety* [3] E_B *tat* E_{Sh} *tada* [4] $E_B E_{Sh}$ *asaṃskṛtās* N *'saṃskṛtā*

yang bla ma dam pa'i gdams ngag gis nyams su myong[1] bzhin du gzhan la 'dri ba de ni mi shes pa nyid du gzung bar bya'o | gang gi phyir chos thams cad rang bzhin med pa nyid yin pas de la ji ltar skye ba yod de | med do | [P 219a] 'di[2] yang bstan pa'i phyir |
[1] D inserts *ba* [2] B *'dir*

> [E_B 122] ([1]Saraha bhaṇaï vaḍha[1]) jāṇaü appā |
> ṇaü so dhea ṇa dhāra[ṇa ja]ppā | (60cd)
> [1] E_{Sh} om.
>
> [B:] | mda' bsnun na re rmongs pa bdag nyid shes par gyis |
> | de'i tshe bsam gtan bsam bya bzlas brjod med | (60cd)
>
> [DP:] | mda' bsnun na re rmongs pa rnams |
> | rang nyid rang gis shes par gyis |
> | de'i tshe na bsam gtan dang |
> | bsam pa dang ni bzlas brjod med | (60cd)

ukta[1]tattvaṃ tat sarvam ātmanaivātmani jānīyāt[2] | na[3] punaḥ tat[4] tattvaṃ dhyeyadhāraṇādir[ū]peṇa jalpitam |
[1] E_{Sh} *uktaṃ* [2] $E_B E_{Sh}$ *jānīta* N *jānāt* [3] E_B *sa* [3] E_BN *sa*

| ces gsungs te | bstan[1] pa'i[2] de nyid thams cad rang nyid la rang gis legs par rtogs par bya ste | yang de'i[3] rnam par rtog pa'i bdag nyid bsam gtan [B 146b] dang bsam bya la sogs pas[4] brtags[5] pa ni ma yin no |
[1] P *brtan* [2] BD *pa* [3] DP *de ni* [4] DP *par* [5] B *brtag*

jaï guru kahaï ki savva vi jāṇī |
mokkha ki[1] labbhaï e[2] viṇu jā[ṇī] | iti | (61ab)
[1] E_B *hi* [2] $E_B E_{Sh}$ *saala* N *saa* (em. according to G)

[B:] | gang tshe bla mas bstan pas thams cad shes |
| de med pas ni thar pa ga la rnyed | (61ab)

[DP:] | gang gi tshe na bla ma yis |
| bstan pa tsam gyis thams cad shes |
| de med thar pa ga la shes | (61ab)

kenacid uktaṃ bhavatīdaṃ yad guruṇā kathitaṃ[1] sarvaṃ[2] na tat sarvaṃ[2] jānīyate[3] | ([4]yad ātmāne[4]) mṛgyate[5] tadā tad vasturūpam[6] ākhyāti | kim aśakyaṃ tasyottaraṃ mokṣaṃ | kiṃ labhyate | guruṇā-uktaṃ tathā[7] vyatikrame[N 68a]ṇa[8] tam amananayā[9] na jānātīti yāvat | tat kathaṃ vijñeyam[10] | abhyāsād iti | sa nābhyāsamātreṇātmagrahāt[11] | tam āha |
[1] N *–ta* [2] N *sarva* [3] E_{Sh} *jānīte* [4] E_{Sh} *yadā yad ātmanā* N *yad ātmane* [5] E_{Sh} *mṛṇyate* N *mṛ .. (nu?)te* [6] E_{Sh} om. *rūpam* [7] E_{Sh} *tasya* [8] E_{Sh} *vyatikrame* N *yati* ||| *na* [9] $E_B E_{Sh}$ *ajānānatayā* N *amananāyā* [10] E_BN *-yād* [11] E_B *cābhyāsamātreṇātmagrahāt* E_{Sh} *cābhyāsamātram ātmagrahāt* N *cābhyāsamātraṃ na* ||| *t*

| ces[1] gsungs te | ’di skad ston pa ni kha cig bla mas bstan pa thams cad ni mi shes te | de ji ltar shes she na | goms pa las shes ([2]so zhes[2]) na | goms pa tsam gyis shes pa ni ma yin te | bdag tu ’dzin pa dang bcas pa’i phyir ro | | de nyid bstan pa’i phyir |
[1] DP *zhes* [2] DP om.

desa[1] bhamaï havvāseṃ[2] laïo[3] |
sahaja ṇa[4] bujjhaï pāpeṃ[5] gahio[6] | iti | (61cd)
[1] E_{Sh} *deśa* [2] E_{Sh} *-se* [3] $E_B E_{Sh}$ *laïje* [4] E_{Sh} *na* [5] E_{Sh} *pāpa* [6] E_B *gāije* E_{Sh} *rāhije*

| ([1]gang yul rnams bgrod cing goms[1]) pas ni |
| lhan [D 198a] cig[2] skyes pa[2] mi shes[3] sdig pas ’dzin | (61cd)
[1] B *gang phyir yul rnams bsgrod par byas* [2] DP om. [3] B *rnyed*

[iha kā]puruṣayoginām[1] ([2]doṣam asti[2]) | svasthānaṃ tyaktvā sarvadeśeṣu bhramaṇaṃ kurvanti | bhakṣābhakṣādihetunā[3] tayā[4] kāyakleśaklamathaṃ[5] na jānanti | ([6]kuto | ’bhyāsād[6]) iti | tad idam anutta[rasahajaṃ] na[7] jānāti

na vyaktīkaroti | kutaḥ | pāpena gṛhītatvāt | tat bhakṣyādidvaityād[8] iti | abhyāsa[rahita iti bhā][N 68b]vaḥ | [E_B 123] tathā coktam |
[1] N *-nā* [2] E_{Sh} *doṣo 'sti* [3] E_BE_{Sh} *bhaktābhaktādhihetunā* N *bha* ||| *dihetunā* [4] E_{Sh} *tena* [5] E_{Sh} *kāyakleśada (śla) m adhvaṃ* [6] N *kuta abhyāsād* [7] E_{Sh} *no* [8] E_BN *-ādvaityād* E_{Sh} *-ādvaitād*

| zhes gsungs te | 'dir skyes bu rnal 'byor pa kha cig rang gi gnas bor nas yul thams cad du (1'khyams te1) | bza' bya dang bza' bya ma yin pa la sogs pa'i [2] ched du byed pa de ni rang gi lus nyon mongs [3] kho nar zad kyi | goms par bya ba ni ci'ang med do | | de'i phyir bla na med pa'i lhan cig skyes pa mi shes pas 'dzin te | ci dran dran tsam la'ang (4rtog pas4) goms pa ni med do zhes dgongs pa'o[5] | | de ltar yang |
[1] DP *'khyam ste* [2] P inserts *don* [3] BD insert *pa* [4] D *rtogs pas* P *rtog pa* [5] D *so*

> yathāgnir dārumadhyastho nottiṣṭhen mathanād vinā |
> tathābhyāsād v[inā bodhir jāyate neha ja]nmani || iti[1] |
> [1] N om.

> | shing gi nang na me yod pa |
> | ma gtsubs bar du 'byung ma yin |
> | de bzhin bla med byang chub ni |
> | ma bsgrubs (1skye ba 'dir yong1) min |
> [1] DP *bar du skye ba*

anayā yadi tāvad abhyāsaṃ kriyate tadā kathaṃ bhāvanādīnāṃ parihāram u[ktaṃ bhavatīti] āśaṅkā[1] kasyacit[2] syāt | tad āha |
[1] E_B *āśaṅkāt* N .. *śaṅkāt* [2] E_B *kasyācit*

| zhes gsungs te | gal te re zhig bsgom par bya ba med na [1] | 'o na bsgom pa dang bzlas pa la sogs pa gsungs pa ji ltar yin snyam pa la | de nyid bstan pa'i phyir |
[1] B inserts *ni*

> visaa[1] ramanta ṇa (2visaahiṃ lippaï2) |
> ūara [haraï] ṇa pāṇī chippaï | iti | (62ab)
> [1] E_{Sh} *viṣaya* [2] E_BN *visaaṃ vilippaï* E_{Sh} *visaa vilippaï*

> [B:] | yul rnams bsten pas yul gyis mi gos te |
> | u tpal blangs kyang chu yis [B 147a] mi reg bzhin |

> [DP:] | yul rnams [P 219b] bstan pas yul gyis na | (62ab)
> | gos par 'gyur ba ma yin te |

| ji ltar chu las u tpa la |
| blangs kyang chu yi ma reg bzhin | (62ab)

yathā pāṇīyamadhye phenaṃ[1] dṛśyate na pāṇīyaṃ gṛhyate hastas[parśāc] ca evaṃ tathā sati parijñāne viṣayāṇāṃ krīḍāṃ karoti pañcakāmādinā tair doṣair na gṛhyate | pu[nar] [N 69a][2] yathā padmapatre jalataraṅgaṃ gṛhītvā tat pānīyair na lipyate | tadu[3]tpannā ca padmapatrāmbhovad iti vacanāt | evam abhyāso yoginaś ca |
[1] E_B *pheṇaṃ* E_{Sh} *pheṇa* [2] N fols. 69–70 are missing [3] E_B *tadu-* E_{Sh} *tado-*

| zhes gsungs te | ji ltar chu'i nang du gru la zhugs nas utpala blangs kyang chus[1] mi gos pa bzhin du | de kho na nyid du shes pa'i rtogs pa yod na 'dod pa'i yon tan lnga la longs spyod kyang nyon mongs pas gos par mi 'gyur ro | | de ltar goms pa'i[2] rnal 'byor pa[3] ni |
[1] DP *chu las* [2] P *ma'i* [3] DP om.

emaï joï[1] mūla saranto |
visahi na vāhaï visaa ramanto | iti | (62cd)
[1] $E_B E_{Sh}$ N *joi*

[B:] | 'di ltar rtsa ba'i rnal 'byor skyabs su 'gro |
| dug gi sngags can dug gis ga la tshugs | (62cd)

[DP:] | 'di lta bu yi bdag nyid kyi[1] |
| rtsa ba'i rnal 'byor skyabs 'gro ba |
| dug gi sngags can dag la ni |
| dug gis tshugs par ga la 'gyur | (62cd)
[1] D *kyis*

([1]īdṛśā yogino[1]) mūlaṃ gurūpadeśasarito 'bhyāsāt saranto jānantas | tadviṣayair na bādhito | yat kiñcit yogināṃ viṣayādirūpaṃ tat sarvaṃ na jātu tasya bādhyakā[2] bhavanti | kiṃ [E_{Sh} 106] jñānaṃ jñeyaṃ jñāpakañ ca | tatprabhavād iti | tasmāt sarvaviṣayāṇāṃ ramaṇāt na bādhyata iti yāvat | tathā coktam |
[1] $E_B E_{Sh}$ *īdṛśena yoginā* (ergative correct?) [2] $E_B E_{Sh}$ *bāhyakā*

zhes gsungs te | 'di lta bu'i rnal 'byor pas rtsa ba ste | bla ma dam pa'i gdams ngag rnam pa thams cad kyis bsgoms na | de la[1] y ul gyi nyes pas mi gos so | de'i phyir | yul rnams kyi ni[1] dri mas mi gos te |
[1] DP om.

bāhyaṃ yat tad asat svabhāvavirahāj[1] jñānaṃ[2] ca bāhyārthavac
chūnyaṃ yat pari[3]kalpitaṃ ca viduṣā tac cāpy[4] aśūnyaṃ matam |
ity evaṃ paribhāvya bhāvavibhavair niścitya tattvaikadhīr
māyānāṭakanāṭanaikanipuṇo yogīśvaraḥ krīḍati || iti |
[1] E_B *svāvavirahāt* [2] E_B *jñānaś* [3] E_BE_{Sh} *yat a-* [4] E_BE_{Sh} *tat api*

| phyi rol gang yin de med de |
| shes pa phyi rol don ltar snang |
| mkhas pa rnams kyis stong btags[1] pa |
| de yang stong nyid du mi 'dod |
[1] BD *brtags*

| 'di ni shes na dngos po dngos med pa |
| de nyid shes[1] na[2] de nyid gcig tu[3] blo |
| sgyu ma mkhan dang gar byed mkhan po ni |
| de bzhin rnal 'byor dbang phyug rol par byed | ces gsungs so |
[1] P *med* [2] DP *pa* [3] DP *pu*

[E_B 124] deva ([1]vi ppajjaï[1]) lakkha vi dīsaï
appaṇu mārīi sa ki karijjaï | iti | (63ab)
[1] E_BE_{Sh}N pijjaï [2] E_BE_{Sh}N *kariaï*

| lha la mchod pa ([1]'bum phrag byas gyur[1]) kyang |
| bdag nyid 'ching 'gyur ([2]de yis[2]) ci zhig bya | (63ab)
[1] DP *'byor byas* [2] DP *des*

yadi tāvad devatārūpeṇotpattis tallakṣaṇaṃ sākṣād[1] dṛśyata iti tadā ātmā mriyate | sā devatā kiṃ kariṣyati[2] | na kiñcid iti yāvat | tasmāt |
[1] E_B *sājñā* [2] E_B *karisyati*

| zhes gsungs te | gal te re zhig lha'i gzugs su mchod cing grub pa mngon ([1]sum du mthong[1]) [D 198b] yang rang nyid 'ching na des[2] lha'i dgos pa ci zhig[3] yod de | cung zad kyang med do zhes pa'o |
[1] DP *du mngon* [2] D *de* P *de'i* [3] P om.

tovi ṇa tuṭṭaï ĕhu saṃsāra |
viṇu abbhāseṃ[1] ṇāhi ṇisāra || iti | (63cd)
[1] E_BE_{Sh}N *āāseṃ*

| de 'dras 'khor ba (1'di ni1) chad min te[2] |
| [B 147b] (3goms pa med par 'byung bar 'gyur ma yin3) | (63cd)
[1] DP *de* [2] DP om. [3] DP *'dir goms med pas 'byung mi nus*

devatākāraṃ yady ātmānaṃ bhavati tad apīdaṃ saṃsāraṃ na naśyati | kutaḥ | yataḥ sarveṣāṃ sattvānāṃ pañcopādānaskandhādyabhāvāt | ālayavijñāne yā pravṛttiḥ sā[1] ca gandharvasattvātmakaṃ | saiva punar āgatiḥ pūrvādyupalambhāt | devatā ca tādṛśī[2] vijñānenopalambhāt | tasmān na naśyati saṃsāraḥ | mithyā ghaṭī[3]yantravat paribhramatīti bhāvaḥ | kin tu tenaiva sati parijñāne tadabhyāsena vinā saṃsāreṣu nāsti niḥsāraḥ[4] | etad evoktena devatābhāvena tāvan na bhavati gurūpadeśaṃ | yasmād abhyāsaḥ kriyate | tato nāsty abhyāsasya[5] viśeṣaḥ | tan na bhavati | samyaggurūpadeśasya tvayā vārttāmātraṃ na[6] śrutaṃ kin tad āha |
[1] E_B *so* [2] $E_B E_{Sh}$ *tādṛśa-* [3] E_B *–ghaṭo-* [4] E_B *nissāraḥ* [5] $E_B E_{Sh}$ *abhāvasya* [6] E_B *na na*

| zhes gsungs te | lha'i gzugs kyi rnam pa[1] rang gis[2] dngos su mngon du byas kyang 'khor ba ni nyams par mi 'gyur ro | | de[3] ci'i phyir zhe na | sems can rnams nye bar len pa'i phung po [P 220a] lnga dang bral nas kun gzhi[4] rnam par shes pa 'ba' zhig tu 'jug pa na[5] bar ma do'i srid pa'i bdag nyid de | sngon kyi las kyi dbang gis yang[6] 'khor bar 'jug go | lha'i rnam pa'ang de dang 'dra ba yin te | rnam par shes pas[7] dmigs (3pa yin3) pa'i phyir ro | de bas na 'khor ba nyams par mi 'gyur te | (8zo chun8) gyi 'khrul 'khor dang 'dra bar 'khor zhes dgongs pa'o[9] | | lha bsgom pa la sogs pa la dgos pa med pa do | | 'o na bsgom pa dang bzlas pa la sogs pa gsungs pa ji[10] ltar yin snyam pa la | 'on kyang de nyid kyi [11] ye shes kyis[12] rtogs[13] pa yod pa yin na | de'i tshe goms pas 'khor ba las 'byung ba (14ma gtogs14) par[7] gzhan gyis ni grol bar mi 'gyur ro snyam du dgongs pa'o[15] | de bas na bla ma dam pa'i gdams ngag gis phrin tsam yang khyed[16] kyis ma thos te | de ji ltar yin pa bstan pa'i phyir |
[1] B *par* D *pas* [2] P *gi* [3] DP om. [4] B *gzhi'i* [5] B *ni* [6] B *de'ang* [7] DP *pa* [8] P *chu zon* [9] DP *so* [10] D om. [11] BD insert *phyir* [12] B *la* DP *kyi* [13] BP *rtog* [14] D *mi rtogs* [15] DP *so* [16] DP *khyod*

aṇimisa[1]-loaṇa-citta-ṇirohem[2] |
pavaṇa ṇirohaï siri-guru-boheṃ | iti | (64ab)
[1] E_{Sh} *-ṣa-* [2] E_{Sh} *–dheṃ* [3] $E_B E_{Sh}$ *ṇiruhaï*

| mig ni mi 'dzum[1] pa (2dang sems 'gags pas2) |
| (3rlung 'gog dpal ldan bla ma'i man ngag gis3) | (64ab)
[1] B *'dzub* [2] DP *dag dang* [3] DP *sems 'gags pa dang rlung 'gags pa | | dpal ldan bla ma'i man ngag yin |*

anena yat kalpitaṃ kudhiyaiḥ kalpanātmakaṃ gurūpadeśaṃ tan na bhavati | yathā nimiṣastabdhalocanaiś cittaṃ ākāśādiṣu nilīnaṃ karoti tena vāyur[1] niro[N 71a]dhito[2] bhavati | śrīgurvādeśata ityādi na bhavati | kuta[3] āha |

[1] E_B *vāyu* [2] E_B *–taṃ* N *-tam* [3] E_BE_{Sh} *kuta evam*

zhes gsungs te | 'dir ni[1] blo ngan pa rnams kyis rnam par rtog pa'i bdag nyid bla ma'i gdams ngag yin [B 148a] no zhes brtags[2] pa ni bla ma'i gdams ngag ma yin no | | ji ltar mig mi 'dzum pa ni cung zad phye zhing mi [(3]'gul ba'o[3)] | | sems 'gags pa ni rnam mkha' la sogs par thim pa'o | | des rlung 'gag par 'gyur te | de[4] ni dpal ldan bla ma'i gdams ngag yin no | | de[1] ci'i phyir zhe na |

[1] DP om. [2] B *brtag* [3] BP *'grub pa'o* [4] P *'di*

pavaṇa vahaï[1] so ṇiccalu [javveṃ |
jo]ī[2] kālu karaï ki rĕ tavveṃ | iti | (64cd)

[1] E_{Sh} *cahaï* [2] E_B *joi*

| gang tshe rlung rgyu [(1]de ni brtan pa na[1)] |
| de[2] tshe rnal 'byor [3] 'chi bdag gis [4] ci [5] bya | (64cd)

[1] DP *mi g.yo ba* [2] DP *de yi* [3] DP insert *pa* [4] DP insert *ni* [5] DP insert *zhig*

[E_B 125] yasmin kṣaṇe vāyuvāhanāyā[1] yogī prāṇaṃ ni[ścalaṃ ka]roti kim atra | tasmin kṣaṇe he mūḍhapuruṣa yogī[2] kālaṃ maraṇaṃ karoti[3] | tasm[ān na] bhava[ti] | kasmān na[4] bhavatīty āha |

[1] E_BE_{Sh} *vāyuvāhanatayā* [2] E_BE_{Sh} om. [3] E_{Sh} *kariṣyati* [4] N om.

| zhes gsungs te | gang gi tshe yid kyi[1] gzhon par gyur pa'i srog rlung[2] brtan par gyur pa de'i tshe [P 220b] kye[3] rmongs pa'i[4] skye bu rnal 'byor pa la[2] 'chi bdag gis ci mi bya ste | 'chi bar mi 'gyur zhes bya ba'i don no[5] |

[1] BD *kyis* [2] DP om. [3] BD om. [4] D *pa* [5] DP *to*

jāu ṇa indīa[1]-visaa-gāma |
tāva hi vipphuraï[2] akāma[3] | i[ti] | (65ab)

[1] N *india* [2] E_BN *viphuraï* E_{Sh} *phuraï* [3] E_{Sh} om.

| [(1]ji srid[1)] dbang po [D 199a] [(2]yul gyi grong la zhen pa na[2)] |
| [(3]de srid[3)] re ba med par [(4]snang zhing[4)] 'phro | (65ab)

[1] B *gang tshe* [2] D *rnams grol zhe na* P *rnam grol zhe na* [3] B *de tshe* [4] DP om.

([1]yāvad indriyaviṣayagrāmaḥ[1]) | tābhyām āsaktiṃ karoti yoginas tāvat na gurūpadeśaṃ vetti | [anāsa[2]][N 71b]ktiś ca vicārāgama[3]yuktyā labhyate | sa cātmā[4]divastur[ū]pa[ṃ na dṛśyate paramārthādibhedena [E_{Sh} 107] tat ka]thaṃ pratyakṣeṣu dṛśyate | bhrāntyā ca bhrāntir nāmālīkaṃ | sa[5] ca ([6]saṃvṛtisatyadarśanāt māyāvat[6]) pratibhāsate | evaṃ māyopamaṃ traidhātukaṃ viśvaṃ | tat[7] kenāgrahaḥ kriyat[e | na kri]yata [iti yāvat] | viśeṣena ca yogīndrasya necchayā aparibhāvitena ca gurūpadeśaṃ sphurate tas[yaivābhyā]sena smaraṇāt ([8]kriyata iti[8]) niścayaḥ |

[1] E_{B} *yāvan nendriyaviṣayagrāmaḥ* E_{Sh} *yāvan nondriyaviṣayagrāmaḥ* N *yāvan nendriyaviṣayagāmaḥ* [2] $E_{B}E_{Sh}$ *āsa-* [3] N *–gamama-* [4] N *cātyā-* [5] $E_{B}E_{Sh}$ *tac* [6] N *sa .. ṛ* ||| yata .. ||| [7] $E_{B}E_{Sh}$ *tataḥ* [8] $E_{B}E_{Sh}$ *kṣapayatīti* N *kriyatīti*

| zhes gsungs te | ji[1] srid du[2] rnal 'byor pa dbang po yul gyi grong khyer la ([3]zhen pa de srid du bla ma dam pa'i gdams ngag mi shes so | | ji srid du dbang po yul gyi grong khyer la[3]) lung dang rigs[2] pas dpyad nas stong pa nyid du ma rtogs pa ([4]de srid[4]) rang bzhin gyis de ltar snang zhing 'dzin pa de sus[5] zlog[6] par nus te | mi nus zhes bya ba'o | de ni[7] goms pa las mi nges par bstan[8] te |

[1] P *de* [2] D *de* [2] B *rig* [3] D om. [4] BP *de'i tshe* [5] P *su yis* [6] DP *bzlog* [7] B *nyid* [8] DP *ston*

aïseṃ visama-sandhi ko païsaï |
jo ja[hiṃ atthi ṇa][N 72a]ü jāva ṇa dīsaï | iti[1] | (65cd) (unmetrical)

[1] E_{B} om.

[B:] | dka' ba'i dgongs pa 'di la su zhig 'jug |
| gang zhig 'dir yod pa ni der mi mthong | (65cd)

[DP:] | ([1]'di ltar[1]) shin tu dka' ba yi[2] |
| dgongs pa la ni su zhig 'jug |
| gang[3] zhig 'di ru yod pa nyid |
| de ni 'di ru ma mthong ste | (65cd)

[1] D *'dir ni* [2] D *yis* [3] P *rang*

īdṛśyī[1] uktalakṣaṇāyāṃ[2] viṣamasandhi[3]vacaneṣu ko puruṣaḥ ([4]praveśaṃ karoti[4]) | kim artham | yo vastu yasmin gurūpadeśasya nāsti yāvan na dṛśyata ātmādibhāvaṃ[5] tāvat | kiṃ[6] sā bhaviṣyati[7] | saṃkṣepataḥ na ([8]bhāvyabhāvakavastur[8]) asti |

[1] E_{Sh} *itīdṛśyā* [2] $E_{B}E_{Sh}$N *-ṇāyā* [3] E_{Sh} *viṣamasaṃni* [4] N *praveśaṅkriyate* E_{B} *yo* [5] E_{Sh} *ātmādi* [6] E_{Sh} *kā* [7] E_{Sh} *bhavati* [8] N *bhāvābhāvavastur*

| zhes gsungs te | gong du bstan pa 'di lta bu'i[1] shin tu dka' ba'i dgongs pa la skyes bu ji ltar 'jug par 'gyur te | mi 'gyur ro | | de[2] ci'i phyir zhe na | dngos po gang zhig gong na med pa'i bla ma'i [B 148b] gdams ngag gis ji srid [(2]mi mthong ba de srid[2)] du 'jug par mi 'gyur ro | sgom[3] pa dang bsgom bya la sogs pa med do zhes pa'o |
[1] B *bu* [2] DP om. [3] D *bsgom*

na bhāvyaṃ bhāvakaṃ vā 'sti bhāvaṃ nāsty eva sarvataḥ |
bhāvyabhāvakabhāvena [(1]jāyate vikṛtākṛtiḥ[1)] ||
[1] E_{Sh} *jāyateti kṛtākṛtiḥ*

tat[1]tyāgo na tu[2] nirvāṇaṃ necchayāpi ca jāyate |
yathā siṃhasyaitat[3] dhyānaṃ necchayā dṛśyate kṣaṇāt[4] || iti |
[1] N *taṃ* [2] E_B *te* [3] E_{Sh} *siṃhasya tat* [4] $E_B E_{Sh}$N *kṣayāt*

[The two verses are not found in the Tibetan.]

[E_B 126] evam ajānatām[1] āha |
[1] N *ajanatāyām*

| de ltar mi shes pa la bstan[1] te |
[1] DP *ston*

[N 72b] paṇḍia saala sattha vakkhāṇaï |
dehahiṃ buddha vasanta [ṇa] jāṇaï ||
avaṇā[1]gamaṇa ṇa teṇa[2] vi[kha]ṇḍia |
tovi ṇilajja[3] bhaṇaï haüṃ[4] paṇḍia || iti | (66)
[1] E_{Sh} *amaṇā* [2] E_BN *teṇa* E_{Sh} *tena* [3] E_{Sh} *-jjaï* [4] N *haü*

| mkhas pa ma lus pa[1] bstan bcos 'chad te[1] |
| lus la sangs rgyas yod par[1] mi[2] shes so[1] |
| [(3]'gro dang 'ong ba gcod par mi nus te[3)] |
| [(1]nga ni[1)] mkhas[4] zhes ngo tsha med par smra | (66)
[1] DP om. B *pas* [2] B *ma* [3] DP *'ong dang 'gro ba gcad mi nus* [4] DP *mkhas pa*

paṇḍitā[1] nānāśāstreṣu vyākhyāna[ṃ] kurvanti | vāgjālamātram eva[2] niṣkevalaṃ narakagamanahetur[3] dravyārthitayā | dehasthita[ṃ] buddhatvaṃ sadgurūpadeśam ajānanād na jānanti hi[4] | akṣaramātram āśritya svarāmnāyāt[5] gurvāmnāyaṃ[6] vinā vyākhyānaṃ kurvanti | taiḥ[7] svayaṃ naṣṭāḥ parān api nāśayanti | kutaḥ | anekaja[N 73a]nmaparamparayā[8] saṃsāre gamanāgamanahetutvān[9] na vināśitaḥ | punar api sa mahānara[kādirū]pe[10] saṃsāre saṃsaratīti[11] cet | tathāpi punar etad arthaṃ kambalācāryeṇokta[m āha] |

[1] E_BN *paṇḍitaiḥ* (ergative?) [2] E_BN *eveti* [3] N *hetu* [4] E_B om. [5] E_B *kharam ajānanāt* E_{Sh} *svaramajānāṣāt* N *ścaramanāyāt* [6] E_BN *-ya* [7] E_BE_{Sh} *te* [8] E_{Sh} *-parasparāyā* [9] E_B *gamanāmanamahetutvān* [10] E_BN *–pa-* [11] N *saṃsarato iti*

| zhes gsungs te | mkhas pa thams cad kyis[1] sna tshogs pa'i bstan bcos 'chad par byed kyang ngag gi[2] (3spros pa3) tsam nyid yin pa'i phyir | nor don du gnyer bas dmyal bar 'gro ba'i rgyu kho na'o | | rang gi lus la yod pa'i sangs rgyas nyid bla ma dam pa'i gdams ngag mi shes shing | yi ge tsam la brten nas bla ma'i brgyud pa med par 'chad par byed pa de[4] dag ni rang nyams shing gzhan yang nyams par byed do | | de[4] ci'i phyir zhe na | skye ba [P 221a] dpag tu med par 'gro ba dang 'ong ba'i 'khor ba'i rgyu nyid yin pa'i phyir ro | | de ltar yang lwa[5] ba can pa'i[6] zhal snga nas |

[1] D *kyi* [2] B *gis* [3] D *spro ba* [4] DP om. [5] P *la* [6] DP *gyi*

(1[va]rṇāḥ padāni1) vākyāni liṅgāni vacanāni ca |
kriyākārakasambandhā[2] vitathatvād[3] a[vāca]kāḥ || (ĀM 151)

[1] E_{Sh} *varṇāpavādāni* [2] E_BN *–bandhād* [3] E_{Sh} *vitathamvād*

(1śloko 'pi1) pañcabhiḥ pādais tribhir (2vā kiṃ nu neṣyate2) |
vākyasya vācyatantra[3]tvāḍ [ḍākinī]samayo bhavet || (ĀM 152)

[1] E_B *śloko hi* E_{Sh} *ślokai [ca]* N *ślokobhiḥ* [2] E_BN *vākyānunīyate* E_{Sh} *vākyo na mīyate* [3] E_BN *vācatantra-* E_{Sh} *vācaka-*

gṛ[1]hītavyeṣu bhāveṣu[2] vidvanmanyaiḥ[3] purātanaiḥ |
pātitaḥ kim asau[4] loka[ḥ śabdasaṃ[N 73b]skāra[5]saṃkaṭe || (ĀM 153)

[1] E_L *gra-* [2] E_BE_{Sh}N *dharmeṣu* [3] E_B *viśvaṃ śūnyeṣu* E_{Sh} *viśvaṃ śūnye* N *vidvatsv anyeṣu* [4] E_L *ayaṃ* [5] E_BN *–saṃsāra-*

eṣā nāseti[1] vaktavye pṛṣṭaḥ ko nāma darśayet |
śiraḥ[2] pradakṣiṇāvartaṃ[3] bhaṅgu[reṇeha pā]ṇinā || (ĀM 154)

[1] E_BN *nāsaiti* [2] E_{Sh} *śivaḥ* [3] N *–varta*

[E_{Sh} 108] śīlāpeṭaka[1]dṛṣṭāntaṃ[1a] lāghavaṃ (2gamitaḥ svataḥ2) |
śabdair ātmā ca lokaś ca śabdadardurarāśibhiḥ[3] || [E_B 127] ityādi vistaraḥ | (ĀM 155)

[1] E_BN *-pīḍaka-* E_{Sh} *vilāṣitaka* [1a] E_{Sh} *-nte* [2] E_B *gamitaṃ svayaṃ* E_{Sh}N *gamita svayaṃ* [3] E_B *–duddhararāśibhiḥ* N *duddharara ||| bhiḥ*

[The corresponding Tibetan is:]

| yi ge tshig dang ngag rnams ni |
| gzung bar bya ba'i chos rnams la |
| mkhas pa'am ni gzhan yang rung |
| sgra ni yongs su sgrub pa la |

| rgan po 'jig rten ci phyir bslad |
| sgra ni gang yin dris pa la[1] |
| thang song[2] ston pa bor nas ni |
| kha cig mgo la bskor nas ston |
[1] D *las* [2] DP *sor*

tato hi punar api nirlajjatayā[1] bhāṣitaṃ | ahaṃ paṇḍito mūrkha e[veti] |
[1] E_{B}N *nirlajjayā*

| zhes [(1]sogs rgyas par gsungs so[1)] |
[1] DP *so*

jīvantaha jo ṇaü jaraï so ajarāmara hoi | iti | (67ab)

| gson po rgas par ma gyur par |
| de ni rgas [(1]shing 'chi bar mi 'gyur[1)] | (67ab)
[1] DP *med 'chi med yin*

anenoktam arthasya dṛṣṭāntaḥ | [yadi tā]vat kvacit puruṣasya ājīvamaraṇaparyantena yadi jarādinā na gṛhyate tadā [1] 'sau ajarāmara[tvaṃ yāti |] [N 74a] evaṃ na dṛśyate kvacit | dṛśyate punaḥ sarveṣāṃ jantūnāṃ[2] jvarādinā gṛhītatvān[3] maraṇāntaṃ hi jīv[itaṃ i]ty ekaṃ | dvitīyaṃ yathā rasajātir[4] jāritasāritamātreṇāṣṭalohān vindhati [(5]yāvan n[ā]tirasaṃ[5)] tathā sattvān maraṇakāle amṛtaṃ na jarati[6] yair ajarāmaraṃ karoti | ā[dā]v eva nirmalamatir bhakṣaṇādinā yāvañ jarati yogī | kenājarāmaraṃ yātīty āha
[1] E_{Sh} inserts *'jārito* [2] E_{B}N *jantavānāṃ* [3] N *gṛhīteṣu* [4] E_{B} *rasa jāti-* E_{B}N *jāti-* N *rasajāti* [5] E_{Sh} om. [6] E_{Sh} *karoti*

| zhes gsungs te | 'di ni gong [B 149a] du bstan pa'i don gyi dpe ste | gal [D 199b] te ma shi bar rgas pa la sogs par ma gyur na de'i tshe de ni rgas shing 'chi bar mi 'gyur ba de lta bu ni gang du'ang ma mthong ngo | | yang na ji ltar dngul chu'i rigs bsad[1] pa du ma bzhus shing bsregs pa tsam gyis lcags srang[2] brgyad[3] gser du sgyur bar byed do | | de bzhin du sems can rnams rgas pa dang 'chi ba

med par byed do | | dang po nyid nas blo gros dag pa'i rnal 'byor pa bza' ba
la sogs pa ji srid du klas⁴ par ⁽⁵'gyur bas⁵⁾ su zhig rgas pa dang 'chi ba med par⁶
mthong zhe na |

¹ P *gsad* ² P *bsrang* ³ BDP *brgya* ⁴ BD *glas* ⁵ B *gyur pas* D *'gyur ba* ⁶ DP *pa*

[guru]uvaeseṃ¹ vimala-maï so para dhaṇṇo koï | iti | (67cd)
¹ E_B –*se* N –*oseṃ*

| bla ⁽¹ma'i gdams ngag¹⁾ dri med blo² |
| de ni gter ⁽³ldan mchog yin no³⁾ |
¹ P *mas bstan pa'i* ² B *pa* ³ P *dang ldan pa'o* (67cd)

yaḥ sadgurūpadeśāt vimalamatin[ā sādhi][N 74b]tam ajarāmaratvaṃ dhar-
masambhoganirmāṇamahāsukhakāyacatuṣṭa⁽¹yaṃ tena¹⁾ sarvasāsravāṇ[āṃ
niro]dhaḥ kṛtaḥ | tena kriyate nānyeneti² | tasmāt sa puruṣo³ dhanyaḥ śreṣṭha
iti⁴ bhāva[ḥ |]
¹ E_B E_Sh -*yabhedena* N –*yatena* ² E_Sh *nānyam iti* ³ N -*ṣa-* ⁴ N *i*

| zhes gsungs te | bla ma dam pa'i gdams ngag gis dri ma med pa'i blo gros kyi
rnal 'byor grub pas¹ skye ba dang 'chi ba med pa ni chos dang | longs spyod
rdzogs pa dang | sprul pa dang | bde ba chen ⁽²po ste |²⁾ sku bzhi'i ngo bo nyid
do | | zag pa dang bcas pa thams cad des 'gog ste | gzhan gyis ni ma yin no | |
de'i phyir | skyes bu de ni gter ldan mchog yin no | zhes ⁽³gsungs so³⁾ |
¹ BD *pa'i* ² DP *po'i* ³ DP *zhes bya ba'o*

[vi]saa-visuddheṃ¹ ṇaü² ramaï kevala suṇṇa carei |
uḍḍia³ vohia⁴ kāu jima paluṭi[a⁵ ta]havi paḍei | iti | (68)
¹ E_B N -*ddeṃ* E_Sh -*ddhe* ² N *ṇo* ³ E_B N *uḍḍī* E_Sh *uḍi* ⁴ E_B *vīhia* ⁵ E_B N
   paluṭṭia

| yul rnams rnam ⁽¹par dag pa ma bsten zhing¹⁾ |
| gang gis stong pa 'ba' zhig ⁽²gis spyad pa²⁾ |
| ⁽³ji ltar³⁾ gzings las⁴ 'phur⁵ ba'i bya rog [P 221b] bzhin |
| bskor⁶ shing ⁽³bskor zhing³⁾ slar yang de ru 'bab⁷ | (68)
¹ P *dag mi sten zhing* ² DP *spyod* ³ DP om. ⁴ DP *la* ⁵ B *'phung* ⁶ P
   skor ⁷ B *'babs*

viśuddha¹viṣayeṣu yaḥ kaścit guror ājñayā pañcakāmopa[bho]gādinā na
ramati so nānuttaraṃ²⁾ prāpnoti | tadvirahān niṣkevalaṃ ⁽³suṇṇa carei iti³⁾
viṣayopasevāmāt[rayā śū][N 75a]nyārthe carati | ⁽⁴atha śūnyamātraṃ carati⁴⁾

na kiṃcid eva sādhayati | kākam[5] iva vohitam[6] ākramya [sa]mudramadhyagata uḍḍīyamānas[7] tatropatiṣṭhati[8] | anyam āśrayam apaśyan [9] punas [E_B 128] ta[trai]va patati | evaṃ bālajātīyāḥ saṃsārakarmaṇā [(10]saṃsāra eva[10)] patanti[11] | [(12]anyaḥ śūnyatādarśanamātrāśrayaṇād[12)] iti tasmāt |

[1] N *viśu-* [2] $E_B E_{Sh}$N *yenānuttaram* [3] E_BN om. [4] E_{Sh} om. [5] E_{Sh} *yathā kākam* [6] E_{Sh} *rohitam* N *vohit-* [7] N *uttīrya manayā* [8] E_B *tatrotiṣṭhati* E_{Sh}N *tatrottiṣṭhati* [9] E_{Sh} adds *na drakṣyati* [10] $E_B E_{Sh}$ *saṃsāre* [11] E_{Sh} *-tati* [12] E_B *anyaḥ śūnyadarśanāt tatrāśrayaṇād* E_{Sh} *anyaśūnyatādarśanāt śrayaṇād* N ||| *darśanamātrāśrayaṇād*

ces[1] gsungs te | skyes bu gang zhig gis[2] rnam par dag pa'i yul 'dod pa'i yon tan rnam pa lnga bla mas gnang ba [2] gang gis thob pa la mi spyod cing | [B 149b] de dang bral ba'i stong pa nyid tsam sgom zhing tha mal pa'i yul 'ba' zhig bsten[3] par byed pa des ni cung zad kyang sgrub par mi byed do | | dper na rgya mtsho chen po'i gru la gnas pa'i bya rog 'phur nas gzhan du 'babs sa ma rnyed tsam na slar yang [(4]de ru[4)] 'ong ba bzhin du | de ltar byis pa'i skye bo rnams 'khor ba'i las kyis[5] 'khor ba nyid du lhung[6] ste | gzhan nyi tshe ba'i stong pa nyid tsam[2] la brten pa'i phyir ro | | de'i phyir |

[1] BP *zhes* [2] B inserts *bla na med pa* [3] D *sten* [4] D *der* [5] P *kyi* [6] P *lhang*

visaā[1]satti ma bandha karu arĕ vaḍha [sara]heṃ vutta[2] |
mīṇa paaṅgama[3] kari bhamara pekkhaha hariṇaha jutta | iti | (69)

[1] E_{Sh} *viśayā-* [2] N *vuttu* [3] E_{Sh} *payagama*

| yul la zhen pas 'ching bar ma byed cig[1] |
| kye hoḥ[2] rmongs pa mda' bsnun gyis [(3]smras pa[3)] |
| nya dang phye [(4]leb glang chen[4)] bung ba dang |
| [(2]'di ni[2)] ri dwags[5] bzhin du blta bar bya | (69)

[1] P om. [2] DP om. [3] DP *ni smras* [4] P *ma leb dang ni* | | *glang po che dang* [5] B *dwag* DP *dags*

viṣayāsakti[ṃ pañcakā][N 75b]mopabhogādinā mā bandhaṃ kuru | mayā saraheṇa[1] [(2]yatnenoktaṃ | yadi ka[2)][roṣi tadā mīno matsyo] rasāsaktaḥ[3] ākāśodakam[4] icchatā[5] pralayaḥ | evaṃ pataṅgo rūpāsaktaḥ pradīpena prala[yaḥ | ka]riṇaḥ sparśeṇa pralayaḥ | bhramaraḥ[6] gandhena pralayaḥ | [(7]mṛgayūthañ ca[7)] śabdena prala[yaḥ] | svayaṃ prekṣatām[8] | kiṃ tat | sarveṣāṃ rāgapūrvaṅgamenotpattitayā |

[1] N *–na* [2] N tops are missing [3] E_B *aśaktā* E_{Sh} *rasāsaktam* N *sā 'saktā* [4] E_BN *kāmodakam* [5] E_{Sh} *-ti* [6] $E_B E_{Sh}$ *–rasya* [7] $E_B E_{Sh}$ *tathā mṛgayūthasya* [8] E_{Sh} *prekṣatā* N *prekṣyayatāṃ*

| zhes gsungs te | yul la zhen pas[1] 'dod pa'i yon tan rnam pa lnga la longs spyod pas 'ching bar ma byed cig[2] ces mda' bsnun gyis smras pa'o | | gal te byed na nya ro la chags pa[3] gnam chu 'dod pas gzhan du 'gro bar[4] gzhan gyis gsod pa dang | phye ma leb gzugs la chags pas mar me la shi ba dang | [D 200a] glang chen [(5]reg bya[5)] la chags pa dang | bung ba dri la chags pa dang | [(6]ri dwags sgra[6)] la chags pas 'chi ba bzhin du | thams cad kyang chags pa sngon du 'gro ba'i phyir ro |

[1] DP *pa'i* [2] B om. [3] P *pas* [4] DP *ba* [5] DP *reg pa* P *rig pa* [6] D *ri dags sgra* P *snyan*

> jatta[1] vi citta[hi] vipphuraï[2] tatta[3] vi [(4]ṇāhi sarūa[4)] | [(5]iti |[5)] (70ab)
>
> [1] E_{Sh} *jattu* [2] E_B *viphphuraï* E_{Sh} *visphuraï* [3] E_{Sh} *tattu* [4] E_BN *ṇāhasarūa* E_{Sh} *sarūva* [5] E_BN om.

> | gang zhig sems [(1]la rnam 'phrul ba[1)] |
> | de ni rang bzhin med pa ste | (70ab)
>
> [1] B *las rnam 'phros pa*

teṣāṃ yatra citte[1] visphuritaṃ gamanaṃ bhakṣaṇādi kāryaṃ [cinti] [N 76a][taṃ tatra nāsti svarūpaḥ | [E_{Sh} 109] ajñātatvād iti] | kutaḥ | lubdhaka[2]kaivarttādīnāṃ visaṃvādanāt[3] [eva kāmika[4]puruṣāṇām ajñā]nād yamakiṅkarādinā[5] māritā bhavanti | punar api grantha[kāreṇātika]ruṇāvaśād uktam |

[1] N *cittena* [2] E_{Sh} *luvaï* [3] E_{Sh} *-vāda* [4] B *kāmaka* [5] N *-dikā*

| zhes gsungs te | gang sems kyi [(1]rnam par 'phrul pa[1)] bza' ba dang bgrod[2] pa la sogs pa de ni rang bzhin med pa ste | mi shes pa las byung ba nyid kyi [B 150a] phyir ro | | sred pa can gyi[3] nya pas nya la sogs pa'i sems can srog gcod par byed pa dang | 'dod pa can gyi skyes bus [P 222a] de ring bud med 'di lta bu spyod[4] do zhes mi shes pas bsam pa'i phyir ro | | gzhan yang gzhung mkhan pos snying rje'i dbang gis bstan[5] pa ni |

[1] DP *rnam 'phrul* [2] DP *'grod* [3] DP *ni* [4] DP *spyad* [5] DP *ston*

> aṇṇa taraṅga ki aṇṇa jalu bhavasama khasamasarū[a | iti |] (70cd)

> | chu yang[1] gzhan la[1] rlabs kyang gzhan yin nam |
> | srid dang[2] zhi ba mkha' mnyam[1] rang bzhin yin[1] | (70cd)
>
> [1] DP om. [2] DP *pa*

yathā[(1]nadyāṃ jalaṃ saiva[1)] taraṅgo [(2]nānyaḥ tathā[2)] [(3]bhavaḥ śama[3)] viśuddhitvāt ś[āntirūpam e]va khasamarūpaṃ nānyaḥ[2] | e[te]na kim [u]ktaṃ syāt | [yo

bhavaḥ saiva nirvāṇaṃ samyaggurūpadeśā][N 76b]d iti jñāninām | [(4]ajñā na j[ānanti[4)] | viṣayaṃ yānti | īdṛśaṃ jñānam |]
[1] E_{Sh} *nadyā jala-* [2] E_{Sh} *nānyathā* [3] E_{B}N *bhavasamāva-* [4] E_{Sh} *ajānanti*

zhes gsungs te | ji ltar chu klung[1] gang yin pa de nyid rlabs dang bcas pa de bzhin du | | 'khor ba rnam par dag pa nyid mya ngan las 'das pa'o | 'dis ci bstan zhe na | bla ma dam pa'i gdams ngag shes pa rnams la 'khor ba gang yin pa de nyid mya ngan las 'das pa'o | | mi shes pa rnams ni de nyid mi mthun par rtog go | | de lta bu'i ye shes ni |
[1] P *rlung*

[kāsu kahijjaï ko suṇaï] kŏ[1] etthu[2] kajjasu līṇa[3] |
duṭhṭhasuru[4]ṅgādhūli jima hiajāa[5] hia[hi līṇa | [E_{B} 129] iti |] (71)
[1] $E_{B}E_{Sh}$N om. [2] E_{Sh} *ettha ka* [3] E_{Sh} *līna* [4] N *suli-* [5] E_{Sh} *-jāta*

| gang la bstan[1] zhing gang du[2] nyan |
| don 'di la ni gang [(3]zhugs te[3)] |
| gdug pa'i khung bu'i rdul bzhin du |
| sems ni de ru nub pa yin | (71)
[1] D *ston* [2] P *la* [3] P *zhig zhugs*

[paramagambh]īraṃ mārgaṃ kasyājñāninaḥ kathyate | ka iha sa puruṣaḥ kathana[yogyaḥ ko vā 'smin[1] kāryeṣu līnaḥ] | [(2]ko nipuṇaṃ[2)] gṛhītvā tatpadaṃ yānti | na kvacit tayoḥ[3] pātram eti[4] | vi[ralāḥ te puruṣapuṅgavāḥ supātrā]ḥ | yathā kvacid durgabhañjanāya bhūmyadho dūrataś [ca su][N 77a]raṅgā[5] dīyate | tat suruṅgikāṇāṃ gamyaṃ nānyeṣu | kutaḥ | tatra[6] saṅkaṭakhanāyā[7] atyantaduṣṭadhūlir[8] bha[vati | yai]s tatkṣaṇāt maraṇaṃ bhavati svalpahṛdayānāṃ | suraṅgikāṇāṃ[9] ca dṛḍhatarahṛdayāt[10] te[ṣāṃ sā] dhūlis taddhṛdayeṣu [(11]līno bhavati[11)] | mṛttikā ca[12] bhūmyāṃ līyate | prathamārambhe kiñcid [dāhyaṃ] tyaktatvād iti | evaṃ pūrvajanmābhyāsikānāṃ teṣāṃ[13] mahāsaṃsāre ca bodhiḥ sa[hṛdayārtham eveti] bhāvārthaḥ | tadguṇāny āha |
[1] E_{Sh} *'smin idaṃ* [2] E_{B} *nipunaṃ* N *nipuṇar* [3] E_{B} *tayo (?)* E_{Sh} *tasya* N *tayo* [4] $E_{B}E_{Sh}$ *eveti* [5] N *–ruṅgā* [6] N *tat* [7] $E_{B}E_{Sh}$ *saṅkaṭakhanāya* [8] N *-dhūtta* [9] N *–nāṃ* [10] E_{B} *-hṛdayatvāt* [11] N *līnā bhavanti* [12] N *ra* [13] N *teṣā*

| zhes gsungs te | mchog tu zab pa'i lam [(1]'di ni[1)] mi shes pa'i gang zag la ji ltar bstan zhing[2] | de bstan du rung ba'i skyes bu ni[3] ga la yod de | med ces pa'o | | gang zhig zhugs ni mkhas pa 'di'i[4] don gzung bar byed pa ni su zhig yod de | med ces pa'o | de lta bu'i dam pa'i skye bu[5] ni kha cig tsam mo | | ji ltar kha cig gzhan gyi[6] mkhar gzhom pa'i ched du thag ring por sa'i 'og nas [(7]khung bu rko ste[7)] |

de lta bu'i[8] rko ba[9] de ni sngon [B 150b] goms pa can gyi gang zag gis nus kyi | gzhan gyis ni mi nus so | de ci'i phyir zhe na | shin tu khung dog mor [(10]brkos pas[10)] de'i nang du[11] shin tu gdug pa'i rdul gyis srog snyi[12] ba rnams de ma thag tu 'tsubs[13] nas 'chi ba'i phyir ro | | sems brtan pa rnams ni | [(14]gong gi[14)] gdug pa'i rdul des 'chi bar mi 'gyur te | sa rkos[15] pa rnams ni khung bu de nyid du thim par 'gyur zhing | dang por[16] rko [D 200b] ba'i dus su cung zad phyir phyung bas so | de ltar skyes [P 222b] bu sngon du goms pas 'khor ba las byang chub chen po 'grub ste | de dag gi[17] ni snod yin pa'i phyir ro | de'i yon tan bstan[18] pa ni |
[1] D om. P *ni* [2] DP *cing* [3] DP om. [4] P *de'i* [5] B *bo* [6] D *gyis* [7] DP *sa brkos te* [8] B *bur* [9] B *ba po* [10] DP *rko bas* [11] D *gi* P om. [12] DP *snyi* [13] B *subs* D *'chubs* P *'tshubs* [14] B *gang du* D *gang gis* [15] DP *brkos* [16] BD *po* [17] P *gis* [18] DP *ston*

> jatta vi païsaï jalahi jalu tattaï sama[rasa hoi |
> dosagu][N 77b]ṇāaracittao[1] vaḍha paripakkha[2] ṇa koi | iti | (72)
> [1] E_B *cittatahā* N *cittaḍ.hā* E_{Sh} *cittatta* [2] $E_B E_{Sh}$ *-vakkha*

> | ji srid[1] chu la chu zhugs pa[2] |
> | de srid[3] chur[4] ni ro mnyam 'gyur |
> | skyon dang yon tan sems rnams[5] ni |
> | [(6]rmongs pa[6)] 'di la mi mthun med | (72)
> [1] B *ltar* [2] DP *na* [3] B *snyed* [4] BD *chu* [5] P *dang* [6] P *blun po*

yathā[1] [yatra samudreṣu jale jalamiśritaṃ bhavati tatra] samarasatā[(2]ṃ yāti[2)] | evaṃ saṃsārādidoṣaguṇāś ca cintitāḥ saparijñāna[sya maharddhika]sya puruṣasya pratipakṣā na bhavanti | kutaḥ | doṣāś ca pañcakāma[3]guṇāḥ | tadviśuddhi[ka]raṇaṃ nānāguruvākyaṃ [(4]nirantarasmaraṇāt | yathā nadyā jalaṃ[4)] nirantarapravāhāt | punar asya spaṣṭatām āha |
[1] E_BN *ta[thā]* [2] E_{Sh} om. [3] E_B *–kāmādi-* [4] N om.

[(1]| zhes gsungs te |[1)] ji ltar rgya mtsho chen po'i chu la chu gzhan zhugs na chu[2] ro mnyam pa bzhin du | 'khor ba la sogs pa'i skyon dang yon tan yongs su shes pa dang ldan pa'i skyes bu chen po la ni mi mthun pa'i phyogs gang yang med do | | de[1] ci'i phyir zhe na | skyon ni 'dod pa'i[3] yon tan rnam pa lnga ste | de dag par byed pa ni bla ma sna tshogs kyi[4] bka'i gdams pa ste | de dran pa'i phyir ro | | yang de nyid gsal bar bya ba'i phyir |
[1] DP om. [2] B *de snyed chu ru* [3] B *po'i* [4] DP *pa'i*

> [suṇṇahiṃ sa]ṅga ma karahi tuhu[1] jahiṃ[2] tahiṃ[3] sama cintassa |
> tila[4]-tusa-matta vi sallatā veaṇu karaï ava[ssa[5] | iti] | (73)
> [1] N *tuha* [2] E_{Sh}N *jahi* [3] E_{Sh} *jahi* N *tahi* [4] N *tiṇa* [5] E_{Sh} *-sa*

| khyed kyis[1] stong par[2] ma zhen cig |
| grogs dag[3] sems ni mnyam par gyis |
| [(4]til phub[4)] tsam gyi zug rngus kyang |
| [5] sdug bsngal nges par 'byin [(6]pa bzhin[6)] | (73)

[1] P *kyi* [2] BD *pa nyid la* [3] B inserts *gang la* [4] B *til gyi phub ma* [5] B inserts *nam yang* [6] B *pas so*

[N 78a] niṣkevalaṃ śūnyatāsaṅgaṃ mā kariṣyasi[1] yenocchedaṃ[2] bhavati | tvam[3] yatra tatra svabhāveṣu vastuṣu sa[matāṃ] cintaya [(4]nātmanā ca[4)] | evam ātmānaṃ[5] ca [(6]paraṃ ca[6)] viśvasaṃgraham ekatāṃ[7] nāpsyasi[8] | nānātvābhāvāt | [ya]di karoṣi | [(9]tadā doṣam[9)] bhavati | yathā tilīyatuṣamātre[10] 'pi cakṣurantargataṃ[11] tasya [12] tat śalyaṃ [E_B 130] bhavati | tena[13] vedanām[14] avaśyaṃ karoti | evaṃ yogendrasya[15] śūnyatā cittamātreṇa śalya[ṃ bha]vati | na sarvāṅgeṣu susthatāṃ prāpyate[16] | yadi tāvat śūnyam aśūnyaṃ[17] dvayam advayaṃ vā na bhāvyate [N 78b] tadā kīdṛśaṃ bhāvyatety āha |

[1] E_B *-ti* [2] E_{Sh} *-do* [3] $E_BE_{Sh}N$ *tvayā* (ergative) [4] E_BE_{Sh} *nātmany eva* [5] N *ātmanaṃ* [6] N om. [7] E_{Sh} *-tva* [8] E_BN *nāpy asi* [9] E_B *adoṣaṃ* [10] E_B *tilīyamātre* [11] $E_BE_{Sh}N$ *vastunāntargatam* [12] E_B inserts *tuṣamadhye kukalaṅka bhavati* | E_{Sh} inserts *joṣamadhye kukalaṅka bhavati* | [13] E_{Sh} *tathā* [14] N *–nā* [15] E_BE_{Sh} *yogīndrasya* [16] E_{Sh} *prāpnoti* [17] N *-nya*

[B 151a] | zhes gsungs te | stong pa nyid 'ba' zhig la ni [(1]zhen par ma byed cig[1)] | des chad par smra bar thal bar 'gyur ro | | gang dang gang dngos po de[2] dang dngos po med pa de dang de la sems mnyam par gyis shig | de ltar bdag dang gzhan sna tshogs kyi dngos pos bsdus pa [3] sna tshogs med par gyis shig | gal te sna tshogs su byed na skyon du 'gyur te | ji ltar til gyi shun pa tsam mig gi nang du zhugs kyang sdug bsngal [(4]chen po[4)] skye ba bzhin du | rnal 'byor gyi dbang phyug gis stong pa nyid la zhen na'ang de dang 'dra'o | gal te stong pa dang | stong pa ma yin pa dang | gnyis ka dang | gnyis ka ma yin pa mi bsgoms[5] na ji lta bur[6] bsgom[7] zhe na |

[1]B *nges par ma zhen cig* [2] P *med* [3] B inserts *dngos po sna tshogs kyi ngo bo gcig tu bya zhing* [4] DP om. [5] BP *sgom* [6] DP *bu* [7] D *sgom*

aïseṃ so para hoi ṇa aïsoṃ[1] |
jima cintāmaṇi-kajja[2]-sa[rīsoṃ[3]] || iti | (74ab)

[1] $E_{Sh}N$ *–so* [2] E_{Sh} *-kaja* [3] E_{Sh} *-so*

| de ltar yin te de nyid[1] ma yin no |
| ji ltar yid bzhin nor bu'i [(2]don dang 'dra[2)] | (74ab)

[1] DP *ni* [2] DP *dgos pa bzhin*

[E_{Sh} 110] īdṛśaṃ[1] nīlapītādyākāram anubhavarūpalakṣaṇaṃ[2)] bhavati | [(3]na tādṛśaṃ sopala[mbha]nirupalambhacittācittakalpanādvaya[4]sarvasāsrava[5]bījā dhārarahitarūpatvāt | kathaṃ jñāyateti[6] cet |[3)] cintāmaṇer[7] iva kārya[8]sadṛśaṃ bhavati | yathā cintāmaṇeḥ sa[rvaṃ][9] vastu na dṛśyate kvacit | punas [(10]tena hastagatena[10)] sarvakāryeṣu cintāṃ karoti jaḍabhāvaś[11] ca | [tathā yo][N 79a]ginām api gurūpadeśaḥ[12] hastagatamaṇim iva necchayā buddhatvādi sādhyatīti bhāvārthaḥ | evam ajānānāṃ[13] paṇḍitānāṃ[14] viharaṇam āha |

[1] E_{Sh} *kīdṛśaṃ* [2] $E_B E_{Sh}$ *anubhavarūpaṃ vā upalakṣaṇaṃ* [3] missing in E_{Sh} [4] $E_B E_{Sh}$ *–yaṃ* [5] E_B *–āśraya-* N *–āsrava-* [6] $E_B E_{Sh}$N *–maṇir* [7] E_B *jñāyate iti* [8] E_{Sh} *kāryaiḥ* [9] E_{Sh} *sarva-* [10] N *tayā hastena* [11] $E_B E_{Sh}$N *-vāś* [12] N *–śa* [13] N *ajānanāṃ* [14] N *paṇḍitānāṃ*

| zhes gsungs te | 'di lta bu'i sngon po dang | ser [P 223a] po [1] la sogs pa'i rnam pa[2] | nyams su myong ba'i ngo bo nyid du mtshon pa yin yang | de lta bu ni ma yin te | dmigs pa dang bcas pa dang | dmigs pa med [(3]par sems pa dang |[3)] sems dang | sems med pa'i rnam par rtog pa gnyis dang | zag pa dang bcas pa'i chos thams cad ni rten med pa nyid[4] yin pa'i phyir ro | | ji ltar [(5]shes she[5)] na | yid bzhin gyi nor bu rin po che dang 'dra bar[6] 'bras bu 'byung ba ni | ji ltar yid bzhin gyi [B 151b] nor bu rin po che las[7] [D 201a] dngos po thams cad 'byung bar mthong yang lag pa na yod pa dang 'dra bar bems po yin yang | rang[8] gis[9] ci bsam[10] pa'i dgos [(11]pa'i don thams cad[11)] byed pa de bzhin du | rnal 'byor pa'ang bla ma'i gdams ngag gi nor bu rin po che lag pa na yod pas | 'dod na yang dag par rdzogs pa'i sangs rgyas kyang[4] sgrub par byed do zhes dgongs pa'o[12] | | de lta bu mi shes pa'i[13] mkhas par rloms pa rnams kyi[14] gnas lugs ston te |

[1] BD insert *dang | dmar po* [2] BDP *pa'am* [3] DP *pa dang* [4] DP om. [5] DP *zhe* [6] DP *bas* [7] DP *la* [8] P *rang rig* [9] D *gi* [10] D *bsams* [11] DP *pa* [12] DP *so* [13] DP *par* [14] B *kyis*

akkaṭa paṇḍia bhantia ṇāsia |
saasam[1]vitti mahāsuhabhāsia[2] | iti | (74cd)

[1] N *–saṃ* [2] $E_B E_{Sh}$N *vāsia*

| [(1]'khrul gzhig mkhas pa ngo mtshar che[1)] |
| rang rig [(2]bde ba chen po'i[2)] bag chags kyis | (74cd)

[1] B *ngo mtshar mkhas pas 'khrul pa gzhig par 'dod* [2] P *bde chen*

akkaṭa ity āścaryaḥ[1] paṇḍitaḥ[2] varṇamātram āśritya [(3]bhrāntyā vināśitaḥ[3)] | [4] vināśiteti yāvat kutaḥ | yataḥ svasaṃvedanaṃ sarvabhāvāntargataṃ[5] nopalabhyate[6] | asaṃvedaneti[7] yāvat | tayā bhrāntyā [(8]anena vyākhyātena[8)] cittācittabhāvena idaṃ svasaṃvi[ttila][N 79b]kṣaṇaṃ mahāsukheṣu bāhyāṅganāsparśeṣu bhāṣitam | punar api tasyaiva bāhyamahāsukhasya dṛḍha[ta]yā[9] vyākhyānam ūcuḥ |

[1] E_B *–aṃ* E_{Sh}N *-a* [2] E_{Sh} *–taiḥ* [3] E_{Sh} *bhrāntir nāśitā* N *bhrāntyā vināśito* [4] $E_B$$E_{Sh}$N *na* is deleted [5] E_{Sh} *-ntagatisāmyāya* [6] E_B *samopalabhyate* E_{Sh} *'labhyate* N *sā nopalabhyate* [7] N *–nā iti* [8] E_{Sh} *anabhyākhyānena* [9] E_{Sh} *[sphuṭātaratayā]*

| zhes gsungs te | ngo mtshar che [1] ni bzhad gad du byed pa'o | | mkhas pa ni dbyangs dang gsal byed la sogs pa la[2] brten nas 'khrul pa gzhig par 'dod de | dngos po la ni mi 'jig[3] go zhes pa'o | | de[4] ci'i phyir zhe na | gang (5gi phyir5) rang rig pas dngos po thams cad nang du gtogs[6] pa de'ang mi dmigs shing mi rig go zhes dgongs pa'o[7] | 'khrul pa de'ang 'di ltar bshad pa 'dis sems dang sems med pa'i rang bzhin gyis 'di ni rang gis[4] rig pa'i (8mtshan nyid8) bde ba chen po'o | | phyi rol gyi yan lag la reg[9] pa'i bde ba de ni kun rdzob tu gsungs so | | yang phyi rol la brten pa'i bde ba de nyid bstan[10] pa'i phyir |

[1] B inserts *ba* [2] D om. [3] B *'jog* [4] DP om. [5] D *gis* [6] BD *rtog* P *rtogs* [7] D *so* P om. [8] P om. [9] DP *rig* [10] D *brten*

savva-rūa[1] tahiṃ[2] khasama karijjaï |
khasama-sahāveṃ maṇa[3] vi [dha]rijjaï | iti | (75ab)
[1] E_B *–rua* [2] E_{Sh}N *tahi* [3] E_{Sh} *gaṇa*

[B:] | rmongs pa chos kun nam mkha' bzhin du gyis |
| nam mkha'i yul du sems kyang gzhag | (75ab)

[DP:] | chos kun nam mkha'i rang bzhin te |
| sems kyang nam mkha'i rang [P 223b] bzhin bzung | (75ab)

[E_B 131] sarvarūpādiviṣayaṃ (1yat tasmin[2] kha1)samaṃ kriyate | manaś[3] ca khasamasvabhāvena dhāryate | tatkṛte |

[1] E_{Sh} *pa* ||| *kha-* [2] $E_B$$E_{Sh}$ *yasmin* N *tasmiṃ* [3] E_{Sh}N *manañ*

| ces[1] gsungs te | [B 152a] gzugs la sogs pa thams cad kyi yul de'ang nam mkha' dang mnyam par bya ba dang | yid kyang nam mkha'i rang bzhin du[2] (3gzhag pa'o3) | | de ltar byas nas[4] |

[1] DP *zhes* [2] D om. [3] DP *bzung bar bya'o* [4] B *na*

(1sovi maṇu tahi1) amaṇu karijjaï |
sahaja-sahāveṃ so paru rajjaï | (75cd)
[1] E_{Sh} |||

| sems de yid med[1] byas ([2]na ni[2]) |
| lhan cig skyes ([3]pa mchog tu[3]) mdzes | (75cd)
[1] DP *med par* [2] DP *nas* [3] B *pa'i rang bzhin mdzes*

tathā so 'pi khasamasvarūpaṃ manaṃ[1] tasminn amanaṃ[2] kriyate | evaṃ yaḥ karoti sa uttamapuru[N 80a]ṣaḥ sahajasvabhāveṣu rajyate krīḍata iti yāvat | evam
[1] E_B *manaḥ* E_{Sh} *manas* [2] E_B *amanaṃ* E_{Sh} *manaḥ*

| zhes gsungs te | nam mkha'i rang bzhin gyi sems de la yid med par ([1]byas te[1]) de ltar gang byed pa de ni skyes bu[2] mchog ste | lhan cig skyes pa mchog tu mdzes pa de la rol zhes bya ba'i don no[3] | | ([4]de ltar yang[4]) |
[1] DP *bya ste* [2] DP *bu'i* [3] DP *to* [4] DP *de ltar mi shes pas*

gharĕṃ[1] gharĕṃ[1] kahiaï[2] sŏjjhuka kah[āṇo |
ṇaü pa]rimuṇia[3] mahāsuhaṭhāṇo | iti | (76ab)
[1] $E_B E_{Sh}$ *ghare* [2] E_{Sh} *kahiyaï* [3] E_B *pari suṇiaü* E_{Sh}N *pa]ri suṇiaï*

[B:] | khyim dang khyim de yi gtam byed pa |
| bde chen gnas ni yongs su shes pa min | (76ab)

[DP:] | khyim dang khyim na[1] de'i gtam |
| brjod pas bde ba chen po yi[2] |
| gnas ni yongs su shes pa min | (76ab)
[1] D *ni* [2] D *yis*

idaṃ kutsitadhīyaiḥ[1] | gṛhe gṛheṣu sattvavañcanāya [vada]nti | īdṛśaṃ śuddhi[2]vyākhyānaṃ yena kathanena tvayādyaprabhṛti śuddhaṃ bhavati | tasmād ([3]anyad eva tadvāhikam[3]) aparaṃ śreṣṭhavyākhyānaṃ mahāsukhasthā([4]nīyaṃ tvayādhigamaṃ[4]) kuruṣva | tasmād [bha]ṅgāpurāṇam eveti | tathā coktam |
[1] $E_B E_{Sh}$ *-dhībhiḥ* [2] E_BN *śuddha-* E_{Sh} *tattva-* [3] N *anya* ||| *dikaṃ* [4] $E_B E_{Sh}$ *yi tvam adhigamaṃ* N *-nīyatvayānādigamaṃ*

| zhes gsungs te | 'dir blo ngan pa rnams kyis khyim dang khyim du sems can rnams bslu bar bya[1] ba'i ched du bshad par[2] byed kyang | de ni kha gtam rnying pa[3] tsam du bas so | de ltar yang |
[1] P *byed* [2] B *pa* [3] D om.

jalaprayātāhipadāni[1] paśyataḥ
khapuṣpamālāracan[āś ca] [N 80b] kurvataḥ |
asūtrakaṃ cāpi paṭaṃ vitanvataḥ
kathaṃ nu[2] lokasya na[3] jāyate trapā | iti | (ĀM 280)
[1] $E_{B}E_{Sh}$ *jalaprapātāni padāni* N *jalaprajātāni padāni* [2] $E_{B}E_{Sh}$ *hi*
[3] E_{Sh} om.

| chu la chu sbrul rjes [D 201b] mthong dang |
| nam mkha'i me tog phreng rgyan dang |
| snal ma med pa'i snam bu rnams |
| 'jig rten ngo tsha med pa yin | (ĀM 280)

kutsitānāṃ doṣatayā[1] paridevanayā[2] sarahetyādi granthakāra[3] āha |
[1] E_{Sh} *doṣaṃ dṛṣyantena* [2] N *–nāyā* [2] N *-am*

| zhes gsungs so | de lta bu'i[1] dman pa dag[2] mthong nas[3] gzhung mkhan po ngo mtshar nas bstan[4] pa ni |
[1] DP *bu* [2] P om. [3] B *bas* [4] DP *ston*

Saraha bhaṇaï jaga cittem̐ vāhia |
[so vi] acitta ṇa[1] keṇavi gāhia | iti | (76cd)
[1] $E_{B}E_{Sh}$N *ṇaü*

| mda' bsnun na re 'gro kun sems khral khur |
| sems med pa[1] sus kyang rtogs pa med | (76cd)
[1] D *pas ni* P om.

[E_{B} 132] mūḍhapaṇḍitaiḥ samastajagan mūrkhalokaṃ ci[ttāci]ttabahuprakāreṇoktalakṣaṇayā[1] vāhitaṃ dāsīkṛtaṃ | madīyopadeśena tac citta[ṃ tyaja]si [(2]acittarūpaṃ prāpsyasi[2)] | na hy etad[3] bhavati | kutaḥ | sa[4] acitta[E_{Sh} 111]lakṣaṇaṃ na [(5]kenacid vidhinā[5)] grāhitaṃ [bhavati | kasmāt] [N 81a] tarhi yasmād[6] acitta[7]rūpasya kāṣṭhapāṣāṇādiṣu kiṃ svasaṃvedanaṃ bhavati | evam acittarūpaṃ ki[ṃ la]kṣyate | na lakṣyateti[8] yāvat | ādāv eva tatsvabhāvatvāt | sa ca |
[1] E_{Sh} *cittacittabahuprakāreṇoktaṃ lakṣaṇena* [2] E_{B}N om. [3] E_{Sh} *tad* [4] E_{Sh} om.
[5] $E_{B}E_{Sh}$ *kena cittavidhinā* [6] E_{B} *kasmāt* E_{Sh} *yasya* [7] E_{Sh} *citta-* [8] $E_{B}E_{Sh}$ *lakṣyate iti*

| ces gsungs te | mkhas pa mngon pa'i nga rgyal can[1] dang rmongs pa'i 'gro ba rnams gong[2] du bstan pa'i sems sna tshogs kyis sems khral khur pa ni khol por byas pas so | | bdag gi[3] gdams ngag gis de lta bu'i sems [B 152b] de mthong na

sems med pa'i ngo bo nyid [(4]'thob par[4)] 'gyur ro | | sems mthong ba dang sems med[5] pa [(6]de cis[6)] mtshon zhe na | mtshon par mi nus zhes bya ste gdod ma nas sems rang bzhin med pa'i phyir ro |

[1] B om. [2] D *gang* [3] P *gis* [4] D *thob par* P *mthong bar* [5] P om. [6] DP *des ci*

> ekku deva vahu āgama[1] dīsaï |
> appaṇu icchem̦ phuḍa paḍihāsaï | iti | (77)
>
> [1] N *āga ..*

> | lha[1] gcig[2] lung ni mang [(3]po'i nang nas[3)] mthong |
> [P 224a] | rang dgar bzhag[4] na gsal por snang | (77)
>
> [1] D *lhan* [2] DP *cig* [3] DP *por* [4] P *gzhag*

ekadevatākāraṃ saṃjñāmātreṇa sa bahvāgameṣu svasvadarśaneṣu ca[1] paśyāmaḥ | saiva[2] cā[3]tmanai[4]vecchayā sphuṭaṃ pratibhāsate [(5]| nānyaḥ[5)] | tathā coktaṃ śrīmaddhevajre |

[1] N om. [2] E$_{Sh}$ *seva* [3] N *ā-* [4] E$_{Sh}$ *–ne-* [5] E$_{Sh}$ *nānā*

| zhes gsungs te | lha[1] gcig[2] gi rnam pa'i[3] ming tsam gyis rang rang gis[4] bstan pa'i lung [(5]mang po las[5)] mthong ste | de ni rang rang gi 'dod pa nyid kyis[6] de dang de'i rnam par snang ste | gzhan du[7] ni[8] ma yin no | | de ltar yang dpal dgyes pa'i rdo rje las |

[1] DP *lhan* [2] DP *cig* [3] BD *par* [4] DP *gi* [5] B *las mang po* [6] DP *kyi* [7] B *du ma* [8] D om.

> svayaṃ hartā[1] svayaṃ [(2]kartā svayaṃ rājā[2)] svayaṃ prabhuḥ ||
> ityādi | (HT I.viii.45cd)
>
> [1] E$_{B}$E$_{Sh}$ *bhartā* N *kartā* [2] E$_{B}$ *hartā rājā* E$_{Sh}$ *harttā svayaṃ rājā* N *hartā*

> | rang gis byed cing rang gis 'phrog |
> | rang nyid rgyal po rang gtso bo'o | (HT I.viii.45cd)

sa ca |

| zhes bya ba la sogs pa gsungs so | de nyid bstan pa'i phyir |

> [N 81b] appaṇu ṇāho aṇṇu[1] viruddho |
> gharĕṃ gharĕṃ sŏ a siddhanta pasiddho || iti | (78ab)
>
> [1] E$_{B}$E$_{Sh}$ *aṇṇa*

| mgon po bdag dang gzhan rnams 'gal |
| khyim dang khyim na grub ([1]pa'i mtha' |
| 'di ni rab tu grags pa yin[1]) | (78ab)
[1] B *mtha' der grags*

ātmātmīyaṃ[1] necchanti[2] | v[inā]śo kutsitakalpanāgrahāt | punar apy anyeṣāṃ bhāvānāṃ[3] nirodhakatvād virodho[tpa]nnatvāt[4] | sa ([5]ghare ghare[5]) ayam siddhāntaḥ[6] prasiddhaḥ[6] | kutaḥ | utpannapralayatvāt | yadi tā[vat] pralayaṃ kasyotpādaḥ | atha cotpādaḥ kiṃ pralayaṃ[7] | tasmād dvayor asatyam | tena [tat] tathoktam[8] | īdṛśaṃ viśiṣṭayoginām āśayaṃ bhavati | ([9]tatsthitānāṃ bhavaty ātmana evaṃ[9]) jñānaṃ gu[rūpa][N 82a]deśāt | yasya nāsti [E_B 133] gurūpadeśaṃ tasya na bhavati | na hy etad[10] buddhabodhisattvānāṃ saṃmatam[8] | teṣā[m bha]gavatoktaṃ hevajre |
[1] N *–ya* [2] $E_B E_{Sh}$ *–ntīti* [3] $E_B E_{Sh}$ N *bhāvanāṃ* [4] $E_B E_{Sh}$ *virodho ['ya]ṃ na syāt* [5] N *ghari ghari* [6] E_{Sh} N *–aṃ* [7] N *–ya* [8] N *-ḥ* [9] $E_B E_{Sh}$ *tatsthitānāṃ bhavaty ātmānam evaṃ* N *kutsitaṃ bhagavaty-ātmanasyaiva* [10] E_{Sh} *tad*

| zhes gsungs te | bdag dang bdag gir 'dzin pa'i sgo nas 'dod pas rang nyid 'ching bar byed pa ni ngan pa ste | rnam par rtog[1] pas yongs su bzung[2] ba'i phyir ro | | gzhan yang dngos po gzhan rnams 'gog pas 'gal ba yin te | dang po[3] skyes pa nyid yin pa'i phyir ro | | khyim dang khyim na[4] grub pa'i mtha' rnams[5] skyes nas 'jig[6] pa ni[7] rab tu grags pa yin te | de[8] ci'i phyir zhe na | skyes nas 'jig pa'i phyir ro | | 'gal ba ni gal te skyes pa yin na 'jig par ji ltar 'gyur [D 202a] zhes pa'o | | de'i phyir gnyis ka mi bden pa zhes bya ba'o |
[1] P *rtogs* [2] B *gzung* [3] B *po'i* [4] DP *ni* [5] P om. [6] D *'jug* [7] DP *'dir* P *pa'i* [8] DP om.

madbhavaṃ[1] hi[2] jagat sarvaṃ madbhavaṃ bhuvanatrayam |
madvyāpitam[3] idaṃ sarvaṃ nānya[mayaṃ] dṛṣṭaṃ[4] jagat || iti |
(HT I.viii.41)[5]
[1] $E_B E_{Sh}$ N *madbhavā* [2] E_{Sh} *hi hi* [3] E_B N *mayā vyāptam* E_{Sh} *mayo vyāptam* [4] E_{Sh} *dṛśyate* [5] The quotation is missing in the Tibetan.

idaṃ kutsi[1]tānāṃ dṛṣṭāntam āha |
[1] N *kucchi-*

dpe ngan pa'i sgo [B 153a] nas bstan pa ni |

ĕkku khāï[1] avara aṇṇa vipoḍaï |
bāhire[2] gaï bhattāraï[3] loḍaï || iti | (78cd)
[1] E_{Sh} *kkhāï* [2] E_B *vāhireṃ* [3] N *bhattāraha*

| gcig ni[1] zos shing gzhan kun bsreg[2] |
| phyi rol song nas khyim bdag 'tshol[3] | (78cd)

[1] DP *nas* [2] P *sreg* [3] DP *tshol*

yathā[1] kaścid[2] annādyā[3]bhakṣaṇaṃ karoti eko[4] 'nyasminn annādyaṃ pralayaṃ kurvanti asādhāraṇatvāt | yathā[5] yoginaḥ ekapuruṣo[6] bhakṣa[yanti |] [N 82b] anyaḥ punaḥ bhoktum icchatāṃ[7] pra[8]lāpenāpi vakṣyati[9] | punar api ghariṇī[10] svasvā[11]minaṃ tyaktvā gṛhā[d bāhyaṃ] gatvā bharttāraṃ prekṣatīti[12] | anyo bahu[13]citta[14]tvād jñānākāreṇai[15]kībhāvād iti | īdṛśī[16] ajñāninām[17] | ekena santuṣṭiṃ karoti ekamātraṃ jānāti na vyāpakaḥ kudhiyām api tādṛśaṃ[18] cittaṃ tena [(19]te naṣṭās[19)] |

[1] E_BE_{Sh} *yadā* [2] N *kathañcit* [3] E_BE_{Sh} *annādya-* [4] E_B *ekam* E_{Sh} *ekam anyam* N *e..m* [5] E_{Sh}N *tathā* [6] E_{Sh} *-ṣaṃ* [7] E_{Sh} *-tā* [8] N *pa-* [9] E_{Sh} *vakṣyati* N *vīkṣyati* [10] E_BE_{Sh}N *gharaṇi* [11] E_B *svasā-* [12] E_BE_{Sh} *prekṣata iti* [13] N om. [14] E_{Sh} *–vi[t]ta-* [15] E_{Sh}N *-ṇe-* [16] E_BE_{Sh} *nedṛśī* [17] E_BE_{Sh} *-nā* [18] E_{Sh} *tādṛśa* [19] E_B *naṣṭāḥ* N *naṣta*

| zhes gsungs te | kha cig rang bza' ba za[1] zhing bza' ba gzhan po thams cad nyams par byed de | gzhan rnams la snying po med pa'i phyir ro | | yang khyim bdag mos rang kyi khyim bor te phyi rol du khyo gzhan po 'tshol[2] ba ni sems ngan pa yin pa'i phyir skyes bu ngan pa rnams kyi sems kyang de dang 'dra'o |

[1] B *zwa* [2] DP *tshol*

āvanta ṇa dīsaï[1] jatta[2] ṇahi[3] acchanta ṇa muṇiaï |
ṇittaraṅga paramesuru[4] ṇikkalaṅka dhāviaï[5] | iti | (79)

[1] E_B *dīssaï* E_{Sh} *dissaï* [2] E_BE_{Sh}*janta* N *jantha* [3] E_{Sh} *ṇaha* [4] E_{Sh} *–saru*
[5] E_BN *dhāhijjaï* E_{Sh} *rohijjaï-*

| [(1]'ong ba bdag kyang mi mthong zhing |
| 'dug pa yang ni [P 224b] mi mthong ngo[1)] |
| rba[2] rlabs med pa'i dbang phyug mchog |
| gos[3] pa med par[4] bsgom par bya | (79)

[1] B *song ba mi mthong 'dug mi mthong* [2] DP *dba'* [3] DP *rnyog* [4] DP *pa*

etat pūrvoktagāhānusāreṇa sudhiyām api īdṛśa āśayaḥ[1] kathyate | yathā ghari[N 83a]ṇī[2] svagṛhe bharttāraṃ bhojayati[3] anyasyāpi bharttārasya[4] bhaktādiṃ sā[5]dhayati | svagṛhān[6] niṣkramya[7] bha[rttāraṃ pa]rīkṣayati[8] | tasmād āvanto 'pi na paśyati[9] gato 'pi [(10]ca na[10)] drakṣyati[11] [E_B 134] svagṛhe

sthito 'pi na [E_{Sh} 112] lakṣaya[ti] | īdṛśaṃ jñānaṃ nistaraṅgaṃ svecchayā parameśvaraṃ niṣkalaṅkaṃ sarvāyāsa[12]rahitaṃ tasya grahaṇaṃ[13] karoti |
[1] E_{Sh} *māyāmayaḥ* [2] E_BN *ghariṇi* E_{Sh} *gharaṇi* [3] E_{Sh} *bhojayati (bhoja)na karoti* [4] E_BE_{Sh} *bharttur* [5] E_{Sh} *sā-* [6] N *sagṛhān* [7] E_B *niṣkamya* N *śodhayati* [8] N *pa]rīkṣati* [9] E_{Sh} *śyati* [10] E_BE_{Sh} *na ca* [11] N *drakṣati* [12] E_{Sh} *sarvāpāya* [13] E_{Sh} *jñānaṃ*

| zhes gsungs te | 'di ni sngon du bstan pa'i tshigs bcad kyi rjes su 'brangs[1] nas blo gros bzang po dag gi bsam gtan 'di lta bu yin no zhes bstan[2] te | ji ltar khyim bdag mos rang gi khyim bdag la bza' ba byin nas | khyim bdag gzhan gyi'ang bza' ba bsgrubs pas rang gi khyim nas byung ste khyo gzhan pa[3] 'tshol ba de ni song ba'ang mi mthong | 'ong pa'ang mi tshor bar[4] | 'dug par gyur pa'ang mi shes so | | de dang 'dra bar rba rlabs med pa'i ye shes ni rang gi yid kyi dbang phyug gi mchog gos[5] pa med cing sdig pa ([4]thams cad[4]) spangs pa de yongs su gzung bar bya'o |
[1] D *'brang* [2] DP *ston* [3] B *po* [4] DP om. [5] DP *rnyog*

anenoktena kiṃ syāt | iha kṣetrajādi[1]yoginīnāṃ svābhāvikaṃ jñānam utpadyate | sā [ca na] kiṃcid vetti | tanmayātmanā paśyati | mayā kṛtaṃ ([2]mayaivotpāditam ityādi[2] vistaraḥ | e[vam e][N 83b]va gurūpadeśād avagantavyam | punar api |
[1] E_{Sh} *–ti-* [2] E_{Sh} *mayevetyādi*

| des[1] ci brjod ce na | 'dir zhing skyes kyi rnal 'byor ma[2] rnams ni rang bzhin gyi[3] ye shes skye'o | | de'ang cung zad mi rig[4] te | thams cad kyis[5] rang bzhin du bdag nyid mthong ste[6] | bdag gis byas shing [B 153b] bdag gis bskyed[7] do zhes bya bar sems so | | de ltar bla ma dam pa'i gdams ngag gis[13] shes par bya'o |
[1] DP *de yis* [2] D *ba* [3] B *gyis* [4] DP *rigs* [5] DP *kyi* [6] DP *bas* [7] D *skyed* [8] P *gi*

> āvaï jāi ṇa cchaḍḍaï[1] tāvahu |
> kahĩṃ[2] apuvva[3]-vilāsi[ṇī] pāvahu || iti | (80)
> [1] E_{Sh}N *chaḍaï* [2] E_{Sh}N *kahi* [3] E_{Sh} *appuvva*

> | gzhan yang 'gro ba[1] dang 'ong ba [1] mi spong[2] |
> | ([3]snga na[3]) med pa'i[1] sgeg mo ([4]gang las[4]) rnyed | (80)
> [1] B inserts *de* (unmetrical) [2] DP *'dor ro* [3] DP *sngar* [4] DP *ga la*

āvanti gacchanti na sā kulaghariṇī[1] tyajanti | etat prasiddhaṃ kāmarūpapī[ṭhādiṣu | ya]thā kaścit puruṣo gṛhe sthitvā tadanyasthānaṃ gamayati | arddhamārgāt punar āgacchati[2] | ta[dvad] yoginījñānaprabhāvād[3] iti | kim etat karoti | kathyate | gacchanto[4] 'pi kasmin sthāne ta[trāpū]rvavilāsinī

saha saṅgaṃ na[5] prāpnoti | tadā māyayā cittakṣatiṃ[6] tena karoti | yā[7] kutrā[8]pūrvavilāsi[nī] [N 84a] na prāpnotīti yāvat | ([9]kiṃ yuktam[9]) ity āha |
[1] N *-ghari* [2] E_{Sh} *gacchati* [3] E_{Sh} *-bhād* [4] E_{B} *gacchato* [5] $E_{B}E_{Sh}$N om. [6] N *cittākṛti* [7] E_{Sh} *tayā* [8] E_{Sh} *bharttā* [9] E_{Sh} *ta*

| ces gsungs te | 'gro zhing 'ong ba la rang gi rigs kyi chung ([1]ma spong[1]) ma yin | khyo dri bar yang ma[2] byed de[3] | de lta ([4]bu ni[4]) kā[5] ma ([6]rū pa[6]) la sogs pa'i gnas rnams na rab tu grags nas yod pa'o | | ji ltar skyes bu kha cig[7] rang gi khyim nas yul gzhan du 'gro ste | song nas kyang lam ([2]phyed nas[2]) phyir ([2]log nas[2]) 'ong ([8]ste |[8]) de lta bu ni rnal 'byor ma'i[9] nus pa yin no | de[2] ci'i phyir de[10] ltar[11] byed ce na | song nas kyang ([12]snga na[12]) med pa'i [D 202b] sgeg mo dang 'phrad[13] nas 'dug par 'dod de | de dang ma[14] 'phrad[13] [P 225a] pas phyir log pa'o | | de[2] ci'i phyir zhe na |
[1] B *ma'ang* DP *ma yang* [2] DP om. [3] DP *do* [4] B *bu'i* [5] BD *ka* P *ka ma pa* [6] D *ru* [7] B inserts *rnams* [8] P *ba* [9] D *ba'i* P *gyi* [10] DP *'di* [11] D *lta bu* [12] DP *sngar na* [13] DP *phrad* [14] D *mi*

sohaï citta ṇirāle[1] diṇṇā |
appaṇarūa[2] ma dekha[ha] bhiṇṇā | iti | (81ab)
[1] E_{B}N *ṇirālaṃ* E_{Sh} *lirāre* [2] $E_{B}E_{Sh}$ *aüṇarua* N *aüṇarūa*

| byang sems dpral ba'i klad rgyas son |
| ([1]rang gi gzugs[1]) dang tha ([2]dad par mi blta[2]) | (81ab)
[1] B *dang po'i gzug snga* [2] DP *mi dad*

tayā[1] yoginībhiḥ sukhacittaṃ śobhanīyaṃ[2] lalāṭasthāne dattaṃ[3] maṇi[4]cchāyā[gṛhaṃ] jñeya[5]vijñānam abhinnarūpatāṃ yāti[6] śarīrasukhayor advayatā bhavati | ekarūpeti [E_{B} 135] yā[va]t | ata eva vakṣyati | yathā ātma[7]rūpaṃ netrādi[8]pṛthaktvena sthitaṃ tayā sthāpite[9] na pṛthagrūpaṃ drakṣyasi[10] | kutaḥ | yasmāt sūtrabandhanādi ekarūpatvaṃ bhavati tasmāt strīpumānrū[paṃ] [N 84b] apṛthag[11]jñānenāviṣṭaṃ sūtravad apṛthag bhavati | evam eva yogināṃ jñānaṃ svabhāvotthitañ ca | na ta[yā[12] kṛteti |] taiś ca sarvakāryakāra([13]ṇaṃ ne[13])cchayā sādhitaṃ bhavati | ([14]sa ca |[14])
[1] E_{Sh} *tābhir* [2] N om. [3] N *datta* [4] E_{Sh} *–ni-* [5] E_{B} *jñeyā-* N *jñayā-* [6] E_{B}N *yāni* [7] $E_{B}E_{Sh}$ *aüna-* N *aḍana-*; Shahidullah (1928, 196) emends to *appaṇa*, Skt. *ātman* [8] N *vetrādi* [9] $E_{B}E_{Sh}$N *sthite 'pi* [10] E_{Sh} *-ti* [11] $E_{B}E_{Sh}$N *pṛthag-* [12] E_{Sh} *tathā* [13] E_{Sh} *sve* [14] E_{Sh} om.

| zhes[1] gsungs te[2] | gang gi tshe rnal 'byor ba'i sems[3] bde[4] ba'i sems de[3] dpral[5] ba'i klad[6] rgyas su phyin nas mdzes te | mi 'dod kyang rang gi gzugs dang tha mi dad par 'gro ste | lus dang bde ba gnyis tha mi dad par 'gyur ro |
[1] DP *ces* [2] D *so* [3] DP om. [4] D *bda* [5] B *dpal* [6] D *glad*

kāa[1]-vāa[2]-maṇu jāva ṇa [bhijjaï |]
sahaja-sahāveṃ[4] tāva[5] ṇa rajjaï | iti | (81cd)
[1] E_{Sh}N *kaya* E_{B} *kāa* [2] E_{Sh} *vāka* [4] E_{Sh} *–ve* [5] E_{Sh} *bhāva*

| gang tshe lus dang[1] ngag yid dbyer med pa[1] |
| lhan cig[1] skyes pa'i[1] rang bzhin de tshe mdzes | (81cd)
[1] DP om.

anenaiva[1] jñānaṃ yāvan na pṛthagjanānāṃ kāyavāṅmanaṃ[2] bhidyate dravī[3]bhavati guruprasādataḥ | sāsravadharmāṇām astamanaṃ[4] na[5] bhavatīti[6] | tā[va]t te[7] sahajasvabhāveṣu na[8] rajyanti | yena yoginīnayam[9] anuttaraṃ prāpyate | tat kiṃ yoginīnayam ity āha |
[1] E_{B} *anena* [2] E_{B} *-no* [3] E_{Sh} *vidravī* [4] Npc *astanamanaṃ* [5] N om. [6] E_{Sh} *ītyarthaḥ* [7] $E_{B}E_{Sh}$ *teṣu* [8] $E_{B}E_{Sh}$N om. [9] E_{B} *yoginīnayam anayam* N inserts in the lower margin in a second hand: *-m anuttaram prāpnoti | tat kiṃ yoginīnaya-*

| zhes gsungs te | ye shes 'dis so so'i skye bo'i lus ([1]ngag yid[1]) dbyer med par chud pa ni bla ma dam pa'i gdams ngag gis der thim par [B 154a] gyur pa'o | | ji srid zag pa dang bcas pa'i chos med par ma gyur pa de srid du lhan cig skyes pa'i rang bzhin mi mdzes te | gang gis[2] bla na med pa'i rnal 'byor ma'i tshul ji ltar 'thob par 'gyur ro[3] | | rnal 'byor ma'i tshul de gang yin zhe na |
[1] DP *dang ngag* [2] P *gi* [3] DP om.

gharavaï khajjaï ghariṇiĕhĭ [ja][N 85a]hi[1] desahi aviāra[2] | iti | (82ab)
[1] E_{B} *–hiṃ* [2] E_{Sh} *avivaāra*

| khyim bdag khyim bdag mo yis zos |
| yul de gang mthong ([1]dag la spyad[1]) mi bya | (82ab)
[1] DP *dpyad*

gharapatir[1] yatra deśe bhakṣaṇaṃ kriyate svagharaṇyā[2] | kṛtam etasmin[3] [deśe] pīṭhādiṣu paśyāmaḥ | īdṛśam avicāritaṃ[4] pṛthagjanair | etat parikalpitaṃ na [yogīndraiḥ] | tāsāṃ[5] bhāvam āha
[1] E_{Sh} *gharaï pati* [2] $E_{B}E_{Sh}$N *gharaṇī ca* [3] E_{B} *etad* N *e* ||| [4] E_{Sh} *avicāra* Nac *avicāri* [5] $E_{B}E_{Sh}$ *teṣāṃ* N |||

| zhes gsungs te | gnas la sogs pa'i yul gang zhig na[1] khyim bdag khyim bdag

mos[2] [(3]za ba de lta bu'i[3)] yul gang dag[4] mthong ba de la spyad par mi bya'o | | de'i dgos pa ni |
[1] D *ni* [2] D *mo yis* P *mo'i* [3] D *za ba lta bui i* P om. [4] DP om.

māie[1] para tahi[2] ki uvaraï visarisa[3] joiṇi[4]cāra[5] | iti | (82cd)
[1] E_{Sh} *māire* [2] E_{B} *tahiṃ* [3] E_{B} *–ria* [4] E_{Sh} *jjhoiṇi* N *joi-* [5] E_{Sh} *cāra*

| kye [(1]gzhan pa de ru 'du bar ga la 'gyur[1)] |
| rnal 'byor [(2]ma yi[2)] spyod pa[3] mi mthun pas | (82cd)
[1] DP | *gzhan po de ru ga la 'du* [2] D *mi* P *ma* [3] DP om.

[E_{B} 136] yatra gha[rapatir māri]taṃ tatra parasya nāsty upacāraḥ | kiṃ tu paratreṣu kṛtam upacāraḥ[1] paratarah[2] | [yoginījñā[3]]na[(4]rūpātmakam[4)] etat | paraiḥ kutsitair māritaṃ bhakṣitaṃ dṛṣṭaṃ carmacakṣuṣā | [E_{Sh} 113] yoginyā ca [na māritaṃ na bha][N 85b]kṣitam api | sahajamayaṃ sahajātmakaṃ sahaje nilīnaṃ kṛtam iti bhāvaḥ | tasmāt visa[dṛśaṃ sarvaśā]streṣu lokavyavahāreṣu yoginīnām ācāraḥ | etad eva spaṣṭayann āha |
[1] E_{Sh} *u[pa]cāraḥ* [2] N *varataraḥ* [3] E_{B} *–śā-* [4] E_{B} *–rūpam ātmakam*

| zhes gsungs te | gang du rang gi khyo yang gsod na gzhan po ga la 'du[1] ste | 'on kyang gzhan rnams kyi[2] mchod par[3] byas na rnal 'byor ma ye shes kyi bdag nyid yin pas de ni mi gsod do | | gzhan ngan pa rnams kyis[4] sha'i mig [(5]gis gsod[5)] par mthong ste | rnal 'byor ma rnams kyis gsod[6] pa[7] ma yin | zos pa[8] yang med do | | 'on kyang lhan cig skyes pa'i ngo bor thim par byas so zhes bya ba'i don no[9] | | [(10]de ni[10)] rnal 'byor ma rnams kyi spyod pa'i lugs[11] thams cad 'jig [P 225b] rten pa'i tha snyad dang mi mthun pa ste | bsam gyis mi khyab pa'o | de nyid gsal bar bya ba'i phyir |
[1] D *'dus* [2] BD *kyis* [3] DP *pa* [4] B *kyi* [5] P *gsad* [6] P *gsad* [7] DP *pa yang* [8] BD *par* [9] DP *to* [10] B *de'i* [11] DP *lung*

gharavaï [khajjaï sa]hajeṃ[1] rajjaï[2] kijjaï[3] rāavirāa |
ṇiapāsa baïṭṭhī[4] citte[5] bhaṭhṭhī[6] joiṇi ma[hu paḍihā]a | iti | (83)
[1] E_{Sh} *–je* [2] E_{Sh} *rasaï* [3] E_{Sh} om. [4] $E_{B}E_{Sh}$ *vaïṭhṭhī* [5] N *citteṃ* E_{Sh} *cinte*
[6] E_{B} *bhaṭṭhī*

| bdag po za zhing lhan cig skyes pa[1] mdzes |
| chags dang chags bral byas nas ni |
| gnyug ma'i [(1]yid kyi[1)] drung du[1] gnas |

| sems nyams [B 154b] [(2]pa yis[2)] [D 203a] rnal 'byor ma ngas[3]
mthong | (83)

[1] DP om. [2] BP *pa yi* D *pa'i* [3] D *ni nga yis* P *ni nga yi*

gharapatibha[1]kṣite sati sahajasvabhāvena rajyate punar api rāgavi[rāgaṃ karo]ti | anyabharttāram āśrayati | rāga[2]virāgaṃ ca rudati | pūrvabharttāraṃ śocayati | nija[sya[3] svapriyasya] [N 86a] pārśve sthitena ca | evaṃ sā yoginī citte bhraṣṭā-acittam iva | mama[4] yogendrasya vā[5] prati[bhāsate | evaṃ] samudāyo yoginījñānam advitīyatvāt | na kriyā[(6]karma tasya[6)] pratibhāsati[7] | karmākarmatena[8] na[9] bā[10]dhyate | sā pṛthagjanānām ābhāsamātram eveti | anyaṃ ca sarvaṃ[11] ci[ttodbhūtaṃ] vikalpanayā[12] sa gharapatiḥ svacittāyattaḥ śarīraḥ sa bhakṣitaḥ | cittaṃ śarīraṃ pīṭhopa[pīṭhādirūpam] | yoginyaḥ[13] prakṛtayaḥ | tannirodhāt prakṛtīnāṃ nirodhaḥ | tadā kim upalabhyate | gu[rūpadeśāj jā][N 86b]nīyād iti | evaṃ vidhāyedaṃ[14] paribhāṣyate[15] |

[1] N *–ra-* [2] E_{Sh}N *rāgaḥ* [3] E_{Sh} *nirasya* [4] N *mayā* [5] N *cā* [6] $E_B E_{Sh}$ *karmatayā* [7] $E_B E_{Sh}$ *pratibhāsaṃ karoti* [8] E_B *karmākarmā-yatena* N *ka* ||| *karmāntena* [9] N added in the upper margin in a second hand [10] E_B *ba-* E_{Sh} *bo-* [11] N *sarva-* [12] E_B *vikalpamanayā* N ||| *lpanayā* [13] E_B *yogibhyaḥ* [14] N *vidhāyarī(?)daṃ* [15] E_BN *-bhāsyate* E_{Sh} *–bhāṣaye*

| zhes gsungs te | rang gi khyim bdag [(1]khyim bdag mos[1)] zos nas lhan cig skyes pa'i rang bzhin du mdzes par byas[2] te | gzhan yang 'dod chags dang 'dod chags dang bral bar byed do | | khyo gzhan yang[3] sngon gyi khyo dang 'dra ba'i sgo nas mya ngan yang byed de | rang gi yid du 'ong ba'i [(4]gan du'ang[4)] 'dug par byed do | | de lta bu'i rnal 'byor ma de ni sems nyams pa ste | rnal 'byor gyi dbang phyug ngas ni 'di[1] bsam gyis mi khyab par mthong ngo | | de [(5]ltar mdor[5)] bsdus pa'i don ni | rnal 'byor ma'i ye shes ni gnyis su med pa yin te | bya ba dang byed [(1]pa med[1)] pa'i rnam par snang zhing | las[1] dge ba dang sdig pa'i rnam pa byed kyang des gnod par mi 'gyur te | phal pa rnams la ni de ltar snang ba'i phyir ro | | yang na thams cad sems kyi rnam 'phrul yin pa'i phyir ro | | khyim bdag sems dbang du gyur pa'i phyir | sems ni lus kyi rnam pa ste | gnas dang nye ba'i gnas la sogs pa'o | | rnal 'byor ma ni rang bzhin te | de bkag pas ci'ang dmigs par mi 'gyur ro | | de ni bla ma dam pa'i gdams ngag gis shes par bya'o |

[1] DP om. [2] DP *bya* [3] DP *yang ste* | [4] DP *gnas na yang* [5] P *la*

khajjaï pijjaï ṇa[1] vichinna[2] [jjaï [(3]citte pa]ḍihāa[3)] |
maṇu bāhira[4] re[5] dullakkha halĕ[6] visarisa[7] joiṇi-māa[8] | iti | (84)

[1] E_{Sh} *na* [2] $E_B E_{Sh}$ *vicinte* N *vicinti-* [3] E_{Sh} *citte paḍḍihāa* [4] $E_B E_{Sh}$N *vāhi* [5] N *reṃ* [6] E_B *haleṃ* E_{Sh}N *hare* [7] E_{Sh} *ria* [8] $E_B E_{Sh}$ *māi*

| za zhing 'thung[1] la bsam mi bya[2] |
| [(3]ji ltar[3)] sems las ci 'byung ba[4] |
| [(5]yid kyi[5)] phyi rol [(6]gyur na sdug bsngal smin[6)] |
| sgyu ma'i rnal 'byor ma ni[7] dpe dang[7] bral | (84)

[1] B *'thungs* [2] B *khyab* [3] B *thogs dag* [4] B *bya* [5] B *yid kyis* DP om. [6] D *gyur pa sdug bsngal 'dzin* P *par sems sdug bsngal 'dzin* [7] DP om.

[E_B 137] ya[t kiṃcit khādayanti] pibantītyādi[1] karma kriyate | [(2]tasya karma sā avicchinnaṃ kriyate |[2)] sa ca yaṃ yaṃ cittena pratibhāsate taṃ taṃ kuryāt [kiṃ tu manavā]hi[3] na kriyate | kiṃ yuktidurlakṣyeṇa[4] | yoginījñānavantasya līnaṃ pūrvavat | vi[sadṛśayogi]nīmārgas tadāśritena[5] sarvaṃ susthaṃ bhavatīti nānyathā | punar āha |

[1] E_{Sh} *-ntīti* [2] $E_B E_{Sh}$ om. N inserts *tasya. ka .. .. avichinnaṃ kriyate* [3] N *-hite* [4] $E_B E_{Sh}$ *–lakṣeṇa* [5] E_{Sh} *tadāśṛtena* N *tadāmṛtena*

| zhes gsungs te | gang cung zad za ba dang [(1]'thung ba[1)] la sogs pa'i bya ba byed pa la ni[2] de ni rgyun mi 'chad par byed de | gang dang [B 155a] gang sems las ci[2] byung ba de bya'o | | 'on kyang [P 226a] sems la gnod pa ni mi bya'o | | sgyu ma'i rnal 'byor [(3]ma de[3)] mtshon par dka'[4] ba'i ye shes dang 'dra bar[5] lhan cig skyes par thim pa ni sngon bzhin no | | rnal 'byor ma'i lam ni thun mong ma yin pa dka' ba'i lam yin pas de'i bdud rtsi thams cad bde bar sgyur[6] na thams cad legs par gnas pa yin te | gzhan du ni ma yin no |

[1] B *'thungs pa* [2] DP om. [3] P *mas* [4] D *dga'* [5] DP *ba* [6] BDP *gyur*

[(1]ia divasa-ṇisahi ahiṇamaï[1)] [N 87a] tihuaṇa jāsu ṇimāṇa |
sŏ citta[2]-siddhi joiṇi sahajā[3]-samvaru-jāṇa[4] | iti | (85)

[1] E_B *ia divasa ṇisahi aïmaṇaï* E_{Sh} *ia davasa ṇasahi* N *chaa .. ṃ .. ṇa* ||| [2] N *cinta-* [3] E_BN *-ja* [4] N *-ṇu*

| 'di ru nyin mtshan dbyer med blo[1] |
| sa gsum [2] gang gi[3] sprul pa yin[4] |
| sems nyid [5] grub pa[5] rnal 'byor ma |
| [(6]lhan skyes[6)] sdom par[7] shes par bya | (85)

[1] P *dag* [2] B inserts *po ni* [3] BDP *gis* [4] DP *des* [5] B inserts *de ni* [6] B *lhan cig skyes pa'i* [7] D om.

[1] evaṃ yaḥ divasaṃ na[2] jānāti rātriṃ ca | abhinna[3]jñānamayaṃ tribhuvanaṃ[4] yasya nirmāṇaṃ sā[5] cittasiddhiḥ yoginī[6] sahajaśaṃ[7]varajñānaṃ

bhavati | ([8]sākṣāt karoti vā[8]) | evam ajānānām āha |
[1] E_{Sh} inserts *punar āha* | [2] $E_B E_{Sh}$ om. [3] E_B *abhi-* [4] E_B *-ṇaṃ* [5] E_B *sa* N *so* [6] E_{Sh}N *yogini* [7] $E_B E_{Sh}$N *–sam-* [7] $E_B E_{Sh}$N *–sam-* [8] Nac *sākṣātkāraṃ karoti*

| zhes gsungs te | gang de ltar nyin mo mi shes shing | mtshan mo'ang mi shes pas | lus ngag yid [D 203b] gsum dbyer med pa'i ye shes kyi rang bzhin sa gsum sprul pa gang yin pa'i sems de ni grub pa'i rnal 'byor ma ste | lhan cig skyes pa'i sdom pa ni ye shes su gyur pa'am | dngos su mngon du byed pa'o |

akkharavāḍhā saala jagu ṇāhi ṇirakkhara koi |
tāva sĕṃ[1] akkhara gholiā[2] jāva ṇirakkhara hoi[3] | iti | (86)
[1] E_{Sh} *se* [2] E_{Sh} *-lijā* [3] E_B *ioi* (?)

| yi ges[1] 'gro ba ma lus pa |
| yi ge med pa gcig kyang med |
| ji srid yi ge rab shes pa |
| de srid yi ge med par 'gyur | (86)
[1] DP *ge'i*

akṣareṣu[1] sakalajagad[2] bādhyate | idaṃ tvayā [3] | athavā—idaṃ ghaṭaṃ[4] | idaṃ paṭaṃ paṇḍitair uktam | yāvajjīvaṃ kriya[te] [N 87b] na paramārthaṃ [5] kiṃcit sādhyate | nirakṣaraḥ ([6]ko 'tra vidyate yena buddhatvaṃ sādhyate |[6]) tāvat saivākṣara[ṃ] gholitaṃ paribhāvanāyā vāgjālaṃ samastam arthataḥ[7] alīkakṛtaṃ yāvan nirakṣaratvaṃ[8] yāti | yāvat naivaṃ kṛtaṃ tāvat[9] kiṃ parama[10]padaṃ prāpnoti | ([11]kiṃ tad | tat[11]) āha
[1] E_B *akṣateṣu* E_{Sh} *ati akṣareṣu* N *akṣare ..* [2] N *-am* [3] $E_B E_{Sh}$ insert *idaṃ mayā* | [4] E_{Sh}N *lataṃ* [5] E_BN insert *na* [6] E_{Sh} om. [7] $E_B E_{Sh}$ *arhitam* N *arthitaḥ* [8] N *nirakṣa* ||| (There is an insertion mark, but the top margin is broken away.) [9] E_B.*yāvat* [10] N *–maṃ* [11] E_B *tad* N *kiṃ tad*

| zhes gsungs te | yi ges[1] 'gro ba ma lus pa la gnod do | 'di ni khyod do | | 'di ni bum pa'o | | 'di ni snam bu'o | zhes mkhas pa rnams brjod de | don dam par ni cung zad kyang[2] med do | | gang gis sangs rgyas nyid grub par byed pa'i yi ge med pa ni gcig kyang med do | | de'i phyir yi ge rab tu shes pa ni yongs su dpyad nas ngag gi spros pa'i dri ma bcom ste[3] brdzun[4] par [B 155b] byas pas ji srid du yi ge med par 'gyur ro[5] | | ji srid de ltar ma byas pa de srid du mchog gi don mi 'thob pa'o | | de gang yin zhes dris[6] na |
[1] DP *ge'i* [2] D om. [3] DP *nas* [4] B *btsun* [5] DP *pa'o* [6] DP *'dri*

jima vāhire[1] tima abbhantaru |
caüdaha[2]-bhuvaṇeṃ[3] ṭhiaü ṇirantaru[4] | iti | (87ab)
[1] $E_B E_{Sh}$N *vāhira* [2] E_{Sh} *caüjaï* [3] E_{Sh} *-ṇe* [4] E_{Sh} *ṇirabharu* N *ṇirantara*

| ji ltar phyi rol de bzhin nang |
| bcu bzhi'i[1] sa la rgyun [P 226b] du[2] gnas | (87ab)
[1] P *bzhi pa yi* [2] P *tu*

[E_B 138] yogendrāṇāṃ yādṛśaṃ bāhyaṃ tādṛśam abhyantaram | kiṃ tarhi jñānākāratvāt | taiś caturdaśabhuvaneṣu ([1]nirantaram anavarāgreṇa[1]) sthita[ṃ] paramakalā[bhāvena][2] [N 88a][3] | sa ca yogī amāvāsyāntena candrakalāmivāśārīratvāt | tenāha |
[1] $E_B E_{Sh}$ *nirantarāvarāgreṇa* N *nirantarā anavarāgreṇa* [2] $E_B E_{Sh}$N *paramakalā[bhāvāt]* [3] N fol. 88 is missing

| zhes gsungs te | rnal 'byor gyi dbang phyug la ji ltar phyi rol bzhin du nang yang ye shes kyi snang ba yin pa'i phyir | des sa[1] bcu bzhi pa la rgyun du thog ma dang tha ma med par gnas te | mchog gi [2] cha med pa'i phyir ro | | de'ang cha ni bcu drug ste | gnam stong gi mthar zla ba'i cha med pa bzhin du lus med pa'i phyir | de bstan[3] pa ni |
[1] DP om. [2] B inserts *don ni* [3] DP *stong*

[E_{Sh} 114] asarīra [kŏi][1] sarīrahi lukko |
jo tahi jāṇaï so tahi mukko | iti | (87cd)
[1] E_{Sh} om.

| lus med lus la gab pa ni |
| gang gis de shes de grol 'gyur | (87cd)

aśarīraṃ sattve sākṣād astam itaṃ bhavati lupto[1] | sa yena jñātaṃ[2] so[3] tasmin mukto[4] bhavati | kutaḥ | yataḥ pratyātmavedako sahajālokaḥ[5] | vedyaṃ cādāv eva notpannaśarīratvāt | nirākāraṃ jñānam etat | tasya saṃjñā sukhapravṛttiḥ | tad amṛtaṃ sahajam iti | puruṣapudgalānāṃ sahajāt ([6]pūrvotpādaḥ |[6]) vināśakāle tatraiva līnaḥ | sukhasya sthitir nāsti asthānatvāt | tasmāt pūrvabhāvaṃ nirākāraṃ jñānaṃ tasyaiva dharmadhātur ityādisaṃjñā | evaṃ yo jānāti gurūpadeśāt sa ihaiva janmani anenaiva śarīreṇa mukto bhavati nānyatheti | anenokte sati granthakārasya tatpari([7]pāla[7])tayā[8] ([9]svaparavastu[9]) na paśyati tenedam udīrayann āha |
[1] $E_B E_{Sh}$ *lukko* [2] $E_B E_{Sh}$ *jñānaṃ* [3] E_BN *sa* [4] $E_B E_{Sh}$ *mukko* [5] $E_B E_{Sh}$ *lokaḥ* [6] $E_B E_{Sh}$ *pūrvotpāda-* [7] $E_B E_{Sh}$ *-ṇāma* [8] E_{Sh} *–nayā* [9] $E_B E_{Sh}$ *svaparas tu*

| zhes gsungs te | lus med pa ni dngos su nub par song bas gab pa ste | de gang gis shes pa de[1] ni[2] grol bar 'gyur ro | ji[3] ltar so so rang gis[4] rig par bya ba'i[5] lhan skyes de[6] ltar 'jig rten pa rnams kyi med pa ste | lus med pa dang | gdod ma nas ma skyes pa'i phyir ro | | 'dir ([7]brjod pas[7]) gzhung mkhan pos rang dang gzhan gyi dngos po ma mthong ba de bstan[8] pa ni |

[1] P *des* [2] D om. [3] B *de* [4] D *gi* [5] B *ba* [6] D *da* [7] B *brjod par bya ba* [8] DP *ston*

siddhir atthu maï paḍhame[1] paḍhiaü |
maṇḍa pibanteṃ ([2]visaraa ĕ maïu[2]) |
akkharam ekka ettha maï jāṇiu |
tāhara ṇāma ṇa jāṇami ĕ saïu | iti | (88)

[1] E$_B$E$_{Sh}$N *paḍame* [2] E$_{Sh}$ *viṇa maï*

| grub par gyur cig nga ([1]yis bton[1]) |
| khu ba 'thungs pas brjed[2] par 'gyur |
| gang gis yi ge gcig shes pa |
| de yi ming ni mi shes so | (88)

[1] DP *yi ston* [2] D *brjod* P *rjed*

[E$_B$ 139] yathā bālatve tv ādāv evā[N 89a]kṣaraśikṣaṇāyopādhyāyasyāgre phalakeṣu siddhir astv ityādinā yāvat sūtradhātvādi[1]vyāka[ra]ṇaparyantaṃ tarkamīmāṃsādi sarvaṃ paṭhitaṃ tadā sarvākṣareṣu na kiṃcit phalaṃ dṛṣṭam ajñānatvāt | punar api sukalyāṇamitrā([2]rādha[2])nāyāṃ satyāṃ parijñānena vicāritaṃ | yaḥ pra[tha]maṃ vākyaṃ siddhir astv iti[3] sa satyaṃ | tatparaṃ yan[4] mayā paṭhitam anyākṣaram asāram | yathā bhaktarandhanāyāṃ sāraṃ gṛhītaṃ maṇḍaṃ[5] samayī pītvā śeṣam asāram[6] | maṇḍam eva sāram | ([7]taṃ pītvānyaṃ[7]) vi[N 89b]smṛtaṃ | gṛhītaḥ siddhir astv[8] iti | etad evākṣaram ekaṃ pūrvoktam[9] jñānam iha mayā jñātam | ([10]tasyānyam anyan[10]) nāmaṃ na jānāmi kīdṛśam iti | avācyatvāt | athavā bālatve[11] nārthaṃ vetti[12] siddhir astu ca | tathāpy asau prau[13]ḍhatve 'pi ca nāsti nāmavarṇā[14]dikhyātiḥ[15] | anye kudhiyaḥ[16] na jānanti[17] | teṣām āha

[1] E$_{Sh}$ *–dhātu-* [2] E$_{Sh}$ *-dhāra-* [3] E$_B$ *īti* [4] E$_{Sh}$N om. [5] E$_B$ *khaṇḍam* [6] N *asāraḥ* [7] N *tatvānyaḥ* [8] N *astur* [9] E$_B$E$_{Sh}$N *pūrvoktajñānam* [10] E$_B$N *tasmin vāmasya* E$_{Sh}$ *tasmin anyam anyan* [11] E$_B$ om. [12] E$_B$ *vatti* [13] N *pro-* [14] N *–vaṇṇā-* [15] N *–ti* [16] E$_{Sh}$ *raktadhiyo* N *–yair* [17] N *jānata*

| zhes gsungs te | ji ltar byis pa'i [D 204a] dus su yi ge slob pa ni[1] slob dpon gyi mdun du ([2]yig shing la[2]) yi ge'i pha ma la sogs pa slob pa'i dus su | dang por[3] 'di grub par gyur cig ces bya ba la sogs pa dang | sgra'i rtsa ba dang | [B 156a] | skad kyi dbyings[4] la sogs pa slob cing dpyod pa la sogs pa thams cad kyi yi ge

rnams la 'bras bu ni gcig kyang ma mthong ba yin te | don mi shes pa'i phyir
ro | | gzhan yang (5dge ba'i bshes gnyen dam pa la bsten pa5) las don yongs su
shes pa6 skye zhing | 'dir dpyad (7tsa na7) dang por8 grub par gyur cig ces bya ba
de (9ni bde bar bklag gi9) | gzhan ni10 snying po med (11par bklag11) pa'o | | ji ltar
zan 'tshed (12par byed12) pa'i dus su snying po khu ba6 blangs nas 'thungs13 te |
[P 227a] gzhan ni snying po med pa'o | 'dir grub (14par gyur cig14) ces bya ba'i yi
ge gcig po de bdag gis shes kyi15 | de'i ming mang bas de'i ming mi shes te | 'di
lta bu yin zhes brjod du med pa'i phyir ro | | ji ltar byis pa'i dus su 'di grub par
gyur cig ces bya ba'i ming shes kyang don mi shes pa bzhin du | ches skyes pa'i
dus na | don shes kyang ming mi shes pa'o |
1 P *na* 2 B *yig shing las* D om. 3 DP *po* 4 P *byings* 5 DP *dam pa'i dge ba'i bshes
gnyen* 6 P om. 7 P *tsam* 8 D *po* P *po'i* 9 D *bde bar bklags kyi* P *bden pa plags kyis*
10 DP *yang* 11 D *pa bkrags* P *pa plags* 12 DP om. 13 D *'thung* 14 B om. 15 DP *kyis*

    ruaṇeṃ1 saala (2vi jŏhi ṇau2) gāhaï |
    kundurukhaṇahi3 (3mahāsuha sāhaï3) | (89ab)
    1 E_Sh -*ṇe* 2 E_Sh *vi jo ṇau* N *jahi ṇa* 2 E_Sh –*ru anaï* N –*rukhaṇaï*
    3 E_B E_Sh -*suhe* N -*suhaï*

sahaja1rūpaṇena sakalaṃ2 tribhuvanaṃ2 patitaṃ | na grāhitaṃ svayaṃ-
bhūjñānākāreṇa vā3vā[cya][N 90a]nāmena4 vā | tadā punar api svayaṃ
naṣṭāḥ5 parān api dhandhāyanti6 | kiṃ tat | kundurukṣaṇeṣu mahā[su]khaṃ
sādhayanti7 | tasmāt te mūrkhadehinaḥ | punar apy āha
1 N –*jā-* 2 E_B E_Sh N -*a-* 3 E_B E_Sh N *cā-* 4 E_B E_Sh –*nām eva* 5 E_Sh N *naṣṭā* 6 E_B *bandhāyanti*
E_Sh *bandhāpanti* 7 E_B N *yatīti*

    | ma lus rang bzhin mi shes gang zhig gis | (89a)

| zhes gsungs te | lhan cig skyes (1pa mi1) shes pas khams gsum du lhung ste
| rang byung gi ye shes sam | brjod du med pa'i rang bzhin du mi rtogs2 pa'i
phyir ro | | gzhan yang des3 rang nyams shing gzhan yang nyams4 par byed do
| | de5 ji lta bur6 zhe na |
1 P *pa'i* 2 D *rtog* 3 D *de yis* P *de'i* 4 B *rmongs* 5 DP om. 6 P *bu*

    [B:] ku ndu ru yi skabs su bde chen bsgrub pa ni | (89b)

    [DP:] kun tu ru'i skad cig la |
    | bde ba chen po sgrub pa ni | (89b)

| zhes gsungs te | ([1]ku ndu[1]) ru'i sgo nas bde chen bsgrub[2] pa[3] ces zer ba ni rmongs pa'i phyir ro |

[1] P *kun tu* [2] D *grub* P *sgrub* [3] D om.

> jima tisio[1] mia[2] tisiṇeṃ[3] dhāvaï |
> maraï[4] [5] sŏsahĭṃ[6] ṇabhajalu[7] kahĭṃ[8] pāvaï | iti | (89cd)

[1] E_{Sh} *tisi* [2] E_{Sh} om. N *sia* [3] E_{Sh} *-ṇe* [4] E_{Sh} *mara* [5] E_BE_{Sh} insert *so* N inserts *su* [6] E_{Sh} *sosena* N *–sosai* [7] E_{Sh} *bhajjalu* [8] E_{Sh} *kahi*

> [B:] | ji ltar ri dwags skom pas smig rgyu'i chu la rgyug |
> | skom pas 'chi ste [B 156b] nam mkha'i chu rnyed dam | (89cd)

> [DP:] | ji ltar ri dags skom pa yis |
> | smig rgyu'i chu la rgyug pa ni |
> | skom 'chi[1] nam mkha'i chu rnyed dam | (89cd)

[1] D *pas 'chi nas*

[E_B 140] yathā ([1]tṛṣṇārtito 'titṛṣṇayā[1]) andhatvena pānīyaṃ[2] dṛṣṭvā[3] dhāvati | tadā cakṣuṣā nīhāramātraṃ na pānīyaṃ[4] | tṛṣṇārttatayā[5] sosena[6] mriyate | ākāśajalaṃ ([7]kutra prāpyateti[7]) yāvat | evam iva kunduruyo[ge][N 90b]na[8] tattvaṃ na prāpyate | mūḍhalokair evaṃ tattvaṃ kva jñeyaṃ kiṃ yuktir vā etad evāha |

[1] E_{Sh}N *tṛṣārttaḥ atitṛṣāyā* [2] N *pāṇīyaṃ* [3] N *dṛṣṭaṃ* [4] E_{Sh} *papaṃ* N *pāṇīyaṃ* [5] E_BE_{Sh}N *tadārttatayā* [6] N *sose* [7] E_BE_{Sh} *kutaḥ prāpyate na prāpyate iti* [8] E_{Sh} *-yoge*

| zhes gsungs te | ji ltar ri dwags[1] skom pas[2] gdungs pas smig rgyu la chur[3] mthong nas de'i ([4]gan du[4]) rgyugs[5] pa las | der[6] chu ma rnyed nas skom pas 'chi ste | nam mkha'i chu ji ltar rnyed par 'gyur te | mi rnyed ces pa'o | ([7]de bzhin[7]) du dbang po gnyis sbyor gyi bde bas ni ([8]de nyid[8]) mi rnyed do[9] | rmongs pa'i[10] 'jig rten pa rnams ni 'di las de[11] nyid rnyed par 'dod de[12] | de nyid bstan pa'i phyir |

[1] DP *dags* [2] P *pa* [3] P *chu ru* [4] P *gnas su* [5] DP *rgyug* [6] DP om. [7] P *bzhan* [8] D om. [9] DP *de* [10] B *pa* [11] D *'di* [12] DP *do*

> [E_{Sh} 115] kandhabhūa[āa]ttaṇaïndīvisaaviāru[1] apa hua |
> ṇaüṇaüdohācchande ṇa[2] tahavi[3] kimpi goppa | iti | (90)[4]

[1] N *viāmerū* [2] E_{Sh} inserts *na* N om. [3] E_BE_{Sh} *kahavi* N *kaha* [4] missing in G

skandhadhātv[1]āyatanendriya[2]viṣa[3]yavikalpaṃ[4] vibhramarūpaṃ paśyati | yatra lakṣyaṃ[5] lakṣaṇaṃ[6] ca na ([7]vidyate tatra[7]) sarvathā marīcijalavad viśvam udakasaṃjñā pratīyate | udakabhāvaṃ ca nāsty eva marīcyābhāsasaṃjñayā | marīcibhrāntim[8] eva hi udakasyābhāsaṃ pratīyata iti | tasmā[n] [N 91a] navanavānyānyadohācchandasā[9] tattvaṃ darśitam | tasmin[10] dohāmadhye tāsu[11] dohāsu[12] kiṃci[d guptaṃ na kṛtaṃ gu]rūpade[(13]śam na[13)] vināśitaṃ syād iti | etad arthaṃ sarveṣāṃ paṇḍitānāṃ kṣamāpaya[tīty āha] |

[1] N *–tu* [2] N *–yaṃ* [3] N *-śa-* [4] $E_{B}E_{Sh}$N *–vikalpa-* [5] N *lakṣya-* [6] N *–lakṣaṃ* [7] $E_{B}E_{Sh}$ *vidyate teṣu* N *vidyettṛṣu* [8] E_{Sh} *–r* [9] $E_{B}E_{Sh}$N *–dohāśabdena* [10] N *tasmi* [11] $E_{B}E_{Sh}$N *kasmin* [12] $E_{B}E_{Sh}$N *doheṣu* [13] E_{Sh} *-śena*

paṇḍialoahu[1] khamahu mahu[2] etthu ṇa kiaï viappu |
jo guruvaaṇeṃ maï [suaü] tahi kiṃ kahami sugoppu[3] | iti | (91)[4]

[1] N *loaehu* [2] N supplied in the margin and partly broken off [3] N *–pu* [4] missing in G

he[1] paṇḍitaloka īdṛśaṃ jñānaṃ guptāguptaṃ may[ā kathitaṃ tathā mama kṣa]māṃ karoṣi[2] | kutaḥ | yataḥ guptasthāne na guptīkṛtaṃ tathāgupta[3]sthāne prakāśitaṃ sattvo[pakāra][N 91b]cetasā tenedaṃ vikalpaṃ[4] na kāryam[5] evaṃ ca sammatam mamaikākinasya[6] na bhavati | kutaḥ | ya[taḥ mayā[7]]pi svaguroḥ[8] sakāśād yad vacanam īdṛśaṃ śrutaṃ | tat kiṃ karoti suguptaṃ prakaṭaṃ ca | [evam u]ktena kiṃ syāt | bhavyasattveṣu [(9]vyaktam abhavyasattveṣu[9)] guptam iti | etad evāha |

[1] E_{Sh} om. [2] N *kurvaṣi* [3] $E_{B}E_{Sh}$ *yathā gupta-* [4] E_{Sh} *vikalpa-* [5] N *kāryā* [6] E_{Sh} *-kino* [7] E_{B} *–mā-* [8] N *–ruḥ* [9] E_{B} om.

(Missing in the Tibetan)

[E_{B} 141] kama[la-kuli]sa vĕvi majjha-ṭhiu jo so suraavilāsa |
ko taṃ[1] ramaï ṇaü[2] tihuaṇĕ[3] kas[sa ṇa pūra]ï āsa | iti | (92)

[1] $E_{B}E_{Sh}$ *ta* N *ḍa* [2] $E_{B}E_{Sh}$ *ṇaha* N *ṇeṃ* [3] $E_{B}E_{Sh}$ *tihuaṇe hi* N *tihuvaṇa hi*

[B:] | rdo rje padma gnyis kyi bar gnas pa |
| bde ba gang gyis rnam rol pa |
| gang gis de ni bstan par mi nus pas |
| sa gsum re ba gang gis rdzogs par byed | (92)

[DP:] | rdo rje padma gnyis par gnas pa[1] | [D 204b]
| bde ba gang gyis rnam rol pa |
| ci ste de bde nus med pas |
| sa gsum re ba ji ltar rdzogs | (92)

[1] DP om.

anenātyantādikarmikāṇāṃ mṛduyogināṃ[1] vā rāgāsaktānā[ṃ ca mahārāgakrī][N 92a]ḍanaiva[2] buddha[(3]tvam upāyena iti[3)] darśitaṃ bhagavatā | tathā iha mayāvatāritaṃ | kamala[kuliśadvayeṣu yat] suratavilāsaṃ ko vīrapuruṣas[4] tatra na[5] ramate[6] | tena tribhuvane[7] kasya na [pūritāśā[8]] | sarveṣāṃ tanmayatvena tatsvabhāvatayā[9] sarvesāṃ[10] mahāmudrāsiddhiḥ pūri[tā bhavati | mahāka]ruṇām[11] āmukhīkaraṇād iti niyamaḥ | kiṃ tv adhimātrendriyāṇāṃ [nedṛśaḥ | kiṃ tad ā]ha | yadi kamalakuliśena tattvaṃ tadātmanā [(12]sukham utpādya[12)] parasya sukhā[nubhavaṃ vinā gate] [N 92b] na sarvatribhuvanasyāśāḥ[13] pūritā bhavanti[14] | buddhajñānam eveti | ta[smān na tādṛśaṃ | buddhajñānaika]kṣaṇe abhisambodhiḥ sarveṣāṃ samānakālatvāt saṃkṣepa[taḥ |]

[1] N *yogīnāṃ* [2] E_{Sh} *-ḍaṇaiva* [3] E_{B} *–tvam upāya iti* E_{Sh} *–tvopāpa iti* N *–tvam upāyaiti* [4] N *-ṣa* [5] $E_{B}E_{Sh}$N om. [6] N *ramanti* [7] N *-nai* [8] $E_{B}E_{Sh}$ *pūrita āsaḥ* [9] N *-vayā* [10] $E_{B}E_{Sh}$N *sarvāṣāṃ* [11] E_{B} *–ruṇāyā* [12] N *sukhotpādā* [13] E_{B} *sarvatribhuvanasya sā* N *sarve tribhuvanasyāsā* [14] $E_{B}E_{Sh}$ *bhavati*

| zhes gsungs te | 'di ni las dang po pa dang dbang po tha ma'i rnal 'byor pa 'dod chags la zhen pa rnams la[1] 'dod chags chen po[2] rol [P 227b] pa'i thabs 'dis sangs rgyas 'grub par bcom ldan 'das kyis bstan[3] to | | de bzhin du [(4]mda' bsnun gyis[4)] de nas phyung ste 'dir bstan pa'o | | rdo rje dang[5] padma gnyis kyi sbyor ba'i bde bas ni[5] dbang po tha ma'i skyes bu rol par byed pa gang yin pa des ni sa gsum gyi re[6] ba yongs su rdzogs par ci ste mi byed de | thams cad de'i rang bzhin gyis thams cad kyi bsam pa phyag[7] rgya chen po yongs su rdzogs par byed de | snying rje chen po mngon du byed pa'i phyir ro zhes dgongs pa'o[8] |

[1] D *las* [2] B *por* [3] D *ston* [4] BD *bdag gis* [5] DP om. [6] DP *bde* [7] P om. [8] DP *so*

> [khaṇa [(1]uvāa-suhaha a]havā ahavā[1)] veṇṇi[2] vi soi[3] |
> gurua-pa[4]sāeṃ puṇṇū[5] jaï viralā jā[naï kovi[6]] | iti[7] | (93)

[1] E_{B}N *uvāasuha ahavā* E_{Sh} *uvāasuha bhahavā* [2] N *veṇṇa* [3] E_{B}N *sovi* E_{Sh} *soï* [4] $E_{B}E_{Sh}$ *gurupāa* [5] E_{B}N *puṇṇa* [6] E_{Sh} *koï* [7] E_{B} om.

> | yang na thabs de[1] skad cig ma |
> | yang na de nyid[2] gnyis med de |
> | bla ma'i [(3]bka' drin[3)] bsod nams kyis |
> | brgya la 'ga' [B 157a] yis shes par 'gyur | (93)

[1] B *kyi* [2] DP *gnyis* [3] P *drin gyi*

[kṣaṇaṃ] cedaṃ[1] upāyasukhasya[2] catuḥkṣaṇabhedāt | athavā-abhinne 'pi [kṣaṇe tattvam upalakṣayet |] sa ca (tac ca?) paramaviramayor madhye [(3]iti bhinnam[3)] eva | pratha[mārambhe vicitrādikṣaṇe utpadyamāne[4] | abhi][N 93a]nnaṃ[5] sahajabhāvaṃ saiva gurupādaprasādena puṇyavaśāt | yaḥ kaścit

tattvaṃ[6] viralo[7] lokaḥ jānā[ti | kaś[8]ci]d iti na sarvasattveṣu sādhāraṇatvaṃ[9] bhavati | tenedaṃ mayā sadgurūpadeśena vyaktī[kṛtaṃ pū]rvoktanyāyāt sarvajaneṣu sādhāraṇam iti |
[1] N *cāyaṃ* [2] $E_B E_{Sh}$ N *sukhasya* [3] $E_B E_{Sh}$ *abhinnam* [4] $E_B E_{Sh}$ *utpādanāyā* [5] E_B N *-nne* [6] E_B *tattva-* N om. [7] N *viralā* [8] E_B *kva-* [9] E_{Sh} *sāratvaṃ*

| zhes gsungs te | skad cig ma ni dga' ba bzhi'i skad cig ma'i bye brag yin pa'i phyir ro | | yang na gnyis su med pa'i dus su de nyid mtshon pa'o | | de'ang mchog dang dga' bral gyi dbus su yin pas tha dad pa ni mgo rtsom pa'i skad cig ma ste | rnam pa sna tshogs pa la sogs pa[1] skyes pa'i dus so | | tha dad pa med pa ni lhan cig skyes pa'i ngo bo nyid de bla ma dam pa'i gdams ngag gi drin gyis skyes bu[2] kha[3] cig gis[4] shes kyi[5] | 'jig rten pa thun mongs pas ni ma yin no | | de'i phyir bdag gis[6] bla ma dam pa'i gdams ngag gi sgo nas gong du bstan pa'i rigs[7] pas skye 'gro thun mong ba rnams la gsal bar byas pa yin no |
[1] B *las* [2] B *bus* [3] B *skad* [4] P *gi* [5] D *kyis* [6] DP *gi* [7] D *rig*

[E_B 142, E_{Sh} 116] gambhīraha[1] uāharaṇeṃ[2] ṇa[ü para][3] ṇaü appāṇa[4] |
sahajāṇanda[5]-caüṭhṭha[6]-khaṇĕ[7] ṇia-saṃveaṇa[8]-jāṇa | iti | (94)
[1] $E_{Sh} E_B$ N gambhīraï [2] E_{Sh} *uvāharaṇe* N *uāharahale* [3] E_{Sh} *pahara* [4] E_{Sh} *adhyaṇṇa* [5] E_B *–ndeṃ* E_{Sh} *-nde* [6] N *caüṭṭha-* [7] E_B N *-kkhaṇa* E_{Sh} *-kkhane* [8] E_{Sh} *saṃvesaha*

| kye grogs [(1]zab mo dang ni[1)] rgya che ba |
| 'di la bdag gzhan yod ma yin |
| lhan cig skyes dga' bzhi pa'i skabs |
| gnyug ma nyams su myong bas shes | (94)
[1] DP *dag zab dang*

evaṃ ca | yat pu[ṇyeṣu] viralā lokā jānanti tat gambhīrasya vicārabalena nirantarasmaraṇatayā[1] pakṣāpakṣa[ṃ nirudhyate |] [N 93b] paramagambhīre tatra na paraṃ nātmanaḥ[2] kiṃcid asti | ādāv eva rahitatvāt | īdṛśaṃ saha[jānanda[3]]caturthakṣaṇe loka[4]parikalpitamadhye nijasaṃvedanaṃ jānāsi[5] | punar api taṃ[6] jānāti [sa eva] hi | asyānuśaṃsām āha |
[1] N *-ṇayā* [2] N *anātmana* [3] $E_B E_{Sh}$ N *-nandena* [4] E_B *lokaḥ* [5] E_{Sh} *–mi* [6] E_B N *tāṃ* E_{Sh} *tā*

| zhes gsungs te | zab mo ni dpyad pa'i stobs kyis rgyun mi 'chad par dran pas phyogs dang phyogs ma yin pa nub par [(1]'gyur ro[1)] | | de ltar mchog tu zab pa de la ni bdag dang[2] gzhan thams cad nyams [P 228a] te | gdod ma nas skye ba med

pa’i phyir ro | | ’di lta bu’i lhan cig skyes pa dga’ ba bzhi’i dus su ([3]dbus su[3]) lhan cig skyes pa nyams su myong ba rtogs par bya’o | | ’di’i phan yon bstan[4] pa ni |
[1] B *gyur pa’o* [2] B om. [3] D om. [4] DP *ston*

> ghorāndhāre[1] candamaṇi jima ujjoa karei |
> paramamahāsuha[2] ekku-khaṇĕ[3] duriāsesa harei | iti[4] | (95)
> [1] E_B *ghorāndhāreṃ* E_{Sh} *ghore ndhare* [2] N *parama* ||| *suha* [3] N *etthukhaṇa* [4] N *ti*

> | mun nag chen [D 205a] por zla shel gyis |
> | ji ltar gsal bar byed pa bzhin |
> | mchog tu bde ba[1] skad cig la |
> | sdig pa ma lus pham byed pa’o | (95)
> [1] B *ba’i*

iha yathā[1] ghorāndhakāramadhye candrakāntamaṇir[2] uddyotanaṃ karoti | yādṛśaḥ[3] sarvacauracaṇḍālādibhir harati | tādṛśaḥ paramamahāsukha [ekakṣa][N 94a]ṇe saṃsāraduścaritāśeṣaṃ harati[4] | tathā |
[1] E_BN om. [2] N *–kāntiya(?)* ||| [3] E_{Sh} *yādṛśa-* [4] E_B *karoti*

| zhes gsungs te | ’dir[1] mun nag chen po’i nang du zla shel gyi nor bu’i snang bas gsal bar byed pa’i [B 157b] dus su rigs ngan dang[2] rkun ma la sogs pas gzhan gyi nor rku bar byed pa bzhin du | mchog tu bde ba chen po[3] mtshan nyid dang bral ba’i skad cig ma’i dus su[2] ’khor ba’i sdig spyod thams cad kyang[2] nyams par byed do | de ltar |
[1] DP *’di* [2] DP om. [3] DP *po’i*

> dukkha-divāara ([1]atthagaü ūvaï[1]) tara-vaï [sukka |
> ṭhi]a[2] ṇimmāṇeṃ[3] ṇimmiaü[4] teṇa-vi maṇḍala-cakka | iti | (96)
> [1] E_{Sh} *atthavi uṭhṭha* [2] E_{Sh} *vijjā* [3] E_{Sh} *-ṇe* [4] E_{Sh} *nirmiaü*

> | sdug bsngal snang byed nub pa na |
> | skar ma pa wa sangs ni ’char |
> | ’di ltar gnas pas[1] sprul pa sprul |
> | ’di ni dkyil ’khor ’khor lo’o | (96)
> [1] D *pa’i*

yathā grīṣmakāladuḥ[khadivāka]raḥ[1] astam ito[2] bhavati | tadā atyantaśītalatvaṃ karoti | tārāgaṇanāyakaś[3] candra[ḥ śukra[4]] utthito bhavati | īdṛśaṃ[5] maṇḍalacakrādi[E_B 143]bhāvanā kriyate | yena nirmāṇas[thitena viśvaṃ]

buddhasaṃvṛttyā[6] nirmāṇaṃ nirmiṇoti[7] | tatsvarūpaṃ[8] maṇḍalacakraṃ [vijñeyād iti bhāvārthaḥ | punar yo][N 94b]ginām kartavyam āha |
[1] N *-ra* [2] N *-aṃ* [3] N *-ka* [4] $E_B E_{Sh}$ *śukraś ca* [5] $E_B E_{Sh}$ *īdṛśa-* [6] E_{Sh} *sāṃsthityā* [7] N *–noti* [8] $E_B E_{Sh}$ N *–pa-*

| zhes gsungs te | ji ltar [(1]sos ka'i[1)] dus su [(2]sdug bsngal[2)] gyi [(3]nyin mtshan[3)] de nub nas shin tu bsil ba'i gtso bo skar ma pa wa sangs 'char te | 'di lta bu'i dkyil 'khor gyi 'khor lo la sogs pa bsgom zhing gnas pa gang gis sna tshogs [4] sangs rgyas kyi sku kun rdzob kyi sprul pa sprul te | de'i ngo bo nyid du dkyil 'khor gyi 'khor lo'ang shes par bya'o zhes bya ba'i don no[5] | | yang rnal 'byor pa'i bya ba bstan[6] te |
[1] DP *so ga'i* [2] B *rdul* [3] P *nyi tshan* [4] B inserts *kyi* [5] DP *to* [6] P *don*

cittahĩṃ[1] citta ṇi[hālu vaḍha[2] saala vi mucca[3] kudiṭṭhi[4] |
parama-mahāsuhe sojjha paru ta]su āattā siddhi[5] | iti | (97)
[1] E_{Sh} *cittehi* N *cittahi* [2] $E_B E_{Sh}$ N *vaḍa* [3] E_{Sh} *–ccaï* [4] E_{Sh} *–diṭhṭhi* [5] E_{Sh} *siddhiḥ*

| rmongs pa sems kyis[1] sems la [(2]ltos shig dang[2)] |
| lta ba ngan pa [(3]thams cad las grol te[3)] |
| [(4]'di ni bde ba chen po mchog[4)] yin te |
| de la [5] dngos grub dam pa yod | (97)
[1] P *kyi* [2] DP *rtogs* [3] DP *kun las grol* [4] DP *mchog tu bde chen 'di* [5] B inserts *gnas na*

cittena cittaṃ tvaṃ[1] vicārayasi | kiṃ tu[2] cittam a[cittaṃ cāsti | pū]rvoktanyāyād [(3]eva dvayor[3)] nāsti | tathā cāha |
[1] N *tvayā* [2] N *ta* [3] E_{Sh} *etayor*

| ces gsungs te | khyod kyi sems kyis[1] sems la[2] dpyod dang | ci sems dang sems med pa sngon du bstan pa'i rigs[3] pas [4] gnyis ka'ang med do | | de ltar yang |
[1] P *kyi* [2] DP om. [3] BP *rig* [4] P inserts *de*

cittam eveha[1] nācittaṃ dvayābhāvān na ki[ṃcana |
na] kiṃcin nāmāpadyeta[2] bhrāntyā sarvam idaṃ jagat || iti[3] |
[1] N *evā* [2] $E_B E_{Sh}$ *nāma vidyeta* (slightly faulty *ma-vipulā*) [3] E_B om.

| sems nyid dam pa sems [1] med [2] nyid |
| gnyis ka med cing[3] cung zad med [4] |

| 'gro [P 228b] ba ma lus 'khrul pa'o[5] |

[1] B inserts *la* [2] B inserts *pa* [3] B *phyir* [4] B inserts *pa'i ming yang med* [5] P *pa yis*

tasmāt sarvaṃ kudṛṣṭaya[ḥ[1] muñcasi[2] tyajasi | saka]lātmajīvapuruṣapudgalādayaḥ sarve kutsitalokavyavahārasaṃvṛtamātram e[tat | tena tat tatho][N 95a]ktaṃ | evaṃ[3] sarve paramamahāsukhe[4] śodhanaṃ kuru | yena paramabhūmilokottarabuddha[saṃvṛteṣu pra]veśaṃ karoṣi[5] | tasya paraṃ[6] śreṣṭhasiddhir[7] āyatā[8] bhavati | tenedaṃ |

[1] E_{Sh} *-dṛṣṭīr* [2] E_{Sh} *muñca* [3] E_B om. [4] $E_B E_{Sh}$N *–sukheṣu* [5] N *kurvasi* $E_B E_{Sh}$ *karoti* [6] E_BN *para-* [7] E_{Sh} *syeṣṭhasiddhir* N *śreṣṭhasiddhi* [8] E_{Sh} *āsannā*

([1]zhes gsungs so[1]) | de lta bu'i lta ba ngan pa bor te | ma lus pa'i bdag dang | skyes bu [B 158a] dang | srog la sogs pa bya ba ngan pa thams cad ni kun rdzob tsam yin pa'i phyir ro | | de ltar bde ba chen po'i rang bzhin du thams cad dag par gyis shig dang | [2] 'jig rten las 'das pa'i mchog thob pa ni de la rag las pa'i phyir ro | | de'i phyir |

[1] P om. [2] BD insert *thams cad*

mukkaü citta-[gaenda] karu ettha viappa ṇa[1] puccha[2] |
gaaṇa-girī-ṇaï-jala piaü tahiṃ[3] taḍa[4] vasa[ï sa]ïccha | iti | (98)

[1] $E_B E_{Sh}$N *ṇu* [2] E_B *–cchā* [3] E_{Sh}N *–hi* [4] N *taṭa*

| sems kyi glang po yan du chug |
| de ([1]ni rtog pas ma 'dris shig[1]) |
| nam mkha'i ri bo chu 'thung dang |
| de yi 'gram du rang dgar zhog | (98)

[1] BD *la bdag ni ma 'dri zhig* comes from *ettha vi appaṇu puccha*

muktaṃ cittagajendraṃ kuru | yathecchayā saṃsāramadhyeṣu krīḍanaṃ ku[ru | a]syedaṃ[1] vikalpaṃ[2] na pṛcchasi | kutaḥ | yataḥ sarve bhāvās[3] tattvātmakās tattvāśritās[4] tattveṣu [nilīnā] [N 95b] bhavanti | kiṃ tu prāṇātipātādi kukarma[5] varjasi[6] | yais tīrthikādi [E_B 144] narakaṃ yānti kā[ruṇikāṇā]ṃ[7] ca daśakuśalakarma[E_{Sh} 117]pathaparipālanayā[8] sarvaṃ susthaṃ bhavati | tena ga[ganagiri]ṇo[9] hastivat sarvavyāpakatveṣu nadyāḥ[10] jalaṃ pibanti | yaḥ ([11]puruṣo yatas tasmin[11]) [taṭe[12]] mahāsukhanadyāḥ[13] śoṣayati | idaṃ mahāsukhe 'pi vikalpamātraṃ tasyāsa[ṅgam iti bhā]vārthaḥ |

[1] E_{Sh} *tasyedaṃ* [2] E_BN *kalpaṃ* E_{Sh} *-kalpa* [3] E_B *bhāvas* N *bhāvā* [4] N *-tā* [5] N *-rman* [6] E_{Sh} *vajjasi* [7] $E_B E_{Sh}$N *kā[ruṇikai]ś* [8] N *-nāyā* [9] $E_B E_{Sh}$N *-ṇā* [10] $E_B E_{Sh}$N *nadyāṃ* [11] E_{Sh} *puruṣa yato 'smin* [12] $E_B E_{Sh}$N *taṭeṣu* [13] E_BN *–dyāṃ* E_{Sh} *-dyā*

| ces gsungs te | 'khor ba'i ([1]nang du[1]) dga' ba'i sems kyi glang po rol du chug | ci'i phyir zhe na | dngos po thams cad de nyid la brten pas de nyid [D 205b] du thim pa'i phyir ro[2] | | 'on kyang mu stegs pa thams cad kyis[3] srog gcod pa la sogs pa byas pas dmyal bar lhung ngo | | snying rje can zhes dge ba bcu'i las kyi lam la gnas[4] pas mtho ris su 'gro zhing bde bar gnas so | sems kyi glang po thams cad la khyab pa'i tshul gyis nam mkha'i chu ([5]'thungs shig[5]) | de'i 'gram du ni bde ba chen po'i chu 'gram mo | | bde ba chen po yin yang mngon par zhen par ma byed ces dgongs pa'o[6] | [7]

[1] B *nags su* [2] D om. [3] P *kyi* [4] DP *yongs su gnas* [5] DP *'thung zhig* [6] DP *so* [7] D inserts *de bzhin du*

visaagaendĕṃ[1] kareṃ[2] gahia jima[3] māraï paḍihāï[4] |
joï[5] kava[ḍiāra[6] jima ti][N 96a]ma tahŏ[7] ṇissari[8] jāi | iti | (99)

[1] E_{Sh} *viṣaagajendra* [2] E_{Sh} *kara* N *kari* [3] E_{Sh} *jaṇi* [4] E_{Sh} *-hāsaï* [5] E_{B} *joi* E_{Sh} *jovi* [6] E_{Sh} *ḍaāra* [7] E_{Sh} *ho* [8] E_{Sh} *ṇisari*

| yul gyi glang po'i snas blangs nas |
| ji ltar gsod pa ltar snang yang[1] |
| rnal 'byor glang po skyong ba bzhin |
| de'i[2] tshe byung nas song ba yin | (99)

[1] B *bas* [2] P om.

tathā viṣayagajendreṣu cakṣurādiṣu sarvavastuṣu[1] gṛhītvā indriyavi[ṣayādi] bhiḥ[2] kareṇa grahaṇām iva dantinā tadā māraṇam iva pratibhāsate[3] | yāvat[4] pratibhā[syati[5] tā]vat kasya viṣayinasya[6] | na[7] svabhāvam etat tasyaiva dṛśyate | na māraṇaṃ kriyate | narakādi([8][ṣu na ca][8]) nīyate | īdṛśaṃ[9] yogendrāṇāṃ kavaḍīkārādyair yādṛśaṃ pratibhāsyati[5] | tādṛśam iva ta[to ni]ḥsaritvaṃ[10] gacchati | sahaje[11] pralīyate[12] | na kavaḍīkārādyās[13] tasya bādhyate lokasya pratibhā[sa eveti |] [N 96b] evaṃ bhakṣyābhakṣeṣu na lipyata iti[14] yāvat | tathā cāha |

[1] N *-vastra* [2] E_{Sh} *–viṣayaiḥ* [3] E_{Sh} *vratinaṃ kuru* [4] E_{Sh}N *tāvat* [5] E_{Sh} *-sate* [6] E_{Sh} *viṣayinaś ca* [7] E_{B}N *ca* E_{Sh} om. [8] E_{B} *-ṣu* [9] E_{Sh} *kīdṛśaṃ* [10] E_{Sh} *–taṃ* [11] E_{B}N *sahajeṣu* [12] N *līyataḥ* [13] E_{Sh} *-dyā* [14] $E_{B}E_{Sh}$ *lipyate iti*

| zhes gsungs te | de bzhin du yul gyi glang po ni dngos po thams cad de | yul dang dbang po lta bur mchus[1] blangs nas gsod pa lta [B 158b] bur snang yang mi 'chi ste | glang po che[2] dang rtse mkhas pas so | | rnal 'byor gyi dbang phyug gis phyir phyung nas gnas su 'gro zhes bya ba'o | de ltar ([2]bza' bya dang[2]) bza' bya ma yin pa[3] de mi rigs so zhes dgongs pa'o[4] | | de ltar [P 229a] yang |

[1] DP *mchu yis* [2] DP om. [3] B *pas* [4] DP *so*

jo bhava so ṇivvāṇa khalu [[(1]bhevu na[1)] maṇṇahu aṇṇa[2] |]
[(3]ekkasahāveṃ[3)] vi[4] virahia[5] ṇimmala[6] maï[7] paḍivaṇṇa | iti | (100)
[1] E_{B} *sa u ṇa* [2] E_{Sh} *paṇṇa* [3] E_{Sh} *eka sahāve* [4] $E_{B}E_{Sh}$N om. [5] N *vevirahia*
[6] E_{Sh} *nirmmala* [7] E_{B} *maïṃ*

| gang zhig srid de mya ngan 'das[1] |
| de la dbye ba ma sems shig |
| rang bzhin gcig pas[2] rnam par spangs[3] |
| dri med de ni nga yis rtogs | (100)
[1] DP *'das pa'o* [2] B *gi* [3] DP *spongs*

nāstiyoginā[ṃ[1]viśeṣādviśeṣaḥsa]ṃkṣepataḥ[2]|yathāyuganaddhakrameṣūktam āryanāgārjunapādena bhavanirvāṇetyādi[nā ca |] [(3]iha etad eva[3)] yat bhavanirvāṇaṃ khalu [E_{B} 145] sarveṣāṃ dvayaṃ dvayavacaneṣu | sa vijñeyaṃ[4] yuga [(5]na[ddham a[5)]dvayaṃ[6]] [(7]tatra na[7)] bhedam anyaṃ vijñeyād iti kiṃ tarhy[8] eka[9]svabhāvena | [(10]ac chāstreṣu[10)] siddhāntaṃ ta[t][11] [N 97a][12] tasmād virahitam[13] ekānekabhāvam | kiṃ tu advayo 'pi nirmalaḥ pratipannaḥ | paramādvayam iti bhāvaḥ | etad eva spaṣṭārtham āha |
[1] E_{Sh} *-nā* [2] $E_{B}E_{Sh}$ *–kṣepaḥ* [3] E_{Sh} *ihāpi tad eva* [4] $E_{B}E_{Sh}$N *vijñeya-* [5] E_{B} *–naddha-* E_{Sh} *–naddhaṃ* N *–naddhā-* [6] E_{Sh} om. [7] $E_{B}E_{Sh}$N *tac ca* [8] E_{Sh} *tu* [9] E_{Sh} *dvayeka* [10] $E_{B}E_{Sh}$ *yad advayaṃ sarvaśāstreṣu* N *ya ya śāstreṣu* [11] E_{Sh} om. [12] N fol. 97 is missing
[13] E_{B} *avirahitam*

| zhes gsungs te | ji ltar 'phags pa klu sgrub kyi zhal snga nas | zung du 'jug pa'i rim pa las | | 'khor ba dang ni mya ngan 'das | | zhes bya ba la sogs pa gsungs pa de bzhin du | 'khor ba dang mya ngan las 'das pa dbyer[1] med pa de ni [(2]gnyis su[2)] med pas[3] zung du 'jug pa zhes bya'o | de nyid gsal bar bstan pa'i phyir |
[1] DP *gnyis su* [2] P *dbyer* [3] B *par* D *pa'i*

gharahi ma thakku ma jāhi vaṇe jahi tahi maṇa pariāṇa |
saalu ṇirantara bohi-ṭhiu kahĩṃ[1] bhava kahĩṃ[1] ṇivvāṇa | ity (101)
[1] E_{Sh} *kahi*

| khyim du [(1]ma 'dug nags su ma 'gro zhig[1)] |
| gang na 'dug kyang sems la ltos |
| ma lus rgyun du byang chub gnas |
| srid gang[2] mya ngan 'das gang yin | (101)
[1] D *ma 'dug nags ma 'gro* P *nags ma 'gro* [2] P *pa*

anena svagṛheṣu sthitiṃ mā kurvantu[1] | vanāntaram api gamanaṃ mā kuru | kiṃ tarhi niścitaṃ dvayasthāneṣu gamyād vikalpaṃ jāyate | kathaṃ kriyatām[2] ity ucyate | yasmin yasmin sthitvā vā caṅkramaṇabhakṣādiṃ kṛtvā tatra manasya paribhāvanaṃ kuru | alīkaṃ manaḥ | sa ca vijñaptiṃ kuru | tac ca pūrvaṃ[3] nirākṛtam asiddhatvāt | tasmāt sakalatraidhātukeṣu nirantarāvyavacchinnapravāhāt bodhisthitaṃ siddham | na kenacid utpāditaṃ svayambhūtvāt | tad iha kudhībhiḥ mūḍhatvena parikalpitam | bhavanirvāṇayor advayoḥ kenedaṃ[4] na syāt uktanyāyād api | tasmin bhavaṃ tasmin nirvāṇaṃ na bhavati | kutaḥ | yataḥ ādāv eva viśvasyotpādaṃ nāsti | tat kim iti dṛśyate | māyāvad iti bhrāntyā pratibhāsamātram eveti | yathā darpaṇādiṣu pratibimbaṃ[5] dṛśyate tad vicārān nopalabhyate | tad bimba[6][N 98a]piṇḍa[(7]parimāṇavattvā[7)]dibhedanā[(8]sambhavam iti[8)] | kasmād bhavanirvāṇayor asambhavam | ta[thā coktam] |

[1] $E_B E_{Sh}$ *kurvanti* [2] $E_B E_{Sh}$N *kriyate* [3] $E_B E_{Sh}$ *pūrve* [4] E_B *kenedhaṃ* [5] E_{Sh} *-bimba* [6] E_{Sh} *viṣva-* [7] E_{Sh} *paramāṇuvandhā* [8] N *–sa bhavati*

| zhes gsungs te | khyim dang nags gnyis gang[1] la'ang nges par gnas par mi bya ste | gnas gnyis po la zhen na rnam rtog skye ba'i phyir ro[2] | 'o na ji ltar bya zhe na | gang dang gang za ba[3] dang | 'chag[4] pa dang | nyal ba la sogs pa'i dus su de la sems yongs su chags par ma byed cig | rdzun[5] pa'i rnam par rig pa tsam du [(6]shes par[6)] gyis shig ces pa'o | de'i phyir mkhas pa[7] ma lus [8] rtag tu rgyun mi 'chad par byang chub la[6] gnas [B 159a] te[9] | gang cung zad kyang skye ba [D 206a] ni med de | rang byung ye shes kyi phyir ro | de ltar yang |

[1] DP *ka* [2] B om. [3] P om. [4] BD *'chags* [5] BD *brdzun* [6] DP om. [7] D *pas* [8] P inserts *pa* [9] DP *pa ste*

> [(1]saṃsāraṃ caiva nirvāṇaṃ[1)] manyante 'tattvadarśinaḥ |
> [(2]na saṃsāraṃ[2)] na nirvāṇaṃ manyante tattvada[rśinaḥ ||] (YṢ 5)
>
> [1] $E_B E_{Sh}$ *nirvāṇaṃ caiva lokaṃ ca* N ||| *va lokañ ca* [2] $E_B E_{Sh}$N *naivaṃ lokaṃ*

> | mya ngan 'das dang 'khor ba nyid |
> | de nyid ma mthong rtog[1] par byed |
> | 'khor ba mya ngan 'das [(2]pa med[2)] |
> | de nyid [3] mthong bas[4] rtog par byed | (YṢ 5)
>
> [1] D *rtogs* [2] B *med pa* [3] DP insert *ma* [4] DP om.

[nirvāṇaṃ ca] bhavaś caiva dvayam etan na vidyate |
parijñānaṃ bhavasyaiva nirvāṇam iti kathya[te || iti |] (YṢ 6)

| 'khor ba dang ni mya ngan 'das |
| gnyis ka yod pa ma yin te |
| 'khor ba yongs su shes pa nyid |
| mya ngan 'das zhes de la bya | (YṢ 6)

[E_B 146; E_{Sh} 118] [tasmāt si]ddhaṃ paramādvayaṃ bodhirūpaṃ sa cāha |

| zhes gsungs so[1] | | de'i phyir byang chub kyi ngo bo nyid ni gnyis su med pa'i ngo bo mchog yin par grub pa'o | | de bstan[2] [P 229b] pa ni |
[1] DP *te* [2] DP *ston*

ṇaü gharĕ ṇau vaṇĕ[1] bohi ṭhiu ĕ[hu[2] pariāṇahu bheu |]
ṇi[3]mmala-citta-sahāvaḍā[4] karahu avikkala[5] seu || (102)
[1] E_BN *vaneṃ* [2] E_{Sh} *eku* [3] N *ni-* [4] E_{Sh} *-ḍa* E_B *-tā* [5] E_BN *avikala*

| byang chub khyim dang nags mi[1] gnas |
| 'di yi dbye ba shes par gyis[2] |
| dri [(3]med sems kyi rang bzhin la[3)] |
| de ni rtog pa med par bya[4] | (102)
[1] DP *na* [2] D *gyas* [3] B *ma med sems ji bzhin pa* [4] B *byos*

[(1]iha uktalakṣaṇā yā[1)] [na ghare na vaneṣu bodhiḥ[2] sthi][N 98b]tam | evaṃ[3] bhedaṃ parijānāsi sandhyābhāṣāntare 'pi gṛhaṃ[4] śarīraṃ vanaṃ viśvaṃ[5] ghaṭapaṭādi[|[6] tatra na bodhiḥ | kutaḥ |] sarve hy asambhavāt | evaṃ bhedaṃ yat dṛśyate lokādi tat sarvam utpannavinā[śinaḥ | nedṛśī bo]dhir avinaṣṭa[(7]tvāc ca[7)] | teneha nirmalacittasvabhāvatāṃ[8] kurvati | yā[9] vi[kalpanā vikalpasi] samastāsaṅgatā tyajasīti vistaraḥ | tair bodhirūpam āyāti tad ā[ha |]
[1] E_BE_{Sh} *idam upalakṣaṇāyāṃ* N *iham uktalakṣaṇāyā* [2] E_BE_{Sh}N *bodhi-* [3] N *eva* [4] E_{Sh}*gṛha* [5] E_BE_{Sh} om. [6] E_BE_{Sh}N *ghaṭapaṭādi[ṣu* [7] E_{Sh} *-tvāt* [8] N *–tā* [9] E_BE_{Sh}N *yair*

| zhes gsungs te | gong du bstan pa'i mtshan nyid kyi[1] byang chub ni khyim dang nags na med pa de lta bu'i dbye ba dgongs pa'i tshig gis shes par bya'o | | khyim ni rang gi lus so | nags ni bum pa dang snam bu la[2] sogs pa'i gzugs so | | de la ni[3] byang chub med do |
[1] P *kyis* [2] P *dang* [3] DP om.

[ehu sŏ a]ppā[1] ehu paru[2] jo[3] paribhāvaï kovi[4] |
teṃ[5] viṇu bandheṃ[6] veṭhṭhi[7] kiu appa vim[ukkaü to vi] || iti | (103)
[1] E_{Sh} *adhya* [2] E_{Sh} *para* [3] N *jā* [4] E_{Sh} *koï* [5] E_{Sh}N *te* [6] E_BE_{Sh} *vandhe* [7] E_{Sh} *bandhi* N *veḍhi*

| 'di ni bdag dang 'di ni gzhan |
| gang gis[1] de ni yongs shes[2] pa |
| dbye (3bas 'ching dang bral bar bya3) |
| des ni bdag nyid grol ba'o | (103)

[1] P *gi* [2] DP *sems* [3] B *ba de yis 'ching dang bral*

[N 99a][1] idam ātmā nedaṃ[2] paraḥ yena kenacid viparibhāvitaṃ tena vinā bandhanena ātmānaṃ viṭaṅkitaṃ[3] vikalīkṛtaṃ | mukto 'pi svabhāvayātaṃ tadā no muktaḥ | tasmāt svaparavibhāgaṃ na kriyata iti yāvat | tad iha |

[1] N fols. 99–101 are missing [2] $E_B E_{Sh}$ *idaṃ* [3] E_B *viṭakitaṃ* E_{Sh} *vitāktiṃ*

| zhes gsungs te | gang gis 'di ni bdag | (1'di ni gzhan zhes gang zag de'i1) phyin ci log tu yongs su bsgom[2] pa de dbye bas 'ching ba med kyang | 'on kyang bdag nyid rnam par bcings pa'o | | [B 159b] de'i tshe bdag nyid grol yang ma grol zhes bya ste | de'i phyir rang[3] dang gzhan gyi char[4] mi rtog go zhes dgongs pa'o[5] | de ltar yang

[1] B *'di na | gang zhes | gzhan zhes bya ba gang des* D *'di na gzhan zhes gsungs te bya ba gang des* [2] P *bsgoms* [3] D *bdag* [4] B *cha* [5] DP *so*

para appāṇa ma bhanti karu saala ṇirantara buddha |
ĕhu[1] se[2] ṇimmala parama-paü citta sahāveṃ suddha | iti | (104)

[1] $E_B E_{Sh}$ *pahu* [2] E_{Sh} *so*

| bdag dang gzhan (1du ma 'khrul zhig1) |
| ma lus (2gdod nas2) sangs rgyas yin |
| de[3] nyid dri med go 'phang mchog |
| sems nyid[4] rang bzhin dag pa'o | (104)

[1] DP *'phrul ma byed* [2] DP *rgyun du* [3] DP *'di* [4] BP *kyi*

[E_B 147] paraṃ cātmānaṃ[1] ca ekasvabhāvaṃ na dvayarūpeṇa bhrāntiṃ[2] kuru | kiṃ tarhi sakalasattvadhātur[3] (4nirantaram ādāv4) eva svabhāvena śuddhaḥ | tadādāv eva paribhāvanayā-anantakamalāvṛtā na buddhātmānaṃ paribhāvayanti | evaṃ dvayarahitena buddhaḥ so nirmalaṃ paramacittaṃ svabhāvato rūpaṃ bodhicittaṃ svabhāvarahitatayā |

[1] E_B *ātmadañ* [2] E_B *bhrāntir* [3] $E_B E_{Sh}$ *-tu* [4] $E_B E_{Sh}$ *nirantarādāv*

| zhes gsungs te | sems can gyi rigs rnams dang po nyid nas sangs rgyas yin te | de nyid dang po nyid nas glo bur gyi rnam par rtog pas bsgos[1] pas ma rtogs te | rang nyid sangs rgyas yin par ma shes so | | de nyid dri ma med pa'i mchog

sems kyi ngo bo nyid du[2] byang chub kyi rang bzhin yin te | dngos po thams cad [3] 'dzin pa spangs pa'i phyir ro |
[1] P *dgos* [2] DP om. [3] B inserts *kyi*

> addaa[1]-citta-[(2]tarūara hi[2)] [(3]gaü tihuvaṇeṃ[3)] vitthāra |
> karuṇā-phullī-phala[4] dharaï ṇāu[5] [(6]paratta uāra[6)] | iti | (105)

[1] E_{Sh} *advaa* [2] E_{B} *-taruaraha* E_{Sh} *-taruruara* [3] E_{Sh} *parāu tihuāṇeṃ* [4] E_{Sh} *phullīaphala* [5] E_{Sh} *ṇāme* [6] E_{B} *paratta ūāra* E_{Sh} *paraüāra*

> | gnyis med sems kyi sdong po mchog |
> | khams[1] gsum ma lus khyab par son |
> | snying rje'i me tog [D 206b] 'bras bu 'dzin |
> | ming ni[2] gzhan la phan pa'o | (105)

[1] DP *sa* [2] P *gis*

ukte sati paropakāraṃ sūcayati | yad advayaṃ cittaṃ yogināṃ tad [(1]taruvaraṃ tu[1)] tarurājaḥ[2] | kalpavṛkṣam iva sarvagatatribhu[3]vanavistāraṃ[4] | sarvaṃ paramādvayam iti bhāvaḥ | tasya karuṇāpuṣpaphulitena tat phullaṃ bhavati | nāmena[5] sa paropakāraḥ | sarveṣāṃ sarvāśāṃ[6] bu[7]ddhatvādi paripūrayatīti te tayā || su***[8]
[1] $E_{B}E_{Sh}$ *dharantu* [2] $E_{B}E_{Sh}$ *bhavarājaḥ* [3] E_{B} *–bhū* [4] $E_{B}E_{Sh}$ *-aḥ* [5] E_{B} *nānena* [6] $E_{B}E_{Sh}$ *sarvāsāṃ* [7] E_{B} *śu-* E_{Sh} *su-* [8] E_{B} not available

[P 230a] zhes gsungs te | de ltar mchog gi don bstan nas | gzhan la phan par[1] bstan[2] te | rnal 'byor pa'i sems gang gnyis su med pa ni dpag bsam gyi shing bzhin du khams gsum ma lus par[1] khyab par son pa ste | thams cad gnyis su med pa zhes bya ba'i don no[3] | | de'i snying rje'i me tog gi 'bras bu'i ming ni gzhan la[4] phan pa ste | thams cad kyi[5] thams cad du sangs rgyas kyi byang chub la sogs pa rgyas par byed pa'i phyir ro |
[1] P *pa* [2] DP *ston* [3] DP *to* [4] B om. [5] B *kyis*

> [(1]suṇṇatarū[2]vara phulliaü karuṇā viviha vicitta |
> aṇṇābhoa paratta phalu ehu sokkha paru citta |[1)] (106)

[1] Not available in E_{Sh} [2] E_{B} *taru*

> | stong pa'i sdong po me tog skyes |
> | snying rje rnam pa sna tshogs 'byung |
> | lhun grub [B 160a] gzhan gyi 'bras bu ste |
> | bde ba 'di ni sems gzhan min | (106)

| zhes gsungs te | de ltar stong[1] pa'i 'bras bu ste[2] snying rje rnam pa sna tshogs kyis mi 'dod bzhin du'ang bsam pa sna tshogs yongs su rdzogs par byed pa'i phyir ro | | 'on kyang yongs su rdzogs pa'i snying rje bstan[3] pa ni |

[1] P *ston* [2] BDP om. [3] DP *ston*

> [(1]suṇṇa-tarū[2]vara ṇikkaruṇa jahĩṃ phulu[3] mūla ṇa sāha |
> tahĩṃ ālambaṇa[4] jo karaï tasu paḍibhajjaï[5] bāha[6] |[1)] (107)
>
> [1] Not available in E_{Sh} [2] E_B *taru-* [3] E_B *puṇu* [4] E_B *ālamūla* [5] E_B *-bhajjāi* [6] E_B *vāha*

> | stong pa'i sdong po snying rje min |
> | gang la rtsa ba lo 'dab med |
> | de la dmigs byed gang yin pa |
> | de ni lhung nas yal ga chag | (107)

| ces gsungs te | stong pa'i [1] sdong po snying rje min pa ni stong pa dang snying rje dbyer med pa'i phyir 'dir dmigs pa med pa'i snying rje la snying rje min pa [2] zhes bya'o | | stong pa nyid kyi sdong po de la rtsa ba dang lo 'dab med de[3] | sgom pa po[4] dang | sgom pa [5] dang | bsgom bya gdod ma nas med pa'i phyir ro | | de la dmigs par byed pa gang yin pa de ni lhung nas yal ga chag[6] pa ni khams gsum gcig pa'i ngo bo nyid yin pas so | | de nyid bstan pa'i phyir |

[1] P inserts *sdong po snyid pa'i* [2] BP insert *ni* [3] DP *do* | [4] D om. [5] DP insert *po* [6] P *chags*

> [(1(2]ekkeṃ bīeṃ vevi[2)] taru teṃ kāraṇě phala ekka |
> e ābhiṇṇā[3] jŏ muṇaï sŏ bhava-ṇivvāṇa-vimukka |[1)] (108)
>
> [1] Not available in E_{Sh} [2] E_B *ekkemvī ekkevi* [3] E_B *abhiṇṇā*

> | sa bon gcig las[1] sdong po gnyis |
> | ltos pa med pas me tog gcig | [2]
> | 'dir ni dbyer med gang mthong ste[3] |
> | srid dang mya ngan 'das las grol | (108)
>
> [1] DP *la* [2] B inserts | *rgyu mtshan de las 'bras bu gcig* | [3] BP *de*

[P 230b] | zhes gsungs te | sa bon gcig las[1] sdong po dang yal ga'i bye brag gnyis skye ste | de ltar rgyu dang 'bras bu rnam pa gnyis su 'gyur te | de'ang 'bras bu las tha mi dad do | | rgyu de lta bu las 'bras bu'o zhes gsungs pa'i phyir [(2]ro | |[2)] sangs rgyas dang 'khor ba dbyer [B 160b] med par mthong ba de ni thar par 'gyur[3] te | gnyis su med [(4]pa'i don[4)] rtogs pa'i phyir ro |

[1] DP *la* [2] DP om. [3] B *gyur* [4] P *par*

[(1][E_B 148] jo atthīaṇa āiaü[2] so jaï jāi ṇirāsa |
khaṇḍasarāveṃ bhikkha varu cchaḍḍahu[3] e gihavāsa |[1)] (109)
[1] Not available in E_{Sh} [2] E_B *ṭhīaü* [3] E_B *cchaḍahu*

| gang zhig 'dod pa [D 207a] can 'ongs[1] tshe |
| de ni re ba med song nas |
| kham phor[2] dum bu blangs nas ni |
| kye hoḥ[3] rang khyim bor la song[4] | (109)
[1] D *'ong* [2] P *por* [3] DP *ho* [4] B *sogs*

[(1] *** [N 102a] †pīḍayād[2] iti | manasi vihāya† tadā sattveṣu karuṇāvantaḥ yasmād āyāti yaḥ kiṃcid arthinaḥ[3] s[o yadi] nirāsaṃ yāti mayā loke na kiṃcit dattam | [(4]tadāpi na[4)] yena kiṃcit siddhaṃ bhavati | tasmā[t tvaṃ] khaṇḍaśarāve[5] bhikṣāṃ karoṣi | na bhogāsaktaṃ bhavasi | tya[6]jasi varam idaṃ gṛhavāsam[7] | yatra[8] [coktaṃ |][1)]
[1] Not available in E_{Sh} [2] E_B *pāḍayād* [3] E_B *athinaḥ* [4] E_BN *tadā yena* [5] E_BN *-sarāveti* [5] N *tyā-* [6] N *-sa* [7] E_B *yathā*

| zhes gsungs te | gong du bstan pa'i don mtha' dag 'khor ba'i longs spyod dag[1] la chags pa med pa de'i tshe rtogs par 'gyur ro | | longs spyod la chags pa dang bu dang tsha bo la sogs pa yang dag par rgyas pa ni sbrul gyi dug dang 'dra[2] bar gnod par[3] byed pa'i phyir ro | | de'i phyir snying rje dang ldan pas 'dod pa can slong pa'i mi 'ongs pa'i tshe | bdag nyid sred[4] pa'i dbang gis cung zad kyang mi ster na | nga la dngos grub mi 'byung ngo zhes bsams nas rang gi khyim nas thon te phyir bor ba'i kham phor blangs nas longs spyod la chags par mi bya'o zhes bya ba'i don no[5] | | de bstan pa'i phyir |
[1] DP om. [2] P *'dri* [3] DP *pa* [4] DP *srid* [5] DP *to*

[(1]para-ūāra ṇa kīaü[2] atthi ṇa dīaü dāṇa |
e[3] saṃsāre [(4]ki vaḍha[4)] phalu varu cchaḍḍahu [a]ppāṇa | iti |[1)] (110)
[1] not available in E_{Sh} [2] E_BN *kīaü* [3] E_BN *ehu* [4] E_BN *kavaṇa*

| gzhan la phan par[1] ma byas shing |
| 'dod pa la ni mi ster ba |
| 'dir[2] ni 'khor ba'i 'bras bu gang |
| de bas ring por byas na rung | (110)
[1] DP *pa* [2] DP *'di*

[(1]kiṃ tena bhogena gṛheṇa vā kriyate yataḥ paropakāraṃ na bhavati | asti [(2]suva[N 102b]rṇā[2)]divastu dānaṃ na dīyate | tac ca tena dhanena evam[3] idaṃ saṃsāre sthitatvāt kiṃ phalaṃ bhavati | na ([4]bhavati | tadā[4]) varam idam ātmānaṃ tyajāmaḥ | kāyajīvitanirapekṣeṇa viharaṣyāmīti bhavaḥ[5] |[1])

[1] Not available in E_{Sh} [2] E_B *-ṇā-* N *ga .. ṇā* [3] N *<eva>m* [4] E_B *bhavati yāvad* N *bhava* ||| *d ā* [5] E_B ...

| zhes gsungs te | gzhan la phan par[1] ma nus na khyim dang longs spyod[2] kyis[3] dgos pa ci yod | gal te gser la sogs pa'i nor yod pa sbyin par mi gtong na 'khor bar gnas pa la nor ([4]des 'bras bu ci yod de |[4]) ([5]'bras bu[5]) med ces pa'o | | de'i tshe rang nyid bor bar[6] byas na rung gi | khyim nas ([7]thon la[7]) lus dang srog la mi blta[8] bar gnas so zhes bya ba'i [P 231a] don no[9] |

[1] DP *pa* [2] P om. [3] DP *kyi* [4] D *der 'bras bu* P *des 'bras bu ci yod de* | [5] B om. [6] DP *ba* [7] D *'thon pa* [8] DP *lta* [9] DP *to*

[samāpte]yaṃ dohākoṣasya pañjikā viṣamapadabhañjikā[1] | dohā abhibhraṣṭavacanasyeti | tenai[t]e[2] koṣitāś[3] chāditāḥ | tattvaṃ bālajaneṣu vismayīkṛtam iti ||

[1] E_B not readable [2] E_B *tene[daṃ]* [3] E_B *–āc*

byis [B 161a] pa'i skye bo rnams kyi ngor do ha mdzod kyi ṭī[1] kā[2] bka' ba'i[3] don 'grel 'di[4] byas pa'o | |

[1] B *ṭi* [2] BDP *ka* [3] P *bka'i* [4] DP om.

([1]kṛtā[2] ceyaṃ mayā [tv atra][3] pañjikā cātmabodhinī |
nāmnāpi sātmavedhī ca gurvāmnāyaprakāśinī ||[1])

[1] not available in E_{Sh} [2] E_BN *kṛtvā* [3] E_B *[asya (?)]*

| rang gis go bar bya ba'i phyir |
| dka' 'grel byas pa 'di yi[1] ni |
| ming ni bdag nyid go byed pa |
| bla ma'i brgyud[2] rim gsal byed pa'o |

[1] DP *yis* [2] B *rgyud*

†([1]anyāṃ ca-[N 103a][2] īkṣapetvā ...[1]) rmāṇy[3] api kuru |†

[1] Not available in E_{Sh} [2] The last folio is missing in N [3] $E_B E_{Sh}$ *kṣamāṃ*

| gang tshe gzhan gyis bltas nas kyang |
| de'i tshe de la phan gyur na |
| de ni[1] sems can phan[2] 'gyur[3] yin |

| de ltar[4] min na bzod par zhu |
[1] D *na* [2] P *don* [3] DP *gyur* [4] DP *lta*

([1]svārthaṃ vāpi parārthaṃ vā sādhitaṃ me śubhaṃ yataḥ |
tena puṇyena loko 'stu jñānabhūmiḥ svayambhuvaḥ ||[1])
[1] E_B reports E_{Sh} only

| rang gi don dang gzhan don du |
| bdag gis 'di byas bsod nams kyis |
| de yis 'jig rten thams cad kun |
| rang byung ye shes thob par shog |

([1]samāpteyaṃ dohākoṣasya pañjikā | granthapramāṇam aṣṭaśatam asya | kṛtir iyaṃ śrī-Advayavajrapādānām iti |][1])
[1] E_B reports E_{Sh} only

do ha mdzod kyi bka' 'grel slob dpon chen po dpal gnyis su med pa'i rdo rjes mdzad pa rdzogs so |

[B:] rgya gar lho phyogs kyi yul ko sa lar sku 'khrungs pa'i rnal 'byor pa chen mar me mdzad ra kṣi ta dang | bod kyi lo tsā ba dge slong ba ris bsgyur ba | slad kyi be ro tsa na ba dzras cung zad bcos te gtan la phab pa'o ||

[DP:] rgya gar lho phyogs yul ko sa lar sku 'khrungs pa'i rnal 'byor pa chen po śrī bai ro tsa na ba dzras bsgyur ba'o || ([1]bkra shis |[1])
[1] D om.

English Translation

Commentary on the *Treasury of Spontaneous Songs*

Homage to the glorious Vajrasattva!

As I continuously pay devoted homage
to the gurus, the protectors of the world,
[this] commentary on the treasury of songs (*dohākoṣasya pañjikā*)
will be written in a tradition that goes back to Saraha.

[This commentary] on what was composed by the venerable Sarojavajra[1]
accords with the tradition of these [masters].
Nothing unprecedented—that is, beyond what
the Buddha taught—is spoken of here.

Those who rely on [the description of] true reality
in accordance with the six systems of philosophy do not understand.
Brahmans and others are useless,
relying as they do on such things as caste distinctions.

Ruined, reproached for [their view of][2] liberation, non-liberation, and
the self,
they wander in the saṃsāra of the six states of existence.[3]
[There,] they lack the two reliable types of cognition,
the direct and inferential.

1. Tib.: "Padmavajra" (*padma rdo rje*). Roerich (1949–53, 856) equates Padmavajra with Saroruha, the author of the *Guhyasiddhi*.

2. Supplied from the Tibetan.

3. Tib.: "[Cultivating] the view of a self, they are deprived of liberation and wander in the saṃsāra of the six states of existence."

Without a proper path,
they keep the company of base friends,[4]
and so virtuous persons
always worship a guru.

Pleasing him brings about liberation
in this world and in the next.
Because of [one's] devotion, [the guru] confers
the entire truth taught by the Buddha.[5]

First of all, the six systems of philosophy are taught here:[6] They are [those of] the brahmans, the followers of Śiva, the Jaina (lit. "Arhats"), the Buddhists, the Lokāyata, and the Sāṃkhya.[7] The author of this text [first] teaches them in this order and [then] randomly. [The passage] from "Brahmans, not knowing [proper] distinction..." (1a) up to "they do not know that dharma and non-dharma are [both] the same and not [the same]"[8] (3d) was taught in order to refute the [views of the] brahmans. There,[9] [Saraha] says:

Brahmans, not knowing [proper] distinction,[10] ... (DK_A 1a)

Brahmans[11] do not know [proper] distinction and further distinction.[12] If someone were to ask here: "How is that? What distinction is the distinction [they do not know]?"[13] Firstly, it is the distinction of caste, since it is said in their scriptures that the caste of the brahmans is the highest among the four

4. Tib.: "In keeping the company of base friends, they are without a proper path."

5. Tib.: "He confers the entire truth taught by the Buddha upon disciples who please [him]."

6. Tib: "...as for the systems, there are six types."

7. In the Tibetan, the Buddhists are listed at the end. The single compound with a *ca* after it and not observing internal sandhi show Apabhraṃśa influence.

8. The relative clause "that dharma and non-dharma are [both] the same and not [the same]" is added in accordance with the Tibetan and not quoted from the end of DK_A 3 in the Sanskrit commentary.

9. Missing in the Tibetan.

10. Tib.: "Brahmans do not know." The independent Tibetan root text has "reality" (*de nyid*), which is also found in Mokṣākaragupta's commentary (only available in Tibetan).

11. Missing in the Tibetan.

12. The Tibetan has only "distinctions."

13. Tib.: "How are they non-knowers of distinction?"

castes. This is to be refuted by valid cognition,[14] canonical scriptures, and reason.[15]

First, let us suppose that one is a brahman by birth because of the [Vedic] statement: "The brahman was [born from] the mouth [of Brahmā]." However, it is then and only then that he is called a brahman and not from the next [generation onward]. How can this be so? In this world, according to direct perception, [a brahman] is born from a womb [and not from a mouth]; so the previous [condition] does not apply.[16] Because the one caste[17] [of brahmans is invalidated, the system of] many [castes] has not been properly considered. Their statement that they [came from] the mouth of [Brahmā] is false, for it is the words of a deceiver.[18] Alternatively, [brahmans may claim that somebody can become a] brahman through a sanctifying ceremony, but it is not like this. Why is it not the case? Such a ceremony [could] be performed even for someone of the lowest birth.[19] Why could somebody like that not be a [brahman] then? He [would] be one.[20] Therefore, caste [can]not be established.

Then, in anticipation of the question, "[Even] in the absence of castes, how can the Vedas not [be accepted as] a self-arisen [revelation]?"[21] [Saraha] says:

> [...] merely recite the four Vedas.[22] (DK_A 1b)[23]

Those who do not know the distinction of castes merely recite the four

14. "Valid cognition" is missing in the Tibetan.

15. This suggests that brahmans *do* know caste distinctions but that such distinctions are fallacious.

16. Tib.: "According to your tradition, brahmans arise from the mouth of Brahmā. When, then, [can] somebody be called a brahman by birth? This [belief] has the undesired consequence that one was a brahman before, but not now because the previous [situation] does not apply; and according to direct valid cognition the present brahman was born from a woman's womb. He has not [the status of] the former brahman [anymore]."

17. "Caste" is missing in the Sanskrit.

18. Tib.: "They are, according to our [Buddhist] canonical scriptures, false words, for the statement that [brahmans] were born from the mouth of Brahmā are the words of a deceiver."

19. The Tibetan translation of this sentence is difficult to construe.

20. The answer is missing in the Sanskrit.

21. The Tibetan must have read *jātyabhāvena* instead of *jātyabhāve na*: "How, then, in the absence of castes can the Vedas [be reliable as] a self-arisen [revelation]? They [can]not be."

22. Apa.: *evaï*; both Bagchi's Sanskrit translation (*vṛthā*) and the Tibetan translate freely: "uselessly."

23. It is strange that this first verse consists of only two *pāda*s (quarters), especially since there is no *maṅgala* verse.

Vedas.[24] [The four Vedas] are the *Ṛg[veda]*, *Sāma[veda]*, *Yajur[veda]*, and the *Atharva[veda]*.[25] This [kind of rote reading] as well as recitation and so forth is not a problem for those of the lowest caste, because neither of them (i.e., brahmans nor those of the lowest caste) understand [the meaning].[26] Furthermore, if [brahmans][27] understand only the words, then, in common with others, they have [merely an understanding of the words].[28] It is the same with the words of the Vedānta that are used in grammar: They are words only, labels used by people, but ultimately, nothing at all [is referred to].[29]

Words (or sounds), whose nature is impermanence, are neither permanent nor self-arisen. How could they be called permanent?[30] They [can]not be,[31] just as the [whole] world does not [truly] exist, since it is impermanent. Thus it (i.e., your concept of a permanent sound) is destroyed,[32] and there is no authenticity in the Vedas. [The brahman contends:] In the absence of an agent there is no contradiction.[33] [When] there is no village, where[34] is [then its] boundary? But how is there no agent? [The brahman] answers: "[Sound] is not produced by human effort because it is self-established." But this is not the case either.

One also perceives directly that the psychophysical aggregates undergo destruction due to dependent arising. Given the absence of the previous, the subsequent does not exist [either].[35] This is because of seeing their illusion-like nature: [They are] a mere accumulation [of causes and conditions], because they have [only] arisen through delusion.[36] Those who do not know that, like-

24. Tib.: "...read the four Vedas, each [group according to] their own."

25. The compound *ṛksāmāyajvatharvāś* with a *ca* after it shows again Apabhraṃśa influence.

26. Tib.: "There is nothing incongruous about those of lowest birth reading them since both brahmans and those of lowest birth are similar in that they read and do not understand the meaning."

27. "brahmans" is supplied from the Tibetan.

28. Supplied in accordance with the Tibetan.

29. Supplied in accordance with the Tibetan.

30. Tib.: "Likewise, how can words (or sounds), whose nature is impermanent, be called permanent and self-arisen?"

31. The negation is added in the Sanskrit on the basis of the Tibetan.

32. This first part of the sentence is missing in the Tibetan.

33. Instead of this objection the Tibetan reads: "Something produced passes out of existence, but according to the Vedas it does not."

34. Skt. *kutaḥ* has not been translated into Tibetan, which incomprehensibly reads: "It is like saying that there clearly is a boundary to a village when there is no village at all."

35. Tib.: "In the absence of a cause there is no fruit."

36. The Tibetan has *'khrul pa* (nominative) instead of Sanskrit *bhrāntyā* (instrumental): "...for

wise, the whole of saṃsāra is mere delusion wander around in the saṃsāra of the six states of existence. Once this delusion is destroyed, all of them will fare well.

Accordingly, the Vedas are merely religious rites.[37] [Brahmans] imagine a result without a cause, [but] then from what does the result arise?[38] This is simply false [logic], and there is much more to say [about this]. Therefore everything performed [by brahmans] is not authentic.[39]

[Saraha] continues:

> **With earthen vessels** and so forth [in their hands,] **they perform fire offerings.** (cf. DK_A 2ab)[40]

What is gained by these fire offerings?

> Useless fire offerings... (DK_A 2c)

[41] There is no [meaningful] fire offering of ghee and the like. Why is that? There is no fruition for those who do not know the ultimate meaning. [This is so because] then even for one of the lowest birth, there would inevitably be such [fruition].

> ...make the eyes burn with pungent smoke. (DK_A 2d)[42]

[such objects are] a delusion, which arises from a mere accumulation of causes and conditions."

37. Skt. *tan na* (or simply *na*) does not fit logically and has not been rendered into Tibetan, either.

38. The Sanskrit is incomplete here: "because they indirectly conceive of an effect in the absence of a cause."

39. Tib.: "In attempting to demonstrate [further] that all the [Vedas] were composed without authenticity..."

40. The complete *pratīka* 2ab is as follows: *maṭṭhīpāṇīkusaha pabitteṃ / gharahi basante aggi huṇante.* "With holy things such as earthen vessels, water, and *kuśa* grass, they perform fire offerings sitting at home." For the sake of convenience, we follow here the numbering of Bagchi (1938, 14–39), who starts with a second verse after two *pāda*s (i.e., 1a and 1b are taken as a complete verse). Here we print the root text in bold to distinguish it from the commentator's insertion.

41. The commentary starts with a Sanskrit translation of the DK_A 2c, which is not repeated here.

42. In the Tibetan translation, line 2a is missing. It has, however, as an extra quotation: "They purify earth and water with earth."

[Useless fire offerings] burn their eyes with very pungent smoke, which[43] will infect them. [Somebody asks]: "Then what is true reality for them?" They[44] say: "Supreme Brahman." They speak of it in different ways, such as the wisdom of Brahman and so forth. In this context, Supreme Brahman means nothing else but sacrifice—that is, [they claim that] they go to Brahmanhood through fire offerings.[45]

This is the fruition of enjoying the objects of the sensual pleasures of heaven, which is their (i.e., the Pūrvamīmāṃsaka's) desired [goal].[46] Because of this,[47] they kill and offer a white goat. As a consequence of this,[48] they will experience the suffering of hell and the like. This is because they have not understood the meaning taught with a hidden intention. Thus it follows that there is Brahman as well as the killing of Brahman,[49] for it is [clearly][50] stated in the [Brahmanical][51] scriptures, "Everything is Brahman."[52]

Likewise, the wisdom of Brahman [can]not be established either. How

43. I.e., taking the feminine relative pronoun (*yayā*) in the sense of the masculine one (*yena*).

44. We are using the plural here for the sake of consistency.

45. The Tibetan of DK_A 2 and the corresponding commentary up to here is as follows:

> [Brahmans] sit at home burning [offerings] in the fire.
> Performing these pointless fire offerings
> harms [their] eyes with smoke. (DK_A 2a–c)

[Furthermore, Saraha] says:

> They purify earth and water with grass. (DK_A 2d)

As for fire offerings, it is asked: "What is gained through making fire offerings?" For those who do not know the [ultimate] meaning, useless fire offerings of butter and so forth [can]not bear fruition. If there were some fruition, there would be fruition even if those of lowest birth performed [them]. Certainly, it is precisely this that pains [their] eyes through the action of making smoke. The smoke from moist wood stings their eyes, so that they become sick and suffer. What then is [true] reality for all of them? They say that it is Brahman and Supreme Brahman. It is also the wisdom of Brahman, which they talk about in different ways. [In this system,] Supreme Brahman is a term [used] only [in the context] of offerings. They believe that there is liberation (i.e., the attainment of Brahmanhood) through fire offerings.

46. Tib.: "They wish for the fruit of enjoying the objects of sensual pleasure in the higher states of existence."

47. Supplied from the Tibetan.

48. I.e., taking up the preceding instrumental of *nipātanā*; Tib.: "through [this] killing."

49. Tib.: "Since everything has the nature of Brahman, they have thus killed [this] Brahman."

50. Supplied from the Tibetan.

51. Supplied from the Tibetan.

52. Tib.: "The nature of Brahman is everywhere."

could that be?[53] If [they say it is] in the *Atharvaveda*, the fourth [Veda], then [I would say] they have neither yogic conduct nor view. [That is why] they[54] do not know. In the three Vedas, even the recitation [of the *Atharvaveda*] is not admitted.[55] This being the case, the statement that [the Vedic tradition] is uninterrupted is utterly false.[56] Now, not everything that has been taught in the [three other Vedas] is [in support of] the wisdom of Brahman.[57] [So,] then these three Vedas do not command reliable authority, given such[58] denial [of authority with regard to wisdom].[59] Likewise, the fourth Veda, the *Atharvaveda*, is not a [reliable authority] either, because of the mutual contradictions.[60] In the absence of canonical scripture, how can the wisdom of Brahman be established? [The truth is,] it [can]not.

Alternatively, they may say that there is the experience [of the wisdom of Brahman[61]]. This is a completely false assertion. Why?[62] When no entities [can] be apprehended, given that they are empty, how can there be a [form of] wisdom [that is aware] of them? There [can]not be.[63] If experience, for its part, is apprehension accompanied by phenomenal content, then it [can only] be accepted as the opposite of wisdom, since no [external][64] entity whatsoever is apprehended [by wisdom].[65] Entities are imagined by the world, and having the nature of what is opposed to wisdom, they are not the ultimate. As for the ultimate in our tradition, it is grasped from the mouth of the guru.

Likewise, there is another [set of] four distinctions of[, or stations in,] a brahman['s life]: the life of chastity, the hermit in a forest, the householder, and the ascetic. These are not acceptable either. Why? Because as a child, one

53. Missing in the Tibetan.

54. The Sanskrit switches from plural to singular subject.

55. Tib.: "As for the fourth [Veda], the *Atharvaveda*, since they do not know yogic conduct, even the recitation of the words of the *Atharva*[*veda*] in three [other] Vedas is not admitted."

56. Tib.: "Since it is interrupted in this case, the words of the *Atharvaveda* are wrong."

57. Tib.: "Since it is said in the *Atharvaveda* that there is nothing at all besides wisdom of Brahman..."

58. The Tibetan reads *des na* instead of *tathā*: "given their denial [of wisdom]."

59. The Tibetan has an added question and answer: "Why is that? It is because of contradictions [with regard to the wisdom of Brahman] within the three Vedas themselves."

60. Tib.: "because it contradicts the [other] three Vedas."

61. Added in accordance with the Tibetan.

62. Missing in the Tibetan.

63. This negation is missing in the Sanskrit.

64. Supplied from the Tibetan.

65. The Tibetan has wrongly analyzed *tadājñānam* as *de tshe de nyid shes pa yin pas.*

does not have the [necessary] determination for keeping [one's vows], [restrictions on] food, and so forth. As in all religious traditions, a life of chastity is to be led with firm conviction for one's whole life. But [children] lack [such] a determination.[66] Moreover, [brahmans] marry and make households. In this case, there is no [fixed] determination either, because they [can again] take up a life of chastity.[67] As a hermit in the forest, again, [a brahman] meditates and recites [mantras]. In this case, there is no fixed determination either since it is possible [for them] to discontinue [doing so].[68] If they wish to take up asceticism, neither brahmans nor outcastes differ in terms of wearing[69] the sacred thread or in what they eat. In some stations [of life], being a brahman amounts to the same thing as being an outcaste. This is true. Why?[70] After looking into the Veda of the brahmans, [we find that] when a female brahman has performed acts [typical] of a thief or an outcaste, [her husband] washes the vagina of this female with ghee and *kuśa* grass and drinks [the runoff], claiming that this purifies [his wife's misdeed].[71] Therefore all [this] is indeed the action of an outcaste.

As to the asceticism [of brahmans], there are three types. [Saraha] says:

> [Some] carry [one] staff, [some] three staves [tied together], and
> [some] are in the guise of a holy man (or the lord).[72] (DK_A 3a)[73]

Dressed as such they roam about.[74] Eventually they abandon such types of asceticism and take up something else. This is what [Saraha] teaches:

66. Tib.: "Because as a child, one does not know [anything] about keeping [one's vows], food, and so forth and because in all religious traditions vows of chastity are firmly taken for one's whole life. But children do not have the [necessary] determination for something like this."

67. The causal clause is missing in the Sanskrit.

68. Again, the causal clause is missing in the Sanskrit.

69. When it comes to wearing a sacred thread they both are equal, because neither one is entitled to wear a thread.

70. Instead of "This is true. Why?" the Tibetan reads: "On some occasions, a brahman precisely is an outcaste."

71. According to the Tibetan; the Sanskrit only has the enigmatic phrase "There is purity through the act of ghee-vagina."

72. Lit.: Bhagavān, i.e., Brahmā or Śiva.

73. The first sentence of the following commentary is only a Sanskrit translation of the Apabhraṃśa, and not repeated.

74. Missing in the Tibetan.

> [Finally] they restrain themselves in the guise of a swan (*haṃsa*).[75]
> (DK$_A$ 3b)

[If one says][76] wisdom is not attained as long as one does not take the guise of the supreme swan,[77] since not all deeds have been abandoned, this is not the case either. Why? It is because they are [still] held by the demons[78] of the imprints of ignorance. This [can] be observed directly. When practicing austerity after abandoning the fire of a householder,[79] they give all their belongings—whatever there is—to their sons, grandsons, and so forth instead of giving it equally[80] to all sentient beings. They remain attached to their own family lineage, not wanting it to perish.[81] Therefore [it is said]:

> Those who are born as fools and propose
> wicked deeds are invariably destroyed.[82]
> Indeed they do not know true reality,
> [because] they are deluded by their previous deeds.

They themselves are destroyed, and they destroy others. In order to teach this, [Saraha] says:

> People are falsely led by [their] falsehood and error.[83] (DK$_A$ 3c)

Through misleading speech, the whole world, [consisting of] stupid people, has embarked on a bad path.[84] This is also expressed in the following:[85]

75. Not recognized as a *pāda* in Tibetan.

76. Supplied from the Tibetan.

77. The guise of the supreme swan symbolizes a purified mind, which has become as white as a swan. We retain this common, although mistaken, translation of the word, which means "goose."

78. Skt. *graha* has not been translated into Tibetan.

79. Tib.: "[their] household."

80. Skt. *sādhāraṇaṃ* has not been translated into Tibetan.

81. This sentence is obscure in the Sanskrit, and translated from the Tibetan.

82. Tib.: "Destroyed and born as fools, they always propose wicked deeds."

83. Tib.: "People are led into falsehood."

84. Tib.: "People are [here] ignorant persons who have entered upon a bad path. 'Confusion' means [what is conveyed] by misleading speech."

85. Tib.: "Moreover, [Saraha] says:"

They do not know that dharma and non-dharma are [both] the same [and not the same].[86] (DK_A 3d)

As to the dharmas here, [usually] they include all things, [but here] they are the cognitive objects of compassion in the form of classes of sentient beings and so forth.[87] Non-dharmas are the opposite, in that they do not enjoy this [status of being cognitive objects of compassion]. Their defining characteristic is [also] the performance of [wrong][88] action and so forth. "Same" means that these are not two [separate categories].[89] [Brahmans] do not know [this] special path.[90] In short, they do not know the [special][91] tenet. [This] must be known in detail from elsewhere. [But] virtue, wrongdoing, and so forth are not the same either.

With respect to refuting[92] those who rely on Śiva, [Saraha] teaches [the verses] starting with "[Śaiva][93] masters smear [their body] with ash..." (4a) up to "take the [guru's] fee [in return]" (5d). In this regard, [Saraha] says:

[Śaiva] masters[94] smear [their body][95] with ash. (DK_A 4a)

[96] Thus, they smear [their] limbs[97] with ash [collected] from outside (i.e., a cremation ground), since they have not [yet] found the certainty that comes from having a body, which is [like] the Illustrious One (i.e., Śiva). Then [Saraha] says:

On their head they wear this pile of braided hair. (DK_A 4b)

86. The addition is in accordance with the Tibetan.

87. Going by the Sanskrit, the compound ending in *ngo bo* depends on *yul* and not *snying rje*.

88. Added in accordance with the Tibetan.

89. I.e., in virtue of sharing the same true nature.

90. Tib.: "'[Brahmans] do not know' means that they do not know the special path."

91. Supplied from the Tibetan.

92. Missing in the Sanskrit.

93. In the commentary on DK_A 4a, the Tibetan has "non-Buddhist masters" for *ayiri* or *aïri*.

94. The etymological derivation of *aïri* is doubtful (Skt. *aiśvara*). Bhayani (1997, 2) proposes *ācāryaiḥ*, Bagchi (1938, 25) *āryaiḥ*.

95. Supplied from the Tibetan.

96. The commentary starts with a Sanskrit translation of the Apabhraṃśa. Tib.: "Non-Buddhist masters from the South smear their body with ash."

97. Tib.: "That is, they cover their body..."

On their head they wear a pile of braided hair, made of various [strands of] hair. Moreover,

> They stay in their homes and light butter lamps. (DK$_A$ 4c)

Putting on a show of religious authority among worldly people, they light butter lamps and stay in their homes.[98]

> Sitting down in the [proper] corner, they ring bells. (DK$_A$ 4d)

They sit in [the corner of] the "powerful" (i.e., Śiva)[99] and ring [their] bells.[100]

> With eyes blinking and the posture of sitting cross-legged
> (DK$_A$ 5a)

This is the greatest simulation of religious authority, [which] they achieve by alternately closing and opening their eyes. "Posture" means the lotus[101] posture of sitting cross-legged or squatting.

> Whispering in their ears, they mislead people. (DK$_A$ 5b)

[The Śaiva yogin] whispers in the ears of ignorant people, who do not know what to adopt or abandon, after they have seen [and are impressed by] the above-mentioned characteristic marks of a [Śaiva] master. [The ignorant people then] testify to each other:[102] "This is a special path. I am following it. People, listen [to me]!"[103]

98. The causal ablative (*sthitatvāc*) does not fit the context. Tib.: "Moreover, putting on a show of religious authority among worldly people,

> They enter their houses and light butter lamps. (DK$_A$ 4c)"

99. Rig pa'i ral gri informs us in his commentary that this corner is in the northwest, where Śiva resides (Schaeffer 2005, 134).

100. The commentary on DK$_A$ 4d being merely a Sanskrit translation of the Apabhraṃśa, the Tibetan merges the two into one.

101. Tib.: "vajra."

102. Originally *phan tshun* must have been placed after *shub shub*, as if at the beginning of a new sentence. The Sanskrit reads: *anyo 'nyam ālocayanti—idaṃ viśiṣṭamārgaṃ tatrāhaṃ lagno 'smi śruṇuta janāḥ* |.

103. Tib.: "The path I am on being very special, you must listen."

> For widows,[104] shaven [women],[105] and other types [of people]...[106] (DK_A 5c)

"Widow" means "one who is without a husband." Shaven [women] are those who observe a monthly fast. "Others" refers to ascetics in various attires. [He plays the trick of whispering in their ears][107] on these who have entered his path. What is so special then about their[108] guru? Therefore [Saraha] said that there could be no liberation.[109] [The sentence continues]:

> He bestows empowerment. (DK_A 5d)

His pretending is clear. What is it?[110]

> It is for the sake of a guru's fee.[111] (DK_A 5d)[112]

Only for the sake of acquiring gifts and motivated by self-interest, they make[113] sentient beings fall [prey to] defilements, because they themselves do not know [any better].[114]

If something is said to the effect that everything is Īśvara (i.e., Śiva), it is not correct. How so? This is to be refuted by means of valid cognition and canonical scriptures, the two admitted proofs.[115] The following is therefore briefly

104. Skt. *raṇḍī* has the connotation of a loose woman.

105. Rig pa'i ral gri has "shaven monks" (see Schaeffer 2005, 134), but the commentary refers to them with both a feminine relative pronoun and a feminine compound (see below).

106. DK_A 5c is counted as two lines in the Tibetan.

107. Tib.: "They will enter their path and praise him to his face."

108. Tib.: "such a."

109. This sentence is missing in the Tibetan.

110. The commentary in between is missing in the Tibetan.

111. Tib.: "He takes the guru's fee [in return]."

112. Following Shahidullah and Bagchi, this is taken together with the preceding *pratīka* as line 5d.

113. Tib.: "In order to acquire gifts for themselves, they bestow empowerments and cause..."

114. The Tibetan concludes the refutation of the Śaiva with the following sentence, which is missing in the Sanskrit: "This refutes those who rely on Īśvara (i.e., the Śaiva)." In the Sanskrit text there is a long refutation of Śaiva theology that is not found in the Tibetan. Given that it is at least double the length of the next longest commentary in the *pañjikā*, and not at all related to the topic of the root text (i.e., bestowing empowerment for a fee), it is safe to say that it is a later interpolation.

115. Thanks to Francisco Sferra, we read *pramāṇāgamayuktibhyām* instead of *pramāṇāgama-*

stated here: Here (i.e., in our system) [this] "everything" is not something that truly exists. How is that so? Because the elements of earth and the rest are everything. These consist of the accumulation of a material form, whose atoms are clustered together. [Indivisible] atoms in turn cannot be cognized, because of their [further] division into six [spatial] parts.[116] Something "really existing" then turns out not to be really existing. [A really existing everything] not being established, how [can] the existence of Īśvara be maintained? In the absence of something to be pervaded (*vyāpya*, the atoms) there can be no pervader (*vyāpaka*, Īśvara).[117]

Or else, if they speak of [Īśvara as a] creator, then we say that this is not [acceptable either]. How so? Things are created gradually or instantaneously but not permanently.[118] Hence, there would be no material thing outside of him nor anything imagined inside him.

[Or] this is said: "He is capable (*śakta*)." [In this case,] should [creation not] depend on space, time, and so forth? If so, [it can]not be instantaneous. What would this [Īśvara] produce? On the other hand, [an Īśvara] who depends on something else would neither be permanent nor [possess his divine] power (*śakti*). [Anything] existent does not possess permanence. Why? At any given time, existent [things] are momentary. It cannot be anything else but the cognitive objects and their possessor (i.e., subject and object).

[Again,] why [are they not permanent]? This is because what the eyes see as form and the like is nothing other than error. Upon analysis, things such as pots and cloths are not seen, because their former [moment] does not exist [any more at the time of perception]. How can atoms and the like,[119] with the defining characteristics as previously stated, become cognitive objects? In the same way as the defining characteristics of the psychophysical aggregates and so forth is not diverging from [that] of atoms in an aggregation.

Next, let us suppose that [the cognitive object] is the manifestation of appearances, such as blue, yellow, and so forth. This does not work either: since it contradicts direct perception, [a cognitive object] itself does not exist. How is that? The activity as perceived and perceiver in visual and other forms

yuktyā ca. The Tibetan did not render *pramāṇa*, and the presence of *pramāṇa* and *yukti* in the same compound is a bit suspicious.

116. This is an echo of Vasubandhu's famous argument. If atoms aggregate, then they cannot be indivisible, because they must make contact or face each other on the four sides as well as above and below. See *Viṃśikā* k. 12ff.

117. Either the author or the transmission is confused about *vyāpya* and *vyāpaka*.

118. Which would follow, if a permanent creator god was at work.

119. Probably the progressive aggregation of atoms that become visible.

of perception is an error. They are imagined (i.e., mentally created) by ignorant people [saying] "This is white," "This is yellow," and so forth.

Moreover, someone (i.e., a Śaiva) says:

> Even something already understood, if not cultivated, goes into oblivion.

In that case, it not being present [anymore at some point], why do you not [accept] then that [everything is only] cognition, like a river stream. Otherwise, how could it be forgotten?[120]

Moreover, who would [go to the length] of creating rugged mountains and massive oceans from these extremely small atoms? Let us suppose that that impossible task could be achieved because of some superpower. But then he would act like a madman, for how could he destroy his painstaking creation at the time of destruction (i.e., at the end of the eon)?

Or else [you may say:] He creates automatically;[121] for example, it is not negated that magnets attract weapons. [End of objection.][122] That, too, is negated in the scriptures of Vijñāna[vāda]. This is because the recollection of the body and so forth is without a basis. As for the body, which is [but] a detestable skeleton, when subjected to analysis, it is not a real [entity]. This is as stated in the following:

> With the scalpel of insight
> separate the flesh from the skeleton! (BCA V.62cd)
>
> And after having split open even the bones,
> look right down into the marrow!
> Examine precisely your own [body]
> [to see] whether there is an essence [to it]! (BCA V.63)
>
> The horror that is the body is full of saliva,
> urine, excrement, tears, blood, sweat,

120. To rephrase this objection: If the external object were permanent, one would not have to continuously cultivate its recognition, because if one has to, everything must be admitted to be a stream of cognition only.

121. Lit. "without control," i.e., in accordance with the karma of the sentient beings, for whom the world is created.

122. We conjecture that a substantial amount of text has been lost here because what follows does not address the opponent's argument.

intestine, fat, and marrow:
through the openings of wounds, it constantly oozes foul [fluids].
(not identified)

Thus consciousness has no firm standing—it is mental imprints alone and arises through the power of ignorance. All faults manifest through that [ignorance].[123] This has been said in the following:

With a self, there is the concept of other.
From the distinction between self and other, attachment and hatred [arise].
All faults arise closely connected
to these two (i.e., attachment and hatred). (PV II.219c–220b[124])

Therefore the defining characteristic of dependent origination is established. Otherwise, if there is dependence on something corporeal that is a deity, that cannot be. If the creator god is without nonexistence (i.e., still exists after producing its effect), what could this deity of yours create that is outside [of it]? For your scriptures state[125] that [the world] consists of him (i.e., Īśvara). But that cannot be.[126]

Or let us suppose that they[, cause and effect, i.e., Īśvara and his creation] are experienced together. But that too cannot be the case, because the existence of an inference with regard to anything existing prior is not established.

Or else, if it is [Īśvara who] causes the state of possession[127] [that manifests] as trembling, shaking, and so forth, then [that would be no better than] expe-

123. We take *taiḥ* in the sense of *tayā*.

124. The counting of chapters and verses follows Steinkellner's (1977) *Verse-Index*.

125. The Śaiva opponent here takes the *mayaṭ* suffix in the sense of *svabhāve*, not *hetau*.

126. Taking *tasmān* in the sense of *tad*.

127. Skt. *āveśa*. For lack of a better English word, we translate *āveśa* as "possession." For this feature, see Sanderson 2009, 133–39, Szántó 2021, 1:380–91. Sanderson identifies *āveśa* as a "hallmark of initiation in the Śaiva Kaula systems, setting them apart from all others," but points out that it is very likely a derivate from those systems' Kāpālika antecedents. He also identifies the yogatantras (via their paradigmatic scripture, the *Sarvatathāgatatattvasaṃgraha*) as the motif's entry into the Buddhist tantric traditions. In Śaivism, experiencing this state is a sign of approval on the part of the deity or deities that the initiation ritual may proceed. The same doctrine was adopted by the Buddhist traditions; e.g., Ānandagarbha states that "If possession does not occur even so, then he must not give him the consecration" (Sanderson 2009, 135). The angle from which our commentator approaches the issue is that such a state was also seen as a proof for the efficacy of the ritual and therefore proof of the very existence of the deity/deities. Such supernatural "proofs" are sometimes called *pratyaya*s.

riencing with our senses the "reality" of a conjurer, because there is support [that is caused by Īśvara]. Moreover, that [possession] happens as a private experience. This is as stated in the following:[128]

> Please tell, what is this state
> of him (i.e., Īśvara) being experienced privately?
> Someone who speaks of something to be known by oneself
> [normally] thinks of its real existence.
>
> But we object to this that in order to create
> a conviction in those other than yourself,
> [you use] his (Īśvara's) private experience:[129] it is impossible to say
> that this [experience] is that (i.e., his activity).
>
> But righteous ones always act without deception.
> Someone who makes himself known must possess something by which he is known,
> and in the absence of that by which he is known,
> the one who makes known does not exist either.
>
> So why do you not accept
> that neither of them exists?

Therefore [the world] is only dependent origination, and its being based on Īśvara stands refuted.[130]

Now comes [a refutation] of the Jaina, [taught in the verses] starting with "They have long nails..." (6a) up to "They torment [themselves] with mere physical austerity" (9d). [Saraha] says:

> They have long nails, and their bodies have [mere] filth as clothing. (DK_A 6a)

Thus are the embodied beings who rely on these worthy ones (i.e., the Jaina). Everyone is consumed by deceit and guile. Wearing filth as clothing and not

128. Not identified.

129. Because of the context, *niścaya* (lit. "ascertainment") is rendered as "conviction" in *pāda* b, and "experience" in *pāda* c.

130. End of the Sanskrit-only part.

knowing the truth themselves, they mostly inflict suffering on their own bodies. [Saraha] says of them:[131]

> Naked and [their] hairs pulled out, (DK$_A$ 6b)

No ultimate purpose whatsoever [is served] by the behavior of ending up naked with their hair pulled out. What is the use of instructing one to behave in such a way? [Saraha] says:

> The Jaina mock the path by the way they look.[132] (DK$_A$ 6c)

[133] In no way [can the true path] be like that. Why? Because of [their] use [of the terms] permanent and impermanent, and further, they do not know the path. Those people who follow their [path][134]

> They have deluded themselves for the sake of liberation. (DK$_A$ 6d)

For the sake of liberation, they delude themselves with the wrong path of wrong acts. They do not attain the goal of liberation.[135] The reason for this will be explained below. [Saraha] says:

> If going naked means liberation,[136]
> then dogs and jackals[137] would have it. (DK$_A$ 7ab)

Why is there no liberation for dogs and jackals?[138] Moreover, [Saraha] says:

131. These four sentences of the commentary are missing in the Tibetan.

132. DK$_T$: "[With the] outfit of [such] a harmful path, the Jaina..."

133. The commentary starts with a Sanskrit translation of DK$_A$ 6c, which is not repeated here.

134. Instead of lines 6bc and their commentary we find in the Tibetan: "Embodied beings rely on deceit and guile and whatever they desire, yet this does not include a path of liberation. Why? Because of [their] use [of the terms] *permanent* and *impermanent* and because they do not know the path. For those who rely on them, there is no way to liberation. Why? Therefore [Saraha says]:"

135. Tib.: "They harm themselves by [engaging in] base acts and by being on a base path. They [may think that they] are acting for the sake of liberation, but they do not attain it."

136. The commentary on 7a is simply a translation of the root text into the Sanskrit. The Tibetan has only translated the root text.

137. Tib.: "donkeys."

138. In the Tibetan, DK$_A$ 7b is not recognized as root text. It reads instead of DK$_A$ 7b and its

> If accomplishment lay in[139] pulling out hairs,[140]
> girls' buttocks [would be liberated]. (DK$_A$ 7d)

This is because young girls constantly pull out unwanted hairs. Why is there no liberation of their buttocks?[141] Or, rather:

> If liberation is seen in the grasping of[142] a [bunch of] peacock feathers, (DK$_A$ 8a)

If a Jaina can be liberated[143] by taking a bundle of peacock feathers [and moving them around with his hands],[144]

> Then elephants and horses [would certainly attain it].[145] (DK$_A$ 8b)

Then elephants and horses would be liberated through having a garland made from a bundle of peacock feathers on their body.[146] The implication is that of course they are not [liberated]. Furthermore,[147]

> If wisdom is [obtained] by picking up the grains scattered [in the fields],[148]
> [why then is wisdom not possible] for horses, elephants, and so forth?[149] (DK$_A$ 8cd)

commentary: "If one is liberated simply by being naked, why are dogs, donkeys, and so forth not liberated also?"

139. Tib.: "If liberation lay in the..."

140. The commentary on 7c, again, is simply a translation of the root text into Sanskrit. The Tibetan has only translated the root text.

141. In the Tibetan, DK$_A$ 7d is not recognized as root text. It reads instead of DK$_A$ 7d and its commentary: "If one [can] be liberated by pulling out hairs, then girls would be liberated because they constantly pull out bad hair."

142. Tib.: "If one [can] be liberated by moving..."

143. Lit.: "If liberation is seen by a Jaina..."

144. Supplied from the Tibetan, which is presented after DK$_A$ 8d.

145. Tib. (presented after DK$_A$ 8d): "Peacocks, yaks (*camara*), and the like would be liberated."

146. The translation of *gūḍhapakṣareṣu* remains tentative.

147. The commentary on line DK$_A$ 8b is missing in the Tibetan.

148. The commentary simply is a translation from Apabhraṃśa into Sanskrit.

149. The Tibetan recognizes only DK$_A$ 8a and 8c as root text and paraphrases DK$_A$ 8b and 8d in its commentary: "'If one can be liberated by moving around a bundle of [peacock] feathers,'

This consequence that they would be [liberated] is unwanted.[150]

> [In this respect,][151] Saraha says: "I do not maintain [that there is any possibility]
> whatsoever [of] liberation for the Jaina."[152] (DK_A 9ab)

Venerable Saroruhavajra[153] says: "The liberation of the Jaina does not appear to me [to be possible] at all."[154] If you ask why, [Saraha] says:

> Bereft of reality, all they achieve
> is causing others [to inflict] physical austerities [on themselves].[155] (DK_A 9cd)

[They are] bereft of reality. What are the other [issues]? Being ignorant themselves,[156] they merely bring other people to a worthless [path] and send them down it.[157] [158] On the one hand,[159] their tenet is that the different types of souls (*jīva*) and so forth have the defining characteristic of permanence, and on the other hand, they state that the lords of the forest have a soul, which is not possible. Why not? When the psychophysical aggregates and the rest pass out of existence,[160] there is impermanence. Under these circumstances, this is one type of soul [for them].[161] The second [type refers to] forest plants—that

(DK_A 8a): If a Jaina liberates [himself] by taking a bunch of peacock feathers and moving them around in his hands, then peacocks, yaks, and the like would be liberated. 'If one [can] be liberated by eating whatever one finds,' (DK_A 8c)[a] why are horses, elephants, and so forth not liberated? This consequence that they would be [liberated] is unwanted."

[a] DK_A 8c is repeated in the commentary and not translated again.

150. Missing in the Sanskrit.

151. Supplied from the Tibetan.

152. Tib.: "through the path of the Jaina."

153. The Tibetan has Saraha instead of Saroruhavajra.

154. Tib.: "I maintain the liberation of the Jaina is not at all [a possibility]."

155. Tib.: "Bereft of reality they harm [others] by [teaching] mere physical austerities."

156. Tib.: "Not knowing anything..."

157. Both verbs are supplied from Tibetan.

158. Next, the Sanskrit text contains a later interpolation, in which the Jaina are refuted on philosophical grounds. There is no Tibetan translation.

159. We are not happy with *yadā*, which is strange Sanskrit.

160. This possibly refers to the trees as well: "when their trunks are cut."

161. That means that the impermanent psychophysical aggregates are considered a soul.

is, grass, groves, and forest. The third one is [divided into] the four elements starting with earth. Thus, we get six types of souls.

All of them are not possible. Why? Because they all [consist of] inanimate elements.[162] In which of them is a soul observed? To put it plainly, it is not. If you say [this] soul is what adheres to human beings, then this has already been rejected in the previous refutation of Īśvara.[163] What follows from having said this? That everything, indeed, has the nature of impermanence. What then is the state of the dependently arisen? Dependent arising has the nature of error,[164] because the world has no stability.

Once this world is left behind, one proceeds to the heavens and other states of existence. For the Buddhists, too, it is like that. Having worked for the benefit of sentient beings in this life and gone on to the next world through a transformation of the psychophysical aggregates, one again accomplishes benefit for sentient beings, again abandons this [existence], and grasps the psychophysical aggregates [of yet another existence]; [this cycling] always resembles the apparent circle made by a whirling firebrand. This [taking on of existence] is through former wishes of compassion.

Yet these [existences] share something special: they are like an illusion. They are neither true nor false. According to the common meaning, a permanent nature [of such a person] is established, but not in the way the Jaina [think], as their liberation has a permanent nature, which is not the case. Why? Because in their scripture, it is said that [their place of] liberation has the form of an umbrella above the threefold world and measures 86,000 Indian miles (*yojana*). This is not established, given the [eventual] destruction of the threefold world. On which basis would the umbrella rest [then]? Hence, [their] liberation does not have a permanent nature. In short, it is impermanent. For a detailed [presentation] one should look somewhere else.

Next, [a refutation of the conduct of Buddhist] ascetics (*śramaṇa*)[165] is taught. It is from "Novices..." (10a) up to "They do not attain any ultimate" (12cd). [Saraha] says:

162. This obviously does not apply to the mental skandhas of the first type of soul.

163. This refers to the deconstruction of the body as a firm basis for consciousness, body and mind being only mental imprints and dependent arising.

164. This reminds one of Vasubandhu's commentary on the *Madhyāntavibhāga*, where the dependent nature (*paratantrasvabhāva*) exists but only as an error (*bhrāntamātra*). See *Madhyāntavibhāgabhāṣya* on III.3 (38_{4-5}): "The dependent characteristic exists but not in reality, because it has the nature of error. Thus it is a reality in terms of the dependent nature" (*paratantralakṣaṇaṃ sac ca na ca tat[t]vato bhrāntatvād ity etat paratantrasvabhāve tat[t]vam*).

165. Tib.: "śrāvaka," but the monks of Mahāyāna are also meant to be included here.

> Novices, monks, and those called[166] *sthavira*—
> [those] ascetics take up the guise of homelessness.[167] (DK_A 10ab)

Novices follow ten precepts; monks follow the highest number of precepts.[168] Ten years after full ordination, [a monk is called] a *sthavira*. All of them promise to become homeless only to become praiseworthy by wearing red robes.[169] But even with their discipline of begging and teaching, they are not supreme.[170] Not knowing true reality for what it is, they harm people through deceit and outward show.[171] This is as the Illustrious One [himself] has said:

> Later, after my passing into nirvāṇa, at the time of fivefold degeneration,[172] the monks who follow my teachings will delight in being deceitful and showing off. Moreover, they will delight in the activities of building, ploughing fields, and trading. They will engage[173] in every[174] wrongdoing and laugh at the teachings. All those who formerly belonged to the retinue of Māra will be reborn in the guise of monks. Among them, the elders (*sthavira*) of the Saṅgha[175] will steal the Saṅgha's food. They will bring it under their control and enjoy it.[176]

And [he relates] much more in detail. For this reason they are not enlightened. How could they be? Those who rely on the Śrāvakayāna flout [their precepts] in the above-mentioned way, and due to this, they will go to hell.[177] By only protecting the precepts with the above-mentioned defining characteristics of

166. This accords with the reading *zhes bya ba'i* (B), which has not been adopted for metrical reasons.

167. Tib.: "take up homelessness in such a way."

168. Tib.: "253 percepts."

169. Tib.: "Monks have promised to become homeless in order to be worshiped by others."

170. The predicate and the preceding *-āpy* is reconstructed from the Tibetan.

171. In the Tibetan this sentence is a causal clause connected to the preceding sentence.

172. I.e., the degeneration of lifespans, the degeneration in terms of defilements, the degeneration of sentient beings, the degeneration of the times, and the degeneration of the view.

173. Tib.: "delight."

174. Skt. *sarva-* has no equivalent in the Tibetan.

175. The Tibetan has *sthaviras* only.

176. This sentence is missing in the Sanskrit.

177. Tib.: "If those who rely on the Śrāvakayāna and possess the above-mentioned defining characteristics flout the precepts, they will go to hell."

the Vinaya, one will only enjoy the heavens[178] and not supreme enlightenment. How so? When the venerable *sthavira* Ānanda passed into nirvāṇa, he did not communicate anything to anyone. The enlightenment of a śrāvaka amounts to [that much] instruction.[179] And if they rely on the Mahāyāna? There is no certainty [for them] either. Why? Because they formerly belonged to the retinue[180] of Māra.

Even if they do good, there is no certainty [this way][181] either. To this, [Saraha] says in the following:[182]

> Some are bogged down in explaining sūtras. (DK_A 10c)

In some cases, a monk is explaining reality [as expounded in sūtras],[183] which he has not studied[184] before, and is again on his way to hell or the like due to his desire for material wealth.

> Some are seen to have dried up through having a mind full of thoughts. (DK_A 10d)

In some cases, [a monk] is thinking [too much] about all the Dharma [teachings]. He talks [about them] as they are constantly on his mind.[185] In some cases, ascetics and others reflect on the words (lit. "letters") of canonical texts and correct them. Looking at them, they do not understand what they read, and so they will take the path to annihilation.[186] Thus, because of [too many] thoughts, they dry up their mind and become sick.

> Yet others run after the Mahāyāna. (DK_A 11a)

178. Tib.: "Even those who do not flout but protect precepts will only attain enjoyment of the higher states of existence..."

179. These two sentences starting with "When the venerable..." are missing in the Tibetan.

180. The Tibetan translated *mārakāyika* as "having been the deities of Māra."

181. Added in accordance with the Tibetan.

182. Tib.: "In order to teach this, [Saraha] says:"

183. Added in accordance with the Tibetan. Another meaning could be that a monk teaches a sūtra without having studied it.

184. Tib.: "seen."

185. Lit.: "has [them] in front of his eyes and looks [at them]."

186. Tib.: "Some read Dharma [texts] never heard of [and] fabricate many concepts. This is not acceptable either. Some ascetics look at many canonical texts and correct them. Not understanding their [true] meaning, they become companions in vice."

Other monks adhere to the [Mantra-]Mahāyāna and accordingly settle with Mantra-Mahāyāna.[187] [Saraha] teaches precisely this[188] [in the following]:[189]

> Some[190] cultivate everything as the maṇḍala circle. (DK_A 11b)

As a result of this, not having heard of the essence of the Mantra-Mahāyāna,[191] they are [followers of nontantric] Mahāyāna only.[192] This too is the cause of going to hell and other [lower states of existence].

Moreover, [Saraha] says:

> Some are engaged in explaining [the meaning][193] of the fourth.[194] (DK_A 11c)

In some cases, monks are engaged in explaining [the meaning of][195] the fourth in terms of the Vaibhāṣika, Sautrāntika, Yogācāra, and Madhyamaka [tenets]. This is nothing but a net[196] of words. Without [an understanding] of true reality[, this is meaningless].[197] Or else, in some cases [monks are engaged] in explaining the fourth on the basis of pith instructions about the coemergent, not knowing its defining characteristic on their own, but looking only in texts.[198] Or if they do know, then why do they give the explanations [they do]? Being thus engaged in self-contradiction, they [all] go to Raurava hell or other [lower states of existence].

187. "Mantra-" is missing in the Tibetan.

188. I.e., taking *tam* in the sense of *tat*.

189. This sentence is missing in the Tibetan.

190. Tib.: "Others."

191. Tib.: "Resorting to the pride of Mantra-Mahāyāna..." (The Tibetans probably read *-garvitam āśritya*.)

192. Skt. *mahāyānamātreṇeti* has not been translated into Tibetan.

193. Supplied from the Tibetan.

194. As explained in the introduction, we believe that Saraha here was referring to the controversial fourth empowerment in the sequence of tantric Buddhist initiations. The commentator exploits the polysemy of the word.

195. Supplied from the Tibetan.

196. Tib.: "many."

197. Supplied from the Tibetan.

198. Tib.: "Or else, [some say] the fourth is the coemergent and are engaged in giving pith instructions on this out of sheer pride of having looked at texts." (The Tibetans probably read *-garva-* instead of *-garbha-*.)

> Investigating, they fall away from the path. (DK_A 11d)

In other cases, some, by investigating, fall away from the [bodhisattva levels and][199] the path[, whose existence they themselves maintain],[200] since the latter is completely nonconceptual.[201] These [types], since they lack any [genuine] compassion, also fall into base paths.

> Some develop concepts about the element of space.
> Still others develop views on emptiness.
> In general, they stand in contradiction.[202]

Some conceptualize and analyze the element of space but do not attain what they themselves maintain.[203] They obsessively cling to a [wrongly] imagined external [whole] possessing parts.[204] Again,

> They who run after a nirvāṇa
> that is apart from coemergent [bliss][205] (DK_A 12a)

Apart from the coemergent, there is no liberation, such as nirvāṇa. They will run after the nirvāṇa of others, merely because they do not understand names and synonyms and [so become] confused.[206] Because of this confusion, they go to lower states [of existence]. Confusion is therefore conceptual thought, while abandoning it is liberation. Thus [they]

199. Supplied from the Tibetan.

200. Supplied from the Tibetan.

201. Tib.: "not an object of analysis."

202. These three *pāda*s are missing in E_B and A. The first *pāda* is found in the Tibetan translation of DK_A: *la la nam mkha'i khams la rtog par byed* |. The second and third *pāda*s are supplied from the standard Tibetan root text: | *gzhan yang stong nyid lta bar byed pa de* | | *phal cher mi mthun phyogs la zhugs pa yin* |. See also Schaeffer 2005, 136. DK_A seems to have lost something in the end between *patanti* | and *kalpitabāhyāṅgasakte sati*, the latter phrase being an incomplete commentary on the second Tibetan line of DK_T 12. All three *pāda*s of DK_T 12 are absent in all Apabhraṃśa root texts.

203. This sentence is missing in the Sanskrit.

204. The Sanskrit is incomplete here: "While obsessively clinging to [wrongly] imagined external parts, [they do] not...."

205. Tib.: "Bereft of coemergent [bliss], they run after another nirvāṇa."

206. Having read *tadaprajñātatvāt*, the Tibetan has: "Not knowing this, they run after the nirvāṇa of others on account of mere synonyms."

do not attain
any ultimate.[207] (DK_A 12b)

When they [only] analyze with logical arguments, [Buddhist] ascetics and the like do not attain any ultimate, such as the śrāvakas' [ultimate, let alone the actual ultimate]. They have only taken vows and control their conduct for the sake of their livelihood.

Here, to sum up, [Saraha] says:

Does one who is pleased by
what[ever practice strikes his fancy]
and takes up the [respective] path[208]
attain liberation? (DK_A 13)

[In the eyes of one] who is pleased by whatever he looks at—that is, only his path, such as the one taught to by the Illustrious One to be Śrāvakayāna and so forth;[209]—those who have entered [their respective provisional] paths (*yāna*) do not, [accordingly,] attain liberation, since [their *yāna*s still] have the defining characteristics of the expression and what is expressed. As long as they do not honor a genuine guru, they, and also *tīrthika*s (i.e., non-Buddhists) can hardly attain [liberation] because [their understanding] lacks true reality.

Now Saraha addresses everybody:[210]

What use are butter lamps?[211] What use are food offerings [to
deities]?[212] (DK_A 14a)

207. This is counted as one line in the Tibetan.

208. Cf. Tib. "path/vehicle" (*yāna*), either because the translators understood *jhāṇa* in this way (as did Advayavajra) or because they had the reading *jāṇa*. However, *jhāṇa* could equally be "wisdom" (Skt. *jñāna*) or "meditation" (Skt. *dhyāna*). Mokṣākaragupta must have had the second meaning in mind, because he talks about the *utpattikrama* stage.

209. I.e., other provisional *yāna*s. Tib.: "To be pleased by whatever one looks at—this is the path of the Śrāvakayāna, as taught by the Illustrious One."

210. According to the Tibetan, the preceding sentence ends with "expressed." Then the Tibetan continues: "As long as one does not honor a genuine guru, it will be difficult to find [liberation]. This is the idea. To ordinary people who have failed to [realize] true reality, including the *tīrthika*s, [Saraha] says:"

211. The Apabhraṃśa has an additional *taha* ("for him").

212. Added according to the Tibetan.

[The meaning here is:] What use is [receiving blessings through] the sight (*darśana*) [of deities] and venerating [them]?[213]

> What is the use of reciting mantras? (DK_A 14b)

What is the use of mantra recitation? What is the use of offering lamps? What is the use of [offering] food? Without wisdom, one can do nothing whatsoever.[214]

> Why do we need to take up the Secret Mantra [Vehicle]?[215]

Why do we need to take up the Mantra [Vehicle], the recitation of mantras? Again, there is not the slightest use in [burning] butter lamps or making divine offerings when not in contact with the [true] reality of wisdom. Likewise,

> [What is the use of] going to bathing places?
> What is the use of going to the forest?[216] (DK_A 14c)

[What is the use of] going to the bathing places like Vārāṇasī and so forth?[217] What is the use of going to the forest for austerities?[218]

> Is liberation attained merely by bathing in water? (DK_A 14d)

In this [line the question is asked whether] liberation can be attained at a bathing place through the purification of immersion in water. It cannot, of course.

> Hey, reject misguided bondage![219] (DK_A 15a)

213. It is difficult to see how butter lamps and food offerings become *darśana* and veneration in the commentary.

214. Tib.: "What use are butter lamps, divine offerings, the recitation of mantras, and so forth when lacking [the realization of] reality? The intended meaning here is that there is not the slightest use."

215. This verse line and the commentary on it are missing in the Apabhraṃśa and Sanskrit. Probably they are a variant translation of DK_A 14b and commentary. DK_T has this line (16b) instead of DK_A 14b.

216. Counted as one line in the Apabhraṃśa.

217. Incomplete in the Sanskrit.

218. The Tibetan has only "forest."

219. This line differs in DK_T: "Hey, whatever has been said is false and wrong—get rid of it!" (*kye lags gang smras brdzun zhing log pa de bor la*).

Hey people! Cast off the misguided bondage taught by false spiritual friends, which means bathing places and the rest!

[But also cast off] the doctrine of the Lokāyata, which will surely send you to hell or similar states of existence. [They claim that] there are no [meaningful] offerings, fire offerings, ascetics, brahmans, or other worlds.

> As long as you live, live comfortably—
> there is nobody outside the purview of death.
> Has anyone ever seen a cremated body
> that later came back to life?[220]

[This must be abandoned,][221] because it is a nihilistic view.[222]

Or the Sāṃkhya say:

> The Sāṃkhya maintain that the permanent cause of the world
> is the primordial source (i.e., *prakṛti*). BCA IX.126cd

Such statements [on the other hand maintain] eternalism.[223] If somebody asks: "Why is it (i.e., eternalism) not considered good?" [Saraha answers:]

> Get rid of any sham![224] (DK_A 15b)

To sum up, [Saraha] is teaching [here] a special form of conduct. Trust in the genuine paths![225] In doing so,[226] one will help oneself and others as well. Leave the wrong path. Abandon it! In this way you[227] will not remain in a sham. On the good path, you will be free from this sham, which [freedom] is nothing but the coemergent.[228]

220. This is a very famous floating verse (although *pāda* b is usually different), commonly quoted, as it is here, as the epitome of the Materialist school, i.e., Cārvāka or Lokāyata. The *locus classicus* is unknown.

221. Supplied from the Tibetan.

222. Skt. "by those with a nihilistic view."

223. Tib.: "assert permanence."

224. Tib: "Get rid of what binds you."

225. This quotation is not in Apabhraṃśa and thus not considered a *pratīka*.

226. I.e., taking *yena* in the sense of *yasmin*.

227. Note that we follow Advayavajra's change from the third to the second person.

228. The Tibetan commentary on DK_A 17b is as follows: "Leave [any] irrational path! Get rid of anything that deludes your mind! In brief, [Saraha] proclaims a special path [when] he says:

Likewise, [Saraha continues:]

> Once you know it thoroughly, there is nothing else [to know].[229] (DK_A 15c)

Once you thoroughly know the coemergent,[230] there is no other liberation at all.

> Even all the types [of liberation imagined] by others are [nothing but] this [coemergent].[231] (DK_A 15d)

The many types of liberation imagined by[232] all others are not something else, for each of them separately is [in reality] the coemergent itself. But not knowing this coemergent, they wander in saṃsāra like a waterwheel.[233] The [coemergent] is attained by attending to a genuine guru.[234] In this coemergent here, expression and expressed [object] are not found.[235] [This is as stated in the following:][236]

> The coemergent is not found through [any of these] three:
> what is expressed, expression, and the relation [between them].
> [Still,] the Illustrious One pointed out [the coemergent] occasionally
> by using words pointing [to it indirectly].

"Trust the genuine paths!" In doing so, you help yourself and others. By these—and by nothing else—you will remain safe from [the] two wrong paths (i.e., the paths of the Lokāyata and Sāṃkhya) and find the coemergent nature."

229. DK_T differs here: "When you understand, this is everything."

230. Tib.: "'It' refers to the coemergent. Once you thoroughly know it...."

231. According to Bagchi's Sanskrit translation; Tib.: "Even all the types [of liberation imagined] by others are nothing but this [coemergent]." DK_T: "Nobody knows anything other than this."

232. Tib.: "of" instead of "imagined by."

233. Tib.: "Therefore it does not exist as something else."

234. The passage "But not knowing" up to "genuine guru" is missing in Tibetan.

235. Tib.: "If it is this way, the coemergent is not found through a relation between an expression and the expressed."

236. Not identified. The passage is not in Apabhraṃśa, and thus not a quotation of Saraha's root text.

Just by looking at texts,
one would not [truly] realize [the coemergent] for the benefit of
sentient beings.
Whatever subject matter one studies,
it is a concept in the form of delusion or similar characteristics.

These topics are not understood.[237]
Through the lineage of the gurus, [one's understanding is] free of
error.[238]

Therefore, [Saraha] says:

This is what you read [and recite].[239] (DK_A 16a)

Whatever reading and recitation [is done, it should furnish insight into] the supramundane, which consists of the coemergent, and not only the supramundane but also the mundane [coemergent]. [Saraha] continues:

[Whatever] is explained in treatises and the Purāṇas [is this].[240]
(DK_A 16b)

Whatever explanation is given in accordance with[241] treatises, the Purāṇas, and so forth, it is all about this very coemergent and [about] nothing else. This is taught [in the following]:

There is no view[242] as long as [the coemergent] has not been
marked.[243] (DK_A 16c)

237. Lit. "seen."

238. Skt. *parvan* is declined as if its stem were *parvā*. *Parvan* literally means "knot," "joint," or the "intersection" of, for example, a bamboo stick. *Guruparvan* can also refer to the intersections of the *gurunadī*, which are gradually identified as the yogin's attention moves along the *gurunadī* to the crown of his head (oral explanation from Kulavadhuta Satpurananda, Santiniketan, Feb. 2012).

239. Completed on the basis of the commentary. DK_T: "...read, maintain, and meditate on."

240. Supplied from the Tibetan. DK_T agrees with the locative *satthapurāṇem*.

241. This requires the insertion of an instrumental in the Tibetan.

242. I.e., the views propounded in treatises and the Purāṇas. The meaning here is that while all these texts reflect some degree of understanding of the coemergent, they crucially do not teach the view necessary for realizing it.

243. Tib.: "[But] with such views it cannot be marked." DK_T: "[In them] there is no view to mark it (the coemergent)."

In this way, as long as people have not marked[244] the coemergent in a manner stated above, they will not see liberation.[245] They destroy defilements from the very moment [they realize it].

How is it seen?[246] [Saraha] says:

> It depends only on the venerable guru.[247] (DK_A 16d)

[The path] is attained only—that is, exclusively—by relying on the most venerable guru.[248] In order to clarify this, Saraha says:

> When the teaching of the guru has entered [one's] heart,[249]
> (DK_A 17a)

When[250] the path taught by the guru has entered [one's] heart and one has realized it,[251]

> it is certainly seen, as if it were placed in [one's] hand.[252] (DK_A 17b)

It is like this: in the rare case in which someone[253] finds a wish-fulfilling jewel, it will certainly display its generosity and so forth through its power.[254] Likewise, in our case, when the nature of the coemergent has been attained, it makes all sentient beings identical to [this nature][255] just like the wish-fulfilling jewel. It makes one abandon everything—money and so forth. Because [people nor-

244. "Marked" (derivate of the root *lakṣ*) here and elsewhere means to ascertain as a target.

245. Tib.: "they do not attain liberation."

246. Tib.: "realized."

247. Shahidullah (1928, 131) completes the missing part of the line on the basis of a quotation from the *Subhāṣitasaṃgraha*: *ekku parū gurupāā pekkhaï*. DK_T: "Yet it only depends on the words of the guru."

248. Tib.: "[The path] is found through devotion to the venerable guru."

249. Counted as two lines in the Tibetan. Tib.: "[For] one into whose heart the teaching of the guru has entered."

250. Taking *yat* in the sense of *yadā*.

251. "And one has realized it" is missing in the Sanskrit.

252. Tib.: "it is like seeing a treasure placed on the palm of [one's] hand."

253. Skt. *kvacit* has not been translated into Tibetan; "person" (*skyes bu*), however, has the indefinite pronoun *kha cig*.

254. The Tibetan has not rendered *taduddeśena*.

255. The addition in brackets is based on the Tibetan.

mally] do not know such a path, the author of the treatise laments in the line starting with "People":[256]

> People are fooled by delusion. (DK_A 17c)

Everybody is fooled by delusion—that is, by error, false *tīrthika*s, and the like.[257]

> The immature [can]not recognize their own true nature.[258]
> (DK_A 17d)

Foolish people [can]not recognize their own true nature, which is the nature of the coemergent.[259] Moreover, they do not worship genuine gurus,[260] so they experience the suffering of the six states [of existence].

This fault applies not only to *tīrthika*s but also to [Buddhist] ascetics (*śramaṇa*). [In order to teach this,][261] [Saraha] says:

> Without wisdom[262] and renunciation[263] (DK_A 18a)

Even when these [Buddhist] ascetics, who are without proper wisdom, take the vow of renunciation and observe the precepts in the tradition of the Vinaya, they will not have success. Why is that?

> they [eventually] live in a home together with a wife.[264] (DK_A 18b)

256. The commentary has "Saraha." In Advayavajra's root text, this line probably started with *Saraha bhaṇaï*.

257. Tib.: "Everybody is fooled by delusion, fooled by the paths of *tīrthika*s and the like."

258. Counted as two lines in the Tibetan.

259. Tib.: "the uncontrived nature, which is the coemergent."

260. Tib.: "for they have not pleased genuine gurus."

261. Supplied from the Tibetan.

262. The Tibetan strangely has "meditation" here, but in its commentary it agrees with the Apabhraṃśa reading "wisdom."

263. Advayavajra must have read Apa. *gahiaü* instead of *rahiaü*. The Tibetan supports *rahiaü*, though, negating "homelessness."

264. Saraha seems to say in lines DK_A 18ab: "Without wisdom and renunciation, they live in a household together with wives."

When he [chooses to] start a household and the rest, then his [marvelous][265] conduct and so forth will be completely corrupted.[266] Once a single promise is violated, all are violated. It is just like fear arising in everyone when they see a person [die][267] from taking poison. That is, when one person dies, the fear of dying from poison arises, even though no one [else] has consumed it.[268] Whatever one consumes,[269] one consumes it [only after] carefully examining it, or by practicing the science of poison. Now if this [possibility of corruption] is not ascertained right from the beginning, a violation [of discipline] will occur.[270] Whatever conduct is adopted [on the basis] of a vow, it [must be] fully [observed] with firm resolve. About [such people], [Saraha] says:

> If they could not liberate themselves by enjoying sense pleasures
> intensively, (DK_A 18c)

If they do not abandon extreme and intense desire for attending to objects [of sensual pleasure],[271] then the author of the treatise,

> [Saraha,] says: "What thorough knowledge can be communicated
> to them?"[272] (DK_A 18d)

What is the use, then, of knowing something other [than liberation through sense pleasures]? What is the use of mentioning [something else]?[273] [It is meaningless,] because not having abandoned joy that lasts but a moment, one [prepares the ground for] the experience of suffering. Or, if one is not liberated through such things as the five sensual pleasures of enjoying objects with

265. Supplied from the Tibetan.

266. Tib.: "...then his marvelous conduct and thus his discipline will be impaired."

267. Added in accordance with the Tibetan.

268. The last part of the sentence starting with "even" is missing in the Tibetan.

269. Tib.: "Whatever little one consumes."

270. Tib.: "Therefore one must analyze carefully right from the beginning; otherwise [discipline] will be violated."

271. The negation in both the Sanskrit and Tibetan does not correspond to the root text here. In his commentary on DK_A 20d, Advayavajra picks up the idea that liberation is attained through the sense pleasures.

272. Tib.: "Is it not through complete knowledge?"

273. The Tibetan combines these two questions: "What is the use of having mentioned something else?"

the complete knowledge [of their true reality], what then is the use of teaching dry knowledge? To be clear, this will not bring liberation.

> If [the coemergent] is directly manifest, what is achieved by meditation?
> Or if it remains hidden, just try to measure that darkness![274] (DK_A 19ab)

If [the coemergent] is directly manifest, what is achieved by meditation? When it [remains] hidden and [can]not be seen, what is seen then in the middle of darkness?[275] What does this teach? Why[276] are all the vows taken, such as that of entering ascetic life? [They are useless] because in the middle of darkness,[277] no fruition of the other world (i.e., nirvāṇa) [can] be seen. What kind [of thing, then,] is [your so-called] direct knowledge [that is found] with inference as cause?[278] Saraha says:[279]

> "I have proclaimed this loudly."[280] (DK_A 19c)

[He meant:] "I do not speak in secret." To all sentient beings I teach [this][281] openly and in a loud voice. What [does he teach]?

> The nature of the coemergent is neither existent nor nonexistent. (DK_A 19d)

"Existent" applies here to any entity whatsoever—that is, [any entity] perceived by the eye and so forth or imagined by the mind. Why? The whole material world has emerged[282] with the coemergent as its nature. By this concept, one

274. Tib.: "... you are set aside by darkness."

275. Tib.: "When it [remains] hidden and [can]not be seen, it is like measuring darkness. Nothing whatsoever [can] be seen."

276. Tib.: "As for vows, why..."

277. Taking the *ca* after *andhakāramadhye* in the sense of *hi*. Tib.: "Like measuring darkness:"

278. "Inference as cause" is missing in the Tibetan.

279. Part of the root text in the Tibetan.

280. Tib.: "I, Saraha, call out as loud as I can."

281. Tib. *de nyid* has no equivalent in the Sanskrit.

282. Following the Tibetan. The Sanskrit has the causative *utpāditam*; we would expect *utpannam*.

is liberated. Therefore, since it is to be realized individually, [the coemergent] is not nonexistent [either].[283] This is as taught [in *Ratnagotravibhāga* I.154]:

> There is nothing to be removed from it
> and nothing to be added.
> The real should be seen as real;
> and seeing the real, you become liberated. (RGV I.154)

How does this [quotation apply]? The reason is as follows: Humans are born on account of bliss. Seeking bliss, they are born from the union of their parents.[284] Since it is something to be realized individually, [bliss] is not nonexistent. Why is that? Because it is inexpressible, given that one is wholly identical with it.[285] The idea is that *this* is [also] the bliss at the end of dying. Therefore, [Saraha] says:

> It is on the basis of [the same bliss through] which one dies, is reborn, and bound[286]
> that one attains great supreme bliss. (DK_A 20ab)

The bliss by which one dies[287] is for this matter [the same bliss] by which one is reborn and, once reborn, bound.[288] This is because one fancies ordinary bliss. Once one has come to know and understand the instruction of a genuine guru,[289] one will accomplish supreme great bliss[290] [on the basis of] this very same [ordinary bliss]. This is the idea [here].

> Saraha says: ["I shout aloud this secret,
> but bound people do not understand. What can I do?"][291] (DK_A 20cd)

283. This sentence is missing in the Sanskrit.

284. This means that sentient beings are attracted by the bliss of their future parents' union. The Tibetan has a question that is missing in the Sanskrit: "Why is [this bliss] not realized [at that time]?"

285. Tib.: "It is because its nature is inexpressible."

286. Tib.: "dies, is born, exists, and is bound."

287. Based on the Sanskrit, *'ching* must be corrected to *'chi*.

288. Tib.: "are born, exist, and are bound."

289. Tib.: "When taken care of by a lineage of genuine gurus..."

290. Lit.: "great bliss succeeds for him" (i.e., taking *sa* in the sense of *tasya*).

291. Translated from the Göttingen manuscript of the root text.

The line beginning with "Saraha" is easy to understand.

[Saraha further] explains this in detail:

> What will meditation do for someone without wisdom?[292]
> How to express what is inexpressible?[293] (DK_A 21ab)

Here, first of all, wisdom[294] is free from the defining characteristics of an expressed [object] and an expressing [subject]. What is it then? It is coemergent wisdom. What is achieved [then] by imagination?[295] Since it is without cause,[296] it [can]not be presented as an effect. To put it plainly, how can an explanation be given [of wisdom,] inexpressible as it is? Likewise, it is said [in *Ālokamālā* 40]:

> For as long as one conceptualizes,
> everything is false.
> That is truth; that is reality as it truly is,
> which is not conceptualized. (ĀM 40)

What is it [then]?[297] It is further said:

> Its (i.e., the mind's) nature is taken to be clear,
> without [mental] forms, and immaculate.
> And it can, in fact, never[298] be realized
> by one who is not a buddha. (ĀM 53)
>
> The Buddha in turn does not know
> the way others do,
> and when it comes to its (i.e., the mind's) interdependent reality,
> he alone knows that. (ĀM 54)

Therefore true reality is not realized by those who are tainted by ignorance. What is this "ignorance"? [Saraha] says:

292. Tib.: "Since [the coemergent] is beyond meditation, what does meditation do?"

293. Tib.: "[True] yoga cannot be expressed by anything."

294. Tib.: "mind."

295. Tib.: "It is not fabricated by thought."

296. Tib.: "beyond cause and effect."

297. This question has not been translated into Tibetan.

298. Skt. *kathañcana* has not been translated into Tibetan.

> The seal of [cyclic] existence has the entire world fooled.
> Nobody [can] realize their own true nature. (DK$_A$ 21cd)

[299] [This] seal of existence is [like] a woman whose heart is full of sin and who deceives sentient beings. She makes the world her slave.[300] Whatever[301] she likes—taking a life or the like—all that she [can] make happen, [driven] by the greed of desire. She makes [everybody] crazy. Therefore nobody [can] realize the uncontrived true nature.

Moreover, people are deluded by these teachings on mantras, tantras, and so forth[302] because of their greed for wealth. [Therefore, Saraha] says:

> There are no tantras, mantras, objects of meditation, or meditation. (DK$_A$ 22a)

The author of the treatise says [this] out of compassion, for liberation is not attained only[303] by means of mantras and tantras. He says:[304]

> Hey you fool! All these are causes of confusion. (DK$_A$ 22b)

Hey, you fool! That [mantras and tantras][305] are the cause of power and wealth[306] in all existences is mistaken. Due to this error, you[307] will experience suffering. Therefore, [Saraha] says:

> Do not ruin [your] already stainless mind through meditation! (DK$_A$ 22c)

299. The first sentence of the commentary is a translation of DK$_A$ 21c into Sanskrit and not repeated here.

300. Missing in the Tibetan.

301. Tib.: "If."

302. Tib.: "Moreover, mantras, tantras, and so forth are taught because of the greed for wealth, and people are deluded by these [teachings]."

303. Taking *rahitatayā* in line with Tib. *tsam po* in the sense of *–mātratayā*.

304. Tib. *de dag gis ni* is a too literal translation of Skt. *taiḥ*, which is short for *tair uktam* "by him it is said." (The plural of the demonstrative pronoun is honorific.)

305. The subject of the sentence ("mantras and tantras") is not mentioned in the Sanskrit and is supplied from the Tibetan.

306. Tib.: "abundant wealth" instead of "power and wealth."

307. Lit.: "they."

Do not ruin the stainless mind by ignorance! Why is it called stainless? The concept of mind is twofold, mundane and supramundane. The mundane [mind] has the defining characteristic of thoughts and has already been refuted. The supramundane [mind] is stainless.[308] It has the defining characteristic of the *dharmakāya* or the form of the coemergent. Therefore, [Saraha] says:

> Rest in bliss and cause yourself no torment! (DK_A 22d)

With this [verse], it has been established that the entire threefold world has the nature of nonconceptual bliss, so do not turn away from yourself as [if you were something] different.[309] Do it then (i.e., rest in it) full of bliss. How? [Saraha] says:

> Eating, drinking, enjoying intercourse,
> summoning the assembly [of adepts][310] with plenty of alcohol (*ali*) and food (*bali*)—
> through this, [these] fortunate people attain [supreme] siddhi.
> [The master] tramples on the heads of the deluded world.[311] (DK_A 23)

Here, [Saraha] also teaches the conduct with elaboration,[312] just like the one engaged in by Indrabhūti: among the five forms of sensual pleasure, the play of intercourse must be performed with food and drink.[313] With the skull bowl and so forth in his hands, [the master] offers the [alcohol and] food (*bali*)[314] and

308. The predicate "stainless" is missing in the Tibetan.

309. Tib.: "Do not ruin yourself! The idea is, Do not abide in suffering!"

310. Skt.: *[gaṇa]cakra*; Tib.: "Always fill (summon?) the assembly, again and again."

311. Apa.: "From 'Eating' up to '[The master] stamps down the heads of the deluded world.'" The full root text is not quoted here and is only available from Mss G and T (as well Sāṅkṛtyāyana, v. 48). In light of Mokṣākaragupta's commentary, DK_T is translated as follows: "Rejoice in eating, drinking, and intercourse, and always filling the cakras, again and again; by [following] such a teaching, the other world (i.e., mahāmudrā) is attained. [The master] stamps down the heads of the deluded world and moves on."

312. This terminology goes back at least as far as Āryadeva's *Sūtaka* (also known as the *Caryāmelāpakapradīpa*); see chapter 9 (Wedemeyer 2007, 277–305).

313. Tib.: "Eat, drink, enjoy the five forms of sensual pleasure, and create the bliss of intercourse!"

314. Skt. *padmabhājana* is a code word for skull bowl (see *Hevajratantra* II.iii.58b). Judging by context, by *bali* he means the five *amṛtas* (excrement, urine, meat/phlegm, menstrual blood,

stands as the deity in the middle of the great assembly.[315] By this means, [these] fortunate people will attain the accomplishment of wisdom, the accomplishment of mahāmudrā."[316] With this [siddhi the master] tramples on the heads of *tīrthika*s and turns them into disciples. He is one whom the world greatly fears.[317] By this [means,] mahāmudrā is attained.

What is the instruction of this [mahāmudrā]? [Saraha] says:

> Where the mind and the winds do not move
> and the sun and the moon do not enter,
> in there, you fool, relax your mind.
> Saraha has given a [simple] instruction. (DK_A 24)

You must relax your mind through the direct reflexive awareness of [your uncontrived] true nature, even in undesirable situations among all kinds of people; [all this is done] in accordance with the guru's instructions.[318] This is where you achieve greatness. In this state,[319] there is no movement of mind or [internal] wind; the sun and the moon do not enter and exit [the *rasanā* and *lalanā* channels].

Not everything stops, though, as a result of conceptual [practice] only.[320] [But this can be misunderstood,] as fools who do not understand the secret language imagine [this instruction] to refer to stopping the mind, the winds, and so forth.[321] But this is not the case. Why? We will explain it here.[322] "To stop" is an expression of "obstruction." What is the use of such painful conduct?[323] As

and semen) and five *pradīpa*s (meats of cow, dog, horse, elephant, and man) dissolved in alcohol. See Szántó 2019a, 289 and 293.

315. Tib.: "As for "satiating the assembly, again and again," [the master] takes up the skull bowl and offers the torma (*bali*), and the persons gathered at the *gaṇacakra* remain as deities."

316. Tib.: "From this comes attainment. Fortunate worldly beings will attain the accomplishment of wisdom, the accomplishment of mahāmudrā."

317. Tib.: "The deluded world relies on such worldly beings as *tīrthika* [teachers]. [The master] stamps down the heads of the deluded world and moves on. This means that he tames them."

318. Tib.: "In accordance with the guru's instructions, all kinds of people experience true reality on their own. You must relax your mind in this [true reality]."

319. Tib.: "In such a state."

320. Tib.: "This is not only the absence of thought."

321. Tib.: "...as when fools do not understand the secret language and thus experience suffering as a result of [the cessation in which] the mind and the winds have equally stopped."

322. Instead of "But this is not the case. Why? We explain it here," the Tibetan continues with "Therefore."

323. Tib.: "What is the use of stopping the wind and the waves?"

long as the body—the vehicle of wind and so forth—exists, one will obstruct or kill it by obstructing the wind.[324] Therefore [our practice] must be understood in accordance with the pith instructions of a genuine guru. "Saraha" and so forth are easily understood. Moreover, wind is bodhicitta and nectar, the blissful nature of mind. Thus the sun and the moon [stand, respectively, for] attachment and freedom from attachment.[325] A falsely imagined coemergent arises in [between] these two.[326] This is not the one that should be accepted.[327]

Having obtained this pith instruction, [Saraha taught a group of dohās] starting from "Do [not] create [duality but] unity!"[328] (DK_A 25a) up to "Seek clarification [about it] from the venerable guru" (DK_A 28d). These are easy to understand. [The verses are as follows:][329]

Do not create duality but unity![330]
Do not make any caste/color distinctions!
The entire three realms, without remainder,
become one great passion.[331] (DK_A 25)

It has no beginning, middle, or end
and is neither [cyclic] existence nor nirvāṇa.
This supreme great bliss[332]
is neither self nor other.[333] (DK_A 26)

Whatever I see in front, behind, and in the ten directions
is always, again, exactly this [great bliss].

324. Tib.: "As long as there is a body, the winds move. The stopping of the winds leads to the absorption of cessation (*nirodhasamāpatti*) or to death."

325. I.e., the joys at the second and third moments.

326. This is a disapproving reference to the attested and still unidentified verse in, for example, Nāgārjuna's *Caturmudrānvaya*: *paramaviramayor madhye lakṣyaṃ vīkṣya dṛḍhīkuru* (Mathes 2015, 391).

327. Tib.: "You should behold the coemergent but not through an intellect that is mentally fabricated by [the power of] these two."

328. Tib.: "Create neither duality nor unity." Skt. *mā* (see DK_A 26a) must have been taken to negate both. The context, however, requires the negation of duality alone.

329. Verses DK_A 25b–28c are only available in DK_T and translated from there.

330. Supported by DK_T 29a: *gnyis su mi bya gcig tu bya ba ste.*

331. DK_T 29cd: "Transform the entire three realms, without remainder, into one great passion, one caste/color."

332. Tib.: "In this supreme great bliss, there is..."

333. This verse is identical with *Hevajratantra* II.v.68 (212_{10-11}).

Today, at this very moment, error is destroyed.
Now I no longer need to ask anyone. (DK_A 27)

Where the senses have dissolved
and where the own-nature [of a self] has been destroyed—
friends, this is the coemergent.[334]
Seek clarification [about it] from the venerable guru. (DK_A 28)

In any case, everything is covered by [this] pith instruction [of the guru].[335] Therefore turn this entire [world] into the nature of the [coemergent].[336] Whenever you have doubt, seek clarification from the venerable guru, and this will free you from it. Then this pith instruction will be given by him.

[Saraha] himself says:[337]

Wherever mental consciousness terminates
and the winds dissolve, (DK_A 29ab)

This is because the mental consciousness terminates, and the winds [automatically] cease and dissolve.[338] It is not only that these two [cease]. [Saraha] continues:

This is supreme great bliss.
Without it one does not get anywhere. (DK_A 29cd)

This is what is taught by this statement: Supreme great bliss is free from even that by which it is attained.[339] Without the pith instructions of a genuine guru, nothing is achieved from teachings in conventional language.[340] Or else, "free"

334. Dergé and Peking of DK_T: "the body of the coemergent" (*lhan cig skyes pa'i lus*), correctly reflecting the Apabhraṃśa reading °*taṇu*.

335. Supplied from the Tibetan.

336. Supplied from the Tibetan.

337. Tib.: "Therefore [Saraha] teaches at this time how to follow pith instructions, which are the precepts of the guru." In the Indian text we have before the actual *pratīka* the superfluous "He taught him: 'Wherever mental consciousness...'" Unfortunately, it is not clear whom Saraha taught.

338. According to the Tibetan. The Sanskrit is simply a translation of the Apabhraṃśa line.

339. The Tibetan negates "attained," which fits with the reading of P: "[All] that by which supreme great bliss is not attained: that I have abandoned."

340. Lit.: "in terms of the relation between what is expressed and expression."

means "not stationary."[341] [Apabhraṃśa] *kahimpi ṇa jāi* means "has not gone anywhere" (*na gataṃ kvacit*). The intended meaning is that it is beyond the reach of words. This is as taught [in the following:]

> [The coemergent] is beyond the reach of words inasmuch as it is
> not the object[342] of the intellect.
> Forget (*dūre*) about understanding the subject matter taught by
> the guru.
> In due order, it will itself step into the heart of the faithful,[343]
> the heart purified by virtues such as compassion.

This is just as [in Saraha's verse:][344]

> Do not make self-awareness[345] into a sham!
> It is bondage [to call it] existence or nonexistence, or higher states
> of existence. (DK_A 30ab)

With your beginningless mental creations, do not call self-awareness "bliss."[346] If you do, you will get confused. Or (*tasmāt*), you may conceptualize it as existent (whose defining characteristics have been taught above), or nonexistent, or higher states of existence[347]—Hey fool, all that is bondage! There is no difference between a golden or an iron chain. Therefore it is indeed something to be abandoned.[348] [This is as stated in *Ālokamālā* 6–7]:

> Even to thoughts of the ultimate,
> the learned should not be attached.

341. Missing in the Tibetan.

342. The Tibetan did not render the instrumental ending (*agocaratayā*).

343. The Tibetan did not understand the idiomatic expression *padaṃ svayam ādadhāti* and translated: "on the level of a faithful mind."

344. Missing in the Tibetan.

345. The Tibetan has a demonstrative pronoun after "self-awareness."

346. Tib.: "It is self-awareness. Friends, do not conceptually fabricate this so-called bliss, which has been imagined throughout beginningless time!"

347. The Tibetan translation does not make sense: "Therefore it exists. The defining characteristics taught above and the defining characteristics of nonexistence are concepts of higher states of existence."

348. Tib.: "Both bind you. Therefore both of them must be completely abandoned."

What[349] is the difference between thoughts,
be they pure or impure? (ĀM 6)

Take the burning nature of fire:
a different fuel does not make a difference.
If touched [by fire], it burns,
even if it was kindled by [cooling] sandalwood. (ĀM 7)

What to make of this? [Saraha] says:

Hey, yogin! Watch your natural mind[350] skillfully!
It is like water poured into water. (DK_A 30cd)

Watch[351] [your] stainless mind skillfully. It is beyond existence and nonexistence or luminous by nature.[352] Hey, you are yogins by virtue of skillful[353] yoga [practice]. And yoga has the defining characteristic of one-pointed mental application[354] or the defining characteristic of knowledge and the object of knowledge. But the [practice needed here] is the same sort of thing as water poured into water. If this is the way it is,[355] [Saraha] says:

Hey, how can you expect[356] liberation through false types of
meditation?
Hey, why[357] do you take into your lap [this] net of illusion?
(DK_A 31ab)

Hey, you fool! Will you realize liberation through false meditation [that deceives] as an illusory net of hairs and the like [would do]? Therefore hard-

349. There is no question particle in the Tibetan.

350. The Tibetan has *gnyug ma yi yid* for *ṇiamaṇa* (Skt. *nijamanas*).

351. I.e., taking the future *drakṣyasi* as an imperative.

352. Tib.: "Hey, yogin! Concentrate one-pointedly on [your] natural mind, and observe [its] luminous nature, which is beyond existence and nonexistence."

353. Tib.: "concentrated."

354. Tib.: "As for one-pointed yoga, the mental application is the one-pointed awareness (*sems*) of the object [of meditation]."

355. Tib.: "It is yoga, if it is the same sort of thing as water poured into and mixed with water."

356. Tib.: "find."

357. I.e., taking the Apabhraṃśa question particle *ki* in this sense. The Tibetan has "how" (*ji ltar*).

ship is difficult to overcome.[358] Why? The entirety of the three realms is a net of illusion. Why do you take it into your lap? This is to say that [these false meditations] cannot be successful."[359]

Still,

> You must trust that the teaching of the genuine guru is true![360]
> Saraha says: "I have spoken in my own words." (DK_A 31cd)

If you believe[361] now that the words of [me, your] guru, are true, I, Saroruha, the supreme guru, have taught this *Dohākoṣa* and so forth.

> If space is pure right from the very beginning, (DK_A 32a)

If you thus believe the pith instructions of the guru, the difficulty associated with the whole of cyclic existence will be cleared away. Why is that?

> you continuously look, and the vision [of it] ceases.[362] (DK_A 32b)

Just like by gazing, by looking without blinking,[363] the distant perception of a mirage of water[364] ceases. In the same way, through an analysis of [cyclic existence], everything here [will be seen] to have the nature [of the exquisite *dharmakāya*][365] and not otherwise. How is it analyzed? By means of what has been directly made manifest through the pith instructions of the guru and through an uninterrupted process. However, this is not[366] a conceptual meditation, which is like the [illusory] net [of hairs].[367] If buddhahood [were attained]

358. Tib.: "Therefore, given such hardships, [liberation] is very difficult to find."

359. Tib.: "'How [can you afford] to take [them] on your lap?' means that [meditation] being of such a nature, realization [through it] is not possible."

360. Apa. *sacceṃ* has no equivalent in the Tibetan.

361. Tib. *yid ches par byas pa* has no equivalent in the Sanskrit.

362. The Tibetan of 32ab is as follows: "Continuously looking at the nature of originally pure space, vision of it ceases."

363. The Tibetan has "again and again" instead of "without blinking."

364. The *ādi* ("and so forth") after "mirage" is out of place and not translated here.

365. Supplied from the Tibetan. "Exquisite" is a simple modifier and does not imply that there is another kind of *dharmakāya*.

366. The negation has not been rendered into Tibetan.

367. This refers to *keśoṇḍuka* in the commentary on DK_A 33ab. The Tibetan must have read *jala* instead of *jālā* and made it mean mirage water.

through [conceptual meditation], it would be produced in terms of dependent [arising]. The exquisite *nirmāṇakāya* arises in[368] this [buddhahood] like light [appearing] when darkness ceases or sunshine is free of shadows. [Everything will be seen to have] the nature of the exquisite *dharmakāya* through the suppression of mental consciousness. The intended meaning is that it (i.e., the *dharmakāya*) is the nature of everything. But [the *dharmakāya*] is not mental consciousness.[369] [Mental consciousness, on the other hand,] is not simply nothing.[370] It is produced in dependence, because of dependent arising.[371]

To those who do not understand in this way, [Saraha] says:

> Thus, although there is no trouble at all,[372]
> the fool does not know[373] this because of the faults [covering his]
> natural mind. (DK_A 32cd)

Thus, although there is no trouble at all—that is, [it takes] no time at all for [the natural mind] to arise, the intended meaning being that all the trouble has already ceased—it is invariably the case that fools and non-Buddhists do not understand this, given their fault of clinging to existence. This is what he teaches: Therefore the Sāṃkhya and the Jaina together with the Vedānt[ins] are [the ones] intended [here], [as they are] known for having false understanding. [Positing] a stable mind that knows the ultimate, they are attached to the view of a universal single self. Because the time of converting [to Buddhism] (*vinaya*) has not yet come for them, the great compassionate ones disregard them. Thus these [groups] tighten the knot of saṃsāra ever stronger. They are indeed to be pitied. For compassionate ones, it is not proper to hate people in the time of trouble. Those who have an eye for Buddhism are aware of [certain] things: they become skilled in recognizing what belongs to saṃsāra and what to nirvāṇa and are not misled [anymore] by clever people following their own self-proclaimed tenets. This is [my] elaboration.[374]

368. Tib.: "from."

369. Missing in the Tibetan.

370. Tib.: "It does not mean that [the *dharmakāya*] is [simply] the pacification and cessation of mental consciousness."

371. This sentence is missing in the Tibetan.

372. I.e., following the commentary. Tib.: "Whose universal destruction is in such space?" This is very likely the result of understanding *āāsa-vikālo* as Skt. *ākāśa-vikāra*. Construing Tib. *dus* is difficult.

373. Tib.: "is deluded."

374. The Tibetan translation of this commentary on DK_A 32cd is comparatively short, breaking

Therefore, [Saraha] says:

> Due to the fault of pride, true reality [can][375] not be realized (lit. "marked"). (DK_A 33a)

Due to [their] fault of pride, [which has arisen from] false knowledge, true reality [can][376] not be realized.[377]

> Through this, these demons spoil the entire path.[378] (DK_A 33b)

Given their defects, the entire path, i.e., the [spiritual] way, is spoiled by them,[379] as if they were people possessed by demons. Therefore, [Saraha] says:

> Everyone in the world is deluded by [their own] meditation.[380] (DK_A 33c)

Everyone in the world refers to their respective path, the path of the non-Buddhists and others like them.[381] Thus:[382]

> No one realizes their own natural state.[383] (DK_A 33d)

One's own natural state is the coemergent, because one is always grounded [in it]. The author of [this] treatise laments that it is not realized by any ignorant, worldly people.[384]

off after the first sentence.

375. Added according to the Tibetan.

376. Added according to the Tibetan.

377. According to the Tibetan, "marked." The Sanskrit has "known."

378. Tib.: "[Their] entire path is undermined." DK_T took Apa. *jāṇu* as *skye bo*, which makes it "He strongly criticizes everybody." Being the first line in DK_T, "he" refers back to "fool" in DK_A 32d.

379. "By them" is missing in the Tibetan.

380. Apa.: "meditation." But in the commentary, we find "path" (*-yānaṃ*), which is also supported by the Tibetan translation of the root text.

381. Instead of the second part of the sentence, the Tibetan reads: "All *tīrthika*s are deluded by their own path."

382. Taking *idam* in the sense of *evam*.

383. Taken as two lines in the Tibetan.

384. The entire commentary in the Tibetan on DK_A 33d is: "The author of [this] treatise is

Moreover,

> The root of the mind [can]not be realized (lit. "marked").
> From the viewpoint of the coemergent, the three (goal, mark, and marker)[385] are false.[386]
> Only a few succeed in living in it.[387]
> Son,[388] you must remain in it![389] (DK_A 34)

In these [lines] a solid pith instruction is made even stronger. "Of the mind" means "of thoughts."[390] [This] is one [point] of the pith instruction. Then, the root [of these thoughts can]not be realized. What is [thus] established through the words of the gurus is the second [point]: The nature of the coemergent [can] not be marked by a marker. Thus the [notion of] a threefold principle of goal, mark, and marker is [both] false and misleading.[391] If these [three] were allowed to stand, then everything would have the nature of the [ordinary] mind and mental factors. As a consequence, the tradition of pith instructions would not be valid.[392] Heroes live on this level (i.e., of the coemergent), but [only] a few wise yogins are successful.[393] Therefore, O son, you must remain on such a level!

On that [level], all phenomena must be dissolved. This is called the ultimate. Precisely this has been said:

> The king of bliss alone gains the upper hand.
> He is causeless and yet always arises for the sake of the world.
> The omniscient one was at a loss for words

surprised."

385. I.e., the coemergent is not a goal, for which an acting subject (marker) could possibly find a mark.

386. "Are false" is missing in the Tibetan.

387. Translated according to the commentary. Saraha must have meant: "In this [coemergent, mind] arises and dissolves."

388. Missing in the Tibetan.

389. Having probably understood *phuḍa* as *sphuṭam*, the Tibetan reads: "It is the coemergent wherein these three are born, dissolve, and evidently abide."

390. Perhaps Advayavajra read *cintaha* instead of *cittaha*.

391. The Peking Tengyur repeats here a part of the commentary on DK_A 16d.

392. Tib.: "would be interrupted."

393. Tib.: "On this level, only a few yogi heroes get liberated."

when it came to expressing his [reality][394] (i.e., that of the king of bliss).[395]

Likewise, [Saraha] says:[396]

Whoever meditates on[397] true reality, which has no base, [should know that]
it [only] becomes evident through the pith instructions of the guru.[398] (DK_A 35ab)

Whoever meditates on[399] true reality, which is without root, [should know that] this reality is [only] known by the jewels of humankind through the pith instructions of the guru.[400]

Saraha says: Fools! You must know [this teaching] well[401]
for the destruction of saṃsāra, which has the nature of mind. (DK_A 35cd)

In these [lines] the author taught it clearly. Whatever[402] the meditation on the nature of mind might be, it is said to be the cause for destroying saṃsāra. This

394. Added in accordance with the Tibetan.

395. The source of this verse cannot be traced, but it is also in Raviśrījñāna's *Guṇabharaṇī*, a commentary on Anupamarakṣita's longer *Ṣaḍaṅgayoga* (Sferra 2000, 143). It is also quoted in the *Sekoddeśaṭīkā* on verse 103, where Nāropa attributes it to Saraha. Moreover, it is the *maṅgala* verse in the *Vyaktabhāvānugatatattvasiddhi* of Yoginī Cintā.

396. Missing in the Tibetan.

397. Mokṣākaragupta glosses *sems pa* with *bsgoms pa*.

398. This translation is in accordance with the Tibetan of Dergé and Peking (DP). If Apa. *viatta* is taken in the sense of *vyartha*, we get: "For those who meditate on true reality, which in truth is without a base, the pith instructions of the guru are pointless."

399. Again following Mokṣākaragupta.

400. There follows a sentence that cannot be construed and is missing in the Tibetan. It is perhaps possible that the last words should be read with Śāstrī and an *avagraha*—i.e., *°yāyino 'siddham*—in which case the meaning would be: "[Although] the pith instruction of the guru was known, it is not brought to success by those going on a path leading hither and thither (i.e., nowhere)." This perhaps shows that Advayavajra was aware of the possibility of reading *viatta* not as Skt. *viditam* but *vyartham*.

401. Tib. (B): "Fools, you must know what Saraha said!" Tib. (DP): "You must know the Dharmas Saraha taught!"

402. Taking *yaḥ kaścid* as *yā kācid*.

then is taught[403] [by Saraha, too]: "Through the pith instructions of the guru, true reality is realized (lit. "marked") with firm ascertainment." The intended meaning is that because saṃsāra has the nature of mind, its destruction also emerges from the mind.[404] Therefore, [Saraha teaches] this reality:[405]

> One's own natural state [of mind can]not be described in words. (DK_A 36a)

One's own natural state,[406] which is characterized by self-arisen [wisdom],[407] cannot be described by others—that is, by non-Buddhists and the like.

So who can describe it? The genuine guru. And this is what [Saraha] teaches [in the next *dohā*]:[408]

> It can be seen through the eyes of the guru's pith instructions. (DK_A 36b)

He says:[409] "I, Saraha, have seen it as a result of the pith instructions of [my] genuine guru, which are based on the teachings of the Buddha and nothing else. [In other words,] I have experienced[410] this through the eyes of[411] the guru's pith instructions. When it comes to describing it, I am unable to speak (lit. 'I am a mute')."[412] [However,] he describes some of its qualities:[413]

> In it (i.e., one's natural state) there is not even the smallest speck of a fault. (DK_A 36c)

In it, there is not a single[414] foothold for fault. Why is that?

403. Taking *uktaḥ* as *uktam*. This introduction is missing in the Tibetan.
404. Tib.: "The intended meaning is that through this the saṃsāra of mind is destroyed."
405. Tib.: "Therefore, [Saraha] says:"
406. Tib.: "nature or natural [state]."
407. Tib.: *shes pa* (Skt. *jñāna*?); missing in the Sanskrit.
408. Tib.: "In order to address [the question] 'By whom is it taught then?' [Saraha] says:"
409. I.e., translating *iti*; missing in the Tibetan.
410. The Tibetan translates *-avagataṃ* as *nyams su myong ba*.
411. "The eyes of" is missing in the Tibetan.
412. This sentence is missing in the Tibetan.
413. Tib.: "Which qualities does somebody like this then have?"
414. Tib.: "...the smallest speck that might offer a..."

It purifies and consumes virtue and wrongdoing. (DK_A 36d)

Because[415] the above-mentioned virtue and wrongdoing must be purified in accordance with the guru's pith instructions, one purifies and consumes [them].

[Saraha] explains how [the teaching] works:[416]

When your own natural mind is completely purified, (DK_A 37a)

Thus all phenomena, rather than being mentally [fabricated],[417] arise naturally. They are not produced by anybody. Just as grass, forests, thickets, and so forth arise naturally and come to an end, so two-footed and four-footed [beasts] arise naturally and come to an end without [the intervention of a] mind. They are not produced by anyone. How [can] this be seen? As to arising and the like, [there is the mistaken view that] I have created this form and so forth. This is the speech of the ignorant, [overpowered as they are] by delusion. The very moment this [deluded view] is abandoned, a purification of all phenomena occurs. And being absorbed [in them] (i.e., identical with them), they are consumed.[418] [Saraha continues:]

the [enlightened] quality of the guru enters [your] heart.
(DK_A 37b)

When the quality of the pith instructions given by the guru has entered your own heart, [and when this is realized,][419] at the moment of purification and the consumption [of all phenomena], you give everything, even [your] body, out of[420] firm conviction, without objecting to the pith instructions of the guru.[421]

415. The Tibetan must have read an absolutive instead of a causal ablative.

416. Lit.: "its conduct."

417. Taking the lead from the Tibetan (*yid la mi byed pa*), we understand *amanaḥ-* in the sense of "not becoming mentally fabricated."

418. The Tibetan commentary on DK_A 37a differs completely here: "Thus no phenomena are mentally fabricated [any longer]. Not having arisen in terms of an own-nature, they do not depend on causes that are different [from themselves either]. When the confusion that exists in the mind has been abandoned, all phenomena become pure, for this is their nature."

419. Supplied from the Tibetan.

420. The *iti* and causal ablative have not been taken into account in the Tibetan.

421. Instead of "without objecting to the pith instructions of the guru" the Tibetan has: "even after realizing the guru's pith instructions."

Not to give anything[422] means not having understood [the pith instructions] due to strong attachment.

> In this way Saraha[423] realized the state of the sage (i.e., his guru) through[424] not becoming mentally engaged. (DK_A 37c)

[The state of the Sage] is thus marked through not becoming mentally engaged.[425]

Alternatively, in this way—that is, through that [practice]—[he realized the state of] the Sage, the Illustrious One, whose nature is the ultimate, as taught by the venerable Saroruhavajra. This [state] has the defining characteristic of the dharmadhātu and is not, like a rabbit's horn, simply the nonexistence of the mind. As taught [in the *Ālokamālā* 142–44]:[426]

> This special state, which is called emptiness,
> cannot be known by someone like me.[427]
> But [the concept of emptiness] does not imply the kind of nonexistence
> that is based only on worldly convention. (ĀM 142)
>
> Its very nature of [ultimate] nonexistence [does not exclude]
> existence on a conventional level.
> [And in an ultimate sense,] of what is there existence and nonexistence
> when [all] phenomena lack an own-nature? (ĀM 143)
>
> As when you say: "You should not be concerned about it,"
> the [person addressed] thinks of what is prohibited [instead].
> Exactly in this way, he realizes something[428] other

422. Tib.: "others."

423. Tibetan (DP) reads "I, Saraha" instead of "Saraha."

424. The Tibetan lacks the instrumental.

425. The commentary includes here the resolving of a compound.

426. Tib.: "Or, rather, such a no-mind is the hero, the Illustrious One. He is the venerable Saroruhavajra. He said that [no-mind] is the ultimate nature, characterized by the dharmadhātu. No-mind is not, like a rabbit's horn, [something] nonexistent."

427. The Tibetan ("Wisdom in such a state—") is difficult to construe. Instead of *ye shes* in line a, we need an equivalent of *avijñeyā*.

428. Tib.: "peace." The Tibetan must have read *sa śāntaṃ* instead of *so 'ntaraṃ*.

> than [what is expressed by] the word "nonexistence." (ĀM 144)

And so on. Or rather, when they say that because of practice, through the suppression of a mind covered by defilements, a distinguished mind in the form of buddhahood is produced, then [we ask:] "To judge by what has been said, how could there possibly be anything?" If you answer: "The ultimate is accomplished for me in everything, since [everything] is based on it," [we reply:] "This is not the case." If one asks how that is, [Saraha] answers:[429]

> I have not seen a single tantra, a single mantra. (DK_A 37d)

There are many kinds of tantras, in which mantras are taught as well as various tenets—[all of] which have been invented in our own and the other [schools]. [In these] I have not seen even a single defining characteristic of a [view, meditation,] an object to be meditated upon, a meditator, or the like.[430] Why? They [have been taught] in order to discipline the world. [But] the special fruition is not produced by them.[431] This is as stated in the following:[432]

> Oh, what is the use of taking up practice?
> This ever-pure original state
> is naturally accomplished.
> Suchness is not born from thought. (*Pañcakrama* II.83)

> The defining characteristic of enlightenment is nonexistence.
> All phenomena are identical with it.
> Therefore one should aspire for it (i.e., enlightenment),[433]
> the conduct being like the raft of one's own psycho-physical aggregates.[434]

Therefore, [Saraha] says:

429. The corresponding Tibetan of this part after the quotation of ĀM 142–44 is: "If asked: 'How is a distinguished mind in the form of a buddha accomplished through the suppression of a mind covered by defilements?' [Saraha] answers:"

430. The sentence is completed on the basis of the Tibetan.

431. Tib.: "[But] I have not seen any particular fruit [produced by them]."

432. Missing in the Tibetan.

433. Tib.: "Therefore the encouragement through conduct..."

434. The source of this verse is untraced.

> Beings are bound by karma.
> Once one is free from karma, the mind is liberated. (DK_A 38ab)

Through the zealous application[435] of abandoning the karma by which people are bound, there is "mind liberation." Liberation comes through the freedom from the thought of an "I" and "mine." Through erroneous meditation, one merely gains notions about the mind.[436] This is bondage, so it [must] be stopped.[437] The idea is that by perfectly knowing [attachment][438] to be this way (i.e., a notion of the mind), there will be instant "mind liberation."

> Through "mind liberation"
> one will attain supreme nirvāṇa, which is complete.[439] (DK_A 38cd)

"Mind liberation" is a *karmadhāraya* compound inasmuch as it is mind and liberation. The [respective] other of the pair is [always] implied.[440] Thus we get that the one not being without the other is the defining characteristic of supreme nirvāṇa.[441]

[Saraha continues:]

> Mind[442] alone is the seed of everything.
> From it, cyclic existence and nirvāṇa spread. (DK_A 39ab)

As long as the above-mentioned nirvāṇa is not attained in such a way (i.e., that mind is already liberated), what is the state of mind?[443] From the mind comes the entire seed of ignorance and the rest. [All phenomena] that have cyclic existence and nirvāṇa as their nature spread beyond control. To be sure,

435. The Tibetan does not translate *-adhimokṣena*.

436. Tib.: "Through a mind in wrong meditation [arises] the notion of characteristic signs."

437. Tib.: "This is bondage."

438. Supplied from the Tibetan.

439. Tib.: "The liberation of mind is not found somewhere else. This is supreme nirvāṇa."

440. Advayavajra must have been led astray by misreading Apa. *aṇūṇaṃ* in the sense of Skt. *anyonyam* instead of Skt. *anyūnam/anūnam*. His understanding seems to be that wherever there is mind, there is liberation; in other words, mind is already liberated.

441. Tib.: "The one not being without the other, this is unquestionably the defining characteristic of supreme nirvāṇa."

442. Tib.: "The true nature of mind" or "mind itself."

443. This would require reading *sems* instead of *bsam* in the Tibetan.

[however,] they do not constitute the stability of cyclic existence.[444] Therefore, [Saraha says:]

> Prostrate to this [mind, which like][445] a wish-fulfilling jewel
> bestows the fruition of desire! (DK$_A$ 39cd)

The distinguishing attribute of supreme nirvāṇa is [its similarity to][446] a wish-fulfilling jewel. Prostrate to it! Why? With this [prostration as] a cause,[447] it bestows the fruition of desire. The desire is great compassion whose nature is to benefit the world.[448] He who fulfills without effort[449] the fruition wished for by that [great compassion] is the guru; therefore he is its (i.e., the mind's) wish-fulfilling jewel.[450]

Likewise:

> When the mind is bound, one is bound.
> When it is liberated, one is liberated. There is no doubt about this.
> (DK$_A$ 40ab)

People are bound through a bound mind, thoughts, and so forth.[451] On the other hand,[452] by knowing these [forms of bondage], they attain liberation. Thus there is a triad of bondage, liberation, and the one liberated from bondage. There is no doubt that among [these three,] liberation is through nondu-

444. Tib.: "When the above-mentioned defining characteristic of nirvāṇa [can]not be found, how [can] one conceive of [it]? [The mind] being unable to purify [itself of] the defining characteristics of saṃsāra and nirvāṇa, which have arisen from this mind—from the seed of all ignorance—they (i.e., saṃsāra and nirvāṇa) appear and spread. These two, however, cannot be presented as the true nature of cyclic existence."

445. Added according to the Tibetan.

446. Supplied from the Tibetan.

447. Tib.: "Because."

448. Tib.: "The desire is to work for the benefit of the world with great compassion."

449. In the light of Skt. *anābhogataḥ*, Tib. *lhun gyis grub pa'i* should be read as *lhun gyis grub par.*

450. Tib.: "This [mind] is like the guru, a wish-fulfilling jewel."

451. Tib.: "A bound mind is [a mind] bound by thoughts and so forth."

452. Tib.: "In a similar way."

ality.[453] Not knowing [this] to be so, foolish people wander in saṃsāra while learned ones are freed. In consideration of this, [Saraha] says:[454]

> Whatever it is that binds fools,
> by the very same [things], the wise swiftly[455] obtain liberation.
> (DK$_A$ 40cd)

Whatever binds foolish worldly people—the enjoyment of the five objects of sensual pleasure and so forth—by these very same things, the wise are swiftly liberated from saṃsāra. Thanks to the guru's pith instructions,[456] they have complete knowledge [of what these objects truly are]. As stated [in the *Hevajratantra*]:[457]

> Through a tiny amount of poison,[458]
> which would kill any living being—
> the one who knows the science of poison
> destroys that very poison with this tiny amount of it. (HT II.ii.46)

Likewise, [Saraha] says:

> Burdened [with many loads], it[459] runs in the ten directions;
> unburdened, it remains immovable. (DK$_A$ 41ab)

A sentient being who is bound by the concepts of an "I" and "mine" runs in the ten directions,[460] drifting through saṃsāra's six states of existence. Likewise, the same sentient being, when liberated on the right path, remains in an immovable state completely free from [the problem of] manifoldness (i.e., cog-

453. Instead of these two sentences (starting with "Thus there is a triad"), the Tibetan has: "Liberation is nondual wisdom. There is no doubt that one will be liberated by it."

454. This sentence is missing in the Sanskrit.

455. Apa. *lahu* (Skt. *laghu*) has not been rendered into Tibetan.

456. Tib.: "the wise who have realized the guru's pith instructions are swiftly liberated from saṃsāra by them (i.e., the objects of sensual pleasure)."

457. This and the following quotation are missing in the Tibetan.

458. This refers to the visualization of the deity's body in order to destroy the mental imprints (*vāsanā*) of our saṃsāric body.

459. The Tibetan has a plural particle.

460. In the Tibetan there is no equivalent of Skt. *daśadiśi dhāvati*.

nitive proliferation). The idea is that one then embodies the *dharmakāya*.[461] [Saraha continues:]

> Friend, this is like a camel!
> This paradox is evident to me. (DK$_A$ 41cd)

This means in brief: A camel[462] runs as fast as it can when heavily loaded, and it cannot be held back.[463] The very moment it is free of [any] load, it remains in one place[464] without moving. Similar to the camel, one's mind rests [when its nature] is directly manifest.[465] Such [a paradox] "is evident to me" refers to the meaning of the simile.[466]

Now [Saraha] teaches what needs to be done.

> Do not think that you [can exist] without breath![467]
> Do not become attached to the clinging caused by difficult
> practices![468] (DK$_A$ 42ab)

"Breath," meaning winds,[469] has the defining characteristic of being exhaled and inhaled through the nostrils. One will never observe oneself without it.[470] Why? Since the body is based on breath, in its absence how [can] there be any continuance of a body?[471] Having thus established in accordance with the instructions of the guru that breath[472] is identical with the [body],[473] where

461. Tib.: "at this time [the sentient being,] which abides in a state of not being moved by [all its] inclinations toward various appearances, embodies the *dharmakāya*. This is the idea."

462. In the Sanskrit commentary *karabha* ("camel") is glossed by the synonym *uṣṭra*.

463. Tib.: "...nobody can hold it back."

464. Tib.: "on the ground."

465. This sentence is incomplete in the Tibetan.

466. This sentence is missing in the Tibetan.

467. Tib.: "winds."

468. Tib.: "Even ordinary yogins should not fix their attention on the tip of nose." Instead of Apa. *saggo*, the Tibetan must have read *ṇāsaggo* (Skt. *nāsāgra*). Apa. *kaṭṭhajoeṃ* was understood as *kṣetrayoginā* by the Tibetans, and *kaṣṭayogena* by Advayavajra.

469. The Tibetan has only "winds."

470. Tib.: "Without it one will neither exist nor die."

471. Tib.: "As long as there is breath, a body remains. Where will the body remain without breath? It will not."

472. I.e., reading *vāyum* instead of *vāyus*.

473. Supplied from the Tibetan.

are their (i.e., the winds') own-natures? They cannot be found.[474] So abandon [breath control]! Do not be attached to painful yoga, which is [only] conceptual![475] This is for sure. How is [this certainty][476] arrived at? [Saraha] says:

> Hey you fools! Orient all your strength toward the coemergent!
> The bondage that stinks of cyclic existence must not be attended to![477] (DK_A 42cd)

Hey, you foolish people! Give up the small goal and go for the big one! What is that? Search out the coemergent! Give top priority to harnessing your strength in order to realize it! [Then he continues with the line starting,] "The bondage that stinks of cyclic existence must not..." The stench[478] of existence means [to repeatedly become] a being in the intermediate state.[479] The bondage of existence, similar to a circle made by a firebrand, comes about through a coming and going of that [being in the intermediate state]. Do not become attached to it![480]

[Saraha continues:]

> Leave this mind and wind here alone;
> they are extremely fickle like a steed![481]
> Abiding in the coemergent nature,
> one becomes stable.[482] (DK_A 43)

This mind and the winds are extremely fickle, like a steed,[483] because they are

474. Tib.: "here one focuses on the body, after the identity of breath and the body is established; apart from that one does not focus on the body."

475. Tib.: "Ordinary yoga is a yoga [practice] that is conceptual by nature."

476. In accordance with Tib. *nges par ji ltar bya zhe na.*

477. Tib.: "Hey, you fools! The coemergent is supreme. Completely abandon your bondage to the mental imprints of cyclic existence!"

478. Tib.: "mental imprints."

479. Advayavajra is trying to play with the similarity between *gandha* and *gandharva.* In the Tibetan, the sequence of the previous and present sentence is in reverse order.

480. Instead of the last two sentences, the Tibetan reads: "Do not become attached to it, and abandon it, because it is like the apparent circle made by whirling a firebrand! This is the idea."

481. Tib.: "Expose its fault, for the mind and the winds are unstable! They are like an extremely fickle steed."

482. Tib.: "When realizing the coemergent nature, the mind thereby becomes stable."

483. Tib.: "cannot be tamed very [easily] and are like a fickle steed."

so similar as if there were nothing between them.[484] Leave them alone! And take up this! What exactly? The stable basis of [relaxing] in the coemergent nature in accordance with the guru's instruction. Based on this, [the coemergent nature] will become directly manifest in a stable way.[485] This is because, as stated [in the *Hevajratantra*]:

> The [coemergent] is realized by oneself from [having accumulated] merit. (HT I.viii.36c)

[Saraha] teaches the distinguishing attribute of this [coemergent in the following]:

> When the [conceptual] mind is stopped,
> [all][486] subtle bondages break.
> Then there is the equal taste in the coemergent.
> [In it] there is neither low caste nor brahman.[487] (DK_A 44)

The very moment the conceptual mind has stopped, all forms of bondage are destroyed.[488] It is not only that one's own bondage no [longer exists],[489] but at this specific time, the equal taste in the coemergent causes everyone to abandon[490] [making distinctions]. At this time,[491] it is established that[492] there is no difference between the lowest caste and the brahman caste. The idea is that the whole world is a single caste in terms of the coemergent.

He then presents the advantage [that is gained from] this. To teach that there is no tenet apart from the coemergent, [Saraha] says:

> Here are the rivers of the gods: here is the Yamunā,

484. The Tibetan does not have an equivalent for the causal clause.

485. Tib.: "Based on the pith instructions of the genuine guru, the abode of the coemergent nature will become unwavering and stable."

486. Supplied from the Tibetan.

487. Tib.: "Wherever there is the equal (i.e., single) taste of the coemergent, there is neither low caste nor brahman."

488. Tib.: "abandoned."

489. Added in accordance with the Tibetan.

490. Tib.: "understand [it]."

491. I.e., taking *tayā* in the sense of *tadā*, which is supported by the Tibetan.

492. Instead of "it is established that," the Tibetan has an extra sentence here: "Therefore this meaning is entirely established."

and here is the meeting of the Gaṅgā with the sea.
Here is Prayāga and here is Vārāṇasī.
Here are the moon and the sun.[493] (DK_A 45)

Thus [here are "rivers of gods" (i.e., *sura-sari*), where] there is perfect (*suṣṭhu*) play.[494] Why? This is because each of them flows uninterruptedly with the coemergent.[495] It is precisely this [play] that is called Yamunā, Gaṅgā, and so forth, and the latter do not refer to [the real rivers] of the bathing places. Rather, Yamunā stands for being based[496] on all paths. Gaṅgā stands for the tendency of flowing to and realizing these [paths].[497] Sāgara[498] stands[499] for the ocean of all pith instructions on meditative concentration. Prayāga stands for nonduality [because here the Gaṅgā and the Yamunā merge]. Vārāṇasī[, too,] stands for nonduality because this is where the two [streams Varaṇā and Asī] merge.[500] Just as the moon and the sun are seized by Rāhu, everything is consumed by the fire of pith instructions.[501]

It is not only that the bathing places [actually] are the coemergent, but [the coemergent is also found] in the major and subsidiary power places.[502] In order to teach this, [Saraha] says:

493. The Tibetan translations differ slightly. B: "This is the Gaṅgā. [This is] the Yamunā. This is where the Gaṅgā flows into the ocean. This is Prayāga and Vārāṇasī. This is the moon, this is the illuminating sun." DP: "This is the river Yamunā. This is the confluence of the Gaṅgā into the ocean. This is Prayāga and this is Vārāṇasī."

494. The meaning of this sentence is not entirely clear, but it seems to transmit an etymology (*nirukti/nirvacana*) of *sura-sari*. Advayavajra understood the verse as follows: *sura-sari* is a collective term, and then *gaṅgā-sāaru* is not interpreted as a compound ("the confluence of the Gaṅgā with the sea") but as two words, "the Gaṅgā and the sea." This seems unnecessarily complicated, and it is more likely that Saraha meant the Gaṅgā by "the river of gods" (*sura-sari*).

495. Tib.: "As to these streams of gods here, in terms of the uninterrupted coemergent [nature] of each of them, they are of a single taste."

496. Lit.: "because of being based..."

497. The Tibetan has here the additional sentence: "'The Gaṅgā flows into the ocean' means that all sentient beings enter into the single taste of emptiness and compassion."

498. Tib.: "...because Sāgara..."

499. Tib.: "because of standing."

500. Lit.: "because their duality is abandoned."

501. The sentence is completed on the basis of the Tibetan.

502. Tib.: "but the [major] and subsidiary places of pilgrimage, too, are the nature of the coemergent."

> [These] sites, the major and subsidiary power places, are here[503] [in the body]. (DK_A 46a)

In a like manner, the major sites, subsidiary sites, and so forth—the twenty-four power places of pilgrimage—all [have the same nature as the coemergent].[504] Therefore it is not necessary to visit [them] in the external [world].

> I have been made to stay at them while wandering.[505] (DK_A 46b)

[506] [This is as] taught in the pith instructions of the yoginīs: The manifold world, which includes the external and internal, is of the nature of [great][507] bliss. This is the idea. What does this teach?[508] One's own body has the nature of bliss, its constituents have the nature of the major power places, and so on,[509] so it is not necessary to visit the external ones. Therefore, [Saraha] continues:

> The bathing places are nowhere else but[510] in the body.
> I have not seen bliss anywhere else.[511] (DK_A 46cd)

The body is the blissful bathing places. They are nowhere else but the body. When this is [seen], one is comfortable.[512] Because I have not seen[513] these blissful bathing places[514] as being somewhere else but in the body, a yogin[515] must therefore [strive to] remain inseparable [from these power places]. Moreover, he must realize these internal power places in accordance with the *[Yoginī] saṃcāra* and other [tantras]. What is more, [they should understand] that this

503. "Are here" is missing in the Tibetan.

504. The sentence is completed on the basis of the Tibetan.

505. Tib. (DP): "[All of them] I visited, and having inspected [them], I understood." B is difficult to construe.

506. The first sentence is a translation of the Apabhraṃśa root text into Sanskrit. The Tibetan repeats here its version of the root text.

507. Supplied from the Tibetan.

508. Tib.: "This teaches the following."

509. From here on, Skt. *pīṭhādi* (Tib. *gnas la sogs pa*) is simply rendered as "power places."

510. Lit.: "similar to."

511. Cf. with the corresponding verse 59 in DK_T, which differs considerably.

512. These first three sentences are missing in the Tibetan.

513. Tib. *mi mthong*; read *na dṛṣṭam* instead of *naṣṭam*?

514. Tib.: "the bathing places as a cause of bliss."

515. Advayavajra's switch from the subject "I" to "a yogin" is a bit awkward.

practice (*saṃcāra*) is pervaded by bliss and not [performed] by the subtle winds alone.[516] Therefore, since it has been established that the power places have the nature of the great bliss of Dharma,[517] a yogin of the perfection stage, who is blessed by the gods of the interior power places, does not need to visit the power places in the external [world]. This is as stated [in the *Abhidhānottaratantra*]:[518]

> The power places numbering twenty-four
> are found here [in the body]!
> Therefore those who know true reality
> should not exhaust themselves by wandering around [in the exter-
> nal ones].[519]
>
> If not in possession of true reality,
> nothing [is gained] from wandering around.[520]
> On the other hand, if they are in possession of true reality,
> there is nothing whatsoever for them in wandering around.[521]

Therefore it is certain[522] that they have the nature of not being separate [from the body]. [Saraha] teaches precisely this[523] [in the following]:

> The cluster of lotuses [in the vajra body], the lotus petals, the lotus
> fragrance,
> the filaments, and the beautiful stalk—[524] (DK_A 47ab)

Abandon [the visualization of the] parts of a lotus [described] in this example! [Your nature] is not like the cluster of individual elements, such as the cluster

516. Tib.: "the abiding in the body alone."

517. Tib.: "supreme great bliss."

518. The verses correspond to chap. 65/68.14–15 in the *Abhidhānottaratantra* (or *Abhidhānottarottaratantra*), which is transmitted with two chapter numerations. The oldest manuscript numbers the first three chapters and then restarts the count, whereas later transmissions and the Tibetan translation numerate continuously.

519. Tib.: "should not wander around [elsewhere] and exhaust themselves."

520. Tib.: "there is not the slightest need to wander around."

521. The last two lines are missing in the Tibetan.

522. Tib.: "the intention is."

523. I.e., taking *tam* in the sense of *tat*.

524. Tib.: "In the middle of the anther on the stalk of a lotus, a very subtle fiber, fragrant and colored." The precise construction of this passage eludes us.

of lotuses, their flowers, petals, leaves, and fragrant pollen, and the beautiful, superior stalks. Likewise:[525]

> Hey, you fools, do not torment yourselves with false notions!
> You must abandon such distinctions![526] (DK_A 47cd)

Hey, you fools, abandon [this visualization that creates] the distinction of the individual elements of the lotus mentioned above![527] Do not torment your mind![528] Therefore do not—according the approach of the various treatises [full] of such senseless expressions—engage in something that is foreign to bliss.

Likewise:

> What is the use of mantra treatises?
> They will go into oblivion.
> Brahmā, Viṣṇu, and Trailokya (i.e., Śiva) will disappear—
> just ask a lowborn person![529] (DK_A 48)

Ask yourself:[530] What is the use of the mantra treatises, which are foreign to the coemergent? Without it,[531] any mantra treatise would vanish.[532] It is like the worthless son of a base family, for [when] the father no [longer] exists, everything—whatever wealth there is—vanishes. Everything is [then] seized by the king and his men.[533] Likewise, without [being in harmony with] true reality, any mantra treatise[534] or Dharma [teaching] will vanish, thanks to those

525. Tib.: "All of them are the same in terms of their lotus nature."

526. Lit.: "duality."

527. "Mentioned above" is missing in the Tibetan.

528. Tib.: "Hey, you fools, a lotus is [divided into] parts through the enumeration of distinct features. Do not torment your mind in such a way!"

529. Tib.: "If you ask yourself: Are the mantra treatises useless because they go into oblivion? Like a lowborn person, Brahmā, Viṣṇu, Trailokya (i.e., Śiva), and everybody devoted to them will disappear." DK_T: "When Brahmā, Viṣṇu, and the three-eyed [Śiva], the illegitimates, who are [considered] to be the support of the world, are worshiped, the least accumulation of karma will be exhausted."

530. Missing in the Tibetan.

531. I.e., reading *tena* instead of *tair*.

532. The Tibetan has the extra sentence: "Do not believe in them, and ask yourself!"

533. Tib.: "It is like the worthless son of a base family not having control over [his] possessions. Or it is like when a father who has no son to protect the family lineage dies, all possessions will be seized by the king and his men."

534. The Tibetan has only "treatise" instead of "mantra treatise."

who are gripped by ignorance. To sum up, once the space-like coemergent is abandoned, from conceptual knowledge [alone] buddha[hood] and the other [states of deities] are not attained, not even in name. In this case,[535] all these treatises will vanish along with the five buddha families and so forth, which are the essence of the coemergent[536]—all of them will disappear. [Even though] all people are devoted to the place where the other [gods]—Brahmā, Viṣṇu, Maheśvara, and the like—are, [among them] there are no knowers of true reality at all.[537] Therefore, without it (i.e., the coemergent), [so-called] knowers of the reality [taught] in all the treatises will be unsuccessful.[538] This is as stated [in the *Caturdevīparipṛcchāmahāyogatantra*]:

> All those who do not know the true reality within the eighty-four thousand
> collections of teachings of the Great Sage will not have success.

Therefore, [Saraha] says:

> Hey, son! Understand that the [art of] extracting the essence of mercury
> is well established but [what the essence is] cannot be understood.
> People reading explanations
> do not know what it is that must be refined.[539] (DK_A 49)

Hey, son! When you do not precisely know the purification process that extracts the essence of mercury, you will be destroyed. Similarly, when you are not aware of the purification process for attachment and other [defilements], you will be destroyed. Do not do it in this way! By playing with desired phenomena and so forth[540] under the influence of attachment and without [an awareness of their] true reality, you will only be taken over by extreme ignorance. This does not apply only to you. Other people who [merely] read and

535. Tib.: "Therefore."

536. The apposition "essence of the coemergent" is missing in the Sanskrit.

537. Tib.: "Likewise, Brahmā, Viṣṇu, Maheśvara, and all people will vanish."

538. Tib.: "Without it, there will be no knower of reality in any of them, and no activity will meet with success."

539. Tib.: "Not knowing the [art of] extracting the essence of mercury, the inseparable [?essence of?] controlled earth is lost. Commentators and readers cannot know it."

540. Tib.: "with the five objects of sensual pleasure."

explain, all of them, are not successful [either]. Why? Because the world does not understand saṃsāra.

With respect to those who know [true reality], however, [Saraha] says:

Hey, son! True reality, this taste of the manifold world,
cannot be taught as being a thing.
[True reality] is the abode of bliss and is without an essence.
The best of worlds (i.e., the nonconceptual world) arises within it.
(DK$_A$ 50)

Hey, disciple! Hey, son! The reality you ponder—its essence (i.e., its experience)—cannot be expressed, just like [ascertaining] that a thing (i.e., a form) is dark blue, yellow, or some other color.[541] What is it then? [True reality] has to be experienced by oneself. Just as[542] it has been stated [in the *Ālokamālā*], "He alone(, i.e., the Buddha,) knows that [interdependence]."[543] Beyond thought, the realm of bliss, the nature of true reality, is the best of worlds.[544] This is the idea. Being naturally accomplished in such a way, it is not attained by meditation. It is attained only through the thorough knowledge of the guru, and not through self-conceit or the like.

This is [also] taught [in the following]:

The intellect stops and the mental consciousness dies.[545]
[What remains] when self-conceit is interrupted
is [like] the miraculous, most subtle phase [of the moon].
Why then fix [one's] meditative concentration on it?[546] (DK$_A$ 51)

Because the coemergent that is conferred by the guru has been directly made manifest, one destroys any fabricated intellect; in other words, one stops recollecting [mental fabrication].[547] The conceptual mind dies—that is, it no longer

541. From here on, the commentary on this verse is available in the Sanskrit only.

542. Reading *yathā* instead of *yataḥ*.

543. *Ālokamālā* 54d.

544. The sequence of *tasmāt* and *yasmāt* is turned around.

545. Tib.: "is pacified."

546. The verse in the Dpal spungs edition (B) has four lines with nine syllables each and accords with the Apabhraṃśa; the corresponding texts in DP consist of five lines with seven syllables each. The last two lines differ from B: "Once the miraculous, subtlest phase [of the moon] is realized, why fix [one's] meditative concentration?"

547. Tib.: "The guru teaches how he will manifest the coemergent and [proceeds to] confer it.

engages in the identification [and perception][548] of external and other objects. In such a state, self-conceit and [other] concepts related to the perception of an "I" and "mine" are broken—that is to say, destroyed. Because[549] of this, it (i.e., the coemergent) is like the sixteenth phase [of the moon], the miraculous, most subtle phase, which does not act as an [external or internal] object.[550] Thus what [can be] achieved here by fixing one's meditation on it? To put it plainly, there is no [need] for[551] anything fabricated by the mind.

That is further specified [in the following:]

> [The subtle phase] rises in cyclic existence and sets in
> dissolution.[552]
> How could it arise, then, when it does not exist? (DK_A 52ab)

Precisely in this state, in which cyclic existence has been devoured, there is also freedom from dissolution.[553] Thus, if something is neither existent nor not existent, how can it come into being again? Surely, it cannot. Having stated this, [however,] does not make [Saraha] into a nihilist. How so? Because there would be the undesired consequence that everything—the defining characteristics of "Buddha" and so forth, which [in reality] are like an illusion—would [then] be subject to existence and nonexistence.[554] But this was taught in terms of nonconceptuality.

> Abandoning both[555] and the meeting point between the two as
> well—
> this amazement will be conveyed by the glorious guru.[556]
> (DK_A 52cd)

Once it is manifest, one is without recollection for as long as the conceptualizing intellect has stopped."

548. Added according to the Tibetan.

549. Skt. *yasmāt* has no equivalent in the Tibetan.

550. Tib.: "... any result of such objects."

551. The instrumental of the abstract suffix in the Sanskrit normally expresses a causal or adverbial relationship; the Tibetan has a *la don*.

552. Tib.: "in the sky."

553. Tib.: "there is neither existence nor nonexistence."

554. Tib.: "Because he taught the defining characteristics of a buddha and so forth, which [in reality] are like illusions in terms of the concept of existence and nonexistence."

555. I.e., the extremes of existence and nonexistence.

556. Tib.: "[This] distinction having been abandoned, [can] there be anything that has arisen?

Once duality has been abandoned, the meeting point between the two (i.e., existence and nonexistence) is not obtained in the middle of supreme [joy] and [the joy] of no joy[, as taught] by those who do not understand the true middle. This is the intended meaning.[557] The correct position is that everything is beyond duality. By avoiding that, too, you abide firmly there, where you will communicate with your teacher by [nodding] heads. The nodding of heads stands for [their common] amazement [at encountering the coemergent].[558]

Accordingly, you adopt the following way of life:

> You may see,[559] hear, touch,[560] eat,
> smell, walk, sit down, and rise;[561] (DK_A 53ab)

[The meaning] here is: whatever things your eyes see, sounds your ears hear, touch[562] [that comes from] the clothes and so forth that you put on your body, food in your mouth, good or bad smell[563] in your nose, [whether] you wander or roam around,[564] sit on your seat, or stand up—

> [you may] linger around and waste time for worldly
> transactions,[565]
> [but do] abandon your conceptual mind. Do not move [prompted
> by] any single aspect [of mind].[566] (DK_A 53cd)

"Linger around" refers to buying, selling, and the like. Spend [your] time with

You must rely on what was taught by the venerable guru."

557. Tib.: "The abandonment of the distinction [between existence and nonexistence] equates to nondual wisdom, that which is apprehended in the middle. Abandonment means that in the position between supreme [joy] and the [joy of] no joy, the very [distinction between existence and nonexistence] is abandoned and not apprehended."

558. Tib.: "Therefore you must abandon all of it and accept with great reverence what is taught by the glorious guru."

559. In the Apabhraṃśa, the verbs are in the second-person plural imperative.

560. According to the Tibetan (*reg pa*).

561. "Rise" is missing in the Tibetan.

562. According to the Tibetan. The Sanskrit has *paridhāna* ("dressing").

563. The Tibetan only has "smell."

564. "...you may wander or roam around," is missing in the Tibetan.

565. Tib.: "and conduct a conversation."

566. Tib.: "Do not move out of [mind's] unitary mode!"

these worldly transactions,[567] but your mind should not move out of [the state of] nondual yoga. Do not turn away from the nature[568] of the [mind's] unitary mode through [engaging the concepts of] action, agent, and so forth—[a mode in which] another type of mind (i.e., a dualistic one) is required! [Otherwise] you will experience the suffering of hell.[569]

[Saraha] therefore teaches that you must remember the pith instructions of a genuine guru:

> Whoever runs around not drinking[570]
> the essence of nectar that is the guru's pith instruction
> will die of thirst in the desert
> of the manifold meanings of treatises.[571] (DK_A 54)

Any wicked man[572] who runs around and does not drink the essence of the nectar that is the guru's pith instructions will be defeated in his ambition to benefit the wide variety of sentient beings. This is like a large group [of traders] who were thirsty and without water in the desert. The leader of [these] traders saw water somewhere in a hidden place. Thinking that being lazy,[573] [traders] will not [walk such a long way to] drink [since] they do not know what is good for them, he did not tell them. Because of that, all of them were afflicted and eventually died.[574]

[Next, Saraha] teaches the distinctive characteristics of pith instructions:

> Completely abandon thought and no-thought
> and abide in the [natural] way of a small child.

567. The plural *tair* does not fit and is taken as *tena*.

568. Skt. *svabhāvena* only makes sense in this way.

569. The Tibetan translation omits a few elements here: "'Talk idly' refers to haggling and the like. As to the unitary mode of mind, it is [the mode in which the mind] does not abandon [the state of] nondual union."

570. Tib.: "Whoever does not drink to his satisfaction..."

571. Tib.: "are like the many visitors dying of thirst in the desert of suffering."

572. Missing in the Tibetan.

573. The letter *ṣī* in Skt. *kauṣīdā* is corrected in the upper margin in a second hand, but we cannot determine what the correction is.

574. Tib.: "It is like a large group of traders who are tortured by thirst and whose leader reveals his knowledge of a place where water is concealed. Those who are diligent rush there, drink the water, and live, but those who lack diligence die." We find this unpacking of the simile more apposite.

> If you are firm in devotion to the teaching of the guru,
> the coemergent will spring up.[575] (DK_A 55)

"Thought" means knowledge, the objects of knowledge, and so forth;[576] "no-thought" means lack of an own-nature and so forth. These two you must abandon.[577] Abide in the [natural] way of a small child. Just be firm in your devotion to the pith instructions of the guru![578] Through this, the coemergent will spring up. By continuously practicing this emerging wave, one will become identical with it.[579]

[Next, Saraha] shows that this complete identification is free from all hindrances and inexpressible:

> It lacks word, referent, comparison, and quality.
> It is spoken of, but not known—this [coemergence] I have
> taught.[580] (DK_A 56ab)

It cannot be apprehended in terms of word or referent.[581] Alternatively, *akṣara* (syllable) here is *a-kṣara* (the supreme indestructible).[582] Its nature[583] is to consist of [great][584] bliss, incomprehensible and indescribable.[585] In this way it is without comparison, not ascertained by a sequence of words, but I, Saroruha,[586] have taught it; in this way, it was taught by me, Saroruha. This is as explained [in the following]:

575. The Tibetan adds: "beyond doubt."

576. Tib.: "...thoughts about knowledge and objects of knowledge..."

577. Tib.: "...are abandoned."

578. Tib.: "Be firm in devotion to the pith instructions of a genuine guru and abide in the [natural] way of a small child!"

579. Tib.: "Through this, the coemergent will arise accordingly, and as you become familiar with it, its nature will become [manifest] as the [real] coemergent."

580. Tib.: "It lacks color, word, supreme quality, and example. [But although it is] inexpressible, I have taught this [coemergent]."

581. Tib.: "color and word."

582. This second meaning of Skt. *akṣara* ("indestructible") was lost in the Tibetan translation.

583. Skt. *varṇa* has been translated into Tibetan as "color" (*kha dog*).

584. Supplied on the basis of the Tibetan.

585. Tib.: "Therefore it is said that it cannot be grasped."

586. Tib.: "Saraha."

> No matter how many concepts arise in the mind, all of them must be abandoned.[587]
> That which takes the form of bliss, that which makes you happy—this, too, is a mere concept.
> Or what is caused by ascetic indifference [is] also [a concept].
> Both are the foremost causes of cyclic existence.[588]
> Except for what has a nonconceptual nature, there is no other nirvāṇa anywhere else—in no [other] thing.[589]

Why is that? [Saraha] answers:

> To whom can this supreme lord (i.e., the coemergent) be taught?
> It would be like a virgin knowing erotic bliss. (DK_A 56cd)

This supreme lord, which is the supreme reality, exists within all sentient beings. Since there is confusion about this,[590] to what ordinary being [can] I teach it, since it does not exist in other tenets? Through words only, they do not understand. Why? [It would be] just like a virgin[591] trying to find out from a confidante[592] [what erotic bliss is]. "To find out" means to form a firm notion [of it]. [The confidante says:] "Erotic bliss is first experienced by you after going to your husband. Then, certainly you will tell it to me directly." Having gone and returned from his house, she is [then] asked by the confidante: "Was it as I said before?" She responds:[593] "You have to learn it directly, at a time when you [can] experience [bliss] together with a husband of your own. Not the slightest arising of bliss can be told to you directly, since it is inexpressible."[594] The pith instructions of the guru are like that, and not only with the [example of] a virgin's bliss; they make you realize reality as it is.[595]

587. Tib.: "purified."

588. Tib.: "Both are not anything. They are main causes of cyclic existence."

589. The source of this verse is untraced.

590. Tib.: "What exists among sentient beings is confusion. The supreme lord, which definitely abides in them, is the supreme reality."

591. I.e., using the singular for the plural.

592. The text changes from plural to singular, so we have chosen to use the singular consistently.

593. The text changes again to the plural: *ta ucuḥ*.

594. The Tibetan abbreviates the detailed presentation of the example in the Sanskrit as follows: "It would be like the arising of [erotic] bliss for a virgin, because [the experience of erotic bliss] cannot be told to others."

595. Tib.: "Likewise, neither can [the coemergent] be realized without the teaching of a genuine guru."

Precisely this is taught [in the following]:

> Into that which is completely devoid of existence and
> nonexistence,
> the entire world dissolves. (DK_A 57ab)

Since ultimate reality is inconceivable,[596] it is free from[597] existence and nonexistence because compassion and emptiness are not two. Into this [supreme reality] the entire world, visualized as Buddha Vajradhara and so forth, dissolves. This is because there is no object [anymore] inasmuch as it (i.e., the world) is completely identical with the [dissolved visualization].

> When the mind has been stabilized in this,
> one is free from cyclic existence and nirvāṇa.[598] (DK_A 57cd)

Once the mind abides without movement as a result of[599] having abandoned the notions of an "I" and "mine" through the stage taught above, it will be liberated from existence[600]—that is, the faults of saṃsāra in its six states of existence. If it is done in any other way, there will be faults, as taught [next]:

> As long as you do not fully know the supreme in yourself,[601]
> how will you attain[602] the unsurpassable body? (DK_A 58ab)

As long as you do not realize the excellent nature of[603] true reality in yourself,[604] given that you are pervaded by it, how should you attain the unsurpassable

596. The Sanskrit has been emended on the basis of the Tibetan.

597. "Being free from" (*rahita*) is usually construed with an instrumental and not an ablative (*bhāvābhāvayoḥ*). Taking the latter as a genitive, the Tibetan becomes incomprehensible.

598. According to the Göttingen manuscript and the Tibetan. Advayavajra must have read "cyclic existence and saṃsāra."

599. The causal connection is not found in the Tibetan.

600. "From existence" (*bhāvāt*) has not been translated into Tibetan.

601. The Tibetan has *bdag gzhan* for *appahiṃ para*, which could be misunderstood as "self and other." "Self" is in the locative, however, and "supreme" for *para* is quite common and also suggested by the commentary.

602. Tib.: "find."

603. The Tibetan did not translate *–rūpaṃ*.

604. Following the root text, *nātmānaṃ* should be changed to *nātmani*. In the Tibetan, we need the locative after *bdag* instead of the instrumental (BD) or genitive (P).

reality of the pervading [body], which is the *nirmāṇakāya*?[605] Overthrowing the clinging to a self, from which the notions of one and many derive, everyone will have such realization. Why? Because [otherwise, the self] would be the unsurpassable true reality. That is the meaning.[606]

Likewise [Saraha] says:

> I have taught this. Do not go astray![607]
> [Because if you do,] you will recognize a self in yourself.[608]
> (DK_A 58cd)

In this way, it was taught by me, Saroruha:[609] "Never confuse it! Through confusion you will recognize a self in yourself. After having abandoned [confusion], there is nothing else [to do]."[610] Therefore, [Saraha] says:[611]

> Do not conceptualize either particles or the smallest particles,[612]
> and erotic bliss shines forth in an uninterrupted way.[613] (DK_A 59ab)

Particles, including the smallest of them, are not conceptualized through meditation. In meditation [practices] that include yoga, erotic bliss[614] appears in an uninterrupted way.[615] If you do so (i.e., conceptualize particles),

605. Tib.: "...why should you attain the unsurpassable reality of great bliss, which pervades your body with its nature of the *nirmāṇakāya* or the *dharmakāya*?"

606. Instead of these two sentences (starting with "Because [otherwise, the self] would...") the Tibetan simply has: "You will not!"

607. The Apabhraṃśa accords with Dpal spungs (B). DP: "Without going astray..."

608. Tib.: "Perfectly realize (B: know) yourself by yourself!"

609. Tib.: "Saraha."

610. Tib.: "In this way it was taught by me, Saraha: Do not confuse it! After having abandoned this [confusion], there is nothing else [to do]. The meaning of this is that you will perfectly realize yourself by yourself."

611. Missing in the Tibetan.

612. Tib.: "Do not conceptualize particles or freedom from particles!" It is possible, however, that in its transmission the Tibetan eventually confounded *bral* for *phran*.

613. The Tibetan differs completely here: "Being continuously fixated on entities, they proliferate." These first two lines of DK_A 59 in the standard Tibetan root text (DK_T 75ab) are as follows: "Entities are not atoms, not non-atoms, not even mind. They have always been without [a basis of] fixation."

614. Skt. *vā* is in an awkward position and should be put after *kriyate*.

615. Tib.: "For him who does not conceptualize particles and freedom from particles, uninterrupted great bliss manifests."

Saraha says: "That is a gross misunderstanding."[616] (DK_A 59c)

This [meditating on particles] is merely conceptual knowledge. With this type of yoga, there will be error and confusion. That is what I say.[617]

Hey, you must know that the ultimate has no roots![618] (DK_A 59d)

Hey, you deluded one![619] You must understand that the ultimate is without roots or affiliation, free from any seed, base, [abode,][620] and so forth.[621] This[622] is as stated in the following:

The nature of being considerate toward others is without root,
and so is the nature of meditation.
The true reality of knowable objects[623] is that they are without root,
and the tathāgatas are without family.[624]

For this reason, [the ultimate] manifests as it is (*svarūpeṇa*) and not how people like it.[625] "Erotic bliss" is used in this sense, namely embracing that [reality].[626]

Such a meaning has been taught [in the following:]

He is at home but she looks [for him] outside.
She sees [him] at home but asks her relatives. (DK_A 60ab)

Just as a certain yoginī has a husband *in* her house and asks outside where he is, or [just as she] sees [her] beloved husband next to her [but still] asks in

616. DP: "This is all Saraha has to say"; B: "Saraha says: 'Seriously think about it.'"

617. Tib.: "True reality is the nonconceptual, free from all thought. In such yoga the mind will not go wrong, because I taught it as being perfect."

618. Tib.: "Hey you friends! You all must know the ultimate!"

619. Tib.: "Hey all you deluded friends!" We have supplied the commentator's understanding.

620. Supplied from the Tibetan.

621. The Tibetan construes "without roots" and "without affiliation" with the "deluded one."

622. Taking *tam* as *tat*.

623. Tib.: "True knowable object."

624. This quotation remains untraced.

625. The instrumental of *icchā* is not realized in the Tibetan: "As for the manifestation of ... and wish for [the ultimate], [this] is not [how it is]."

626. Tib.: "[The ultimate comes to] be known well in virtue of not being attached to it."

the house where he is,[627] so do [people abandon][628] the true reality that dwells in their own body and go asking for another form of wisdom outside themselves.[629] This is pure ignorance.

Again, thanks to the instructions of the guru, one sees and experiences one's self-experience. Then some bystander might ask how is this reality, and [the guru] will say it is non-knowledge. This is the type of non-knowledge you must grasp, because all [other] things are conditioned. What is there to know?[630] Thus [Saraha] again reinforces [the same idea in the dohā] starting with "Saraha":[631]

> Saraha says: "Fool! You must know [true reality in yourself] on your own!
> It [can]not be addressed in terms of an object of meditation or meditation."[632] (DK_A 60cd)

This true reality taught [above] must be realized entirely in oneself by oneself. To be sure, true reality [can]not be addressed in terms of an object of meditation or meditation and so forth.[633]

> Is it possible to understand everything the guru says?
> [Can] liberation be attained without having understood everything?[634] (DK_A 61ab)

Someone said the following: "Not everything taught by the guru [can] be fully understood,[635] [but only] that which is sought on one's own reveals true real-

627. The Tibetan simply reads: "Just as some women leave their husbands back home and ask their relatives [outside where he is]..."

628. Supplied from the Tibetan.

629. Tib.: "and go asking for another [one]."

630. Instead of the last two sentences, the Tibetan has: "To experience [something] on the basis of the pith instructions of a genuine guru but to ask somebody else how true reality is [constituted]—this must be considered sheer ignorance. When [the guru has pointed out] that all phenomena lack an own-nature, how could there be [true] arising?"

631. Tib.: "In order to teach this..."

632. Tib.: "Then [you will see that] it is not meditation, an object of meditation, or a formula."

633. Tib.: "It [can]not be imagined through meditation, an object of meditation, or the like, [all of which] by nature are [mere] concepts of this [true reality]."

634. Tib.: "When taught by the guru, everything is understood. Where can liberation be attained (DP: known) without this?"

635. From here on, the remaining part of the sentence and the following question and answer

ity as it is. Is liberation impossible after such a [revelation]? [Answer:] What do you achieve [by saying this]? Disregarding and not contemplating what the guru taught, you do not understand. This much is the meaning. How can it be understood? Through regular practice? Through regular practice one will not [understand it,][636] for there is [still] a clinging to a self." In order to teach this, [Saraha] says:

> Traveling [from] country [to country], occupied by [useless types of] practice,
> you will not understand the coemergent, caught up as you are in harmful deeds. (DK_A 61cd)

Here bad yogins have the following flaw: They leave their native place[637] and travel to all [manner of] countries. They do not know the exhaustion of the body's defilements because of [thinking about things permitted] to be eaten and not to be eaten.[638] Why? Because of their practice.[639] Not knowing this unsurpassable coemergent, they do not[640] actualize it. Why? This is because of being caught up in harmful deeds [and] because of the duality [of thinking about what one is or is not permitted] to eat and so forth. The idea is that they lack [genuine] practice.[641] It is as stated [in *Pañcakrama* II.86]:

> Just as fire does not spark from wood without friction,[642]
> so too is there no enlightenment in this life without practice.[643]

are missing in the Tibetan. The Tibetan translation continues with "Through regular practice?"

636. Supplied from the Tibetan.

637. Instead of "Bad yogins..." the Tibetan commentary starts with: "Some people here including yogins leave their native place..."

638. Tib.: "They only end up defiling their body for the sake of things [both] edible and non-edible."

639. Tib.: "But there is nothing to be practiced."

640. The negation is missing in the Tibetan.

641. Tib.: "However much they recollect and conceptualize—by this [alone] they will not become familiar [with the coemergent]. This is the idea."

642. The first half of the verse is identical with *Yogakuṇḍali-Upaniṣad* 14cd, and *Yogaśikhā-Upaniṣad* 76ab.

643. This verse is in Sanskrit and thus not part of the root text.

Because of these [lines,] someone may doubt: "If that much practice is performed, how could it be taught that meditation and so forth are abandoned?"[644] This is addressed [in the following]:[645]

> Though taking delight in objects of sensual pleasure, one is not sullied by them.
> Though one plucks a lotus, one is not touched by water.[646] (DK_A 62ab)

Foam is seen amid water, but one does not get to the water even when [the foam] is touched by one's hands. Likewise, when properly knowing [the true reality] of objects, one [may] engage in the play with the five sensual pleasures, but one is not overtaken by the [resulting] faults. Again, it is like a wave of water spilling over a lotus leaf while the [leaf] does not get sullied. This is because it is stated in scriptures: "They (i.e., faults) have arisen from it (i.e., the object), and still they are like the lotus leaves and the water."[647] The practice of a yogin is also like this:

> Moving along with the [poison transforming] source in this way,
> The yogin is not troubled by poisonous (objects) when delighting in them.[648] (DK_A 62cd)

Such a yogin,[649] practicing in line with the flow of the guru's pith instructions, moves to—that is, knows—the [poison-transforming] source. Thus he is not bound by objects [of sensual pleasure]. Whatever objects there are for the yogin, none of them ever become troublesome for him. What is the use [then] of knowledge, object of knowledge, and knower? [They do not impose themselves,]

644. Tib.: "If that much practice is not performed, why are meditation, recitation, and the like taught?"

645. Tib.: "In order to teach this, [Saraha] says:"

646. Translated in accordance with the commentary. The original intent of DK_A 62b probably is: "Although the water grasps the lotus, it does not stick to it." This is also supported by DP of the Tibetan root text (DK_T 78b): "Just as water does not stick to the petals of a lotus."

647. Tib.: "Having gone to the middle of a body of water by boat, one plucks a lotus without being sullied by water. Likewise, when in possession of realization, which is the knowledge of true reality, one [can] enjoy the five objects of sensual pleasure without being sullied by defilements."

648. Tib.: "Taking refuge in the connection (*yoga*) with the root (i.e., true reality) in this way, how does poison affect those in the possession of mantras against poison?"

649. In the Sanskrit, singular and plural endings are used promiscuously in this paragraph for the subject and the words depending on it. The singular is used consistently throughout here.

because of its (i.e., the source's) power. To make this [perfectly] clear: therefore, he is not bound by delighting in any object.[650] This is is as stated [in the following]:[651]

> External [objects] do not exist; they lack [independent]
> existence.[652]
> As for knowledge, [it does not exist either,] just like external
> objects.
> Whatever a clever person conceptualizes as empty [like that],
> we say that this is not yet [true] empti[ness].[653]
>
> Having ascertained and understood in this way,
> the master yogin, whose intellect [dwells] in true reality alone
> and who is uniquely skilled in the display of illusion,
> plays with the richness of objects.[654]

[Next, Saraha] says:

> The deity is generated and even the goal is seen.[655]
> You kill yourself. What good does it do you?[656] (DK_A 63ab)

When the deity is seen directly with its marks, having arisen in its [complete] form, then you kill yourself (lit. "the self dies"). What will this deity do [to you]? To put it plainly, nothing at all.[657] Therefore, [Saraha] says:[658]

650. The Tibetan commentary on DK_A 62cd is comparatively short: "When such a yogin entirely cultivates the root, which is the pith instruction of the genuine guru, he does not get sullied by the faults of objects. Therefore he does not get sullied by the stains of objects."

651. Missing in the Tibetan. The source of this Sanskrit quotation is not identified.

652. The second part of the sentence is missing in the Tibetan.

653. Supplied from the Tibetan.

654. I.e., dramatic sentiment (*bhāvavibhava*). The Tibetan must have read *vibhāvair* instead of *vibhavair* and construed the instrumental with *niścitya*: "Having ascertained and understood existence and nonexistence..."

655. Tib.: "Although you offer the deity, one lakh has been given" (i.e., some type of deity yoga has been performed 100,000 times).

656. Tib.: "You [only] bind yourself. What good does it do you?"

657. Tib.: "Even if you worship the form of a deity to such an extent [that] you see [the deity itself] directly, what is the use of [such] a deity if you [thereby] bind yourself [to it]? There is none." Tib. *'ching* is probably a corruption of *'chi*.

658. Missing in the Tibetan.

> Saṃsāra is not uprooted then,[659]
> [but] without practice there is no departure [from saṃsāra].[660]
> (DK_A 63cd)

Even if you make yourself into the form of a deity itself [i.e., making it directly manifest],[661] this *saṃsāra* here is not [thereby] uprooted. Why is that? For the following reason: Since [sentient beings then] would not have the five psychophysical aggregates of appropriation, [their remaining] function, based on the ground consciousness, amounts to that of a being in the intermediate state (*gandharvasattva*). However, given their previous grasping, [they] will return again. The deity itself, too, is just like that, for it is visualized through consciousness. And so saṃsāra is not uprooted. The [underlying] idea is that [the deity as well] meaninglessly turns around like an irrigation waterwheel.

[Objection:] But, by the same reason, without practice[662] there is no departure from within the realms of saṃsāra, [even] having full knowledge [of how meaningless it is]. [Answer:] To start with, there is no [departure from saṃsāra] through the aforementioned deity practice. It is due to the guru's pith instruction that practice is performed.

[Objection:] Then we do not differ on the issue of practice. [Answer:] That is not possible. So, you have not [rightly] heard even a single message from the pith instructions of a genuine guru. What are they [then]?

[Saraha] gives [the example of a practice that does not work]:[663]

> With eyes unblinking and by immobilizing the mind, [one may think]

659. Tib.: "Saṃsāra is not uprooted by means of such [worship]."

660. According to the Tokyo manuscript (which is the oldest we have and the only one not from Nepal), this concludes the entire *Dohākoṣa*.

661. Addition in brackets supplied from the Tibetan.

662. It is not clear what *tad* in *tadabhyāsena* refers to.

663. The Tibetan commentary on DK_A 63cd differs slightly: "Even if the form of a deity is itself made directly manifest, saṃsāra is not [thereby] uprooted. Why is that? When sentient beings are without the five psychophysical aggregates of appropriation, and only [their] ground consciousness is operative (i.e., as a consequence of their having actualized the deity), they are [still] in an intermediate state of existence, and under the influence of previous karma, they return to saṃsāra. Even [in] the form of the deity, one is like that because it is visualized through consciousness. This is why saṃsāra is not uprooted. The [underlying] idea is that [the deity as well] wanders in a circle like an irrigation waterwheel. There is no purpose in meditating on deities. You may wonder why meditation, recitation, and the like were taught. Well, only if there is realization through the wisdom of reality [can] practice lead to one's departing saṃsāra; otherwise one will not be liberated. This is the idea. In order to show how this can be, [Saraha] says:"

> the winds are stopped, [mis]understanding[664] the venerable
> guru.[665] (DK_A 64ab)

By this, [the following is taught]: What is imagined by those of poor intellect—that the guru's pith instructions are conceptual by nature—is not the [the guru's pith instruction],[666] namely that the mind is dissolved in space and so forth by those with a fixed, unblinking gaze. Because of this, [they think] that winds are stopped[667] in accordance with the pith instructions of the venerable guru. This is not the case.[668] Why? [Saraha] teaches it in the following way:

> The [life] wind flows. When it becomes immovable,
> the yogin breathes his last. What is the point then? (DK_A 64cd)

When the yogin stabilizes the life wind [by blocking it] from its natural wind flow, what happens then? In that moment, hey, you fool, the yogin breathes his last—that is, he dies. That [breath retention] does not work. Why is that? [Saraha] says:[669]

> As long as there are neither objects nor sense faculties,
> the [guru's instructions] become clear on their own.[670] (DK_A 65ab)

As long as there are all[671] the objects and sense faculties, the yogin will be attached because of these two, and he will not understand the pith instructions of a genuine guru. Freedom from attachment is attained through analysis, scripture, and logic. But he does not see what the self and so forth truly are in terms of the divisions into the ultimate and so forth. All the more so, he

664. Tib.: "in accordance with."

665. Tib.: "...on account of the pith instructions of the venerable guru."

666. Supplied from the Tibetan.

667. Tib.: "Just as 'the unblinking gaze' means that when one opens the eyes a little, it [becomes] immovable, 'cessation of mind' means that it dissolves in the sky and similar [realms]."

668. The negation is missing in the Tibetan.

669. The Tibetan commentary on DK_A 64cd are as follows: "When the life wind, which is the mind's vehicle, has been stabilized—hey, you fool—does the yogin then die? What is meant [here] is that he does not."

670. Tib.: "As long as one is attached to the village of the objects of sense faculties, for that long [the mind] appears and spreads without hope."

671. The Tibetan takes the plural marker *grāma* literally as "village" (*grong khyer*).

will not see directly [what truly is].[672] Confusion leads to confusion, and this is false. Because of seeing relative truth, it appears as illusion. Thus the manifold, three-tiered world is like an illusion. Who is becoming attached to it? To put it plainly, no one. In particular, for the best of the yogins, the guru's pith instructions become clear on their own without contemplating them. And it is only through that practice[673] that [the guru's instructions] are [truly] brought to mind. This is certain.[674]

[The text continues:]

> Who would get involved with this twisted[675] intent?[676]
> One fails to see what and where [an object truly] is.[677] (DK_A 65cd)

Who will engage with words of such a twisted intent? What is the meaning of the words that have been explained above in this way? The thing that is not in the guru's instructions—the reality of a self and so forth—will one ever really find it there? In brief, there are no such things as an object of meditation and a meditator.[678] [Thus, it is said:]

> Nowhere do [such things as] an object of meditation, a meditator,
> or meditation exist.
> Anything born from these three has the nature of distortion.

672. I.e., taking *pratyakṣeṣu* as *pratyakṣam*.

673. I.e., of not becoming attached to sense faculties and objects.

674. The Tibetan differs considerably here: "As long as a yogin is attached to the village [consisting] of objects and sense faculties, he will not understand the pith instructions of a genuine guru. As long as one does not analyze [this] village [consisting] of objects and sense faculties on the basis of scripture and logic and realize that it is emptiness, [the objects] will naturally appear in such a way, and one will cling [to them]. Who can stop them [then]? This means that it is not possible. It is taught that there is no certainty from [merely] becoming familiar with it."

675. Tib.: "difficult."

676. "Intent" (Skt. *sandhi*, Tib. *dgongs pa*) normally refers to the ultimate meaning behind a teaching that may prove provisional and is delivered simply on account of the disciple's present spiritual level and needs.

677. Going by the commentary, Advayavajra must have read: "No matter what [the object], as long as it is not there (i.e., covered by pith instructions), it [can]not be understood." Rig pa'i ral gri understands, however: "At that time, yogin, you must settle into a nonconceptuality in which whatever an object is and where an object is are not seen" (Schaeffer 2005, 157).

678. Tib.: "How does one understand the very difficult intent taught above? Nobody will. Why is that? As long as any particular subject is not seen in accordance with the pith instructions of the unsurpassable guru, it will not be understood. There are no such things as an object of meditation and a meditator."

Their abandonment, however, is not nirvāṇa. Nor does it arise
just because you want it.
You will not instantly become a lion because you meditate that
you are one.[679]

For those who do not know that, [Saraha] teaches:

The learned ones explain all the treatises[680]
[but] do not know the buddha within [their own] body
and [can][681] not break [the chain of] coming and going.
Still they claim shamelessly, "I am a learned man." (DK_A 66)

The learned ones[682] explain the various treatises. Since these are only verbal elaborations, they are just a cause for their going to hell due to their greed for wealth. They do not know [anything][683] since they do not know the pith instructions of a genuine guru about the buddha existing within [their own] bodies. [Still,] relying on mere words and the transmission of verbal instructions,[684] they give explanations without [having received] the transmission from a guru. They have destroyed themselves and harm others as well. Why is that? Not [only] are they destroyed because of the coming and going in saṃsāra in an immeasurable chain of lives,[685] but they also circle in [a part of] saṃsāra that is characterized by realms such as the great *naraka* [hell]. This is how things stand,[686] and this (i.e., the learned ones' mistake) is also addressed by Kambala[pāda in *Ālokamālā* 151–55]:

Syllables, words, statements,
gender, number,
and action-agent relationships
are devoid of meaning, not referring [to anything real]. (ĀM 151)

679. These two verses are missing in the Tibetan. The source of the original is untraced.

680. Tib.: "All the learned ones explain the [various] treatises..."

681. Supplied from the Tibetan.

682. Tib.: "All the learned ones..."

683. "They do not know [anything]" is missing in the Tibetan.

684. "And the transmission of verbal instructions" is missing in the Tibetan.

685. Tib.: "This is because of being the cause for the saṃsāra of coming and going in an immeasurable [chain of] lives."

686. Missing in the Tibetan.

Why not accept a verse
in three or even five verse quarters?
[The number is arbitrary], like the order of a ḍākinī, because the statement
[merely] depends on [the meaning] to be expressed. (ĀM 152)

If it is [concrete] things that need to be perceived,
why have ancient [grammarians],
who pass for intelligent, exposed this world
to the pitfall of Sanskrit grammar? (ĀM 153)

When asked, you could simply answer:
"This is [my] nose,"
and, bending your arm,
point to it with your hand. (ĀM 154)

By [the use of] words that admit a multitude
of intonations, both you and [other] people are,
of your own accord, reduced to a [level of] insignificance
comparable to a casket of stones.[687] (ĀM 155)

Then they shamelessly claim: "I am learned," even though they are stupid.[688]
[Next, Saraha] says:

Anyone alive who does not age
would be free from old age and death. (DK_A 67ab)

This exemplifies the meaning taught above. If someone is not afflicted by old age and the like at any time during his entire life until the end, then he would be free from old age and death. No such thing [can] be observed anywhere. This is the first [half of the dohā, i.e., 67ab]. It is seen that life has death as its end, for all sentient beings are [eventually] seized by fever and other such [maladies].[689]

[As for] the second [half, below], just as the element of mercury, as soon as it has been deoxidized and distilled (*jāritasārita*), [can] penetrate the eight met-

687. For an edition and translation of these verses see Lindtner 2003, 63–64. Our translation mainly follows his.

688. "Even the stupid ones" is missing in the Tibetan.

689. The part starting with "This is the first" is missing in the Tibetan.

als until [they] become gold,[690] so too does the nectar of not aging and dying prevent sentient beings from aging, [even] when [their] time of death [will have come]. From early on until he is old, the yogin has a stainless intellect, thanks to his consumption [of pith instructions] and so forth. Who becomes free from aging and dying?[691] [Saraha] says:

> He whose intellect [becomes] stainless by [following]
> the guru's pith instructions. Who is more fortunate?[692] (DK_A 67cd)

His stainless intellect, by which[693] freedom from aging and death is attained according to the pith instructions of a genuine guru, terminates all bad influences. [This freedom has the nature of] the four *kāyas*, namely the *dharma*[*kāya*], *saṃbhoga*[*kāya*], *nirmāṇa*[*kāya*], and [*kāya* of] great bliss.[694] All contamination is terminated by this [freedom]. [His stainless intellect] does this and nothing else. Therefore, [such a] person is most fortunate. This is the idea.[695]

[Next, Saraha] says:

> Those who do not embrace the pure objects [of cognition]
> but concern themselves only with [their being] empty
> are like a crow that has flown away from a ship:
> it circles[696] but [has to] land on it again. (DK_A 68)

Someone who does not embrace the pure objects by enjoying them as the five objects of sensual pleasure, as instructed by the guru, would thereby not attain the unsurpassable. Because of lacking these [pure objects], he attends to

690. Tib.: "Just as the element of mercury transforms the eight metals into gold without exhausting [itself], only by burning [the metals]..."

691. Tib.: "Who observes that a yogin of a stainless intellect gets old and dies, as long as his consumption [of pith instructions] and so forth have been limitless right from the beginning?"

692. The Tibetan is in the declarative.

693. I.e., taking the initial *yaḥ* as *yena* depending on *vimalamatinā*.

694. The corresponding Tibetan of the first part up to here is as follows: "As to the [attainment of] freedom from birth and death through the yoga practice of an intellect, which [becomes] stainless by [following] the pith instructions of a genuine guru, it has the nature of the four *kāyas*, namely the *dharma*[*kāya*], *saṃbhoga*[*kāya*], *nirmāṇa*[*kāya*], and [*kāya* of] great bliss."

695. Tib.: "Therefore he said that [such a] person is most fortunate."

696. Tib.: "circles and circles."

[impure] objects and concerns himself only with [their state of] being empty. He will not accomplish anything at all by merely concerning himself with empti[ness].[697] It is like a crow that rides on a ship in the middle of the ocean: it takes off and lands on it.[698] Not seeing another place, it lands there again. Likewise, foolish beings, through their saṃsāric[699] deeds, fall into saṃsāra [again] because they merely rely on [an intellectual] view of emptiness.[700] Therefore:

> Do not create bondage [by] clinging to objects.
> Hey, you fools! [This is what] Saraha says.
> Look at the fish, the moth, the elephant,
> the bee, and the herds of deer![701] (DK_A 69)

I, Saraha, explicitly say:[702] "Do not create bondage [by][703] clinging to objects, by enjoying the five objects of sensual pleasure!"[704] If you do so, it is like a fish attached to taste. In its craving for rainwater[705] it gets killed.[706] A moth is attached to forms and dies in a flame. An elephant is brought to his end[707] by tangible objects [placed in a trap], a bee by smell, and a deer by sound. Look yourself! What is it? For all of them [there is death], owing to an event preceded by attachment.[708]

697. Tib.: "Someone who does not enjoy what is attained by what the guru instructed—namely, the five pure objects of sensual pleasure—[someone who thus] merely meditates on emptiness, which is free from these [objects], and attends only to ordinary objects will not accomplish anything at all."

698. Tib.: "A crow on a ship in the ocean, for example, flies away, and not finding another place to land, it returns back to the [ship]."

699. Missing in the Tibetan.

700. Tib.: "an inferior type of emptiness."

701. Tib.: "It is like the fish, the moth, the elephant, the bee, and the deer—look at [what happens to them]!"

702. Tib.: "Saraha explicitly says."

703. According to the Tibetan (B).

704. In the following, each of the five animals are attracted to one of the five objects of the sense faculties.

705. Or, when fish come to the surface to breathe? The underlying idea must be that when fish come to the surface and repeatedly gape, they are extracting *rasa* from the air or rainwater.

706. The Tibetan has "killed by others," presumably other fish?

707. Tib.: "is attached to."

708. The structure of the Tibetan translation is as follows: "If you create bondage by attachment...it is like [the various animals] dying through attachment, because all [their deaths] are preceded by attachment."

[Saraha continues:]

> Whatever manifests in the mind
> lacks an own-nature. (DK$_A$ 70ab)

Whatever manifests in the mind[709]—whatever action is thought of, such as going or eating—all lacks an own-nature.[710] This is because [these manifestations have arisen][711] from ignorance. How is that?[712] Because of the inappropriate behavior of hunters and fishermen[, animals get killed. Likewise,] people filled with desire[713] get killed out of ignorance, and the agent of killing is the servant of the god of death and so forth.[714] Moreover, out of great compassion, the author taught:

> Are waves and water different?
> Cyclic existence and calmness [share] the nature of being like
> space. (DK$_A$ 70cd)

Just as in a river the water is the same as the wave and not different,[715] in the same way, [cyclic existence] has the nature of nothing but quiescence, because the ultimate pure nature of cyclic existence is calmness—it is similar to space and nothing else. What does this teach? Cyclic existence is precisely nirvāṇa. Knowledgeable people [realize this] through the pith instructions of the genuine guru. The ignorant ones do not understand, and they go for objects.[716]

Such wisdom [is addressed in the following:]

709. The commentary translates the Apabhraṃśa into Sanskrit.

710. The Tibetan after "Whatever manifests in the mind" is much shorter here: "—food, movement, and so forth—lacks an own-nature."

711. Supplied from the Tibetan.

712. Missing in the Tibetan.

713. We interpret the genitive plural as a partitive genitive (i.e., a plain nominative).

714. Tib.: "This is because a greedy fisherman kills fish and other such sentient beings while a desire-filled man, [overpowered] by ignorance, thinks that today he will enjoy such and such a woman."

715. In the Sanskrit, the gender has not been used consistently.

716. The Tibetan commentary on DK$_A$ 70cd is as follows: "Just as that which is a river has waves, the purity of saṃsāra is nirvāṇa. What is taught by this? For those who understand the pith instructions of a genuine guru, nirvāṇa is nothing if not saṃsāra. Those who do not understand conceive these [two] as being opposed [to each other]." Note that the Tibetan probably read *viśamaṃ* (*mi mthun par*) instead of *viṣayaṃ*, which can mean either objects of sensual pleasure or reifying saṃsāra and nirvāṇa.

> To whom is it taught? Who will listen?
> Who is absorbed in [its] application?
> [Saṃsāric states] arisen in the heart dissolve [back] into it
> like the dangerous dust of a tunnel [dissolves into the miner's heart].[717] (DK_A 71)

To which ignorant person [can] this profound path be taught? Where are those who are suitable for instruction? There is no one.[718] Who is absorbed in [its] application? Who takes [the teachings] skillfully and follows his (i.e., the guru's) footsteps?[719] Nowhere does anyone become a vessel for these two.[720] [Such] great persons who are appropriate vessels are few. [Suppose] someone digs an underground tunnel from far away in order to overrun an enemy castle. And that can be achieved only by miners and no one else.[721] Why is that? In the case of such narrow digging, invasive dust is produced that immediately [suffocates and][722] kills those with delicate health.[723] As miners have an extremely stable heart,[724] the dust is dissolved in their heart, and the [bits of] earth [on their body] fall down to the ground.[725] [This works] because the first [thing they do] when they start [digging] is to burn (i.e., abandon) some [impurities from their heart]. Likewise, for someone with experience from former lives, there is enlightenment in the great *saṃsāra*. The idea is that one [must] have the heart for it.[726]

The qualities of this [enlightenment] are taught [in the following]:

717. Tib.: "To whom is it taught? To whom should one listen? Who penetrates its intent? [Saṃsāra] dissolves into the mind like the dust of a tunnel [into the pores of the skin]." The first part of the Tibetan root text (DK_A 71ab) differs: "If you correctly employ what is taught, what you heard, in accordance with the intent."

718. This sentence is missing in the Sanskrit.

719. Tib.: "Where is the expert who [can] penetrate its intent?"

720. I.e., the teaching and the practice. Instead of this sentence the Tibetan has only: "There is nobody."

721. Tib.: "Such digging can only be undertaken by someone with previous experience and not by anyone else."

722. Supplied from the Tibetan.

723. Lit.: "of a small heart"; the Tibetan has *srog snyi ba*.

724. Tib.: "mind."

725. Tib.: "They are not killed by the dangerous dust because, in the case of miners, [the dust] is dissolved into [their] pores."

726. Tib.: "Likewise, through previous experience, some accomplish great enlightenment from within saṃsāra, because it is an appropriate vessel for them."

As long as you pour [only] water into water,
its taste remains the same.
Pondering[727] faults and qualities,
O fool, is not an antidote.[728] (DK_A 72)

It is as follows: When pouring water into the water from the great oceans, the water [will still] have the same taste. In a similar way, one may ponder over the faults and qualities of saṃsāra and so forth, but this will not become an antidote [to overcome saṃsāra, even] for someone who thoroughly knows this and has great power.[729] Why is that? It is because the faults are the objects of the five sensual pleasures, while the teachings of the various gurus are the means of purifying them.[730] It is because [the sensual pleasures] are constantly remembered [as pointed out by the guru]—in other words, because of their continuous flow (i.e., presence), like the water of a river.[731]

In order to make this clear, [Saraha] says:

Do not become attached to empti[ness]!
[Friends!][732] Think of this or that [appearance] as equal!
Even the mere husk of a sesame seed
becomes a thorn and inevitably gives rise to painful experience.
(DK_A 73)

Do not become attached to emptiness alone! The [unwanted consequence][733] of doing so is nihilism.[734] You could keep on thinking about the sameness with regard to things, which have an own-nature, but they do not [exist] in

727. Apa. *–cittao*, Tib. *sems rnams*.

728. This is the oldest attested verse, quoted in Bhavabhaṭṭa's (mid-tenth century) *Catuṣpīṭhanibandha* on *Catuṣpīṭhatantra* III.4.11 (MS Kaiser Library 134 [pc], fol. $39b_2$). Thus, if we accept that Saraha knew the *Hevajratantra* (ca. 900 CE), we can place him at the beginning of the tenth century.

729. The Tibetan has no equivalent for *cintitāḥ* and reads: "[Even] a great being with complete knowledge of faults and qualities of saṃsāra and so forth has no antidote whatsoever."

730. In other words, liberation does not result from distinguishing faults from qualitites but from recognizing faults for what they truly are.

731. This second causal clause is missing in the Tibetan.

732. Supplied from the Tibetan.

733. Supplied from the Tibetan.

734. Lit.: "annihilation."

terms of a self![735] In this way, you will not obtain the oneness that encompasses everything—the self as well as the other—because they (i.e., things) are not really different.[736] If you do [continue in this way],[737] you will have the fault [of being attached to emptiness].[738] Even the mere husk of a sesame seed, if inside the eyes, becomes a thorn for you[739] and inevitably causes a [strong] sensation of pain. Likewise, emptiness [understood] in terms of mind-only becomes a thorn for a master of yoga (*yogendra*). Clarity in every aspect [of emptiness] will not be attained.[740]

If one does not meditate [on phenomena as] being empty, not empty, a combination of both, or neither of the two, then how is one to meditate? [Saraha] answers:[741]

> [You may think] it is like that, but[742] this is not the case.
> It is like the activity of a wish-fulfilling jewel. (DK_A 74ab)

You may think that [cognition] is like that—that it has forms that are blue, yellow, and so forth and that it is characterized by having the nature of experience—but this is not the case. This is because [cognition] has the nature of being without a basis for the seeds of all bad influences, such as conceptualizing things as dualities—having an object and not having an object or being mind and no-mind. How is [this to be] understood? It is like the activity of a wish-fulfilling jewel. Even though not[743] everything [can] be seen everywhere [to be coming] from a wish-fulfilling jewel, when it is in one's hand it bestows

735. Tib. "Keep on thinking about the sameness with regard to these and those entities and non-entities!"

736. This amounts to a description of the Yogācāra tenet—a nondual mind empty of self and other.

737. I.e., continue thinking in terms of distinct entities with an own-nature.

738. In the Tibetan this statement differs completely: "Likewise, it must be [realized] that [everything] included in the [categories of] entities—you yourself and other [external objects—manifest] no diversity [among them]. If you take them to [constitute] a diverse multitude, this is a fault."

739. We do not accept Bagchi's insertion *tuṣamadhye kukalaṅka bhavati* and suggest on the basis of the Tibetan to correct *vastunāntargataṃ* to *cakṣurantargatam*.

740. The Tibetan here is as follows: "Just as the mere husks of sesame seeds cause great pain when they are put into the eyes, so too does a master of yoga [experience] similar [difficulties] when attached to emptiness."

741. Missing in the Tibetan.

742. Apa. *para*.

743. There is no negation in the Tibetan.

all results that are wished for, even though it is insentient. Likewise, a yogin holds in his hand a precious jewel, the guru's pith instructions, which can, if wished for,[744] bestow buddhahood. This is the idea.

For the proud paṇḍitas who do not understand it in such a way, [Saraha] explains:[745]

> Oh, how strange! The paṇḍita has been destroyed by his
> confusion.[746]
> [Therefore,] it is taught that great bliss must be experienced by
> oneself.[747] (DK_A 74cd)

"Strange" means "astonishing."[748] Relying merely on the written word,[749] the paṇḍita comes to ruin through confusion.[750] As for this coming to ruin,[751] where does it come from?[752] It is [simply] because he does not apprehend self-awareness, which is contained in everything existent. To put it plainly, he has no sensation [of it].[753] Because of this confusion—which has been explained in this way as having the nature of [conceptualized dualities, such as] mind and no-mind—the defining characteristic of self-awareness is mentioned in terms of great bliss.[754] [The bliss aroused from] contact with an actual woman [is taught to pertain to the level of apparent truth].[755]

744. The Sanskrit has a negation, which does not make sense: "...[even] if not...," unless the meaning is "*volens nolens.*"

745. Tib.: "[Saraha] teaches the true state of the proud paṇḍitas who do not understand it in such a way."

746. Tib.: "...claims to destroy confusion."

747. I.e., reading in accordance with the commentary Apa. *bhāsia* instead of *vāsia*. The Tibetan translation of the root text (*bag chags kyis*) supports *vāsia* in compound, even though the *kyis* is difficult to construe. DK_A 74d would then be: "Self-awareness is permeated by great bliss."

748. Tib.: "provoking laughter."

749. Lit.: "letters"; Tib.: "vowels, consonants, and so forth."

750. Tib.: "The paṇḍita claims to destroy delusion."

751. Tib.: "He does not refute (i.e., destroy) entities."

752. Tib.: "Why is that?"

753. The Tibetan for the last two sentences is: "...not apprehend, i.e., not aware, with self-awareness of what is contained in all entities. This is the intent."

754. I.e., taking the locative plural as a locative singular. In the Tibetan there is a nominative.

755. The addition in brackets is supplied from the Tibetan.

Again, in order to teach how to stabilize[756] this bliss,[757] which is based on external [causes], [Saraha] says:

> All forms[758] should be made space-like in that [great bliss],[759]
> and the mental consciousness should be placed in this space-like nature. (DK_A 75ab)

All objects, starting with form, should be made space-like in that [great bliss].[760] Even mental consciousness is placed in this space-like nature. Once that has been done, [Saraha] says:

> And that mind, too, [should be] made into no-mind within that [great bliss].
> That supreme [being] shines forth within coemergent nature.[761] (DK_A 75cd)

In a like manner,[762] the mind, in its space-like nature, [should be] made into no-mind within that [great bliss]. Whoever practices in this way is a supreme being. To be precise, "shines forth" means "plays" within the coemergent nature.

Likewise, [Saraha] says:

> In every house there is talk of purity,[763]
> [yet] the place of great bliss is not properly known. (DK_A 76ab)

In every house people of base intention, in order to cheat people, say: "Such is the explanation of purity. Based on these words, you will be pure beginning from today. You must realize the supreme explanation, which is truly different from that [which others say]. It brings about that [purity], which is the con-

756. Lit.: "with stability."

757. Following the Tibetan, we read "bliss" instead of "great bliss."

758. Tib.: "phenomena."

759. I.e., taking up great bliss qua self-awareness in DK_A 74d.

760. "In that" is missing in the Tibetan.

761. DK_A 75cd is quoted in the *Fragment with Apabhraṃśa Citations*. Tib. (B; DP are not metrical): "If this mind is taken to be no-mind, the coemergent is very beautiful."

762. Missing in the Tibetan.

763. Tib.: "In every house they talk about it."

ducive basis for great bliss." Therefore this[764] [talk] is only some old wives' tale. It is as taught [in *Ālokamālā* 280]:

> To have seen serpents'[765] traces in water,
> created garlands of sky flowers,
> and woven pieces of threadless cloth—
> how can these people not feel shame[766] [when they claim such things]? (ĀM 280)

The author is taken aback at seeing [people] of such base [intention] and teaches, beginning with "Saraha":[767]

> Saraha says: The world is overpowered by [conceptual] mind:[768]
> no one realizes no-mind. (DK_A 76cd)

The entire world (stupid people) is overpowered (enslaved) by confused paṇḍitas with their sundry [prattle] about mind and no-mind, which we have already explained.[769] [Thus they say:] "According to my instructions, you abandon the [conceptual] mind,[770] and you attain the nature of no-mind."[771] This is not the case.[772] Why? The defining characteristic of no-mind cannot be perceived by any [discursive] method. Why is that? Well, is there a reflexive awareness in such [insentient] things as wood and stones, which have the nature of no-mind? Has anybody identified such a nature of no-mind? It cannot be identified! It is because [wood and stones] have had that [insentient] nature throughout beginningless time.[773]

764. The corresponding Tibetan is incomplete: "Although people of base intention give explanations in every house in order to cheat people, this..."

765. Tib.: "water serpents."

766. Tib.: "People do not feel shame..."

767. "Beginning with Saraha" is missing in the Tibetan.

768. Tib.: "Everybody bears his mental burden:"

769. Tib.: "Proud *paṇḍitas* and deluded people bear [their] mental burden, which consists of the above-mentioned manifold [appearances in the] mind. They are enslaved by it. Therefore..."

770. Tib.: "If you look at such a [tormented] mind according to my instructions..."

771. From here on, the Tibetan is incomplete.

772. For the remaining part of the commentary starting with "This is not the case," the Tibetan has the following: "[How can] you see the mind and identify [it as] no-mind? It is said that it cannot be identified, because the mind does not have an own-nature in the first place."

773. It should be noted that Advayavajra takes "no-mind" in its literal sense (i.e., as insentient)

The one divinity is seen in many textual traditions.
It clearly manifests in accordance with our own preference.
(DK$_A$ 77)

It is only because of [our various] notions[774] of the appearance of the one divinity that we see it [differently] from within the numerous textual traditions and in accordance with[775] our respective views. It clearly manifests in accordance with our own preference and not otherwise. This is also as stated in the *Hevajratantra*:

One is oneself the destroyer,
the creator,[776] the king, and the lord (i.e., *sahaja*). (HT I.viii.45cd)

In order to teach this [Saraha] says:

The self (*ātman*) is the lord, and everything external is opposed to it.
This [Śaiva] tenet is common[777] in every house. (DK$_A$ 78ab)

[Wise people] do not desire a "self" and "mine." [Otherwise] there will be ruin because one will be carried away by contemptible thoughts.[778] Moreover, [if God were absolute, this] would obstruct the existence of other things (i.e., things other than God). This is because there would be a contradiction in how they have arisen.[779] In every house this [Śaiva] tenet[780] is common. [It is false.] Why? Because [things indeed appear to] arise and pass out of existence.[781] If there is, to start with, a passing out of existence, whose arising [are we talking about]? Or, if there is arising, what is [its] passing out of existence?[782] Therefore

and not in the sense of nonconceptual mind (as suggested by the Tibetan).

774. Tib.: "names."

775. Based on the Tibetan, we take the locative as instrumental.

776. The Tibetan has the reverse order: "...the creator. The destroyer..."

777. Lit.: "established." The word is missing in the Tibetan.

778. Tib.: "Clinging to a 'self' and 'mine,' desire binds oneself and makes oneself contemptible because one is carried away by thoughts."

779. Tib.: "Moreover, there would be a contradiction through the obstruction of other things because [other things] would have arisen prior to him."

780. The Tibetan wrongly qualifies "tenet" with "that things arise and pass out of existence."

781. From here on, the Tibetan is incomplete.

782. Instead of these two questions the Tibetan reads: "As to being hostile, if [the other] had

neither is true.[783] This is why it is taught in this way. Such is the intent of distinguished yogins. Those who are settled in this [truth] have acquired [such] wisdom about the [real nature of the self] on the basis of the pith instructions of a guru.[784] Those without such pith instructions do not have it. This was [initially] not approved of by the buddhas and bodhisattvas. To the [theists, however,][785] the Illustrious One taught in the *Hevajratantra*:

> This entire world is born from me.
> The threefold world is born from me.
> The whole visible world is pervaded by me;
> it consists of nothing else.[786] (HT I.viii.41)

To these contemptible people he gives the following example:[787]

> [It would follow that] one eats food, and [all][788] others digest the food.
> Having gone outside, she looks for [another] man. (DK_A 78cd)

It is just as if one person eats food and others digest the food and so forth. [This is absurd,] because it cannot be shared [in this way].[789] Or, suppose a person is feeding yogins, and another [yogin] wishing to eat will speak, prattling, ["I have not eaten"].[790] Or, the mistress of the house abandons her husband and goes out looking for [another] man.[791] [As for the notion of] "other," [it occurs] because of the mind being manifold, but [in fact everything] is one

arisen, how could it pass out of existence [and be hostile]?"

783. Here, the Tibetan commentary on DK_A 78ab stops.

784. Or, according to the reading of Skt. (N): "Such is the intent of distinguished yogins: To recognize the Self within the lord (i.e., Śiva) is a comtemptible view."

785. If the quoted *Hevajra* verse is a valid objection to Śaiva theism, it must have been commonly understood that the anthropomorphic Buddhist ultimate (Heruka) is *sahaja*, taken in the sense of dependent arising and emptiness.

786. This verse is not found in the Tibetan.

787. Tib.: "He teaches with unfortunate examples."

788. Supplied from the Tibetan.

789. The line is pointing out the absurd consequence that God eats (i.e., destroys) the world and the souls digest it.

790. This example points to the problem of reifying categories. If you feed yogins as a real unit, there should not be another hungry yogin left.

791. Advayavajra understands DK_A 78d as: "[Or] having gone outside, she looks for [some other] provider of nourishment."

in terms of wisdom. Such are [the kinds of behavior] of the ignorant. There is satisfaction in one: [the good mistress of the house] knows only one [husband] without [being available] everywhere. Those of poor intelligence, however, have a mind [deluded by "self" and "other"] such that they are destroyed by it.[792] [Thus, it is said:]

> He is not seen to come or go,
> nor is he perceived to abide.
> She runs after the unwavering
> and unstained supreme lord.[793] (DK_A 79)

Continuing the idea of the previous verse, [Saraha] teaches that even clever people entertain such ideas.[794] [It would absurdly follow that when,] for example, the mistress of the house feeds the man of her own house, she would [simultaneously] prepare food for a man of another house. She would leave home and look for [her][795] husband. Or then he may then come, [but this] is not seen [by her]. He may leave,[796] [but this] is not noticed [by her]. He may stay [home], [but this is] not known [to her]. Such type of knowledge [as that held by the nondualist Śaiva] perceives[797] him (i.e., the lord) as unwavering, being the supreme lord by his own accord and unstained—that is to say, free of all trouble.

What is taught by this? In our system, for yoginīs who are born in the sites of pilgrimage and other power places,[798] it is a natural wisdom that arises. She does not cognize anything [in a dualistic way, but] she [entirely][799] sees in perfect identity [with *sahaja*]. She thinks: "[Everything] is produced by me, cre-

792. Tib.: "So somebody, having eaten his own food, [proceeds to] destroy all the other food, since others have no meaningful purpose [to him]. Or, that the mistress of the house should leave her husband and search outside for some other men is due to such a base state of mind. Indeed, that is how the mind of base people [in perceiving a 'self' and 'other'] is."

793. The second part of the verse differs in the Tibetan: "The unfluctuating supreme lord must be meditated upon as being unstained."

794. Tib.: "that this is the meditation of those with superior intelligence."

795. Tib.: "another."

796. In the Tibetan, "come" and "leave" are in reverse order.

797. The Tibetan did not understand here that the knowledge of a Śaiva system is being described and distorts the intent by using "must be preceived."

798. I.e., women born in power places, such as the twenty-four power places of Cakrasaṃvara. See Templeman 1989, 121n88.

799. Supplied from the Tibetan.

ated by me," and more in detail. This is how it should be taken in accordance with the pith instructions of the guru.

[Next, Saraha] says:

> He comes and goes, not [being able] to abandon [his own wife].
> How will he win the extraordinary woman?[800] (DK_A 80)

He[801] comes and goes,[802] not [being able] to abandon his own wife. She does not even ask [her] husband [to stay].[803] This[804] is quite common in power places such as Kāmarūpa. It is just as if someone were to leave home for another country and return after having gone halfway. Such is the power of the yoginī's wisdom.[805] What does it do? It is said: Even after going to some [other] place, he [wishes but] does not[806] have intercourse with an extraordinary woman. At that time, he suffers in mind[807] because of his delusion. Where is that extraordinary woman? He does not find her. Is [that] appropriate?[808] [Saraha] says:

> When the [bodhi]citta[809] is set at the forehead, it shines.[810]
> Do not see it as separate from your own body. (DK_A 81ab)

800. The meter changes here from *dohā* to *pādākulaka*.

801. The Sanskrit text continues to switch between third-person plural and third-person singular. The singular is used here throughout.

802. Again the sequence differs in the Tibetan.

803. This sentence has no equivalent in the Sanskrit.

804. Tib.: "Such [practice]."

805. Ignoring that *prabhāva* is in the ablative and following the Tibetan, except that the Tibetan has only "yoginī," not "yoginī's wisdom."

806. The negation is supported by the Tibetan and also the context, according to which it is fruitless to seek *sahaja* bliss outside one's body, metaphorically referred to as one's own house.

807. I.e., taking *tena* as an ergative, referring to the yogin.

808. Tib.: "Why would he do that? After leaving [home], he meets an extraordinary woman and wishes to remain [with her]. Unable to meet her, he returns home. Why is that?" The extraordinary woman stands for blissful levels in and above the yogin's future excrescence (*uṣṇīṣa*) on top of the head, to which he ascends. The own wife stands for his body, to which the yogin is forced to return. Oral explanation given by Kulavadhuta Satpurananda, Santiniketan, Feb. 2012.

809. The Tibetan reads *byang sems*.

810. This fits well Satpurananda's explanation of DK_A 80, where the extaraordinary woman stands for bliss levels in the space above his body. Shahidullah (1928, 156) reads *lirāre* (Skt. *lalāṭe*) instead of *ṇirāle*, which is supported by Tib. *dpral pa*.

Through the[811] yoginī (i.e., the extraordinary woman),[812] blissful [bodhi]citta shines as it is set at the forehead, like a house [becoming beautiful] through the light refracted through a jewel.[813] Object of knowledge and knowledge become inseparable, and body and bliss will not be different, which is to say they become of one nature. For this reason alone, [Saraha] will speak. It is as follows: your body (*rūpa*) abides with separate parts, such as eyes. When the [bodhicitta] is set by her (i.e., the yoginī), you will not see separate body [parts]. Why? The cloth woven of threads becomes one single piece. Therefore, [in a like manner,] when the bodies of women or men are pervaded by the wisdom of nondistinction, then there is no sense of separation [anymore], as in the case of the thread [and the woven cloth]. This is how the wisdom of the yogins is. Moreover, it arises from [their] nature, and it is not produced by her (i.e., the yoginī). They spontaneously achieve the cause of all fruits.[814]

[Saraha continues:]

> As long as [the distinction between] body, speech, and mind is not destroyed,
> [people] will not shine within the coemergent nature.[815]
> (DK$_A$ 81cd)

As long as through this wisdom[816] and the kindness of the guru, ordinary people's [distinction into] body, speech, and mind is not destroyed, does not melt [into the coemergent][817]—that is, as long as [their] base influences have not dis-

811. The yoginīs are repeatedly referred to by the instrumental of feminine and masculine demonstrative pronouns in the singular and plural. This is clear from the context here, and it is impossible that such an inconsistency is a mere oversight or due to a poor command of Sanskrit grammar.

812. Following *tayā* further down, we take *yoginībhiḥ* as a singular.

813. Lit.: "the shadow of a jewel."

814. The Tibetan commentary on DK$_A$ 81ab is comparatively short: "When the [bodhi]citta of the yogin, the blissful mind, has reached [his] forehead, it looks beautiful. Even if he does not wish it, it comes to be ever more inseparable from his own body. Body and bliss [indeed eventually] become inseparable."

815. Tib.: "When body, speech, and mind are not separate [from bodhicitta] the coemergent nature shines."

816. Based on the Tibetan, we emend *jñānaṃ* to *jñānena*.

817. Tib.: "Through this wisdom, the inseparably contained body, speech, and mind of ordinary people melt into the [coemergent] through the instructions of a genuine guru."

appeared—they do not[818] shine within the coemergent nature. For this reason, the unsurpassable tradition of yoginīs will be attained.[819]

What is this tradition of yoginīs? [Saraha says:]

> In some[820] places the mistress of the house
> eats the husband unbeknown.[821] (DK$_A$ 82ab)

In [some][822] locations a husband [appears to] be eaten by his own wife.[823] We see this in such power places as sacred sites. [But] such [a perception] is unbeknown to ordinary people.[824] It is not [wrongly] imagined [in this way] by the masters of yogins (*yogīndra*).

Their (i.e., the yoginīs') true state [Saraha] teaches [next]:[825]

> And when she has killed him,[826] whom else will she honor? [No one].
> The conduct of the yoginīs is at odds [with worldly convention]. (DK$_A$ 82cd)

Where her [own] husband is killed, there will be no honoring of others.[827] But she renders supreme honor to others.[828] This is the nature of the yoginīs' wisdom.[829] Other ordinary [persons] see with their human eyes that [a man] gets

818. Following the Apabhraṃśa of the root text, the negation particle must be inserted. This is also supported by the Tibetan translation of the commentary, even though the Tibetan does not have the negation in its root text.

819. In the Tibetan *yena* is not understood as a relative pronoun introducing a causal clause, and *ji ltar* ("how") is added, making it a question: "By whom and how is this unsurpassable tradition of yoginīs attained?"

820. Lit.: "which."

821. Tib.: "But such a perception should not be taken at face value."

822. Supplied from the Tibetan.

823. Based on the Tibetan, we emend *svagharaṇī ca* into *svagharaṇyā.*

824. Tib.: "... such a perception should not be taken at face value."

825. Tib.: "As for the purpose of these [lines]:"

826. This first part of the line is missing in the Tibetan.

827. Tib.: "whom else will she honor?"

828. The image is that under normal circumstances such a woman would be a widow and not able to honor anyone anymore, but the yoginī, inasmuch as she is *sahaja,* continues to honor others, being available to all yogins.

829. The Tibetan connects and extends the two sentences: "But when she renders supreme honor to others, they do not get killed, because this is [only] the nature of the yoginī's wisdom."

killed and eaten, but yoginīs neither kill nor eat [anyone]. It is rather that he[830] who is full of the coemergent and whose nature is the coemergent is dissolved into the coemergent.[831] This is the idea. Therefore the yoginīs' conduct is at odds with all treatises and worldly convention.[832]

To make this clear, [Saraha] says:

> The husband is eaten and becomes radiant within the
> coemergent.[833]
> Passion and dispassion is performed [again],[834]
> and she stands next to her own[835] [husband] being broken in her
> mind.
> [Such] a yoginī appears to me.[836] (DK_A 83)

Once her [own][837] husband is eaten and becomes radiant within the coemergent nature, she starts [the cycle of] passion and dispassion again and looks for other men.[838] She cries for [previous forms of] passion and dispassion, mourning former husbands.[839] She stands in front of her own beloved one.[840] Thus the yoginī [appears to] be broken in her mind—as if she had no mind.[841] This is how she appears to me or the masters of yoga.[842]

To sum up, the wisdom of a yoginī is such because it is without duality. What needs to be done and action do not[843] appear to him [anymore]. He

830. I.e., ignoring the neuter endings.

831. The Tibetan abbreviates: "It is rather that he dissolves into the coemergent nature."

832. The Tibetan adds: "It [can]not be comprehended."

833. Tib.: "and the coemergent shines."

834. I.e., a state of relaxation after union, in which passion is only remembered ("passion"), as its intense form has ceased ("dispassion").

835. Even though unmetrical, Tib. *gnyug ma'i drung du gnas* corresponds better to the Apabhraṃśa.

836. Tib.: "As the [desirous] mind is losing out, I see the yoginī."

837. Supplied from the Tibetan.

838. The last part of the sentence starting with "and" is missing in the Tibetan.

839. Tib.: "She also causes pain through other husbands, former husbands of sorts."

840. I.e., the husband is directly confronted with his *sahaja.*

841. The yoginī is the *sahaja* mind, in which or rather through which all dualistic conceptuality is broken.

842. This sentence is incomplete and incomprehensible in the Sanskrit: "It appears to me, the master of yoga or..."

843. The Tibetan has no negation particle and did not translate *tasya* ("for him"). The Dpal

is not bound by virtuous and unvirtuous actions. This [being eaten] is only the appearance for ordinary people.[844] Everything else [too] has arisen from mind through discrimination.[845] The husband is [thus] overpowered by his own mind, and [his] body [only appears to be] eaten.[846] It is [his own] mind [that manifests] a body, a sacred place, a subsidiary sacred place, and so forth. The yoginīs are [simply] the true nature [of all this projection]. Stopping the [yoginīs], one stops the natural energies (*prakṛti*[847]).[848] What is apprehended then?[849] [All] this must be learned through the pith instructions of a genuine guru.

Having thus settled this issue, the following is elucidated:[850]

> She eats and drinks, not conceptualizing
> whatever comes to mind.[851]
> [Does this] affect her mind? Hey, the path of the yoginī is difficult to fathom[852]
> and way beyond compare! DK_A 84

Whatever[853] act she performs—eating, drinking, and the like—she does without interruption.[854] She does whatever comes to mind.[855] But this does not

spungs edition (B) inserts a *pa med* after *bya ba dang byed*: "[Things] appear without [the concept of] what needs to be done and action." Otherwise one would have to understand: "What needs to be done and action [may still] appear, but...."

844. Tib.: "No matter what wholesome deeds or wrongdoings she engages in, she is not harmed by it, for [only] to ordinary beings does this [distinction (i.e., wholesome and not)] appear in the way it does."

845. Tib.: "This is because, among other things, everything is [only] a projection of the mind."

846. Tib.: "Because the husband is overpowered by his own mind..."

847. I.e., the eighty *prakṛti* of the Ārya school. See Tomabechi 2006, 72–73.

848. Tib.: "one would not apprehend anything."

849. This question is missing in the Tibetan.

850. In the Tibetan there is no introduction to the next verse.

851. The Tibetan is difficult to construe here. It differs considerably from DK_T.

852. See the commentary below where *kiṃ tu manavāhi na kriyate* is translated by *'on kyang sems la gnod pa ni mi bya'o* |. The Tibetan must have taken *-vāhi* as *bāhya* ("outside"), read *dukkha* (nonmetrical) instead of *dullakkha*, and translated: "When one [is busy with objects] outside the mind, suffering increases."

853. Tib.: "However slight the..."

854. Advayavajra understood Apa. *vichinna* in the sense of "interrupted" instead of "conceptualizing."

855. Tib.: "Whatever comes to mind must be done."

affect her mind. What is the use of something so difficult to fathom by reason? For those who have the wisdom of the yoginīs, [all] is dissolved, as [explained] before.[856] The path of yoginīs is way beyond compare, [but] he who follows it will be all right.[857] It cannot be otherwise.

Again, [Saraha] says:[858]

> She who does not distinguish day and night
> and whose emanation is the threefold world
> that is the accomplishment of mind, the yoginī,
> the wisdom that is coemergent highest bliss (*śaṃvara*).[859]
> (DK$_A$ 85)

She who thus knows neither day nor night, who is endowed with a wisdom that does not distinguish [day and night],[860] and whose emanation is the threefold world, that is the yoginī, the accomplishment of mind, the wisdom of the coemergent highest bliss. Or, [the epithets are meant to refer to the yogin,] who makes it directly manifest. To those who do not know it in such a way, [Saraha] says:[861]

> The whole world is obsessed with words / the indestructible (*akṣara*),
> but everybody is illiterate.[862]

856. The Tibetan equivalent of this question and answer differs: "As [explained] before, this illusionary yoginī dissolves into the coemergent, like [her] wisdom [itself], which is difficult to fathom."

857. Tib.: "Since the path of yoginīs is extraordinary, it being a difficult path, all will be well [only] when its elixir has turned everything into bliss."

858. Missing in the Tibetan.

859. Reading *saṃvara*, the Tibetan has *sdom pa* ("binding").

860. Tib.: "wisdom inseparable [from body, speech and mind]." The commentary deviates here from the root text. One would expect an explanation of *abhinnamati* and not only an attribute (*abhinnajñānamayam*) qualifying the threefold world.

861. Tib.: "This mind, which thus knows neither day nor night and whose wisdom-nature of inseparable body, speech, and mind emanates the threefold world, is the yoginī of accomplishment. The binding of [this] coemergent [nature] has become wisdom—that is, one makes it directly manifest."

862. Lit.: "there is no one who is not illiterate." The verse must be also understood with the following second meaning: "Everyone is obsessed with the indestructible, but there is no one who realizes the indestructible."

> [But] once words are thoroughly understood[863] [for what they truly are],
> one will get past words (becoming truly illiterate). (DK_A 86)

The whole world is obsessed with words. The learned ones say: "This is you," "This is a vase," or "This is a woven cloth."[864] They do this for their entire life,[865] and nothing of the ultimate is achieved.[866] Those who are the [truly] illiterate achieve buddhahood.[867] Reflecting [on words,] the entire net of words is definitely proven false; once words are thoroughly understood, one will get past words.[868] As long as this has not been done, what ultimate meaning could be attained?[869]

What is it [like]?[870] [Saraha] teaches it:

> As it is outside, so it is within.
> [The masters of yoga] abide on the fourteenth level continuously. (DK_A 87ab)

For the masters of yoga, the outside is as within. What then is the purpose of representations (*ākāra*)[871] of knowledge?[872] [The masters of yoga] abide on the fourteenth level continuously without beginning or end, in the manner of the supreme [invisible] phase of the moon.[873] This is because the yogin[874] is [then]

863. Tib.: *rab shes pa*. Apa. *gholiā* is not clear. Is it related to Skt. *ghūrṇitākṣara*?

864. The bizarrely phrased *idaṃ tvayā* perhaps refers to the *mahāvākya*s of the Upaniṣads such as *tat tvam asi*. The vase (*ghaṭa*) and the cloth (*paṭa*) are typical examples for objects in the outside world (cf. English "tables and chairs").

865. This first part of the sentence is missing in the Tibetan.

866. Tib.: "exists."

867. Tib.: "Nobody is the [truly] illiterate, who accomplishes buddhahood."

868. Tib.: "Therefore words [must] be thoroughly understood; by careful analysis the stains of verbal fabrication are overcome and proven false. This is when one gets past words."

869. Tib.: "...the ultimate meaning is not attained."

870. The question is missing in the Sanskrit.

871. Tib.: "appearance."

872. I.e., taking *jñānākāratvāt* in the sense of *jñānākāratvena*. The Tibetan took it as a causal clause but ignored *kiṃ tarhi*.

873. I.e., reading *paramakalābhāvena* instead of *paramakalābhāvāt*. The Tibetan has "because the supreme phase of the moon does not exist," which does not fit the context. The Tibetan also specifies here that there are sixteen phases.

874. "The yogin" is missing in the Tibetan.

without a body, just like the supreme phase of the moon[, which is not visible] at the end of the new moon.[875] Therefore, [Saraha] says:[876]

> The exquisite[877] bodiless is hidden in the body.
> Whoever realizes it is liberated. (DK_A 87cd)

The exquisite is hidden in a sentient being, which means it (i.e., the body) has clearly disappeared. One is liberated in that [true state] by which it[878] (i.e., the bodiless) is known. Why is that? This is because the appearance of the coemergent must be recognized by oneself.[879] And this should [have] happened at the beginning before one has obtained a body.[880] It is knowledge without representations. The activity of bliss indicates it.[881] The nectar it yields is the so-called coemergent. People are born from the coemergent, and when they die, they are absorbed into it again. The bliss, [however,] is not constant, for it lacks a basis. Therefore, before birth, knowledge without representations is called *dharmadhātu* and the like. Whoever realizes this in accordance with the guru's pith instructions is liberated in this life through this very body, and not in any other way.

Having taught [this] in this [verse], the author, by conclusion, does not see [the body and bodiless] as separate (lit. "self" and "other") things. Therefore this [is what Saraha] expressed:[882]

> First, I [could] read [the sentence]: "May there be realization!"
> [Later,] I drank the essence [of its meaning] and [the rest] became
> pointless.

875. This refers to the sixteenth phase of the moon, the miraculous, most subtle phase (*paramakalā*).

876. Tib.: "This, [Saraha] teaches in the following:"

877. Missing in the Tibetan.

878. I.e., changing the *sa* into a neuter form.

879. I.e., taking *pratyātmavedako* in the sense of *pratyātmavedanīyo*.

880. Namely, when one is still in the intermediate state. See Advayavajra's commentary on 21cd, where one is attracted by the bliss of one's future parents. The translation of this sentence remains tentative.

881. Lit.: "is its indicator."

882. The Tibetan commentary on DK_A 87cd is much shorter: "'Bodiless' means 'having truly disappeared,' wherefore it is hidden. He who knows it is liberated. The coemergent, which must be directly realized by each person individually, does not exist for worldly beings as it [really] is, for it is bodiless and has never arisen. Having taught [this] here [means that] the author does not see the existence of a "self" or "other." This is taught in the following:"

> I understood the unique letter / unchangeable [bliss][883] then
> but not its name [anymore], my friend.[884] (DK_A 88)

It is similar to when one is a child: to learn the alphabet at the very beginning, one [writes] in front of the teacher on a wooden slate the sentence "May there be realization!" and so forth. Only then is everything studied, from the letters[885] and the verbal roots up to grammar plus the [tenets of] Tarka and the Mīmāṃsā. In all these letters, not a single result is seen, because of not understanding [the meaning]. But then, while attending a good spiritual friend, [everything] is discussed with thorough knowledge, and [my] first sentence, "May there be realization!" [proves] to be true. Whatever other scriptures I read after that became pointless. It is similar to distilling [fermented] rice and obtaining the distillate: the holder of the vow drinks the distillate, and the rest is pointless. The distillate is the essence. What has been grasped is [the sentence] "May there be realization!" Only this unique unchangeable [bliss][886] mentioned above have I understood in this life. But I do not know the various other names for it, because it is ineffable. Or else, [it can be said that] as a child, one knows [the sentence] "May there be realization!" but when fully grown [and understanding the meaning], one does not think [any longer] about nouns, syllables, and so forth.

Others are stupid and do not understand. For them, [Saraha] says:[887]

883. Saraha profits here from the double meaning of Apa. *akkhara* (Skt. *akṣara*) as "letter" and "unchangeable [bliss]." The unique letter in the sense of unchangeable bliss is also the letter *a*, which stands for luminous emptiness (see Mathes 2015, 246–47).

884. Tib.: "Through which I came to know the single word, its name I do not know [anymore]."

885. Skt. *sūtra* refers here to the *Śivasūtras*—i.e., the alphabet.

886. According to Mokṣākaragupta's understanding. In any case, the result of "May there be realization!" is the understanding of unchangeable bliss.

887. Tib.: "It is as when I was a child learning the alphabet. When I learned in front of the teacher [to write] words such as *father* and *mother* [in their physical shape of] letters on a wooden slate, and [when I wrote] for the first time sentences, such as "May there be realization," I learned and analyzed the strokes of the letters, the roots of the words, and so forth. In all these letters I did not see a single result because of not understanding [the meaning]. Then, by attending to a genuine spiritual friend, a true understanding of the meaning arose; when I analyzed, I read for the first time the [sentence] "May there be realization" in a meaningful way. Otherwise, I would have continued reading without [grasping] the essential [meaning]. When preparing food one takes and drinks the broth and [leaves] the rest (such as bones), which has no essence. Then I understood the unique letter / unchangeable [bliss] of [the sentence] "May there be realization" but not its names, as there were too many of them. This is because it cannot be expressed as being such [and such]. As a child I knew the names [for what is referred to by the sentence] "May there be realization" but not the meaning. Having grown up, I know the meaning but not [its] names."

> Those who do not grasp [*sahaja*] completely [but only] through analysis[888]
> [try] to accomplish great bliss during the [four] moments of erotic bliss.[889] (DK$_A$ 89ab)

By [wrongly] analyzing the coemergent, the whole threefold world is made to fall. [In other words,] it is not grasped in the shape of self-arisen wisdom or in terms of the inexpressible name.[890] They are ruined then, and they delude others.[891] By what means?[892] During the moments of erotic bliss, they [try to] accomplish great bliss.[893] Therefore they are foolish people.[894]

> It is just like the thirsty deer that runs [toward the water of a mirage][895]
> and dies of thirst. Where could it find [such] water in the sky?[896] (DK$_A$ 89cd)

It is just like [a deer] tormented by thirst. Blinded by extreme thirst, it sees water and runs [toward it].[897] Its eyes do not see water but only mist. Thirsty and desiccated, it dies.[898] To put it plainly, where would it find water in the sky?[899] Likewise, true reality is not found through [the bliss of][900] erotic union.

888. The Tibetan mistook Apa. *ruaṇeṃ* ("by analyzing") as *rang bzhin* ("nature").

889. Skt. *kunduru* with the meaning of erotic bliss is first attested in the *Hevajratantra*; see II.iii.60b, where it is taken as "union of the organs" (*indriyayoga*).

890. Tib.: "Somebody who does not know the coemergent is lost in [the saṃsāra of] the threefold world, since he has not realized self-arisen wisdom or the inexpressible nature."

891. Tib.: "On account of this he ruins himself and others."

892. Tib.: "How is that?"

893. The Tibetan takes this sentence as a quotation of DK$_A$ 89b and repeats it in a paraphrase. Our translation follows the Sanskrit, in which *pāda*s 89a and 89b are presented together at the beginning of the commentary.

894. Tib.: "[This is wrong,] for to claim that one will accomplish great bliss through erotic union is a delusion."

895. Supplied from the Tibetan.

896. Instead of the question word *kahiṃ* ("where"), the Tibetan has a simple question particle.

897. Supplied from the Tibetan.

898. Instead of the last two sentences the Tibetan reads: "Not finding water there, [the deer] dies of thirst."

899. Tib.: "How could such water of the sky be found? It [can]not be found."

900. Supplied from the Tibetan.

Where [in the world] could deluded sentient beings realize true reality in such a way?[901] With what reasoning could one even begin?[902]

This is precisely what [Saraha] teaches [next]:[903]

> An[904] investigation of the psychophysical aggregates, elements, sense fields,
> sense faculties, and objects [shows that] they are [like] the water [of a mirage].
> Within these ever-newer dohā verses,
> nothing has been hidden. (DK_A 90)

[Saraha] sees as erroneous the conceptualization of psychophysical aggregates, elements, sense fields, sense faculties, and objects. Where neither the object marked by its defining characteristic nor a defining characteristic is present, the notion of water, like the water in a mirage, [may] be applied to anything at any time.[905] [But] it is not real water, given one's understanding that the mirage is a [mere] appearance. The deception of a mirage, however, creates the appearance of water.

In such a way[906] true reality is taught in ever-newer, ever-different dohā verses. Nothing is kept hidden in the contents of the dohās. The pith instruction of the guru should not be destroyed. This is the meaning. By way of an apology to all paṇḍitas, [Saraha] says:

> Hey, you paṇḍitas! I apologize.
> Nothing has been mentally fabricated here.
> Do I speak about what I received as a teaching from [my] guru
> as something to be kept completely secret? (DK_A 91)

Hey, you paṇḍitas! I have taught the kind of knowledge that is both hidden and not. So please forgive me! For I have not kept secret what should have been secret, and I have elaborated on those things that are not secret. So do

901. Tib.: "Deluded people claim that true reality [can] be found from it."

902. This question is missing in the Tibetan.

903. Tib.: "In order to teach that..."

904. DK_A 90–91 and Advayavajra's commentary on these verses have not been translated into Tibetan and are probably a later insertion.

905. I.e., reading *tatra* instead of *teṣu*, which is Bagchi's conjecture of *-tṛṣu*.

906. The *tasmān* does not make sense here, there being no causal relationship to the previous paragraph.

not make this differentiation [into secret and not secret]. And I am not alone in this practice [of revealing everything]. How so? Because I heard these words openly from my guru. Did he [say, "This is] secret," [and "This is] open? [No, he did not]. So what does [the author] intend to say with this? That [these] topics will be clear to those who are worthy and will remain secret to those who are unworthy.

In the following, [Saraha] teaches precisely this:

> The play of erotic bliss between lotus and thunderbolt—
> who does not rejoice in it?
> Whose expectation is not fulfilled [by it]
> in the threefold world?[907] (DK_A 92)

Through this [the following is intended:] It was taught by the Illustrious One that through [appropriate] means—the play of great attachment—buddhahood [is attained]. [This was meant] for the beginners or yogins of lower[908] capacities and for those fixated on attachment. Such [an approach] has been introduced by Saraha[909] here. Which noble being does not rejoice in the play of erotic bliss [between] lotus and thunderbolt? Whose expectations in the threefold world are not fulfilled by it?[910] The accomplishment of mahāmudrā is possible[911] for everybody since each and every thing (including erotic bliss) is identical with it (i.e., mahāmudrā), [or rather] has its nature.[912] This is certain[913] because great compassion is made directly manifest [in the process].

But[914] [the practice] for those with superior faculties is not like that. What is it, then? If true reality is [realized] through the lotus and the thunderbolt, then once bliss has been generated by oneself, there is no experience of bliss

907. Tib. (DP): "The erotic bliss between lotus and thunderbolt, with which you play—since it cannot [bestow uncontaminated] bliss, how [can] expectations within the threefold world be fulfilled [by it]?" The last two lines in B differ slightly: "by which it (i.e., true bliss) cannot be shown. The hope of what person in the threefold world is [then] fulfilled?"

908. The Sanskrit has "extremely low."

909. Skt.: "me." The Tibetan (BD) confirms that this is Saraha (*mda' bsnun*).

910. Tib.: "But why are the expectations within the threefold world not fulfilled by this play with the bliss of erotic union, in which people of lower capacities are involved?"

911. Lit.: "is fulfilled."

912. Tib.: "...mahāmudrā, which [should be] everybody's hope, [can] be fulfilled."

913. Tib.: "This is the intent..."

914. From here on, the commentary on DK_A 92 has not been translated into Tibetan.

for others. When proceeding [in this way,] the hope of the threefold world is not fulfilled. [The desired goal is] buddha wisdom only. Therefore it is not like [erotic practice]. Complete enlightenment [happens] in a single moment of buddha wisdom. In short, [it differs] because each and every thing [is realized] at the same time.

> The moments are [only] the bliss of the means (i.e., the male practitioner);
> or rather, this [bliss] is differentiated.[915]
> [Or the goal is marked] thanks to the merit that comes through the kindness of the guru.
> Few are those who come to know [it in this way].[916] (DK_A 93)

This is because that moment of bliss of the means is divided into four moments. Alternatively, you may say that true reality must be identified in an undifferentiated moment. But then you cite the passage "[the goal must be marked] between supreme [joy] and [the joy of] no joy."[917] So indeed, it is differentiated when, beginning with the first, the moments of the manifold and so forth arise. [But] the undifferentiated [character] is the state of the [real] coemergent. [It can be marked] through the power of merit [accumulated] through the kindness of the venerable guru. Few are those who know true reality [this way]. "[Few] are those who..." means that [this method] is not common to everyone.[918] Therefore, for the reason mentioned in [verse 93], I have publicly made this clear to everyone in accordance with the instructions of the genuine guru.[919]

Likewise, [Saraha] says:

> By calling to mind[920] the profound,

915. Tib.: "The means is momentary, or else it is not differentiated."

916. The translation accords with Advayavajra's understanding. Read on its own, the root verse says: "[Make up your mind:] either the moments belong to the bliss of the 'male adept' (*upāya*), or they belong to both (male and female adepts)."

917. The Tibetan translation of *virama* is *dga' bral*.

918. Tib.: "It is momentary because of a division of momentary [bliss] into four joys. Moreover, reality [can be] identified [only] at the [crucial] moment of nonduality. Because this [happens] between supreme joy and [the joy of] no joy, the state of being differentiated is when, beginning with the first, the moments of the manifold and so forth have arisen. [Its] undifferentiated [character] is the state of the coemergent."

919. This sentence is missing in the Sanskrit.

920. I.e., reading Apa. *uāharaṇeṃ* instead of Ms G's *uāra hale*, which coincides with the

> [one realizes] that there is neither self nor other.[921]
> During coemergent joy in the fourth [moment],
> it is known by experiencing [the goal] as one's own natural state.
> (DK$_A$ 94)

And since things stand so: that [coemergent bliss], which few people know, [even] among those who have merit,[922] destroys[923] partiality by virtue of having analyzed[924] the profound—namely, having constantly called it to mind.[925] In this,[926] the supremely profound, all [distinctions between] the self and other do not exist at all,[927] for it lacks [such distinctions][928] in the first place. In this way, during coemergent joy[929] at the fourth moment, notwithstanding[930] what is imagined by [other] people,[931] you know your own awareness.[932] And again, the same thing will be experienced again.[933]

[Next, Saraha] teaches its benefit:

> Just as the jewel of the moon
> shines forth in frightful darkness,

Tibetan; see next note.

921. Tib.: "O friends, [the teaching] is both profound and vast. In it you cannot find other and self."

922. This still glosses the previous verse.

923. This requires an active form of *ni-rudh*. The text is not consistent, however, in using the instrumental for the subject in a passive construction.

924. Skt. *vicāra*. Already in Theravāda practice, *vicāra* operates together with *vitakka*. While *vitakka* has the function of redirecting the mind to its object of concentration, *vicāra* keeps the attention on it (Sferra 2000, 29). "Calling to mind" must be seen in this light.

925. Tib.: "When you are continuously aware of the profound by virtue of having analyzed it, biased states of mind subside."

926. Tib.: "Likewise, in this..."

927. Tib.: "vanish."

928. Tib.: "For they have never arisen..."

929. In the root text, "coemergent joy" is in the nominative. In his Sanskrit translation, Bagchi puts it into the locative.

930. Lit.: "in the middle of."

931. I.e., those who identify the goal between supreme joy and the joy of no joy. The Tibetan does not mirror the compound *lokaparikalpitamadhye*.

932. Tib.: "During the fourth [moment] such coemergent joy must be realized as a [genuine] experience of the coemergent." The Tibetan does not mirror the compound *lokaparikalpitamadhye*.

933. This sentence is missing in the Tibetan. The *sa eva* is taken in the sense of *tathā*, in an allusion to *caturthaṃ tat punas tathā*.

supreme great bliss takes away[934]
all wrongdoings in one moment. (DK_A 95)

Here, it is like being in the middle of frightful darkness when the jewel of the moonstone[935] [starts to] shine forth. Just as outcastes, thieves, and such persons rob[936] [the wealth of others at this moment],[937] so too does supreme great bliss take away all the wrongdoing of saṃsāra in one moment.[938] Likewise,

The sun of suffering sets,
and the leader of stars, the semen,[939] appears.
Abiding in this[940] emanating [meditation, the yogin]
emanates the circle of the maṇḍala. (DK_A 96)

When the sun of the summer season of suffering sets, a real cooling sets in; the leader of the multitude of stars, the moon—[that is,] the semen—comes forth.[941] In such a way, meditation on the circle of the maṇḍala and the like[942] (i.e., the moon and the stars) is performed, whereby [the yogin] abiding in the emanating meditation performs an emanation of the entire world following the convention that [sentient beings] are buddhas.[943] The circle of the maṇḍala, [too,][944] it should be known, has the nature of this [semen]. This is the idea.

Again, [Saraha] teaches what the yogins have to do:

934. Tib.: "destroys."

935. This is a code word for drops of semen.

936. I.e., taking the instrumental plural (*sarvacauracaṇḍālādibhiḥ*) as an ergative. The third person singular (*harati*) should then be changed into the plural (*haranti*).

937. Supplied from the Tibetan.

938. Tib.: "at the moment of freedom from defining characteristics."

939. The commentary takes the moon as the leader of the stars, thereby according fairly well with the context of DK_A 95. Only those familiar with tantric code language will correctly understand, then, that *śukra* here means semen and not the planet Venus, which is normally considered the leader of the stars. The Tibetans obviously read Venus (as *pa wa sangs* suggests).

940. The Tibetan has *'di ltar* for *tena*: "Abiding thus, he emanates the emanating [meditation]. This is the *maṇḍalacakra*."

941. Tib.: "The leader of the multitude of stars, the [planet] Venus comes forth."

942. The Tibetan (like Bagchi) takes *īdṛśa* out of the compound: "Meditation on such a circle of the maṇḍala and the like is performed..."

943. This corresponds to the *maṇḍalarājāgrīsamādhi* or the *binduyoga* in Jñānapāda's *Samantabhadrasādhana*, verses 109–10.

944. Supplied from the Tibetan.

Hey, you fools! Observe [your] mind with [your] mind.
Abandon wrong views, all of them!
Get pure in supreme great bliss!
For such [a person][945] supreme accomplishment comes about.[946]
(DK$_A$ 97)

You observe the mind with [your][947] mind. But do mind and no-mind exist? According to the logic taught above neither of the two exist.[948] This is as taught [in the following]:

This mind here is not the no-mind;[949]
because[950] neither of them exists at all,
there should not even be a name for what is not anything,
[but] the entire world is [overcome] with confusion.[951]

Because of this [observation], you abandon (i.e., give up), wrong views,[952] as[953] all [these notions of] a self, living being, man, person, and so forth are but the relative [truth] of contemptible worldly conventions. And so [wrong views] have been taught like this.[954] In this way you must purify everything [and dissolve it] into the nature of great bliss. In doing so you enter the supreme-level, supramundane buddha relative truths.[955] Thereafter, supreme accomplishment is attained.[956]

Therefore [Saraha] says the following:

945. The Göttingen manuscript reads the locative *tahi* instead of the genitive *tasu*: "In this [supreme bliss]..."

946. Tib.: "It is precisely this that is supreme great bliss. In it there is genuine accomplishment."

947. Supplied from the Tibetan.

948. The Tibetan introduces the sentence with *ci*: "But according to the logic..."

949. Tib.: "The genuine nature of mind is no-mind..."

950. The Tibetan did not honor the causal clause.

951. This verse is not in Apabhraṃśa and thus not part of the root text.

952. This requires *kudṛṣṭi* to be in the accusative plural. The Tibetan has: "wrong views of this kind."

953. The sense of a causal relation is taken from the Tibetan.

954. This sentence is missing in the Tibetan.

955. The commentator seems to distinguish between two kinds of relative truth here: one that belongs to saṃsāra and one that has soteriological value.

956. Instead of the last two sentences the Tibetan simply has: "Because the supramundane supreme accomplishment depends on this."

Let the elephant of the mind wander freely!
Don't ask for options!
Let it drink the river water of the sky mountain,
and let it rest on its banks according to its wish! (DK_A 98)

Free the elephant of the mind! Let it play in the middle of saṃsāra as you wish! Do not long for the [mere] idea of it![957] Why is [this a valid teaching]? Because all entities have the nature of [true] reality, are based on [true] reality, and dissolve into it. [Thus] you [naturally] abandon bad actions, such as taking life, which sends *tīrthika*s and others to hell. All compassionate ones[958] are doing well by guarding the path of the ten virtuous deeds. Like an elephant they[959] drink in the water of the mountain river—namely, their all-pervading state, which is the sky. Someone dries up on the bank of the river of great bliss—attachment toward even great bliss being nothing more than conceptualization. This is the idea.[960]

Seized by the huge elephant[961] of sense objects [with] its trunk,
he, it appears, was going to be killed.
[But] the yogin, who is taking little bits [of the sense objects],
somehow escapes from it.[962] (DK_A 99)

All entities, the eyes and so forth, being the elephant of objects,[963] it appears that he is going to be killed by the elephant, seized by the trunk of sense faculties and objects. As long as [an object] manifests, to which subject does it

957. This sentence is missing in the Tibetan.

958. Reading genitive instead of instrumental, and *bhavanti* instead of *bhavati*.

959. Skt. *tena* could reflect an ergative construction, but then it should be in the plural.

960. Because in this case, great bliss becomes conceptual and out of reach. One thus becomes like someone who stands at the shore without being able to drink the water.

Tib.: "Let the elephant of the mind, which is happy in the forest of *saṃsāra*, play [freely]! Why is [this a valid teaching]? It is because all entities are based on [true] reality and dissolve into it. All *tīrthika*s, however, fall into hell because [they do] such [things] as taking life. Compassionate persons, [those] on the path of the ten virtuous deeds, go to the higher states of existence and [there] dwell happily. May the elephant of the mind drink the water of the sky in such a way that it (i.e., the mind) pervades everything! 'On its bank' means 'on the bank of the waters of great bliss.' The idea is that even though it is great bliss you should not become attached to it."

961. The Tibetan has only *glang po* for *gajendra* ("huge elephant").

962. Tib.: "Like an elephant keeper, the yogin escapes in the same moment."

963. According to the Tibetan. The locatives in the Sanskrit could be an attempt to formulate an absolute locative.

belong? It is not seen to have an independent existence. It neither kills nor leads to hells and similar realms. And it is in this way that [the consumption of sense objects] appears for the masters of yoga—they take small bites [of the sensory world] precisely so that they can escape it, [viz.] by merging into coemergent bliss. These small bites [of the sensory world] do not hinder them; nevertheless, this is how it appears to ordinary people.[964] This is to say, [the yogin] is not tainted by [concepts of] what is edible and not.

Likewise, [it is said:]

> What is cyclic existence is indeed nirvāṇa as well.
> Do not take them to be separate!
> [Reality] is without a single own-nature, too.
> [This][965] stainless [nonduality] I have realized. (DK_A 100)

In brief, for yogins there are no distinctions whatsoever. This is as stated in Ārya Nāgārjuna's [*Pañcakrama*], in the [chapter called] *Yuganaddhakrama*, starting with "cyclic existence and nirvāṇa"[966] (*Pañcakrama* V.2a). Here, what is referred to as "cyclic existence and nirvāṇa" everyone takes to be two [separate things] according to [the conventions of] dualistic speech. That [duality][967] should be known as an indivisible union, [which means that it is] nondual [in reality]. It should be known that there is no other distinction [possible]. How then to speak of a single nature?[968] The final tenet in the treatise is that [true reality] is without this—that is, [beyond] the state of one and many. Nevertheless, nonduality is also stainless, as [I] have realized. The idea is that this is supreme nonduality.[969]

In order to make this clear, [Saraha] says:

964. Tib.: "Likewise, the elephant of sense objects stands for all entities. [The elephant keeper] is seized by the [elephant's] trunk the way the senses [are by] sense objects, but he does not die, even though it appears as if he were going to be killed. This is because he is an expert in playing with the elephant. [Similarly,] the master of yogins escapes and regains stability."

965. Supplied from the Tibetan.

966. *Pañcakrama* V.2a: *saṃsāro nirvṛtiś ceti.*

967. Advayavajra takes *dvaya* as a masculine word.

968. Namely, that even saṃsāra and nirvāṇa are not of a single nature. The second meaning could be that reality is without a single own-nature.

969. The Tibetan simply reads: "This is as stated in Ārya Nāgārjuna's [*Pañcakrama*], in the [chapter called] *Yuganaddhakrama*, starting with "saṃsāra and nirvāṇa" (i.e., *Pañcakrama* V.2a). Accordingly, the inseparability of saṃsāra and nirvāṇa is nonduality and thus called an indivisible union."

Neither remain at home nor go into the forest!
Wherever you are, [simply] look at the mind!
It is entirely and continuously grounded in enlightenment.
Where [then] is cyclic existence and where is nirvāṇa? (DK_A 101)

This [verse teaches] that you should not remain in your house. Do not go inside the forest either. Why? It is certain that thoughts arise from spending time in these two places. What to do then? It is explained: Wherever you are, whatever you do—whether walking or eating—you must look at the mind in every situation! The mind is false. You must take [all] that[970] to be cognition only.[971] This has been repudiated before because it cannot be established.

Therefore, in the entire threefold world, [mind] is established as being uninterruptedly grounded in enlightenment. Being self-arisen [wisdom], it is not generated by anything. It is [falsely] imagined by those of low intellect in their bewilderment. Cyclic existence and nirvāṇa being nondual, this [mind] should not be [created] through anything, because of the reasoning above. There is neither cyclic existence nor nirvāṇa in it. Why? Because the manifold [world] has not been produced in the first place. Why can you see it? It is like an illusion, a mere appearance caused by delusion. It is like, for example, a reflection in a mirror: upon analysis it is not apprehended [as anything]. It does not truly occur with distinct features, such as being a disk or an orb of definite size and so forth.

From what does it follow then that cyclic existence and nirvāṇa do not [truly] occur?[972] This is as stated [in *Yuktiṣaṣṭikā* 5–6]:

Those who think in terms of saṃsāra and nirvāṇa
do not see reality,
[whereas] those who think neither in terms of saṃsāra nor
nirvāṇa
see reality. (YṢ 5)

Nirvāṇa and cyclic existence—

970. Taking *sa* in the sense of *tat*.

971. Following the Tibetan, we read *tac ca vijñaptimātraṃ kuru* instead of *sa ca vijñaptiṃ kuru*.

972. The corresponding Tibetan commentary is comparatively short: "Whether house or forest—in neither of the two should one obstinately abide, since thoughts arise when one becomes attached to either of them. What to do, then? Whatever you do—whether eating, walking, or sleeping—your mind should not become too attached to it (i.e., these activities). Be aware that [these] are only false representations! Therefore all experts continuously abide in enlightenment. Being self-arisen [wisdom], it is not generated by anything."

> this duality does not exist.
> Thorough knowledge of cyclic existence—
> this is called *nirvāṇa*. (YṢ 6)

Therefore it [can] be established that supreme nonduality[973] is the nature of enlightenment.

He further says:

> Enlightenment depends[974] on neither house nor forest;
> you must understand the distinction [being made] with these
> [words figuratively].
> You [must] become steeped in the stainless nature of mind,
> because it is nonconceptual![975] (DK_A 102)

Here,[976] enlightenment with the above-mentioned defining characteristics is found[977] in neither house nor forest. In other instances of intentional language, you [need to] understand the difference between such [words]: *house* means "[one's own][978] body," and *forest* means "the [outside] world [of objects],[979] such as a pot or cloth." In neither can one obtain enlightenment.[980] Why? Because neither of them truly occurs. Everything, the world and so forth—that which is seen as having such distinctive features—is subject to arising and destruction. Enlightenment is not so, for it [can]not be destroyed. Therefore here one [must become] steeped in the stainless nature of mind! In brief, whatever you conceptualize, give up all those attachments! You will thereby attain enlightenment.

This [Saraha] says [in the following]:

> This is the self, and this the other.
> Whoever cultivates [this way of thinking]

973. Tib.: "the supreme nature of nonduality."

974. Lit.: "is based [on]."

975. Tib.: "Do not create concepts about the stainless nature of mind!"

976. Missing in the Tibetan.

977. Reading *sthitā* instead of *sthitam*.

978. Supplied from the Tibetan.

979. Skt. *viśva*; the Tibetan has material forms (*gzugs*).

980. From here onward, the Tibetan translation is missing.

has created bondage, even without fetters [in the first place].[981]
So[982] you must save yourself! (DK_A 103)

Whoever mistakenly conceptualizes [the notion of personhood],[983] saying, "This is the self," "That is the other,"[984] which is marked (i.e., spoiled),[985] [may initially] not have been bound [by this distinction].[986] Even though liberated, one is not so when taking recourse to [the notion of] selfhood.[987] The intent is not to conceptualize in [two] parts, oneself and the other. Likewise [it is said:]

Do not confusedly make self and other [two different things]!
Everybody has always been a buddha:
this is the stainless supreme level,
the naturally pure mind. (DK_A 104)

Do not confusedly make "self" and "other" into two different things when they have one nature![988] It is rather that the entire realm of sentient beings—[every single one]—by their nature has been a buddha[989] without interruption from beginningless time.[990] With regard to "This" and so on: covered by the limitless stains caused [by concepts][991] from beginningless time, [sentient beings] have not cultivated their identity as buddhas.[992] Truly, in that one is free from duality, the buddha is by nature the stainless supreme mind. [Its] form is bodhicitta, free from an own-nature.[993]

981. Tib.: "Needs to break loose from the bondage of [such] distinctions."

982. Taking Apa. *kiu* in the sense of Skt. *kim u*.

983. The additions in brackets are supplied from the Tibetan.

984. Tib.: "This is the self, this the other..."

985. The Tibetan simply has: "binds himself."

986. Supplied from the Tibetan.

987. Tib.: "At this time he is not free, even though [his true] nature is free."

988. This sentence is missing in the Tibetan.

989. Bagchi reads *śuddhaḥ* instead of *buddhaḥ* (N is not available). The corresponding root text has *buddha*, however, which is also supported by the Tibetan. It is interesting to note here that in a sutta from the Aṅguttara Nikāya, called *Loke*, the word *suddho* in an older or original version was replaced by *buddho*. See Rhys Davids 1933, 910–11.

990. Lit.: "from the beginning."

991. Tib.: "adventitious concepts."

992. Lit.: "the buddha-self"; Tib.: "they do not realize this, and [so] they do not know that they are [already] buddhas themselves."

993. Tib.: "The utterly stainless nature of [their] mind is the essence of [their] enlightenment.

The supreme tree of nondual mind
pervades the entire threefold world!
It bears the flower and fruit of compassion.
This is what is called benefit for others. (DK_A 105)

Having taught this,[994] he now teaches benefit for others. The nondual mind of the yogins is the supreme tree—that is, the king of trees. Like a wish-fulfilling tree, it pervades the entire threefold world. The idea is that everything is [this] supreme nonduality. With its opened flowers of compassion it is fully blossomed. Its name is *benefit for others*. For each and every being, all the hopes, buddhahood and the rest, are fulfilled.[995]

The supreme tree of emptiness[996] has blossomed
in many kinds and shapes of compassion.
It brings fruit to others without effort.
The supreme[997] mind is of such bliss.[998] (DK_A 106)

The fruit of emptiness is [described] thus because, given the manifold compassion [within it], it [is able to] fulfill manifold wishes, even without intending to do so.

Moreover, [Saraha] teaches fully perfect compassion:[999]

The tree of emptiness, which is not [genuine] compassion,
will have no roots or leaves.
If someone turns [emptiness] into an object,[1000]
such a person will fall and break his limbs. (DK_A 107)

This is because [this nature] is free from grasping at any entities."

994. Tib. supplies "the Supreme Benefit/Aim/Truth."

995. The Sanskrit text still has *te tayā* || *su* and then breaks off. *Su-* must be the beginning of DK_A 106. Tib.: "The supreme goal having thus been taught, Benefit for Others proceeds to be taught. The nondual mind of the yogins pervades the entire threefold world like a wish-fulfilling tree. The idea is that everything is [this] nonduality. The name of its fruition, which is the flowers of compassion, is Benefit for Others because [the nondual mind] causes the enlightenment of a buddha and so forth to blossom (i.e., become fully manifest) for the sake of all."

996. Lit.: "empty tree."

997. Apa. *paru* (Skt. *param*) means here "supreme" and not "other."

998. Tib.: "This [ordinary] bliss [here] is not the supreme mind."

999. There is no commentary on verses DK_A 106–8 in the Sanskrit.

1000. I.e., tries to climb an empty tree.

As for the tree of emptiness[1001] without compassion: since emptiness[1002] and compassion are inseparable, here it is compassion without an object that is meant by "without compassion."[1003] This tree of emptiness is without roots and leaves because meditator, meditation, and object of meditation have never existed. As for the statement that whoever sets his sights on [and climbs] this [tree] will fall and break both arms, this is because it has the single nature of the threefold world.

In order to teach this, [Saraha] says:

> Two trees [come] from the same seed;[1004]
> therefore they bear the same [type of] fruit.[1005]
> Whoever knows[1006] their inseparability
> is liberated from [both] cyclic existence and nirvāṇa. (DK_A 108)

[Suppose that] two individual trees and [their] branches have grown from the same seed. Thus there would be a [single] cause and a twofold fruit. The [cause] is not separate from [its] fruit, for it has been said: "[This] fruit is from a cause similar [to it]." Whoever sees that the Buddha and saṃsāra are not separate will be liberated, for he [then] realizes the meaning of nonduality.

> If a beggar comes
> and leaves without having [his] hopes [fulfilled],
> it is better[1007] to go begging with a cracked bowl
> and leave the household.[1008] (DK_A 109)

1001. Lit.: "empty tree." Note that two lines further down *stong pa'i sdong po* is taken up by *stong pa nyid kyi sdong po*.

1002. Lit.: "the empty."

1003. The commentary suggests that the tree of emptiness is without the lower types of compassion that still need objective support. The last two *pāda*s then mean that if somebody generates compassion with objective support he will fall and break his limbs.

1004. The Tibetan has the extra line: "Irrespective [of their duality], they [display] the same [type of] flower."

1005. The first two lines (DK_A 108ab) are translated from the Tibetan. The context requires two individual trees grown from one seed. The Apabhraṃśa, however, reads: "One seed and one tree—therefore there is one fruit."

1006. Tib.: "sees here."

1007. I.e., it is better to become a beggar oneself than to be rich and stingy.

1008. Tib.: "[Then] take chunks [of food] in a bowl [and say:] Hey, you'd [do better to] abandon your household."

One comes to realize all the above-mentioned points once one is no [longer] attached to the possessions of saṃsāra. This is because attachment to possessions and to enriching [one's] sons, relatives, and so forth is as harmful as a snake's poison.[1009] This is why compassionate persons get close to sentient beings.[1010] When a beggar leaves without having received what he was looking for, [you come to realize:] "I have not given anything to the world." Through this [stinginess] nothing whatsoever is accomplished. Therefore you had better put the alms in a cracked bowl, and you will not be attached to possessions [anymore]. It is better that you abandon this household.[1011] In this respect[1012] [Saraha] says:

> Others are not helped.
> The needy are not given [alms].
> O fool,[1013] what fruit do you [expect] in this saṃsāra?
> It is better to renounce [this] self.[1014] (DK_A 110)

If others cannot be helped, what is the use of a house and possessions? When one has gold and so forth and does not give it away, since one will remain in saṃsāra, what fruit do you expect from this wealth? There will be none. Then we[1015] had better abandon our [cherished] self. The idea is that we live at home but without concern for our body and life.[1016]

This commentary on the *Dohākoṣa*, which is an analysis of the difficult words, is ended. The dohās are in the Apabhraṃśa language, which conceals (encrypts) these [verses]. True reality is presented so that ignorant people are perplexed.[1017]

1009. Translated from the Tibetan. The Sanskrit is missing up to here.

1010. The Tibetan of this sentence is incomplete.

1011. Tib.: "Therefore, when compassionate beings are overpowered by greed and do not give anything when a beggar approaches [them], you think, 'I lack accomplishment.' Then, leaving your house, you take up the bowl left outside and [resolve] that you will not be attached to possessions [anymore]. This is the idea."

1012. Tib.: "In order to teach this..."

1013. This is our diagnostic conjecture, not reflected in the transmission. Missing in the Tibetan.

1014. Tib.: "Therefore it is better to throw [your cherished self] far away."

1015. This is a plural of humility.

1016. Tib.: "Then it is good that we renounce our [cherished] self. The idea is that we should leave home with no concern for life and limb."

1017. Tib.: "I have composed this *Dohākoṣaṭīkā* as a commentary on difficult points for foolish

This commentary I have here composed
for my own understanding.
Called Self-Understanding,
it illuminates the teaching of the guru.

When others study it as well,
it will benefit them.
This is what is meant by benefiting sentient beings.
If not, I beg your pardon.[1018]

By the merit I have accumulated
for the sake of myself and others,
may the entire world attain
the level of the wisdom of the self-arisen!

This commentary on the *Dohākoṣa* is ended.[1019] The quantity of *granthas* in this [text] is eight hundred. This work is of the venerable Śrī-Advayavajra.[1020]

Translated by the great yogin from the land of Southern Kosala (i.e., the inner part of modern-day Orissa), Dīpaṃkararakṣita, and the Tibetan translator-monk Ba ri. Later it was slightly corrected and finalized by Vairocanavajra.[1021]

[worldly] people."

1018. The Sanskrit of this verse in incomplete.

1019. This strange repetition points to a complex transmission history of the commentary.

1020. Tib.: "The *Dohākoṣapañjikā*, composed by the great master Advayavajra, is completed."

1021. The colophon in the Peking Tengyur only provides the information that the commentary was translated by Śrī-Vairocanavajra: "Translated by the great yogin from the land of Kosala in South India, Śrī-Vairocanavajra."

Part 2. The Root Texts

Annotated Diplomatic Edition of the *Mūla* Manuscripts

THIS CHAPTER CONTAINS an annotated formatted diplomatic transcript of two Apabhraṃśa *Dohākoṣa* manuscript witnesses that have never been used before in works dealing with Saraha. By *formatted* we mean that we parsed the text, adding spaces between words, a feature not observed in the witnesses, which use the so-called continuous script (*scriptio continua*). We use the abbreviations G and T for these two sources, which are also discussed in the introduction and were frequently referenced in the annotation to the foregoing presentation of Advayavajra's commentary:

- G = Ms Niedersächsische Staats- und Universitätsbibliothek, Göttingen Xc 14/16 (A copy of the photographs taken on behalf of Rāhula Sāṅkṛtyāyana, the full set of which was originally deposited in Patna). *Praemittit*: [$1b_1$] [*siddham*] namaḥ sarvajñāya ||.
- T = Ms Tokyo University Library no. 517. *Praemittit*: [$16b_4$] [*siddham*] namo vajraḍākāya ||.

"Sāṅkṛtyāyana" denotes the manuscript from a Tibetan private collection (at Sa skya) published on plates 1–6 in Sāṅkṛtyāyana 1957 (whose numeration we follow when referring to this version). The *incipit* is missing along with the entire first folio.

The primary aim here is to point out that Advayavajra's readings are not always the ones seen in other transmissions; these variations are discussed where appropriate. We have also included a good number of testimonies—that is, places where certain dohās are quoted—and here, too, the readings vary. Further, it is also important to take note of these quotations because they may show which verses were more popular and influential. While we also used unpublished manuscript material, the list of testimonies is likely not exhaustive, nor does it intend to be. The readings and formatting of the testimonies have been transcribed as they were printed by the editors, and we have formatted the unedited ones. The readings of manuscripts before correction have not been noted separately.

The transcription of the letter व in the manuscripts has been standardized, but it should be noted that its phonetic quality is not always entirely clear, as it sometimes denotes a labial plosive (i.e., *b*), sometimes a *w*-like glide between vowels. The scribe of G uses an interesting and rare combination of cerebral *d* and *h*, which we transcribe as *d.h* to distinguish it from the aspirated cerebral (i.e., *ḍh*). Note that the scribe sometimes reverses the order, thus *h.d.* The various types of *daṇḍa*s (e.g., half, left-slanting) are not distinguished, although in G they are especially helpful, because they signal *pāda* breaks. Illegible or lost syllables (e.g., where the edge of the folio is broken) are marked with +.

Some, mostly regular, phonological/spelling differences, which are not pointed out separately below include:

- T usually spells word-initial metrically long *a* as *ā* (e.g., 1a, 2a, 2c).
- T geminates the negation particle (e.g., *ṇṇa* in 3d or *ṇṇā* in 17c), sometimes word-initial *ṇ* as well (e.g., *ṇṇagnā* in 7a), but this does not affect the metrical quantity of the preceding syllable.
- T occasionally geminates *jha* (e.g., 20a, 20b) and degeminates *tha* (e.g., 47a).
- Nasalization of word-final *e* and *i* are much rarer in T.
- T has a slight preference for the *ma-śruti* instead of the *ba-śruti* in certain cases (e.g., 1b, 5a, 6c, 9a).
- T contains a higher number of (possibly scribal) Sanskritisms (e.g., 5d, 14a, 58a, 58c); this feature is rarer in G (e.g., 2b).

The numeration of the verses is entirely our own. Because of a one-folio lacuna in the Tokyo manuscript, the numbers are uncertain after the text resumes on folio 20. We also signal the folio and line changes within the text in square brackets.

Uncertain readings are followed by a bracketed question mark. Scribal corrections are given in footnotes, where superscript *pc* and *ac* mark, respectively, the readings after and before correction.

Other abbreviations and sigla used in the edition

ø	Missing verse
DK_A	*Dohākoṣa* verses in Advayavajra's *Dohākoṣapañjikā*
DKP_A	*Dohākoṣapañjikā* by Advayavajra

The Göttingen and Tokyo Manuscripts

bamhaṇehiṃ ajāṇantahi bheu |
evam me paḍhiaü e caüveu | [G1 = DK_A 1]

A] *Ajāṇantahi* seems to be a valid equivalent for *ajāṇantahĭṃ/ajāṇaṁtĕhĭṁ.* B] *Evam* might read *evem* (not entirely clear whether the scribe meant to write a *śirorekhā* over the *v*). The *me* creates a metrical problem, unless it is to be read as short with the previous *a/e* also read as short. As for the meaning, it could possibly be construed as a *genitivus incommodi*—i.e., with a sense of disapproval.

bāhmaṇehiṃ ajāṇaü bheu bheu |
emaṃ paḍhiaü e caüveu || [T1]

A] While *bheu bheu* is most likely a dittography, the DKP_A might mirror it when it glosses it as *bheda* and *prabheda.*

The meter is *pādākulaka*, but it is somewhat odd that the verse apparently consists of a single line. However, this type of *in medias res* beginning without anything resembling an obeisance verse is not uncommon in the genre, as Kāṇha/Kaṇhu also begins in this manner (cf. Shahidullah 1928, 71).

---

maṭṭhīpāṇīkusaha pabitteṃ |
gharahiṃ basanteṃ agni huṇanteṃ [$1b_2$] ||
kajjeṃ birahia huvaṃbahahomeṃ |
akkhi jaṭāiu kaḍuveṃ dhūmeṃ | [G2 = DK_A 2]

B] The double *daṇḍa* is perhaps justified if the line is to be read with the previous line-verse.

C] For *huvaṃ°* read *hua°*; either a slip of the pen or an unwarranted *aluk-samāsa*. *jaṭāiu*, a significant variant for DKP_A's (conjectured) *ḍahāvia*, probably stems from *jaḍa*, "the eyes are made numb with pungent smoke."

māṭṭīpāṇīkusaha pabitte
gharehiṃ basante aggi huṇa[$16b_5$]nte |
kāje birahia huaüese
akhkhi jajyaü (?) kaḍueṃ dhume | [T2]

C] *Huaüese* perhaps to be emended to *huavaüese*. In general this *pāda* is corrupt.
D] *Jajyaü* possibly corrected to *jaḍḍāü*? The intended meaning is unclear. *dhume* must be corrected to *dhūme/dhūmeṃ*.

---

daṇḍi tidaṇḍi bhagaüvabeseṃ |
viṇayā hoia haṃsaüveseṃ ||
micche[$1b_3$]hiṃ jaga vāhia bbhulleṃ |
dhammādhamma ṇa jāṇia tulleṃ || [G3 = DK_A 3]

A] Correct *tidaṇḍi* to *tidaṇḍī* for the meter or recite thus.
B] Note the double *daṇḍa* again; this could suggest that the verses were read with different constructions. Correct *hoia* to *hoai* or *hŏiaï*.
C] Correct *bbhulleṃ* to *bhulleṃ* or dismiss as an orthographical variant; the *bbh* cannot lengthen the vowel before it.
D] There is a small mark under the line suggesting that the reading ought to be parsed as *jāṇi atulleṃ*.

dāṇḍi[1] tidāṇḍī bhagaveṃ vese
binayā hoiae hansaüdeśeṃ |
[$17a_1$] micchehiṃ jaga vāhia bhulle |
dhammādhamma ṇṇa jāṇia tulle || [T3]

B] *Hoiae* cannot possibly be correct. Correct to *hoai*.

---

1. dāṇḍi] T^{ac}, dāṇḍī T^{pc} (unmetrical)

aïriehi uddhūlia cchāreṃ |
sīsasu vāhia e jaḍabhāreṃ |
ghara[1b$_4$]hiṃ païsī dīvā jālī |
koṇahi vaïsī ghaṇṭhī cālī | [G4 = DK_A 4]

A] *Aïriehi*'s *i* must count as long or emend the word to *aïriehiṃ*; *cch* does not make position; it is probably a mere orthographical variant.

aïriehiṃ uddhūlia cchāreṃ
sīsasu vāhia e jaḍabhāreṃ |
gharehi vaïsī divā jālī |
[17a$_2$] koṇehi vaïsī[2] ghaṇṭī cālī | [T4]

C] The reading *vaïsī* for *païsī* is less preferable because of the *punaruktidoṣa*. *divā* must be corrected to *dīvā* or read thus. The correction in D is a trace of the scribe's confusion regarding these readings.

---

akkhi nivesī āsaṇa bandhī
kaṇṇahiṃ khusakhusāi jaṇa dhandhī [1b$_5$] ||
raṇḍī muṇḍī aṇṇa vi veseṃ
dikkhijaï gurudakhiṇaüveseṃ || [G5 = DK_A 5]

B] For the sake of the meter, read *khusakhusaïṃ*?
C] It is possible that *veseṃ/vese* originally stood for *veśyā*—i.e., "prostitute."
D] Parsing the text as *guru dakhiṇa*°, "to gain a subject," is also possible.

akkhi nimesī asaṇa bāndhī
kāṇṇehiṃ khusahusāi jaṇa dhāndhī ||
rāṇḍī muṇḍī aṇṇa vi vese
dikkhijaï guruda[17a$_3$]kṣiṇarese | [T5]

A] For *asaṇa*, read *āsaṇa*.
B] Same problem as above with the middle of the *pāda*.
D] It is difficult to make sense of the reading °*rese*. Perhaps it is nothing more than a simple corruption of °*uese*.

2. vaïsī] T^{pc}, pavaïsī T^{ac}

---

dīhaṇakha jjaï maliṇeṃ veseṃ
ṇagnala hoia upāḍia keseṃ |
[1b$_6$] khavaṇa jāṇa viḍambia eseṃ
appaṇu vāhia mokkhagaveseṃ | [G6 = DK$_A$ 6]

A] Understand *jjaï* as a relative pronoun. The reduplication is to maintain the meter. Perhaps T's reading is preferable.
B] The ligatures *gna* and *gga* look very similar, so the reading *ṇagnala* is understandable. Alternatively, emend *hoia* to *hoi* to avoid too many absolutives.
C] Here we must agree with Advayavajra in reading an instrumental *khavaṇehi/khamaṇehi.*
D] Note the variant "in search of liberation" instead of "for the sake of liberation."

dīhaṇakhā[3] jeṃ maliṇe vese
ṇṇagnala huaü uppāḍia keseṃ |
khamaṇa jāṇa viḍambia vese
appaṇu vāhia mokkhaüdde[17a$_4$]śeṃ || [T6]

B] The double *p* does not make position.
D] The double *d* does not make position.

---

jaï ṇagnā via hoi mutti
tā suṇaha siālaha |
lomupāḍa[2a$_1$]neṃ[4] atthasiddhi
tā juïṇiambaha | [G7 = DK$_A$ 7]

C] Note the variant "[if there is] accomplishment of purpose (Skt. *artha*)" instead of "if there is (Skt. *asti*) accomplishment."
D] For *jui°*, read *juaï°*, a banal omission.

jaï ṇṇagnā avi hoi mutti
tā suṇaha siālaha |

3. °ṇakhā] T^{ac}, °ṇakkha T^{pc} (sic!)
4. lomupādaneṃ] G^{pc}, lomupādateṃ G^{ac}

lomopāḍaṇe atthi siddhi
tā juaïṇiamba |[5] [T7]

D] The scribe omitted the final °*ha*.

For the metrical issue of the break being placed not after the thirteenth but the fourteenth *mora* in some of the dohās, see Shahidullah 1928, 61.

---

picchīgahaṇeṃ ḍhiṭṭha mokkha
tā barahituraṅgaha |
ubbheṃ bhoaṇeṃ hoi jāṇa
tā kariha tu[2a$_2$]raṅgaha | [G8 = DK$_A$ 8]

A] The meaning of *ḍhiṭṭha* is somewhat doubtful; *dṛḍha* would not be apposite here, so it is probably a spelling variant of *ḍiṭṭha* (Skt. *dṛṣṭa*).
B] Both here and in T, we have a different animal: Advayavajra has "elephant and horse" (translated into Tibetan as "peacock and yak"), whereas the two manuscripts seem to read "peacock (Skt. *barhin*) and horse." Given that elephants and horses appear in the second line, this reading is perhaps the original one.
C] The reading *ubbheṃ* and *ubbhe* in T are corruptions of the rare word *uñcheṃ*. The word *jāṇa* means *jñāna* according to Advayavajra, but for that we would normally expect *jhāṇa*. It is possible that here "the path" or "the vehicle" [to liberation] (Skt. *yāna*) is meant.

piñchīgahaṇe diṭṭha mokkha
tā barihituraṅgaha |
[17a$_5$] ubbhe bhoaṇe hoi jāṇa
tā karihi turaṅgaha | [T8]

D] For *karihi*, read *kariha*.

Saraha bhaṇaï khavaṇāṇa mokkha
mahu kiṃpi ṇa bhāvaï |

5. °ṇiamba |] T^{pc}, °ṇiambā T^{ac}

tattarahiakāāṇa tāva
para kevala sāhaï || [G9 = DK_A 9]

D] Advayavajra understood *para* as "others," but it could also be an adjective to *tāva*—i.e., "supreme pain." It is not entirely clear how to understand the finite verb here. The corresponding Skt. root could be *sādh* ("to achieve") or *sah* ("to bear"). Sāṅkṛtyāyana's manuscript reads *vāha*+—i.e., *vāhaï* ("to deceive").

Saraha bhaṇaï khamaṇāṇaṃ[6] mokkha
mahuṃ kimpi ṇa bhāvaï
+ + + +i + +āa tāva
para kevala sāhaï || [T9]

Cf. Sāṅkṛtyāyana 8cd–9ab. The testimony of the Sa skya manuscript begins with the last syllable of the first quarter.

---

cellu [$2a_3$] bhikhkhu jeṃ tthaviraüvesemṃ
bandehiṃ pavvaïaü vesemṃ |
kovi sutattavakhāṇa baïṭho
koi cittaikkara sosaï diṭṭho || [G10 = DK_A 10]

A] Read *cellu* as *cellū*. The *tth* does not make position.
C] There are several ways to scan this quarter, but perhaps the easiest solution is to read *vaïṭṭho* for *vaïṭho*.
D] The reading *cittaikkara* is very doubtful. Because this quarter is so poorly attested, we could not judge what the original reading may have been and decided to follow Advayavajra.

[$17b_1$] cellu bhikhkhu je tthaviraüddeśe
bandehiṃ pāvvaï uesemṃ |
ke vi sutāntavakkhāṇaï ba+ i +
+ + + + + + + + + d+ṭṭho | [T10]

Cf. Sāṅkṛtyāyana 9cd–10ab. Most of the verse is illegible in the manuscript.

---

6. khamaṇāṇaṃ] T^{pc}, khamaṇajāṇaṃ T^{ac}

[2a$_4$] aṇṇatahiṃ mahā[7]jhāṇa hi dhāviu
maṇḍalacakkateṃ saala vibhāviu ||
kovi vakkhāṇa caüṭṭhihi laggo
kovi ṇihā[2a$_5$]laṇamagnahi bhaggo || [G11 = DK$_A$ 11]

A] Advayavajra seems to have read *maha°* possibly for the meter, but one might also scan the beginning of the quarter as *aṇṇatahĭṃ mahā°*. The reading *°jhāṇa* seems to suggest Skt. *jñāna* or *dhyāna*.
C] Read *vakkhāṇa* as *vakhāṇa* (see C in the previous verse) or *vakhāṇĕṃ* or understand *kkh* as not making position. It is very likely that we have to emend *caüṭṭhihi* to a genitive *caüṭṭhaha*.
D] For *°magnahi*, read *°maggahi*.

aṇṇataṃhi mahājāṇaṃ hi vāviu
[17b$_2$] maṇḍalacakkateṃ saala vibhāviu ||
kevi vakkhāṇa caüṭṭhahiṃ laggaü
kevi nihāla nāsāggahiṃ bhāgaü || [T11]

A] For *vāviu*, read *dhāviu*; in this type of script, the two letters can be easily confused for each other.
D] It is difficult to make sense of this reading. If genuine, it must refer to some kind of yogic practice, one in which one focuses on the tip of the nose.

Cf. Sāṅkṛtyāyana 10cd–11ab. Most of the second line is illegible in the manuscript.

---

sahaja cchaḍḍi ṇivvāṇa hi dhāviu |
ṇaü paramattha[8] ekka teṃ sāhiu || [G12 = DK$_A$ 12]

A] The *ḍḍ* does not make position, but the *cch* does. The logic of the statement would make the presence of a relative pronoun in the first quarter desirable, hence our diagnostic conjecture in the DKP$_A$ edition.
B] The end of *paramattha* must be read as long: *paramatthā*. Alternatively, we might translate as "they achieve anything except one thing—ultimate reality."

7. mahā°] G^{pc}, maha° G^{ac}

8. paramattha] G^{pc} (The missing *ra* is added in the lower margin in the scribal hand.), pamattha G^{ac}

sahaja cchāḍī ṇṇivāṇa vi dhāviu |
ṇṇaü paramāttha ekka te [17b_3] sāhiu | [T12]

Quoted without attribution (*tad uktam*) in Vibhūticandra's *Amṛtakaṇikoddyotanibandha* (ed. p. 120):

sahaja iha nivvāṇa hi dhāviu |
nacca paramathe ekatte sāhiu ||

Cf. Sāṅkṛtyāyana 11cd.

---

jo jasu jeṇa hoi santuṭṭho
mo[2a_6]kkha ki labbhaï jhāṇapaviṭṭho || [G13 = DK_A 13]

A] The reading *hoi* (and *a* in T) are probably both traces of *hoia*.
B] For the various possible meanings of *jhāṇa*, see note 208 in the translation of the commentary.

jo jasu jeṇa a saṃtuṭṭhaü |
mokkha ki lābbhaï jhāṇapaïṭṭhaü || [T13]

Cf. Sāṅkṛtyāyana 12ab. The line is illegible after *jeṇa*.

---

kiṃ taha dīveṃ kin tahi vejeṃ
kin taha kijjaï mantaha seveṃ |
kin taha tittha tapovaṇa jāi
[2b_1] mokkha hi labbhaï pāṇī hoi || [G14 = DK_A 14]

A] Emend *tahi vejeṃ* to *taha ṇivejjeṃ*.
D] Emend *hi* to *ki*. Emend *pāṇī hoi* to *pāṇiṇahāi*.

kin taha dīpeṇa kin taha ṇṇibĕjjeṃ
kin taha kijjaï mantaha sebeṃ |
kin taha [17b_4] titha tapova jāi
mokkha ki lābhaï pāṇiṇṇahāi || [T14]

C] Emend *tapova* to *tapovaṇa.*

Cf. Sāṅkṛtyāyana 12cd–13ab.

---

karuṇarahia jo suṇṇahi laggo
ṇaü so pāwaï uttima maggo ||
ahavā karuṇā ke[$2b_2$]vala bhāvaï
jammasahasreṃ mokkha ṇa pāwaï || [G15 = DK_A ø]

D] °*sahasreṃ* is very likely a scribal Sanskritism; read °*sahasseṃ*.

[not transmitted in T]

Translation: "He who is stuck in emptiness bereft of compassion will not obtain the supreme path. Equally, if he cultivates only compassion [without emptiness], he will not obtain liberation even after one thousand rebirths."

Quoted with attribution (*tad āha Sarahaḥ*) in Vibhūticandra's *Amṛtakaṇikoddyota* (ed. p. 123):

karuṇā rahia jo suṇṇa hi laggu
ṇaü so pāvaï uttima maggu |
ahavā karuṇā kevala bhāvaï
janmasahasse mokkha ṇa pāvaï ||

Quoted without attribution (*tathā*) in the *Subhāṣitasaṃgraha* along with the next verse (Bendall ed., part II, p. 8):

karuṇā chaḍḍi (?) jo suṇahiṃ la – –
so pāvaï uttima mā – – – ||
˘ havā karuṇā kevala bhāvaï
jamma-sahassahi mokkha ṇa pāvaï ||

Cf. Sāṅkṛtyāyana 16cd–17ab.

---

jo uṇa veṇṇa vi joḍaṇa sakkaï
ṇaü bhava ṇaü ṇivvāṇahi thakkaï [$2b_3$] || [G16 = DK_A ø]

Translation: "On the other hand, he who is able to unite the two (i.e., emptiness and compassion) will reside neither in cyclic existence nor in nirvāṇa."

[not transmitted in T]

Quoted in Vibhūticandra's *Amṛtakaṇikoddyota* (see note to previous verse):

suṇṇa karuṇa jaï jouṇa sakkaï |
ṇaü bhave ṇaü ṇivvāṇe thakkaï ||

Quoted in the *Subhāṣitasaṃgraha* (see note to previous verse):

suṇṇa-karuṇa jaï jouṇu sakkaï |
ṇo bhavaṇo ˘˘vāṇeṃ thakkaï ||

Cf. Sāṅkṛtyāyana 17cd.

---

cchaḍḍaü re ālikkā dhandhā
so mucchaha jo ticchaï bandhā ||
tasu pariāṇaṇa aṇṇa ṇa koi
avareṃ gantheṃ savva vi [2b$_4$] sovi | [G17 = DK$_A$ 15]

AB] The last words are reversed here (also in T and in the Tibetan translation of the *mūla*). The word *dhandhā* means something like the English idiom "smoke and mirrors." For example, in Hindi *Gorakh-dhaṃdhā* means "a difficult puzzle; an intricate toy, or machine; a labyrinth, maze," and therefore "a complicated task or problem," figuratively "a trying existence" (McGregor, *The Oxford Hindi–English Dictionary*, s.v.). The compound originally referred to some sort of mechanical puzzle associated with Gorakṣa, the famous Nāth. D] The reading *ganthem̥* suggests "books." This was perhaps connected to (or, if a scribal variant, inspired by) the following verse. Advayavajra must have read something like Skt. *gaṇanā* or another word meaning "heap" or "collection" (cf. Skt. *gaṇa*). Alternatively, it is possible that he, too, read *gantheṃ*, because in the verses he cites, the second refers to bookish knowledge explicitly.

chāḍḍahu re ālikkā dhandhā
so muñcahu jahiṃ ācchaï dhāndhā |

tasu pariaṇaü aṇṇa (?) na kovi
avare [17b$_5$] gālu sāvva vi sovi || [T15]

C] The reading is probably *aṇṇa*, but it looks more like *aṇu*.
D] It is difficult to make sense of the reading *gālu*.

Quoted without attribution (*tad uktam*) following G12 in Vibhūticandra's *Amṛtakaṇikoddyota* (ed. p. 120):

punastāpariāṇai aṇṇa na ko vi |
avareṃ geṇṇeṃ savva vimovi ||

Cf. Sāṅkṛtyāyana 13cd–14ab. Much of the first line is illegible.

---

sovi paḍhijjaï sovi guṇijjaï
sātthapuṇehiṃ vakkhāṇijjaï |
ṇāhi se diṭṭhi je tāva ṇa lakkhaï
[2b$_5$] ekka varaṃ gurupāā pekkhaï | [G18 = DK$_A$ 16]

B] Emend °*puṇehiṃ* to °*purāṇehiṃ*.

sovi paḍhijjaï[9] sovi guṇijjaï
sathapurāṇe vakkhāṇijjaï |
ṇṇā hi so diṭṭhi jo taha[10] ṇa lakkhaï |
etu vi varagurupāa apekkhaï || [T16]

CD] With these readings, the meaning would be: "There is no view that is not marked/seen in this [coemergent], but this [understanding] depends on the venerable, perfect guru."

Quoted without attribution (*tad uktam*) following the previous verse in Vibhūticandra's *Amṛtakaṇikoddyota* (ed. p. 120):

sovi paṭṭijjei movi guṇijjaï |
satthapurāṇai hiṃ bujjhāṇijaï |

9. sovi paḍhijjaï] T^{pc} (in a second hand), so ḍhijjaï T^{ac}
10. taha] T^{pc}, tāha T^{ac}

nāhi so diṭṭha jo tāuṇa lakkhaï |
ekke vara guru pāā pekkhaï ||

Quoted with attribution (*tathā Saraha-pādāḥ*) in the *Subhāṣitasaṃgraha* (Bendall ed., part I, p. 384):

soi paḍhijjaï soi guṇijjaui sa[t]thogame so vakkhāṇij[j]aï |
ṇāhiṃ diṭṭhi jo tāu ṇa lakkhaï ekkuvara-guru-pāā pekkhaï |

Cf. Sāṅkṛtyāyana 14cd–15ab. The second and third quarters are almost entirely illegible.

---

jaï guruvattaü hiaahi païsaï
ṇiccia hatthatha ṭhaviaü dīsaï |
sara[2b$_6$]ha bhaṇaï jaga bandhia āleṃ
ṇiasahāva ṇaü lakkhia bāleṃ || [G19 = DK$_A$ 17]

C] This line is read slightly differently in all the transmissions: Advayavajra reads "people are fooled by delusions," G reads "people are bound by delusions," and T reads "people are fooled by delusions."
D] *Ṇia°* must be read as *ṇīa°*. Emend *ṇaü* to *ṇa*.

[18a$_1$] jaï guruvutaü hiaṃhi païsaï
ṇṇicaa hatthaü ṭṭhābiaü dīsaï |
Saraha bhaṇaï jaga dhāndhī āleṃ
ṇiasahāva ṇṇa lakkhia bāleṃ || [T17]

Cf. Sāṅkṛtyāyana 15cd–16ab. Much of the verse is illegible.

---

jhāṇadīṇa pavvajjeṃ rahio
gharahi vasa[3a$_1$]nte bhaje sahio |
jaï bhiḍi visaa ramanta ṇa muccaï
Saraha bhaṇaï pariāṇa ha vuccaï || [G20 = DK$_A$ 18]

A] The reading *°dīṇa* is perhaps a corruption of *°hīṇa*, although it could perhaps be meaningful: "poor in knowledge."

B] For *bhaje*, read *bhajje/bhajjeṃ/bhājje/bhājjeṃ*.
C] The *ha* must be emended to *ki*.

jhāṇahīṇa pavva[18a_2]jje rahiaü
gehe vasante 'bhājje sahiaü |
jaï bhiḍi visaa ramante ṇṇa muñcaï
Saraha bhaṇaï pariāṇa ki vuccaï || [T18]

B] The *avagraha* is very surprising: perhaps the scribe thought that the intended meaning was "without a wife"?

Quoted without attribution in the anonymous *Yuktipradīpa*,[11] Ms 2b_2:

viṇu jhāṇeṃ viṇu pāthājjeṃ (?)
geha vasante sama gharabhajjeṃ |
jaï vaḍha viṣaya ramante na muccaï |
bhaṇaï Saraha pariāṇa ko vuccaï ||

And with a variant (?) of the second line on Ms 2b_{4-5}:

biṇu jhāṇe viṇu pāthājjeṃ (?)
geha vasanteṃ sama ghare bhajjeṃ |
eeṃ jaï puṇu ejjaṇu saccaï |
aiaï sīmo jaḍi kāha na ruccaï |

Cf. Sāṅkṛtyāyana 18.

---

jaï paccakkha ki [3a_2] jhāṇeṃ kijjaï
aha parokkha andhāra mavijjaï |
Saraha bhaṇaï maï kaḍḍhia rāva
sahajasahāva ṇa bhā[3a_3]vābhāva || [G21 = DK_A 19]

B] There is a metrical problem with this quarter. Accepting T's reading with *ndh* not making position is tempting ("or else, your meditation will just try to measure darkness"?). However, for Advayavajra, we need something with *parokkha*, which obviously is not only clearly glossed but attracted by *paccakkha*.

11. See note 14 in the introduction above.

CD] Read the rhyming syllables with an extension: *rāvā*/°*bhāvā*.

jaṃï pacakkha ki jjhāṇeṃ kīaï
[18a$_3$] ahavā jjhāṇa andhāra mavīaï |
Saraha[12] bhaṇaï maeṃ kaḍḍhia rāva
sahajasahāva ṇṇa bhāvābhāva || [T19]

A] The *anusvāra* in *jaṃï* is perhaps nothing more than a smudge.

Cf. Sāṅkṛtyāyana 19.

---

jallaï maraï uvajjaï bajjhaï
tallaï paramamahāsuha sijjhaï |
Saraha bhaṇaï haü pukkara[3a$_4$]mi
pasuloa ṇa jāṇaï ki kkarami || [G22 = DK$_A$ 20]

jallaï maraï uajjaï bājjhaï
tāllaï paramamahā[18a$_4$]suha sijjhaï |
Saraha bhaṇaï haüṃ phukkarami
vaḍḍhaloa ṇṇa bujjhaï ki kkarami || [T20]

D] Note the variant for *pasu*° (Skt. *paśu*), *vaḍḍha*°, which should be read as *vaḍha*°, "fools."

Cf. Sāṅkṛtyāyana 20.

---

jhāṇarahia ki kījaï jhāṇeṃ
jo avāha tahiṃ kāi vakhāṇeṃ |
bha[3a$_5$]vamuddeṃ jeṇa saala vi vāhiu
ṇiasahāba ṇaü keṇa vi gāhiu || [G23 = DK$_A$ 21]

jhāṇarahia ki kīaï jjhāṇe
jo avācca taṃhi ki vakkhāṇeṃ |
bhūamuddeṃ sa[18a$_5$]ala jaga vāhiu
ṇṇiasahāva sa hi keṇa nna gāhiu || [T21]

12. Saraha] T[pc], sarahe T[ac]

The entire verse is strained with metrical problems, and this perhaps explains the wildly fluctuating readings. Shahidullah did his best to make this work as a *pādākulaka*, but it is entirely possible that the verse was originally composed in another, rarer meter.

Cf. Sāṅkṛtyāyana 42.

---

manta ṇa tanta ṇa dhea ṇa dhāraṇa
savva vi [3a$_6$] re vaḍha vibbhamakāraṇa |
asamalacitta ma jhāṇeṃ kharaḍaha
suha acchanteṃ ma appaṇa jhagaḍaha || [G24 = DK$_A$ 22]

tānta ṇṇa mānta ṇṇa dhea ṇṇa dhāraṇa
sāvvaï re vvaḍha vibbhamakāraṇa |
asavalacitta ma jjhāṇe kharaḍaü
[18b$_1$] suhe acchante mma appaṇa jharaḍaü || [T22]

Quoted with attribution (*Sarahapādā api*) in Ratnarakṣita's *Padminī*, a commentary on the *Saṃvarodayatantra* (Buddhist Library, Nagoya Ms Takaoka CA17, fol. 21b$_{7-8}$):

manta ṇa tanta ṇa dheya ṇa dhāraṇa
savva vi re vaḍha vibhamakāraṇa |
asamalacitta ma jhāṇe kharaḍaha
suhe acchante appāṇa sagaḍaha ||

Cf. Sāṅkṛtyāyana 43.

---

khāanteṃ pībanteṃ [3b$_1$] suraa ramanteṃ
alibalibahala cakka pasaranteṃ |
emaï siddhi jāṇa paraloaha
matthahi pāva deï pasulovaha || [G25 = DK$_A$ 23]

D] The last compound is transmitted in various ways: here we have the word for "beast" (*pasu*, Skt. *paśu*), otherwise a Śaiva idiom for bound souls. T and possibly the Sa skya manuscript, as well as N of the DKP$_A$, read "ghosts" (*bhūa* or *bhua*, Skt. *bhūta*). Advayavajra seems to have read "frightened" (*bhaa*, Skt. *bhaya* in the meaning *bhīta*).

khānte pibante suraa ramante
alicalibahalaṃ cakka phurante
evehiṃ siddhi jāi paraloaha
māthe pāa daï bhūalo[18b_2]aha || [T23]

B] The reading °*cali*° is a copying mistake for °*bali*°.

Depending on which readings we accept as genuine, there could be several metrical patterns in play. Shahidullah had to reconstruct most of the verse and opted for a *pādākulaka*.

Cf. Sāṅkṛtyāyana 48.

[3b_2] jahi maṇa pavaṇa ṇa sañcaraï
ravi sasi ṇāhi pavesa |
tahi vaḍha citta visāma karu
sarahem̩ kahia uesa [G26 = DK_A 24]

jahi maṇa pavaṇa ṇṇa saṃcaraï
ravikiraṇaho ṇṇāhiṃ paveśa |
tahi vaḍḍha citta visāma kuru
sarahem̩ kahia uddeśa || [T24]

B] Note the variant: not "the sun and moon" but "the rays of the sun."

Cf. Sāṅkṛtyāyana 49.

[3b_3] ekka karu mā bhiṇṇa karu
mā karu vaṇṇavisesa |
ekkem̩ raṅgem̩ raṅgiā
tihuvaṇa saalāsesa[13] || [G27 = DK_A 25]

13. saalāasesa] G^{pc}, saalāasesa G^{ac} (The cancellation mark is very faint but just about visible above the *a*.)

A] The *u* in *karu* must be read as long. Note the variant *bhiṇṇa* for *veṇni*—i.e., "distinction" instead of "two." The meaning is more or less the same.

eka karu mā veṇṇi karu
mā karu va[18b_3]ṇṇavisesa
eke rāñje rañjiā
tihuṇa saalāsesa | [T25]

D] Emend *tihuṇa* to *tihuaṇa/tihuvaṇa*.

Cf. Sāṅkṛtyāyana 50.

āi ṇa anta [3b_4] ṇa majhu tahi
ṇaü bhava ṇaü ṇivvāṇa |
ehu so paramamahāsuhao
ṇaü para ṇaü appāṇa || [G28 = DK_A 26]

A] For *majhu*, read *majjhu*.

āi ṇṇa anta ṇṇa majjha tahi
ṇṇaü bhava ṇṇaü ṇṇivāṇa |
ehu so paramamahāsuhaü
ṇṇaü para ṇṇaü [18b_4] appāṇa || [T26]

B] For *ṇṇivāṇa*, read *ṇivvāṇa* for the meter.

This famous verse is paralleled in *Hevajratantra* II.v.68. The direction of the borrowing is unclear for the time being. It is difficult to ascertain which source a particular author had in mind when quoting this couplet without attribution. See, e.g., Abhayākaragupta's *Āmnāyamañjarī* chap. 5, Vibhūticandra's *Amṛtakaṇikoddyota* (ed. pp. 131, 178), Kuladatta's *Kriyāsaṃgrahapañjikā* chap. 6, and several *sādhana* texts.

Cf. Sāṅkṛtyāyana 51.

---

aggeṃ paccheṃ dasa[3b_5]disahi
jaṃ jaṃ jovami sovi |

evvem̩ tuṭṭaï bhantaḍī
ṇāha ṇa pucchami kovi || [G29 = DK_A 27]

ageem̩ pāccheem̩ daśadiśehim̩
jam̩ jam̩ joami sovi
eve tuṭṭī bhāntaḍī
ṇṇāha ṇṇa pucchami kovi || [T27]

Quoted without attribution (*tad uktam*) in *Fragment with Apabhramśa Quotations*, Tokyo University Library no. 312 (old no. 230), Ms fol. 12b:

aṅgem̩ pacchen daśadiahi jañ jañ jovami soi |
evven tuṭṭaï bhantaḍī ṇāha ṇa pucchaï koi ||

Cf. Sāṅkṛtyāyana 52.

---

indī jattha vilīa gaü
ṇaṭṭhaü appa[3b_6]sahāva |
so hale sahajānandataṇu
phuḍa pucchaha gurupāva || [G30 = DK_A 28]

C] Scan either *sŏ halē* or *sō halĕ*.

indī jatha vilaa[14] gaü
ṇṇaṭṭha vi appasahāva |
so [18b_5] hale sahajāṇandataṇu
phuḍa pucchaü gurupāu || [T28]

BD] Note that the scribal forms should rhyme in pronunciation: °*sahāva*/°*pāva* or °*sahāu*/°*pāu*.

Quoted without attribution in Abhayākaragupta's *Abhayapaddhati* (Ms. A, National Archives Kathmandu 5–21 = NGMPP reel no. A 48/2, fol. 14a; Ms B, Asiatic Society Calcutta G3827, fol. 38a; transcripts courtesy of Harunaga Isaacson):

14. bilaa] T^{pc}, balea T^{ac}

indī yattha vilīna gaü (gaḍa B) naṭṭha (naṭṭa B) vi appasahāva |
so hale sahajāṇandagaï phuḍu pucchaha gurupāva (°pāca A) ||

Quoted without attribution (*tad uktaṃ*) in Kuladatta's *Kriyāsaṃgrahapañjikā*, chap. 6:

indrī jattha vilīya gaü ṇatthā appasahāva |
so hale sahajānanda taṇu phuḍa pucchaha gurupāḍa ||

Cf. Sāṅkṛtyāyana 29.

---

jahi maṇa maraï pava ho kkhaa jāi |
ehu sa paramama[4a$_1$]hāsuha rahia kahiṃ ppi ṇa jāi || [G31 = DK$_A$ 29]

B] A syllable dropped out, read *pava* as *pavaṇa*. The pronoun *sa* was perhaps cancelled by the scribe, but the mark is barely legible.

jahi maṇa maraï pavaṇa ho khaa jāi |
eso paramamahāsuha Saraha kahi ppi ṇu jāi || [T29]

D] Note the variant "Saraha does not go anywhere" or perhaps "Where is it that Saraha does not go?"

The identity of the meter is doubtful. Shahidullah calls it a *pādākulaka*, but this is simply because he had thought that the verse was lacunose form and therefore reconstituted much of it. G does not split the verse quarters in any way.

Cf. Sāṅkṛtyāyana 30.

---

saïsaṃvitti ma karahu re dandhā
bhāvābhāva sugati re bandhā |
ṇiamaṇa muṇahu re [4a$_2$] ṇiuṇeṃ jāi
jima jala jalahi milanteṃ soi || [G32 = DK$_A$ 30]

C] For *jāi*, read *joi* (also see next note).
CD] Both endings must be read as long—i.e., *joī/soī*.

saeṃsaṃbitti [19 *missing* (lacuna of one folio)] [T30]

Cf. Sāṅkṛtyāyana 88cd–89ab.

---

jhāṇeṃ mokkha ki cāhu re āleṃ
māājāla ki lehu re koleṃ |
[4a$_3$] varaguruvaaṇa pah.ḍijjaha succeṃ |
Saraha bhaṇaï maï kahiaü vacceṃ || [G33 = DK$_A$ 31]

C] For *succeṃ*, read *sacceṃ*.

Cf. Sāṅkṛtyāyana 89cd–90ab.

---

paḍhameṃ jaï āāsa visuddho
cāhanteṃ cā[4a$_4$]hanteṃ diṭṭhi ṇiruddhā |
evveṃ jaï āāsavikālo
ṇiamaṇadosa ṇa bujjhaï bālo || [G34 = DK$_A$ 32]

B] For *ṇiruddhā*, read *ṇiruddho*.

The first line is quoted with attribution (*śrīSarahapādair uktam*) in Nāropa's *Sekoddeśaṭīkā* (Sferra 2006, p. 139):

mūḍhā antarāla parimāṇaha
tuṭṭaï mohajāla jaï jāṇaha |
paḍhame jaï āāsa visuddho
cāhaṃte cāhaṃte diṭṭhi ṇiruddho ||

The same can be found with a slightly different attribution (*śrīSarahavīrair uktam*)[15] in Raviśrījñāna's *Amṛtakaṇikā* (ed. p. 35):

15. This attribution is curious. While Raviśrījñāna very likely borrowed the quotation from the *Sekoddeśaṭīkā*, we do know of a Sarahavīra, son of Bhaṭṭa, from a different source; see the

mūḍho antarālaparimāṇaha |
tuṭṭai mohajāla guru pucchia jāṇaha ||
paḍhame yai āāsa visuddho |
cāhaṃte cāhaṃte diṭṭhi ṇiruddho ||

Cf. Sāṅkṛtyāyana 33.

---

ahimaṇadūseṃ ṇa lakkhi[4a$_5$]a tatta
dūsaï saala jāṇa so datta |
jhāṇeṃ mohia saala vi loa
ṇiasahāva ṇaü lakkhaa kovi a || [G35 = DK$_A$ 33]

A] The ending must be read as long—i.e., *tattā*.
B] All transmissions of this line lack a *mora* in the second *gaṇa*. As a diagnostic conjecture, one might reasonably propose *dūsaï a* (Skt. *ca*) *saala*. In the DKP$_A$ we opted for another tentative solution: to read an instrumental pronoun at the beginning of the line. However, it is possible that this was originally part of the *pañjikā*, not the root text. For *datta*, read *detta*, with the second syllable lengthened.
D] The are several occurrences in the root text where *ṇia* (Skt. *nija*) must be read as *ṇīa* (cf., e.g., G19d above). For *ṇaü*, read *ṇa* for the meter's sake.

Cf. Sāṅkṛtyāyana 34.

---

ci[4a$_6$]ttaha mūla ṇa lakkhiaü
sahajeṃ ttiṇṇi jāṇa vitattha |
tahiṃ uvajjaï vilaïjjaï
vasiaü kahi phuḍa ettha || [G36 = DK$_A$ 34]

B] The word *jāṇa* seems to be an intrusion: neither the meaning nor the meter sanctions it, and it is not seen in any other transmission. Perhaps it was originally a gloss that became part of the constituted text. This would suggest that

colophon of a work simply called the *Svādhiṣṭhānakrama*, Ms National Archives Kathmandu 5-6905 = NGMPP reel no. A 48/12.

the postulated glossator thought that "the three" refers to the three vehicles, as *jāṇa* is mentioned in the previous verse.
CD] The DKP_A gives a somewhat artificial reading of this line; it is possible that the author was trying to make sense of a line that he had in a corrupt form. The third *pāda* is metrically impossible, but perhaps it bears a trace of the original meaning, which must have been something like "[the mind] arises and dissolves in that (i.e., *sahaja*)." The reading *kahi* as well seems to be corrupt, unless *tahiṃ* also was *kahiṃ*, in which case we have a series of rhetorical questions: "Where does it arise? Where does it dissolve? Where does it abide?" The last two words may have been a separate sentence, "This is clear." In the DKP_A edition, we were constrained to follow Advayavajra's gloss, *putra*, which seems artificial.

Cf. Sāṅkṛtyāyana 27.

[$4b_1$] mūlarahia jo cittaï tatta
guruuvaesaha etta viatta |
Saraha bhaṇaï vaḍha jāṇahu caṅgeṃ
ciarūasaṃsāraha bha[$4b_2$]ṅgeṃ || [G37 = DK_A 35]

AB] Read the endings lengthened—i.e., *tattā/viattā*.
D] In spite of the fact that it creates a syncopation at the beginning of the *pāda*, we must emend to *cittarūa*°.

Cf. Sāṅkṛtyāyana 29 (note, however, that the second half is quite different).

ṇīasahāva ṇaü kahiaü vaaṇeṃ
dīsaï guruüesaṇha ṇaaṇeṃ |
ṇaü tasu dosa jeṃ ekka vi ṭhāi
dhammā[$4b_3$]dhamma so soh.ḍī khāi || [G38 = DK_A 36]

A] Here G spells out that *ṇīa*° must be read with a long *-i*, as it should be in the DKP_A edition, too. For *ṇaü*, read *ṇa*.
B] The intrusion of the *ṇ* in the genitive ending is surprising.
CD] Read the endings as long: *ṭhāī/khāī*.
D] The reading *soh.ḍī* is surprising; we expect an absolutive or a participle here.

Cf. Sāṅkṛtyāyana 90cd–91ab.

ṇiamaṇa saccem̥ sohia jaccem̥
guruguṇa hiaem̥ païsaï taccem̥ |
evam aṇem̥ muṇi sarahem̥ gā[4b$_4$]hiu[16]
tatta manta ṇaü ekka vi cāhiu || [G39 = DK$_A$ 37]

A] For *saccem̥*, read *savvem̥*, although the reading is not meaningless: "in truth," or "earnestly."
AB] The rhyme must be read as *javvem̥/tabbem̥*; this reading is very likely a copying mistake.
C] For *aṇem̥*, read *amaṇem̥*.
D] For *tatta*, read *tanta*. The reading constituted in the DKP$_A$ edition is perhaps smoother, but here too, with a syncopation, we can see the quarter as metrical.

Cf. Sāṅkṛtyāyana 36.

---

bajjaï kammeṇa jaṇo
kammavimukkeṇa hoi maṇamokkham̥ |
maṇamukkhaṇa a[4b$_5$]ṇūṇṇam̥
pāvijjaï paramaṇivvāṇem̥ || [G40 = DK$_A$ 38]

A] The reading *vajjaï* can be conceived of as a spelling variant of *vajjhaï*.
C] °*Mukkhaṇa* must be corrected to °*mokkheṇa*. For *aṇūṇṇam̥*, read *aṇūṇam̥*.
D] The oblique-case °*nivvāṇem̥* must be corrected on account of syntax to °*ṇivvāṇam̥*.

Cf. Sāṅkṛtyāyana 24.

---

ciekka saalabīam̥
bhavaṇivvāṇā vi jattha viphuranti |

16. gāhiu] G^{pc}, gahiu G^{ac}

tam̩ cintāmaṇirūvam̩
[$4b_6$] paṇamaha icchāphalam̩ dei || [G41 = DK_A 39]

A] Read *ciekka* as *cīekka* or emend to *cittekka*.
B] The locative *jattha* is perhaps smoother than the genitive; the transmissions and the testimonies attest both in more or less equal measure.

Quoted with attribution (*uktam̩ ca Sarahapādaiḥ*) in Ratnarakṣita's *Padminī* (Buddhist Library, Nagoya Ms Takaoka CA17 fol. $22a_{4-5}$):

cittaika sakalabījam̩ bhavaṇirvvāṇa vi jassa visphurinti |
tañ cintāmaṇirūam̩ paṇaraha icchāphalam̩ dei ||

Quoted without attribution (*tad uktam*) in *Fragment with Apabhram̩śa Quotations*, Tokyo University Library no. 312 (old no. 230), Ms fol. 12a–b:

citteka saalabīam̩ bhabaṇibbāṇā bi jattha biphuranti |
tañ cintāmaṇirūam paṇamaha jo icchāphalan dei ||

Quoted with attribution to the title (*Dohākośe 'py uktam*) in the *Subhāṣitasam̩graha* (Bendall ed., part II, p. 12):

cittekku saalabīam̩ bhava-nivvāṇa jahi vipphuḍant'assu |
tam̩ cintāmaṇi-rūam̩ paṇamaha icchāhalam̩ deï ||

Cf. Sāṅkṛtyāyana 23.

---

cittem̩ bajjem̩ bajjaï
mukkem̩ mukkei ṇatthi sandeho |
bajjanti jeṇa vi jaḍā
lau pariṇamucca[$5a_1$]nti teṇa te vi buhā || [G42 = DK_A 40]

B] The scribe put his *pāda*-marker after *mukkem̩*, but this is incorrect, because the meter is *gāthā*/*āryā*.
D] For *pariṇamuccanti*, read *parimuccanti*. The *te* must be deleted.

Quoted without attribution (*tad uktam*) in *Fragment with Apabhram̩śa Quotations*, Tokyo University Library no. 312 (old no. 230), Ms fol. 12b:

citte bajjeim bajjaï mukkem mukkei ṇatthi sandeho |
bajjanti jeṇa bi jaa lahu parimucanti teṇa vi buddhā ||

Cf. Sāṅkṛtyāyana 91cd–92ab.

baddho dhāvaï dahadihahiṃ
mukko u ṇiccala ṭhāi |
emai karahā pekkhu sahi
vivaria mahu paḍ.hihāi || [G43 = DK_A 41]

B] The *u* does not have any justification, unless we read it as Skt. *tu*, but then the previous word has to be read as *mukkŏ*.
C] *karahā* is lengthened purely for metrical reasons.

Cf. Sāṅkṛtyāyana 26.

[$5a_2$] pavaṇarahia appāṇa cintaha
kaṭhajoaṇā saṅge ma vindaha |
are vaḍha sahajagaī para rajjaha
mā bhavagandhaba paḍ.hivajjaha || [G44 = DK_A 42]

A] The *ma* before *cintaha* must have dropped out.
D] Emend °*gandhaba* to °*gandhabandha*.

[manuscript resumes: $20a_1$] + + + + + + + rajjaü
mā bhavagandhabandha paḍivajaü || [T*42]

The readings fluctuate wildly for this verse, and we suspect that Advayavajra's interpretation is slightly artificial in parts. The intended meaning may have been something along these lines: "Do not think that you can exist without breath. Do not partake in (imperative of Skt. *vid*, i.e., *vindati/e*) attachment by means of difficult yogic practices (instrumental of Skt. *kaṣṭa-yoga*)! O fool! Rather (Skt. *param*; alternatively "intensively"), take pleasure (imperative of Skt. *rañj*) in the ways of the coemergent (Skt. *sahaja-gati*), and do not dedicate yourself (imperative of Skt. *prati-pad*) to bondage reeking of existence!"

Cf. Sāṅkṛtyāyana 93cd–94ab. The first half may be interpreted as follows:

"Do not split yourself (imperative of Skt. *bhid*) holding the breath! Do not seek difficult yogic practice [by focusing] at the tip of your nose!"

> [5a$_3$] ehu maṇa mallaha pavaṇa tuṅga sucañcala |
> sahajasahāvaṭhā vasahi homu ṇiccala || [G45 = DK$_A$ 43]

B] The word *tuṅga* should perhaps be emended to *turaṅga*. It is not meaningless as it is ("mighty" or "strong"), but comparing the mind to a fickle steed is common.

> ehu ṇṇiamaṇa sacala cāra taraṅga saṃcala
> melahiṃ sahāvaṭṭhā vasaï dosaï ṇṇiccala || [T*43]

The identity of the meter was already questioned by Shahidullah. It seems that this verse was garbled in transmission at a very early date.

Cf. Sāṅkṛtyāyana 94cd. Here, too, the readings are quite different.

> javveṃ maṇa atthamaṇa jāi
> tasu [5a$_4$] uṭṭaï bandhaṇa |
> tavveṃ samarasa sahajeṃ vajjiaü
> ṇa suddha ṇa bamhaṇa || [G46 = DK$_A$ 44]

B] The locative pronoun *tasu* could make sense ("in that," i.e., "in the mind"), but *taṇu* seems to be the better reading. Emend *uṭṭaï* to *ṭuṭṭaï*.

C] All sources transmit this *pāda* in a hypermetrical form (even though in this version of the dohā we should have fourteen *morae*). The closest to an acceptable solution is the Sa skya manuscript, which reads *tavveṃ samarasahi majjheṃ*. If the suffix *hi* is read as long, the meter works. The meaning would be: "Then, in the middle of one taste, there is no *śūdra* and no brahman." It is possible that at some point this *pāda* was glossed and that the glosses garbled the transmission.

D] Emend to the first *ṇa* to *ṇaü*, for the sake of the meter, and *suddha* to *sudda*, as Skt. *śuddha*, "pure," does not make good sense.

[20a$_2$] jeve maṇu akṣamanta jāi
taṇu tuṭṭaï bandha
tavveṃ samarasa rahiamajjhā
ṇaü sudda ṇṇa bāhmaṇa || [T*44]

A] The reading *akṣamanta* is very likely a severe corruption.
B] Emend *bandha* to *bandhaṇa*.
C] The reading *rahiamajjhā*, "bereft of middle," is difficult to construe.

Cf. Sāṅkṛtyāyana 95.

etthu se surasari jamuṇā
etthu se gaṅgāsā[5a$_5$]aru |
etthu paāga vaṇārasi
etthu ye canda divāaru || [G47 = DK$_A$ 45]

D] Emend *ye* to *se*.

ethu se surasaï somaṇāha ethu gaṅgāsāaru
vā[20a$_3$]rāṇasi paeāle ethu se canda divāaru | [T*44]

The meter (*mahānubhava*) is unique in the collection, if we accept the readings of G and possibly Advayavajra. The readings of the Sa skya manuscript and Tokyo suggest another metrical form and with the crucial variant *somaṇāha/sovaṇāha* (i.e., Somanātha) instead of the river Yamunā. There is a possibility that the original verse was by an author who was still aware of the significance of the famous Somanātha temple in Gujarat and that the verse was recomposed in Gangetic India. However, it is equally possible the verse (a dohā?) was garbled in transmission early on and the transmission sought to repair it in this way.

Cf. Sāṅkṛtyāyana 96.

khetta piṭṭha upapiṭṭha
etthu maï bhamaï paviṭṭhao |
dehāsarisa suti[5a$_6$]ttha
maï puha vibhamanta ṇa diṭṭhao || [G48 = DK$_A$ 46]

B] Note the variant *paviṭṭhao*, possibly "entered."
C] The variant *sutittha* is elegant and probably better than the reading of DK_A.
D] Emend *puha* to *suha*. The *pāda* is otherwise severely hypermetrical and corrupt. This and other fluctuations may be because the meter (*soraṭṭhā*) is somewhat rare in the collection and therefore more susceptible to corruption in the hands of a less learned scribe.

khetta piṭṭha upapiṭṭha
ethu maï bhamaa samiṭṭhao
dehāsarasamasarisa titha
maï suaü ṇṇaü diṭṭhao || [T*46]

B] The meaning of the variant *samiṭṭhao* (also witnessed by the Sa skya manuscript) is "obscure."
C] The *pāda* is severely hypermetrical; it can be suspected that the nonsensical first word is an uncorrected dittography.
D] Note the variant: "I have never heard of or seen." However, one must conjecture that a *ṇa* was lost after *maï*.

Cf. Sāṅkṛtyāyana 97.

---

saṇḍapuiṇidalakamala-
gandhakesaraṇāleṃ |
chaḍḍahu veṇṇi ma karaha
sosa ṇa lagaü va[$5b_1$]ḍha āleṃ || [G49 = DK_A 47]

B] Note the variant without °*vara*°, which, although clearly read by Advayavajra, makes the line hypermetrical (if indeed Shahidullah is correct in stating that this pattern is *rolā*).

[$20a_4$] sarapuhaaṇidalukamala-
gandhakeśaravaraṇṇāle
cchāḍahu[17] veṇṇi mā karahu
sosa lāggahu vaḍha āleṃ || [T*47]

17. cchāḍahu] T^{pc}, cchāḍahahu T^{ac}

A] Emend °*puhaaṇi*° to a form with one less *mora*.
C] Correct *mā* to *ma*.
D] Emend *sosa* to *sosa na*.

Cf. Sāṅkṛtyāyana 98.

---

kā manthasanthavakhāṇaha
puiha kulahīṇao |
bamha viṭṭhu tahiloa
saala jahi jāi vilīṇao || [G50 = DK_A 48]

A] The reading becomes meaningful ("What is the use of explaining *mantraśāstra*") if we emend to *kā mantasatthavakhāṇehi* (*tth* not making position), but then the meter suffers. Unfortunately the same is true of the constituted *pāda* in DKP.
B] It seems that we must emend to *jāi pucchaha/pucchahu* throughout, with *cch* not making position. If the meaning is indeed Skt. *kṣayaṃ yāti*, we have here a rare instance of *kārikā*-style syntax.
D] For *jāi*, read *jaï*.

ka mmātu sāndhu khae
jāe pujahu kulahīṇa[20a_5]e |
bahma viṭṭhu taïloa
saala jahi jāi vilīṇao || [T*48]

AB] The first line is very corrupt; see notes above.

Cf. Sāṅkṛtyāyana 99.

---

are putta bojja [5b_2] rasa-
ramaṇa susaṇṭhi avejja |
vakkhāṇa paḍhantahiṃ jagahiṃ
ṇa jāṇia sejjā || [G51 = DK_A 49]

B] Correct °*ramaṇa* to °*rasaṇa*.
D] Emend *sejjā* to *sojjha*, but the pāda is still hypometrical.

are putta bojjhu re
susathaaü abhejja |
vakkhāṇa paḍhantāmiu jagaṃhi
ṇṇi āṇiu mijja || [T*49]

BD] The transmission seems hopelessly corrupt.

Cf. Sāṅkṛtyāyana 56.

---

are putta tatta vicittarasa
kahuṇu ṇa sakkaï [5b$_3$] vatthu |
kapparahia suhaṭhāṇu
varu jjagu ūaggaï tatthu || [G52 = DK$_A$ 50]

A] Note that the more natural reading is Skt. *vicitra*, "of manifold taste," but Advayavajra opted for Skt. *vicintita*.

[20b$_1$] are puta tatta vicittarasa
kahaṇṇa ṇṇa sakaï vathu |
karppu(?)rahia suṭṭhāṇaü
jaga uajaï tathu || [T*50]

CD] A corrupt transmission.

Cf. Sāṅkṛtyāyana 104 (*pāda* d is very different).

---

buddhi viṇāsaï maṇa maraï
tuṭṭhaï jahiṃ māṇa |
so [5b$_4$] māāmaa paramakalu
tahiṃ kiṅ kijjaï jhāṇa || [G53 = DK$_A$ 51]

B] Emend *māṇa* to *ahimāṇa*.
D] This phrasing is slightly different: "What will meditation do regarding that?"

buddhi viṇāsaï maṇa maraï
tuṭṭhaï jaṃhi ahimāṇu |
so [2ob$_2$] māāmaa paramakalu
taṃhi ki bajjhaï jjhāṇu | [T*51]

Cf. Sāṅkṛtyāyana 61.

---

bhavahiṃ uvajjaï khaahi ṇivajjaï
bhāvarahia puṇu ka[5b$_5$]hia uvajjaï |
veṇṇi vivajjia joū vajjaï
atthaha siraguruṇāha kahijjaï || [G54 = DK$_A$ 52]

B] Correct *kahia* to *kahi*.

bhaba ubbhājjaï (?) khaeṃhi ṇṇivajjaï
bhāvarahia puṇṇa kahi ujjaï |
vevi vivajjia jou ajjaï
athaha śi[2ob$_3$]riguruṇāhe[18] kahijjaï[19] || [T*52]

B] Emend *ujjaï* to *uajjaï*.
C] Emend *ajjaï* to *vajjaï*.

Cf. Sāṅkṛtyāyana 62.

---

dekkhaha suṇaha parīsaha khāhu
ji[5b$_6$]gghahu bhamahumahu baïṭṭahu ṭhāhu |
ālamālavyavahāreṃ bollaha
maṇa cchuḍu ekkākāra ma calaha || [G55 = DK$_A$ 53]

B] Emend *bhamahumahu* to *bhamahu*, an uncorrected dittography.
C] The Sanskritism °*vya*° is widely attested in the transmission. The reading *bollahu* seems to have the same meaning as *pellahu*, glossed in the DKP$_A$ as "to spend time."

18. °guruṇāhe] T^{pc}, °gurupāṇāhe T^{ac}
19. kahijjaï] T^{pc}, kahiṃjjaï T^{ac}

dekkhaü suṇaü païsaü sāu
jigghaü[20] bhamaü baïṭṭhaü uṭṭhāu |
ālamālavyavahāre bollaü
maṇa cchuḍa ekākā[20b$_4$]re mā cālaü || [T*53]

A] If *païsaü* is kept, the *i* must be lengthened. Emend *sāu* to *khāu*.

Quoted without attribution (*uktaṃ ca*) in *Fragment with Apabhraṃśa Quotations*, Tokyo University Library no. 312 (old no. 230), Ms fol. 9a:

dekhahu suṇṇahu parīsahu khāhu |
jigghahu bhamahu baïṭhahu ṭhāhu ||
ālamālavyavahārem bolahu |
maṇa cchaḍa (?) ekākāra ma ccallahu ||

Cf. Sāṅkṛtyāyana 63.

---

guruuvaeso ami[6a$_1$]arasa
dhavahi ṇa pīaü jehiṃ |
bahusatthatthamarutthalihiṃ
tisia maruvvaü tehiṃ || [G56 = DK$_A$ 54]

guruuaesem amiarasa
ovahi ṇṇa pibiao jjaṃhi
bahusattāthamaruthili
tisihiṃ maniccao ttehiṃ || [T*54]

B] Emend *ovahi* to *dhavahi*.
D] Emend *maniccao* to *marivvao* or some similar spelling variant.

Quoted with attribution (*tathā Saraha-pādāḥ*) in the *Subhāṣitasaṃgraha* (Bendall ed., part I, p. 384):

guru-uvaesaha amia rasu havahi ṇa pīaü jehi |
jaha satthe[ṇa] marutthalihiṃ tisia mariaü tehi ||

20. jigghaü] T^{pc}, jiṅghagghaü T^{ac}

Cf. Sāṅkṛtyāyana 44.

---

cintācinta vi parihara
tima atthaha jima bā[6a$_2$]la |
guruvaaṇeṃ diḍhabhanti karu
hoihaï sahaja ullālu || [G57 = DK$_A$ 55]

A] Emend *parihara* to *pariharahu.*

cittācitta vi pariharahu
tima acchaha ji[20b$_5$]ma bāl+ |
g+r+vaaṇehi diḍhabhalli[21] karu
hoi sahaja ullāla || [T*55]

C] Emend °*bhalli* to °*bhatti.*

Cf. Sāṅkṛtyāyana 64.

---

akkharavaṇṇopamaguṇarahio
bhaṇaï ṇa jā so e maï kahi[6a$_3$]o |
so paramesara kāsu kahijjaï
suraa kumārī jima uppajjaï || [G58 = DK$_A$ 56]

akṣaravaṇṇopama guṇe rahiae
bhaṇaï ṇṇa jāi so amaṃ kahiao |
so [21a$_1$] parameśvara kāsu kahijjaï
suraa kumārī jima uajjaï || [T*56]

Cf. Sāṅkṛtyāyana 65.

ṇa ttam vāeṃ guru kahaï
ṇa ttam bujjhaï [6a$_4$] sīsa |

21. °bhalli] T^{pc}, °mabhalli T^{ac}

sahajāmiarasa ekku jaï
kāsu kahijjaï kīsa || [G59 = DK_A ø]

[not transmitted in T]

Translation: "The guru will not explain it with words, and the disciple will not understand it. Since the coemergent is one and of the taste of immortality (*pun*: of endless delight), who will explain it to whom?"

Quoted without attribution (*yad āha*) in Vibhūticandra's *Amṛtakaṇikoddyota* (ed. p. 179):

ṇaü taṃ vāahi guru kahaï ṇaü taṃ bujjaï śīṣa |
sahaja amia rasu saala jagu kāsu kahijjaï kīṣa ||

Quoted with attribution to "another tantra/treatise" (*tad uktaṃ tantrāntare*) in Kuladatta's *Kriyāsaṃgrahapañjikā* chap. 6:

ṇa taṃ vāe guru kaha ṇa taṃ bujja sīsa |
sahajāvatthā amaarasa kāsu kahija kīsa ||

This dohā verse is transmitted in another Saraha collection, see stanza 9 in Bagchi 1938, 12–13. Some readings were silently corrected by the editor, as the manuscript (National Archives Kathmandu 1–1633 = NGMPP reel no. A 21/13, fol. 2a) reads *sahaja*° for *sahajā*° and *kāmu* for *kāsu*.

Cf. Sāṅkṛtyāyana 77.

---

bhāvābhāveṃ jo parihīṇo
tahi jaga saala ase[$6a_5$]sa vilīṇo |
javveṃ tahi maṇa ṇiccala thakkaï
tavveṃ bhavaṇivvāṇahi mukkaï || [G60 = DK_A 57]

bhāvābhāvehi jo paricchinnao
taṃhi jaga tiasāsesa viliṇṇa + |
jevve taṃhi maṇa ṇṇica[$21a_2$]la thākaï
tavveṃ bhavasaṃnsārahiṃ mukkaï || [T*57]

A] Note the variant *paricchinnao*, which conveys the same meaning.
B] The reading *tiasā*° is puzzling. Perhaps "all three worlds"?

D] The reading °*saṃnsārahiṃ* must be a corruption attracted by *bhava*°. All the other witnesses have the equivalent of *nirvāṇa*.

Cf. Sāṅkṛtyāyana 66.

---

jāva ṇa apā para pariāṇahi
tāva ki [6a$_6$] dehāṇuttara pāvasi |
emaï tahio bhanti ṇa kavvā
appahi appā bujjhasi tavvā || [G61 = DK$_A$ 58]

A] The phrasing here is slightly different: "As long as you do not recognize yourself as the supreme reality."
C] Emend *tahio* to *kahio*.

jāva ṇṇa appaü para pariāṇasi
tāva ki dehāṇuttara pāvasi |
e dhammā kahiao bhāva
appaü appā bujjha[21a$_3$]hiṃ tāvā || [T*58]

C] This quarter seems corrupt, unless the meaning is "This teaching I have taught with relish" (correct to *dhamma* ... *bhāveṃ*), but then *tāvā* becomes difficult to construe.

Cf. Sāṅkṛtyāyana 67.

ṇaü aṇu ṇa paramāṇu vicittao
[6b$_1$] aṇavarabhāvahi phuraï sorattao |
bhaṇaï Saraha bhiḍi etta vimattao
ari ṇikollī bujjhaha paramatatthao || [G62 = DK$_A$ 59]

aṇu paramāṇu na rua vicittao
aṇavarabhāvaha pharaï sanātao |
Saraha bhaṇaï bhiḍi putta vimāntao
are ṇṇikolli bajjhahu mittao || [T*59]

B] Note the variant subject: "the eternal one."

C] Note the variant *putta*, a vocative for "son."
D] The last two words seem to be corrupt.

Cf. Sāṅkṛtyāyana 68.

---

meheṃ accha[6b$_2$]ï bāhira pucchaï
paï dekkhaï paḍivesī pucchaï |
Saraha bhaṇaï vaḍha jāṇaha appā
ṇaü so dhea ṇa dhāraṇa jappā || [G63 = DK$_A$ 60]

A] Emend *meheṃ* to *geheṃ*.

[21a$_4$] ghareṃ ācchaï bāhire ācchaï
paï dekhiï paḍavesaha pucchaï
Saraha bhaṇaï vaḍha[22] jāṇahu appā
ṇṇaü so dhia dhāraṇa appā || [T*60]

A] Note the variant for *pucchaï*, perhaps attracted by the first indicative, but also meaningful ("sometimes in the house, sometimes outside").
D] The second *ṇa* dropped out.

Cf. Sāṅkṛtyāyana 69.

---

jaï [6b$_3$] guru kahaï ta savva vi jāṇī
mokkha ki labbhaï e viṇu jāṇī |
desa bhamaï bavkāseṃ laïo
sahaja ṇa bujjhaï pā[6b$_4$]peṃ gahio || [G64]

C] Note the variant for "practice"; perhaps cf. Hindi *bakvās*, "idle chatter"?

jaïṃ guru ka[21a$_5$]haï[23] savva vi jāṇī
mokkha na cchāḍaï appaü vāṇī |

22. vaḍha] T^{pc}, vaḍhu T^{ac}
23. kahaï] T^{pc}, kahahaï T^{ac}

deśa bhamaï habbhāse laïao
sahaja ṇṇa bujjhaï pāveṇṇa gaḍhiao | [T62]

B] The variant is somewhat obscure: "Liberated, will you not give up on your own words?" (?).

Cf. Sāṅkṛtyāyana 70.

---

visaa ramatta ṇa visaahiṃ lippaï
ūvala haraï ṇa pāṇī cchippaï |
emmaï joī mūla sara[$6b_5$]ttao
visahiṃ ṇa vāhaï visahi ramattao | [G65 = DK_A 62]

visaa raman+a ṇ+a + [$21b_1$]saaṃhiṃ lippaï
uala haraï ṇṇa pāṇī cchippaï |
emaï joi mūla sarāttao
viṣaa ṇṇa bājjhaï viṣaa ramantao | [T*62]

D] Note the variant for "troubled," "deluded," or "bound."

Quoted with attribution to the title (*Dohākośe 'py uktam*) in the *Subhāṣita-saṃgraha* (Bendall ed., part II, p. 12):

visaa ramanta ṇa visaeṃ lippaï |
ūala harei ṇa pāṇī chippaï ||
emaï joī mūla saranto |
visaa ṇa bāhaï visaa ramanto ||

Cf. Sāṅkṛtyāyana 71.

---

deva pi ppajaï lakkha vi dīaï
appaṇu mārī kī sa karijaï |
mā viṇu [$6b_6$] tuṭṭaï ehu saṃsāru
viṇu ābhāseṃ lohi ṇisāru || [G66 = DK_A 63]

AB] Perhaps in the original this was a critique of external practices: "You venerate deities, give hundreds of thousands [of coins for charity], and [even] kill yourself [in ritual suicide], but what good do these do?"
C] Emend *mā viṇu* to *tovi ṇa* or some such formulation.
D] The reading *lohi* is corrupt; emend to *ṇāhi*.

deva vi ppajaï lakkha [21b$_2$] + + aï
appaüṃ mārī ki sa kīrīaï[24] |
tovi ṇṇa tuṭṭaï ehu saṃnsāru
viṇu abbhāse ṇṇāhi nisāru || [T*63]

kṛtir iyaṃ dohākoṣa Sarahapādānāṃ || [*fleuron*] || [T *explicit*]

Cf. Sāṅkṛtyāyana 72.

---

aṇimisaloaṇacittaṇirohеṃ
pavaṇa ṇirohaï siriguru[7a$_1$]bohyeṃ (?) |
pavaṇa cahaï so ṇiccala javveṃ
joi kālu karaï ki re tavveṃ || [G67 = DK$_A$ 64]

C] *Cahaï* is a copying mistake for *vahaï*.
D] Read *joī* for *joi*.

The first line is quoted with attribution (*Sarahapādāś ca*) preceded by two other lines that are not in this recension in Raviśrījñāna's *Amṛtakaṇikā* (ed. p. 31):

aṇimisa loaṇa cia ṇiroheṃ |
pavaṇa ṇiruhaï siriguruvoheṃ ||

The first line is quoted without attribution (*tad uktam*) in Vibhūticandra's *Amṛtakaṇikoddyota* (ed. p. 185):

aṇimiṣaloaṇa cīa ṇiroheṃ |
pavaṇa ṇiruhaï sadguru voheṃ ||

24. kīrīaï] T^{pc}, kīriaï T^{ac}

---

jāu ṇa indīvisaa marāma
tāva ki e hi phuraï akā[$7a_2$]ma |
aïsī visami sandhi ko païsaï
jo jahi atthi jāhi ṇa dīsaï || [G68 = DK_A 65]

A] *Marāma* is an attractive reading ("as long as we do not kill the objects of the senses"), so *gāma* is perhaps an old corruption: the syllable *ma* probably dropped out, and then *rā* was misread as *ga* and then lengthened to *gā*.
B] This reading, *ki e hi*, is difficult to make sense of without exegetical help. It is possible that the original intent and meaning of the first line was different from how Advayavajra understood it. The quarter seems to be hypometrical in every transmission, if Shahidullah is right that this is an *aḍillā* verse.
D] The reading *jāhi* seems to be corrupt.

---

paṇḍia saala sattha vakkhāṇaï
dehahi buddha vasanta [$7a_3$] ṇa jāṇaï |
avaṇāgamaṇa vi jeṇa vikhaṇḍia
tovi ṇilajja bhaṇaï haü paṇḍia || [G69 = DK_A 66]

C] This reading, without the negation particle but *api*, is probably original, so the caustic critique of the learned was phrased slightly differently. There are perhaps two ways to understand this: (a) Even those who have refuted coming and going (i.e., beginners in Madhyamaka philosophy) shamelessly claim that they are learned. (b) Those who refute such obvious (or silly?) things as coming and going shamelessly claim that they are learned. Either way, this seems to be a reference to Nāgārjuna's *Mūlamadhyamakakārikā* chap. 2.

---

jīvantaha jo ṇaü jjara[$7a_4$]ï
so ajarāmara hoi |
guruūesem̩ vimalamaï
so para dhaṇṇā koi || [G70 = DK_A 67]

A] The *jja* does not make position.

D] For *dhaṇṇā*, read *dhaṇṇo*, probably a copying mistake.

---

visaavisuddheṃ ṇaü ramaï
keva[7a$_5$]la suṇṇa carei |
uḍḍia vohiattha thaü jima
balibali tahi jayantei || [G71 = DK$_A$ 68]

CD] This second line looks quite corrupt, so it is advisable to look to Advayavajra for help. Although the subject ("the crow") seems to be missing, unless the word beginning with *bali* is a trace of some synonym based on "*bali* eater," perhaps the adjective *vohiattha* ("situated on a ship") preserves something of a more original reading.

---

visaāsatta ma bandha karu
are vaḍha saraheṃ vutta |
[7a$_6$] mīṇa paaṅgaha kari bhamaï
pekkhaha hariṇaha jutta || [G72 = DK$_A$ 69]

A] DKP$_A$ seems to have understood *visaāsatti* as an instrumental. This *bahuvrīhi* is perhaps preferable and conveys the same meaning.
C] Both *paaṅgaha* and *bhamaï* seem to be inferior readings; cf. the testimony below.

Quoted without attribution (*yad āha*) in Vibhūticandra's *Amṛtakaṇikoddyota* (ed. p. 132; the editor was probably mistaken in typesetting *are* as *a re*):

visaāsatti ma bandha kuru a re vaḍha saraheṃ vutta |
mīṇa paaṅgama kari bhamara pekkhaha hariṇaha jutta ||

---

jatta vi cittaha vipphuraï
tatta vi ṇāhasarūa |
aṇṇa taraṅga ki [7b$_1$] aṇṇa julu
bhavasama khasamasarūa || [G73 = DK$_A$ 70]

B] The variant *ṇāhasarūa* is noteworthy. It could be a simple copying mistake of the DKP_A's reading (*ṇāhi sarūa*), but it could also be a genuine variant, having the sense of "[all these things] are of the nature of the protector (*nātha*—i.e., the *iṣṭadevatā* the tantric yogin is supposed visualize himself as)." Note that this is also the form cited in Vibhūticandra's testimony below.
C] The variant *julu* is probably a copying mistake.

Quoted without attribution (*iti vacanāc ca*) in Vibhūticandra's *Amṛtakaṇikoddyota* (ed. p. 123; the first line of the text has to be parsed differently, although **vināśasvarūpam* is not entirely impossible):

jata vi cittahi viphphuraï tatta viṇāha sarua |
aṇṇa taraṅga ki aṇṇa jalu bhavasama khasama sarua ||

---

kāsu kahijjaï ko suṇaï
ho etthu kajjasu līṇa |
duṭṭasulugnadhūli jima
hiaḍ.hā ta[$7b_2$]hi avalīṇa || [G74 = DK_A 71]

B] The reading *ho* is a corruption of *ko*.
CD] Unfortunately, the readings of G do not help in elucidating this notoriously difficult line. The third quarter is hypometrical. The fourth is metrical but is missing the element ("dust" in the comparison) of the state of being born in the heart. See DKP_A. The reading *sulugna* is very likely a copying mistake for *sulugga*, the Middle Indic form for the rare Sanskrit word *suruṅga*.

---

jattaï païsaï jalahi jalu
tattaï samarasa hoi |
dosaguṇāaracittaḍ.hā
vaḍha paḍ.hibakkha ṇa koi || [G75 = DK_A 72]

C] Note that the end of this quarter fluctuates rather wildly in transmission and testimony. Here we should understand an abstract noun, °*cittatā*, "The idea that the mind has the aspects of faults and qualities."

Quoted without attribution in Bhavabhaṭṭa's *Catuṣpīṭhanibandha* ad *Catuṣpīṭhatantra* 3.4.11 (Ms Kaiser Library no. 134, fol. $39b_2$):

jattiu païsaï jalehi jalu tattiuṃ samarasa hoi |
doṣaguṇāara cittao baḍha paḍibakkha ṇa ko bi ||

Quoted without attribution in Śrībhānu's *Amṛtadhārā* (Ms fol. $12a_5$ in Sferra 2020, 378n18):

jettiuṃ païsaï jalahiṃ jalu tettiuṃ samarasu hoi |
dosaguṇāara citta üa vaḍha paüivakkha na ko vi ||

The first line is quoted in a corrupt form without attribution in Vibhūticandra's *Amṛtakaṇikoddyota* (ed. p. 126):

yattu viṣaa saa jalahi jala |
tattu visamarasa hoi ||

[$7b_3$] suṇṇahi saṅga ma karahi tuhu
tahi tahi sama cittamsa |
tiṇatusamatta vi llaḍ.hā
veaṇu karaï avassa || [G76 = DK_A 73]

B] *Cittamsa* is a slip of the pen for *cittassa*.
C] This quarter is corrupt: *tiṇa*° can be easily explained as a wrongly copied *tila*°, whereas *llaḍ.hā* is missing the initial *akṣara*, *sa*°.

The second line is quoted without attribution (*uktaṃ ca*) in Raviśrījñāna's *Guṇabharaṇī* (Sferra 2000, p. 76):

tilatusamatta vi salladā veaṇu karaï avassa ||

---

aï[$7b_4$]so so para hoi ṇa aïso
jima cintāmaṇikajjasarīso |
ākaḍha paṇḍia bhantia ṇāsia
saasamvi[$7b_5$]tti mahāsuhavāsia || [G77 = DK_A 74]

D] For this variant reading (also reflected in the Tibetan), see note to DKP_A translation.

---

savvarūva je khasama karijjaï
khasamasahāveṃ maṇa vi dharijjaï |
so vi maṇū tahi aṇu karijjaï
[$7b_6$] sahajasahāveṃ so para rajjaï || [G78 = DK_A 75]

A] Note the variant, a nominative relative pronoun for the locative pronoun. See note in DKP_A translation.
C] For *aṇu* read *amaṇu*.

Quoted with attribution (*Sarahapādair api*) in a somewhat different form in Raviśrījñāna's *Guṇabharaṇī* (Sferra 2000, p. 80):

savvabhāva vaḍha khasama karijjaï
khasamasahāveṃ cīa dharijjaï |
so vi cīa acīa dharijjaï
tenāṇuttarabohi lahijjaï ||

Quoted without attribution (*uktaṃ ca*) in *Fragment with Apabhraṃśa Quotations*, Tokyo University Library no. 312 (old no. 230), Ms fol. 8a:

sarvarūa tahi khasama karijaï
khasamasahāvem maṇa hi dharijaï |
so vi maṇū tahi amaṇu karijjaï |
sahajasahāveṃ so paru rajjaï ||

Quoted without attribution (*tad uktam*) in Vibhūticandra's *Amṛtakaṇikoddyota* (ed. p. 144):

savvarua tahiṃ khasama karijjai |
khasama sahāveṃ maṇa vi gharijjai ||
so vi maṇu tahi amaṇu karijjai |
sahaja sahāveṃ so paru rajjaī ||

---

gharĕ gharĕ kahiaï sojjukahāṇo
ṇo parimuṇiaï mahāsuhaṭhāno |
Saraha bhaṇa[8a$_1$]ï jaga cittem̩ vāhia
so vi citta ṇaü keṇa vi gāhia || [G79]

A] Perhaps read *sojjhu°*; cf. G 99c.
B] *Parimuṇiaï* is one *mora* too long.
D] The most likely reading is our conjecture, **so vi acitta ṇa*. This harmonizes with the intended explanation of the DKP$_A$, and it is perfectly metrical in the sense that it does not differ from the non-syncopated *pādākulaka* lines commonly employed in the text.

Cf. Sāṅkṛtyāyana 128.

---

ekku deva bahu āgama dīsaï
appaṇu icchem̩ phuḍ.ha parihāsaï || [G80 = DK$_A$ 77]

Although consisting of a single line, this must be a self-standing verse, because the meter (*aḍillā*) is different from that of both the previous and the next stanzas (*pādākulaka*). Cf. however Sāṅkṛtyāyana 121ab, seemingly to be construed with the first line of the next verse.

---

appaṇu [8a$_2$] ṇāho aṇṇa viruddho
ghare ghare so vi siddhanta pasiddho ||
ekku khāi avara aṇṇa poḍ.haï
bāhira gaï bhattāraha loḍ.haï | [G81 = DK$_A$ 78]

B] The *vi* (Skt. *api*) is an insignificant variant of *a* (Skt. *ca*).
C] The quarter is short one *mora*. One should add either an enclitic *vi/a* or a verbal prefix after *aṇṇa*.
D] The form *bhattāraha* is curious, inasmuch as even Sanskrit spells it as *bhaṭṭāraka*.

For the first line, cf. Sāṅkṛtyāyana 121cd.

ā[$8a_3$]vanta ṇa dīsaï jatta
ṇāhi acchanta muṇijjaï |
ṇittaraṅga paramesaru
ṇikalaṅka dhāvijjaï || [G82 = DK_A 79]

B] This verse quarter poses a metrical problem: read *ṇa hi ... muṇiaï.*
C] Here the last syllable must be lengthened to *paramesarū.*
D] This verse quarter, too, poses a metrical problem: read *ṇikkalaṅka dhāviaï.*

āvai jāi ṇa cchaḍa[$8a_4$]ï tāvahu
kahi appuvvavilāsi pāvahu | [G83 = DK_A 80]

B] The *pp* does not make position. One must conjecture *°*vilāsinī.*

sohaï citta ṇirālae diṇṇā
addhaarūa ma dekkhahu bhiṇṇā ||
kā[$8a_5$]avācamaṇa jāva ṇa bhijjaï
sahajasahāveṃ tāva ki rajjaï || [G84 = DK_A 81]

A] Scan as *ṇirālaĕ* or emend to *ṇirāle.*
B] The variant for *appaṇa rūa* (Skt. *ātmano rūpam*) is *addhaa-rūa* (very likely Skt. *advayarūpam*).
D] Note that instead of the negation, here we have a rhetorical question: "How will they shine within coemergent nature? [They will not.]"

aïsa uvese jaï phuḍa jāṇahu |
tā pparu sattagrarū[$8a_6$]vaa ṇa pamāṇaha || [G85 = DK_A ø]

This verse is not transmitted anywhere else in Indic sources. The meaning is difficult to make out, as the second line seems corrupt. The first line and the first two words of the second line perhaps mean "If, by virtue of this pith instruction, you know clearly, then the supreme...." Cf. Kāṇha's Dohā 24c (Shahidullah 1928, 79): *aïsa uese jaï phuḍa sijjhaï.*

---

gharavaï khajjaï gharaṇiehiṃ
jahi desahi aviāra |
māie para kaseṃ uvvaraï
visaria [8b$_1$] joiṇicāra || [G86 = DK$_A$ 82]

C] The quarter is metrical only if we read *kasĕṃ* (likely an interrogative pronoun to express the rhetorical question) and if *vv* is not making position.

---

gharavaï khajjaï sahajeṃ rajjaï |
kijjaï rāavirāa |
ṇiapāsa baïṭṭhī citteṃ bhaṭṭhī |
joiṇi mahu paḍ.hihā[8b$_2$]a || [G87 = DK$_A$ 83]

For the meter (*marahaṭṭhā*), which is used only here, see Shahidullah 1928, 66.

---

khājjaï pijjaï vicirintijjaï (?)
cittaṃ jo paḍ.hihāa |
maṇu bāhira dullakkha hale
visarisa joiṇimāa || [G88 = DK$_A$ 84]

A] We cannot make sense of the third verb, which is unmetrical.
B] Perhaps emend to *citte*?

[8b$_3$] aïadarisaṇa jahiṃ ṇamaï
tihuvaṇa jasu ṇimmāṇa |
sŏ cittasiddhi joiṇi
sahajā samvaru jāṇa || [G89 = DK$_A$ 85]

A] This verse quarter seems quite corrupt, although it is metrical.
B] Although this is not reflected in the transmission, for the sake of the meter one must read °*siddhī joinī*.

D] Although DKP_A seems to read this as a compound, perhaps we have to understand "the yoginī, who is the coemergent, should be known as/is the gnosis of highest bliss."

---

akkha[$8b_4$]ravāḍhā saala jagu
ṇāhi ṇirakkhara koi |
tāva so akkhara gholaaï
jāu ṇirakkhara hoi || [G90 = DK_A 86]

Cf. Sāṅkṛtyāyana 25.

---

jima bāhira [$8b_5$] tima abbhattaru
caüdahabhuaṇeṃ ṭhiaü ṇirantara |
asarīra sarīrahiṃ lukko
jo jahiṃ jāṇaï so tahiṃ mukko || [G91 = DK_A 87]

A] While not reflected in the transmission, for the sake of the meter we have to read *bāhīre*.
B] Emend *ṇirantara* to *ṇirantaru* for the sake of the rhyme.
C] See the conjecture *kŏi* in DKP_A 87c, which was inspired by the testimony below.

Quoted without attribution (*tad uktaṃ*) in *Fragment with Apabhraṃśa Quotations*, Tokyo University Library no. 312 (old no. 230), Ms fol. 13a:

jiman bāhira tima abhāntara |
caüdahabhubaṇe ṇṇiaü (?) ṇirantara ||
asarira koi sarīrahi lukko |
jo ttahi jāṇaï so ttahi mukko ||

---

siddhir a[$8b_6$]su maï paḍhameṃ paḍhiaü
maṇḍa pibanteṃ vissaria e maï |
akkharam ekka ettha maï jāṇiu
tāhara ṇāma ṇa keṇa vi jāṇi[$9a_1$]u || [G92 = DK_A 88]

A] The metrical pattern is slightly unusual at the beginning, but this was probably dictated by the formula's pattern. The reading *asu* must be a corruption of *atthu*.
B] Here it is the latter half that poses metrical problems. One must conjecture *maïu* for the rhyme, but this makes the quarter hypermetrical unless it is read as *visaria ĕ*.
C] Once again, the syncopated metrical pattern is unusual for the author's usage of the *pādākulaka*.
D] The end of the quarter is very likely a scribal slip, using a cliché instead of the author's intimate vocative.

For this custom of beginning the alphabet with *siddhir astu*, see Halhed 1778, 23–24, and Takakusu 1896, 170–71.

---

ruaṇa saala vi jahi ṇaü sāhaï[25]
kundurukhavaṇahi mahāsuha sāhaï |
jima tisio miatisaṇeṃ dhāvaï
maraï [9a$_2$] sosahiṃ ṇabhajalu kahi pābaï || [G93 = DK$_A$ 89]

A] Two emendations are necessary: *ruaṇeṃ/ruaṇe* for *ruaṇa*, and *gāhaï* for *sāhaï*.
B] Read °*khaṇahi* for °*khavaṇahi*; the mistake was perhaps prompted by a memory of G6c.
C] While this is not how Advayavajra understood the verse, it is quite likely that here *miatiṣaṇeṃ* was originally a compound, a locative of the word for "mirage," and the subject was not a deer (which is only ever so slightly suggested by Advayavajra and supplied by the Tibetan translations) but simply a person tormented by thirst.

In light of these new readings, we can ascertain that the meter is *pādākulaka* and not *aḍillā*, as Shahidullah (1928, 159) thought.

Quoted without attribution (*tad āha*) in Vibhūticandra's *Amṛtakaṇikoddyota* (ed. p. 124):

> ruaṇe saala vi johi ṇaü gāhaï
> kunduru khaṇahi mahāsuha sāhaï |

25. sāhaï] G^{pc}, sāhii G^{ac}

jima tisio mia-tisiṇeṃ dhāvaï
maraï so sosahiṃ ṇabhajalu kahiṃ pāvaï ||

The verse is followed by a helpful mini-commentary:

> ruaṇeṃ bhāvanāyāṃ sarvadharmaśūnyatāṃ yo na gāhate samāpattau sa kiṃ mahāsukhaṃ sādhayati | yathā tṛṣito mṛgatṛṣṇāṃ dhāvati sa śuṣyati nabhasi jalābhāvād iti |

> "How will one who does not fathom the emptiness of all phenomena in 'analysis'—that is, during meditation—accomplish great bliss in sexual union? [He will not.] This is just as 'A thirsty man who runs toward a mirage will become dehydrated because there is no water in the sky.'"

---

kamalakulisa vevi majjhaṭhiu
jo so suraavilāsa |
ko taṃ ramaï tihuvahiṃ
kassa [9a$_3$] ṇa pūria āsa || [G94 = DK$_A$ 92]

C] The *pāda* omits *ṇaü*. Emend to *tihuvaṇahiṃ*.
D] Note the participle *pūria* instead of the indicative.

Note that this and the following seven verses also survive in a single-leaf fragment with a gloss. This unfortunately very obscure text was published in Sāṅkṛtyāyana 1957, (68)–(69). In spite of its shortcomings, there are three noteworthy features about this fragment. (1) Sāṅkṛtyāyana states that the script was *kuṭilā* or *vartula*, and he conjectures that it may date from twelfth-century Magadha. This is significant, because if the statement is correct, this document is the only one, next to Ms T, that hails from India proper and not Nepal. (2) The dohās are numerated 76 to 83. To our knowledge this is the only time we can see this feature before the advent of modern editions, though the range does not match any of the recensions known to us. (3) The commentary in broken Sanskrit is interlinear, which also seems to be unique. Unfortunately, we do not have more of this precious document because the chaplain at Sa skya from whom Sāṅkṛtyāyana had bought the manuscript was in the habit of giving out little pieces of it to the pious as blessed victuals.

ṇava ṇavāasuha
ahavā veṇṇi vi so |
guruapasāeṃ puṇṇa jaï
viralā jāṇaï koi || [G95 = DK_A 93]

A] The line is unusually corrupt: *ṇava ṇa* must read *khaṇa u°* (which would be impossible to restore without other witnesses), then *°suha* is a corruption of *°suhaha* through haplography. Immediately after this, there is another, longer haplography, as *ahavā* must be read at the end of the quarter too.
B] Emend *so* to *soi*, as this is needed both for the rhyme and the *mora* count.
C] Emend *puṇṇa* to *puṇṇu* read long or *puṇṇū*.

[$9a_4$] gaṃbhīraï ūāra hale
ṇaü para ṇaü appāṇa |
sahajāṇasahajāṇanda caüṭhakhaṇa
ṇiasamveaṇa jāṇa || [G96 = DK_A 94]

A] The DKP_A most likely read *uāharaṇeṃ*, but this reading coincides with the extracanonical Tibetan translation. The final *°i* in *gaṃbhīraï* is unclear and perhaps corrupt. The *e* in *hale* is short.
C] The present reading *sahajāṇasahajāṇanda* is an uncorrected dittography; read *sahajāṇanda*. Correct *caüṭha* to *caüṭṭha/caüṭhṭha*.

The second line is quoted in Raviśrījñāna's *Amṛtakaṇikā* (ed. p. 63) in a very curious way. First we have this quotation attributed to Saraha: *uktaṃ ca—sahajāṇanda caüṭṭhao so kī buccaṇa jāī* || *iti Sarahapādaḥ* |. Then we have this line, but attributed to Līlāvajra: *sahajāṇanda ca catukkhaṇa ṇia samveaṇa jā[ṇa]* || *iti līlāvajraś ceti* ||.

[$9a_5$] ghorandhāreṃ ca maṇi
jima ujjoa karei |
paramamahāsuha ekkukhaṇa
duriāsesa harei || [G97 = DK_A 95]

A] The *ṇḍa* in *candamaṇi* dropped out, hence the corrupt reading.
C] Emend *khaṇa* to *khaṇe*, read with a short *-e*.

Quoted with attribution to the title (*Dohākośe 'py uktam*) in the *Subhāṣitasaṃgraha* (Bendall ed., part II, p. 12):

> ghora aṃdhāreṃ candamaṇi jima ujjoa karēi |
> parama mahāsuha ekkukhaṇĕ duriāsesa harēi ||

---

dukkhadivāara a[$9a_6$]tthamiu
uvaï tārāvaï sukka |
ṭhia ṇimmāṇeṃ ṇimmiaü
teṇa vi maṇḍalacakka || [G98 = DK_A 96]

B] Read *ūvai taravaï.*

This meter (*ullāla*) is unique in the collection, as pointed out by Shahidullah (1928, 65).

Quoted without attribution (*tad uktaṃ*) in *Fragment with Apabhraṃśa Quotations*, Tokyo University Library no. 312 (old no. 230), Ms fol. 12a:

> duḥkkhadivāara athaviu uvaï tarāvaï mukka |
> ṭhia nimmāṇeṃ ṇṇimmiaü teṇa vi maṇḍalacakka ||

---

cittehiṃ citta ṇihāla vaḍha
sa[$9b_1$]ala vi muccahu diṭṭhi |
paramamahāsuha sojjhu paru
tahi āattā siddhi || [G99 = DK_A 97]

B] Note the variant with the meaning "abandon [all] views," instead of "abandon wrong views." Misreadings of *h* and *k* are not rare; cf. G74b.
CD] This reading seems to suggest: "Supreme bliss is the highest purity; in that, supreme accomplishment comes about."

---

mukkaü cittagaenda karu
ettha viappa ma puccha |
[9b$_2$] gaaṇagirīṇaïjala piaü
tahi taḍ.ha vasiu suiccha || [G100 = DK$_A$ 98]

For the image of the mind elephant, cf. Sāṅkṛtyāyana 134cd–135ab.

---

viagaendeṃ kare gahia
jima māraï paḍ.hi[9b$_3$]hāi |
joī kavaḍiāra jima
tahi puṇa ṇissari jāi || [G101 = DK$_A$ 99]

A] A syllable dropped out from *via*°; read *visaa*°.
D] Note *puṇa* for *tahŏ*, which seems to be the *lectio difficilior.*

Quoted with attribution to the title (*Dohākośe 'py uktam*) in the *Subhāṣita-saṃgraha* (Bendall ed., part II, pp. 12–13):

visaa-gaenda-kareṃ gahia māria jima paḍihā[i] |
joī kavaḍīāra jima tima ṇīsāri jāi ||

---

jo bhava so ṇivvāṇa khalu
bheu ma maṇṇahu a[9b$_4$]ṇṇa |
ekkasahāveṃ ve virahia
ṇimmala pah.ḍivaṇṇa || [G102 = DK$_A$ 100]

C] Read *vi* for *ve.*
D] The word *maï* after *ṇimmala* seems to have dropped out.

---

gharahi ma thakka ma jāhu maṇa
jahi tahi maṇa pariāṇa |
[9b$_5$] saala ṇirantara bohiṭhiu
kahi bhava kahi ṇivvāṇa || [G103 = DK$_A$ 101]

A] For *maṇa*, read *vaṇa*. Intervocalic *m* and *v* do fluctuate, but this is rare at the beginning of a word.

ṇaü ghare ṇaü vaṇe bohi ṭhiu
ehu pariāṇahu bheu |
ṇi[9b$_6$]mmalacittasahāvaḍ.hā
karahi avikkala seu || [G104 = DK$_A$ 102]

---

ehu se appā ehu paru
jo paribhāvaï ko vi |
teṃ viṇu bandheṃ veḍhi kiu [10a$_1$]
appa vimukkaü to vi || [G105 = DK$_A$ 103]

C] Here the work of the original scribe ends; the next folio is an addition penned by another hand. The second scribe repeated *pāda* c thus: [*siddham* symbol] *te viṇu bandheṃ veḍhi kiu*.

---

para appāṇa ma bhanti karu
saala nirantara buddha ||
ehu se nimmala paramapaü
citta sahāṃveṃ suddha || [G106 = DK$_A$ 104]

B] There is a small smudge above the first syllable of *nirantara*: it is possible that this is a tilde-like sign, which is meant to change the quality of the consonant (i.e., *n* to *ṇ*). Note, however, that the scribe spells *ṇimmala* as *nimmala* in the next quarter.
D] The first *anusvāra* in *sahāṃveṃ* is intrusive; read *sahāveṃ*.
This verse is also transmitted as Tillopāda's *Dohākoṣa*, verse 13 (Bagchi 1938, 5 and 64).

---

advaacittataruvara pha
sa[10a$_2$]ü tihuaṇa vitthāra ||

karuṇāphullīphula dharaï
ṇaü paratattaüāra || [G107 = DK_A 105]

A] *Advaa°* can also be read as *adhaa°*. The reading *pha* is puzzling; it is very likely a corruption of *hi*. The *u* in *°taruvara* must be emended or read as long for the sake of the meter.
B] For *saü*, read *gaü*.
D] This *pāda* seems corrupt; read *ṇāu paratta uāra*.

This verse is also transmitted as Tillopāda's *Dohākoṣa*, verse 12 (Bagchi 1938, 4 and 64).

Quoted without attribution (*uktaṃ ca*) in *Fragment with Apabhraṃśa Quotations*, Tokyo University Library no. 312 (old no. 230), Ms fol. 9b:

advayacittatarūvara hi gaü tihuvaṇa vithāra |
karuṇāphulīphala dharaï ṇāu paratta uāra ||

---

suṇṇatarūvara phulliaü
karuṇā viviha vicitta ||
aṇṇābhoa paratta phulu
ehu sokha [$10a_3$] paru titta || [G108 = DK_A 106]

D] For *titta*, read *citta*; most likely a copying mistake.

This and the following verses up to the end were not treated by Shahidullah, so here we lose his valuable identifications of the meter. All the remaining verses are dohās.

Quoted without attribution (*tad uktaṃ*) in *Fragment with Apabhraṃśa Quotations*, Tokyo University Library no. 312 (old no. 230), Ms fol. 9b:

suṇṇatarūvara phuliaü karuṇā viviha vicitta |
āṇābhoa paratta phulu ehu sokha paru citta ||

---

suṇṇatarūvara ṇikkaruṇa[26]
jahi phula mūla ṇa sāha |
tahi ālambaṇa jo karaï
tasu paḍibhajjaï bāha || [G109 = DK_A 107]

Quoted without attribution (*tad uktaṃ*) in *Fragment with Apabhraṃśa quotations*, Tokyo University Library no. 312 (old no. 230), Ms fol. 10a:

suṇṇatarūvara ṇikaruṇa jahi phula mūla ṇa sāha |
tahi ālambana jo karaï tasu paḍibajjaï bāha ||

---

ekkaṃ bīeṃ vevi taru
teṃ kāraṇa phala [$10a_4$] ekka |
e ābhiṇṇā jo maṇaï
bhavaṇivvāṇavimukka || [G110 = DK_A 108]

A] For *ekkaṃ*, read *ekkeṃ*.
C] The correlative pronoun *so* seems to have been dropped. The quarter could still be metrical and convey the same sense.

Quoted without attribution (*tad uktaṃ*) in *Fragment with Apabhraṃśa Quotations*, Tokyo University Library no. 312 (old no. 230), Ms fol. 10a:

ekke bīaṃ veṇṇi taru te kāraṇe phala eka |
e ābhiṇṇā jo munaï so bhavanivvāṇavimukka ||

---

jo atthīaṇa āiaü
so jaï jāi ṇirāsa |
khaṇḍasarāeṃ bhikkha varu
cchantrahi e gahapāsa || [G111 = DK_A 109]

D] For *cchantrahi*, read *cchaḍahi* or *cchaḍahu*. The variant *gahapāsa* is also meaningful: "the fetters of the household."

26. ṇikkaruṇa] G^{pc} (not in the scribal hand), ṇiccha(?)ruṇa G^{ac}

---

para[10a$_5$]üvaāra ṇa kkīiaü
atthi ṇa dīaü dāṇa ||
e saṃsāreṃ havaṇu phala
varu cchantrahu appāṇa || o || [G112 = DK$_A$ 110]

A] The gemination of *k* is unlikely to be correct, because here we expect a *gaṇa* of four *morae*. There are various ways in which one can make this quarter metrical—e.g., *paraūāra ṇa kīaū, paraüvaāra ṇa kīaū.*
C] The third word is puzzling in all the transmissions; hence, we offer the diagnostic conjecture *ki vaḍha.*
D] For *cchantrahu* (or perhaps just *cchantahu*), read *chaḍḍahu*, as in G111b. The *ccha* does not make position.

---

dohākoso amatoti kidi esā siriSarahapāassa || [G *explicit*]

The word for "is finished" should be read as **samatto tti.*

Sāṅkṛtyāyana's Manuscript Obtained from Sa skya

Abbreviations and sigla in this edition

+	illegible or lost syllables
(!)	the word is printed thus, but its value is doubtful
(¯)	mātrā supplied by the editor
<>	insertion
ac	ante correctionem
pc	post correctionem

The Sa skya Manuscript

[bramhaṇeṃhi ma jānantahi bheu |
evaï paḍhiaü e ccaüveu ||
maṭṭi (pāṇi kusa laī paḍhantaṃ |
gharahiṃ baïsī aggi huṇantaṃ || 1
kajje virahia huaavaha homeṃ |
akkhi ḍahāvia kaḍuaeṃ (!) ghūmeṃ |
ekadaṇḍi tridaṇḍī bhaava(¯)ṃ beseṃ |
viṇuā hoiaï haṃsa ueseṃ || 2
micchehiṃ jaga vāhia bhulleṃ |
dhammādhamma ṇa jāṇia tulle ||
aïriehiṃ uddūlia cchāreṃ |
sīsasu vāhia e jaḍa-bhāreṃ || 3
gharahī baïsī dīvā jālī |
koṇahiṃ baïsī ghaṇṭā cālī ||
akkhi ṇivesī āsaṇa bandhī |
kaṇṇehiṃ khusakhusāi jaṇa dhandhī || 4
raṇḍī-muṇḍī aṇṇavi beseṃ |
dikkhijjaï dakkhiṇa-uddeseṃ ||
dīhaṇakkha jaï maliṇeṃ beseṃ | |
ṇaggala hoi upāḍia keseṃ || 5
khabaṇehiṃ jāṇa viḍaṃbia beseṃ |
appaṇa bāhia mokkha ubeseṃ ||
jaï ṇaggāvia hoi mutti,
tā suṇaha siālaha || 6
lomupāḍaṇeṃ atthi siddhi,
tā jubaï ṇiambaha |
picchīgahaṇe diṭṭha mokkha
(tā moraha camaraha) || 7
ucche bhoaṇeṃ hoi ja ṇa,
tā kariha turaṅgaha |

thus far reconstructed from Bagchi

Saraha bhaṇaï khabaṇāṇa] mokkha,
mahu kimpi na bhāvaï || 8cd
tatta-rahia kāa(˜) na tāva,
para kevala sāhaï | 9ab

[1 deest] [2a1]kṣu
mahu kimpi ṇa bhāwaï |
tattarahiakāa
para kewala wāha +

cellu bhikkhu je tthavira uesem̩ |
(vandehia pabbajjiu besem̩ || 9cd
koi suttam̩ta bakkhāṇa baïṭṭho |
kovi) citta karua maï diṭṭho || 10ab

+ + + kṣu je thawi + ra ues+m̩
wam̩dehi + + + + + +
+ + + + + + + + + + + +
+ + + [2a2]ttekarūa maïm̩ diṭṭho |

aṇṇu tahi mahājāṇe dhāviu |
maṇḍala cakka . . mavi nādheu || 10cd
(tasu pariāṇem̩ aṇṇa na koi |
abare (ga)aṇe sajjaï soī || 11ab

aṇṇatahim mahājāṇe dhāwiu
maṇḍala + + + saala wi bhāwiu |
kewi wakṣāṇa + + + + + +
+ + + + + + + + + + + [2a3] ||

sahaja cchāḍī ṇibbāṇehim̩ dhāviu |
ṇaü paramattha ekavi sāhiu || 11cd
jo jasu jeṇa hoi santuṭṭha |
mokkha ki labbhaï jhāṇa-paviṭṭha || 12ab

sahaja cchāḍī ṇiwwāṇehim̩ dhāviu
ṇaü paramattha eka wi sāhiu |
jo jasu jeṇa + + + + +
+ + + + + + + + + + +

kintaha dīpe kintaha ṇevejje |
kintaha kijjaï mantaha bhāveṃ || 12cd
kintahi ntittha tapovaṇa jāi |
mokkha ki labbhaï (pāṇī nhāi || 13ab

> + n taha dī + + + + + + +
> + [2a4]n taha kijjaï mantaha seweṃ |
> kin tahin titthatapowaṇajā +
> + kṣa ki labhaï pāṇi + + +

cchaḍḍahu re ālīkā bandhā) |
so muñcahu jo (acchahu dhandhā) || 13cd
tasu pariāṇahu aṇṇa ṇṇa kovi |
avare gāṇṇe sabbaï sovi || 14ab

> + + + + + + + +
> so muñca + + + + + + +
> [2a5] tasu pariāṇahu aṇṇa ṇṇa kowi |
> awareṃ gāṇṇeṃ (?) sawwa + + +

sovi paḍhijjaï sovi guṇijjaï |
sattha-purāṇe bakkhāṇijjaï || 14cd
nāhi so (diṭṭhi jo tāu ṇa la(kkhaï) |
ettavi varagurupāā pekkhaï || 15ab

> + wi paḍhijjaï sowi gu + + +
> + + + + + + + + + jjaï |
> nāhi + + + + + [2a6] lākṣaï
> etta wi waragurupāā pekṣaï ||

jaï (guru-vutta)ho (hiahi paīsaï |
ṇiccia hatthe ṭhaviaü dīsai || 15cd
Saraha bhaṇaï jaga-vāhia āleṃ |
ṇia sahāva ṇa lakkhia bāleṃ || 16ab

> ja + + + + + + + + + + + + + +
> + + + + + + + + + + saï |
> Saraha bhaṇaï jaga + + + + +
> + + + [2b1]hāwa ṇa lakṣia wāleṃ ||

karuṇa-rahia jjo suṇṇahiṃ laggā |
ṇaü so pāvaï uttima maggā || 16cd
ahavā karuṇā kevala sāhaa |
so jaṃmantareṃ mokkha ṇa pāvaa || 17ab

karuṇarahia jjo suṇṇahiṃ laggo
ṇaü so pāwaï uttima māggo
ahawā karuṇā kewala jhā(?) + + a
jaṃmantareṃ mokṣa ṇa pāwaa |

jaï puṇa veṇṇavi joḍaṇa sākkaa |
ṇaü bhava ṇaü ṇivvāṇeṃ thākkaa || 17cd

jaï puṇu we[2b2]ṇṇa wi joḍaṇa sākkaa
ṇaü bhawa ṇaü ṇiwwāṇeṃ thākkaa ||

jhāṇa-hīṇa pabbajjeṃ rahi(a)ü |
gahī vasanteṃ bhājjeṃ sahi(a)ü ||
(jaï) bhiḍi visaa ramante ṇa muccaa |
Saraha bhaṇaï pariāṇa ki ruccaa || 18

jhā(?) + + + + wwajjeṃ rahio,
gehā wasanteṃ bhājjeṃ sahio |
+ +i bhiḍi wisaa ramante ṇa muccaa ||
Saraha [2b3] bhaṇaï pariāṇa ki uccaa ||

jaï paccakkha ki jhāṇe kīaï |
ahavā jhāṇa andhāra sādhiaa ||
Saraha bhaṇaï maï kaḍḍhia rāva |
sahaja sahāu ṇaü bhāvābhāva || 19

jaï paccakṣaṃ ki jhāṇeṃ kīaï,
ahawā jhāṇa andhāra māwiaa |
Saraha bhaṇaï maï kaḍḍhia rāwa,
sahajasahā[2b4]wa ṇaü bhāwābhāwa ||

jā llaï uvajjaï tā llaï bājjaï |
tā laï paramamahāsuha sijjhaï ||
Saraha bhaṇaï mahu (ki) kkarami |
pasū loa ṇa bujjhaï kī karami || 20

jāllaï uwajjaï tāllaï wājjaï
+ālaï paramamahāsuha sijjhaï |
Saraha bhaṇaï hamu phukkarami,
pasuloa ṇa wujjhaï kī [2b5] karami ||

ekkeṃ sāñcia dhaṇaa paüru,
avare ndiṇṇa saāi ||
kāla gacchanteṃ veṇṇi gaü,
bhaṇato bhaṇṇo kāi || 21

ekkeṃ sañcia dhaṇaa paüru,
awaren diṇṇa saāi |
kāla gacchanteṃ, weṇṇi gaü
bhaṇato bhallo (?) kāi ||

pāṇi calaṇi raa gaï,
jīva dare ṇa saggu |
veṇṇavi panthā kahia maï,
jahiṃ jāṇasi tahiṃ laggu || 22

pāṇi ca teṇa (?) ṇiraa gaï
jīwa dare ṇa gaṇṇu |
weṇṇu [2b6] wi panthā kahia maïṃ,
jahiṃ jāṇasi tahiṃ lāggu ||

cittekka citta saala bīa
bhava-ṇivvāṇā jamma viphuraṃti |
taṃ cintāmaṇirūaṃ paṇamaha
icchāphalandei || 23

citteka saalawīaṃ,
bhawaṇiwwāṇā jassa wiphurati |
taṃ cintāmaṇirūaṃ paṇamahi
icchāphalan dei ||

bajjhaï kammeṇa jaṇo
kammavimukkeṇa hoi maṇamukko |
maṇamokkheṇa aṇuaraṃ
pāvijjaï parama (ṇi)vvāṇaṃ || 24

> [3a1] wajjhaï kkammeṇa jaṇo
> kammawimukkeṇa hoi maṇamukṣo |
> maṇamokṣeṇa aṇuaram
> pāwijjaï parama wwāṇaṃ ||

akkhara bāḍā saala jagu,
nāhi ṇirakkhara koi |
tāva se akkhara gholiaï,
jāva ṇirakkhara hoi || 25

> akṣarawāḍā saalajagu
> nāhi ṇirakṣara koi |
> tāwa se [3a2] akṣara gholiaï
> jāwa ṇirakṣara joi ||

baddho dhāvaï dasa disahiṃ,
mmukko ṇiccala ṭṭhāa |
emaï karahā pekkha sahi,
vivaria mahu paḍihāa || 26

> waddho dhāwaï dasadisihim
> mukko ṇiccala ṭṭhāa |
> emaï karahā pekṣu sahi
> wiwaria mahu paḍihāa (pc, pajihāa? ac) ||

cittaha mūla ṇa lakkhiaï,
sahajeṃ tiṇṇavi tattha |
kahiṃ uajjaa vilaa jāa,
kahiṃ vasaa phuḍa etthu || 27

> cittaha mūla ṇa [3a3] lakṣiaï
> sahajeṃ tiṇṇi wi tattha |
> kahiṃ uajjaa wilaa jāa
> kahiṃ wasaa phuḍa etthu ||

mūla-rahia jo cintaï tātta |
guru-āesaha etta viātta ||
Saraha bhaṇaï ṇiu(ṇa)ttaṇeṃ jāṇahu |
evvahiṃ para(ma) mahāsuha māṇahu || 28

mūlarahia jo cintaï tātta
guruāesaha etta wiānta |
[3a4] Saraha bhaṇaï ṇiu tteṇaṃ jāṇahu
ewwahiṃ paramahāsuha māṇaha ||

indī jattha vilīa gaü,
ṇaṭṭho appa sahāva |
so haleṃ sahajānanda taṇu,
phuḍa pucchaha gurūpāṃva || 29

indī jattha wilīa gaü
ṇaṭṭho appasahāwa |
so haleṃ sahajānanda taṇu
phuḍa pucchaha gu[3a5]rupāwa ||

jahi mmaṇa maraï,
pavaṇaho tahi khaa jāi |
ehu so paramamahāsuha,
Saraha kahihaü jāi || 30

jahim maṇa maraï
pawaṇaho tahi laa jāi |
ehu se paramamahāsuha
Saraha kahi phuḍa jāi ||

jahiṃ icchaï tahi jāu maṇa,
ahavā niccala ṭṭhāi |
addhugghāṭī loaṇeṃ,
diṭṭhīvisāme koi || 31

jahiṃ icchaï tahi jāu maṇa
ahawā ṇiccala ṭṭhā[3b1]i |
addhugghātīloaṇeṃ
diṭṭhivisāme kāiṃ |

jaï uāa uāeṃ dhāhaa |
ahavā karuṇā kevala sāhaa ||
jaï puṇu veṇṇivi joḍaṇa sakkaa |
tabbeṃ bhava-ṇivvāṇahi mukkaa || 32

jaï uāa uāeṃ dhāhaa,
ahawā karuṇā kewala sāhaa |
jaï puṇu weṇṇiwi joḍaṇa sakkaa,
tawweṃ bhawaṇiwwāṇahiṃ mukka[3b2]a ||

paḍhameṃ jaï āāsa visuddha |
cāhanteṃ-cāhanteṃ diṭṭhi ṇiruddha ||
ese jaï āāsa vi kālo |
ṇia maṇa doseṃ ṇa bājaï bālo || 33

paḍhume jaï āāsa wisuddha,
cāhanteṃ cāhanteṃ diṭṭhi ṇiruddha |
ese jaï āāsa wikālo
ṇiamaṇadoseṃ ṇa wājaï wālo ||

ahimāṇa doseṃ ṇa lakkhia tātta |
dūsaï saala jāṇa so detta ||
jhāṇeṃ mohia saalavi loa |
ṇia sahāva na lakkhia kovi || 34

ahimāṇadose ṇa lakṣia [3b3] tātta |
dūsaï saalajāṇa so detta |
jhāṇeṃ mohia saala wi loa |
ṇiasahāwa na lakṣia kowi ||

canda-sujja ghasi ghālaï ghoṭṭaï |
so āṇuttara etthu paaṭṭhaï ||
evvahiṃ saala jāṇa ṇigūḍho |
sahaja sahāve ṇa jāṇia mūḍho || 35

candasujja ghasi ghālaï ghoṭṭaï |
so āṇuttara e[3b4]tthu paaṭṭhaï |
ewwahiṃ saalajāṇa ṇigūḍho
sahajasahāwe ṇa jāṇia mūḍho ||

ṇia maṇa sācceṃ sohia jabbeṃ |
guru-guṇa hiahi mpaïsaï tabbeṃ ||
eva muṇevi ṇu saraheṃ gāiva |
manta ṇa tanta ṇa ekkavi gāhiva || 36

ṇiamaṇa sācceṃ sohia jawweṃ,
guruguṇa hiahim païsaï tawweṃ |
ewa mu[3b5]ṇe wiṇu saraheṃ gāiwa,
manta ṇa tanta ṇa ekka wi gāhiwa ||

so guṇa-hīṇo ahavā ṇirakkhara |
sirigurupāe ndiṇṇu mo vākkhara ||
tasu cāhenteṃu (!) hami ṇa dīsa |
sarūa cāhenteṃu (!) hami ṇa kīsa || 37

so guṇahīṇo ahawā ṇirakṣara
sirigurupāen diṇṇa mo wākṣara |
tasu cāhenteṃ u hami ṇa dīsa
sarūa [3b6] cāheṃteṃ u hami ṇa kīsa ||

saalahi tattasāra so vuccaa |
Saraha bhaṇaï mahuṃ sovi ṇa ruccaa ||
jaï puṇu aha-ṇisi sahaja païṭṭhaï |
amaṇāgamaṇa jeṃ tahi ṇevāṭṭaï || 38

saala hi tattamāra so wuccaa |
Saraha bhaṇaï mahuṃ so wi ṇa ruccaa |
jaï puṇu [4a1] ahaṇisi sahaja païṭṭhaï
amaṇāgamaṇa jeṃ tahi ṇewāṭṭhaï ||

bhāvābhāveṃ veṇṇi na kājja |
antarāla ṭṭhia pāḍahu bājja ||
viviha paāreṃ cittavi apiva |
sovi citta ṇa keṇavi apiva || 39

bhāwābhāweṃ weṇṇi na kājja
antarāla ṭṭhia pādahu wājja |
wiwihapaāreṃ (pc, °wyaāreṃ ac) citta wi apiwa
so wi [4a2] citta ṇa keṇa wi apiwa ||

indī visaa u asaṃṭṭhāu,
saeṃ samvittie jatthā |
ṇia cittanteṃ kāla gaü,
jhāṇa mahāsuha tattha || 40

indī wisaaü asaṃṭṭhiu
saeṃsamwittie jatthuṃ |
ṇiacitan teṃ kālagaü
jhāṇa mahāsuha tatthu ||

patta musāriu masi miliu,
hovi lihe nā khīṇu |
jāṇiu teṃ visa paramapaü,
kahi (aï kahi) līeṇu || 41

patta musāriu masi miliu
howi lihe [4a3] no khīṇu |
jāṇiu teṃ wisa paramapaü
kahiṅ gaü kahi līeṇu ||

jhāṇa-rahia ki kīaï jhāṇeṃ |
jo avācca tahiṃ kia vakkhāṇe ||
bhua mu(d)de saala jaga vāhiu |
ṇia sahāva ṇa keṇavi ṇāhiu || 42

jhāṇarahia ki kīaï jhāṇeṃ
jo awācca tahiṃ kia wakhāṇeṃ |
bhuamude saalajaga wāhi[4a4]u
ṇiasahāwa ṇa keṇawi gāhiu ||

manta ṇa tanta ṇa dhea ṇa dhāraṇa |
savvavi re baḍha vi(b)bhama-kāraṇa ||
asamala cīa ma jhāṇeṃ kharaḍaha |
suha acchanteṃ ma appaṇa jhagaḍaha || 43

manta ṇa tanta ṇa dhea ṇa (pc, ṇa ṇa ac) dhāraṇa
sawwa wi re waḍha wibhamakāraṇa |
asamalacīa ma jhāṇeṃ kharaḍaha (gloss: mā kuruḥ?)
suheṃ acchanteṃ ma appaṇa [4a5] jhagaḍaha ||

guru-vaaṇa-amia-rasa,
dhavahiṃ ṇa piviaü jahiṃ |
bahu sātthāttha-marutthalihiṃ,
tisia maribbo ttehiṃ || 44

guruwaaṇaamiarasa
dhawahiṃ (gloss: sāmakheyaṃ?) ṇa piwiaü jehiṃ |
wahusāttāthamarutthalihiṃ
tisia mariwwo tehiṃ ||

maṇa nimmala sahajāvatthe gaü,
ariula nāhi mpavesa |
e teṃ cīehu phuḍa sathāviaü,
so jiṇa nāhiṃ visesa || 45

maṇa nimmala sahajāvattha/the gaü,
ariula nāhim pawesa |
[4a6] eteṃ wīeṃ phuḍa saṃthawiaü
so jiṇa nāhiṃ wisesa ||

jima loṇa vilijjaï pāṇiehiṃ,
tima jaï cittavi ṭṭhāi |
appā dīsaï parahiṃ sama,
tattha samāhie kāi || 46

jima loṇa (?) wilijjaï pāṇiehiṃ |
tima jaï citta wi ṭṭhāi |
appā dīsaï parahiṃ sama
tattha samāhieṃ [4b1] kāi ||

jovaï citta ṇa āṇaï bamhā |
avara ko vijjaï pucchaï amhā ||
ṇāmehiṃ saṇṇa a-(sa)ṇṇa paārā |
puṇu paramatthemṃ ekāārā || 47

jowaï citta ṇa āṇaï wamhā |
awara ko wijjaï pucchaï amhā |
ṇāmeṃhiṃ saṇṇa aṇṇapaārā
puṇu paramatheṃ ekāārā ||

khanteṃ-pīvanteṃ suraa ramante |
āli-ula bahalaho cakka pharante ||
evahi siddhi jāi paraloaha |
māthe pāa dei bhualoaha || 48

khāanteṃ piwanteṃ suraa [4b2] ramante
āliula wahalaho cakka pharante |
ewahi siddhi jāi paraloaha |
māthe pāa daï bhualoaha ||

jahi maṇa pavaṇa ṇa saṃcaraï,
ravi-sasi ṇāhiṃ pavesa ||
tahiṃ baḍha citta visāma karu,
saraheṃ kahia uesa || 49

jahi maṇa pawaṇa ṇa saṃcaraï
rawisasi ṇāhiṃ pawesa
[4b3] tahiṃ waḍa citta wisāma karu
saraheṃ kahia uesa ||

ekka karu mā veṇṇi karu,
mā karu viṇṇi visesa |
ekkeṃ raṃge rañjiā,
tihuaṇa saalāsesa || 50

ekka karu mā weṇṇi karu
mā karu wāṇṇawisesa,
ekkeṃ raṃga rañjiā
tihuaṇa saalāsesa ||

āi ṇa anta ṇa majjha tahiṃ,
ṇaü bhava ṇaü ṇivvāṇa |
ehu so paramamahāsuha,
ṇaü para ṇaü appāṇa || 51

āi [4b4] ṇa anta ṇa majjha tahiṃ
ṇaü bhawa ṇaü ṇiwwāṇa |
ehu so paramamahāsuha
ṇaü para ṇaü appāṇa ||

aggeṃ paccheṃ dasa diseṃ,
jaṃ jaṃ joami sovi |
evveṃ tu dīṭhanta ḍī,
ṇāha ṇa pucchami kovi || 52

aggeṃ paccheṃ dasadiseṃ
jaṃ jaṃ joami sowi |
ewweṃ tuṭhṭī (!?) bha[4b5]ntaḍī
ṇāha ṇa pucchami kowi ||

bāhareṃ sāda ko dei,
abhintare ko ālavaï |
sāddhaha sāddha ko melavaï,
ko āṇei ko lei || 53

wāhareṃ sāda ko dei |
abhintare ko ālawaï |
sāddhaha sāddha ko melawaï
ko āṇei ko ṇei ||

appā parahiṃ ṇa melaviu,
gamaṇāgamaṇa ṇa bhāgga |
tusa kuṭṭaṃte kāla gaü,
cāula hattha ṇa lāgga || 54

appā parahiṃ ṇa melawiaü
[4b6] gamaṇāgamaṇa ṇa bhāgga | (gloss: sakhī; here?)
tusa kuṭṭaṃte kālagaü
cāula hātheṃ ṇa lāgga ||

ravi-sasi veṇṇavi mā kara bhāntī |
bamhā-viṭṭhu mahesara bhāntī ||
gāḍhāliṅgamāṇa so rājja varu,
jaga uppajjaï tatthu || 55

rawi sasi weṇṇi wi mā kara māntī |
bamhā viṭṭhu mahesara bhāntī |
gāḍhāliṅgamāṇa so rājja [5a1] waru
jaga uppajaï tatthu ||

are putta tojjha (tatta),
rasu susaṃṭṭhiu bhojja |
vakkhāṇanta paḍhantānia,
jagahiṃ ṇiā-ṇia sojjha || 56

are putta tojjhu
rasu susaṃṭṭhi<u> bhejju |
wakṣāṇanta paḍhantānia,
jagahiṃ ṇiāṇia sojjhu ||

adha-uddha māggavareṃ païsarei |
canda-sujja vei paḍiharei ||
vañcijjaï kālahutaṇaa gaï |
ve viāra samarasa karei || 57

adhaüddha māggawareṃ païsarei |
candasujja wei [5a2] paḍiharei |
vañcijjaï kālahutaṇaa gaï
we wiāra samarasa karei ||

ko pattijjaï kasu kahami,
ajjaü kiaü arāu |
pia-dansaṇeṃ hale ṇaṭṭha ṇisi,
saṃjhāsaṃ huḍa jāu || 58

ko pattijjaï kasu kahami
ajjaü kiaü arāu |
piadansaṇeṃ haleṃ ṇaṭṭhaṇisi
saṃ[5a3]jhā saṃphuḍa jāu ||

suṇṇavi appā suṇṇa jagu,
ghareṃ-ghareṃ ehu akkhāṇa |
taruara-mūla ṇa jāṇiā,
sarahe hiṃ kia vakkhāṇa || 59

suṇṇa wi appā suṇṇa jagu
ghare ghareṃ ehu akṣāṇa |
taruaramūla ṇa jāṇiā
sāhehiṃ kia wakṣāṇa ||

jaï rasāalu païsarahu,
aha duggamahu āāsa |
bhiṇṇāāra muṇa tuha,
kaha mokkha-habbāsu || 60

jaï rasāalu païsarahu
[5a4] aha duggamahu āāsu |
bhiṇṇāāra muṇa tuha,
kaha mokṣa hawwāsu ||

buddhi viṇāsaï maṇa maraï,
tuṭṭaï jahiṃ ahimāṇa |
so māāmaa paramapaü,
tahiṃ ki bajjaha jhāṇa || 61

buddhi wiṇāsaï maṇa maraï
tuṭṭhaï jahiṃ ahimāṇa |
so māāmaa paramapa[5a5]ü
tahiṃ ki wajjhaï jhāṇa ||

bhava uekkhaï khaehi ṇivajjaï |
bhāva-rahia puṇu kahiṃ uajjaï ||
vei-vivajjia jo uajjaï |
acchahu siriguruṇāheṃ kahijjaï || 62

bhawa uekṣaï (gloss: ālambane) khaehi ṇiwajjhaï,
bhāwarahia puṇu kahiṃ uajjaï |
wei wiwajjia jo uajjaï,
acchahu siriguruṇāheṃ kahijja[5a6]ï ||

dekkhaü suṇaü paīsaü sāddaü |
jighghaü bhamaü baīsaü uṭṭhaü ||
ālamāla bavahāreṃ bollaü |
maṇa cchaḍu ekāāre mma calaü || 63

dekṣaü suṇaü, paisau, sādaü,
jigghaü, bhamaü, waïsaü, uṭṭhaü |
ālamālawawahāreṃ wollaü,
maṇa cchaḍu ekkāārem ma calaü ||

cittācitta vi pariharahu,
tima acchahu jima bāla |
guru-vaaṇeṃ diḍha bhatti karu,
hoihaï sahaja ullāla || 64

cintācinta wi, pariharahu,
[5b1] tima acchahu jima wāla |
guruwaaṇe diḍhabhatti karu
hoihaï sahaja ullāla ||

akkharavāṇo paramaguṇeṃ rahiaü |
bhaṇaï ṇaṃ jāi so maï kahiaü ||
so paramesara kāsu kahijjaï |
suraa kumārī jima uajjaï || 65

akharawāṇo paramaguṇeṃ rahiu |
<bhaṇaï ṇaṃ jāi so maï kahiu>
so paramesara kāsu kahijjaï
suraa kumā[5b2]rī jima uajjaï ||

bhāvābhāveṃ jo paricchiṇṇaü |
ta(hiṃ) jaga tia sahāva vilīṇaü ||
jabbeṃ tahi maṇa ṇiccala thākkaï |
tabbeṃ bhava-ṇivvāṇehi mukkaï || 66

bhāwābhāweṃ jo paricchiṇṇaü
ta jaga tia sahāwa wilīṇaü |
jawweṃ tahi maṇa ṇiccala thākkaï,
tawweṃ bhawaṇṇiwwāṇahi mukkaï ||

jāva ṇa appaüṃ para pariāṇasi |
tāva ki dehāṇuttara pāvasi ||
emaï kahiu bhānti ṇa bhāvā |
appaü appā bujjhahi tāvā || 67

jāwa ṇa appaüṃ para [5b3] pariāṇasi
tāwa ki dehāṇuttara pāwasi |
emaï kahiu bhānti ṇa bhāwā
appaü appā wujjhahi tāwā ||

aṇu-paramāṇu ṇa rūa vicittaü |
aṇavara bhāvahu phuraï saraïu ||
Saraha bhaṇaï bhiḍi ettavi māntaü |
are ṇikollī bujjhahu mittaü || 68

aṇu(gloss: thira)paramāṇu ṇa rūa wicittaü |
aṇawara [5b4] bhāwahu phuraï saraiu |
Saraha bhaṇaï bhiḍi ettawi māntaü,
are ṇikollī wujjhahu mittaü ||

āgge ācchaa bāhire ācchaa |
paï dekkhaa paḍavesī pucchaa ||
Saraha bhaṇaï baḍha jāṇahu appā |
ṇaü so dhea ṇa dhāraṇa jāpā || 69

āgge āccha, wāhire ācchaa,
paï dekṣaa, pahavesī [5b5] pucchaa |
Saraha bhaṇaï baḍha jāṇahu appā,
ṇaü so dhea ṇa dhāraṇa jāpā ||

jaï guru kahaï sabba vi jāṇī |
mokkha ki cchaḍaï appaṇu bāṇī ||
desa bhamaï hābbāse laïu |
sahaja ṇa bujjhaï pāveṃ gahiu || 70

jaï guru kahaï sawwa wi jāṇī,
mokṣa ki cchaḍaï appaṇu wāṇī |
desa bhamaï hāwwā[5b6]seṃ (gloss: icchā?) laïu
sahaja ṇa wujjhaï pāweṃ (gloss: pāpena) gahiu ||

visaa ramante ṇa visaahiṃ lippaï |
uala harantеṃ ṇa pāṇī cchappaï ||
emaï joi mūla sagatto |
visaa ṇa bājjhaï visaa ramanto || 71

wisaa ramante ṇa wisaahiṃ lippaï
uala (gloss: utpala) haranta ṇa pāṇī cchuppaï |
emaï joi mūla sagatto
visa[6a1]a ṇa wājhhaï wisaa ramanto ||

deva pudijjaa lakkhavi dijjaa |
appauṃ mārī kīsa karijjaa ||
tahavi ṇa tuṭṭaï ehu saṃsārū |
viṇu ābhāseṃ ṇāhi nisārū || 72

dewa pudijjaa lakṣa wi dijjaa,
appaüṃ mārī kīsa karijjaa |
taha wi ṇa tuṭṭaï ehu saṃsāru,
wiṇu ābhāseṃ ṇāhi nisāru ||

bhāvābhāvaha bhāvaṇuratto |
pasua majjhe te gaṇianti satto ||
jhāṇe jā kia mokkhāvāsa |
so bhava-rākkhasakero dāsa || 73

[6a2] bhāwābhāwaha bhāwaṇuratto
pasua majjhe te, gaṇianti satto |
jhāṇe jā kia mokṣāwāsa
so bhawarākṣasakero dāsa ||

dhariaü haṃsa maï kahiaü bhea |
adha-uddha dui pakkhāṃ cchea ||
pakkhavihuṇṇe kahavi jāa |
deha maḍha jaï ṇiccala ṭṭhāa || 74

dhariaü haṃsa maïṃ kahiaü bhea
adhaüddha du[6a3]i pakṣāṃ cchea |
pakṣavihuṇṇe kahawi jāa,
deha maḍha laï ṇiccala ṭṭhāa ||

paṃḍia saala sattha vakkhāṇaa |
dehahiṃ buddha vasanta ṇa jāṇaa ||
amaṇāgamaṇa ṇa ekka vi khaṇḍia |
taü ṇilajja bhaṇaï haṃu (!) paṇḍia || 75

paṃḍia saalasattha wakṣāṇaa |
dehahiṃ buddha wasante ṇa jāṇaa,
amaṇāgamaṇa ṇa [6a4] ekka wi khaṇḍia
taü ṇilajja bhaṇaï haü paṇḍia ||

jattaï cittahu viphuraï,
tattaï ṇāhu sarūa |
aṇṇa taraṃga ki aṇṇa jalu,
bhava-sama kha-sama sarūa || 76

jattaï cittahu viphuraï
tattaï ṇāhasarūa |
aṇṇa taraṅga ki aṇṇa jaṇu
bhawasama khasama sarū[6a5]a ||

ṇa ttaṃ vāeṃ guru kahaï,
ṇaü taṃ bujjhaï sīsa |
sahaja sahāvā haleṃ amiarasa,
kāsu kahijjaï kīsa || 77

ṇa ttaṃ wāeṃ guru kahaï
ṇa ttaṃ bujjhaï sīsa |
sahajasahāwā haleṃ amiarasa,
kāsu kahijjaï kīsa ||

jattaï païsaï jaleṃhi jalu,
tattaï samarasu hoi |
dosaguṇāara cittatā,
baḍha paḍivakkha ṇa hoi || 78

jattaï païsaï jaleṃhi jalu
tattaï sama[6a6]rasu hoi |
dosaguṇāaracittatā,
waḍha paḍiwakṣa ṇa lei ||

cchaḍḍaha je sahaje sahaja buddhie laïu |
viviha paāra pavañcā sahiu ||
ekka kahavi ṇa kīaī vāsaṇa |
ehu āṇatta saala jiṇa-sāsaṇa || 79

cchaḍaha je sahaje sahaja buddhie laïu
wiwihapaāra pawañcā sahiu |
ekka kahiaawi ṇa [6b1] kīaï wāsaṇa
ehu āṇatta saalajiṇasāsaṇa ||

mukkāvathi je saala jagu,
ṇāhi ṇibaddho kovi |
mūḍhahi mohe pamattiaï,
satthāvattha je sovi || 80

mukkāvathi je saalajagu,
ṇāhi ṇiwaddho kowi |
mūḍhahi moha (gloss: [illegible]) pam/sattiaï
satthāwattha je sowi ||

cittaha pasara ṇirantara dekkhī |
loha moha je kahiu(u)ekkhī |
jakkha-rūa jima cittaera vibhāa |
māyājāla je tima paḍihāa || 81

cittaha pa[6b2]sara ṇirantara dekṣī
loha moha je kahiu ekṣī
jakṣarūa jima cittaera wibhāa |
māājāla je tima paḍihāa |

saalaho ehu sāhāñcia dekkhahu |
tahimbi līṇa citta uekkhahu ||
sahajeṃ sahaja vi bujjhaï jabbeṃ |
antarāla gaï tuṭṭaï tabbeṃ || 82

saala ho ehu sahāñcia dekṣaha |
tahim wi [6b3] līṇa citta uekṣaha |
sahajeṃ sahaja wi wujjhaï jawweṃ
antarālagaï tuṭṭaï tawyaṃ (!) ||

riddhi-siddhi haleṃ veṇṇi na kājja |
pāpa-puṇṇa tahiṃ pāḍahu bājja ||
so a(¯)ṇuttara bujjhahi jabbeṃ |
Saraha bhaṇaï jaga sijjhaï tabbeṃ || 83

riddhisiddhi haleṃ weṇṇi na kājja
pāpapuṇa tahiṃ pāḍahu wājja |
so a[6b4]ṇuttara wujjhahi jawweṃ
Saraha bhaṇaï jaga sijjhaï tawweṃ |

gurua vaaṇa saṃsiddhaü jabbeṃ |
indiāla sabba tuṭṭaï tabbeṃ ||
Saraha bhaṇaï a(¯)ṇuttara dhāmma |
hari-hara-buddha ehuvi kāmma || 84

gurua waaṇa saṃsiddhaü jawweṃ,
indiāla sawwa tuṭṭaï tawweṃ |
Saraha bhaṇaï aṇuttara dhāmma |
hari[6b5]harawuddha je ehawi kāmma ||

sabbāāravarottama kovi |
suṇaha siāla ba sattu leṃ sovi ||
suddhie "(?)" jāṇia jabbeṃ |
jiṇa-guṇa-raaṇa pāvia tabbeṃ || 85

sawwāārawarottama kowi,
suṇaha siāla wa sattaleṃ sowi,
suddhieṃ jāṇia jawweṃ
jiṇaguṇaraaṇa pāwia tawweṃ ||

ahavā mohe so pariāṇiu |
mokkhaha buddhie jāi sammāṇiaü ||
hatthahi kaṅkaṇa ṭṭhiaü ṇṇāi |
guṇa-dosa-viakkhaṇa dappaṇahiṃ ṇa jāṇaï || 86

ahawā moheṃ so [6b6] pariāṇiaü |
mokṣaha wuddhieṃ jāi sammāṇiaü |
hatthahi kaṅkaṇa ṭṭhiaü ṇṇāi |
guṇadosaviakṣaṇadappaṇahiṃ ṇa jāṇaï ||

buddhaha saala maṇe dei
mukkā malla māṇa so bājjhaï |
jāṇaha paramāttha na atthā cchiṇṇaṃ
sabbocchiṇṇaṃ pecchaha sabbaṃ || 87

wuddhaha saalamaṇe de[7a1]i
mukkā malla māṇa so wājjhaï ||
jāṇaha awya (?) (gloss: paramāttha?) <na> atthā cchiṇṇaṃ |
suwwocchiṇṇaṃ pecchaha sawwaṃ |

sā hoha subbocchinnaṃ
abbocchinnaṃ manu āṇaṃtaṇa || 88ab

sā (?) ho (?) ha (?) suwwocchinaṃ,
awwocchina muna āṇaṃtaṇa ||

saesaṃvitti mā karahu re dhāndhā |
bhāvābhāva sugati reṃ bāndhā | 88cd
ṇia maṇa maṇahu re ṇehueṃ joi |
jima jala jalehi milante soi || 89ab

saesaṃwitti mā karahu re dhāndhā |
bhāwābhāwa [7a2] sugati reṃ bāndhā |
ṇiamaṇa maṇahu re ṇihueṃ joi |
jima jala jalehi milante soi ||

jhāṇa mokkha ki cāhu re āleṃ |
māājāla ki cāhu re koleṃ || 89cd
varaguruvaaṇa pattijaï sācceṃ |
Saraha bhaṇaï maï kahiaü vācceṃ || 90ab

jhāṇa mokṣa ki cāhu reṃ āleṃ
māājāla ki cāhu re koleṃ |
waraguruwa[7a3]aṇa patti<jaï> sācceṃ |
Saraha bhaṇaï maïṃ kahiaü wācceṃ ||

ṇia sahāva ṇa laddhaa vaaṇeṃ |
dīsaï guru-āese ṇaaṇeṃ || 90cd
ṇaü tasu dosa je ekkavi ṭṭhāa |
dhammādhamma je mohī khāa || 91ab

ṇiasahāwa ṇa lakṣaa (?) waaṇeṃ
dīsaï guruāese ṇaaṇeṃ |
ṇaü tasu dosa je ekkawi ṭṭhāa
[7a4] dhammādhamma je mohī khāa ||

citte baddhe bajjhaï
mukke mukkaï ṇatthi sandeho | 91cd
bajjhanti jeṇa jaḍā
parimuñcanti teṇa budhā || 92ab

citte waddhe wajjhaï
mukke mukkaï ṇatthi sandeho |
wajjhanti jeṇa jaḍā
parimuñcanti teṇa budhā ||

baddho gamaï dasa disehi,
mukko ṇiccala ṭṭhāa | 92cd
emaïkarahā pekkhu sahi,
vivaria mahu paḍihāi || 93ab

> bāddho gamaï dasadisehi,
> mukko [7a5] ṇiccala ṭṭhāa |
> emaïṃ karahā pekṣu sahi
> wiwaria mahu paḍihāi ||

pavaṇa dhari appāṇa ma bhindaha |
kaṭṭha-joa nāsāgga ma vindaha || 93cd
are baḍha sahaja gaï para rajjaha |
mā bhava-gandha-bandha paḍibajjaha || 94ab

> pawaṇa dhari appāṇa ma bhindaha |
> kaṣṭhajoa nāsāgga ma windaha |
> are waḍha sahaja gaï pa[7a6]ra rajjaha |
> mā bhawagandhawandha paḍiwajjaha ||

ehu nia maṇa sabala cātara sa cala |
melahiṃ sahāva ṭṭhāa vasaï dosa-ṇimmala | 94cd

> ehu niamaṇa sawala cātara sañcala
> melahiṃ sahāwa ṭṭhāa wasaï dosaṇimmala |

jabbeṃ maṇa atthamaṇu jāi,
taṇu tuṭṭaï bandhaṇa |
tabbeṃ sama rasahi majjhe,
ṇaü sudda ṇa bāmhaṇa || 95

> jawweṃ maṇu atthamaṇu jāi
> ta[7b1]ṇu tuṭṭaï wandhaṇa |
> tawweṃ samarasahi majjheṃ
> ṇaü sudda ṇa wāmhaṇa ||

ethu se surasaï sovaṇāha,
ethu se gaṅgāsāaru |
vāraṇasi paāga ethu,
se cānda-divāaru || 96

ethu se surasaï sowaṇāha,
ethu se gaṅgāsāaru,
wārāṇasi paāga ethu
se cāndadiwāa[7b2]ru |

khetta piṭṭha uapiṭṭha,
ethu maï bhamia samiṭṭhaü |
dehāsarisa tittha,
maï suṇaü ṇa diṭṭhaü || 97

khettapiṭṭhaüapiṭṭha
ethu maï bhamia samiṭṭhaü
dehāsarisa tittha
maï suaü ṇa diṭṭhaü ||

saru puḍaaṇi dalu kamala,
gandha-kesara vara ṇāleṃ |
cchāḍahu veṇṇimā karahu se,
mā lāggahu baḍha āleṃ || 98

saru puḍaaṇi dalu kamala
gandhakesara waraṇāleṃ |
cchāḍahu we[7b3]ṇṇi mā karahu se
mā lāggahu waḍha āleṃ |

kāmānta sānta khaa jāa,
ettha pujjahu kulahīṇaü |
bāmha-viṭṭhu-taïloa,
jahiṃ jāi vilīṇaü || 99

kāmānta sānta khaa jāa
etthu pujjahu kulahīṇao |
wāmhawiṭṭhutaïloa
jahiṃ jāi wilīṇao ||

jaï ṇaü visaahiṃ līliaï,
tahu buddhatta ṇa kehiṃ |
seu-rahia ṇava aṅkurahiṃ,
tarusampatti ṇa ja(˜) u || 100

jaï ṇa[7b4]ü wisaahiṃ lāliaï |
taü wuddhatta ṇa kehiṃ |
seurahia ṇawa aṅkurahiṃ
tarusampatti ṇa jaüṃ |

jatthavi tatthavi jahavi tahavi,
jeṇa teṇa hua buddha |
saesaṅkappe ṇāsiaü,
jagu sahāvahi suddha || 101

jatthawi tatthawi jahawi tahawi
jeṇa teṇa hua buddha |
sae[7b5]saṅkappeṃ ṇāsiaü
jagu sahāwahiṃ suddha ||

sahaja kappa pare vevi ṭhiu,
sahaja leu re suddha |
kaapaapāṇī pīsa laü,
rāahansa jima duṭṭha || 102

sahaja kappa pare wewi ṭhiu
sahaja lehu re suddha |
kaapaapāṇī pīsa laü,
rāahansa jima duṭṭha ||

jaga upapāaṇe dukkha bahu,
uppaṇṇaü tahiṃ suhasāra |
uppaṇa uppāa ṇahiṃ,
loa ṇa jāṇaï sāra || 103

jagaüppāaṇe du[7b6]kṣa wahu
uppaṇṇaü tahiṃ suhasāra |
uppaṇa uppāa ṇahiṃ
loa ṇa jāṇaï sāra ||

are putta tatta vicitta rasu,
kahaṇa ṇa sakkaï vattu |
kappa-rahia suha ṭṭhāṇa kuha |
ṇia sahāveṃ seviu ekkaha || 104

are putta tatta wicittarasu
kahaṇa ṇa sakkaï wattu |
kapparahiasuhaṭṭhāna[8a1]kṣaha
ṇiasahāweṃ sewiu ekṣaha |

kamaṇe so guṇahi dhariaü |
ahavā ekovi ṇa dhariaü ||
suṇṇāsuṇṇa vi bujjhaï jatthu |
guru ṇṇaü vaṇṇa vi bhuṃjaï tatthu || 105

kamaṇe so guṇahi dhariaü
ahawā ekowi ṇa dhariaü ||
suṇṇāsuṇṇa wi bujjhaï jatthu |
guru ṇṇaü waṇṇa wi juṃjaï tatthu |

buddha vi vaaṇeṃ ettavi dhamma |
loācāreṃ ettavi kamma ||
saala tatta sahāveṃ dekkhaha |
loācāra je tahiṃ uekkhaha || 106

buddha [8a2] wi waaṇeṃ etta wi dhāmma |
loācāreṃ etta wi kāmma ||
saala <wi> tatta sahāweṃ dekṣaha |
loācāra je tahiṃ uekṣaha |

evahiṃ buddha-rūa haleṃ kovi |
sahaja sahāveṃ sijjhaï sovi ||
suaṇe jima varakāmiṇi māṇiu |
raï-suha tahiṃ paccakkhahiṃ samāṇiu || 107

ewahiṃ buddharūa haleṃ kowi,
sahajasahāweṃ sijjhaï [8a3] sowi ||
suaṇe jima warakāmiṇi māṇiu |
raïsuha tahiṃ paccakṣehiṃ samāṇiu |

evahiṃ buddha-ruahu laḍa sijjhaï |
pajjopāeṃ kahavi ṇa bajjhaï ||
jaï maṇa sahaja ṇirantareṃ pāvaï |
indī visaahi khaṇavi ṇa dhāvaï || 108

ewahiṃ buddharūahu laḍa sijjhaï
pajñopāeṃ kahawi ṇa wajjhaï ||
ja[8a4]ï maṇa sahaja ṇirantareṃ pāwaï |
indī wisaahiṃ khaṇa wi ṇa dhāwaï |

tahiṃ so vi dea e caüriddhī |
Saraha bhaṇaï jiṇa-bimba vi siddhī || 109ab

tahiṃ so wi dea e caüriddhī
Saraha bhaṇaï jiṇawimwa wi siddhī ||

dohā-saṅgama maï kahiaü,
jehu vibujjhia tattha | 109cd
ehu saṃsāra haleṃ lehu,
jahiṃ jāṇijjaï tattha || 110ab

dohāsaṅgama [8a5] maïṃ kahiaü
jehiṃ wiwujjhia tattha |
ehu saṃsāra haleṃ lehu
jahiṃ jāṇijjaï tattha ||

gahi guṇa dhamma saṃsāra
ahavā satthattha ṇiatthaṇeṃ | 110cd
tahi bhāsia dohākosaṃ
tattha cciakandhaaṃ samattaṃ || 111ab

gahiū ṇa dhamma saṃsāra
ahawā satthattha ṇiatthaṇeṃ,
tahi bhāsia do[8a6]hākosaṃ
tattha cciakandhaaṃ samattaṃ ||

jaï kahami tojjhu kuhaṇa ṇa jāi |
ahavā kahami jaṇakera maṇapattaa ṇa jāi || 111cd

jaï kahami tojjhu kahaṇa ṇa jāi |
ahawā kahami jaṇakera maṇapattaa ṇa jāi |

jaï pamāeṃ vihi baseṃ,
baḍha laddhaü bheu |

jaï caṇḍāla-ghareṃ bhuñjaï,
taavi ṇa laggaï leu || 112

jaï pamāeṃ wihi waseṃ
baḍha la[8b1]ddhaü bheu |
jaï caṇḍālaghareṃ bhuñjaï,
tawia, ṇa lagaï leu ||

sahaja-sahaja mu māṇahu āleṃ |
jeṃ puṇu bandha hoi bhavapāseṃ ||
are baḍha āsā kahavi ṇa kājja |
dasa (?sada)guru kiraṇe pāḍahu bājja || 113

sahaja sahaja ma, māṇahu, āseṃ,
jeṃ puṇu wandha hoi bhawapāseṃ |
are waḍha, āsā, kaha wi ṇa kājja
dasagu[8b2]rukiraṇeṃ pāḍahu wājja ||

saaṃ-saṃveaṇa tatta baḍha,
loeṃ taṃ kāi maṇanti ||
jo maṇa-goareṃ pāviaï,
so paramattha na honti || 114

saeṃsaṃweaṇa tatta waḍha
loeṃ taṃ kāi maṇanta |
jo maṇagoareṃ pāwiaï
so paramāttha na honti ||

ṇia sahāva gaaṇa-sama,
appā para ṇaü soi |
sahajāṇanda caüṭṭhaü,
so kī vucca ṇa jāi || 115

ṇiasahāwa gaaṇasama,
appā para [8b3] ṇaü māi (?) |
sahajāṇanda caüṭṭhao
so kī wucca ṇa jāi ||
n.b. sahajānanda as the fourth!

viṇa bajje jima cchāntī jāvatia,
maṇa māākera sahāva |
saala visaa ṇa sahāveṃ sijjhaa |
pajjopāeṃ kahavi ṇa bājjhaa || 116

> wiṇa wājje jima cchāntī jāwatia
> saṇa māākerasahāwa | sic
> saalawisaa la sahāweṃ sijjhaa, sic
> pa[8b4]jñopāeṃ kaha wi ṇa wājjhaa ||

jiṇavara-vaaṇaṃ pattijjahu sācceṃ |
Saraha bhaṇaï maï kahiaü vācceṃ ||
sahajeṃ sahaja vi vāhia jabeṃ |
acinta joeṃ sijjhaï tabbeṃ || 117

> jiṇawarawaaṇeṃ pattijjaha sācceṃ |
> Saraha bhaṇaï maï kahiaü wācceṃ |
> sahajeṃ sahaja wi wāhia jawweṃ |
> acintajoeṃ [8b5] sijjhaï tawweṃ ||

jima jala-majjheṃ candaḍā,
ṇaü so sācca ṇa miccha |
tima so maṇḍalacakkaḍā,
ṇaü heḍaï ṇaü khitta || 118

> jima jalamajjheṃ candaḍā,
> ṇaü so, sācca ṇa miccha |
> tima so maṇḍalacakkaḍā,
> ṇaü heḍaï, ṇaü khitta ||

citta deva je saala hi rājjaï |
para-cittanta cāuli bhuṃjaï ||
cittahiṃ saala jaga jo dīsaa |
sahaja sahāveṃ kimpi ṇa dīsaa || 119

> citta dewa je saala hi rājjaa,
> paracinte [8b6] nte cāuṇi rujaï | sic
> cittahiṃ saalajaga jo dīsaa,
> sahajasahāweṃ kimpi ṇa dīsaa ||

cittahiṃ citta jaï lakkhaṇa jāi |
cañcala maṇa pavaṇa thira hoi ||
citta thira jo ṇimmala bhāva |
tahiṃ ṇa païsaï bhāvābhāva || 120

> cittaṃhiṃ citta jaï lakṣaṇa jāi |
> cañcalamaṇapawaṇa thira [9a1] hoi ||
> citta thira jo ṇimmalabhāwa
> tahi ṇa païsaï bhāwābhāwa ||

ehu deva bahu āgama dīsaa |
appaṇa icchеṃ phuḍa paḍihāsaa ||
appaṇu ṇāho para viruddho |
ghare-ghare so siddhāṃta pasiddho || 121

> ehu dewa wahuāgama dīsaa
> apaṇṇa icchеṃ phuḍa paḍihāsaa |
> appaṇu ṇāho para wiruddho
> [9a2] ghare gharеṃ so siddhānta pasiddho ||

hiahiṃ kāca maṇi laï tuṭṭho |
bohimaṇḍala mahāsuha ṇa païṭṭho ||
samvara citta-rāa diḍha cāṅgo |
jāva ṇa daṃsaa visaa bhujaṃgo || 122

> hiahiṃ kācamaṇi laï tuṭṭho |
> wohimaṇḍala mahāsuha ṇa païṭṭho |
> samwaracittarāa diḍha cāṅge
> jāwa ṇa daṃsaa wisaabhujaṅge ||

pañjare jima pagi pakkhi ṇicañcala |
tima maṇa rāu lagaï suṭhu vañcala ||
so jaï laïaï aïnta virālеṃ |
calaï na bullaï ṭṭhiaï nirālеṃ || 123

> [9a3] pañjare jima pagi pakṣi ṇicañcala
> tima maṇarāu la<gaï suṭhu wañcala>
> so jaï laïaï aïnta wirāle |
> calaï na wullaï ṭṭhiaï nirālеṃ ||

cintācinta ṇa kiaü maï,
ṇaü pariāṇia kīsa |
bujjhaho jo guṇavanto,
veṇṇi kariā sīsa || 124

cintācinta ṇa ki[9a4]aü maïṃ
ṇaü pariāṇia kīsa |
bujjhaho jo guṇavanto
weṇṇi kariā mīsa ||

jaï ṭṭhāṇa ṇa gheppaï duṭṭha maṇu,
indī kāi carei |
pasughareṃ coraha manta ṇa pecchaï,
jo taïloa harei || 125

jaï ṭṭhāṇa ṇa gheppaï duṭṭhamaṇu
indī kāiṃ carei |
pasughareṃ co[9a5]raha manta ṇa pecchaï
jo taïloa harei ||

cchāācchāahiṃ jaï so païṭṭho |
deha vasanto citta ṇa diṭṭho ||
jo so jāṇaï ṇia maṇa ṭṭhāṇā |
saala jaga bhavati bhava suiṇā || 126

cchāāchāahiṃ jaï so païṭṭho
deha wamanto citta ṇa diṭṭho |
jo so jāṇaï ṇiamaṇaṭṭhāṇā |
saalajaga bha[9a6]vati (?) bhavasuiṇā ||

ṇibbāṇeṃ ṭṭhia jhāṇe rājaï |
āṇṇa mānda āṇṇa āu saha kījaï ||
ṇaü so jhāṇeṃ ṇaü pabbājeṃ |
geha vasaṃteṃ samarasa bhājjeṃ || 127

ṇiwwāṇeṃ ṭṭhia jhāṇeṃ rājaï |
āṇṇa mānda āṇṇa āu saha kījaï |
ṇaü so jhāṇeṃ ṇaü pawwājeṃ
geha wasanteṃ samarasa bhājjeṃ |

ghare-ghareṃ kahiaa sojjhu kahāṇo |
ṇaü pariāṇia mahāsuha ṭṭhāṇo ||
Saraha bhaṇaï jaga citteṃ vāhiu |
sovi acinta ṇa keṇavi gāhiu || 128

gha[9b1]reṃ ghareṃ kahiaa sojjhu kahāṇo |
ṇaü pariāṇia mahāsuhaṭṭhāṇo |
Saraha bhaṇaï jaga citte nāhiu, sic?
so wi ācinta ṇa keṇa wi gāhiva || sic

e je karuṇa muṇantī māgahi,
diḍha lāggaï teṃ bhava-pāsa |
aï aṇṇo so aṇakkharu ṇava,
suṇṇahiṃ citta ṇirāsa || 129

e je karuṇa [9b2] muṇantī māgahī,
diḍha lāggaï teṃ bhawapāsa |
aï aṇṇo aṇakṣaru ṇawa
suṇṇahi citta ṇirāsa ||

jima jalehiṃ sasi disaï cchāā |
tima bhava paḍihāsaï saalavi māā ||
aïso citta bhamante ṇa diṭṭho |
bhava ṇivvāṇa ṇirantareṃ païṭṭho || 130

jima jaleṃhi sasi disaï cchāā,
tima bhawa paḍi[9b3]hāsaï saala wi māā |
aïso citta bhamante ṇa diṭṭho
bhawa ṇiwwāṇa ṇirantareṃ païṭṭho ||

anto ṇattha suiuaā ṇaṭṭho kāla duiu |
eko vi so jānivvo jeṇa kammasaü ||
ṇijia sāso ṇihanda-loaṇo
saala viāra vimukko maṇo || 131

anto ṇāttha suioā ṇaṭṭho kāla duio |
eko [9b4] wi so jāṇiwwo jeṇa kammakhao hoi || !
ṇijia sāso ṇihandaloaṇo |
salawiārawimukko maṇo |

jo e āvattha gaü so
joi ṇatthi saṃdeho | 132ab

> jo e āwattha gao so
> joi ṇatthi sande[9b5]ho ||

ṇiṭṭhura suraa saṃ pāṇia,
kamala-kulisa sampatti || 132cd
khaṇe-khaṇe kiṃ vibohia
ṇivvāṇa saesamvitti | 133ab

> ṇiṭṭhura suraa saṃ pāṇia recte: suraarasaṃ
> kamalakulisasampatti |
> khaṇakhaṇehiṃ wiwohia
> ṇiwwāṇa saesamwitti ||

vevi koḍi ṇa ratto,
kahi mpuṇa lakkha k.hāṇa (!) || 133cd
taha vevi rahia ṇiuṇo,
aṇuttara bohi viṇṇāṇa || 134ab

> wewi koḍi ṇa ratto
> kahim puṇu lakṣa kahā[9b6]ṇaṃ |
> taha wewirahia ṇiuṇo
> aṇuttarawohiwiṇṇāṇaṃ

rasu paribhuñja ṇa mūla-rasa,
kamalavaṇeṃ paṇa majjaï | 134cd
bahu santāveṃ saaleṃ,
citta-gaenda ṇa rajjaï || 135ab

> rasu paribhuñja ṇa mūlarasa
> [10a1] kamalawaṇeṃ paṇa majjaï | ghaṇa?
> wahusantāweṃ saaleṃ
> cittagaenda ṇa rajjaï ||

ālaataru umalaï,
hiṇḍaï jaga cchācchānda | 135cd
gammāgamma ṇa jāṇaï,
matto citta-gaanda || 136ab

    ālaataru umalaï
    hiṇḍaï jaga cchācchānda |
    gammāgamma ṇa jāṇaï
    ma[10a2]tto cittagaanda ||

jaï jaga pūria sahajāṇande |
ṇāccahu gāahu vilasahu caṅge | 136cd
jaï puṇu gheppahu vāsaṇa vinde |
taha phuḍa bājjhahu e bhava-phānde || 137ab

    jaï jaga pūria sahajāṇande
    ṇāccahu gāahu vilasahu caṅge |
    jaï puṇu gheppahu wāsaṇa winde |
    taha phuḍa wājjhahu e bhawa[10a3]phāṇḍe ||

samatā kāmiṇi aṇuha ṇivāsa |
samarasa bhoaṇa amvara vāsa || 137cd
tahi puṇu kimpi ṇa dīsaï āntara |
sama gaü cittarāa ṇirantara || 138ab

    samatā kāmiṇi aṇuha ṇiwāsa
    samarasabhoaṇa amwara wāsa |
    tahi puṇu kimpi ṇa dīsaï āntara,
    samagaü cittarāa ṇirantara ||

suṇṇa ṇirañjaṇa parama paü,
suiṇomāa sahāva | 138
bhāvahu-citta sahāvatā,
jaü ṇāsijjaï jāva || 139ab

    [10a4] suṇṇa ṇirañjaṇa paramapaü
    suiṇo māasahāwa |
    bhāwaha, cittasahāwatā
    ṇaü ṇāsijjaï jāwa ||

ravi-sasi bandhaṇa gaü jabbeṃ |
uare araï taleṃ kharaï ṇa tabbeṃ | 139cd
dekkhaï ravi pari ta buddha viṇṇāṇā |
uare araï taleṃ ṇāhi mokkharaṇā || 140ab

rawisasibandhaṇagaü jawweṃ
uareṃ araï [10a5] taleṃ kharaï ṇa tawweṃ
dekṣaha <|ra|>wiparitabuddhaviṇṇāṇā |
uare araï taleṃ ṇāhi mokṣaraṇā ||

ṇaübhava ṇaü ṇibbāṇe diṭṭhiaü,
mahāsuha bājja | 140cd
jo bhāvaï maṇu bhāvaṇe,
so para sāhaï kājja || 141ab

ṇaü bhawa ṇaü ṇiwwāṇe diṭṭhiau
mahāsuha wājja |
jo [10b1] bhāwaï maṇu bhāvaṇeṃ
so para sāhaï kājja ||

akkhara-vaṇṇa-vivajjia,
ṇaü so vindu ṇa citta | 141cd
ehu so paramamahāsuha,
ṇaü pheḍia ṇaü khitta || 142ab

akṣarawaṇṇawiwajjia
ṇaü so windu ṇa citta
ehu so paramamahāsuha
ṇaü pheḍia ṇaü (pc, ṇaüṃ ac) khitta ||

jima paḍibimba-sahāvatā,
tima bhāvijjaï bhāva | 142cd
suṇṇa ṇirañjaṇa paramapaü,
ṇa tahiṃ puṇṇa ṇa(ü) pāva || 143ab

jima paḍiwimwa[10b2]sahāwatā
tima bhāwijjaï bhāwa |
suṇṇa ṇirañjaṇa paramapaü
ṇa tahiṃ puṇṇa ṇa pāwa ||

pañca kāmaguṇa bhoaṇehiṃ,
ṇicinta thiyehiṃ | 143cd sic
ebbeṃ labbhaṇa paramapaü,
kimbahu bollia ehiṃ || 144ab

pañcakāmaguṇabhoaṇeṃhi
ṇicintathiaehiṃ |
ewweṃ labbhaï [10b3] paramapaü
kim wahu wollia ehiṃ ||

haüṃ puṇu jāṇami jeṇa maṇu,
cchāḍaï cintā-tātta | 144cd
jo dujjaa paḍia maṇu,
ṇaü so bujjhaï tātta || 145ab

haü puṇu jāṇami jeṇa maṇu
cchāḍaiṃ cintātātta |
jo dujjaa paḍia maṇu
ṇaü (pc, ṇattha? ac) so wujjhaï tātta ||

dhea ṇa dhāraṇa manta tahiṃ,
ṇaü tahiṃ siva (a) satti | 145cd
lakkhālakkha viṇāhi ntehiṃ,
ṇaü tahiṃ bhāva-pasatti || 146ab

dhea ṇa dhā[10b4]raṇa manta tahiṃ
ṇaü tahiṃ siwa satti |
lakṣālakṣa wiṇāhin tahiṃ
ṇaü tahi bhāwapasatti ||

naü tahiṃ ṇindā ṇaü siviṇa,
ṇaü jāgara susutta | 146cd
bhāvābhāva-ṇibandaṇu,
ṇaü tahiṃ thakkaa citta || 147ab

naü tahiṃ ṇindā ṇaü siwiṇa recte: ṇiddā
ṇaü jāgara susutta |
bhāwābhāwaṇiwandhaṇu
[10b5] ṇaü tahi thākkaa citta ||

ṇaü jāiaï ṇaü saraï,
ṇaü avitthiṇṇa vi hoi | 147cd
ṇaü karāvaï ṇaü karaï,
heu viāraha tovi || 148ab

ṇaü jāiaï ṇaü saraï ṇaü maraï sic
ṇaü awitthiṇṇa wi hoi |
ṇaü karāwaï ṇaü karaï
heu viāraha towi ||

jasu āi ṇa ānta,
ṇaü jāṇia majjha | 148cd
tasu kahi kijjaï kahasu maï,
joihiṃ pujjā kajja || 149ab

jaswā (?) ṇa [11a1] āi ṇa ānta
ṇaü jāṇia majjha |
tasu kahi kijjaï kahasu maïṃ
joihiṃ pujjā kajja ||

vaṇṇa-āāra pavāṇa-rahia,
akkhuru veu aṇanta | 149cd
ko pujjaï kaha pujjiaï,
jāsu āi ṇa anta || 150ab

waṇṇaāāra pawāṇarahia
akṣaru weu aṇanta |
ko pujjaï kaha pujja[11a2]aï
jasu āi ṇa anta ||

sahi saṃSaraha kahiṃ tuhu,
ettha kahijjaï tatta | 150cd
ṇaüṇa viāra karantahiṃ,
ṇaü katthavi paramāttha || 151ab

sahi saṃSaraha kahiṃ tuhu
etthu kahijjaï tatta |
ṇiuṇaviāra karantahi (pc, karantahiṃ? ac)
ṇaü katha wi paramāttha ||

jima kelataru sohaṇehi,
ṇaü pāvijjaï sāru | 151cd
tima bhua tatta viāraṇeṃ,
dīsaï ehu saṃsāru || 152ab

jima kailataru sohaṇehiṃ sic
[11a3] ṇaü pāwijjaï sāru |
tima bhuatattaviāraṇeṃ
dīsaï ehu saṃsāru ||

banda ṇa dīsaï etthu haleṃ,
ṇaü so mokkha sahāva | 152cd
buddha saṃyoga paramapaü,
ehu se mokkha-sahāva || 153ab

wanda ṇa dīsaï etthu haleṃ
ṇaü so mokṣasāhāwa |
buddhasaṃyoga [11a4] paramapaü,
ehu se mokṣasahāwa ||

jeṇa pasavaï hiaa pajjora,
teṇa kisevi eṇa | 153cd
saguṇa païsaï tiasa jaṇu,
bhāvaü citta maṇeṇa || 154ab

jeṇa ṇa pasavaï hiaapañjara
teṇa ki sewieṇa |
saguṇa païsaï tiasa jaṇu,
bhāwaü ccitta maṇeṇa ||

ṇipuṃkho (?) vāṇo vāṇavāso ettha kāraṇeṃ,
kimpi ṇa jāṇo aṇusaraï | 154cd
suṇṇahi majjhe suṇṇa paü,
tahi sandhāṇa païsaraï || 155ab

[11a5] ṇipuṃkho wāṇo waṇiwāso (pc, wāṇiwāso ac) etthu kāraṇeṃ
kim pi ṇa jāṇo aṇusaraï |
suṇṇahi majjheṃ suṇṇa paü
tahiṃ sandhāṇa païsaraï ||

sabba dhamma je khasama karīhasi |
khasama sahāveṃ cīa ṭṭhavīhasi || 155cd
sovi cīa acīa karīhasi |
evahi so aṇuttara gamīhasi || 156ab

sawwadhamma je khasa<ma> karīhasi |
[11a6] khasamasahāweṃ cīa ṭṭhawīhasi |
so wi cīa, acīa karīhasi,
ewahi so aṇuttara gamīhasi ||
n.b. similarity to that famous upadeśa!

ṇaaṇa duhahu aṇupama ṇibandhaha |
ṇia gaï ṇia maṇeṃ jaï bhiḍi bandhaha | 156cd
Saraha bhaṇaï eha dui pāvahu |
turia dukkha miccu ṇivārahu || 157ab

gaaṇa duhahu aṇupama ṇiwandhaha,
ṇiagaï ṇiamaṇeṃ [11b1] jaï bhiḍi wandhaha |
Saraha bhaṇaï eha dui <pā>wahu |
turia dukṣa, miccu ṇivārahu ||

ehu ghareṃ ṭṭhia mahilā maṇusā |
ehu ṇa dīsaï bhaṇa sahi kaïsā | 157cd
pāseṃ pāsa bhamante acchaha |
Saraha bhaṇaa tasu ghariṇī ṇecchaa || 158ab

ehu ghareṃ ṭṭhia mahilā maṇusā,
ehu ṇa dīsaï bhaṇa sahi kaïsā |
pāseṃ pā[11b2]sa bhamante acchaa
Saraha bhaṇaa, tasu, ghariṇī ṇecchaa ||

saṅke khāddhaü saala jagu,
saṅkā ṇa keṇavi khāddha | 158cd
jeṃ saṅkā saṅkiaü,
so paramattha vi laddha || 159ab

saṅke khāddhaü saalajagu,
saṅkā ṇa keṇa wi khāddha |
jeṃ saṅkā saṅkiaü
so parama<t>tha wi laddha ||

malla ādi uatti kamma,
jo bhāvaï uatti | 159cd
so ṇava dhammia bappaḍo,
cchāḍahu aliā tatti || 160ab

me[11b3]lla, ādi uatti kamma
jo bhāwaï uatti |
so ṇawa dhammia wappaḍo
cchāḍahu aliā tātti ||

maraṇa maranta pavaṇa tallayeṃ gaaü,
tihuaṇe sahala samāu | 160cd
maṇa-taṇeṃ jo paḍihāsaï |
Saraha bhaṇaï so tatta ṇa gavesaï || 161ab

maṇa (pc, maraṇa ac) marantu pawaṇa tallaeṃ gaaü |
tihua[11b4]ṇeṃ saala samāu |
maṇataṇeṃ jo paḍihāsaï,
Saraha bhaṇaï mo tatta ṇa gawesaï ||

tella-khiccaḍaḍa akkhara sārā |
bhava-ṇibbāṇa kimpi ṇa dūrā || 161cd
saṃsāra aṇupalambha ṇibbāṇa |
ehu boha ṇa dhea ṇa dhāraṇa || 162ab

tellakhiccaḍaï akṣara sārā
bhawaṇiwwāṇeṃ kimpi ṇa [11b5] dūrā |
saṃsāraaṇupalambha ṇiwwāṇa |
ehu woha ṇa dhea ṇa dhāraṇa |

a-dasaṇa dasaṇa jattivi tāṇa |
tettivi mātam (?) bhava-ṇivvāṇa || 162cd
a-musiāraha tatteṃ kāla |
ehu uesa ṇa jāṇaï bāla || 163ab

adasaṇa dasaṇa jetti wi tāṇa |
tetti wi māttam ṇiwwāṇa (pc, bhawaṇiwwāṇa ac) |
amusiāraha tatteṃ kā[11b6]la
ehu uesa ṇa jāṇaï wāla ||

guñjā-raaṇa majjheṃ dīpa ujāla |
cañcala thira kari pavaṇa ṇivāra || 163cd
jo baḍha mūlaha sāra vi jāṇaï |
tā kī kāla-vikāla vilāggaa || 164ab

gujjāraaṇa majjheṃ dīpa ujāla |
cañcala thira kari pawaṇa ṇiwāra |
jo waḍha mūlaha sāra wi jāṇaï/jāgaï
tā kī kālawikāla wi[12a1]lāggaa ||

ṇādaha binduha antareṃ jo,
jāṇaï tia tia bhea | 164cd
so paramesara paramaguru,
uttāraï taïloa || 165

ṇādaha winduha antareṃ jo
jāṇaï tia tia bhea |
so paramesara paramaguru
uttāraui taïloa ||

kṛtir iaṃ Sarahapādāṇāṃ

kṛtir iaṃ Sarahapādāṇāṃ || ||
[12b] (In *dbu med* script:) sa ra ha'i glu

The Standard Tibetan Root Text

Abbreviations in this edition

ø	Missing verse
om.	omittit/omittant
B	Dpal spungs edition of *Indian Mahāmudrā Works* (*Phyag chen rgya gzhung*), vol. *oṃ*, 142b2–151a4
D	Dergé Tengyur, Tōh. no. 2224, *rgyud 'grel*, vol. *wi*, 70b5–77a3
G	Ms Niedersächsische Staats- und Universitätsbibliothek Göttingen Xc 14/16. Praemittit : [1b$_1$] [*siddham*] namaḥ sarvajñāya ||
GT	G and T
D2258	*Dohākoṣapañjikā* by Mokṣākaragupta in the Dergé Tengyur, Tōh. no. 2258, *rgyud 'grel*, vol. *wi*, 265a2–283b1.
DK_{AT}	Tibetan translation of *Dohākoṣa* verses in Advayavajra's *Dohākoṣapañjikā*
P	Peking Tengyur, no. 3068, *rgyud 'grel*, vol. *mi*, 74b6–81b8
T	Ms Tokyo University Library no. 517. *Praemittit*: [16b$_4$] [*siddham*] namo vajraḍākāya ||.

Variant readings have not been recorded in the following cases:

shad against double *shad*

yang against *'ang*

Do ha mdzod kyi glu

[B 142b; D 70b; P 74b] || rgya gar skad du | do ha ko ṣa gī ti |
bod skad du || do ha mdzod kyi glu |

'jam dpal gzhon nur gyur pa la phyag 'tshal lo |

| dug sprul lta bu'i skal med ni |
| nges par skye bo dam pa la |
| skyon gyi dri mas 'go[1] pa'i phyir |
| mthong ba tsam gyis 'jigs par byos | 1 (ø DK_{AT}, ø GT)
[1] DP *dgod*

| de nyid mi shes bram ze ni |
| gyi na rigs byed bzhi[1] dag 'don | 2 (DK_{AT} 1, GT 1)
[1] D *gzhi*

| sa chu ku sha[1] dag byed dang |
| khyim na gnas shing me la bsreg[2] |
| don med sbyin sreg byed pa ni |
| du bas mig la gnod par byed[3] | 3 (DK_{AT} 2, GT 2)
[1] B *sha'i* [2] P *bsrig* [3] BDP *bas*

| dbyu gu dbyug gsum legs ldan gzugs |
| tha dad pa dang ngang[1] pas bstan[2] pa [P 75a] dag[3] |
| chos dang chos min ([4]mi shes par mnyam[4]) zhing |
| 'gro ba rnams ni[5] brdzun[6] pa nyid du gol | 4 (DK_{AT} 3, GT 3)
[1] BD *dad* P *dang* [2] B *bsten* [3] D *dang* [4] DP *shes par mi mnyam* [5] B *la* [6] BP *rdzun*

| ([1]e ra'i[1]) thal bas[2] lus la byugs[3] nas su |
| mgo la ral pa'i [D 71a] khur bu khur bar byed |

| khyim du mar me sbar[4] nas gnas |
| mtshams su 'dug nas dril bu 'khrol | 5 (DK$_{AT}$ 4, GT 4)
[1] P *i ri* [2] B *ba* [3] B *bsgos* [4] D *btang* P *btan*

| skyil krung bcas nas mig [(1]btsums te[1)] |
| rna bar shub shub skye bo slu bar byed |
| khyo med skra med 'di 'dra gzhan la ston |
| dbang rnams bskur zhing bla ma'i yon rnams len | 6 (DK$_{AT}$ 5, GT 5)
[1] P *btsum ste*

| sen mo ring zhing lus la dri mas g.yogs | [B 143a]
| gos dang bral zhing skra ni 'bal bar byed |
| nam mkha'i yid can gnod byed lam gyi gzugs |
| thar pa'i ched du bdag nyid 'gro byed slu[1] | 7 (DK$_{AT}$ 6, GT 6)
[1] B *bslu*

| gcer bu[1] gal te grol 'gyur na |
| khyi dang wa sogs cis mi grol |
| spu btogs pas ni grol 'gyur na |
| bud med spu btogs grol bar 'gyur | 8 (DK$_{AT}$ 7, GT 7)
[1] DP *bus*

| mjug spu [(1]bslangs pas[1)] grol 'gyur na |
| rma bya g.yag sogs grol bar 'gyur |
| langs te za bas grol 'gyur na |
| rta dang glang po ci phyir min | 9 (DK$_{AT}$ 8, GT 8)
[1] DP *bslang bas*

| mda' bsnun na re nam mkha'i yid can la |
| thar pa nam yang yod pa ma yin zer |
| bde pa'i de nyid dang ni bral gyur zhing |
| lus kyi dka' thub 'ba' zhig tsam ldan pas | 10 (DK$_{AT}$ 9, GT 9)

| dge tshul dge slong gnas brtan zhes bya ba'i[1] |
| ban+de rnams ni de ltar rab byung nas |
| kha cig mdo sde 'chad par byed cing 'jug[2] |
| la la ro gcig sems kyi tshul 'dzin mthong | 11 (DK$_{AT}$ 10, GT 10)
[1] D *bas* [2] B *'dug*

| kha cig theg chen de la rgyug byed cing |
| de ni gzhung lugs tshad ma'i bstan bcos yin | (ø $\mathrm{DK}_{\mathrm{AT}}$, ø GT)
| gzhan yang dkyil 'khor 'khor lo ma lus bsgom |
| kha cig bzhi pa'i don 'chad pa la zhugs |
[(1]| kha cig dpyad cing bltas pas lam las nyams |[1)] 12 ($\mathrm{DK}_{\mathrm{AT}}$ 11, GT 11)
[1] BDP om.; supplied from $\mathrm{DK}_{\mathrm{AT}}$

| la la nam mkha'i khams la rtog par snang |
| gzhan yang stong nyid [(1]lta bar[1)] byed pa de |
| phal cher mi mthun phyogs la zhugs pa yin | 13 (ø $\mathrm{DK}_{\mathrm{AT}}$, ø GT)
[1] DP *ldan par*

| lhan cig skyes bral gzhan gang gis |
| mya ngan 'das gang sgom byed pa |
| de dag 'gas [P 75b] kyang don dam ni |
| cig shos 'grub par mi 'gyur ro | 14 ($\mathrm{DK}_{\mathrm{AT}}$ 12, GT 12)

| gang zhig [B 143b] gang la mos par gyur pa des |
| bsam gtan gnas pas thar pa thob bam ci | 15 ($\mathrm{DK}_{\mathrm{AT}}$ 13, G 13, T 15)

| mar me ci dgos lha bshos de ci dgos |
| de la ci bya gsang sngags bsten[1] pa ci zhig dgos |
| 'bab stegs 'gro dang dka' thub mi dgos te |
| chu la zhugs pas thar pa thob [D 71b] bam ci | 16 ($\mathrm{DK}_{\mathrm{AT}}$ 14, G 14, T 16)
[1] BDP *bstan*

| snying rje dang bral stong pa nyid zhugs gang |
| des ni lam mchog rnyed pa ma yin no |
| 'on te snying rje 'ba' zhig bsgoms[1] na yang |
| 'khor ba 'dir gnas thar pa thob mi 'gyur | 17 (ø $\mathrm{DK}_{\mathrm{AT}}$, G 15, ø T)
[1] P *bsgom*

| gang yang gnyis po sbyor par nus pa des[1] |
| 'khor par mi gnas mya ngan 'das mi gnas | 18 (ø $\mathrm{DK}_{\mathrm{AT}}$, G 16, ø T)
[1] B *de*

| kye lags | gang smras [(1]brdzun zhing[1)] log pa de bor la |
| gang la zhen pa yod pa de yang thong |

| rtogs par gyur na thams cad de yin te |
| de las[2] gzhan pa sus kyang shes mi 'gyur | 19 (DK$_{AT}$ 15, GT 17)
[1] B *rdzun pas* [2] D *la*

| klog pa de yin 'dzin dang sgom pa'ang[1] de yin te |
| bstan bcos snying la 'chad pa'ang de yin no |
| de[2] mi mtshon pa'i lta ba yod min te |
| 'on kyang gcig pu[3] bla ma'i zhal la ltos pa yin | 20 (DK$_{AT}$ 16, GT 18)
[1] DP *pa* [2] B *des* [3] DP *bu*

| bla mas[1] smras pa gang gi snying zhugs pa |
| lag pa'i mthil du gnas pa'i gter mthong 'dra |
| gnyug ma'i rang bzhin byis[2] pas ma mthong bar |
| 'khrul pas byis[2] pa[3] bslus[4] zhes[5] mda' bsnun smra | 21 (DK$_{AT}$ 17, GT 19)
[1] D *ma'i* [2] B *bus* [3] D *ba* [4] P *slus* [5] P *shes*

| bsam gtan med cing rab tu 'byung ba med |
| khyim na gnas shing chung ma dag dang lhan cig tu |
| gang zhig yul gyi dga' bas bcings las mi grol na |
| mda' bsnun nga[1] ni de nyid shes pa yin zhes smra | 22 (DK$_{AT}$ 18, GT 20)
[1] D *da*

| gal te mngon du gyur na bsam gtan ci |
| gal te lkog tu gyur na mun pa 'jal | [B 144a]
| lhan cig skyes pa'i rang bzhin de nyid ni |
| dngos dang dngos po med pa ma yin te |
| mda' bsnun 'o dod[1] rtag tu 'bod par byed | 23 (DK$_{AT}$ 19, GT 21)
[1] D *dong*

| gang zhig blangs nas skye shi gnas gyur pa |
| de nyid blangs nas bde chen mchog grub ces |
| skad gsang mthon pos[1] mda' bsnun smra byed kyang |
| byol song 'jig rten [P 76a] mi go ji ltar bya | 24 (DK$_{AT}$ 20, GT 22)
[1] P *bos*

| bsam gtan bral bas ci zhig bsam byar yod |
| brjod du med gang ji ltar bshad du yod |
| srid pa'i phyag rgyas 'gro ba ma lus bslus |
| rang bzhin gnyug ma lus kyang blangs pa med | 25 (DK$_{AT}$ 21, GT 23)

| rgyud med sngags med bsam bya bsam gtan med |
| de kun rang yid 'khrul bar byed pa'i rgyu |
| rang bzhin dag[1] pa'i [(2]sems la[2)] bsam gtan dag gis mi bslad de[3] |
| bdag [(4]gi de nyid bde[4)] la gnas shing gdung bar[5] ma byed cig | 26 (DK$_{AT}$ 22, GT 24)

[1] D *ngag* [2] B *sems nyid la* | [3] D *da* [4] B *nyid de* [5] P *ba*

| za zhing 'thung[1] la gnyis[2] sprod kyis dga' zhing |
| rtag tu yang dang yang du 'khor lo 'gengs |
| chos 'di lta bus 'jig [D 72a] rten pha rol 'grub 'gyur te |
| rmongs pa 'jig rten [(3]mgo bor[3)] rdog pas mnan nas song | 27 (DK$_{AT}$ 23, GT 25)

[1] B *'thungs* [2] D *gnyid* [3] DP *mgon por*

| gang du rlung dang sems ni mi rgyu zhing |
| nyi ma zla ba 'jug pa med gyur pa |
| mi shes pa dag gnas der[1] dbugs phyung cig[2] |
| mda' bsnun[2] gyis ni man ngag thams cad bstan nas song | 28 (DK$_{AT}$ 24, GT 26)

[1] DP *de* [2] D *zhing* [2] P *bsnun*

| gnyis su mi bya gcig tu[1] bya ba ste |
| rigs la bye brag dag tu ma 'byed par |
| khams gsum ma lus 'di dag thams cad ni |
|'dod chags chen po gcig tu kha dog 'gyur[2] | 29 (DK$_{AT}$ 25, GT 27)

[1] BP *tu'ang* [2] DP *sgyur cig dang*

| der ni thog ma dbus mtha' med |
| [(1]srid min[1)] mya ngan 'das pa min |
| bde ba [B 144b] chen po mchog 'di la |
| bdag dang gzhan du yod ma yin | 30 (DK$_{AT}$ 26, GT 28)

[1] DP *ji srid*

| mdun dang rgyab dang phyogs bcu ru |
| gang gang mthong ba de de nyid |
| de ring [1] da ltar 'khrul pa chad |
| da ni su la'ang dri [(2]mi bya[2)] | 31 (DK$_{AT}$ 27, GT 29)

[1] D inserts *nyid du mgon po* P inserts *nyid du mgon pos* [2] DP *bar mi bya'o*

| dbang po[1] gang du nub gyur cing[2] |
| rang gi ngo bo'ang[3] nyams par 'gyur |

| grogs dag de ni lhan cig skyes[4] |
| bla ma’i zhal las gsal par bris | 32 (DK_{AT} 28, GT 30)
1 B om. 2 B *tsa na* 3 D *bor* P *bo* 4 DP *skyed pa’i lus*

| yid ni gar ’ching rlung gar dengs | (DK_{AT} 29ab, GT 31ab)
| sa ([1]steng ’di na[1]) yan lag gnas |
| de ni rmongs pas[2] mtshams su[3] yongs shes bya |
| gti mug rgya ([4]mtsho ’chad pa[4]) gang shes [P 76b] pa |
| ’di ni bde chen mchog yin te | (DK_{AT} 29c, GT 31c)
| sa ra ha yis bstan nas ’gro | 33[4]
1 D2258 *gsum ’di la* 2 B *las* 3 B om. 4 B *chad* 4 DK_{AT} 29d and GT 29d are missing

| kye ho ’di ni rang rig yin pa ste |
| ’di[1] la ’khrul pa ma byed cig |
| dngos dang dngos med bde par gshegs pa’i ’ching pa ste |
| srid dang mnyam nyid tha dad ma ’byed par | (missing in DK_{AT} and G)
| gnyug ma’i yid ni gcig tu gtod[2] dang rnal ’byor pa |
| ([3]chu la[3]) chu bzhag bzhin du shes par byos | 34 (DK_{AT} 30, G 32a, ø T)
1 D *yid* 2 P *sdod* 3 D *tshul*

| bsam gtan brdzun[1] pas thar pa rnyed min no |
| sgyu ’phrul[2] dra bas ji ltar pang[3] du ’khyud |
| bla ma dam pa’i bka’ yi[4] bden[5] par[6] yid ches par[7] |
| nga yis brjod du yod min zhes ni mda’ bsnun smra | 35 (DK_{AT} 31, G 33, ø T)
1 B *rdzun* 2 DP *lus* 3 P *par* 4 BD *yis* 5 BD *bde* 6 DP *bar* 7 B *na*

| gdod nas dag pa nam mkha’i rang bzhin la |
| bltas shing bltas shing mthong pa[1] ’gag[2] par ’gyur |
| de lta bu nyid dus su ’gog par ’gyur |
| gnyug ([3]ma’i yid[3]) la skyon gyis byis[4] pa bslus | 36 (DK_{AT} 32, G 34, ø T)
1 D *ba* 2 P *’gags* 3 DP *ma nyid* 4 B *bus*

| skye[1] bo ma lus lhag par sun ’byin cing |
| nga rgyal skyon [D 72b] gyis de nyid mtshon mi nus |
|’jig rten ma lus bsam gtan gyis rmongs ’gyur |
| gnyug ma’i rang bzhin sus kyang mtshon ([2]du med[2]) | 37 (DK_{AT} 33, G 35, ø T)
1 D *skyo* 2 B *ma yin*

| sems kyi rtsa [B 145a] ba mi[1] mtshon te |
| lhan cig skyes pa rnam gsum gyis[2] |

| gang las[3] de skyes gang du nub |
| gang du gnas 'gyur[4] gsal bar mi shes so | 38 (DK$_{AT}$ 34, G 36, ø T)
[1] B *rang bzhin mi* D *min* [2] DP *gyi* [3] P *la* [4] B *gyur*

| rtsa ba bral pa'i de nyid gang sems pa |
| bla ma'i man ngag ([1]thob pa[1]) de yis chog |
| ([2]'khor ba'i[2]) rang bzhin sems kyi ngo bo nyid yin zhes |
| rmongs rnams mda' bsnun gyis smras tse ne[3] shes par byos | 39 (DK$_{AT}$ 35, G 37, ø T)
[1] D *mthong ba* P *mthon pa* [2] D *khro pa'i* [3] B *ner* N *ni*

| gnyug ma'i rang bzhin tshig gis mi brjod kyang |
| slob dpon man ngag mig gis mthong bar 'gyur |
| chos dang chos min mnyes nas zos pa yis[1] |
| 'di la nyes pa rdul tsam yod ma lags | 40 (DK$_{AT}$ 36, G 38, ø T)
[1] P *yi*

| gnyug ma'i yid ni gang tshe sbyangs gyur pa |
| de[1] tshe bla ma'i yon tan snying la 'jug par 'gyur |
| 'di ltar rtogs nas mda' bsnun glu len te |
| sngags dang rgyud rnams gcig[2] kyang [P 77a] ([3]ma mthong ngo[3]) | 41 (DK$_{AT}$ 37, G 39, ø T)
[1] B *de'i* [2] B *kyis* [3] B *ngas ma mthong*

| 'gro rnams las kyis so sor bcings gyur te |
| las[1] las grol na yid ni thar pa yin |
| rang yid[2] grol na nges par gzhan med de |
| ([3]mchog gi mya ngan 'das pa thob[3]) par 'gyur | 42 (DK$_{AT}$ 38, G 40, ø T)
[1] P *la* [2] DP *rgyud* [3] B *mya ngan 'das pa'i mchog nyid 'thob*

| sems nyid gcig pu kun gyi sa bon te |
| gang las[1] srid dang mya ngan 'das 'phro ba |
| 'dod pa'i 'bras bu ster bar byed pa yi |
| yid bzhin nor 'dra'i sems la phyag 'tshal lo | 43 (DK$_{AT}$ 39, G 41, ø T)
[1] DP *la*

| sems bcings pas ni 'ching[1] 'gyur te |
| de nyid grol na the tshom med |

| blun po gang gis 'ching 'gyur ba |
| mkhas rnams de yis myur du grol | 44 (DK$_{AT}$ 40, G 42, ø T)
[1] BD *'chings*

| sems ni nam mkha' 'dra bar gzung bya ste |
| [(1]nam mkha'i rang bzhin nyid du sems gzung[2] bya[1)] |
| [(3]yid de yid ma yin par byed 'gyur[3)] na |
| des [B 145b] ni bla med byang chub thob par 'gyur | 45 (ø DK$_{AT}$, ø GT)
[1] B *chos rnams kun kyang nam mkha' mnyam par blta* [2] P *bzung* [3] B *sems de bsam mi khyab bsam*

| mkha'[1] 'drar byas na rlung ni rnam par 'ching |
| mnyam nyid yongs su shes pas rab tu thim |
| mda' bsnun gyis smras nam zhig nus ldan na |
| mi rtag g.yo ba myur du spong bar 'gyur | 46 (ø DK$_{AT}$, ø GT)
[1] DP *mkhas*

| rlung dang me dang dbang chen 'gags pa na |
| bdud rtsi rgyu ba'i[1] dus su rlung ni sems la 'jug |
| nam [D 73a] zhig sbyor bzhi gnas gcig la ni zhugs pa na |
| bde chen mchog ni nam mkha'i khams su mi shong ngo | 47 (ø DK$_{AT}$, ø GT)
[1] D *ba'i*

| khyim dang khyim na de yis gtam [(1]smras kyang[1)] |
| bde chen gnas ni yongs su shes pa min[2] |
| 'gro kun bsam pas sun 'byin mda' bsnun smra |
| bsam gyis mi khyab grub pa 'ga' yang med | 48 (ø DK$_{AT}$, ø GT)
[1] DP *smra yang* [2] DP *med*

| srog chags thams cad kun la yang |
| de nyid yod de rtogs[1] pa med |
| thams cad ro mnyam rang bzhin pas |
| bsam pas ye shes bla med pa'o | 49 (ø DK$_{AT}$, ø GT)
[1] P *rtog*

| kha sang de ring de bzhin sang dang gzhan |
| [(1]don rnams phun sum tshogs par skye bo[1)] 'dod |
| kye ho bzhin bzang[2] snyim pa chus bkang pa |
| 'dzag[3] [P 77b] pa bzhin du nyams pa ma tshor ro | 50 (ø DK$_{AT}$, ø GT)
[1] B *skye bu don rnams phun sum tshogs par* [2] DP *bzangs* [3] DP *'dzags*

| bya ba byed dang bya [(1]ba mi[1)] byed pa |
| nges par rtogs na [(2]'ching dang grol ba med[2)] |
| yi ge med las 'chad par [(3]yod 'dod pa[3)] |
| gang zhig rnal 'byor brgya la 'ga' yis mtshon | 51 (ø DK_{AT}, ø GT)
[1] B *bar mi* D *ba min* [2] B *mi 'ching mi gtong ngo* [3] B *yid 'jug par*

| 'jur bus bcings pa'i sems 'di ni |
| glod na grol bar the tshom med |
| [(1]dngos po gang gis[2] rmongs pa[3] 'chings[1)] |
| mkhas rnams de yis rnam par grol | 52 (ø DK_{AT}, ø GT)
[1] B *gang gis rmongs pa 'ching ba'i dngos* [2] D *gi* [3] D *pas*

| bcings pa dag ni phyogs bcur 'gro ba rtsom[1] |
| [(2]btang bar[2)] gyur na mi g.yo brtan par gnas |
| go bzlog[3] rnga mo lta bur bdag gis rtogs |
| bu khyod rnams kyang rang la 'tshol[4] [B 146a] te ltos | 53 (DK_{AT} 41, G 43, ø T)
[1] B *rtsol* [2] D *mthong bar* P *thos sar* [3] B *ldog* [4] DP *cher*

| kye lags dbang pos[1] ltos shig dang |
| 'di las ngas ni ma rtogs[2] so |
| las zin pa yi skyes bu yi |
| drung du sems thag gcad par byos | 54 (ø DK_{AT}, ø GT)
[1] DP *po* [2] D *gtogs*

| rlung bcings pa la rang nyid ma sems kyis[1] |
| shing gi rnal 'byor sna rtser ma 'dug cig |
| e ma'o | ma yengs[2] lhan cig skyes pa mchog chags byos |
| srid pa'i sna rtser 'ching ba [(3]yang dag[3)] spang | 55 (DK_{AT} 42, G 44, T 43)
[1] BP *kyi* D *skye* [2] DP *yin* [3] B *yongs su*

| 'di na[1] [(2]yid dang rlung ni g.yo phyir phyar |
| shin tu mi srun pa yi rta 'dra thong[2)] |
| lhan cig skyes pa'i rang bzhin rtogs gyur na |
| de yi[3] [(4]bdag nyid brten[5] par gyur pa[4)] yin | 56 (DK_{AT} 43, G 45, T 44)
[1] D *ni* [2] DP *yid 'dus pa la rlung gi rlabs | | g.yo zhing 'phyar la shin tu mi srun* (P *bsrun*) *'gyur* [3] D *yis* [4] B *yid ni brtan par 'gyur ba* [5] BP *brtan*

| gang tshe yid ni nye par 'gags gyur na |
| [1] lus kyi 'ching ba rnam par 'chad [D 73b] [(2]par 'gyur[2)] |

| gang la[3] lhan cig skyes dang[4] ro mnyam pa |
| de la[3] [(5]dman pa'i[5)] rigs dang[6] bram ze med | 57 (DK$_{AT}$ 44, G 46, T 45)
[1] B inserts *de tshe* [2] B om. [3] DP *tshe* [4] B *pa* [5] B *rmongs* [6] B inserts *ni*

| 'di ni zla ba[1] rgya mtsho nyid dang ni |
| 'di na[2] gaṅgā'i rgya mtsho nyid[3] dang ni[3] |
| wā[4] rā[5] ṇa[6] sī[7] pra yā[8] ga[9] [(10]yin te[10)] |
| 'di ni zla ba gsal byed nyid | 58 (DK$_{AT}$ 45, G 47, T 46)
[1] B *ba'i* [2] B *la yang na* D *ni* [3] B om. [4] D *bā* P *ba* [5] BP *ra* [6] B *ṇā* [7] P *se* [8] BP *ya* [9] DP *gha* [10] BDP *ya ti*

| zhing kun gnas dang nye ba'i gnas sogs su[1] |
| phyin te bltas[2] pa'i rtogs pa[3] gang smra ba |
| lus dang [(4]dran pa'i mu na gnas pa'i mtsho[4)] |
| dge ba nga yis[5] [(6]nges par yang dag[6)] mthong | 59 (DK$_{AT}$ 46, G 48, T 47)
[1] DP *pa* [2] P *ltes* [3] P *par* [4] DP *dra ba'i mu gnas gzhan na med* [5] P *yi* [6] B *gang dag nges par*

B has two extra lines:
| nga yis rmi lam du yang mthong ba med |
| ri bo'i khrod du gnas te bag yod byos | 59.1 (ø DK$_{AT}$, ø G, ø T)

| 'dab ldan padma'i sdong po ge sar gyi dbus na |
| shin tu phra ba'i snal[1] ma dri dang kha dog ldan |
| bye brag [(2]bor cig[2)] rmongs pa mya ngan gyi[3] |
| [(4]gdungs [P 78a] pas[4)] 'bras bu med par ma byed cig | 60 (DK$_{AT}$ 47, G 49, T 48)
[1] DP *rnal* [2] DP *'ongs shing* [3] BD *gyis* [4] B *gdung bas* D *gdungs pa'i*

BD: | gang tshe[1] tshangs pa khyab 'jug mig gsum dang |
| 'jig rten ma lus thams cad gzhir gyur pa |
| rigs med de la [B 146b] mchod na las kyi yang |
| mtha' yi tshogs ni yang dag zad par 'gyur | 61 (DK$_{AT}$ 48, G 50, T 49)
[1] B *du*

P: | gang tshe tshangs pa khyab 'jug mig gsum 'jig rten ma lus gzhir gyur pa |
| mig med de la mchod na las kyi mtha' yi tshogs ni yang dag zad par 'gyur | 61

| kye ho bu nyon rtsod pa'i ro ni dag par yang dag gnas shes pa |
| 'gro ba 'chad cing 'don la sogs pas[1] de ni shes par nus[2] ma yin[3] | 62 (DK$_{AT}$ 49, G 51, T 50)

[1] B *pas* [2] B *nus pa* [3] B *yin no*

| kye ho bu nyon de nyid sna tshogs kyi[1] |
| ro 'di bstan par nus[2] pa ma yin te |
| bde ba'i gnas mchog rtog [3] spangs te[4] |
| 'gro ba nye par skye pa nyid bzhin no | 63 (DK$_{AT}$ 50, G 52, T 51)
[1] BDP *kyis* [2] B *'thod* [3] BP insert *pa* [4] BP *nas ni*

| blo ni rnam 'gags yid ni [(1]rab zhi ba[1)] |
| gang du mngon pa'i nga rgyal chad pa'o |
| de nyid sgyu ma'i rang bzhin mchog tu rtogs[2] pa ste |
| de la bsam gtan 'ching ba des ni ci byar yod | 64 (DK$_{AT}$ 51, G 53, T 52)
[1] DP *pham gyur pa* [2] D *rtog*

| dngos por [(1]skyes pa[1)] mkha'[2] ltar [(3]rab zhi na[3)] |
| dngos po rnam spangs phyi nas ci zhig skye |
| gdod nas skye med rang bzhin yin pa la |
| de ring dpal ldan bla ma [(4]bstan pas rtogs[4)] | 65 (DK$_{AT}$ 52, G 54, T 53)
[1] P *skye ba* [2] D *mkha'i* [3] DP *rang bzhin na* [4] B *mgon pos bstan pa yi | | dbye ba rnam spangs de la gnas par byos*

| mthong dang thos dang [(1]reg dang dran[1)] pa dang |
| [(2]za snom 'khyam[2)] dang 'gro dang 'dug pa dang |
| cal col gtam dang lan smra gyur pa la |
| sems so zhe na gcig gi rnam pa la mi bskyod[3] | 66 (DK$_{AT}$ 53, G 55, T 54)
[1] B *dran dang reg* D *rig dang dran* [2] B *zas skom 'chams* [3] B *spyod*

| gang zhig bla ma'i man ngag bdud rtsi'i chu |
| gdung sel bsil[1] ba ngoms par mi 'thung pa[2] |
| de ni bstan bcos don mang mya ngam gyi |
| thang la skom pas gdungs te 'chi bar zad | 67 (DK$_{AT}$ 54, G 56, T 55)
[1] D *bsal* [2] DP *par*

| bla mas bstan pa brjod min na |
| slob mas go ba ma yin te |
| lhan cig [D 74a] skyes pa bdud rtsi'i ro |
| gang gis ji ltar bsten[1] par bya | 68 (ø DK$_{AT}$, ø G, ø T)
[1] P *bstan*

| [1] tshad mar 'dzin pa'i dbang gis su |
| blun pos bye brag rnyed pa ste |
| de tshe rdol[2] pa'i khyim du rol |
| 'on kyang dri mas mi [B 147a] gos so | 69 (ø DK_{AT}, ø G, ø T)
[1] B inserts *gal te* P inserts *gang gis* [2] BP *gdol*

| gang tshe slong na srang kha'i kham phor gyis spyod de |
| bdag ni rgyal po yin na slar yang ci byar yod |
| dbye ba rnam par spangs nas de nyid gnas pa la |
| rang bzhin [P 78b] mi g.yo btang snyoms lhun gyis grub |
| mya ngan 'das pa la gnas srid par mdzes | 70 (ø DK_{AT}, ø G, ø T)

| nad gzhan dag la sman gzhan gtang mi bya |
| bsam dang bsam bya rab tu spangs nas su |
| ji ltar bu chung tshul du gnas [(1]par bya[1)] |
| bla ma'i lung la bsgrims te rab[2] 'bad na |
| lhan cig skyes pa 'byung bar the tshom med | 71 (DK_{AT} 55, G 57, T 56)
[1] B *bya zhing* [2] B *gus*

| kha dog [(1]yi ge yon tan[1)] dpe bral ba |
| smra ru mi btub[2] de ni bdag gis[3] gyin[4] mtshon |
| gzhon[5] nu ma yi bde ba snying la[6] zhen pa bzhin |
| dbang phyug dam pa de ni su la bstan nus sam | 72 (DK_{AT} 56, G 58, T 57)
[1] DP *yon tan yi ge* [2] D *btung* [3] P *gi* [4] BP *gyi na* [5] P *gzhin* [6] B *la'ang*

| dngos dang dngos med yongs su bcad pa gang[1] |
| der ni 'gro ba ma lus rab tu thim par 'gyur |
| gang tshe yid ni mi g.yo rang[2] gnas brtan pa ste[3] |
| de tshe 'khor pa'i dngos po las ni rang grol 'gyur | 73 (DK_{AT} 57, G 60, T 58)
[1] DP *dang* [2] B *rab* [3] B *bya* P *de*

| gang tshe bdag gzhan yongs su shes med na[1] |
| de tshe bla med lus [(2]su grub pa nyid[2)] |
| de ltar [3] bstan[4] pa nyid la[5] nges par ma 'khrul par |
| rang gis rang la legs par [(6]shes par byas nas ni[6)] | 74 (DK_{AT} 58, G 61, T 59)
[1] D *ni* [2] DP *ni thob par 'gyur* [3] B *nga yis* [4] P *brtan* [5] DP *las* [6] B *bstan te shes par byos*

| rdul min rdul bral ma yin sems kyang min |
| dngos po de dag gdod nas zhen pa med |

| mda' bsnun gyis[1] smras de tsam zhig tu zad |
| kye ho ma lus dri med don dam shes par byos | 75 (DK$_{AT}$ 59, G 62, T 60)
[1] D *gyi*

| khyim na gnas[1] pa phyi rol song nas 'tshol[2] |
| khyim bdag mthong nas khyim mtshes[3] dag la 'dri[4] |
| mda' bsnun gyis smras bdag nyid shes par byos |
| blun pos [B 147b] bsam gtan bsam bya bzlas brjod min | 76 (DK$_{AT}$ 60, G 63, T 61)
[1] B *yod* [2] DP *tshol* [3] DP *tshes* [4] D *dri*

| [(1]gang tshe[1)] bla mas bstan cing [2] thams cad shes byas kyang |
| bdag gis yongs su brtags pas [3] thar pa [(4]thob bam[4)] ci |
| yul rnams bgrod cing gdung bas nyen byas kyang |
| lhan cig skyes pa mi rnyed sdig pas 'dzin | 77 (DK$_{AT}$ 61, G 64, T 62)
[1] B *gal te* [2] B inserts *bden par* [3] B inserts *ma rtogs* [4] B *rnyed dam*

| yul rnams bsten pas yul gyis mi gos so |
| utpal [(1]'dab ma[1)] chu yis ma reg bzhin |
| gang [(2]yang 'di ltar rtsa ba [2)] [D 74b] skyabs su 'gro[3] |
| dug gi sngags can dug gis ga la tshugs | 78 (DK$_{AT}$ 62, G 65, T 63)
[1] B *blangs kyang* [2] DP *ltar rtsa ba rnal 'byor* [3] B *song*

| lha la mchod pa [P 79a] khri phrag byin byas[1] kyang |
| bdag nyid [(2]'ching 'gyur de yis[2)] ci zhig bya |
| de 'dras 'khor ba 'di ni 'chad min te |
| [(3]gnyug ma'i rang bzhin ma rtogs rgal mi nus[3)] | 79 (DK$_{AT}$ 63, G 66, T 64[4])
[1] DP *nas* [2] DP *de yis* (P *yi*) *'ching 'gyur* [3] B *'dir goms ma gtogs ma lus brgal ma yin* [4] This is the last verse in T.

| mig ni mi 'dzums sems ni[1] [(2]'gog pa dang[2)] |
| rlung 'gog pa[3] ni dpal ldan bla mas rtogs |
| gang tshe rlung rgyu[4] de ni mi g.yo ste |
| 'ching ba'i tshe na rnal 'byor pas ci bya | 80 (DK$_{AT}$ 64, G 67)
[1] D *kyang* P om. [2] B *'gags pa na* D *mi 'gog dang* P *'gog dang* [3] B *par* [4] D *rgyud*

| ji srid dbang po yul gyi grong la lhung[1] |
| de srid rang nyid las med[2] rab tu rgyas |
| khyed cag da lta[3] ci byed [(4]gar 'gro[4)] soms[5] dang kye |
| de ni shin tu dka' ba'i dgongs pa[6] 'jug |

| gang zhig gang la gnas pa ni |
| de ni de ru mi mthong ste | 81 (DK$_{AT}$ 65, G 68)
[1] B *lhung ba na* [2] B *ngan* [3] D *ltar* [4] DP om. [5] D *sam* [6] B *pas*

| mkhas pa thams cad bstan bcos 'chad pa yis |
| lus la sangs rgyas yod par ma rtogs[1] so |
| glang chen lobs[2] nas sems tshags tshud[3] ([4]pa ltar[4]) |
| der[5] ni 'gro 'ong chad[6] nas ngal[7] ba ste |
| 'di ltar rtogs na gang du 'ang dri sa med |
| ([8]mkhas pa[8]) ngo tsha med ([9]smra mkhas pa nga[9]) | 82 (DK$_{AT}$ 66, G 69)
[1] P *gtogs* [2] P *lam* [3] DP *chud* [4] DP *pas na* [5] B *de* [6] B *bcad* [7] B *dal* [8] DP *de ltar* [9] B *pas de ma rtogs*

| gson pa gang zhig rnam par ma gyur pa |
| de ni rgas shing 'chi bar 'gyur ram ci |
| bla mas bstan pa'i[1] dri med blo gros ni |
| de nyid gter yin gzhan pa gang zhig lo[2] | 83 (DK$_{AT}$ 67, G 70)
[1] D *pa* [2] D *po*

| yul nyid rnam [B 148a] par dag ste bsten[1] bya min |
| stong pa 'ba' zhig gis ni spyad par bya |
| ji ltar gzings las 'phur pa'i bya rog bzhin[2] |
| bskor[3] zhing bskor[3] zhing slar yang de ru 'bab[4] | 84 (DK$_{AT}$ 68, G 71)
[1] D *bstan* [2] B *ni* [3] DP *skor* [4] B *babs*

| thag pa nag po'i dug sbrul bzhin |
| mthong ba tsam gyis sdang[1] par 'gyur |
| grogs dag skye bo dam pa ni |
| yul gnyis skyon gyis bcing[2] par 'gyur | 85 (ø DK$_{AT}$, ø G)
[1] B *bsdang* P *sdangs* [2] P *bcings*

| yul la zhen pas 'ching bar ma byed cig |
| kye ho rmongs pa mda' bsnun gyis smras pa |
| nya dang phye leb glang chen bung ba dang |
| 'di ni ri dwags[1] bzhin du blta[2] bar bya[3] | 86 (DK$_{AT}$ 69, G 72)
[1] DP *dags* [2] DP *bya* [3] DP *byos*

| gang zhig sems las rnam 'phros pa[1] |
| de srid[2] mgon po'i rang bzhin te |

| chu dang rlabs dag gzhan yin nam |
| srid dang mnyam nyid[3] nam mkha'i rang bzhin no | 87 (DK_{AT} 70, G 73)
[1] P *pas* [2] B *bzhin* [3] DP *zhing*

| [P 79b] gang zhig bstan[1] te gang thos pa |
| dgongs pa gang [D 75a] yin dam par skyol ba na |
| [(2]gdug pa'i lkungs sa[2)] [(3]sa yi[3)] rdul bzhin brlag |
| snying ga nyid du nub par [(4]gyur pa[4)] yin | 88 (DK_{AT} 71, G 74)
[1] P *bsten* [2] DP *nyi zer lkugs pa* (P *sa*) [3] P om. [4] B *'gyur ba*

| ji ltar chu la chu bzhag na |
| de snyed[1] chu ru ro[2] mnyam 'gyur |
| skyon dang yon tan mnyam ldan sems |
| mgon po sus kyang [(3]mtshon ma[3)] 'gyur |
| rmongs pa dag la gnyen po gang yang med| 89 (DK_{AT} 72, G 75)
[1] D *rnyed* [2] D *ru* [3] DP *mthong mi*

| nags la mched pa'i [(1]me lce[1)] bzhin |
| gdong du [(2]babs pa[2)] 'di ltar snang ba kun |
| sems[3] kyi rtsa ba stong pa nyid du lhan cig byos | 90 (ø DK_{AT}, ø G)
[1] B *me 'bar* D *lce* [2] DP *bab ba'i* [3] P *khyod*

| gal te yid du 'ong ngam snyam[1] pa'i sems |
| snying la bab pa gces par [(2]byas na ni[2)] |
| til gyi shun pa tsam gyi zug rngus kyang |
| [(3]nam yang[3)] sdug bsngal 'ba' zhig byed par zad |[4] 91 (DK_{AT} 73cd, G 76cd)
[1] B *mnyam* [2] B *bya ba yis* [3] DP *nams kyang* [4] B inserts | *grogs po phag dang glang por ltos* |

| de ltar yin te[1] [B 148b] de ltar[2] ma yin no |
[(2]| grogs po phag dang glang chen ltos |[2)]
| ji ltar yid bzhin nor bu'i dgos pa bzhin |
| 'khrul pa zhig pa'i mkhas pa ngo mtshar che |
| rang la rang rig bde ba chen po'i bag chags gzugs | 92 (DK_{AT} 74, G 77)
[1] B *no* [2] B om.

| thams cad de tshe mkha' mnyam byed par 'gyur |
| ka la ku ṭa smos su mi[1] rung ste |
| rang bzhin mkha' mnyam yid kyis 'dzin pa yin |

| yid de yid ma yin par byed 'gyur na |
| rang bzhin lhan cig skyes pa mchog tu mdzes | 93 (DK_{AT} 75, G 78)
[1] DP *ci*

Repetition of verse 48:

| khyim dang khyim na de ni brjod pa[1] te |
| bde chen gnas ni yongs su shes pa min |
| 'gro kun sems khral [(2]khur par[2)] mda' bsnun smra[3] |
| de ni bsam med sus kyang rtogs [(4]ma yin[4)] | 94 (DK_{AT} 76, G 79)
[1] DP *min* [2] B *khyer ba* D *khur ba* [3] DP *'dra* [4] B *pa min*

| bde gsang yan lag yongs su spangs pa na |
| bsgom dang mi sgom dbyer med bdag gis mthong |
| yul gyis mtshon pas gzhan dag bsam par byed |
| de nyid bsam pas ma rtogs[1] rang gzhan[2] 'gags par 'gyur | 95 (ø DK_{AT}, ø G)
[1] P *gtogs* [2] P *bzhin*

B: | kye ma rnal 'byor bsgom pa 'dris |
| mgo snying lte gsang rkang lag spangs de ngas mthong ba'o |
| bsam pas yul ni mtshon par byed |
| gzhan dag bsams pas rlung 'gag 'gyur | 95 (ø DK_{AT}, ø G)

| gal te sems kyis sems ni mtshon du 'gro |
| [(1]rlung dang yid[1)] ni mi g.yo brtan par gnas |
| ji ltar lan tshwa chu la thim pa ltar |
| de [P 80a] ltar sems ni rang bzhin la thim 'gyur |
| de tshe bdag dang gzhan ni mnyam par mthong |
|'bad de bsam gtan byas pas ci byar[2] yod | 96 (ø DK_{AT}, ø G)
[1] DP *rnam rtog dang* [2] P *byas*

| lha[1] cig la ni lung rnams [(2]mang por[2)] mthong |
| rang[3] gi 'dod pa[4] mang po [5] gsal bar snang | 97 (DK_{AT} 77, G 80)
[1] DP *lhan* [2] DP *ma lus* [3] P illegible [4] P *pa'i* [5] B inserts *so sor*

| mgon po bdag nyid gcig pu gzhan rnams 'gal |
| [D 75b] khyim dang khyim na[1] grub mtha' de grub bo |
| gcig zos pas ni [(2]gzhan kun[2)] 'tshim[3] |
| phyi rol song nas khyim bdag 'tshol[4] | 98 (DK_{AT} 78, G 81)
[1] D om. [2] DP *thams cad* [3] D *tshig* P *'tshig* [4] D *chol* P *tshol*

| 'ongs[1] kyang ma mthong phyin kyang med |
| 'dug par gyur kyang ngo ma shes |
| rba[2] rlabs med [B 149a] pa'i dbang phyug mchog |
| rnyog pa med pa'i bsam gtan 'gyur |
| chu dwangs[3] mar me rang gsal gcig tu zhog | 99 (DK_{AT} 79, G 82)
[1] B *'ong* [2] D *dba'* P *dpal* [3] DP *dang*

| 'gro 'ong nga yis mi len mi 'dor ro |
| gang yang snga na med pa'i sgeg mo dang phrad nas | 100 (DK_{AT} 80, G 83)

| nyal ba'i sems ni gzhi med pa la brten |
| rang gi gzugs[1] dang tha dad ma blta[2] cig |
| de ltar sangs rgyas lag tu gtod pa yin | (ø DK_{AT}, ø G)
| gang tshe lus dang ngag yid dbyer med pa |
| lhan cig skyes pa'i rang bzhin de tshe mdzes | 101 (DK_{AT} 81, G 84)
[1] B *sems* [2] D *lta*

| khyim bdag [(1]zos nas[1)] khyim bdag mo longs spyod |
| yul ni gang [(2]mthong ba de[2)] spyad par bya | (DK_{AT} 82ab, G 84ab)
| nga yis[3] rtsed mo byas pa la | (ø DK_{AT}, ø G)
| bus[4] pa rnams ni a[5] thang chad | (ø DK_{AT}, ø G)
| a ma bzhag nas bu de skye mi 'gyur | [6] (differs from DK_{AT} 82c, G 84c)
| [7] rnal 'byor spyod pa dpe dang bral [(8]ba ste[8)] | 102 (DK_{AT} 82, G 86)
[1] B *dang ni* [2] DP *zag mthong ste* [3] P *yi* [4] B *byis* [5] B *sha* [6] B inserts | *me ni sbra ba nyid la rkyen gyis 'bar* | | *kye ho gzhan na yod ma yin* | | *'on te gzhan la gnas sam ci* | [7] DP insert *des ni* [8] DP om.

| bdag po za zhing rang bzhin mdzes |
| chags pa'i [(1]yul gyis[1)] gang ba'i sems de nyid |
| chags dang chags bral byas[2] nas gnyug[3] mar zhugs |
| sems nyams pas na rnal 'byor [(4]ma ngas[4)] mthong | 103 (DK_{AT} 83, G 87)
[1] DP *spyod des* [2] DP *spangs* [3] DP *dbu* [4] DP *ngas ma*

| za zhing 'thung[1] la bsam [(2]du med par gyur[2)] |
| grogs mo[3] 'di ni[4] sems la gang snang ba |
| phyi rol [(5]sems la mtshon med bdag[5)] gis 'dzin |
| sgyu ma'i rnal 'byor ma[6] ni dpe dang bral [(7]pa ste[7)] | 104 (DK_{AT} 84, G 88)
[1] B *'thungs* [2] B *pa'ang med* P *du med* [3] B *dag* [4] B *na* [5] B *par sems sdug bsngal dag* [6] DP *pa* [7] B om.

| sa gsum du yang [(1]dri med mi gnas mi ’byung ste[1)] |
[(2]| me ni spra[3] ba nyid la rkyen gyis ’bar |[2)]
| zla ba chu [P 80b] ’dzag nor bu rang dbang med[4] |
| thabs kyis rgyal srid kun la dbang bsgyur ba |
| sems nyid de nyid grub pa’i rnal ’byor ma[5] | (DK$_{AT}$ 85c, G 89c)
| lhan chig skyes pa’i [B 149b] sdom par shes par bya | 105 (DK$_{AT}$ 85d, G 89d)
[1] B *dri ma med* [2] B om. [3] P *pra* [4] B *min* [5] DP *ma’o*

| yi ge [1] ’gro pa ma lus pa |
| yi ge med pa gcig kyang med |
| ji srid yi ge med gyur pa |
| de srid yi ge rab tu shes | 106 (DK$_{AT}$ 86, G 90)
[1] B inserts *pa yi* [2] P *ba’i*

| snag tsha mnyes pas klag tu med |
| [(1]rig byed don med[1)] ’don pas nyams |
| dam pa[2] soms[3] dang cig shos mi shes na |
| gang nas shar cing gang du nub | 107 (ø DK$_{AT}$, ø G)
[1] B *rtsol med rig byed* D *rag byed don med* [2] B *pas* [3] DP *sems*

| ji ltar phyi rol de bzhin nang |
| bcu bzhi pa yi [D 76a] sa la[1] rgyun du gnas |
| lus med lus la sbas pa ste[2] |
| [(3]gang gis de shes de grol[3)] ’gyur | 108 (DK$_{AT}$ 87, G 91)
[1] P *las* [2] P *med* [3] DP *de shes de yis* (P *yi*) *grol bar* B *gang gis de shes de grol*

| [(1]nga yis grub pa’i yi ge dang po bton[1)] |
| khu ba ’thungs pas nga[2] ni brjed par gyur[3] |
| gang gis yi ge gcig shes pa |
| de yi[4] ming ni mi shes so | 109 (DK$_{AT}$ 88, G 92)
[1] D *sgrub yig bzhi las* (P *la*) *dang po bdag gis ston* [2] B *ngas* [3] B *’gyur* [4] BDP *yis*

| [(1]nags khrod[1)] gsum ni[2] yi ge gcig |
| [(3]yi ge[3)] gsum gyi dbus na lha |
| gang zhig gsum [(4]las ’babs[4)] pa ni |
| gdol pa rig byed [(5]de bzhin no[5)] | 110 (ø DK$_{AT}$, ø G)
[1] DP *rkyen bral* [2] B *na* [3] DP *zag med* [4] DP *po zag* [5] B *bzhi yang ngo*

| ma lus rang bzhin mi shes gang[1] |
| kunduru yi skabs su bde chen bsgrub[2] ba ni |

| ji ltar skom[2] pas smig [(3]rgyu'i chu snyegs[3)] bzhin |
| skom nas 'chi ste[4] nam mkha'i chu rnyed dam | 111 (DK$_{AT}$ 89, G 93)
[1] DP *pas* [2] D *sgrub* D *sgom* [3] B *rgyu snyegs pa* [4] DP *yang*

| rdo rje padma gnyis kyi bar gnas pa |
| bde ba gang gis[1] rnam par bskyed[2] pa ni[3] |
| ci ste de bstan[4] nus pa med pas na |
| sa gsum [(5]re ba gang gis rdzogs par 'gyur[5)] | 112 (DK$_{AT}$ 92, G 94)
[1] B *gi* [2] DP *rol* [3] D *yin* [4] DP *bden* [5] B *gang du rdzogs su re ba lags*

| yang na thabs kyi bde ba skad cig ma |
| yang na de nyid gnyis su 'gyur ba ste |
| bla ma'i drin gyis slar yang ni |
| brgya la[1] 'ga' yis[2] shes par 'gyur | 113 (DK$_{AT}$ 93, G 95)
[1] B *las* [2] P *yi*

[1] | grogs dag zab mo[2] dang ni rgya che ba |
| gzhan min[3] bdag nyid ma yin no[4] |
| lhan cig skyes dga' bzhi pa'i [B 150a] dus |
| gnyug ma nyams su myong bas[5] shes | 114 (DK$_{AT}$ 94, G 96)
[1] B inserts | *kye* [2] DP *pa* [3] DP *med* [4] B *te* [5] DP *bar*

| mun nag chen por zla ba'i[1] nor bu ni[2] |
| ji ltar 'char bar byed pa bzhin |
| mchog tu bde chen skad [(3]cig gcig la ni[3)] |
| [4] sdig pa ma lus pham[5] par[6] byed pa'o | 115 (DK$_{AT}$ 95, G 97)
[1] D *ba* [2] P *bzhin* [3] B *cig la* [4] DP insert *bsam* [P 81a] *pa'i* [5] DP *phan* [6] B om.

| sdug bsngal snang byed nub pa na |
| skar ma'i bdag po gza' dang mnyam du shar |
| 'di ltar gnas pas sprul [(1]pa sprul[1)] |
| de ni dkyil 'khor 'khor lo dam pa'o | 116 (DK$_{AT}$ 96, G 98)
[1] B *pa sprul pa dang* D *par sprul*

| kye ho rmongs pa[1] sems kyis sems la rtogs[2] na ni |
| lta ba ngan pa thams cad las ni [(3]grol 'gyur te[3)] |
| mchog tu bde ba chen po'i[4] dbang gis ni[5] |
| de[5] la gnas na dngos grub dam pa'o | 117 (DK$_{AT}$ 97, G 99)
[1] DP *pa'i* [2] DP *brtags* [3] DP *rang grol 'gyur* [4] B *po de yi* [5] P *na*

| sems kyi glang po yan du chug |
| de ni bdag nyid ([1]la dris shig[1]) |
| nam mkha'i ri bo chu 'thung[2] dang |
| de yi 'gram du zhog cig rang dga' bar | 118 (DK_{AT} 98, G 100)
[1] DP *dris la gcig* [2] B *'thungs*

| yul gyi glang ([1]po'i dbang po'i[1]) lag pas blangs nas su |
| ji ltar gsod par rang dbang [D 76b] snang bar 'gyur |
| rnal 'byor ba ni glang po skyong ba bzhin |
| de nyid nas ni ldog par 'gyur pa yin[2] | 119 (DK_{AT} 99, G 101)
[1] B *po dbang po'i* DP *po'i dbang po* [2] P *bzhi*

| gang zhig 'khor ba de ni mya ngan 'das par nges |
| ([1]yul gyi[1]) dbye ba[2] gzhan du sems ([3]par ma byed cig[3]) |
| rang bzhin gcig gis[4] dbye ba rnam par spangs[5] |
| dri ma med pa nga yis[6] rab tu rtogs | 120 (DK_{AT} 100, G 102)
[1] DP om. [2] B *bas* [3] DP *pa* (P *dpa'*) *ma yin te* [4] BP *gi* [5] B *spang* [6] B *yi*

| yid kyi[1] de nyid dmigs dang bcas |
| dmigs med[2] stong pa nyid yin la[3] |
| gnyis la skyon ni yod pa ste |
| rnal 'byor gang gis sgom pa min | 121 (ø DK_{AT}, ø G)
[1] BD *kyis* [2] DP *pa* [3] B *no*

| sgom pa[1] dmigs bcas dmigs med de |
| sgom dang mi sgom tha snyad med |
| bde ba'i rnam pa'i [B 150b] rang bzhin no |
| rab tu bla med rang 'byung ba |
| bla ma'i dus thabs bsten pas shes | 122 (ø DK_{AT}, ø G)
[1] B *bya*

| nags su ma 'gro khyim du ma 'dug par |
| gang yang de ru yid kyis yongs shes nas[1] |
| ma lus rgyun du byang chub rtogs[2] pas[3] gnas |
| 'khor ba gang yin mya ngan 'das pa gang | 123 (DK_{AT} 101, G 103)
[1] B *na* [2] BDP *rtag* [3] DP *par*

| yid kyi[1] dri ([2]ma dag na[2]) lhan cig skyes ([3]pa ste[3]) |
| de tshe ([4]mi mthun phyogs[4]) kyi[5] 'jug pa med |

| [(6]ji ltar rgya mtsho dang bar gyur pa la |
| chu bur chu nyid yin te de nyid thim par 'gyur[6)] | 124 (ø DK$_{AT}$, ø G)
[1] B *ni* [2] B *med* D *ma dag la* [3] B *pa'i gnas skabs so* P [4] B *'gro ba'i rigs la* [5] D *kyis* [6] B *de tsam zhig la nges par gnas pa ni* | | *de ni rgyal ba yin te bye brag med*

| [(1]nags dang khyim na byang chub gnas pa med[1)] |
| [P 81b] de[2] ltar [(3]dbye ba[3)] yongs su shes [(4]nas su[4)] |
| dri ma med pa'i sems kyi rang bzhin gyis |
| ma lus mi rtog pa ru brten par 'os[5] | 125 (DK$_{AT}$ 102, G 104)
[1] B *rtogs pa nags dang khyim na gnas pa min* [2] B *'di* [3] D *byed pa* [4] B *na* [5] B *byos*

| de ni[1] bdag yin gzhan yang de [(2]yin no[2)] |
| gang bsgom[4] yongs su bsgom pa gang |
| dbye ba de nyid 'ching dang bral bar bya[3] |
| 'on kyang bdag nyid rnam par grol pa'o |[5] 126 (DK$_{AT}$ 103, G 105)
[1] B *nyid* [2] B *nyid yin* D *bzhin no* [3] B *byas* [4] P *bsgoms* [5] B has the extra line | *ji ltar rgya mtsho mthong phyes bzhin* |

| bdag dang gzhan du 'khrul pa ma byed dang[1] |
| [(2]thams cad snga nas[2)] gnas pa'i sangs rgyas te |
| [(3]sems ni ngo bo nyid kyis dag pa na[3)] |
| de nyid dri med mchog gi go 'phang ngo | 127 (DK$_{AT}$ 104, G 106)
[1] B *cig* [2] DP *ma lus rgyun du* [3] B om.

| gnyis med sems[1] kyi sdong po dam pa ni |
| khams[2] gsum ma lus kun tu khyab par song[3] |
| snying rje'i me tog gzhan phan[4] 'bras bu 'dzin |
| [(5]ming ni mchog tu[5)] gzhan[6] la phan pa'o | 128 (DK$_{AT}$ 105, G 107)
[1] P om. [2] B *sa* [3] B *son* [4] B *don* [5] B *de la ming ni* [6] P *gnas*

| stong pa'i sdong po dam pa me tog rgyas |
| snying rje rnam[1] pa sna tshogs du mar ldan |
| lhun gyis grub pa phyi ma'i 'bras bu ste |
| bde ba 'di ni gzhan pa'i sems min no | 129 (DK$_{AT}$ 106, G 108)
[1] DP *dam*

| stong pa'i sdong po dam pa'i snying rje min |
| gang la slar yang rtsa ba me tog [D 77a] lo 'dab med |

| de la dmigs par [B 151a] byed pa gang yin pa |
| der lhung bas ni yan lag med[1] par 'gyur | 130 (DK$_{AT}$ 107, G 109)
[1] B *'chag*

| sa bon gcig las[1] sdong po gnyis |
| rgyu mtshan de las 'bras bu gcig |
| de yang dbyer med gang sems pa |
| de ni 'khor [(2]dang mya ngan 'das rnams grol[2)] | 131 (DK$_{AT}$ 108, G 110)
[1] BDP *la* [2] B *ba'i 'bras bu gang yin lo*

| gang zhig 'dod pa can gyi skye bo [(1]'ongs pa'i[1)] tshe |
| de ni [(2]re ba med na gal te 'gro ba ni[2)] |
| [(3]phyi sgor bor ba'i kham phor blangs nas su |
| de bas khyim thab bor nas bsdad pa rung[3)] | 132 (DK$_{AT}$ 109, G 111)
[1] B *'ong ba'i* [2] B *gal te 'gro na re ba med* [3] B *kham phor dum bu slong ba'i mi | | phyi sgor bor ba blangs nas su*

| gzhan [(1]la phan pa'i[1)] don ni mi byed pa[2] |
| 'dod pa po la [(3]sbyin pa[3)] mi ster ba |
| 'di ni 'khor ba'i 'bras bu gang yin lo |
| de bas bdag[4] nyid bor bar byas na rung | 133 (DK$_{AT}$ 110, G 112)
[1] B *gyi* [2] B *la* [3] B om. [4] B *rang*

| rnal 'byor gyi dbang phyug chen po dpal sa ra ha [(1]chen po[1)]'i zhal snga nas [2] mdzad pa'i[3] do ha mdzod ces bya ba de kho na nyid rnal du mtshon pa don dam pa'i yi ge rdzogs so ||
[1] B om. [2] B inserts *kyis* [3] DP *pa*

Only in B: || rgya gar gyi mkhan po ba dzra pā ṇi'i zhal snga nas dang | lo tsā ba rma ban chos 'bar gyis bsgyur ba'o | slad kyi 'brog mi jo sras dang dge slong tshul khrims rgyal bas zhu dag byas te gtan la phab pa'o ||

Part 3. Mokṣākaragupta's Commentary

Edition of the Tibetan

In his commentary, Mokṣākaragupta does not quote the root verses in full but only the first syllable(s) followed by a *la sogs pa* ("and so forth"). Occasionally, he also gives a range of the root text in the form of "from that syllable(s) to these syllables(s)." Still, it was possible to identify, with the exception of verses 62 and 85, the 133 verses of the standard Tibetan root text (DK_T). A translation of DK_T has been inserted in the respective parts of the commentary. In most cases the readings of the root texts match the ones in the commentary. In the few cases in which they do not, this is documented, and the translation is adapted to Mokṣākaragupta's understanding. To make comparison easier, the verses matching the ones in Advayavajra's commentary (DK_A) are provided in brackets. To give an example, "2 (DK_A 1)" means verse 2 of the standard Tibetan root text, which is verse 1 in Advayavajra's commentary. The verses corresponding to DK_A profit from our analysis of the Apabhraṃśa root texts.

Other abbreviations in this edition

om.	omittit/omittant
B	Dpal spungs edition of *Indian Mahāmudrā Works* (*Phyag chen rgya gzhung*), vol. *āḥ*, 161a5–189b1
D	Dergé Tengyur, Tōh. no. 2258, *rgyud 'grel*, vol. *wi*, 265a2–283b1
P	Peking Tengyur, no. 3103, *rgyud 'grel*, vol. *mi*, 295b1–317b8

Variant readings have not been recorded in the following cases:

shad against double *shad*

yang against *'ang*

Do ha mdzod kyi bka' 'grel

|| rgya gar skad du | do[(1]hākoṣapañji[1)]kānāma | bod skad du | do ha mdzod kyi dka' 'grel zhes bya ba | [(2]'jam dpal gzhon nur gyur pa[2)] la phyag 'tshal lo ||
[1] B *ha ko ṣa pany+tsi* D *ha go ṣa pany+tsi* P *ha ko ṣa pany+tsi* [2] B *dpal rdo rje sems dpa'*

| stong pa snying rje ro mnyam pa |
| lhan cig skyes pa de la 'dud |

| gang zhig zhal gyi bdud rtsi yis[1] |
| 'gro ba'i 'chi bdag 'joms mdzad pa |
| bla ma'i zhabs la phyag 'tshal te | [B 161b]
[1] P *yi*

| do ha mdzod kyi dka' 'grel ni |
| rmongs pa'i blo gros sad byed pa |
| 'gro la phan phyir bri bar bya |

DK_T 1
| sngags kyi theg pa 'dir rdzogs pa'i byang chub ni bla ma la rag las pa yin no | | zhes gsungs pas dang por bla ma brtag par bya'o | | de la bla ma dam pa ma yin pa bsten[1] pa ni bdag nyid nyams par byed pas | de'i skyon bstan pa ni | dug sbrul zhes bya ba la sogs pas bstan te | dper na [(2]sos ka'i[2)] tshad pas nyen pas dug sbrul la grib mar 'khrul te drung du phyin na bdag nyid gsod par byed pa bzhin du | bla ma ngan pa rnams la bla mar 'du shes nas sdug bsngal gyis nyen nas de'i drung du phyin na[3] | de bsten pas | de'i skyon lta ba ngan pa dang spyod pa ngan pa [(4]'go bas[4)] | | de dag sbrul bzhin du bltas te spang bar bya'o |
[1] P *brten* [2] D *so ga'i* P *so ka* [3] B *te* P *nas* [4] BP *'gos pas*

DK$_T$ 2–4

| sbrul[1] lta bu'i bla ma de gang yin snyam pa la | | de nyid mi shes bram ze zhes pa nas | | brdzun[2] pa nyid du gol zhes pa'i bar gyis[3] bram ze ba[4] bstan te | gyi na rig byed ces pa nas | | me la bsreg[3] gi bar ni khyim na gnas pa'o[4] | | dbyu gu nas tshig gzhan gyis ni dka' thub la gnas pa bstan te | dbyu gu ni brtul zhugs [(5]so | | 'dul ba dang ngang pas[5)] bstan pa'ang[6] de nyid do |

[1] B *dug sbrul* D *sprul* [2] BP *rdzun* [3] P *gyi* [4] P *pas* [3] D *sreg* [4] B *pa bstan la* DP *pa'o* [5] D *'dul ba dang pos* [6] B *pa*

DK$_T$ 5–6c

| e ra'i[1] thal ba nas gzhan la ston gyi bar gyis ni dbang phyug pa bstan te go sla'o | [D 265b]

[1] B *ri'i*

DK$_T$ 7–10b

sen mo ring zhing[1] nas[2] thar [P 296a] pa nam yang yod ma yin zer ba'i bar gyis mchod 'os pa bstan te go sla'o | [B 162a]

[1] B om. [2] P om.

DK$_T$ 10d–11

| lus kyi dka' thub 'ba' zhig tsam nas rang[1] sangs rgyas kyi tshul 'dzin gyi bar gyis[2] ni | theg pa chung ngu la zhugs [(3]pa bstan no[3)] |

[1] DP om. [2] D *gyi* [3] DP *pa'o*

DK$_T$ 12ab

| [(1]theg pa chen po[1)] de la rgyug[2] byed ces pa[3] nas | | tshad ma'i bstan bcos yin [(4]gyi bar[4)] gyis ni rgyu'i theg pa la zhugs par bstan to |

[1] B *theg chen* [2] B *rgyur* DP *rgyu* [3] DP om. [4] D om.

DK$_T$ 12c

| kha cig dkyil 'khor 'khor lo ma lus bsgom [(1]zhes pa[1)] ni 'bras bu'i theg pa la zhugs pa rtog[2] pa'i rnal 'byor la[3] gnas pa bstan to |

[1] DP om. [2] B *rtogs* [3] B *pa*

DK$_T$ 13a

| nam mkha'i khams la rtog[1] par snang[2] | [(3]zhes pa[3)] ni phyi rol pa dang [(4]man ngag[4)] thun mong ba ste | nam mkha' la lta[5] ba dang | dus la lta[5] ba dang | phyogs la lta[5] ba'o | | de la dang po ni [6] nam mkhar[7] sprin med pa la glo bur du sprin[8] byung bas de mi rtag par lta[5] ba dang | dus kyi 'gyur bas mi rtag par lta[5] ba dang | phyogs ni[9] nyi ma shar nub kyis mi rtag par lta[5] ba'o |

[1] BD *rtogs* [2] BD *nang ba* [3] DP om. [4] D *yang dag* P *yang* [5] B *blta* [6] B inserts *rgyu* [7] DP *mkha'i* [8] D om. [9] B *nas*

DK$_T$ 12d

| bzhi ba'i don 'chad pa ni bzhi pa gsum pa'i don du go nas sangs rgyas pa'i bde ba la brten pa'o |

DK$_T$ 14a

| de dag las kha cig ni de kho na nyid dang bral ba'o | | kha cig de ([1]kho na[1]) nyid ma nor ba dang bral ba'o | | de ltar bla ma dam pa ma yin pa de dag shes nas spangs la | | de dag las bzlog[2] pa'i ([3]bla ma dam pa[3]) de kho na nyid ma nor ba la zhugs shing de ston par nus pa rnams bsten par bya'o |

[1] D om. [2] B *ldog* [3] D *bla ma'i* P *dam pa'i bla ma'i*

DK$_T$ 15ab

| de nas[1] de kho na nyid kyi don btsal bar bya'o | | de la dang por de kho na nyid ma yin pa shes par bya ba'i phyir de'i mi mthun pa dmigs pa dang bcas [B 162b] pa'i bsam gtan kun shes nas spang bar bya ba ni | gang zhig gang la zhes pa la sogs pas ([2]bstan te[2]) | | de la gang zhig ni gang zag go | | gang la ni yi dam gyi lha lta bu de la'o | | mos par gyur pa ni des bdag grol bar byed do zhes lhag par dad pa'o | | bsam [P 296b] gtan [3] gnas pa ni de la bskyed ([4]rim gyi[4]) sgo nas bsgom pa'o | | thar pa mi thob pa ni | sangs rgyas nyid du mi 'gyur ba ste | dpal dgyes pa'i rdo rje las | lha med sngags kyang[5] yod ma yin | | zhes gsungs pa dang | mtshan yang dag par brjod pa las | | [D 266a] bdag gir mi 'dzin ngar mi 'dzin | | zhes gsungs pas so |

[1] B *las* [2] DP *ston to* [3] B inserts *la* [4] P *rims kyi* [5] D *kyi*

DK$_T$ 16ab

| mar me ci dgos lha bshos ([1]de ci[1]) dgos | | de la ci bya gsang sngags bsten[2] pa de ci dgos | | zhes pa ni mchod pa dang bzlas pas mnyes pas mi grol ba'o |

[1] B *ci la* D *de la* [2] DP *brten*

DK$_T$ 16cd

| 'bab stegs nas thob bam ci'i bar gyis lha rten ([1]lta bas[1]) mi grol ba ste | [2]

[1] B *la bltas pas* [2] B inserts *go sla'o* |

DK$_T$ 17

'o na de kho na nyid ji lta bu yin snyam pa la | snying rje dang bral ba[1] zhes bya ba la sogs pa smos te | de'i don ni 'di yin te | stong pa dang snying rje ro mnyam pa'o | | de la stong pa gang zhe na | sgyu ma'i rnam par snang ba ste dngos pos stong pa'o | | de ni rnam pa thams cad kyi mchog dang ldan pa'i stong[2] pa'o | | ([3]de yang[3]) mtshan yang dag par brjod pa las | gzugs med gzugs bzang dam pa ste | | sna tshogs gzugs can yid las skyes | | zhes gsungs pa dang |

[1] B *zhing* [2] P *ston* [3] B *de'ang*

'di nyid las | sgyu ma'i [B 163a] rnal 'byor pa[1] ni mchog tu rtogs | | zhes gsungs pas so | | de ni mngon sum du mthong ba yin gyi[2] chad pa'i stong pa'am rtag[3] pa'i stong pa lta bus[4] mngon du ma mthong ba ni ma yin te | rdo rje gur las | gal te stong nyid thabs yin na[6] | | de tshe sangs rgyas mi 'byung ngo | | rgyu las[7] 'bras bu gzhan min pas | | zhes gsungs pas so | | snying rje ni mi 'bral ba ste | zag med kyi bde ba'o | | de ni sdug bsngal dang bral ba tsam yang ma yin gyi[8] | mi dmigs pa'i bde ba'o | | ([9]de yang[9]) bde mchog las | lha dang mi yi bde ba yis | | bsdus[10] byas rdo rje 'dzin pa yi[11] | | bcu drug char yang mi phod do | | zhes [P 297a] pa dang | 'di nyid las | gang yang brten[12] par nus ([13]pa nas[13]) | | zhes gsungs so[14] |

[1] BP *ma* [2] D *gyis* [3] B *blos brtags* [4] B *bu* [5] D *gyur* [6] D *no* [7] D *la* [8] D *gyis* [9] B *de'ang* [10] B *'dus* [11] P *yis* [12] B *bstan* [13] BP *pas na* [14] B *pas so*

DK$_T$ 18a

| snying rje dang bral nas thob par mi 'gyur gyi[1] bar[2] gyis ni | kha yar ba lam ma yin pa dang | gang yang gnyis po la sogs pa ni ro mnyam[3] pa lam du bstan te | 'bras bu dang mthun pa'i lam bsgom dgos pas so |

[1] D *gyis* [2] BDP *par* [3] BDP *nyams*

DK$_T$ 19

| de nyid ma bcos pa'i lha ste | thams cad kyi[1] don gyi snying por bstan[2] pa ni kye lags gang smras zhes pa[3] la sogs pa ste | kye lags ni bod pa'o | | gang smras [4] ni [D 266b] bla ma dam pa ma yin pa rnams kyis[5] gong du ston pa'o | | brdzun[6] pa ni don med do | | log pa ni gnyug ma mi mtshon pa'o | | gang la zhen pa yod pa de yang thong | | zhes [B 163b] pa ni yi dam gyi lha yin zhes 'dzin pa de thong zhes pa'o | | rtogs[7] par gyur na thams cad de yin te | | zhes pa ni lhan cig skyes pa de rtogs na[8] brtan g.yo thams cad de yin te | [9] lhan cig skyes pa'i rang bzhin 'ba' zhig yin pa'o | | de las gzhan zhig[10] sus kyang shes mi 'gyur | | zhes pa ni lhan cig skyes pa las gzhan logs[11] nas lha gang gis kyang mi shes pa'o |

[1] B *kyis* D om. [2] DP *ston* [3] B *bya ba* [4] B inserts *pa* [5] D *kyi* [6] B *rdzun* [7] DP *rtog* [8] D *nas* [9] D inserts *zhes pa ni* [10] D *gyis* P *gyi* [11] D *log*

DK$_T$ 20

| 'o na gzhan thams cad spang ngam snyam pa la | klog pa zhes pa la sogs pa smos te | lhan cig skyes pa de ye nas kun la gnas pas rtogs na thams cad de rang

las ma 'das pa'o | | de lta bu'i de kho na nyid de thabs gang gis rtogs par bya snyam pa la | de mi mtshon pa'i lta ba yod min te | zhes pa la sogs pa smos te | de ni lhan cig skyes pa'o[1] | |mi mtshon pa ni mi[2] mtshon[3] pa'i lta ba grub mtha' gang yang med de | kun nas ston kyang bla mas ma[4] mtshon na mi rtogs[5] ste | de dag ni mtha' drug gis[6] rgyas btab pas so |

[1] DP *so* [2] P om. [3] B *ston* [4] DP om. [5] D *rtog* [6] B *gi*

DK_T 21

| bla ma'i man ngag gis ji ltar mtshon na | lag [(1]mthil gyi[1)] nor 'dra bar[2] mngon sum du gsal por mthong ste | bla [(3]ma [P 297b] yis[3)] ni man ngag gang gis de mngon sum du 'gyur ba'i thabs ston gyi | don de dngos su brjod nus pa ni ma yin te | brjod du med [4] gang ji[5] ltar bshad du yod ces pa dang | bla mas bstan[6] pa ma yin zhing | | zhes gsungs pa'i phyir ro | | de ltar na dbang bzhi pa kho nas rtogs so | | ma[7] mtshon par mi [B 164a] rtogs pa ni gnyug ma'i rang bzhin zhes bya ba la sogs [(8]pas bstan[8)] te | lhan skyes de ye nas [(9]rang la[9)] gnas kyang rtog pa'i bag chags bzhi pos dkrug pa'i phyir mi rtogs so |

[1] DP *gi* [2] P *bas* [3] B *mas* P | [4] DP insert *de* | [5] DP *'di* [6] P *brtan* [7] P om. [8] DP *pa ston* [9] D om.

DK_T 22

| de rtogs pa'i gang zag ni shes pa ci la yang mi dmigs shing spyod pa gang [1] yang blang dor med do zhes bstan[2] pa ni bsam gtan med cing zhes pa[3] la sogs pas[4] bstan[5] te go sla'o |

[1] P inserts *la* [2] P *ston* [3] B *bya ba* [4] P *pa* [5] D *ston*

DK_T 23

| [(1]lhan skyes ye shes[1)] de dbang gsum pa'i nyams myong [D 267a] gis mi rtogs sam[2] snyam pa la de dag dgag pa'i phyir | gal te mngon sum gyur na zhes bya ba la sogs pa smos so | | gal te mngon sum gyur na bsam gtan ci | | zhes pa ni gsum pa'i dus su lhan cig skyes pa de mngon sum du mthong na bsgom[3] ci dgos zhes pa'o | | gal te lkog tu gyur na mun pa 'jal | | zhes pa ni |gal te ma mthong na bsgom du med de rtog[4] pas mos par zad de | mun khung gi gzugs lta[5] ba bzhin no | | yang na gsum pa'i bde ba de lhan skyes de[6] rnal ma ma[2] yin te | rnal ma de ni dngos po ma yin te | rdul phra rab las 'das pa'o[7] | dngos med min te mig sngar snang bas so | | yang na dngos dang dngos med min ni | | dngos po ni bde ba'i nyams so | | dngos med ni stong pa'o | | min ni tha dad min te ro mnyam pa'o | | 'di ni de las bzlog [(8]pa ste[8)] | | 'di ni dngos po'i rtog pa'o | [B 164b] | de yang he badzra las | gang phyir 'byung ba che bde ba[9] | | des na bde ba de nyid min | | zhes pa dang klu sgrub kyis bcos ma las ma bcos pa [10] ji ltar 'byung ste | zhes gsungs pa'i [P 298a] phyir ro | | yang na | gal te mngon sum gyur na bsam

gtan ci | | zhes pa la sogs pa'i don ni mngon sum [11] gyur na ste | dngos po ni bsgom[3] mi dgos te | mngon du gyur pas so | | dngos med ni bsgom[3] du mi rung ste ma mthong bas so | | de ni lkog tu gyur na mun pa 'jal [12] te | mun khung gi gzugs la sems pa bzhin no | | de[13] bas na lhan cig skyes pa nyid ni | | dngos dang dngos med min te | stong pa dang snying rje ro mnyam pa'o |

[1] B *lhan cig skyes pa'i ye shes* P *lhan skyes* [2] D om. [3] P *sgom* [4] BD *rtogs* [5] B *la blta* [6] B om. [7] DP *pa dang* [8] B *pa'o* [9] B *ba'o* [10] B inserts *ni* [11] B inserts *du* [12] B inserts *ba* [13] D *da*

DK_T 24

| de ltar lhan cig skyes pa de spyir bstan nas | da ni de nyid bye brag tu phye ste bstan pa'i phyir | gang zhig blangs nas zhes bya ba la sogs pa smos te | de la gang zhig nas[1] ji ltar bya ba'i bar gyis ni rgyu'i lhan skyes te | gang zhig ni rtsa ba'i 'od gsal ba[2] mi shigs pa'i thig le'o | | blangs pa ni de la brten nas rtogs pa skye ba'o | | de'i dbang gis skye zhing 'chi bar byed[3] pas so | | yang na ye shes kyi rlung gis sems can skye zhing [D 267b] des srog zad par byas nas 'chi ba[4] ster ro | | de nyid blangs nas bde chen mchog 'grub[5] ces pa ni | rtsa ba'i 'od gsal de ma dag na 'khor bar skye[6] la | de dag na[7] nyi ma lta bur [B 165a] 'char la | de shar na de las[8] zag med kyi bde ba 'grub pa'o | | gzhan ni go sla'o |

[1] B *blangs nas skye 'chi'i gnas gyur pa | | zhes pa nas mi go* [2] P om. [3] D *byad* [4] D *bar* [5] DP *grub* [6] D *skyes* [7] D *ni* [8] DP *la*

DK_T 25

| da ni rgyu'i ([1]lhan cig skyes pa[1]) de rtogs par bya ba'i phyir | lam gyi lhan cig skyes pa ston par bzhed nas | bsam gtan bral ba ni bsam pa'i yul las 'das pa dang | brjod du med pa ni tha snyad las 'das pa'o | | ma brjod na rtogs sam zhe na | ma yin te | srid pa'i phyag rgya ste | rtog pa'i rgyu rlung la zhugs pa'i dbang gis ([1]lhan cig skyes pa[1]) de mi rtogs pas | bla ma dam pa'i gdams ngag la ltos dgos so[2] |

[1] P *lhan skyes* [2] B *pa'o*

DK_T 26

| gdams ngag kyang rtog[1] pas bsgom pa ma yin par ston pa ni | rgyud med sngags med [P 298b] ces bya ba la sogs pa'o |

[1] P *rtogs*

DK_T 27

| gdams ngag de gang yin na | za zhing ni bde ba'o | | 'thung ba ni shu kra'o | | gnyis sprod ni steng 'og gi rlung 'thab[1] pa'i drod ([2]skye ba'o[2]) | | rtag tu yang dang yang du 'khor lo 'gengs | | zhes pa ni | rtsa dbu ma'i steng byang ([3]chub kyi[3])

sems smad khrag gis gang bas byang sems phyir shor bas lus shed[4] nyams pa la sogs pa'o | | de nas byang sems kha gyen du 'dren pa'o | | shu kra la gyen du bltas te 'khor lo drug rim gyis 'gengs pa'o | | 'jig rten pha rol la sogs pa ni go sla'o |

[1] B *'thabs* [2] DP *kyis so* [3] B om. [4] P *sems*

DK$_{\mathrm{T}}$ 28

| de ltar bde ba'i bsam gtan bstan nas | stong pa [1] bstan pa'i phyir | [(2]gang du[2)] rlung dang sems ni zhes bya ba la sogs pa smos te | rlung mi rgyu ba ni dbu mar rlung bcings pa'o | | de yang sems ma bcings na[3] mi 'grub[4] pas sems [(5]bcings pa ni mi rtog pa la bzhag[5)] pa'o | | [B 165b] | nyi zla ni g.yas g.yon gnyis kyi rlung ngo | | 'jug [(6]pa med[6)] 'gyur ba ni dbu mar zhugs pa'o | | gzhan ni go sla'o |

[1] B inserts *nyid* [2] B om. [3] D *ni* [4] D *grub* [5] P *ni mi rtogs pa la gzhag* [6] B *par mi*

DK$_{\mathrm{T}}$ 29

| gnyis med kyi bsam gtan ni gnyis su mi bya'o[1] zhes bya ba la sogs pas ston[2] te | de la | gnyis su mi bya gcig tu bya ba ste | | zhes bya ba ni g.yas g.yon gyi rlung a ba dhūtīr[3] gcig [D 268a] tu byas pa'o | | rigs [4] ni kha dog lnga'i rlung tha dad du mi bya bar ye shes kyi rlung kha dog gcig tu byas pa'o | | yang na rigs la[5] bye brag ni thabs kyi rigs dang | shes rab kyi rigs tha dad du mi bya bar e vaṃ[6] ro mnyam du bya'o | | khams gsum ni lus ngag yid gsum mo | | 'dod chags chen po ni bde ba chen por ro mnyam pa'o |

[1] D *bya* [2] B *bstan* [3] D *dhūtī'i* [4] B inserts *la bye brag* [5] DP *las* [6] BDP *baṃ*

DK$_{\mathrm{T}}$ 30

| bde ba chen po de ji lta bu yin zhe na | der[1] ni thog ma ste dga' ba dang | | bar [(2]ma ni[2)] mchog tu dga' ba dang | | tha ma [3] dga' bral[4] ste de rnams spangs pa'o | | srid min ni dga' ba dang mchog tu dga' ba ste | 'khor [P 299a] [(5]ba'o |[5)] mya ngan las 'das pa ni dga' bral lo | | ma yin ni[6] de gnyis spangs pa'i lhan cig skyes pa'o | | de ni thag bcas kyi bde ba'o | | yang zag med kyi bde ba'i dbang du byas nas | thog ma ni skye ba | bar ma ni gnas pa[7] | tha ma ni 'jig pa ste | zag med kyi bde ba ni rgyu las ma skyes pa'o | | srid min ni ma zhu ba dang | dpral ba ni[6] gnas pa ma yin pa'o | | mya ngan la 'das pa min[8] [B 166a] ni | rdo rje nor bu nas ma 'phos pa'o | | de ltar phab la[9] ma pho[10] ba'o | | gzhan ni go sla'o |

[1] B *de* DP *des* [2] B *ma ste* P *ni* [3] B inserts *ste* [4] P *ba* [5] DP *ba dang* [6] DP *na* [7] DP *pa'o* [8] B *ma yin* D *min na* [9] B *pa las* [10] B *'phos*

DK$_{\mathrm{T}}$ 31

| gnyis med kyi dus der gzung 'dzin gyis 'brel pa chad pa ni | mdun dang[1] zhes pa la sogs pas ston[2] te | mdun ni mi[3] rtog pa'o | | rgyab ni ye shes so | | phyogs bcu ni phyi'i phyogs so | | gang gang mthong ba de de nyid | | ces pa ni | ci[4]

snang ba de[5] de nyid de bde chen nyid do | | de ring mgon po nga[6] ltar 'khrul pa chad | | ces pa la[7] | de ring ni rtogs pa'i dus so | | mgon po nga[6] ltar ni nang du rtogs pa'i nyams bzhin phyi'i[8] gzung ba'i 'khrul pa chad pa'o | [(9]| de nyid du shes pa'o |[9)] | da ni su la'ang 'dri bar mi bya'o zhes bya ba ni | | 'khrul ba chad pas na bde ba'i don gzhan la mi 'dri ba'o |

[1] D *ni* P *na* [2] B *bstan* [3] DP om. [4] B *cir* [5] B om. [6] DP *da* [7] B *la* [8] D *phyir* [9] P om.

DK_T 32

| dbang po gang du la sogs pas ni 'dzin pa'i 'brel pa chad pa ston[1] te | dbang po ni 'dzin pa'i rtog pa'o | | gang du ni lhan cig skyes pa gang du'o | | nub pa ni 'brel pa chad pa'o | | de yang[2] ji ltar chad na | rang gi ngo bo[3] nyams par[4] 'gyur | [D 268b] zhes pa ste | rang gi ngo bo grub pa[5] med par shes pa'o | | gzung 'dzin gyi 'brel pa chad pas mthong ba de'i[6] ming ci yin na[7] | lhan cig skyes pa'i lus te sku'o | | de ni bla ma'i zhal las shes so |

[1] B *bstan* [2] B *'ang* [3] B *bo'ang* [4] DP *pas* [5] B *par* [6] P *de ni* [7] B *zhe na*

DK_T 33

| bla ma'i zhal las thob pa de'i tshe yid 'ching ste | mi rtog[1] pas so | | rlung dengs pa ste[2] dbu mar thim pa'o | | gar shes pa ste thabs shes pa'o | | lhan skyes de la [B 166b] 'khrul pa [P 299b] bsal[3] ba'i phyir | sa gsum zhes bya ba la sogs pa smos te | de la sa gsum ni snang ba gsum mo | | 'di la zhes pa ni 'dir zhes pa'o | | yan lag thams cad ni 'khor 'das so | | gnas ni gzhi'o | | de ltar snang ba gsum po de ni rmongs pa'i rgyu yin pas bzhag[4] la | snang ba gsum dang ldan pa'i sems kyi rnam pa 'khor ba yin pas [(5]spangs pa[5)] dang | sangs rgyas kyi snang ba stobs yin te | | da ltar mi thob pas de gnyis dbang po'i rim pas mtshams te rnal 'byor pas 'od gsal bsgoms zhes pa'o | | mtshams ni gzhi[6] 'od gsal gyi bdag nyid yongs su shes pa'o | | 'od gsal de'i[7] gti mug ste | mi shes pa'i mtsho chad par byed pa'o | | gal te 'od gsal gang yin ba de shes na'o | | des ni sems can gyis rig[8] pa'i shes pa myong ba ni rtog[9] pa yin pas de lhan skyes ma yin par bstan to |

[1] D *rtogs* [2] DP *de* [3] D *gsal* [4] P *gzhag* [5] B *spang ba* [6] B *gzhan* D *bzhi* [7] B *des* [8] D *rigs* [9] D *rtogs*

DK_T 34

|'o na snang ba 'di nyid la lhan cig yin nam[1] snyam pa la | lan du kye ho[2] zhes pa[3] la sogs pa smos te | kye ho[2] ni kye [(4]ma ste[4)] ngo mtshar ba'o | | 'di ni rang gis[5] rig pa ste | 'di la 'khrul par ma byed cig | ces pa ni snang ba 'di nyid ni gong[6] gis gsum zhes pa snang ba dang | mched[7] pa dang | nye bar thob [(8]pa ste[8)] | 'khor ba brgyud[9] mar 'gro ba rtog pa'i snang ba[10] ste | 'di la lhan cig skyes pa yin no zhes 'khrul par ma byed cig ces pa'o | | de ci'i phyir zhe na | [B 167a] de dngos dang dngos med kyi rtog pa gnyis ka 'ching ba nyid du bde bar gshegs pas gsungs pas

so | | de lta bu'i[11] lam ma nor ba de la blo ji ltar gzhag snyam pa la | gnyug ma'i yid ni zhes [D 269a] pa[3] la sogs pa smos te | gnyug ma'i yid ni ([12]lhan skyes so[12]) | | gcig tu gtod[13] dang[14] zhes pa ni | | bsgom bya sgom byed gnyis spangs la mi [P 300a] dmigs pa la gzhag pa'o | | dpe ji ltar bzhag na | chu la chu bzhag[15] bzhin du ste | chu rgyu 'od gsal stong pa la | | chu bzhag[16] ste mi rtog par bzhag[17] pa'o |

[1] DP om. [2] B *hoḥ* [3] B *bya ba* [4] D *ma de* P *mas te* [5] P *gi* [6] BD *gang* [7] P *mchod* [8] BDP *pas te* [9] D *rgyud* [10] D om. [11] DP *bu* [12] B *lhan cig skyes pa'o* [13] BP *sdod* D *stong* [14] B om. [15] D *gzhag* [16] P *gzhag* [17] BDP *gzhag*

DK$_T$ 35

| bcos ma'i rnal 'byor gyis mi grol bar bstan pa'i phyir | bsam gtan brdzun[1] pa zhes pa la sogs pa smos te | bsam gtan brdzun[1] pa ni rtog pa'i rnal 'byor ro | | sgyu 'phrul dra[2] ba ni las kyi phyag rgya'o | | ji ltar pang du 'khyud de ma 'khyud par spongs[3] zhes pa'i don to[4] | | de nyid spangs[5] pa'i 'thad pa bstan pa'i phyir | bla ma dam pa'i zhes bya ba la sogs pa smos te | bla ma dam pa'i bka' yi[6] bden par yid ches pa ([7]| | de yis ni sa ra ha yis[7]) so | | brjod du yod pa min zhes mda' bsnun smra | | zhes pa la |

[1] B *rdzun* [2] B *drwa* [3] B *spang* [4] B *no* [5] B *spang* [6] B om. D *yis* [7] B *ni sa ra ha pas*

DK$_T$ 36a–37a

sgra dang yi ge'i yul ma yin pas na | | yul ji lta bu la bzhag[1] snyam pa la | gdod nas dag pa'i zhes bya ba la sogs pa smos te | gdod nas dag pa'i nam mkha' ni sprin med pa'i nam mkha'o | | bltas shing bltas shing mthong ba dgag par 'gyur | | zhes pa ni | khengs [B 167b] pa'i lta stangs kyis bltas na mthong ba 'gag pa ni gzung 'dzin gyis 'brel pa chad pa'o | | de lta bu yi dus su 'gog byed ci[2] | | zhes ([3]pa ni[3]) rlung bzhi rim[4] gyis 'gag[5] pa'o | | de yang[6] dang po[7] sangs rgyas kyi[8] rgyud las | | nam mkha'i sprin bral ba ni khengs pa'i lta bas blta[9] | | zhes gsungs pas so | | de'i don ni 'di yin te | nyin par bla gab med par 'dug ste | sprin med pa'i nam mkha' la khengs pa'i lta bas blta[9] zhing | yid mi rtog pa la bzhag na rlung rim gyis 'gags nas rtags 'char ba'o | | 'di ni gdams[10] ngag dam pa ste | gsal bar bla ma'i zhal las shes par bya'o | | de lta bu'i[11] lhan cig skyes pa de rang la gnas na mi rtogs[12] pa'i rgyu ci yin snyam pa la | gnyug ma'i yid ces [P 300b] bya ba la sogs pa smos te | gnyug ma'i yid ni lhan skyes ma bcos pa'o |

[1] BP *gzhag* [2] P *cing* [3] BDP *pa'i* [4] P *rims* [5] P *'gags* [6] B *'ang dpal* [7] B *po'i* [8] D *kyis* [9] P *lta* [10] B *man* [11] D *bu* [12] D *rtog*

DK$_T$ 37b–d

[D 269b] nga rgyal skyon ni nga dang ngar 'dzin pa'i skyon gyis bsgribs pa'o | | gzhan gyi skyon gyis mi rtogs[1] par ston ni[2] | | 'jig rten ma lus bsam gtan gyis rmongs te | | zhes pa la rtog pa'i rnal 'byor mtshan bcas ston pa'i[3] bla ma'i skyon gyis mi rtogs[4] pa dang | gzhan yang stong pa nyid rtog par ston pas kyang mi rtogs te | lhan skyes de skye 'gags rnams kyis brtags na de'i rang bzhin mi shes so |

[1] P *rtog* [2] D *to* [3] P *pa* [4] DP *rtog*

DK$_T$ 38 & 39

| lhan cig skyes pa de rtogs pa las ci 'byung snyam pa la [B 168a] de'i phyir don gyi lhan skyes rnam par dag pa'i 'bras bu bstan[1] par bzhed nas | rtsa ba zhes bya ba la sogs pa smos te | de la rtsa ba dang bral ba ni | rgyus ma skyes | rkyen gyis mi 'gags[2] | ngo bo gang la yang mi brten[3] pas so | | de nyid mi 'gyur ba ste lhan skyes so | | gang sems pa[4] ni lhan skyes gang yin pa de bsgoms pa[5] | 'khor ba'i rang bzhin ni sems nyid kyi rnam rtog tsam yin pas | sems mtshon pa'i ([6]bla ma'i[6]) gdams ngag des chog gi[7] gzhan gyis[8] ci bya zhes pa'o |

[1] B *ston* [2] P *'gag* [3] D *rten* [4] BD *dpa'* [5] BDP *na* [6] P om. [7] DP *pas* [8] P *gyi*

DK$_T$ 40

| lhan skyes de gang gis kyang brjod par bya ba ma yin na | bla mas ji ltar mtshon snyam pa la de'i phyir rang bzhin gnyug ma brjod bya ma yin te | slob dpon man ngag mig gis mthong bar 'gyur | | zhes bya ba la sogs pa smos so | | de'i don ni brjod bya ma yin du zin kyang | thabs bstan pas dang po dbang po'i mngon sum gyis sgyu ma lta bu'i lus mthong bar 'gyur te | dper na mun khung gi rdzas brjod pas mi mthong ([1]yang | mthong[1]) ba'i thabs mar me ston pa lta bu'o | | des[2] ni 'bras bu'i lhan skyes mngon sum du gyur par bstan te | de nyid nyes pa dang bral bar bstan pa'i phyir | chos dang chos min zhes bya ba la sogs pa smos te | de la [P 301a] chos ni dge ba[3] dang | chos min ni mi dge ba'o | | mnyes par[4] khyad par med ([5]pa ro[5]) | | zos pa ni rtogs[6] pa'o | | de ltar de ni las rgyu 'bras dang bral ba'o |

[1] DP om. [2] DP *dpes* [3] DP *ba'i chos* [4] B *pa ni* D *pas ni* [5] BD *pa'o* [6] BDP *rtog*

DK$_T$ 41

| yang de [B 168b] la[1] sangs rgyas kyi yon tan 'byung bar[2] bstan pa'i phyir | gnyug ma'i zhes bya ba la sogs pa smos te | gnyug ma'i yid ni [D 270a] lhan skyes so | | sbyangs pa ni rtog pa'i rlung dag par byas pa'o | | bla ma'i yon tan snying la 'jug pa ni[3] | | ([4]gong ma[4]) mchog gi yon tan stobs dang mi 'jigs pa la sogs pa rang la 'char ba'o | | glu len ni dga' nas so | | sngags dang rgyud rnams gcig kyang ma mthong ngo | | zhes pa ni ma mthong mod | don rtogs pas chog ces pa'o |

[1] B *las* [2] P *bas* [3] D *na* [4] B *gang la*

DK_{T} 42

| de ltar[1] lhan cig skyes pa de mdor bstan nas | de nyid [2] rgyas par bshad pa'i phyir | 'gro ba rnams las kyis zhes bya ba la sogs pa smos te | de la 'gro rnams [(3]thams cad[3)] las kyis so sor bcings[4] gyur te[3] | | zhes pa[5] la dge mi dge'i las ni rang gi rnam rtog tsam ste | | des na rang gi rtog pas sprul pa yin gyi[6] | las rgyur smra ba ni ma yin no | | de skad du yang[7] rdo rje phreng ba las | | khams gsum rlung gi[8] sprul pa ste | | rmi lam rmi ba bzhin du blta | | zhes gsungs so | | rnam par rtog pa de nyid ni rtsa ba'i 'od gsal te | de dag na rtog pa kun [(9]'gag ste[9)] | de dag pa'i gnas skabs la mya ngan las 'das pa zhes bya'o | | de skad du yang[7] | 'khor ba yongs su shes pa na | | mya ngan 'das zhes de la bya | | zhes gsungs so |

[1] DP om. [2] B inserts *kyang* [3] B om. [4] B *'ching bar* [5] B *bya ba* [6] D *gyis* [7] B *'ang* [8] B *gis* [9] BP *'gags te*

DK_{T} 43

| de ltar[1] na sems nyid gcig pu[2] kun gyi sa bon te zhes bstan pa'o | | sems nyid gcig pu de nyid dpyad par [B 169a] bya ste | rang rig rtog med la bya'am 'on te gzhan zhig[3] yin [(4]dang po ni ma yin te[4)] | de ni lta ba'i gnas lugs yin te | de ni 'khor ba'am mya ngan las 'das pa gang yang [5] byas pa [P 301b] ma yin te byed pa dang bral bas so | | gzhan ni ma yin te | [(4]sems las ma gtogs pa'i gzhan med do[6] snyam na de ni bden te | dang po lta ba'i gnas lugs ni | | lam du gyur pa ma yin te | |[4)] rgyud du ma las bkag pas so | | 'o na gang la bya na mi shigs pa la bya[7] ste | de ni rtsa ba'i 'od gsal zhes bya | rnam rtog byang chub sems zhes bya | ma dag pa'i dus na ma rig pa zhes pa'o[8] | | de ni rgyud rnams su a zhes bya ba'i brdas bstan te | mtshan yang dag par [D 270b] brjod pa las | rdzogs pa'i sangs rgyas a las byung | | a ni yig 'bru kun gyi mchog | don chen yi ge dam pa yin | | srog chen po ste skye ba med | | ces pas so | | a zhes pas kyang sems skye med mtshon nam[9] snyam na | de ma yin te | rdo rje snying po rgyan gyi rgyud las | snying ga'i dbus na mi shigs[10] pa | | 'bar zhing mar me dag dang mtshungs | | a ni mi 'gyur dam pa'o | | zhes pa dang | he badzra las[11] | [(12]lte bar[12)] phyag rgya chen po ni | | dbyangs yig dang po'i[4] rang bzhin te | | blo chen sangs rgyas rnams [(13]kyis brtags[13)] | | zhes gsungs pas | skye med la a'i brdas[14] [B 169b] bstan pa ma yin te | skye med ni thun mong du grags pas | brda[15] don med du 'gyur ro |

[1] B *lta* [2] D *po* [3] D *ci* [4] P om. [5] DP insert *ma* [6] B *pas so* [7] DP om. [8] P *bya'o* [9] DP *no* [10] P *gshigs* [11] B *las kyang* [12] BD *de ltar* [13] D *kyi rtags* [14] D *brda* P *brda'* [15] P *brda'*

DK_{T} 44

| de ltar rgyu'i lhan cig skyes pa bstan nas | da ni de mngon du bya ba'i phyir thabs kyi lhan cig skyes pa ston[1] te | sems bcings pa ni zhes bya ba la sogs pa smos te | sems ni mi shigs pa'i thig le'o | | bcings pa ni rtog pa'i rlung [(2]rgyu bas[2)] so | | 'ching 'gyur ni 'khor bar 'gyur ba'o | | de nyid grol nas[3] mya ngan 'das par

'gyur ro | | 'ching ba'i rgyu gang yin zhe na | blun po gang gis 'ching 'gyur ba | | mkhas pa de yis[4] myur du grol | | zhes gsungs so[5] | | blun po ni mi shes pa'i 'gro[6] ba'o | | gang gis 'ching[7] 'gyur ni rlung gis so | | thabs shes pa'i[8] mkhas pa ni | rlung de nyid kyis myur du ste | tshe 'di nyid la sangs rgyas ster ba'o | | de yang[9] he badzra las | gang dang [P 302a] gang gis 'jig rten 'ching 'gyur ba | | de dang de yis mkhas pa [(10]myur du[10)] grol | | zhes gsungs so |

[1] B *bstan* [2] B *rgyus pas* [3] P *ni* [4] P *yi* [5] P *te* [6] D *grol* [7] P om. [8] D *pas* [9] B *'ang* [10] DP *yongs su*

DK$_T$ 45

| 'ching ba las thar pa'i thabs de gang yin snyam pa la | sems ni zhes bya ba la sogs pa gsungs te | sems ni nam mkha' lta bur gzung bya ste | | zhes pa ni | sems rtog med du gzhag[1] pa'o | | chos rnams kun kyang nam mkhar mnyam par blta | | zhes pa ni | chos [2] thams cad sems kyi snang ba yin pas nam mkha' dang mnyam [(3]pa ste[3)] | de gdod ma nas ma grub pa'o | [4] | [D 271a] rtog med de las [B 170a] cir 'gyur zhe[5] na | | sems de bsam gyis mi khyab pa ste | mi rtog par[6] lhun grub tu gzhag na | bla na[5] med de sgyu ma'i rang bzhin du rtogs[7] par 'gyur ba'o | | de yang[8] dpal gsang ba 'dus pa las | dngos po med [(9]par bsgom pa min[9)] | | bsgom par bya ba sgom pa min | | de bas dngos po dngos med pas | | bsgom pa dmigs su med [(10]pa yin[10)] | | zhes pa'o[11] | | de'ang[12] he badzra las kyang | sgom pa po med bsgom bya med | | ces gsungs pa dang | 'di nyid las | bsam gtan dag gis ma bslad | ces gsungs pas so |

[1] P *bzhag* [2] B inserts *rnams* [3] DP *pas te* [4] D inserts *| sems ni nam mkha' lta bur gzung bya ste |* [5] DP om. [6] D *pa* P om. [7] D *rtog* [8] B *'ang* [9] B *la bsgom pa'i dngos* P *par bsgom pa'i dngos* [10] B *pa'o* [11] B *gsungs so* [12] DP om.

DK$_T$ 46

| sems [1] mi rtog pa la bzhag[2] na rlung gang du 'ching snyam pa la | nam[3] mkha' 'drar byas nas zhes pa[4] la sogs pa gsungs te | mkha' 'drar byas nas ni sems[5] mi rtog par byas nas so | | de cis bya[6] na rlung ni[7] rnam par rtog pas[8] bcings pas so | | [(9]de ltar 'ching ni[9)] | mnyam nyid de | yul dang yul can ro mnyam pa'o | | de shes pas ni rab tu thim | | zhes pa ni | rlung gcig la gcig thim nas 'od gsal du 'jug pa'o | | mda' bsnun[10] gyis smras sogs ni phan yon te | go sla'o |

[1] B inserts *ni* [2] P *gzhag* [3] BP om. (B blank space) [4] B *bya ba* [5] D om. [6] DP *byas* [7] B *gis* [8] B *pa* [9] B *ji ltar 'ching na* (P *na*) [10] P *snun*

DK$_T$ 47

[(1]| rab tu thim pa'i tshul gyis de nyid [2] bstan pa ni |[1)] rlung dang zhes bya ba la sogs pa smos te | rlung ni 'og gi dri chu'i rtsa'o | | me ni steng gi g.yas pa'o

| | dbang chen ni ’og gi dbus [P 302b] ma dri chen gyi rtsa na gnas pa’i rlung [B 170b] ngo | | steng du[3] du dhū tī’o | | bdud rtsi rgyu ba ni steng du zla ba’i bdud rtsi rgyu ba’i rlung | ’og tu g.yas byang chub sems kyi rtsa’o | | dus ni[4] mi ’da’ ba’o | | de lta bu’i sems de [5] ’od gsal du ’jug pa’o | | yang na [(6]sa’i rlung[6)] chu la thim | [(7]chu me la thim | me rlung la thim | rlung[7)] sems ’od gsal du ’jug go | | chu ni kha bskang[8] ste bstan pa’o | | bdud rtsi rgyu ba’i dus su zhes pa ni | snyoms ’jug gi dus su yang rlung[9] sems de rtsa[10] dbu mar gzhug[11] go | | yang na de ltar rlung dbu mar zhugs na | srog rtsol gyi mes[12] dpral ba’i haṃ bzhu nas | bdud rtsi byang chub kyi sems ’dzag ste | | de las bde ba skye’o | | de ltar yang gsungs pa | sa ni chu la thim pa ste | | chu ni me la thim par ’gyur | | me ni rlung la thim pa ste | | rlung ni rnam par [D 271b] shes la ’jug | rnam shes de ni ’od gsal ba’o | | zhes pa’o | | de ltar bcings pa las bde ba skye bar bya ba bstan pa’i phyir | nam zhig ces bya ba la sogs pa smros te | de la nam zhig ni gang gi tshe’o | | sbyor ba bzhi ni steng ’og gi rlung bzhi’o | | yang na ’byung ba bzhi’i rlung ngo | | gnas gcig ni a va[13] dhū tīr zhugs pa’o | | yang na sbyor ba bzhi ni dga’ ba bzhi’o | | gnas gcig la zhugs pa ni lhan cig skyes pa la’o | | nam mkha’i[14] khams su mi shong ba ni | | bde ba des chos thams cad la khyab par shes ba’o |

[1] P om. [2] D inserts *smra* | | [3] B *ni* [4] DP om. [5] B inserts *dag* [6] D *sa* [7] DP *me la me | rlung la rlung* | [8] B *bskangs* [9] BD om. [10] D om. [11] B *’jug* [12] P *me dang* [13] DP *ba* [14] BD *mkha’*

DK$_{T}$ 48

| de rtogs dka’ bar bstan pa’i phyir | | khyim dang zhes bya ba [B 171a] la sogs pa smos te | ’gro kun bsam bas sun ’byin [1] | | zhes pa ni rang gi rnam rtog gis bsgribs nas sun ’byin pas de mi rtogs[2] pa’o | | yang na rang gi rnam rtog ngan pas gzhan dam pa’i lam ston pa sun ’byin cing ’dug pas so | | gzhan ni go sla’o |

[1] BP insert *pa* [2] D *rtog*

DK$_{T}$ 49

| de[1] ni rtogs par dka’ yang bsgrub par mi[2] nus pa ma [P 303a] yin par bstan pa’i phyir | sems can thams cad kun la yang | | zhes bya ba la sogs pa smos te | thams cad ro mnyam rang bzhin ni lhan cig skyes pa yod par khyad par med pa’o | | de’i ming ni bsam yas ye shes bla med pa’o | | zhes pa’o | | gzhan ni go sla’o |

[1] DP *des* [2] DP om.

DK$_{T}$ 50

| sgrub pa la zhugs pa rnams kyang le lo’i dbang du gyur pas mi rtogs par bstan pa’i phyir | de ring zhes bya ba la sogs pa smos te go sla’o |

DK_T 51

| de ltar na de nyid rtogs[1] pa'i gang zag dkon pas | sgrub pa la 'bad par byos shig[2] ces bstan pa'i phyir | bya ba byed dang zhes bya ba la sogs pa smos te go sla'o |

[1] D *rtog* [2] D *cig*

DK_T 52

| de ltar na rlung [(1]bcing ba[1)] de yang[2] sems ma bcings na mi 'grub pas sems mi[3] rtog[4] pas [(5]bcings par[5)] bstan pa'i phyir 'jur bus bcings pa'i sems 'di ni zhes bya ba la sogs pa smos te | de la 'jur bus bcings pa ni rtog pas sgribs pa'i sems de'o | | glod na grol bar the tshom med | | ces bya ba ni | mi rtog pa la bzhag na rtog pa'i[6] bcings pa las grol bar gdon mi za'o | | [B 171b] rtog pa'i rtsa ba gang yin zhe na | gang gis [D 272a] rmongs pa zhes [7] smos te | gang gis ni rlung gis so | | rmongs pa ni thabs dang bral ba'o | | 'ching ba'i dngos po ni de las byung ba'i rtog pa'o | | mkhas pa[8] rnams ni thabs dang ldan pa'o | | de yis zhes pa ni mi[8] rtog pa de [(9]bsgoms pas[9)] rnam par grol bar ni rtog pa'i rtsa ba'i rlung dbus su 'jug par 'gyur ro |

[1] DP *bcings pa* [2] B *'ang* [3] DP om. [4] P *rtogs* [5] B *bcing bar* [6] B *pas* [7] B inserts *pa* [8] P om. [9] D *yis sgom pa yes* P *yi sgom pa yi*

DK_T 53

| bcings pa dang grol[1] ba [(2]de dpe yis[2)] gsal bar bstan pa ni | bcings [(3]pa rnams[3)] ni zhes bya ba la sogs pa smos te | dper na | [(4]bcings pa[4)] rnams ni[5] grol[6] bar rtsol la | ma bcings pa rnams grol bar mi rtsol lo | | de bzhin du [(7]bcings pa[7)] ni rtog [P 303b] pas[8] bzung[9] na'o | | [(10]thong bar[10)] gyur na ni mi rtog pa la bzhag[11] na'o[12] | | go bzlog[13] pa'i chos ni bcings na grol[6] la[14] | thong[15] na sdod do | | bdag gis bzlog[13] pa'i gdams ngag rtogs[16] pa'o | | rang la tshol[17] te ltos zhes pa ni | sems 'dzin sdod[18] na zhes[19] pa'o |

[1] P *grol ba'i grol* [2] B *de'i dpe* P *de dpe'i* [3] D *pa'i rnam pa* [4] D *bcing ba* [5] DP om. [6] P *'grol* [7] B *bcing ba* [8] P *pa yis* [9] B *gzung* [10] DP *thongs par* [11] BP *gzhag* [12] DP *go* [13] B *ldog* [14] B *ba la* [15] DP *thongs* [16] BD *rtog* [17] P *tshor* [18] BDP *'dod* [19] P *zhen*

DK_T 54

| de ltar bcings pa dang grol ba'i rgyu bstan nas | da ni thabs bstan [(1]par bya ste[1)] | kye lags zhes bya ba la sogs pa smos te | de la dbang pos[2] ltos shig ces pa ni khengs pa'i lta bas nam mkha' sprin med pa la ltos shig pa'o | | 'di las[3] ngas ni [(4]ma rtogs[4)] zhes pa ni | | yid kyis mi brtag[5] go zhes pa'i don to[6] | | las zin [(7]pa yi[7)] skye bo yi[8] | | zhes pa ni rtog pa bkag pa yis so | | drung du ni nam mkha' sprin [9] med du'o | | sems thag bcad pa ni rtog[10] pa [B 172a] thag bcad pa'o | | des ni 'di skad ston pa yin te | nyin mo'i sbyor bas bla gab[11] med pa'i nam mkha' dri ma med pa la[12] bltas pas | me 'bar ba dang | glog dang | zla ba dang | nyi ma

dang | sgra gcan gyi rnam pa mthong la | mtshan mo'i rnal 'byor gyi[13] mtshan ma lnga 'byung ste | du ba dang | smig rgyu dang | mkha' snang dang | mar me dang | nam mkha' lta bu'o | | de dag ni rlung dbu mar zhugs pa'i rtags yin no | | de yang he badzra las | bsam pa thams cad yongs spangs te | | nyi ma gcig tu yongs su brtag[14] | | gal te mtshan ma ma byung na | | de tshe nga yi rdzun[15] tshig yin | | zhes pa dang | dang po'i[16] sangs rgyas kyi rgyud [D 272b] las kyang | sprin med nam mkha' la ni khengs pa'i lta bas blta | | zhes pa la sogs pa gsungs so | | 'di nyid las 'og nas | mig ni mi 'dzum[17] sems 'gog na | | rlung 'gog pa ni dpal ldan bla ([18]mas rtogs[18]) | zhes pa dang | gdod[19] nas rang bzhin dag pa'i nam [P 304a] mkha' la | | bltas shing bltas shing mthong ba 'gag par 'gyur | | zhes gsungs te | gsal por bla ma'i zhal[20] las shes par bya'o |

[1] B *pa'i phyir* [2] DP *po* [3] DP *la* [4] D *ma rtog* [5] B *rtogs* D *rtag* [6] B *no* [7] DP *pa'i* [8] B *yi* [9] B inserts *la* [10] B *rtogs* [11] D *gang* [12] DP om. [13] BD *gyi* [14] D *rtog* P *rtags* [15] D *brdzun* [16] DP *po* [17] D *'dzums* [18] D *ma'i rtog* P *ma'i rtogs* [19] B *gdengs* [20] P *zhel*

DK$_T$ 55

| da ni thabs dang thabs ma yin pa'i khyad par bstan pa'i phyir | rlung bcings pa la rang nyid ma[1] sems kye | | zhes pa[2] la sogs pa smos[3] te | de la rlung bcings pa ni rlung grangs[4] pa lta bu'o | | shing[5] gi rnal [B 172b] 'byor ni[6] des don med pa'o | | sna rtse ni rtog pa'i rnal 'byor steng[7] 'og gi sna rtser sems 'dzin pa'o | | ma 'dug[8] kye zhes pa ni ma sgoms[9] shig ces pa'o | | 'o na gang bsgom[9] na | e ma hoḥ[10] ([11]ma yengs[11]) zhes pa ni | rtog pa'i rnal 'byor thabs ma yin gyi[12] zhog la | lhan cig skyes pa mchog ni[13] mi rtog pa la gnas par gyis shig ces pa'o | | rtog pa'i rnal 'byor de thabs ma yin par bstan pa'i phyir | srid pa'i sna rtser zhes pa la sogs pa smos te | srid pa'i sna rtser bcings pa yongs su spang | | zhes pa ni | srid pa'i sna rtser gtad pa ni[14] ([15]'ching ba yin pas[15]) de yongs su spang[16] zhes pa'o |

[1] D *la* P om. [2] B *bya ba* [3] DP *gsungs* [4] B *grang* D *grags* [5] D *mi gang zhig* P *mi gang shing* [6] B om. [7] B *te* [8] B *sems* [9] P *sgom* [10] D *ho* P *'o* [11] BD *ma yin* P *yin* [12] DP *gyis* [13] DP om. [14] DP om. [15] D *bcing bar* P *'ching bas* [16] D *spangs*

DK$_T$ 56

| spang pa de ci'i phyir zhe na | 'di ni yid[1] 'dus pa las rlung gis brlabs pas g.yo zhing 'phyar la shin tu mi srun[2] par 'gyur pa'i phyir ro | | lhan skyes de bsgrub pa ci'i phyir zhe na | lhan cig skyes pa'i rang bzhin gyi[3] rtogs pa la gnas na brtan[4] par 'gyur ba'i phyir ro |

[1] D *yongs su* P *yid yongs su* [2] P *bsrun* [3] B *gyis* [4] DP *bstan*

DK$_T$ 57

| yid mi g.yo ba la dgos pa ci yod snyam pa la | yid ni nye bar 'gags[1] gyur na | | lus kyi ([2]bcing ba[2]) rtog[3] pa dang | | sdug bsngal 'chad[4] par 'gyur ba'o | | der ma

zad kyi | bde stong ro mnyam du 'gyur bar bstan pa ni dbus su lhan cig skyes dang ro mnyam pa[5] ste | [6] dbus ni mtha' dang bral ba ste | stong pa dang | lhan skyes bde bar ro mnyam na gdol pa [P 304b] ste | ma reg[7] pa[8] na stong [B 173a] pa dang | bram ze ste bde ba tha dad med pa'o |

[1] B *'gag* [2] D *bcings pa* [3] DP *rtogs* [4] D *chad* [5] B om. [6] B inserts *zhes pas* [7] P *rig* [8] B *pas*

DK_T 58–59

| de ltar [D 273a] | srid pa'i sna rtser thabs ma yin zhing | lhan skyes thabs su bstan nas | lhan skyes de ni phyi rol na[1] mi gnas shing rang gi lus la gnas par bstan pa'i phyir | 'di na [2] zla ba zhes bya ba la sogs pa smos te | lus dang dran pa'i mu na gnas pa'i mtsho | | zhes pa la lus ni lus la gnas pa'o | | dran pa ni man ngag la gnas pa'o | | mtsho ni bde ba mi zad pa'o | | gzhan ni go sla'o |

[1] BD om. [2] B inserts *bsil ba'i*

DK_T 60

| lhan skyes de rang la yod pas gnas gzhan las mi btsal bar bstan pa'i phyir | 'dab ldan zhes pa la sogs pa smos te | 'dab ma dang ldan pa'i ge sar gyi dbus na gnas pa ni | kha[1] ga mu kha'o | | shin tu phra ba ni a va[2] dhūtī'i rtsa'o | | dri ni utpal gyi dri lta bu'o | | kha dog ni dmar po'o | | dri dang kha dog dang ldan pa'i bye brag ste | las kyi phyag rgya dang | rang 'od kyi rig ma la brten par mi bya'o |

[1] B *khā* [2] D *ba*

DK_T 61

| lhan skyes de nyid ma bcos pa'i lha yin pas phyi'i lha mchod pa la mi ltos par bstan pa'i phyir | gang du tshangs pa zhes bya ba la sogs pa smos te go sla'o |

DK_T 62

not commented upon

DK_T 63

| lhan skyes[1] de rtogs[2] pa'i yon tan bstan pa'i phyir | kye ho[3] zhes bya ba la sogs pa smos te | bde ba'i gnas mchog rtog pa spangs pa de ngas mthong zhes pa la | bde ba'i gnas ni [B 173b] rgyu ste stong pa'o | | rtog pa spangs pa ni mi rtog pa'i lam ste[4] ngas mthong zhes pa ni mngon sum du'o | | 'gro ba nye bar skye bar byed pa ji[5] bzhin no zhes [6] pa ni ma las[7] bu skye ba dang 'dra bar zag med kyi bde ba skye'o |

[1] D *cig* [2] B *rdzogs* D *rtog* [3] B *hoḥ* [4] DP *de* [5] DP *nyid* [6] B adds *gsungs* [7] DP *la*

DK_T 64

| blo rnams 'gag ni yul gyi rtog pa'o | | yid [(1]rab zhi[1)] ni yul can gyi rtog pa'o | | gang du mngon pa'i nga rgyal chad pa ni de [P 305a] nyid kyi zhen pa chad pa'o | | de nyid sgyu ma'i rang bzhin mchog tu rtogs[2] pa[3] zhes bya ba ni de ltar yul dang yul can gyi 'brel pa chad na chos thams cad sgyu ma ltar mthong ba'o |

[1] DP *rang bzhin* [2] D *rtog* [3] B om.

DK_T 65

| rtog pa chad pa'i tshul bstan pa ni | dngos po zhes bya ba la sogs pa smos te | dngos po skye ba ni yul du snang ba'i rtog pa'o | | mkha' ltar gyi rtog pa gang zhe na [1] | | dngos po rnam spangs phyi[2] na ci zhig skye | | zhes pa ni | yul gyi rtog pa chad[3] na yul can gyi rtog pa chad[3] pa'o | | de'i phyir bla mas bstan pa'i dbye ba [(4]rnams spangs pa ni[4)] yul dang yul can gyi [D 273b] dbye ba tha dad spangs pa ni bral ba ste | mi rtog pa la gnas par [(5]bya ba'o[5)] | | yang na sgyu ma lta bu la gnas par byos shig ces pa'o |

[1] DP insert *zhes pa'o* [2] D *phyir* [3] P *'chad* [4] B *rnams spangs nas* | | *zhes pas* D *rnam spang pa ni* P *rnam spangs ni* [5] DP *byos shig ces pa'o*

DK_T 66

| de la ji ltar rnam par gnas par bya snyam pa la mthong dang zhes bya ba la sogs pa smos te | [(1]mig la sogs pa'i dbang po lngas mngon sum du gyur pa de la mig ma yengs pa dang yid ma yengs par bltas pas de'i mthar nyams skye [B 174a] bar 'gyur |[1)] | sems so zhe na gcig gi rnam pa las mi 'da' zhes pa ni spyod lam la sems 'jug pa ni | gcig gi rnam pa ste sgyu ma la sems ma g.yos pa'o |

[1] DP om.

DK_T 67

| da ni de lta bu[1] ston pa'i bla ma [(2]la bsten par bstan[2)] pa'i phyir | gang zhig bla ma'i man ngag ces bya ba la sogs pa smos te | de la bla ma'i man ngag bdud rtsi la sogs pa dang bral ba ni | sdug bsngal gyis[3] 'dzin par bstan te go sla'o |

[1] B *bur sus* [2] B *de bsten par bstan* D *la brten* P *la bsten par brtan* [3] P *gyi*

DK_T 68

| bla mas bstan pa zhes bya ba la sogs pas[1] ni lhan cig skyes pa[2] ni rtogs[3] par bstan te go sla'o | | tshig 'di ni 'og ma dang 'brel te bla mas bstan du med cing | slob mas mi go ste |

[1] B *pa* [2] P *pas* [3] B *mi rtog*

DK$_T$ 69

'on kyang bla ma'i gdams ngag la bden par 'dzin pa'i dbang gis bye brag rnyed [1] pa ste | blun pos kyang mngon sum du mthong bar 'gyur ro | | de mthong na bzang ngan dang | che chung dang | gtsang mi gtsang [P 305b] gi rtog pa thams cad [(2]spangs te[2)] | gdol pa'i khyim ste de la rol yang[3] dri mas ma gos pa ni de'i nyes pas ma reg pa'o |

[1] B inserts *las* [2] D *spang ste* P *spangs pa ste* [3] B *kyang*

DK$_T$ 70

| de ltar blun pos kyang mngon sum du byed pa'i yon tan bstan nas dman pa mchog tu gyur pa bstan pa ni | gang tshe zhes pa[1] la sogs pa smos te | srang khar bor[2] ba'i kham phor du[3] slong ba po'i sprang phor yin yang man ngag [4] thob pa'i rnal 'byor pa de ni rang la dbang [(5]chen pos[5)] rgyal [B 174b] po yin na | slar yang ci byar yod ni[6] dman pa'i [(7]spyod pas[7)] gnas med de lhan cig skyes pa'i rtogs[8] pas 'gal[9] zhes pa'o | | de yang[10] gzhi mal stan chen po [(11]la sogs[11)] pa'i sngas ni [(12]rnal 'byor[12)] la khrid ces pa la sogs pa nas | rnal 'byor pa nyid rgyal po yin | | zhes bya ba'i bar du gsungs pa'o[13] | | mya ngan 'das la mi gnas srid par mdzes | | zhes pa ni lus[14] 'khor ba na 'dug mod kyang[14] sems sangs rgyas su 'dug pas so |

[1] B *bya ba* [2] D *por* [3] DP om. [4] D insert *ma* [5] BP *che bas* [6] P *na* [7] D om. [8] D *rtog* [9] BD *'gag* [10] B *'ang sa* [11] DP *lag* [12] DP *'bol* [13] DP *pas so* [14] DP om.

DK$_T$ 71

| de lta bu'i rnal 'byor pa[1] de[2] 'khor ba na gnas na ci'i tshul gyis gnas snyam pa la | ji ltar bu chung tshul du gnas bya zhing | | zhes gsungs te | bu chung gi tshul ji [D 274a] ltar bur[3] zhe na | bsam dang bsam bya rab tu spangs nas su | | zhes pa'o[4] | | bsam pa ni rtog pa'o | | bsam bya ni brtags[5] pa'o | | de ltar rab tu spangs pa ni rtog pa mtha' dag spangs pa'o | | rtog pa spangs pa de ci'i phyir zhe na | nad gzhan dag la sman gzhan gtang mi bya | | zhes gsungs te | de'i don ni ngan pa spong[6] ba la ngan par brtag[7] pas mi [(8]spong ste[8)] | cir[9] yang ma brtags par bzhag [10] na ngan pa'i rtog pa [(11]spangs pa'o[11)] | | 'o na bsgom[12] pas spang bar bya 'am snyam [(12]pa la[12)] | bla ma'i lung la bsgrims te gus 'bad na | | zhes gsungs te | bla ma'i lung bzhin du gus par 'bad par bya'o | | de [P 306a] las lhan cig skyes pa 'byung bar [B 175a] 'gyur ro |

[1] DP om. [2] DP *des* [3] DP *bu* [4] B *pas* [5] B *brtag* [6] B *spang* [7] B *brtags* P *rtags* [8] D *spongs te* [9] DP *ci* [10] B inserts *pa* [11] DP *spong ba'o* [12] D *na* P *bsgoms* [13] DP *na*

DK$_T$ 72

| lhan skyes smra ru mi btub pa de ji ltar 'byung bar[1] bstan pa ni | kha dog[2] ces[3] pa la sogs pa smos[4] ste | kha dog[2] ni[4] mi 'byed[5] yi ge[6] mi 'dri | yon tan mi 'tshol[6]

| dpe mi bshad do | | gzhan ni go sla'o | | lhan skyes de gzhan la bstan du mi btub pa ni | gzhon nu (7ma yi7) zhes pa la sogs pa smos te go sla'o |

[1] DP *ba* [2] DP *ton* [3] DP *shes* [4] DP om. [5] DP *byed* [6] B *ger* [7] DP *tshol* [7] DP *ma'i*

DK$_T$ 73

| de lta bu'i rnal 'byor pa ni | rtog pa dang sdug bsngal las grol bar bstan pa'i phyir | dngos dang zhes bya ba la sogs pa smos te | dngos po ni yod pa | dngos med[1] ni med pa | spangs[2] pa ni de las 'das pa'o | | der[2] ni 'gro ba ma lus rab thim 'gyur | | zhes pa ni der ro[3] mnyam pa'o | | gang tshe yid ni mi g.yo brtan pa[4] ni mi rtog (5pa la'o5) | | de[6] tshe 'khor ba'i dngos po rang grol 'gyur | | zhes pa ni | rtog pa dang sdug bsngal las so |

[1] D *po* [2] D *spang* [2] DP *des* [3] DP om. [4] B *par zhes pa* [5] B *pas so* [6] B *de'i*

DK$_T$ 74

| sdug bsngal dang bral bar ma zad kyi | yon tan khyad par can 'byung bar bstan pa'i phyir | gang tshe zhes bya ba la sogs pa gsungs te | bdag gzhan yongs su shes min na | zhes pa ni | bdag gzhan gyi rtog pa spangs pa'o | | bla ma'i lus su grub pa nyid | | ces pa ni gong ma'i sku thob pa'o | | de ltar bstan pa nyid la zhes pa[1] la sogs pa ni | bla ma'i man ngag las yon tan de dag 'byung bas[2] de la 'bad par bya'o [B 175b] zhes gdams pa'o |

[1] B *bya ba* [2] DP *ba*

DK$_T$ 75

| bla mas bstan pa'i lam nyams su blangs pa'i phan yon ni | rdul med ces pa la sogs pa smos te | de la rdul med ni rdul phra rab kyis bsdus [D 274b] pa ma yin pa'o | | rdul bral min ni gzugs su snang ba med pa ma yin no | | sems kyang min ni gzugs su snang ba'o | | de ltar na dmigs par bya ba'i yul ni sgyu ma lta bu'i lus so | | de bas na dngos po 'di dag ni 'di ltar snang ba kun (1gdod ma1) nas [P 306b] ma grub pas mthong yang zhen pa med pa'o | |gzhan ni go sla'o |

[1] D *gdong* P *gdod*

DK$_T$ 76a–c

| de lta bu de rang la yod kyang bla mas ma bstan na mi go bar bstan pa ni | khyim na yod pa zhes bya ba la sogs pa (1smos te1) | khyim na yod pa zhes bya[2] ba ni rang la yod pa'o | | phyi rol song nas 'tshol[3] zhes bya[2] ba ni gzhan du'o | | dpe bstan pa ni | khyim bdag [4] mthong (5khyim de rang5) khyim bdag che ge mo mthong ngam zhes 'dri'o |

[1] DP *ste* [2] BP om. [3] DP *tshol* [4] B inserts *ni* [5] B *khyim bdag de rang la* D *nas khyim de rang* P om.

DK$_T$ 76d–77b

| bla mas bstan kyang rang gis[1] ma bsgoms na mi rtogs[2] par bstan pa ni | blun pos[3] zhes bya ba la sogs pa smos te go sla'o |

[1] P *gi* [2] DP *rtog* [3] BDP *po'i*

DK$_T$ 77cd

| rang gis bsgom[1] pa de'ang[2] bde bar gnas pas 'grub par bstan pa ni | yul rnams bgrod cing zhes bya ba la sogs pa smos te | de la yul rnams bgrod cing gdung bas nyen[3] byas kyang ni[4] | thos pa btsal ba'i yul rnams su 'phyan[5] cing dka' bas gdungs[6] kyang zhes bya ba'i [B 176a] don to[7] | | de ni mtshon pa tsam ste | dka' thub gzhan yang gzung[8] ngo | | gzhan ni go sla'o | | 'o na gang gis 'grub na bde ba la longs spyod pas 'grub po zhes kha bskang ngo |

[1] P *bsgoms* [2] DP *yang* [3] D *nyan* [4] B *zhes pa ni* P om. [5] B *phyin* D *mkhyen* [6] D *gdung* [7] B *no* P *te* [8] P *bzung*

DK$_T$ 78

| des mi 'ching ngam snyam pa la | yul rnams bsten pas yul gyis[1] mi[2] gos te yul dang yul can ro mnyam par shes pas so | | dpe ji lta bur[3] snyam pa la | utpal blangs kyang zhes pa ste go sla'o | | mi 'ching ba'i rgyu ci snyam pa la | 'di ltar zhes bya ba la sogs pa smos te | gang 'di zhes pa ni bsgrub pa'o | | 'di ltar zhes pa ni gang gi phyir zhes pa ste | rtsa ba rlung gi[4] skyabs su 'gro bas de'i phyir ro | | de la rtsa ba ni sgyu lus so | | rlung gi[4] skyabs su 'gro ba ni | rlung dag pa las[5] sgyu lus 'byung ba'o | | mi 'ching ba'i[6] dpe bstan pa ni dug gis[7] zhes smos te go sla'o |

[1] P *gyi* [2] P *ma* [3] DP *bu* [4] B *gis* [5] DP *la* [6] B *ba de'i* [7] P *gi*

DK$_T$ 79

| de ltar rang la yod pa'i[1] ma bcos pa[2] sgyu ma lta bu nyid mi 'ching ba'i rgyur[3] bstan nas | gzhan dad pa'i[4] lha la mchod pas mi grol bar bstan pa ni | lha la mchod pa zhes pa la sogs pa[5] smos[6] te go sla'o |

[1] DP *pa* [2] D *pas* P *par* [3] DP *rgyu* [P 307a] *ru* [4] DP *pa* [5] P *pas* [6] DP *ston*

DK$_T$ 80

| da ni sgyu ma'i lus [D 275a] de[1] mngon sum du bya ba'i phyir | thabs kyi dam pa lta stangs skyon med dang (2bcas par bstan2) pa'i phyir | mig ni zhes pa la sogs pa gsungs te | de la mig mi 'dzums pa ni khro bo'i blta ba'o | | sems 'gags pa ni de'i stobs kyis rtog pa 'gags pa'o | | rlung [B 176b] 'gag[3] pa[4] ni rlung lnga rim gyis a va[5] dhū tī'i lam la zhugs pa'o | | rlung ma 'gags na skyon ci yod ce na | gang tshe rlung rgyu de ni mi g.yo ste | | zhes pa ni[6] rlung ni 'khor ba'i rtsa ba yin pas ji srid du rlung rgyu ba de srid du 'khor ba las ma 'da'o[7] | | 'chi ba'i tshe na zhes pa ni 'chi ka'i dus su'o | | rnal 'byor mas ni ci bya zhes bya ba la | rnal

'byor ma ni sgyu ma'i rnal 'byor ma'o | | ci bya zhes pa ni rang la yod kyang phan mi[8] thogs zhes pa'o |

[1] DP om. [2] B *bcas pa bstan* D *bstan pa bcas* [3] P *'gags* [4] D *pas* [5] D *ba* [6] B *la* [7] DP *'das pa'o* [8] P *ma*

DK$_T$ 81a–d

| 'khor ba las ji ltar mi 'da' snyam pa la | ji srid dbang po yul gyi zhes pa la sogs pa smos te | don ni 'di yin te | thur sel gyi rlung rgyu ba'i stobs kyis shu kra thur du lhung la | rakta ni[1] gyen du smin na[2] des dbang po'i sgo sad par byed do | | de nas shes[3] pa srog la zhon nas[4] rtog pa kun skyed[5] do | | de ltar yang dgongs pa lung ston pa las | | ji srid 'jig rten brtag pa dang | | 'jig rten brtag pa sna tshogs pa | | rnam rtog byang chub sems zhes pa | | rlung las rtag tu 'byung ba yin | | zhes gsungs so | | de ltar na 'khor ba'i rtsa ba ni rlung yin pas de dgag par bya dgos la | de yang yid bcings pa la rag las[6] so | | yid bcings pa yang[7] rnam par mi rtog par[8] bsgom pa la rag las[6] [P 307b] pa'o[9] | phan yon gyi tshul gyis yid mi rtog par gzhag[10] [(11]par bya ba[11)] ni khyed cag ces pa la sogs pa ste | de la [(12]da ltar[12)] ci byed ces pa ni bya rgyu med pa[13] rang du gcig ces pa'o | | gar 'gro soms[14] [B 177a] dang kye zhes pa ni 'gro sa rang du gcig ces pa ste | de ltar na bya byed spangs la mi rtog par gzhag pa'o | | de ni shin tu dka' ba'i dgongs pas 'jug | ces pa la shin tu dka' ba ni bya byed spong[15] pa ste dka' ba'o | | dgongs pas 'jug ces pa ni thabs dang ldan na mi rtog par ngang gis 'jug pa'o |

[1] D om. [2] B *pa* [3] BD *zhes* [4] DP *pas* [5] B *bskyed* [6] D *lus* [7] B *'ang* [8] DP *pa* [9] D *pas* [10] B *bzhag* [11] DP *pa gsungs pa* [12] D *de* P *de ltar* [13] DP om. [14] P *som* [15] B *spangs* D *stong*

DK$_T$ 81ef & DK$_T$ 82ab

| de ltar rtog[1] med la zhugs nas rang gis[2] rang sems[3] mi rtogs[4] par bstan pa ni | gang zhig ces pa la sogs pa [(5]smos te[5)] | gang zhig ni sangs rgyas [D 275b] so | | gang la ni rang las so | | de ni sangs rgyas so | | de ru ni rang la'o | | ma mthong zhes pa ni sgyu[6] lus med na mi mthong ba'o | | gzhan ni go sla'o | |

[1] P *rtogs* [2] DP *gi* [3] DP *bzhin* [4] BDP *rtog* [5] DP *ste* [6] DP *rgyu*

DK$_T$ 82c–f

da ni nyams su blang ba'i thabs de nyid dpe'i sgo nas rgyas par bstan [(1]pa'i phyir[1)] | glang chen lobs[2] nas zhes bya ba la sogs pa smos te | glang po che 'tsho ba'i ri khrod pas glang chen lob[3] na blo bde bar gnas pa bzhin du sems kyi rtog pa btang na sems tshags su tshud pa[4] de | sems mi[5] g.yo bas [(4]so |[4)] der ni zhes pa ni rtsa dbu[6] ma der ro | | 'gro 'ong ni rlung 'gro 'ong ste | de bcad na rtsa dbus su dal ba'o | | de ni sems mi rtog pa la rnal du gzhag pa dang | rlung dbu mar rnal du gzhag pa'o | | chos ci dgos zhes pa ni rtog pa'i rnal 'byor mi dgos pa'o[7] |

| ngo tsha med smra mkhas pa nga[8] | | zhes pa ni 'dzem[9] pa med par smra ba'i mkhas pa[10] zhes pa'o |

[1] B *pa ni* [2] D *lob* P *loms* [3] P *lom* [4] DP om. [5] DP *ni* [6] DP *dbus* [7] B *zhes pa'o* [8] B *de* P *dang* [9] P *'dzom* [10] BD *pa'o*

DK$_{T}$ 83

| gson pa gang zhig ces pa la sogs [B 177b] pas ni | rnal ma'i bdud rtsi [(1]'thung nas[1)] 'chi ba med pa thob par bstan[2] te | gson po ni gzhon [P 308a] nu'i gnas skabs lta bu | khyad[3] kyi[4] rnam par ma gyur na mi rgas mi 'chi'o | | gzhan yang gson po gang zhig ni srog rlung ngo | | rnam par ma gyur pa ni | khyad[3] kyi[4] [5] dbu mas ma brkus na ste | srog thams cad dbus su bcug pas rku[6] rgyu med na skye 'chi med par 'gyur ro | | de nyid las 'od gsal gyi[7] ye shes skye bar[8] bstan pa ni | bla mas bstan pa[9] zhes bya ba la sogs pa [(10]smos te[10)] | dri med blo gros ni 'bras bu 'od gsal ba'o | | de nyid gter yin te | de skyes pa'i dus na gter te rin po che'o |

[1] B *'thung na* [2] DP *ston* [3] B *khad* [4] BP *kyis* [5] B inserts *khang kyis* P inserts *khyad kyis* [6] B *brku* [7] DP om. [8] D *ba* [9] DP *pas* [10] DP *ste*

DK$_{T}$ 84

| de ltar sems rnal du bzhag[1] pa phan yon dang bcas pa bstan nas | sems bcos pa'i thabs bstan pa'i phyir | yul nyid rnam par dag pa ste | | zhes pa la sogs pa gsungs te | de la yul nyid ni rnal ma la blo bzhag[2] pa'i tshe | yul gzhan gyi[3] rnam par rtog pa mi 'byung ba'o | | rnam par dag pa ste zhes pa ni rnal ma'i don to[4] | | bsten[5] bya min zhes pa[6] ni tshur la bkug pa slar rnal mar bzhag[2] pa ma yin [7] zhes pa'i don to[4] | | 'o na ji ltar bya snyam[8] pa la | stong pa 'ba' zhig gis ni dpyad par bya | | zhes gsungs te | yul gang du [D 276a] 'phros pa de yang[9] stong pa rang[10] yin pas tshur[11] la dgug mi dgos zhes par dgongs pa'o | | de'i dpe bstan pa'i phyir | ji ltar gzings las 'phur pa'i bya rog ni | | zhes pa la sogs pa [B 178a] gsungs te | de'i don ni dper na gzings la bzhag pa'i bya rog bzung[12] bas mi thub par 'gro ba la | de btang bas gar phyin kyang[13] tshur[14] song [15] 'chag[16] sa ma rnyed de | slar la der 'bab[17] pa bzhin du yul la 'phros[18] pa'i sems kyang de dang 'dra'o | | gar 'phros[18] kyang de nyid las ma g.yos pas so | | yul [P 308b] gcig la dmigs pa[19] mi[20] zhen par[21] shes pa glod[22] la bzhag[1] pa'o |

[1] BD *gzhag* [2] BP *gzhag* [3] BD om. [4] B *no* [5] P *sten* [6] B *bya ba* [7] B inserts *te* [8] P *mnyam* [9] B *'ang* [10] DP om. [11] D *chul* [12] P *gzung* [13] B *yang* [14] BD *chur* [15] B inserts *bas* [16] BD *'chags* [17] B *'babs* [18] P *'phos* [19] P *pas* [20] P *ma* [21] D *pas* [22] B *srod*

DK$_{T}$ 85

not commented upon

DK_T 86

| yul gcig la zhen pa'i nyes pa bstan pa'i phyir | yul la zhen [(1]pas zhes bya ba[1)] la sogs pa smos te go sla'o | | yang na tshig 'dis ni rnal 'byor pas 'dod yon la zhen pa'i skyon bstan pa'o |

[1] P *pa la*

DK_T 87

| gzhan yang lhan skyes de nyid las 'byung bar shes pas | sems [1] bcos pa'i thabs bstan pa'i phyir | gang zhig sems las zhes bya ba la sogs pa smos te | gang zhig ni rtog pa'o | | sems las rnam[2] 'phros pa[3] | zhes pa[4] ni rtog pa byung ba kun no | | de srid[5] mgon po'i rang bzhin te zhes pa ni rtsa ba'i 'od gsal ba nyid rtog par shar ba ste | dper na chu dang rlabs bzhin no | | srid dang mnyam nyid nam mkha'i rang bzhin no zhes pa ni | don de srid[6] pa ni 'khor ba'i rtog pa'o | | mnyam nyid ni mya ngan las 'das pa ste rtsa ba'i 'od gsal lo | | nam mkha'i rang bzhin ni[7] gnyis ka skye med do |

[1] B inserts *ma* [2] DP *rnams* [3] BDP *pas* [4] B *bya ba* [5] DP *nyid* [6] P *srid srid* [7] P om.

DK_T 88

| de ltar shes pa'i phan yon bstan pa'i phyir | gang zhig bstan te zhes bya ba la sogs pa gsungs te | [B 178b] de la gang zhig bstan pa ni man ngag gang zhig bla mas bstan pas[1] | gang zhig thos gyur zhes pa ni slob mas thos pa'o | | dgos pa gang yin na grub ba'o | | dam par skyol ba ni mthar phyin pa na'o | | gdug pa ni nyon mongs so | | [(2]skungs sa[2)] ni rtsa ba'i sems so | | rdul bzhin brlag ni rtsa ba nas dag pa'o | | de gang du dag na snying ga nyid du nub ste | mi shigs thig [(3]ler ro[3)] |

[1] B *pa* [2] D *bkug pa* P *skug sa* [3] DP *le'o*

DK_T 89

| der ji ltar thim par 'gyur zhe na | ji[1] ltar [D 276b] chu la chu bzhag pa | | de snyed[2] chu ru ro mnyam 'gyur | | zhes pas bstan[3] te | dper na chu nang du chu blugs pa ni |chur ro gcig pa bzhin du | [P 309a] rtsa ba'i sems su thim par 'gyur pa'o | | yang na 'dis ni gnyis med ro mnyam ston te | chu ni[4] stong pa'o | | chu bzhag pa ni snying rje'o | | chur[5] ro mnyam pa ni gnyis med du bya ba'o | | de nyid ye nas ro gcig tu bstan pa'i phyir | skyon dang zhes bya ba la sogs pa smos te | de la skyon ni rtsa ba'i sems mi shigs pa'o | | yon tan [6] ni[7] sems kyi ngo bo 'od gsal ba'o | | mnyam ldan ni gnyis po'i ro mnyam pa'o | | sus kyang mtshon ma gyur zhes[8] pa ni | | thabs dang bral ba gang gis kyang [(9]mi rtogs[9)] pa'o | | gzhan ni go sla'o |

[1] P *de* [2] D *srid* P *nyid* [3] DP *ston* [4] DP om. [5] B *chu ru* P *chu* [6] DP inserts *gyi ngo bo* [7] P *sems mi shigs pa'o | | yon tan gyi ngo bo ni* [8] B *ces* [9] D *ma rtog* P *ma rtogs*

DK$_T$ 90

| da ni [(1]lhan skyes[1)] de rang ye nas ro mnyam du gnas pas spyod lam ci snang yang thug[2] phrad du myong bar bstan pa ni | nags la mched pa'i me bzhin zhes pa la sogs pa ste go sla'o |

[1] B *lhan cig skyes pa* [2] P *thugs*

DK$_T$ 91

[B 179a] | [(1]lhan skyes[1)] de ma rtogs pa'i skyon bstan pa'i phyir | gal te yid du 'ong ba la zhes bya ba la sogs pa smos te | de la yid du 'ong ba ni yid dang 'thad[2] pa'i dngos po la'o | | snyam[3] pa'i sems ni stong pa dang ro mnyam pa'i sems ma skyes na | de la dngos por zhen pas sdug bsngal bskyed[4] do | | tshig gi don ni go sla'o |

[1] B *lhan cig skyes pa* [2] D *mi 'gag* P *'gal* [3] BDP *mnyam* [4] D *skyed*

DK$_T$ 92

| stong par zhen[1] pas mi 'ching ba'i phyir | stong [(2]pa gang yang 'dra ba[2] snyam pa la | grogs dag phag dang glang por[3] ltos | | de ltar yin te de ni ma yin no | | zhes gsungs te[4] | phag pa dang glang po ni phyogs [(5]'ga' 'dra yang[5)] | phag ni glang po ma yin no | | de bzhin du stong par 'dra yang[6] theg pa gzhan gyis[7] brtags pa'i stong pa ni lam ma yin no zhes pa'i don no | | stong pa des 'khrul pa ji ltar spang[8] zhe na | ji ltar yid bzhin nor bu zhes pa la sogs [P 309b] pa smos te | dper na smyon pa'i[9] lus la rin po che btags[10] pas smyon pa'i[9] 'khrul pa bshig pa[11] bzhin du | stong pa'i rtog pas kyang dngos po'i 'khrul pa bshig pa'o | | stong pa de bde ba'i gnas su bstan pa'i phyir | rang rig pa zhes pa[12] la sogs pa smos te | rang la rang rig bde ba chen po'i bag [D 277a] chags gzugs de bde ba'i rgyu'o | | yang na de ma dag na bag chags te | ma rig pa zhes bya'o[13] | | de nyid dag na gzugs te stong pa'i gzugs su gyur pa'o |

[1] DP *shes* [2] D *par 'dra'ang* P *na gang yang 'dra'am* [3] DP *po* [4] DP *pa ste* [5] B *'dra'ang* P *'gas 'dra yang* [6] B *'ang* [7] P *gyi* [8] DP *spong* [9] DP *ma'i* [10] P *brtags* [11] D *nga* [12] P *bya ba* [13] P *bya*

DK$_T$ 93

| de rtogs[1] pa las cir 'gyur zhe na [B 179b] thams cad ces pa la sogs pa smos te | thams cad ni phyi nang ngo | | de'i[2] tshe ni stong [(3]pa rtogs[3)] pa de'i tshe'o | | mkha' mnyam byed par 'gyur ba ni nam mkha' dang mnyam par mthong ba'o | | stong gzugs nyams su myong ba de ni tshig gis mtshon mi nus par bstan pa'i phyir | [(4]kā la kū ṭa[4)] zhes bya ba la sogs pa smos te | [(4]kā la ku ṭa[4)] ni nyams su myong ba'i ming ngo | | smos su mi rung ba ni tshig gis mi mtshon pa'o | | 'o na gang gis mtshon na | rang bzhin nam mkha' ni stong pa de rtog pa dang bral te

| yid kyis[5] 'dzin pa yin [6] zhes pa ni des myong ba'o | | 'o na yid yod dam zhe na | yid de yid med byed 'gyur te | | rang bzhin lhan cig skyes pa mchog tu mdzes | | zhes gsungs so[7] | yid de[8] zhes pa ni dag pa'i yid do | | yid med byed ces pa ni ma dag pa'i yid do | | dag pa'i yid de gang yin na | rang bzhin lhan cig skyes pa mchog tu mdzes te stong gzugs so |

[1] D *rtog* [2] DP *de* [3] B *par rtogs* D *pa rtog* [4] B *ka la ku tra* DP *kā la ku ṭa* [5] BD *kyi* [6] B inserts *gyi* [7] BD *te* [8] B om.

DK$_T$ 94

| de nyid rtogs dka' bar bstan pa'i phyir | | khyim dang khyim na de brjod[1] pa ste | | zhes pa la sogs pa gsungs te | [2] khyim na gnas pa ni khyim mo | | nags[3] na [P 310a] gnas pa ni[4] khyim min no | | de'i don brjod pa ni stong pa'o | | bde chen gnas ni de'i rgyu stong pa ste | de'i drin gyis bde ba 'char ba'o | | de'i phyir de rnams kyis stong par ma shes na | 'gro kun sems [B 180a] 'phrul gyur pa ste | sems 'khrul pas[5] dngos por zhen par gyur pa'o | [6] | de ni bsam med sus kyang rtogs ([7]ma yin[7]) | | zhes pa ni[8] bsam med kyi[9] lhan skyes de[10] | thabs gang[11] dang bral ba'i gdams[12] ngag [13] gis kyang mi rtogs pa'o |

[1] BD *nyid gnas* [2] B inserts *khyim dang khyim na de nyid ni brjod pa ste |* [3] P *gnas* [4] P *na* [5] DP *nas* [6] P inserts *| sems 'khrul nas dngos por zhen par gyur pa'o* [7] B *pa min* [8] B *la* [9] B *ni* [10] P *te* [11] B om. [12] B *man* [13] B *gang*

DK$_T$ 95

| stong pa de 'gro bas ma mthong na | | rnal 'byor pas ji ltar mthong snyam pa la | kye ma zhes pa la sogs pa smos te | mgo snying lte gsang ([1]rkang lag[1]) spangs pa ste | | ngas mthong ba'o[2] zhes pa ni gzugs med pa'i gzugs ([3]de ngas[3]) mthong ba'o | | de yang[4] | gzugs med gzugs bzang dam pa ste | | sna tshogs gzugs can yid [D 277b] las skyes | | zhes [5] gsungs so | | stong pa de thabs gang gis mthong bar 'gyur snyam pa la | bsam pas yul ni zhes pa la sogs pa gsungs te | bsam pa ni mi rtog[6] pa'i bsgom[7] pas yul ni mtshon par byed ces pa'o | | yul du snang ba stong pa'i gzugs mtshon par byed pa ste | mthong bar 'gyur ba'o | | stong gzugs de mi rtog pa'i dbang gis ji ltar mthong bar 'gyur snyam pa la | gzhan dag bsam pas rlung 'gag 'gyur | | zhes smos te | gzhan dag ni mi rtogs[8] pa'o | | bsam pa ni blo de[9] la gzhag pa'o | | rlung 'gag 'gyur zhes pa ni rlung dbus su 'jug par 'gyur ro[10] | | 'dis ni 'di skad du ston pa yin te | 'khor ba'i rtsa ba ni rlung yin pas de [P 310b] dbus su zhugs te dag [B 180b] par byas nas gzung 'dzin gyis 'brel pa chad nas[11] stong pa'i gzugs mthong bar 'gyur ro |

[1] DP om. [2] DP *ste* [3] D *te des* P *te ngas* [4] B *'ang* [5] P inserts *pas* [6] P *rtogs* [7] P *sgom* [8] BP *rtog* [9] B *bde* [10] B *ba'o* [11] B *de*

DK$_T$ 96

| rlung [(1]’gag pa’i[1)] thabs de nyid gsal bar bya pa’i phyir | gal te sems kyis[2] zhes bya ba la sogs pa smos te | mi rtog[3] pa’i sems kyis stong pa’i sems mtshon du ’gro ba ni | mthong ba rgyu des rlung dang | yid ni [(4]mi g.yo rab tu[4)] brtan par ’gyur te | rang bzhin du thim pa’o | | yid kyi rtog pa rang bzhin gnyug ma la thim pa’i dpe bstan pa ni | ji ltar lan tshwa chu la zhes [(5]bya ba la sogs[5)] pa gsungs te go sla’o |

[1] B *’gags pas* [2] D *kyi* [3] P *rtogs* [4] DP om. [5] BD *pa*

DK$_T$ 97

| bsam gtan mi dgos na[1] | sangs rgyas kyis[2] bsam gtan mang po ci’i phyir bstan snyam pa la | [(3]lha gcig[3)] la ni lung rnams mang por[4] mthong | | zhes pa la sogs pa gsungs te | de la [(3]lhan cig[3)] la zhes pa ni | de kho na nyid[5] gcig pa’o | | lung rnams mang po mthong ba ni de kho na nyid de[5] brda du ma’i sgo nas bstan pa’o | | rang gi[5] ’dod pa [(6]mang po[6)] so sor [(5]gsal bar[5)] snang | | zhes pa ni | dper na sna rtser yungs kar zhes pa lta bu ni rtog pa la dga’ ba rnams kyis steng ’og gi sna rtser thig le bsgoms pas mthong la | de kho na nyid la mos pa rnams kyis rlung byang chub sems su mthong ba’o |

[1] B *ni* [2] P *kyi* [3] D *lhan cig* [4] D *po* [5] DP om. [6] D *yis*

DK$_T$ 98

| des ji ltar mthong ba[1] de ltar mthar thug pa ma yin te | mgon po ni lhan skyes te | des sa ra ha gcig pu[2] dang mthun gyi[3] | rtog pa la gnas pa gzhan rnams dang ni ’gal lo | | don la ’gal na [B 181a] de [D 278a] thams cad nor ram snyam [(4]pa la[4)] khyim dang zhes smos te | rang rang[5] gi skal ba dang mthun pa tsam gyis grub [6] mtha’ ni ma nor ba nyid do | | de ltar sangs rgyas kyis ci dang ci bstan pa rnams ni de [P 311a] kho na nyid las brtsams te bstan gyi | rtog pa’i bsgom pa las [(7]brtsams te[7)] ni ma yin no | | da[8] ni sems de ci bde bar rtogs pas chos thams cad rtogs[9] pa’i dpe[10] bstan[11] pa ni | gcig zos[12] pas ni gzhan kun tshim | | zhes pa ste | de la gcig ni rnam shes so | | zos pas ni bde ba’i ros bsgyur ba’o | | gzhan kun ni phung po bzhin[13] no | | tshim pa ni bde ba’i ros tshim pa’o | | yang na gzhan kun tshig ces pa ste | dper na shing gcig mes ’tshigs[14] pas ’phros[15] zos nas gzhan nags tshal ’tshig[16] pa bzhin du’o | | lhan skyes de ngo ma [(17]shes na[17)] btsal bas mi rnyed par bstan pa ni | phyi rol song nas zhes pa[18] la sogs pa smos te | de la phyi rol song nas zhes pa ni rang la yod pa ngo ma shes par ro | | khyim bdag ni lhan skyes so | | ’tshol[19] ba ni btsal bas mi rnyed pa zhes pa’o |

[1] P *ba’o | | des ji ltar mthong ba* [2] DP *po* [3] D *gyis* [4] DP *na* [5] B om. [6] B inserts *pa’i* [7] B *brtsam ste* [8] D *de* [9] D *rtog* [10] P *bde* [11] DP *ston* [12] B *bros* [13] BP *bzhan* [14] DP *tshig* [15] BP *’phro* [16] DP *tshig* [17] P *mtshon* [18] B *bya ba* [19] DP *tshol*

DK$_{T}$ 99

| de nyid bshad[1] pas ni 'ongs[2] kyang ma mthong zhes pa la sogs pa smos te go sla'o | | de[3] gang gis rnyed snyam na rba rlabs med pa'i[4] zhes bya ba la sogs pa smos te | rba rlabs med pa ni rtog med do | | rtog pa ni sdug bsngal gyi rnyog pa'o[5] | | de dang bral [(6]ba'i bsam gtan ni[6)] rnam [B 181b] par mi rtog pa'i bsgom pa'o | | bsam gtan de nyid kyi dpe bstan pa ni chu dwangs[7] zhes pa[8] la sogs pa smos te | [9] chu dwangs[10] pa dang mar me rang gsal ba bzhin du rtog pas ma bslad par zhog ces pa'o |

[1] B *bshar* [2] D *'on* [3] BP om. [4] DP *pa* [5] P *ma'o* [6] DP *ba ni bsam gtan* [7] DP *dang* [8] B *bya ba* [9] P inserts *go sla'o* [10] D *dangs* P *dang*

DK$_{T}$ 100–101

| 'gro 'ong nga yis mi len mi 'dor ro | | zhes pa ni de'i tshe spyod lam gang yang mi dgag par gzhag[1] pa'o | | de yang[2] [3] dgyes pa'i rdo rje las | | [(4]gnyid ni spang bar[4)] mi [(5]bya zhing[5)] | | dbang po rnams ni dgag mi bya | | zhes [P 311b] gsungs so | | da ni stong pa'i gzugs de nyid kyi dpe bstan pa'i phyir snga na sngon med pa'i zhes bya ba la sogs pa gsungs te | dper na mi zhig[6] rmi lam na gzhon nu ma dang nyal bar rmis na | de[7] ni rang gi sems nyid der snang ba ste [D 278b] log[8] na med do | | de bzhin du sgyu ma'i lus 'di rang gi sems nyid der snang ba'o | | yang na rmi lam gyi gzhon nu ma la bsten[9] pa'i bde ba ni | gzhon nu ma dang tha mi dad de ro gcig pa'o | | de bzhin du rang gi sems ni yul can bde ba gzugs ni lus sgyu ma'o | | tha dad ma blta[10] zhig ces pa ni bde stong [11] mnyam par gyis zhes pa'o | | de yang[2] dang po'i[12] sangs rgyas kyi rgyud las kyang | gzhon nu ma yi pra las ni | | snga na med pa'i gzugs mthong ngo[13] | | zhes [(14]bya ba[14)] gsungs pa dang | | byang chub pa'i rgyud las kyang | | 'ja' tshon lta bu'i lus nyid ni | | de nyid sgom[15] pas[16] thob[17] [B 182a] par 'gyur | | zhes gsungs pa dang | klu sgrub kyis kyang | 'di nyid rdzogs pa'i rim pa ste | | sgyu ma lta bu'i ting 'dzin de | | zhes pa'o[18] | | rang gi sems ni gzugs dang zhes pa ste | gzugs de nyid gsal bar bstan[19] pa ni gal te lus dang zhes pa la sogs pa ste | rdo rje gsum [20] dbyer med pa ni stong pa'i gzugs te | de yang[2] he badzra las | sems dpa' srid pa gsum gcig pa | | zhes gsungs pas so | | yang na 'dis bde ba bstan pa yin te | lus ngag yid gsum gyi rtog pa 'gag pa ni lhan skyes kyi dga' ba'o |

[1] D *bzhag* [2] B *'ang* [3] B inserts *dpal* [4] BP *yid kyang 'gag par* D *yid kyi dag par* [5] B *byed cing* [6] B inserts *gis* [7] B *da* [8] BP *logs* [9] DP *brten* [10] DP *lta* [11] B inserts *ro* [12] P *por* [13] P om. [14] B om. [15] BP *bsgoms* [16] B *par* [17] B *'thob* [18] DP *pas so* [19] DP *ston* [20] B inserts *nyid*

DK$_{T}$ 102

| stong pa[1] nyid [(2]rtogs pas[2)] ni yul du[3] snang ba thams cad thug phrad du stong par mthong bar bstan pa ni | khyim bdag ces pa la sogs pa [(4]smos te[4)] | dper na

khyim bdag pho mo bag tsha [P 312a] med par longs spyod pa bzhin stong par brtag mi dgos par yul du snang ba rnams (5la spyod par bya'o5) | | yang na rtog med du yul la [6] spyod pa'i dpe bstan pa'o | | da ni gong gi don de dag bstan kyang | gzhan [7] gyis mi go bar bstan pa ni | nga yis zhes pa la sogs pa (4smos te4) | nga yis rtsed mo byas pa la | | zhes pa ni (8smyon pa'i8) tshig tu smras pa la'o | | byis pa rnams ni sha thang chad de[9] mi rtogs[10] pa zhes pa'o | | me ni spra ba nyid la 'bar | | zhes pa ni rang kho nas rtogs par zad ces pa'o | | yang na | | nga yis[11] [B 182b] rtsed mo byas pa la | | byis pa rnams ni sha thang chad | | ces pa[12] ni | lhan cig skyes pa nga yis rtsed mor byas pa ni | rnam [D 279a] par 'phrul pa la byis pa ma rtogs pa rnams 'khor bar khrid pa'o | | me ni spra ba nyid la [13] 'bar | | zhes pa ni mkhas pa rnams ni rtogs[14] pa'i spra ba de[1] nyid la me ye shes 'bar ba'o | | de ltar bcings pa bstan nas | da ni byang chub [15] sems ma bcings na mi 'gyur ba'i bde ba med la | de med na sangs rgyas mi 'byung pas mi 'gyur ba'i bde ba bsgrub pa'i phyir byang chub sems (16bcing bar16) bstan pa ni | (17e ma17) zhes pa la sogs pa gsungs te | gzhan na ni yod [18] ma yin zhes pa ni | | gzhan yin nam 'on te rang yin zhes pa'o | | 'on te gzhan na gnas sam ci zhes pa na | gzhan na yod dam | 'on te rtag tu yod ces pa'o | | lan du rnal 'byor (19spyod pa19) dpe dang bral ba ste zhes pa ni | yod min med min zhes bya ba la sogs pa'i[20] spros pa dang bral ba'o |

[1] P om. [2] D *rtog pa* [3] DP om. [4] DP *ste* [5] DP *spyod pa'o* [6] B inserts *longs* [7] B inserts *dag* [8] P *smyo ba'i* [9] B *ces pa ni de ni* [10] BD *rtog* [11] P *yi* [12] D *nga* [13] B inserts *rkyen gyis* [14] B *rtog* [15] B inserts *kyi* [16] D *bcings pa* P *bcings* [17] B *kye ma hoḥ* [18] B inserts *pa* [19] DP *'di ni* [20] B *pa ni*

DK$_T$ 103

| de gang las 'byung[1] zhing rang bzhin ji lta bu[2] zhe na | bdag po za zhing rang bzhin mdzes | | zhes smos te | bdag po za zhes pa ni ye shes kyi rlung ngo | | [P 312b] rang bzhin mdzes zhes pa ni | | de dag ni sgyu ma'i rnam pa yid du 'ong ba'o | | des ci byed ce[3] na chags pa'i yul gyis gang ba'i sems de nyid ces smos te | chags pa'i zhes pa zag bcas kyi bde ba'o | | yul gyis gang ba ni yul [B 183a] yid du 'ong (4bar zhen pa'o4) | | sems (5de nyid ces pa5) ni rtog pa'i sems[6] bde ba ste[7] spong[8] ba'o | | ji ltar spong[8] zhe na | chags dang chags bral byas nas gnyug mar zhugs | | zhes smos te | de la chags pa ni dpral bar gnas pa'o | | chags bral ni thig le mkha' la ltung ba'o | | byas nas zhes pa ni phab lam 'phos[9] ba ni ro mnyam pa'o[10] | | gnyug mar zhugs pa ni de las 'bras bu'i lhan skyes su 'gyur ba'o | | sgyu ma'i rnal 'byor ma de[11] thabs cis mthong zhe na | sems nyams pas na rnal 'byor ma ngas mthong | | zhes smos te | sems nyams pa ni gzung 'dzin gyi rtog pa 'gags [12] na | rnal 'byor (13ma ngas13) ni sgyu ma'i rang bzhin du[3] mthong ngo |

[1] DP *byung* [2] B *bur* [3] DP om. [4] DP *ba'i bde ba'o* [5] DP *nyid de zhes pa* [6] DP om. [7] B *de* [8] B *spang* [9] D *spro* P *pho* [10] P *pa ni* [11] P om. [12] D inserts *pa* [13] D *mas* P *pa*

DK$_T$ 104

| za zhing 'thung[1] la bsam pa'ang med | | ces pa ni bsam [D 279b] pa 'di gnyis tsam las ma gtogs pa gzhan spangs la bsgom par bya'o zhes pa'o | | de'i tshe sems la snang ba rnams ji[2] ltar blta[3] snyam pa la | grogs mo[4] 'di ni[5] zhes pa la sogs pa smos te | rang gi sems la snang [(6]ba dang[6)] phyi rol tha dad du rtog[7] na sdug bsngal [(8]gyis 'dzin no[8)] zhes pa'o[9] | | sgyu ma'i rnal 'byor 'di ni dpe dang bral | | zhes pa ni | sems la gang snang ba de sems sgyu ma'i snang bar [(10]blta ba'o[10)] | | bya ba 'di tsam zhig tu rab bsams la | zhes pa ni | snang ba'i bya ba sgyu ma tsam du bya ba'o | | rtsom pa gang la dbye[11] med pa yi blo | | zhes pa ni | | rtsom rgyu med pas rtsol pa spangs la glod la gzhag[12] [B 183b; P 313a] pa'o |

[1] D *mthong* [2] B *ci* [3] DP *lta* [4] B *dag* [5] BP *na* [6] DP *ba'i* [7] DP *rtogs* [8] B *gyis zin pa'o* D *byas 'dzin no* [9] B *so* [10] DP *lta'o* [11] BP *dbyer* [12] B *bzhag*

DK$_T$ 105

| sa gsum gang du dri ma med | | ces pa ni des lus ngag yid gsum rnam par dag par 'gyur ro | | de ltar byang chub kyi sems [(1]bcing ba'i[1)] thabs stong pa nyid bstan nas | da ni des ji ltar [(2]'ching ba'i[2)] dpe bstan pa'i phyir | zla ba chu 'dzag ces pa la sogs pa gsungs te | zla ba chu 'dzag nor bu rang dbang med ces pa ni | dper na chu shel ni zla ba'i 'od dang phrad na[3] rang dbang med par 'dzag pa'o | | thabs kyis rgyal srid kun la dbang sgyur ba | | zhes pa ni | dpe de bzhin du stong pa'i thabs kyis rgyal srid kun ni mi 'gyur ba'i bde ba'o | | dbang sgyur ba ni ji ltar 'dod pa rang dbang du byed pa'o | | sems nyid de ni grub pa'i rnal 'byor ma | | zhes pa ni shes rab stong pa'o | | lhan cig[4] skyes pa'i thabs bde ba'o | | sdom par shes par bya zhes pa ni de gnyis ro mnyam du sdom par shes par bya'o |

[1] BD *bcing pa'i* P *bcings pa'i* [2] B *bcings pa'i* [3] DP *nas* [4] D om.

DK$_T$ 106

| da ni mi 'gyur ba'i bde ba'i mtshan nyid bstan pa'i phyir | | yi ge [(1]pa yi[1)] zhes pa la sogs pa smos te[2] | de la yi ge [3] tha snyad dam brda'am mtshan ma'o | | 'gro ba ma lus zhes pa ni 'gro ba thams cad do | | yi ge med pa gcig kyang med | | ces pa ni | sems can la mtshan ma med pa gang yang med do | | ji srid yi ge med gyur pa | | zhes pa ni[4] mtshan ma'i rtog pa 'gags na zhes pa'o | | de srid yi ge rab tu shes | | zhes pa ni | mtshan ma 'gags[5] na tha snyad kun [B 184a] shes pa'o | | yi ge med pa yi ge yin | | zhes pa ni | brda[6] yi ge ste brda med na yi ge [7] a ste [P 313b] stong pa'i gzugs su rig ces pa'o | | [D 280a] | yang na de srid yi ge rab tu shes | | zhes pa ni | yi ge ni akṣara[8] ste mi 'gyur ba'i bde ba shes pa'o | | yi ge gang zhe na | yi ge med pa[9] yi ge yin | | zhes smos te | yi ge ni rtog pa ste de[10] med pa'o | | yi ge yin zhes pa ni | mi rtog pa'i bde ba'o | |

dang po'i[11] sangs rgyas las kyang | mi 'gyur las skyes 'gyur ba spangs pa'i bde ba nyid | | ces gsungs so |

[1] D *pa'i* P *pa'i* [2] P *pa te* [3] B inserts *ni* P inserts *tha snyad de* [4] P om. [5] D *'gag* [6] B *brda'i* P *brda' yi* [7] B inserts *ni* [8] D *akṣa* [9] B *pa'i* [10] DP om. [11] P *po*

DK$_T$ 107

| phyi rol pa'i yi ge la zhen pa dgag pa'i phyir | col[1] med rig byed 'don[2] pa nyams | | zhes pa ni | des don dam pa'i oṃ zhes 'don pa de nyams pa ste | 'khor bar sdug bsngal bar 'gyur ro | | de ltar yi ge med na yang[3] | | rang gi lus la rang bzhin gyis gnas pas rtogs su rung bar bstan pa'i phyir | dam pa soms dang zhes pa la sogs pa smos te | dam pa soms dang cig shos mi shes [4] na | (5| zhes pa la |5) cig shos ni stong gzugs te mi shes pa ni ma rtogs na rtog pa rnams kyang gang nas skye ba dang gnas pa dang | gang du 'gag[6] pa mi shes so |

[1] P *bcol* [2] DP *'dod* [3] B *'ang* [4] P inserts *pa* [5] P om. [6] P *'gags*

DK$_T$ 108

| de shes na ji ltar phyi rol gyi rtog pa de bzhin du nang ste stong gzugs so | | bcu bzhi pa'i[1] sa la (2rgyun du2) gnas zhes pa ni | snying ga'i[3] dbus na gnas pa'o | | de ni gzugs med kyang lus su gnas pa'o | | gang gis [B 184b] de shes pa'i mi de grol bar 'gyur ro | | yang na bde ba dang sbyar na cig shos ni[2] bde ba'o | | gang nas shar ba ni dpral ba nas so | | gang du nub pa ni nor bu las[2] 'das pa'o | | ji ltar phyi rol de bzhin nang | | zhes pa ni | shu kra de ni phyi rol gyi zla ba ni[4] tshes gcig (5dkar po'i5) yar ngo [P 314a] nas tshes bco lnga la[2] nya gang ba'o | | (6yar ngo'i6) tshes gcig shar nas gnam stong la zla ba zad pa'o | | de bzhin du shu kra yang[7] dpral bar dkar po'i tshes gcig shar nas nor bu'i nang du nya gang ba'o | | de nas nor bur[8] gnas nas bcu drug gi cha nag po'i tshes gcig la[2] nor bu shar nas | gtsug tor du gnam stong rdzogs pa'o | | bcu bzhi pa'i[1] sa la (2rgyun du2) gnas zhes pa ni rang bzhin gyi[9] gnas lugs te | go bzlog pa ni lam du 'gro ste | shu kra de 'pho ba'i bag chags (10spang ba10) ni kha gyen du bltas nas 'khor lo drug dang bar du[11] drug ste bcu gnyis (2so |2) [D 280b] rin po che'i 'khor lo dang | ba rā[12] ṭa ka rtog med (13kyi sa13) ste bcu bzhir rim gyis 'grims[14] nas sa bcu dag par 'gyur ro | | de yang[7] he badzra las | | bde ba chen po ā li'i gzugs | | de yi cha ni rnal 'byor ma | | gang phyir bcu drug cha med pas | | 'bad pa kun gyi lhag ma spang | | zhes gsungs so | | lus med lus la gnas pa ni | | de yi dbang gis ma skyes pa ste | de yang[7] he badzra las | lus gnas lus las me skyes pa'o | | zhes [B 185a] gsungs pas so | | gang gis de shes de yid[15] grol | | zhes pa ni | sa bcu bgrod pa'i ye shes de'o |

[1] B *pa yi* [2] DP om. [3] B *gi* [4] B om. [5] DP *shar ba'i* [6] B *tshes bcu drug la mar ngo'i* D *mar po'i* [7] B *'ang* [8] DP *bu'i* [9] BD *gyis* [10] B *spangs pa* [11] P om. [12] BDP *ra* [13] P *kyis* [14] B *'grems* [15] B *yis*

DK_T 109

| bde ba de gang las ji ltar byung snyam na | | nga yis sgrub pa'i yi ge dang po bton | | zhes pa[1] la sogs pa gsungs te | sgrub pa'i yi ge dang po ni stong gzugs so | | bton pa ni rig pa'o | | khu ba 'thungs pas nga[2] ni brjed[3] par gyur | | zhes pa ni |stong [(4]pa de'i[4)] drin gyis khu ba 'thungs ba ni | | 'pho ba spangs pas nga ni brjed par gyur[5] | | zhes pa ste[6] | sems kyi rtog pa 'gags [7] nas bde bar [(8]'gyur [P 314b] ba'o[8)] | | de'i rang bzhin ji lta bur[9] zhe na | gang gis zhes pa la sogs pa gsungs so[10] | | yi ge gcig shes[11] pa ni mi 'gyur ba'i bde ba'o | | yang na a ste stong gzugs so | | de yi ming ni mi shes so | | zhes pa ni | mtshan ma'am 'du shes kyi chos nub pa'o |

[1] B *bya ba* [2] BP *ngas* [3] D *brjod* [4] DP *pa'i* [5] B *'gyur* [6] DP *ni* [7] D inserts *pa* [8] D *gyur pa'o* [9] DP *bu* [10] B *te* [11] D *ces*

DK_T 110

| nags khrod gsum ni lus ngag yid gsum mo | | yi ge gcig ni a[1] ste gzhom med do | | yi ge gsum gyi dbus na lha | | zhes pa ni | rlung dgang[2] dgug rengs gsum [3] ni yi ge oṃ āḥ hūṃ gsum gyi[4] [(5]gzhom med[5)] dag gi dbus na lha ste[6] stong gzugs su 'gyur ro | | gang zhig gsum las[7] 'babs[8] pa ni | | zhes pa ni lus ngag yid gsum [9] las 'byung ba'i chags pa ste[10] stong pa'i drin gyis gdol pa[11] rig byed ces pa ni rtog med kyi[12] dga' ba bzhi po[12] 'char ba'o |

[1] D *ā* [2] BD *dag* [3] B inserts *gyis* [4] D *gyis* [5] B *'joms byed de* [6] B om. [7] DP *la* [8] D *bab* P *'bab* [9] B inserts *mo | | lus ngag yid gsum* [10] DP *de* [11] BDP *pa'i* [12] DP om.

DK_T 111

| de [B 185b] ltar zag med kyi bde ba bstan nas zag bcas 'gyur ba'i bde ba spang ba'i phyir | ma lus rang bzhin mi shes gang | | zhes [(1]smos te |[1)] 'od gsal gyi rang bzhin mi shes pas | kun du ru ni las [(2]rgya las[2)] | [(3]bde chen[3)] ni zag med kyi bde ba'o | | ji [D 281a] ltar skom[4] pas smig rgyu[5] bsnyeg[6] pa bzhin | | skom[7] nas 'chi ste nam mkha'i chu rnyed dam | zhes pa ni bde ba'i rnam pa 'dra yang[8] don mi 'dra ba la 'dra bar 'khrul nas skom par 'chi ste | sdug bsngal gyis bzung nas bde chen mi rnyed do |

[1] DP *pa ni* [2] D *rgyas pas* [3] B *bde ba chen po* [4] P *sgom* [5] DP *rgyur* [6] D *bsnyag* [7] B *sgom* [8] B *'ang*

DK_T 112

| ci ste mi rnyed ce na | rdo rje padma gnyis kyi bar gnas pa | | zhes gsungs te | rdo rje dang[1] padma gnyis kyi bar du gnas pa'i bde ba'o | | bde ba gang gis rnam par bskyed pa ni | zhes pa ni | de gnyis bde bar rnam par rang mthun[2] yang | zhes pa'o | | ci ste de bstan[3] nus pa med pas na | | zhes pa ni zag med kyi bde ba

de bskyed[4] [P 315a] pa'i nus pa med pas na | sa gsum [(5]re ba gang gis rdzogs par 'gyur[5)] | | zhes pa ni lus ngag yid gsum po de ji ltar 'dag ces pa'o |

[1] P om. [2] P *'thun* B *bstan* [3] D *snyed* P *bskyed* [4] B *ji ltar bstan* D *skyes* [5] B *gang du rdzogs su re ba lags*

DK$_{T}$ 113

| yang na rdo rje padma'i bde ba de med na yang[1] | zag med kyi bde ba de[2] ji ltar [(3]skye ste | mi skye[3)] zhes pa'o | | kun du ru'i bde ba de ci ste | rnal ma'i bde ba ma yin zhe na | thabs kyi bde ba skad cig ma | | zhes pa gsungs te | skad cig ma yin pa dang[4] | yang na de nyid gnyis su 'gyur ba ste | | zhes pa [(5]smos te[5)] shes rab ma las[6] skyes pa'i ye shes de shes rab ye shes yin na | thabs las skyes pa'i [B 186a] ye shes kyang shes rab thabs kyi ye shes su 'gyur ro | | bla ma'i drin gyis slar yang ni | | brgya lam[7] 'ga' yis shes par 'gyur | | zhes pa la[8] | slar yang zhes pa ni shes rab ye shes de sems can kun la skye yang thig le gsum pa'i[9] mthar skyes pa'i lhan cig skyes pa ngo shes pa ni brgya [(7]lam na[7)] 'ga' tsam gyis[10] shes par 'gyur ba'o | | de bas na slar yang zhes pa ni phyi nas te | thig le gsum gyi mthar ro |

[1] B *'ang* [2] BD om. [3] D *skyes* [4] B *dag* [5] DP *ni* [6] P *lus* [7] B *las* P *la* [8] D *smos te* [9] P *po'i* [10] P *gyi*

DK$_{T}$ 114

| da ni bde stong zung du 'jug pa bstan pa'i phyir | [1] grogs dag ces pa la sogs pa smos te | grogs dag ni bod pa'o | | zab mo ni bde ba'o | rgya che ba ni stong pa'o | | gzhan min ni tha dad min pa'o | | bdag nyid ma yin pa ni gcig nyid kyang ma yin te | gnyis ma grub pa'o[2] | | yang na stong pa nyid ces gcig pu la sbyar te zab pa ni rtogs dka' ba'o[2] | | rgya che ba ni stong pa[3] nyid gcig pur[4] rtogs na chos kun rtogs pa'o | | gzhan min ni rang [D 281b] gis[5] rig pas so | | bdag nyid min pa[3] ni rtogs[6] pa'i bdag nyid ma yin pa'o[7] | | de lta bu de dus na ma skye na | | lhan [P 315b] cig skyes dga''[8] bzhi pa'i dus | | zhes pa la sogs pa smos te | lhan cig skyes pa'i dga' ba ni bzhi pa'i dus te | snang ba gsum la ltos pa'i bzhi pa'i dus kyi 'od gsal gyi ngo bo nyid do | | gnyug ma nyams su myong bas shes | | zhes pa ni | dus rtag tu yod pa'i lhan cig skyes pa [B 186b] de'o |

[1] B inserts *kye* [2] DP *pas so* [3] DP om. [4] DP *pu* [5] P *gi* [6] B *rtog* [7] B *te* [8] B *pa*

DK$_{T}$ 115

| de shar ba'i yon tan bstan pa'i phyir | | mun nag ces pa la sogs pa smos te | [(1]bde ba chen po'i dus[1)] ji ltar mun pas g.yogs pa la | zla ba shar bas mun pa'i tshogs dus gcig la 'joms pa ltar bde ba chen po shar ba'i [(1]dus gcig na[1)] | sdig pa ma lus pham [(2]par byed[2)] | | [(3]zhes pa smos te[3)] | rtog[4] pa thams cad 'joms par byed do |

[1] P om. [2] B *skad cig la* [2] B *byed pa'o* [3] DP *ces pa ste* [4] P *rtogs*

DK_T 116

| sdug bsngal snang byed ni[1] rtog pa nub pa'o | | [(2]skar ma'i[2)] bdag po ni mi[3] rtog pa'i ye shes so | | bza' dang mnyam du shar zhes pa ni[4] | nang gi bza' ye shes kyi rlung dang dus gcig tu shar ba'o | | des cir 'gyur zhe na | 'di ltar gnas pas sprul pa sprul pa dang | | zhes pa ni[5] sprul pa 'byung ba dang | de ni dkyil 'khor 'khor lo dam pa'o | | zhes pa ni [(6]ma bcos pa'i dkyil 'khor ro |[6)]

[1] D *na* [2] DP *sgrol ma'i* [3] D *me* [4] P *na* [5] B *ste* [6] P om.

DK_T 117

[(1]| kye [2] ho zhes pa ni ci yang bod pa'o | | des ci ltar 'gyur na[3] sems kyis[4] zhes pa ni | rang gi sems kyis so | | sems la zhes pa ni rang bzhin rtog med ci yang[5] ma yin pa la | rtogs[6] ces pa ni de la sems bzhag pa'o | | lta ba ngan pa thams cad las [(7]ni grol gyur te[7)] zhes pa ni[1)] cir[8] yang ma yin na sgro 'dogs skur 'debs kun las grol bar 'gyur ro[9] | | mchog tu bde ba chen po'i[10] dbang gis ni | | zhes pa ni[11] | mchog tu bde ba chen po ni zag med kyi dga' ba ste | de'i dbang gis ni mthus so | | [(12]de la gnas na[12)] dngos grub dam pa ni sangs rgyas kyi go [B 187a] 'phang grub pa'o |

[1] P om. [2] D inserts *ma* [3] D om. [4] D *kyi* [5] B *'ang* [6] BP *rtog* D om. [7] D *grol* [8] DP *ci* [9] B *ba'o* [10] B *po de yi* [11] B *la* [12] DP om.

DK_T 118

| de ltar bde stong dbyer med kyi yon tan bstan nas | da ni stong pa dang bde ba la sems bzhag pa'i thabs bstan pa'i phyir | sems kyi glang po zhes bya ba la sogs pa smos te | sems kyi glang po yan du chug | [D 282a] ces pa ni | nan tshir[1] du mi dgag ces pa'i don to | | da ni bdag [P 316a] nyid la dris shig ces pa ni | sems rang lugs su zhog cig ces pa'o | | de la rtogs pas ma dris cig | ces pa ni | de'i[2] tshe mtshan ma yid la mi bya'o | | da ni sems bde ba la bzhag pa'i thabs bstan pa'i phyir nam mkha'i ri bo zhes pa[3] la sogs pa smos te | de la nam mkha' ni spyi bo'o[4] | | ri bo ni lus[5] so | | chu 'thung ni shu kra'i bde ba myong ba'o | | de'i 'gram du zhog ces pa ni | gnyug ma'i dbang po'i rtsar bzhag pa'o | | rang dga' bar[6] ni ci bde bar[7] bag yangs su'o |

[1] B *btsir* [2] D *'di'i* [3] B *bya ba* [4] P *bo* [5] P *lugs* [6] D *bas* P *ba* [7] DP om.

DK_T 119

| ji ltar gzhag[1] snyam pa la | yul gyi glang[2] po'i[3] zhes pa la sogs pa smos te | yul gyi zhes pa ni phyi rol gyi glang po che rgyal po'i lag pas khrid nas ji ltar bskyod[4] par snang yang zhes pa ste | rang gang dga' bar bskyod[4] pa ltar rnal 'byor pa yang[5] sems kyi glang po la dbang [(6]sgyur bar[6)] byed do[7] | | rnal 'byor pa

ni glang po [(8]skyong ba[8)] bzhin | | zhes pa ni ma bsgrims ma [(9]gtad pas[9)] so | | de nyid nas ni ldog par 'gyur ba yin | | zhes pa ni rang log tu 'gyur ba'o |

[1] P *bzhag* [2] DP *dbang* [3] D *po* [4] B *spyod* P *skyod* [5] B *'ang* [6] DP om. [7] B *pa'o* [8] DP *bskyod pa* [9] B *btang bas*

DK_T 120

| dbyer med du gzhag[1] par bya ba'i thabs bstan pa'i phyir | [B 187b] gang zhig 'khor ba zhes pa[2] la sogs pa smos te | gang zhig 'khor ba de ni mya ngan 'das par nges | | zhes bya ba ni 'khor ba rang la thar pa'o | | yul gyi dbye bas gzhan du sems [(3]par ma byed cig | ces[3)] pa ni | yul lnga'i dbye bas phyi rol tu mi lta'o[4] | | de ci'i phyir zhe na | rang bzhin gcig pa gis[5] [(6]zhes pa la sogs pa smos te | rang bzhin gcig pa[6)] ni yul dang yul can tha mi dad du'o | | dbye ba rnams spangs [(6]pa ni tha dad kyi dbye ba spangs[6)] pa'o | | dri med ni gnyis 'dzin med pa'o |

[1] P *bzhag* [2] P *bya ba* [3] DP *pa ma yin te zhes* [3] B *blta ba'o* [4] B *gi* P *ni* [5] D om. [6] P om.

DK_T 121

| dbyer med kyi 'thad ba bstan pa'i phyir | yid [P 316b] kyi[1] de nyid ces pa[2] la sogs pa smos te | dmigs bcas ni snying rje'o | | dmigs med ni stong pa'o | | gnyis la skyon yod ni ma 'dres na'o[3] |

DK_T 122

| bde ba'i rang bzhin ni ro mnyam du'o | | rab tu bla med [(4]rang 'byung[4)] ba | zhes[5] pa ni | gang dang yang ma 'grogs par byung[6] ba'o | | gzhan ni go sla'o |

[1] B *kyis* [2] B *bya ba* [3] B *pa'o* [4] P *rab 'byung* [5] D *ces* [6] P *gyur*

DK_T 123

| da ni gnyis med la gnas pa [(1]zhes pa[1)] la gnas la nges pa med par [D 282b] bstan pa'i phyir | [(2]nags su ma[2)] 'gro zhes pa[3] la sogs pa smos te | gang yang de[1] ru zhes pa ni nags dang khyim du'ang[4] shes[5] pa ni[6] mnyam par ro | | ma lus rgyun du [(7]byang chub[7)] rtogs pas gnas | | zhes pa ni gnyug ma'i rang bzhin no | | gzhan ni go sla'o |

[1] P om. [2] D *gsum* [3] B *bya ba* [4] D *du 'ongs* P *du yong* [5] BD *zhes* [6] B *ste* [7] DP om.

DK_T 124

| de la gnas pa'i yon tan bstan pa'i phyir | de tshe dgra'i[1] zhes pa la sogs pa smos te |

DK_T 125
mi rtog pa ni[2] rtog[3] pa'i rigs la mi 'jug pas na'o[4] | ([5]dgra'i rigs la mi 'jug pa'o |[5]) |'di [B 188a] ltar dbye ba yongs shes na | | zhes pa ni bzang ngan mnyam par ro |

DK_T 126
| dbye ba de[6] ni yongs su 'ching dang bral par bya[7] || zhes pa ni | gnyis kyi 'du shes spangs pa'o | | tha dad du snang ba de nyid[6] ji[8] ltar yin zhe na | [9] ji ltar rgya mtsho mthong phye bzhin | | zhes pa ni | chu dwangs[10] pa'i nang du byad kyi gzugs brnyan snang ba bzhin no |

[1] B *'gro ba'i* [2] DP *de* [3] D *rtogs* [4] DP *na* [5] BP om. [6] P om. [7] DP *byas* [8] B *ci* [9] B inserts *rgya mtsho me tog dang 'dzin pa chod la | mig gis bltas na legs par mthong ngam dris pa dang | mthong ste | me tog gcig pu 'dug zer ro | de yin nam min rtog na | yang rlung dang 'phrad par byas kyang sngar ltar song ngo | | me tog bsal te bltas pas rang gi byad gzugs brnyan la klu byung snyam ste brgyal lo | de bzhin du snang ba thams cad sems yin pas sems 'khrul te 'khor bar 'khyams pa'o | | yang na bar do la sbyor ro |* [10] DP *dangs*

DK_T 127
| bdag dang gzhan du 'khrul par ma byed dang[1] | | zhes pa ni gcig la gnyis su 'khrul pa'o | | de ltar thabs kyi lhan cig skyes pa bzhi bstan nas | da ni 'bras bu'i lhan cig skyes pa rgyas par bstan pa'i phyir | thams cad snga nas[2] ([3]gnas pa'i sangs rgyas te[3]) | | zhes bya ba la sogs pa smos te | sems ni ngo bo nyid ([4]kyis dag[4]) | ces pa ni ye nas so |

DK_T 128
| gnyis med du[5] ni ro mnyam du'o | | ma lus khyab [P 317a] par song ni sems can gyi don du'o | | ([6]de yi[6]) ming ni gzhan la phan pa'o (128d) zhes pa ni | don la bdag[6] gzhan med ces bya'o |

[1] B *cig* [2] BP *na* [3] DP *med pa yi* P *med pa'i* [4] P *kyi bdag* [5] P om. [6] DP om.

DK_T 129
| sna tshogs du mar[1] dang ldan zhes pa ni | phrin las [B 188b] sna tshogs pa'o | | lhun gyis grub pa ni ma btsal bar ro | | phyi ma'i 'bras bu ni thams cad la'o | | bde ba 'di ni gzhan pa'i sems min[2] no zhes pa ni zag bcas min pa'o |

[1] D *ma* [2] DP *mi mngon*

DK_T 130
([1]da ni[1]) bzlog[2] pa'i sgo nas bstan pa'i phyir | | stong pa'i sdong po dam pa zhes pa la sogs pa smos te | stong pa'i sdong po med na snying rje'i yal 'dab med do

zhes pa'i don to[3] | | da ni dmigs par 'dzin pa'i skyon bstan pa'i phyir | de la dmigs par byed pa gang yin pa | | zhes pa la sogs pa smos te | de la dmigs par byed pa ni gnyis med de la rtog pas mtshan mar 'dzin pa'o | | der lhung bas[4] ni zhes pa mtshan mar 'dzin pas [D 283a] lhung pa'o | | yan lag chad par 'gyur zhes pa ni | 'khor bar nyon mongs pa'o |

[1] DP om. [2] B *ldog* [3] B *no* [4] DP *ba*

DK_T 131

| mtshan med du[1] rtogs pa'i yon tan bstan pa'i phyir | sa bon [(2]de las[2)] zhes pa la sogs pa smos te | sa bon gcig pa ni rang bzhin[2] gi sems so | | [(3]sdong po[3)] gnyis zhes pa ni bde stong gnyis so | | rgyu mtshan de las 'bras bu gcig | ces pa ni ro mnyam du'o | | de yang[4] dbyer med ni 'dres pa'o | | gang sems pa ni bsgom pa'o | | de ni 'khor ba dang mya ngan las 'das par grol [5] zhes pa ni | mi gnas pa'i mya ngan las 'das pa thob pa'o |

[1] P om. [2] DP om. [3] D *stong pa* [4] B *'ang* [5] B inserts *ba'o*

DK_T 132

| de lta bu'i gang zag de la 'dod pa can [(1]gyi skye bo[1)] ni don du gnyer ba'o | | [(1]gang zhig[1)] slong pa[2] po ni[1] 'ongs pa'i tshe | de ni gal te 'gro na re ba med | | ces pa ni | 'gro ba gang la yang[3] lan la re ba med [P 317b] par ster ba'o | | [(1]da ni[1)] rang don [B 189a] med par[4] gzhan don mi 'grub par bstan pa ni | kham por dum bu zhes bya ba la sogs pa smos te |

[1] DP om. [2] P *po* [3] B *'ang* [4] B *pas*

DK_T 133

ji ltar slong[5] mo pa ni | gzhan gyi don mi byed [6] gzhan la phan mi 'dogs pa'o | | 'dod pa po la mi ster ba ni sbyin pa mi gtong ba'o | | 'khor ba'i 'bras bu gang yin lo[7] | | zhes pa ni 'khor bar skyes pa don med du byas pa'o | | de bas rang nyid dor bar byas na rung | | zhes pa ni bdag don du gnyer ba bor na rung zhes pa ste | gzhan don bya'o zhes pa'o | | yang na bdag gzhan gyi don byed[8] kyang ma zhen[9] na | 'khor ba'i nyes pas mi gos par [(10]bstan to[10)] | gzhan gyi don ni mi byed la[11] | zhes[12] pa ni phan 'dogs pa'i 'du shes mi byed pa'o | | 'dod pa po la mi ster ba ni sbyin pa'i zhen pa med pa'o | | [(13]'di ni[13)] 'khor ba'i 'bras bu gang yin lo[14] | | zhes pa ni | de la 'khor bas mi gos pa'o | | de bas rang nyid bor[15] bar byas na rung | | zhes pa ni ngar 'dzin gyi zhen pa [(16]spang ba'o[16)] | | kham por dum bu la sogs pa ni | dper na slong ba po la byin pa'i lan la[17] mi re ba bzhin du blta[18] bar bya'o zhes pa'o |

[1] DP om. [2] P om. [3] B *'ang* [4] DP *par* [5] P *slongs* [6] DP insert *pa ni* [7] P *la'o* [8] DP *med*

[9] D *zhe* [10] DP *ston te* [11] DP *pa* [12] D *zhen* [13] DP om. [14] P *la'o* [15] D *por* [16] DP *spangs pa'o* [17] D om. [18] P *lta*

| bla ma'i zhal gyi bka' drin gyis[1] |
| cung zad snying po'i don bshad par[2] |
| bdag gis[3] dge ba gang bsags pas |
| 'gro kun snying po'i don rtogs shog |
[1] P *gyi* [2] D *pa* [3] D *gi*

do ha mdzod kyi dka' 'grel slob dpon chen po thar pa'i 'byung gnas sbas pas mdzad pa rdzogs [D 283b] so || || rgya gar gyi [B 189b] mkhan po rgyal ba'i lha dang | rgya lo tsā bas bsgyur pa'o ||

English Translation

Commentary on the Treasury of Spontaneous Songs

In Sanskrit: *Dohākoṣapañjikā*
In Tibetan: *Do ha mdzod kyi bka' 'grel*

Homage to the youthful Mañjuśrī!

I bow to the coemergent,
this equal taste of emptiness and compassion!

Homage at the feet of the guru,
who conquered with his oral nectar
Death's subjugation of sentient beings!

To benefit sentient beings,
I will wake up my dull intellect
and write this *Commentary on the Treasury of Spontaneous Songs.*

> Like poisonous snakes, unworthy [gurus]
> will certainly tarnish good people
> with the stains of their faults.
> One should fear the mere sight [of them]![1] 1

Since it has been said that in Mantrayāna perfect enlightenment depends on the guru, one must first investigate the guru. Since relying on an inauthentic guru causes one's destruction, [Saraha first] teaches the faults of [fake gurus] in the verse starting "[Like] poisonous snakes." Oppressed by the heat that precedes the monsoon, for example, one [can] mistake a poisonous snake for a shadow, draw near, and be killed. Likewise, one [can] take fake gurus for genuine ones and, oppressed by suffering, approach them. By then relying on them,

1. It should be noted that Mokṣākaragupta does not quote the verses of the root text in full. Their translation is from the edition of the standard Tibetan root text (DK$_T$).

one gets tarnished by their wrong views and conduct, so one should regard them as poisonous snakes to be avoided.

Brahmans, not knowing true reality,
merely recite the four Vedas. 2 (DK_A 1)

[With] earthen [vessels], water, and *kuśa* grass,
they sit at home performing fire offerings.
These useless fire offerings
burn their eyes with pungent smoke. 3 (DK_A 2)

[Some] carry [one] staff, [some] three staves [tied together], and [some] are in the guise of a holy man.
Some teach in terms of the difference [between self and soul][2] and the swan.
They do not know right any more than wrong
and lead people into falsehoods. 4 (DK_A 3)

One wonders who these snake-like gurus are. From "Brahmans not knowing true reality" up to "and lead people into falsehoods," [Saraha] teaches that they are the brahmans. "Merely recite the [four] Vedas" until "they sit at home performing fire offerings" (3b) refers to [brahman] householders. The remaining words, starting "[Some] carry [one] staff," teach about those who follow asceticism. "Staff" stands for the vows [of asceticism]. The [brahmans] include those who [maintain] discipline and teach through [the example of] the swan.

[Śaiva] masters smear their bodies with ash.[3]
On their heads they wear this pile of braided hair.
They stay in their homes and light butter lamps.
Sitting in the right corner, they ring bells. 5 (DK_A 4)

With eyes blinking and the posture of sitting cross-legged,
they mislead people, whispering in their ears.
They teach widows, shaven [women],[4] and other types [of people],
bestow empowerments, and take the guru's fee. 6 (DK_A 5)

2. See Schaeffer 2005, 133–34.

3. Following the Apabhraṃśa. Lit.: "Smearing [their] body with the ash of masters."

4. In his commentary, Advayavajra refers to them with both a feminine realtive pronoun and a femine compound.

From "[Śaiva] masters [smear their bodies with] ash" (5a) until "teach others" (6d),[5] he teaches [that the fake gurus] are the Śaiva. [These lines are] easy to understand.

They have long nails, and their bodies have [mere] filth as
clothing.
Naked and [their] hairs pulled out,
the Jaina, [with the] outfit of [such] a harmful path,
deceive themselves for the sake of liberation. 7 (DK_A 6)

If going naked means liberation,
then dogs and foxes would have it.
If liberation lay in pulling out hair,
girls' buttocks would be liberated. 8 (DK_A 7)

If liberation is seen in the grasping of a [bunch of] peacock
feathers,
peacocks and yaks[6] [would certainly attain it].
If one can be liberated by eating whatever one finds,
why are horses and elephants not liberated? 9 (DK_A 8)

Saraha says: "For the Jaina there is
no possibility of liberation at all." 10ab (DK_A 9ab)

From "They have long nails" until "no possibility of liberation," he teaches that [the fake gurus] are the Jaina. [These lines] are easy to understand.

Bereft of blissful reality,
with only physical austerity, 10cd (DK_A 9cd)

novices, monks, and those called *sthavira*—
[those] ascetics take up homelessness.
Some are bogged down in explaining sūtras.
Some cling to the system of the single-flavored mind. 11 (DK_A 10)

5. Mokṣākaragupta must have had a different version of this verse, whose last line reads: *dbang rnams bskur zhing bla ma'i yon rnams len.*

6. Apa.: "elephants and horses."

From "with only physical austerity"[7] until "cling to the system of the single-flavored mind (i.e., the pratyekabuddhas)," he teaches that [the fake gurus] are those who have taken up the Hīnayāna.

> Yet others run after the Mahāyāna.
> This [Mahāyāna] is [that of] the textual tradition, the treatises on valid cognition. 12ab

From "[Yet others] run after the Mahāyāna" until "the treatises on valid cognition," he teaches that [the fake gurus] are those who have entered the causal vehicle.

> Some cultivate everything as the maṇḍala circle.
> Some are engaged in explaining the meaning of the fourth [empowerment].[8]
> Investigating, they fall away from the path. 12cde[9] (DK_A 11)

> [Some] develop concepts about the element of space.
> Still others develop views on emptiness.
> In general, they stand in contradiction. 13

With "[Some] develop concepts about the element of space" (DK_T 13a), he teaches that [the fake gurus] are those who share instructions in common with non-Buddhists. They look at space, look at time, and look at directions. As for the first among these, because clouds arise suddenly in the cloudless sky, they regard [space] as impermanent. They also regard [time] as impermanent because of [its] temporal changes, and directions [as impermanent] because the sun rises in the east and sets in the west.

> [Some] are engaged in explaining the meaning of the fourth.[10] 12d

As for "[some] are engaged in explaining the meaning of the fourth," [some] understand the fourth in terms of the third and rely on it as Buddhist bliss.

7. Line 10c should have been the beginning here.

8. Line 12d is only quoted after line 13a.

9. The line 12e was probably unknown to Mokṣākaragupta.

10. DK_T 12d is repeated here to fit the commentary.

> Some among them are bereft of true reality. 14a[11] (DK_A 12)

"Some among them are bereft of true reality" means some are bereft of an unmistaken [realization of] true reality. Recognize that these fake gurus are like this and shun them! Different from these are the gurus who unmistakenly realize true reality and can teach it—you must rely on them.

> Does he who is pleased by whatever [practice strikes his fancy]
> and takes up the [respective] meditation attain liberation? 15ab
> (DK_A 13)

Then one must search to find out what true reality is. First, to understand what true reality is not, one must know and abandon all forms of focused concentration that do not accord with true reality. In this respect [Saraha says:] "Does he who is pleased by whatever [practice strikes his fancy]" and so forth. "Does he who" refers to a person, "by whatever" refers to the chosen deities and the like, and "strikes" means that he really believes that this [which strikes his fancy] liberates him. "The meditation" here refers to generation-stage meditation. As for not attaining liberation, this means to not become a buddha, because in the *Hevajratantra* [I.v.11b] it is said: "There is neither mantra nor deity." And in the *Nāmasaṃgīti* [VI.12c] it is said: "[Sugata,] without 'mine,' without 'I.'"

> What use are butter lamps? What use are food offerings to
> deities?
> Why do we need to take up the Secret Mantra [Vehicle]? 16ab

As for "What use are butter lamps? What use are food offerings to deities? Why do we need to take up the Secret Mantra [Vehicle]?" these questions make the point that one is not liberated by delighting [deities] through offerings and recitation.

> Going to bathing places and penance—this is not needed.
> Is liberation attained by bathing in water? 16cd (DK_A 14)

From "[Going to] bathing places" up to "Is [liberation] attained?" [teaches] that one is not liberated by looking (*darśana*) at images of deities.[12]

11. The standard Tibetan root text (DK_T) reads "bereft of coemergent [bliss]."

12. Mokṣākaragupta's explanation seems to be misplaced and fits better lines DK_T 16ab.

[Trying to] understand emptiness without compassion,
one will not find the supreme path.
Cultivating only compassion on the other hand,
one will remain here in saṃsāra and not attain liberation. 17

One may ask then, What is true reality? Saraha says: "[Trying to understand emptiness] without compassion" and so forth. The meaning of this is that empti[ness] and compassion are of equal taste. What is empti[ness] here? Illusory appearances, which are empty of entities or existence. It is also the empti[ness] endowed with all supreme aspects. In the *Nāmasaṃgīti* [VIII.3ab] it is said: "[Discriminative wisdom is] formless, of lovely form, and supreme; it appears in many forms and is made of mind...."[13]

This is also because it is said in this [*Treasury of Spontaneous Songs*]: "The yogin of illusion realizes the supreme."[14] This is directly seen, but it is not the case that something like a nihilistic or eternalist empti[ness can]not be directly seen. In the *Vajrapañjara* it is said: "If emptiness were the means, then there would be no buddhahood, because the result would not differ from the cause."[15] Not being devoid of compassion is uncontaminated bliss. Not only is it empty of suffering, but also it is the bliss free of any referent object. This is also clear from the [*Cakra*]*saṃvara*[*tantra* 1.15]:

The bliss of gods and men
combined cannot be compared
to the [bliss of] the sixteenth digit of the moon[16] [produced[17]]
by Vajradhara[18] (i.e., coemergent wisdom).[19]

13. See Wayman 2006, 86.

14. This verse line could not be identified, but it has similarities to DK_T 64c.

15. D 419, *Āryaḍākinīvajrapañjara*, fol. 31a.

16. *Digit* is a technical term for a moon phase, which stands for the drop having reached the crown of the head (i.e., enlightenment). In common usage the phrase "something does not even equal the sixteenth digit" means that it is less then nothing, as the sixteenth digit is a black nothingness. It should also be noted, as our second reviewer remarks, that in some cases, authors refer to the sixteenth digit as the most important: it is the only one that is always present—which never decays, so to speak—and in fact permits the regeneration of the moon.

17. Supplied from the Tibetan in the Dergé Tengyur.

18. According to Bhavabhaṭṭa's *Cakrasaṃvaravivṛti* (27_{4-5}): "The vajra stands for a stainless intellect. Being subtle, it is [like] a filament. *Vajrakaṇikā* is a *karmadhāraya* compound and stands for coemegrent wisdom" (*vajraṃ nirmalā buddhiḥ, tad eva kaṇikā sūkṣmatvāt | vajraṃ ca kaṇikā ceti vajrakaṇikā, sahajaṃ jñānam ity arthaḥ*).

19. *Cakrasaṃvaratantra* 1.15 (26_{19-20}): *divyamānuṣyatāsaukhyam piṇḍīkṛtya tad eva ca | tad eva*

In this very [text] it is [also] said: "Who can be supported [by the two, emptiness and compassion]…."[20] From "[Trying to understand emptiness] without compassion" to "not attain [liberation]," a few [say that here Saraha teaches that this] is not a path.

> Being able to unite both of them,
> one abides in neither saṃsāra nor nirvāṇa. 18

As to "[Being able to unite] both of them," the equal taste [of emptiness and compassion] is taught to be the path. This is because one must cultivate a path that accords with the result.

> Hey, whatever has been said is false and wrong. Get rid of it!
> Whatever you are attached to—abandon it!
> When you understand, this is everything.
> Nobody knows anything other than this. 19 (DK_A 15)

It is the deity of uncontrived reality. Teaching it as the essential meaning of everything, [Saraha says,] "Hey, whatever has been said" and so forth. "Hey" is an exclamation. "Whatever has been said" means "by the above-mentioned fake gurus." "False" means "meaningless." "Wrong" means "without the identification of one's own-nature." "Whatever you are attached to—abandon it!" means "abandon the fixation that [your true nature] is the chosen deity!" "When you understand, this is everything" means that when you realize the coemergent, everything immovable and movable is this. It is the coemergent nature exclusively. "Nobody knows anything other than this" means that no deity, whoever it might be, knows anything but the coemergent.

> This is what you read, maintain, and meditate on.
> [Whatever] is explained in treatises and Purāṇas is this.
> [In them,] there is no view to mark it (i.e., the coemergent).
> Yet it only depends on the words of the guru. 20 (DK_A 16)

vajrakaṇikayā kalāṃ nārghanti ṣoḍaśīm ||. The Tibetan in the Dergé Tengyur (D 368, fol. 212a) is as follows: *lha dang mi yi bde ba ni* | | *bsdus byas rdo rje 'dzin pa yis* | | *de lta bur ni byed pa yi* | | *bcu drug char ni mi phod do* |. The quotation in Mokṣākaragupta's commentary is shorter and is similar to the three-*pāda* verse 1.15 in Gray's (2012, 54_{3-4}) edition: *dīvyamānuṣyatāṃ saukhyaṃ piṇḍīkṛtya vajrakaṇikayā* | *kalā nārghanti ṣoḍāśīm* ||.

20. Similar to DK_T 18a.

To those who wonder about abandoning everything else, he says: "[This is what] you read" and so forth. Since the coemergent has always been in everything, it is not [found] beyond everything when realized. To those who wonder by which means such a true reality is realized, he says: "There is no view to mark it," and so forth. "It" stands for the coemergent. "No [view to] mark" means that a view to mark it is not found in any tenet. Although taught everywhere, it is not realized when not marked by the guru. The six limits[21] characterize these [tenets].

> Saraha says: "[For] one into whose heart the teaching of the guru
> has entered,
> it is like seeing a treasure placed on the palm of [one's] hand.
> Not seeing their true nature,
> the immature are fooled by delusion." 21 (DK_A 17)

How is [the coemergent] identified (lit. "marked") through the pith instructions of the guru? You see it directly and clearly like a jewel in the palm of your hand. Following the pith instructions, the guru teaches the means (*upāya*) by which it becomes directly manifest, even though it cannot be explicitly stated. This is because he said [in DK_T 25b]: "How to explain what is inexpressible?" and in [DK_T 68a]: "The guru [can]not teach [it]."[22] Thus it [can] only be realized from the fourth empowerment. It is not realized without identification and taught with expressions such as "their true nature." Although the coemergent has always been in them (i.e., beings), they do not realize it because of the four types of mental imprints,[23] which are conceptual.

> Without meditation and renunciation
> they [eventually] live in a home together with a wife.
> [Yet,] if they are not liberated from the bondage [of objects] by
> enjoying objects,
> I, Saraha, say that they do not know true reality. 22 (DK_A 18)

A person realizing this is not aware of any knowledge and does not adopt or

21. I.e., the views of the provisional and the definitive meaning, the implied and the not implied, and the literal and the not literal.

22. DK_T 68a: "If the guru's message was inexpressible," reading *brjod min na* instead of *bstan pa ma yin zhing*.

23. I.e., the mental imprints of expression (*mngon brjod*), viewing a self (*bdag lta*), the factor of becoming (*srid pa'i yan lag*), and the concordant type (*rigs mthun pa*).

abandon any conduct. This is taught in [the verse] starting "Without meditation." It is easy to understand.

> If [the coemergent] is directly manifest, what [is achieved] by meditation?
> Or if it remains hidden, just try to measure that darkness.
> The nature of the coemergent
> is neither existent nor nonexistent.
> Alas, [I,] Saraha have proclaimed this loudly. 23 (DK_A 19)

To refute those who wonder whether coemergent wisdom is not realized through the experience of the third empowerment, he teaches [the verse] starting "If [the coemergent] is directly manifest." [The line] "If [the coemergent] is directly manifest, what [is achieved] by meditation?" means that if one directly sees the coemergent at the time of the third empowerment, why is it necessary to meditate? The line "Or if it remains hidden, just try to measure that darkness" means that if it is not seen, there is nothing to meditate upon. It boils down to conceptual belief, just like looking at the reflection of darkness. Again, the bliss of the third [empowerment], this coemergent, is not genuinely natural. The genuinely natural [bliss] is not existent in the sense of not being made of atoms. It is also not nonexistent because it manifests directly.[24]

Another meaning of [the line] "is neither existent nor nonexistent" is as follows: "existent" refers to the experience of bliss, and "nonexistent" to it being empty. "Neither" [means here that bliss and emptiness] are not separate, being of the same taste. [If] the one [bliss] is opposed to the other [emptiness], this is conceptualizing [its] existence.[25] This is because it is said in the *Hevajratantra* [I.x.40cd]: "Therefore bliss is not called true reality, the great elements being bliss."[26] And Nāgārjuna['s *Caturmudrānvaya* says]: "How can the uncontrived [coemergent] arise from the contrived [practice of uniting with a *karmamudrā*]?"[27] Or else, the meaning of "If [the coemergent] is directly manifest, what [is achieved] by meditation?" is as follows: If directly manifest, the [already] existent does not need to be meditated upon, because it is manifest. It is not appropriate[, however,] to meditate on the nonexistent, because it is

24. Lit.: "in front of the eyes."

25. The erotic bliss of the third empowerment is here taken to be existent (in the sense of consiting of or arising from the great elements). Genuine coemergent bliss, however, is taken to neither exist nor not exist.

26. *Hevajratantra* 125_2: *tasmāt saukhyaṃ na tattvākhyaṃ mahābhūtaṃ yataḥ sukham* |.

27. See Mathes 2015, 121.

not seen. "Or if it remains hidden, just try to measure that darkness"—this is like thinking about the extent (*gzugs*) of darkness. Therefore the nature of the coemergent is neither existent nor nonexistent. It is the equal taste of empti[ness] and compassion.

> It is on the basis of[28] [the same bliss through] which one is born,
> dies, and exists
> that one attains great supreme bliss.
> Even though Saraha shouts aloud this secret,
> bound people[29] do not understand. What can I do? 24 (DK_A 20)

The coemergent has been taught in general. Now it is taught in a differentiated way. To do so, [Saraha] says: "It is on the basis of [the same bliss through] which" and so forth. From "[It is on the basis of the same bliss through] which" to "What can I do?" [he teaches] the causal coemergent. "Which" is fundamental luminosity, the indestructible drop. "On the basis of" means "based on which realization arises." It causes one to be born and die. Again, the wisdom wind causes sentient beings to be born, and causing the life force to end, it [also] delivers death. As for [the line] "that one attains great supreme bliss," when this fundamental luminosity is not purified, one is born in saṃsāra; when purified, it rises like the sun. Once it has risen, uncontaminated bliss is obtained from it. The rest is easy to understand.

> Since [the coemergent] is beyond meditation, what is there to
> reflect upon?
> How to explain what is inexpressible?
> The seal of [cyclic] existence deludes the entire world.
> Nobody, without exception, [can] realize their own true nature.
> 25 (DK_A 21)

Then, to realize the causal coemergent, [Saraha] wishes to teach the path's coemergent. "Beyond meditation" means "beyond objects of thoughts." "Inexpressible" means "beyond the conventional." Is it realized without being expressed? No. "The seal of [cyclic] existence" means that through the power of entering the causal winds of concepts, one does not realize [the coemergent]. It is necessary to rely on the pith instructions of the genuine guru.

28. Taking *blangs nas* in the sense of *brten nas* in DK_{AT}.

29. Apa. *pasuloha*.

There are no tantras, mantras, objects of meditation, or
meditation.
All these are causes of confusing one's mind.
Do not ruin the naturally pure mind through meditation.
Rest in the bliss of your own true reality and cause yourself no
torment! 26 (DK_A 22)

About the teaching that pith instructions are not [about] conceptual meditation, [Saraha] says: "There are no tantras, mantras," and so forth.

Eating, drinking, enjoying intercourse,
and always filling the cakras, again and again—
by [following] such teaching, the other world (i.e., mahāmudrā) is
attained.
[The master] tramples on the heads of the deluded world and
moves on. 27 (DK_A 23)

What are these pith instructions? "Eating" refers to bliss, "drinking" to semen; "intercourse" refers to the heat of bringing the upper and lower winds together. "And always filling the cakras, again and again": Filling the bodhicitta (i.e., white drops) of the upper central channel with the blood [element] in the lower part, [the bodhicitta can] get lost, which would impair the body's strength and so forth; thus bodhicitta must be drawn upward. Seeing to it that the semen [moves] upward, the six cakras are gradually filled. "[By following such teaching,] the other world" and so forth is easy to understand.

Where the winds and the mind do not move
and the sun and the moon do not enter,
ignorant ones, in this position you must relax!
Saraha has given all instructions and gone away. 28 (DK_A 24)

Once blissful meditation has been taught in such a way, he teaches [the reflections of] empti[ness].[30] To do so, [Saraha] says: "Where the winds and the mind" and so forth. "The winds do not move" means that they are bound in the central [channel]. If the mind is not bound, this will not be accomplished. When bound, mind rests without concepts. The sun and the moon stand for

30. Further down in the text, it becomes clear that "empty" refers to the Kālacakra concept "reflections of emptiness" (*śūnyatābimba*), which emerge from emptiness when the winds have entered the central channel.

the right and left winds. As for "do not enter," it means that they have [already] entered the central [channel].

> Do not create duality but unity!
> Do not make any caste/color distinctions!
> Transform the entire three realms, without remainder,
> into one great passion, one caste/color.[31] 29 (DK_A 25)

With "Do not create duality" and so forth [Saraha] teaches nondual meditation. "Do not create duality, but unity!" means that the right and left winds are united in the *avadhūtī* (i.e., central channel). As for "caste/color," the winds of the five colors are not separated out but united into the single color of the wisdom wind. Again, as for the differentiation of caste/color, without distinguishing the caste/color of means and the caste/color of insight, one should take them to have the equal taste of *evaṃ*.[32] The three realms are the three of body, speech, and mind. "Great passion" is the equal taste of great bliss.

> It has no beginning, middle, or end
> and is neither [cyclic] existence nor nirvāṇa.
> In this supreme great bliss,
> there is neither self nor other.[33] 30 (DK_A 26)

Of which kind is this great bliss? "Beginning," here, refers to joy, "middle" to supreme joy, and "end" to [joy of] no joy. [Great bliss] is free of these. "Neither [cyclic] existence" refers to joy and supreme joy—that is, saṃsāra. Nirvāṇa is the [joy of] no joy. "Nor" means that it is the coemergent beyond the two (i.e., saṃsāra and nirvāṇa); it is the ascertained bliss. Alternatively, concerning uncontaminated bliss, "beginning" would be its arising, "middle" its abiding, and "end" its passing out of existence. However, uncontaminated bliss has not arisen from a cause. "Neither [cyclic] existence" means [bliss] does not melt away, nor does it abide at the forehead. "Nor nirvāṇa" means that it is not [based] on the release [of semen] from the jewel. [The semen] descends but is not released. The rest is easy to understand.

31. I.e., following DP, which is, however, unmetrical.

32. I.e., the union of *prajñā* and *upāya* either on a physical or acoustic level (Mathes 2009, 93–94).

33. This verse is identical with *Hevajratantra* II.v.68 (212_{10-11}).

Whatever I see in front, behind, and in the ten directions
is always, again, precisely this [great bliss].
Today, a lord like me destroys error.[34]
Now I no longer need to ask anyone. 31 (DK_A 27)

At the time of nonduality, relating in terms of perceived and perceiver is cut. This is taught in "[Whatever I see] in front" and so forth. "Front" is the nonconceptual, "behind" is wisdom, and the "ten directions" are the external directions. "Is always, again, precisely this [great bliss]" means: whatever appears is always again this—i.e., great bliss. "Today, a lord like me destroys error" means that today is the time of realization. A lord like me destroys, in accordance with internal realization, the error of externally perceived objects. They are known as this [great bliss]. "Now I no longer need to ask anyone" means that because error has been cut through, I do not ask others about bliss.

Where the senses have dissolved
and where the own-nature [of a self] has been destroyed—
friends, [this is] the coemergent.
Seek clarification [about it] from the venerable guru. 32 (DK_A 28)

The [verse] starting "Where the senses" teaches severing the relation between [perceived and] perceiver. The senses are the concepts of the perceiver. "Where" refers to the coemergent, "dissolved" to severing the relation. Again, how is it cut? [He says:] "the own-nature [of a self] has been destroyed." [This means that] one comes to know the nonexistence of an own-nature. Since the relationship between the perceived and perceiver has been cut, what is the name of this seeing? It is the coemergent body or *kāya*. "Seek clarification [about it] from the venerable guru."

Where mental consciousness terminates, where the winds
  dissolve,
there is here in the three grounds[35] the basis of [all] parts [of
  saṃsāra and nirvāṇa].
[Still] deluded, [yogins] must know it in terms of merging.
To know that the ocean of bewilderment has dried up—
this is supreme great bliss.
Saraha has taught this and gone away. 33 (DK_A 29)

34. According to Mokṣākaragupta; DK_T reads: "Today, at this very moment, error is destroyed."
35. According to Mokṣākaragupta; DK_T reads: "in this ground."

When you receive oral [clarification] from the guru, the mental consciousness is bound in the sense of becoming nonconceptual. "The winds dissolve" means that they melt into the central [channel]. Knowing "where" indicates knowing the means. To remove error about the coemergent, [Saraha] says: "[there is, in] the three grounds" and so forth. Here, "three grounds" means "three appearances." *'Di la* means "here" (*'dir*). "All parts" means saṃsāra and nirvāṇa. *Gnas* means "basis." Because these three appearances[36] are the cause of obscuration, they are discarded. Because the aspect of the mind, which is endowed with the three appearances, is saṃsāra, it is abandoned, and the appearance of the Buddha strengthens. Because this is not attained now, the two (i.e., saṃsāra and nirvāṇa) are merged according to one's ability. This is called the yogin's cultivation of luminosity. As for merging, it is the complete knowledge of what has the nature of foundational luminosity. Luminosity dries up his (i.e., the yogin's) bewilderment, the ocean of ignorance. When there is luminosity, there is knowledge. Because sentient beings' experience of awareness-knowledge is [still] conceptual, it is taught to be not the coemergent.

> Hey! This is self-awareness.
> Do not confuse it!
> Existence and nonexistence are bondage for a sugata.
> Without separating what is the same as cyclic existence,
> turn solely toward your natural mind, yogin!
> Know it to be like water poured into water. 34 (DK_A 30)

Well, one may wonder, then, whether these appearances are the coemergent. As an answer [Saraha] teaches the [verse] starting "Hey!" "Hey" is an exclamation expressing surprise. "This is self-awareness. Do not confuse it!" means this very appearance is the three mentioned above: appearance, increase, and full attainment. Being the continuous flow of saṃsāra, they are conceptual appearances. Do not confuse them by thinking that they are the coemergent! Why is that? Because the Sugata said that both the concepts of existence and nonexistence are bondage. To those who wonder how to direct their intellect to such a path without going wrong, [Saraha] says: "[turn solely toward] your natural mind," and so forth. "Your natural mind" is the coemergent. As for "solely toward," one rests without a cognitive object beyond object of meditation and meditator. What would that be like? Like water poured into water. The substance of water stands for empty luminosity. Pouring water means to pour [the mind into the coemergent] without concepts.

36. Not clear, but probably the appearances of the desire, form, and formless realms.

Through false types of meditation, liberation is not found.
How can you take on your lap the net of illusion?
Trusting in the truth of the genuine guru's teaching,
Saraha says: "I have nothing to say." 35 (DK$_A$ 31)

To show that there is no liberation through contrived yoga, [Saraha] teaches the verse starting "[Through] false types of meditation," which are conceptual yoga. "The net of illusion" refers to *karmamudrā*. "How can you take on your lap" means that you should not embrace but abandon [a consort]. To teach that it is proper to leave her, he says: "[Trusting in the truth of] the genuine guru's," and so forth. "Trusting in the truth of the genuine guru's teaching, he"[37]—that is, Saraha—says: "I have nothing to say."

Continuously looking at the nature
of originally pure space, the vision of it ceases.
Is there universal destruction at this time?[38]
Fools are deluded about their own natural mind. (DK$_A$ 32)
They strongly criticize everybody. 36a–37a

For those who wonder how [the coemergent] can be positioned as an object—it not being the object of speech and words—[Saraha] teaches [the verse] starting "[Continuously looking at the nature of] originally pure space." The originally pure space is the cloudless space. "Continuously looking [at the nature of originally pure space], the vision of it ceases," means that when looking with a fixed gaze, the vision [of it] ceases—i.e., the relation between perceived and perceiver gets cut. "Is there universal destruction at this time?" means that four [vital] winds gradually cease. This is also because it is said in the [*Param*]*ādibuddhatantra*: "The cloudless sky—look at it with a fixed gaze!"[39] This means that when you look with a fixed gaze at the cloudless sky, which is without cover in the daytime, and the mental consciousness becomes nonconceptual, the winds gradually cease and the signs occur. This is a genuine instruction. It must be clearly known from the guru's mouth. To those who wonder why such a coemergent is not realized when it is in oneself, [Saraha] says: "Fools are deluded about their own natural mind [because of the faults

37. "He" (Tib. *de yis*) is missing in the root text.

38. I.e., following Mokṣākaragupta's quotation of the line. The standard Tibetan root text (DK$_T$ 36c) reads: "Universal destruction is just like that."

39. See *Laghukālacakratantra* 5.116a: *ākāśaṃ stabdhadṛṣṭyā jaladhararahitaṃ yoginālokanīyam.*

that cover it]," and so forth. "Their own natural mind" is the uncontrived coemergent.

> Due to the fault of pride, true reality cannot be realized.
> Everyone in the world is deluded by [their own] meditation.
> No one realizes their own natural state. 37b–d (DK_A 33)

"The fault of pride" means that they are hindered by the fault of clinging to an "I" and "mine." As for the statement that they do not realize [the coemergent] because of additional faults, [he says:] "Everyone in the world is deluded by [conceptual types of] meditation." This means that they do not realize it because of the fault of [their] guru teaching a form of conceptual yoga with symbolic attributes. On top of that, they do not realize [the coemergent] because emptiness is [only] taught conceptually. If the coemergent is analyzed in terms of arising and passing out of existence, its nature [can]not be known.

> The root of the mind [can]not be realized (lit. "marked").
> They do not understand clearly
> the coemergent in terms of three aspects, as that
> from which they are born, into which they dissolve, and where they abide. 38 (DK_A 34)

> Whoever meditates on true reality, which has no base, [should know that]
> it [only] becomes evident through the pith instructions of the guru.
> The nature of saṃsāra is the essence of mind.
> Fools! You must know everything Saraha said. 39 (DK_A 35)

For those who wonder what arises from realizing the coemergent, he agrees to teach the real coemergent, the fruit of purity, and then teaches [the verse] starting "[Whoever meditates on true reality, which has no] base." [True reality] is without a base because it has not arisen through causes, it is not terminated by conditions, and it is not based on [having] any [kind of] an own-nature. This unchanging true reality is the coemergent. "Whoever meditates" (*gang sems pa*) means [whoever] meditates on the coemergent. As for [knowing] "the nature of saṃsāra," since it is only a concept of the mind itself, the pith instructions of the guru who points out the mind are enough. What would be the use of anything else?

Although one's own natural state [of mind can]not be described
in words,
it [can] be seen through the eyes of the guru's pith instructions.
Having purified[40] and consumed virtue and wrongdoing,
there is not even the smallest speck of a fault. 40 (DK_A 36)

For those who wonder how a guru can identify the coemergent even though it cannot be expressed by anything, [Saraha] says: "[Although] one's own natural state [of mind can]not be described in words, it [can] be seen through the eyes of the guru's pith instructions" and so forth. This means that although inexpressible, the illusory body comes to be seen in the first moment of direct sensory cognition through showing the means [for realizing it]. When telling you about things in the dark, for example, they are not seen, but there are means to [make them] visible, such as a lamp. It is taught that through it, the fruition coemergent[41] becomes directly manifest. To teach that true reality is without mistakes, [Saraha] says: "[Having purified and consumed] virtue and wrongdoing" and so forth. *Chos* is here virtue, and *chos min* wrongdoing. "Having purified [them]" means that they are not different [anymore]. "Consumed" means "understood." Thus they are beyond karma, cause, and result.

When your own natural mind is completely purified,
the [enlightened] quality of the guru enters [your] heart.
Realizing so, [I,] Saraha, sing [this] song.
I have not seen a single tantra, a single mantra. 41 (DK_A 37)

Moreover, to teach that the buddha qualities arise within it, [Saraha] teaches [the verse] starting "[When] your own natural." "Your own natural mind" is the coemergent. "Purified" refers to having purified the winds of thoughts. As for "The [enlightened] quality of the guru enters [your] heart," it means that the higher supreme qualities such as the [ten] strengths and the [four] fearlessnesses arise in oneself. Out of joy, "[I,] Saraha, sing [this] song." "I have not seen a single tantra, a single mantra" means that he has not seen [them in the process]; realizing the goal was enough.

40. Lit.: "smoothened." The Apabhraṃśa equivalent is *sohia*, "purified."

41. This specification of coemergent suggests some sort of causal coemergent, which could be the "image of the [real] coemergent" (*sahajachāyā*) in Nāgārjuna's *Caturmudrānvaya* (see Mathes 2015, 120 and 394).

Beings are bound by karma.
Once one is free from karma, the mind is liberated.
When one's mind is free, there is certainly no other [bondage].
One will attain supreme nirvāṇa. 42 (DK_A 38)

Having thus summarized the meaning of the coemergent, it is [now] explained extensively. To this end, [Saraha] teaches [the verse] starting "Beings [are bound] by karma." As for this first line of the verse, virtuous and unvirtuous forms of karma are one's thought only. They manifest through one's thought, but this is not the position of taking karma as the cause. Similarly, the *Vajrāvalī* teaches: "The three realms are the manifestation of the [vital] winds. One sees the realms as if dreaming a dream."[42] Thoughts themselves are fundamental luminosity. When purified, all thoughts stop. In its pure state, [saṃsāra] is called nirvāṇa. This is as taught in [*Yuktiṣaṣṭikā* 6cd]: "Thorough knowledge of saṃsāra is called nirvāṇa."[43]

Mind alone is the seed of everything.
From it, cyclic existence and nirvāṇa spread.
To prostrate to this mind, which like a wish-fulfilling jewel,
bestows the fruition of desire! 43 (DK_A 39)

Thus [Saraha] teaches: "Mind alone is the seed of everything." This "mind alone" must be analyzed. It is nonconceptual self-awareness. Or instead, it is something else, as [self-awareness] is not the primary [topic under analysis]. [Mind] is the abiding mode of seeing. It is not made into anything constituting saṃsāra or nirvāṇa, because it is free of making and is not anything other [than mind]. When you think it is not anything else apart from mind, this is true.

As for [mind's] initial, abiding mode of seeing, this is not the path, because it is refuted in many tantras. If one wonders then, what [the initial abiding mode of seeing] refers to, it is the indestructible. It is called fundamental luminosity, [non-?]conceptual bodhicitta. When not [yet] purified, it is called ignorance. In the tantras, it is taught by the symbolic [letter] *a*, because in *Nāmasaṃgīti* [V.1b–2a] it is said: "The perfect Buddha has arisen from the

42. Not identified, but if our author really knew Abhayākaragupta's great opus, it would put Mokṣākaragupta in the late 11th or early 12th century.

43. Except for saṃsāra instead of "cyclic existence" (*bhava*), the quote matches *Yuktiṣaṣṭikākārikā* 6cd (see *Yuktiṣaṣṭikākārikā* 14_2: *parijñānaṃ bhavasyaiva nirvāṇam iti kathyate*).

letter *a*. It is at the beginning of the alphabet. Its significance is great: it is the supreme letter, of great strength, free from arising."[44]

If one wonders whether the [letter] *a* signifies a nonarising mind, this is not the case. In the *Vajrahṛdayālaṃkāranāmatantra* it is said: "In the middle of the heart is the indestructible one, blazing like a pure lamp. It is the genuinely unchanging [letter] *a*."[45] In the *Hevajratantra* [II.iv.40d–41b] it is said: "[Semen is itself Nairātmyā, and bliss is the nature of Nairātmyā. Her bliss] is mahāmudrā located at the navel [center]. She (Nairātmyā) is of the nature of the first vowel (*a*). The buddhas conceive of her as great intelligence [personified]."[46] Therefore nonarising is not taught by the symbolic [letter] *a*. Since [the letter *a*] is generally known as nonarising, this is not referred to [by *a* in its] symbolic meaning.

> When the mind is bound, one is bound.
> When it is liberated[, one is liberated.] There is no doubt about this.
> Whatever it is that binds fools,
> by the very same [things], the wise swiftly obtain liberation. 44 (DK_A 40)

Having thus (i.e., in verse 43) taught the causal coemergent, he now teaches the coemergent of the means to make it manifest—namely, [the verse] starting "[When] the mind is bound." "Mind" refers [here] to the indestructible drop; [it is] "bound" by the flowing conceptual winds. "One is bound" means one is [in] saṃsāra. Once this [mind] is liberated, one [attains] nirvāṇa. What is the cause of being bound? He says: "Whatever it is that binds fools, by the very same [things], the wise swiftly obtain liberation." "Fools" are ignorant beings; "whatever binds" are the winds. As for the wise knowing the means, they are swiftly liberated by these winds, which bestow buddha[hood] in this very life. This is also said in the *Hevajratantra* [I.ix19ab]: "By the very same thing by which the world is bound, the wise are swiftly liberated."[47]

44. *Nāmasaṃgīti* 68_{1-5}: *saṃbuddho 'kārasambhavaḥ | akāraḥ sarvavarṇāgryo mahārthaḥ paramākṣaraḥ || mahāprāṇo hy anutpādo*. The last three of these four *pāda*s are also quoted in Maitrīpa's *Amanasikārādhāra* (see Mathes 2015, 247).

45. Quotation not found in Dergé Kangyur, D 451.

46. *Hevajratantra* 180_{9-11}: [*karpūram eva nairātmyāsukhaṃ nairātmyarūpiṇyan | tasya saukhyaṃ*] *mahāmudrā saṃsthitā nābhimaṇḍale || ādisvarasvabhāvā sā dhīti buddhaiḥ prakalpitā* |.

47. The quotation is similar to *Hevajratantra* I.ix.19; see 110_5: *yena tu yena badhyate lokas tena tu tena tu bandhanaṃ muñcet* |.

The mind must be taken to be like the sky.
All phenomena, too, must be seen to be the same as the sky.[48]
When the "conceptual mind" (*yid*) is turned into no-mind,[49]
unsurpassable enlightenment will thereby be attained. 45

To those who wonder what are the means to find liberation from bondage, [Saraha] teaches [the verse] starting "The mind." "The mind must be taken to be like the sky" means that the mind rests in nonconceptuality. "All phenomena, too, must be seen to be the same as the sky" means that being appearances of the mind, all phenomena are the same as the sky. They have never existed in the first place. What do we get from nonconceptuality? [Since] the mind is inconceivable, if one places it without effort in a nonconceptual [state], this unsurpassable [mind] is realized in terms of its illusory nature. This is as said in the *Guhyasamājatantra* [II.3]: "Once the nonexistent [reflections are seen], meditation does not exist [anymore]. Meditation [then] is no meditation at all. This means that if the object of meditation[50] is not real, [this] cannot be called 'meditation.'"[51] In the *Hevajratantra* [I.v.11a], it is said: "There is neither meditator nor object of meditation."[52] In this very [*Dohākoṣa*, verse 26c] it is said: "Do not ruin the naturally pure mind with your meditation!"

Having made it like the sky, the winds are controlled.
Being fully aware of sameness, they subside.
Endowed with the power spoken of by Saraha,
unstable impermanence will soon be abandoned. 46

To those who wonder where the winds are bound when the mind rests in nonconceptuality, [Saraha] teaches [the verse] starting "Having made it like the sky." "Having made it like the sky" means "having made [the mind] nonconceptual." What will make this happen? Thoughts bind the winds. They are bound in such a way [through the idea of] sameness, the equality of object and subject. "Being [fully] aware of sameness, they subside" means that after one wind has subsided into the other, they [all] enter luminosity. "Endowed

48. This line corresponds to the reading of the Dpal spungs edition (B).

49. B: "When the mind is considered inconceivable."

50. We suggest reading *bhāvyo* instead of *bhāvo*, wherefore we need *bsgom bya* instead of *dngos po* in the Tibetan.

51. GST 11_{17-18}: *abhāve bhāvanābhāvo bhāvanā* (Tib. *bsgom par bya ba*) *naiva bhāvanā | iti bhāvo na bhāvaḥ syād bhāvanā nopalabhyate |*.

52. *Hevajratantra* 55_1: *nāsti bhāvako na bhāvyaḥ*.

with the power spoken of by Saraha" and so forth refers to the benefit. It is easy to understand.

> When wind, fire, and earth have stopped,
> at the time the nectar flows, the winds enter the mind.
> When the [winds of the] four yogas enter the single place,
> the sky element cannot contain this supreme bliss. 47

Precisely this is being taught through the subsiding [winds]. [Saraha thus] teaches [the verse] starting "[When] wind." "Wind" corresponds to the lower channel of urine, "fire" to the right [channel] above, and "earth" to the central [channel] below. The latter corresponds to the [earth] wind abiding in the [central] channel of feces [below]. [The central channel] above corresponds to the [*ava*]*dhūtī*. The flowing of nectar corresponds to the wind of the moving moon nectar above. Below [it becomes] the channel of bodhicitta on the right. "Time" means [as long as the flow] has not passed. Such a mind enters luminosity. Or else, the earth wind subsides in the water [wind], the water [wind] in the fire [wind], and the fire [wind] in the wind [of the wind element], and the wind [of the wind element] enters the luminous mind. It is taught that the water [element] is filled up. "At the time the nectar flows" means that at the time of union, too, this wind enters the mind, the central channel. Or else, when the wind enters the central channel, the fire of the life force melts the *haṃ* at the forehead, the nectar, bodhicitta, drips, and from this, bliss arises. Likewise, it has been said [in the *Sarvatathāgataguhyatantra*]: "Earth subsides in water, water in fire, and fire in wind. The wind enters consciousness, and consciousness enters luminosity."[53]

To teach that bliss arises from such binding [of the elements], [Saraha] says: "When [the four yogas]" and so forth. "When" means "at the time of," and "the four yogas" refers to the four winds above and below [the navel]. Alternatively, they are the winds of the four elements. "The single place" is the *avadhūtī*. Or else, the four yogas are the four joys, and "enter the single place" means that they enter the coemergent. As for "the sky element cannot contain," it is known that this bliss pervades all phenomena.

> In every house they talk about it,
> [yet] the place of great bliss is not properly known.
> Saraha says, "The whole world is bogged down by thought:
> the inconceivable is not realized at all." 48 (DK_A 76)

53. See Dergé Kangyur, D 453, fols. 110a–b.

To teach that this [bliss] is difficult to realize, [Saraha] teaches [the verse] starting "In every house." "The whole world is bogged down by thought" means that being hindered by its thoughts, [the whole world] is bogged down and does not realize [the inconceivable]. Moreover, it remains detrimental to the teacher of the genuine supreme path because of its base thoughts. The rest is easy to understand.

> In all living beings
> true reality exists, but it is not realized.
> Everything having the nature of the same taste,
> wisdom is unsurpassed by thought. 49

To teach that although [the coemergent] is challenging to realize, it is not impossible, [Saraha] teaches [the verse] starting "In all living beings." "Everything having the nature of the same taste" means that [everything] is not different in terms of existing as the coemergent. Its name [here] is inconceivable, unsurpassable wisdom. The rest is easy to understand.

> Yesterday, today, and in the future,
> people claim that things are the best.
> Hey, folks, like water trickling from full cupped hands,
> you do not feel the loss. 50

To teach that being lazy, practitioners do not realize [the coemergent], [Saraha] teaches [the verse] starting "[Yesterday,][54] today." This is easy to understand.

> Whether you perform actions or when [the coemergent]
> is realized [together with it], there is neither bondage nor
> liberation.
> [Yet,] it is beyond words, so who among a hundred yogins
> identifies it, claiming that it can be explained? 51

Thus people realizing this [coemergent] are rare. To teach that they must exert themselves in practice, [Saraha] teaches [the verse] starting "[Whether] you perform actions." This is easy to understand.

54. The only other verses containing "today" would be 31 (in the third line) and 65 (in the fourth line). In both cases, the word is not close to the beginning of the verse. Mokṣākaragupta must have read verse 51 without "yesterday" at the beginning.

When this mind, tangled with knots, is relaxed,
it will be liberated beyond doubt.
Through the objects (i.e., winds), by which fools are bound,
experts will be liberated. 52

It is impossible for the winds' binding to constrain the mind, since the mind [can only] be bound nonconceptually. To teach this, [Saraha] teaches [the verse] starting "[When] this mind, tangled with knots." "Tangled with knots..." refers to a mind hindered by thoughts. "...is relaxed, it will be liberated beyond doubt" means that when left in a nonconceptual [state], [the mind] will certainly be liberated from the bondage of thoughts. What is the root of thoughts? [Saraha] answers: "[Through the objects,] by which fools." "[The objects,] by which" refers to "winds." "Fools" are those lacking [skillful] means. "Binding objects"[55] means that thoughts arise from them. "Experts" possess [skillful] means. "Through the" means that being liberated through nonconceptual meditation, the wind in the channels of thoughts enters the central [channel].

Burdened [with many loads], it runs in the ten directions;
unburdened, it remains immovable.
This paradox is evident to me. It is like a camel.
Children, you must find out for yourselves! 53 (DK_A 41)

Clarifying bondage and liberation through examples, [Saraha] teaches [the verse] starting "Burdened." Those loaded [with a burden] seek to become free [from it]. Unburdened, they do not seek to become free. Likewise, you are bound when seized by thoughts. Getting rid [of them] means to rest in nonconceptuality. The paradox is that when [the camel] is loaded, it [seeks] liberation, while it remains [immovable] when unloaded. This paradoxical instruction is evident to me. "You must find out yourself!" is when you stop clinging to the mind.

Hey, look with your sense faculty!
Apart from that, I have not realized [anything].
At the feet of a noble being without karmic activity,
you must become certain about your mind. 54

Since the reasons for bondage and liberation were taught, the means must be

55. Tib. *'ching ba'i dngos po* is not in the standard Tibetan root text.

addressed now. [Saraha] teaches [the verse] starting "Hey." "Look with your sense faculty!" means "Look with a fixed gaze at the cloudless sky." "Apart from that, I have not realized [anything]" means that [Saraha] has not analyzed this with his mental consciousness. "[At the feet] of a noble being without karmic activity," which happens through the termination of thoughts. "At the feet of" refers to the cloudless sky. "Become certain about your mind," means "become certain about your thoughts."

Therefore the following has been taught: Gazing at the unveiled stainless sky during day yoga, you see blazing fire, lightning, the moon, the sun, and eclipses (Rāhu). Then the five signs of night yoga occur. They are like smoke, a mirage, a firefly, a lamp, and the sky.[56] They are signs of the winds having entered the central [channel]. In the *Hevajratantra*, it is said: "Once all thoughts are abandoned, one has fully ascertained them in a single day. If the signs do not occur, I will have lied."[57] In the *Paramādibuddhatantra* and other canonical sources, it is said: "Look with a fixed gaze into the cloudless sky!" In this [*Dohākoṣa*, Saraha] says further down (DK_T 80ab): "The eyes unblinking, the mind stopped, and the winds stopped—[this] is realized through the venerable guru."[58] [In DK_T 36ab, too,] he says: "Continuously looking at the nature of originally pure space,[59] the vision of it ceases." You must seek clarification [about it] directly from the guru.

> Do not think of yourself binding the winds!
> [Follower of] ordinary yoga,[60] do not remain [with your mind] fixed on the tip of your nose!
> Hey, orient yourself without distraction toward the supreme coemergent!
> Completely abandon this binding at the tip of the nose of cyclic existence! 55 (DK_A 42)

To distinguish [the *sahaja* approach] from what it is not, [Saraha] teaches [the verse] starting "Do not think of yourself binding the winds!" "Binding the winds" refers [to practices] such as counting the [movements of] winds. As for "ordinary yoga," nothing is achieved by it. "Tip of your nose" stands for con-

56. Even though the Kālacakra influence is evident, the enumeration of the five signs of night yoga differs from the usual six signs during the night.

57. Verse not identified. The first line accords with *Hevajratantra* II.ii.9a.

58. These two lines differ from Advayavajra's understanding. See below.

59. Translated according to DK_T 36ab.

60. I.e., taking *shing* in the sense of "field," and "yoga of the field" as "ordinary yoga."

ceptual yoga with the mind fixed on [places] above and below the tip of the nose. "Hey,[61] do not remain" means "Do not meditate!" You may ask, meditate on what? "Hey, [orient yourself] without distraction!" indicates that since conceptual yoga is not the means, you should abandon it; "supreme coemergent" means rest without concepts! To teach that conceptual yoga is not the means, he said: "Completely abandon this binding at the tip of the nose of cyclic existence!"[62] Because concentration on the tip of the nose of cyclic existence is bondage, he said: "Completely abandon [it]."

> Expose its fault, for the mind and the winds are unstable!
> They are like an extremely fickle steed.[63]
> When realizing the coemergent nature,
> you stabilize yourself through it. 56 (DK_A 43)

You may ask, why abandon [them]? Contracting the mind, [its waves] surge through the winds. Expose [this fault of their] becoming unstable! This occurs because they are extremely fickle. You may ask, why realize the coemergent? Because abiding in the realization of the coemergent nature, you become stable.

> When the [conceptual] mind is stopped,
> the bondages of the body will break.
> Wherever there is the equal taste of the coemergent,
> there is neither low caste nor brahman. 57 (DK_A 44)

For those who wonder what is the use of a stable mind, [Saraha teaches that] when the [conceptual] mind is stopped, the body's bondages, thoughts, and suffering will break. Not only that, the teaching that one will be of equal taste with bliss and emptiness means that one is in the middle, free from extremes. There is no difference between an untouchable outcaste (empti[ness]) and a brahman (bliss) when [resting in] the equal taste of empti[ness] and coemergent bliss.

> Here are the moon and the sea.
> Here is [the meeting] of the Gaṅgā with the sea,

61. "Hey" is missing in the Tibetan root text.

62. The commentary first presents the first syllables of this line and then repeats it in full.

63. Translated from the Dpal spungs edition (B). D and P read: "This contracts the mental consciousness and the waves of wind churn, rise, and become fickle."

Vārāṇasī, and Prayāga.[64]
Here are the moon and the sun.[65] 58 (DK_A 45)

Some speak of realization because of[66] having visited and seen
all sites, the major and subsidiary power places.
It is an ocean [of bliss] abiding in the boundary region of the body
and mindfulness.[67]
[This] virtue I have definitely and correctly seen. 59 (DK_A 46)

After teaching that the means is not [to remain fixated] on the tip of the nose but [to remain] in the coemergent, [Saraha] teaches that the coemergent is not external but abides in your own body. To do so, he teaches [the verse] starting with "Here are the moon." "[But] there is no other boundary region [like the][68] body and mindfulness": "body" is [short] for abiding in the body, "mindfulness" stands for abiding by pith instructions, and "the ocean" is inexhaustible bliss. The rest is easy to understand.

In the middle of the anther on the stalk of a petaled lotus,
there is a very subtle fiber, fragrant and colored—
Abandon [such] distinctions, you fools! Do not turn the fruit,
through the pain of [such] suffering, into nothing! 60 (DK_A 47)

Existing in oneself, the coemergent does not need to be sought elsewhere. To teach this, [Saraha] teaches [the verse] starting "[In the middle of the anther on the stalk of] a petaled [lotus]." "In the middle of the anther on the stalk of a petaled [lotus]" is the "sky-goer face" [channel].[69] The "very subtle [one]" is the *avadhūtī* channel. The fragrance is like the *utpala* [flower channel]. [Its] color

64. The *ya ti* after *pra yā ga* does not make sense.

65. The verse seems to be corrupt. DK_{AT} 45 reads (B): "This is the Gaṅgā. [This is] the Yamunā. This is where the Gaṅgā flows into the ocean. This is Prayāga and Vārāṇasī. This is the moon, this is the illuminating sun." D and P read: "This is the river Yamunā. This is the confluence of the Gaṅgā into the ocean. This is Prayāga and this is Vārāṇasī."

66. I.e., reading the homophone *bltas pas* instead of *bltas pa'i*, which is supported by B of DK_{AT} 46b.

67. This line follows the Dpal spungs edition and Mokṣākaragupta's commentary. D and P read: "There is no other boundary region like the body."

68. Supported by the reading of D and P.

69. I.e., the channel of the semen below the navel. See *Sekoddeśa*, verse 50 (Sferra 2006, 150).

is red. The distinction of having a [certain] fragrance and color means that one does not need to rely on a *karmamudrā* or a consort of one's own caste.

> Where[70] Brahmā, Viṣṇu, and the three-eyed [Śiva],
> the illegitimates,[71] who are [considered to be]
> the support of the world, are worshiped,
> the least accumulation of karma will be exhausted. 61 (DK_A 48)

This coemergent being one's naturally innate gods, one does not rely on offerings to external gods. To teach this, [Saraha] teaches the verse [starting] "Where Brahmā." The rest is easy to understand.

> Hey, listen son! The [art of] purifying wished-for mercury[72]
> is known to be well established.
> Worldly people[, however],
> such as commentators and readers, cannot know it.[73] 62 (DK_A 49)

> Hey, listen son! This taste of the manifold world
> cannot be taught.
> I have seen that [this] supreme abode of bliss is without concepts.
> It is like giving birth to a sentient being. 63 (DK_A 50)

To teach the qualities of realizing the coemergent, [Saraha] teaches [the verse] starting "Hey." As for "I have seen that [this] supreme abode of bliss is without concepts," the abode of bliss is the cause, "empti[ness]."[74] "Without concepts," refers to the nonconceptual path. "I have seen" means "directly." "It is like giving birth to a sentient being" means that contaminated bliss arises just as when a child is born from a mother.

> The intellect stops, and the mental consciousness is completely
> pacified.
> [What remains] when self-conceit is interrupted [then]

70. The root text has "when."

71. P: "The ones without eyes."

72. Based on DK_{AT} 51, we suggest reading *rtsol ba'i ro* instead of *rtsod pa'i ro*. Rig pa'i ral gri comments on the verse on the basis of "taste of debate" (Schaeffer 2005, 152).

73. Verse 62 does not have a commentary.

74. I.e., the reflections of emptiness (see the commentary on verse 92 below).

is realized [to be like] the miraculous most subtle [phase of the moon].[75]
Why then fix [one's] meditative concentration on it? 64 (DK_A 51)

Stopping the various states of the intellect refers to the conceptual constructs of objects, the complete pacification of the mental consciousness [focused] on the subject's conceptual constructs. "When self-conceit is interrupted" means to sever one's adherence to them. "Is realized [to be like] the miraculous most subtle [sixteenth phase of the moon]" means that when the object-subject relation is severed, all phenomena are seen to be like the miraculous [phase].

[The subtle phase] rises in [cyclic] existence[76] and dissolves in the sky.
How could it arise after it has not existed?
By its nature, it has never arisen.
Abide by the abandonment of distinction[77] taught by the glorious guru today! 65 (DK_A 52)

As for the teaching on how conceptual constructs are severed, [Saraha] teaches the verse starting "[It rises in cyclic] existence." "Rises [in[78] cyclic] existence"[79] refers to conceptual constructs manifesting as objects. One may ask, what are conceptual constructs that resemble the sky? [Thus Saraha] asks: "How could it arise after it has not existed?" When the conceptual constructs of objects are severed, the subject's conceptual constructs are severed [as well]. Therefore the abandonment of distinctions taught by the guru is an abandonment free from the distinctions of object and subject. You must abide in nonconceptuality. Abide in what is like the miraculous [subtle phase].

You may see,[80] hear, touch, remember, eat, smell,
walk, go, sit down, linger around, and conduct a conversation;
in case you wonder whether this is [only] mind,
do not move out of its unitary mode. 66 (DK_A 53)

75. Added in accordance with the *Apabhraṃśa* and DK_{AT} 51c.

76. Apa.: *bhava*; DK_{AT}: *srid pa*.

77. Advayavajra explains that this refers to existence, nonexistence, and the meeting point between the two.

78. The commentary has *dngos po* instead of *dngos por*.

79. I.e., taking *dngos po* in this context here consistently in the sense of Apa. *bhava*, DK_{AT} *srid pa*.

80. In the Apabhraṃśa, the verbs are in the second-person plural imperative.

For those who wonder how to abide in this [nonconceptuality], [Saraha] teaches [the verse] starting "[You may] see." Looking without distraction—with the eyes[81] as well as the mental consciousness—at what directly manifests through the five sense faculties, the eyes and the rest, eventually leads to experience. "In case you wonder whether this is [only] mind, do not move out of its unitary mode" means that the mental application in the course of life involves not letting the mind move out of its unitary mode, [the realization that everything] is illusory.

> Whoever does not drink to his satisfaction
> the refreshing cool water of the guru's pith instruction
> will suffer and die of thirst
> in the desert of the manifold meanings of treatises.[82] 67 (DK_A 54)

Now to instruct that one must rely on the guru who shows such [a path, Saraha] teaches [the verse] starting "[Whoever does not drink to his satisfaction the refreshing cool water of the] guru's pith instruction." It teaches that bereft of the nectar of the guru's pith instructions one is seized by suffering. The rest is easy to understand.

> If the guru's message was inexpressible,
> the disciple would not understand.
> [But] who will rely in which way
> on this nectar-like taste of the coemergent? 68

[The verse] starting with "[If] the guru's message" teaches that the coemergent [can be] realized. The rest is easy to understand. This verse is related to what follows: [The coemergent] cannot be taught by the guru, and the disciples do not understand.

> Clinging to the means of valid cognition,
> [even] fools find the details [of the master's teaching].
> Then you [may] eat in the house of a peasant
> but are not sullied by stains. 69

Well then, by taking the guru's instructions to be true, one finds the details. Even fools come to see them directly. When seeing them, all concepts about

81. Looking with the eyes stands for all five sense perceptions.

82. Atiśa quotes this verse in his *Bodhipathapradīpa* commentary (see Eimer 1978, 183).

good or bad, big or small, clean or dirty are abandoned. Then one [may] eat in the house of a peasant without being sullied by stains. This means one remains unimpaired by his faults.

> When begging, [the yogin] goes with a bowl from the street.
> If he were a king, what would he do with it later?
> Having abandoned distinctions, he abides in true reality
> in effortless equipoise, its nature unwavering.
> Abiding in nirvāṇa, he is beautiful in cyclic existence. 70

The qualities that can be made directly manifest in such a way even by fools have been taught. Next, the inferior is taught to be supreme [by the verse] starting "When." [Given a yogin] with a begging bowl from the street (a poor beggar's bowl) who has obtained pith instructions, if he were a king because of his great power, what would he do with [this bowl] later? This means that being without a place to stay because of inferior (i.e., yogic?) conduct contradicts [the yogin] having realized the coemergent. "Pillows of a great residence and so forth, with a comfortable bed:"[83] This has been taught from "having been brought to the yogin"[84] up to "the yogin himself is the king."[85] "Abiding in nirvāṇa, he is beautiful in cyclic existence" means that although the body is still in saṃsāra, the mind abides as a buddha.

> Completely abandon the thinking and the thought
> and abide in the [natural] way of a small child.
> No other medicine should be prescribed for [any] other disease.[86]
> If you are firm in devotion to the teaching of the guru,
> the coemergent will spring up beyond doubt. 71 (DK_A 55)

If such a yogin [can] abide in saṃsāra, how does he do so? To those who wonder, [Saraha] says: "And abide in the [natural] way of a small child." How is that? He says: "Completely abandon the thinking and the thought." "Thinking" means "to conceptualize"; "thought" refers to the imagined, "Completely abandon" to the complete abandonment of conceptualizing. Why is that? He says: "No other medicine should be prescribed for [any] other disease." As for leaving the negative behind, it is not abandoned through investigation. Rest-

83. Not identified.

84. Not identified.

85. Not identified.

86. In the standard Tibetan root text, this line comes before "Completely abandon...."

ing without imagining anything, negative thoughts are left behind. For those who then wonder whether these are abandoned through meditation, [Saraha] says: "If you are firm in devotion to the teaching of the guru." You must strive with devotion in accordance with the teachings of the guru. From that, the coemergent will spring up.

> It lacks color, word, quality, and comparison.
> [Still,] I keep identifying this inexpressible [coemergence].
> It would be like a virgin attached to erotic bliss.
> To whom can this supreme lord (i.e., the coemergent) be taught?
> 72 (DK_A 56)

As for the teaching how the coemergent springs up when it cannot be expressed, [Saraha] teaches [the two lines] starting "[It lacks] color." Colors are not distinguished, words are not used, qualities are not sought, and comparisons are not explained. The rest is easy to understand. As for the fact that the coemergent cannot be taught to others, [Saraha] teaches [the two lines] starting "[It would be like] a virgin."

> Into that in which "entity" and "non-entity" are abandoned,[87]
> the entire world dissolves.
> When the mind is immovable and stabilized, resting in itself,
> one will liberate oneself from the cyclic existence of saṃsāra. 73
> (DK_A 57)

To teach that such a yogin is free from conceptualizing and suffering, [Saraha] teaches [the verse] starting "[Into that in which] entity and non-entity." "Entity" (*dngos po*) means "existence"; "non-entity" (*dngos med*), "nonexistence"; and "abandoned," "beyond." "Into that [...] the entire world dissolves" means that in it [everything] is of the same taste. "When the mind is immovable and stabilized, resting in itself" indicates [resting] in nonconceptuality. "One will liberate oneself from the cyclic existence of saṃsāra"—that is, from conceptualizing and suffering.

> When the self [and] other are not known at all,
> this is accomplishment in terms of [having] the body of the
> guru.[88]

87. According to Mokṣākaragupta. The standard Tibetan root text has "completely severed."

88. We follow the commentary that does not take *bdag gzhan* in the sense of the "supreme in

Thus I have taught. Do not go astray!
Perfectly know yourself by yourself! 74 (DK$_A$ 58)

To teach that [the yogin] is not only free from suffering but also that particular qualities arise, [Saraha] teaches [the verse] starting "When." "When the self [and] other are not known at all" means that [all] conceptual constructs of self and other are abandoned. "This is accomplishment in terms of [having] the body of the guru" means to have attained a supreme body (*sku*). As for "Thus I have taught" and the rest, since these qualities arise from the guru's pith instructions, it is advised to eagerly engage in them.

Entities are not particles, not non-particles, not even mind.
They have always been without [a basis of] fixation.[89]
This is all Saraha has to say.
Hey, you all must know stainless ultimate! 75 (DK$_A$ 59)

Regarding the benefit of practicing the path taught by the guru, [Saraha] teaches [the verse] starting "[Entities] are not particles." "Not particles" means not to be composed of subtle atoms. "Not non-particles" excludes that they do not appear as form. "Not even mind" refers to [their] appearance as form. Therefore what one has to focus on is the illusory body. Thus these entities, everything appearing in such a way, have never existed in the first place. Thus [the yogin] does not get attached, although he sees [them]. The rest is easy to understand.

He is at home, but she looks [for him] outside.
She sees [her] landlord at home but asks her relatives.
Saraha says: "You must know [the coemergent in yourself] on
your own!" 76a–c (DK$_A$ 60a–c)

Teaching that although such an [illusory body] exists in oneself, it cannot be understood if not taught by the guru, [Saraha] says [the lines] starting "He is at home." "He is at home" means that [the coemergent] exists in oneself. "But she looks [for him] outside,"—that is, somewhere else. To give an example, she

yourself." See DK$_A$ 58ab (Apa.): "As long as you do not fully know the supreme in yourself, how will you attain the unsurpassable body?"

89. DK$_A$ 59ab (Apa.): "Do not conceptualize either particles or the smallest particles, and erotic bliss shines forth in an uninterrupted way."

sees [her] landlord at home but asks her relatives whether they have seen the landlord of her house.

> Fools cannot address it in terms of meditation or an object of meditation.
> When I thoroughly investigate, although the guru has taught
> and made everything known, will liberation be attained by that?[90]
> 76d–77b (DK_A 60d–61b)

Teaching that although the guru has taught it, it is not realized without meditation, [Saraha] says [the lines] starting "Fools." This is easy to understand.

> Traveling [from] country [to country], tormented by pain,
> you will not understand the coemergent, caught up as you are in harmful deeds. 77cd (DK_A 61cd)

Teaching that one succeeds in this meditation by comfortably staying [at home, Saraha] teaches [the lines] starting "Traveling [from] country." "Traveling [from] country [to country], tormented by pain" means to wander, tormented by hardships, the sought-after countries one has heard about. This is only an indication, for other hardships will also be met. The rest is easy to understand. If [one asks], "Well then, by what does one succeed?" it is to be added that one succeeds by enjoying bliss.

> Though taking delight in objects of sensual pleasure, one is not sullied by them.
> Although the water grasps the lotus, it does not stick to it.
> When it comes to those who take refuge in the root (i.e., the illusory body),
> where does poison affect those in possession of mantras against poison?[91] 78 (DK_A 62)

For those who wonder whether one is not bound by this [bliss], [it says:] "Though taking delight in objects of sensual pleasure, one is not sullied by

90. DK_A 60d–61b: "It [can]not be addressed in terms of an object of meditation or meditation. Is it possible to understand everything the guru says? [Can] liberation be attained without having understood everything?"

91. DK_A 62cd: "Moving along with the [poison-transforming] source in this way, the yogin is not troubled by poison (objects) when delighting in poison (objects)."

them." This is because one comes to know that object and subject share the same taste. What is an example? "Although [the water] grasps" and so forth. This is easy to understand. For those who wonder what the cause for not getting bound is, [Saraha] teaches "[Whoever] thus." "Whoever"[92] refers to accomplished ones; "thus" means "therefore": thus takes refuge in the root because of that. The root is the illusory body. Giving an example of not being bound, [Saraha] teaches "[where does] poison" and so forth. This is easy to understand.

> Although you make tens of thousands of offerings to the deities,
> you [only] bind[93] yourself. What good does it do you?
> Through such [worship], saṃsāra is not uprooted,
> and your natural state is not realized. You cannot cross over. 79
> (DK$_A$ 63)

Once he has taught that the illusion-like uncontrived [body] that exists in ourselves is not the cause of bondage, [Saraha] teaches that there is no liberation through offerings to deities in whom others believe, saying "[Although you make tens of thousands of] offerings to the deities" and so forth. This is easy to understand.

> The eyes unblinking, the mind stopped,
> and the winds stopped—[this] is realized through the venerable guru.[94]
> As long as the winds flow, one does not move [out of saṃsāra].
> When dying,[95] what will the yoginī [in ourselves] do?[96] 80
> (DK$_A$ 64)

To teach the supreme means along with the faultless gaze for the sake of making this illusory body manifest, [Saraha] teaches [the verse] starting "The eyes." Here, "eyes unblinking" refers to a wrathful gaze. "The mind stopped" means to forcefully stop thoughts. "The winds stopped" means that the five winds

92. Reading *gang yang* for *gang 'di*.

93. The Apabhraṃśa has "kill."

94. Apa. (in accordance with Advayavajra): "With eyes unblinking and by immobilizing the mind, [one may think] the winds are stopped, [mis]understanding the venerable guru."

95. Tib. *'ching ba* must originally have been *'chi ba*, as the Apabhramśa reads: "The yogin breathes his last. What is the point then?"

96. According to Mokṣākaragupta. The standard Tibetan root text reads: "What will the yogin do?"

gradually enter the *avadhūtī* path (i.e., channel). What is wrong with not stopping the winds? "As long as the winds flow, one does not move" [means that because] the winds are the root of saṃsāra, one does not transcend saṃsāra as long as they flow. "When dying" means "at the time of dying." "What will the yoginī do?" The yoginī is the illusory yoginī. "What will [she] do?" means that even though she exists in oneself, she will be of no use.

> As long as one is attached to the village of the objects of sense faculties,
> for that long [the mind] will not go beyond itself and spread completely.[97]
> Hey, think about what you are doing[98] and where you are going now!
> Take up this very difficult thought! 81a–d (DK_A 65)

For those wondering how it is that one does not transcend saṃsāra, [Saraha] teaches "as long as [one is attached to the village of the] objects of sense faculties" and so forth. The meaning is as follows: When the semen descends through the power of the downward-moving wind and the blood surges upward, the sense faculties' gates are activated. Then the consciousness rides the life wind (*srog*) and produces all the thoughts. In the *Saṃdhivyākaraṇatantra*, it is said: "As long as the world is conceptualized, there is manifold conceptualization. Thoughts and so-called bodhicitta constantly arise from winds."[99] Since in this way the root of saṃsāra is the winds, they need to be stopped, and this depends on binding the mental consciousness. The latter, in turn, depends on nonconceptual meditation. The necessity of resting the mental consciousness beneficially without concepts is taught in the line "[Hey, think about what] you [are doing now!]" "What you are doing now" means that the only [instruction] for you is that there is nothing to do. As for "Hey...think where you are going" means the only place to go is yourself. Having thus abandoned things to do, one rests without concepts. What is very difficult in "Take up this very difficult thought" [refers to] it being difficult to abandon things to do. "Take

97. Apa.: "As long as there are neither objects nor sense faculties, the [guru's instructions] become clear on their own." The Tibetan translation of the *pratīka* in Advayavajra's commentary is: "As long as one is attached to the village of the objects of sense faculties, for that long [the mind] appears and spreads without hope."

98. B adds: "and where you are going."

99. Cf. D 444, fol. 168b: | *ji srid 'jig rten gtags pa dang* | | *de bzhin btags pa sna tshogs rnams* | | *rnam rtog byang chub sems shes pa'i* | | *rlung las rtag tu 'byung ba yin* |. Translated in accordance with Mokṣākaragupta's reading.

up this very difficult thought" means that if in possession of the means, one easily engages in the nonconceptual.

> Which [buddha] in whomever—
> he is not seen there.
> All the learned ones explain the [various] treatises
> [but] do not know the buddha within [their own] body. 81ef & 82ab (DK_A 66ab)

Thus abiding in the nonconceptual, [Saraha] teaches in [the lines] starting with "Which" that they have not realized their mind on their own. "Which" refers to buddha, "in whomever" to themselves; "he" [again refers] to buddha, and "there" to them. "Is not seen" means that without [the realization of] the illusory body, [the buddha within] is not seen. The rest is easy to understand.

> Once an elephant is trained, its mind is well organized.
> In it, [any] movement is severed, and it relaxes.
> If you understand it in this way, there is no need to ask anything.[100]
> Being shameless, [scholars still] claim: "I am a learned man." 82c–f (DK_A 66cd)

Now, to teach the means of practice in detail through examples, [Saraha] teaches [the lines] starting "Once an elephant is trained." When mountain people who keep elephants train them, [the elephants] remain peaceful. Likewise, when the thoughts of the mind are abandoned, the mind is well organized. This is because the mind is not fickle [then]. "In it" means in the central channel, and "movement" the movement of the winds: having been severed, [the winds] repose in the central channel. This is the mind resting at ease without concepts; the winds rest at ease in the central channel. Which Dharma practice is needed [for that]? You do not need conceptual yoga. "Being shameless, [scholars still] claim: 'I am a learned man'" refers to scholars who claim this without hesitation.

> Anyone alive who does not change
> would be free from old age and death.

100. The two lines with the elephant are missing in the Apabhraṃśa and DK_{AT}. Instead of the fifth line, DK_{AT} 68c, reads: "And cannot break [the chain of] coming and going." Since this nicely lines up with lines 82ab, the example with the elephant is probably a later insertion.

The stainless intellect taught by the guru
is a treasure of true reality; what else [do you want]? 83 (DK_A 67)

In [the verse] starting "Anyone alive," [Saraha] teaches that you become immortal by drinking the nectar of the natural state. "Alive" is as if you were young. And if there is no recognizable change, you do not age and die. Moreover, "anyone alive" also refers to the vital wind. Being without change then means [the vital wind] is not recognizably stolen by the central [channel]. Because the entirety of the vital [wind] has entered the central [channel], nothing is left to steal. In this case, there is neither birth nor death. Teaching that luminous wisdom arises from this, [Saraha] says: "[The stainless intellect] taught by the guru" and so forth. "Stainless intellect" is fruition luminosity. "[It] is a treasure" means that when it has arisen, this is a treasure, a precious jewel.

The very objects themselves are pure and should not be attended to.
You should take them as empty only.
It is like a crow that has flown away from a ship:
it circles and circles but [has to] land on it again. 84 (DK_A 68)

[Saraha] thus teaches us to rest the mind at ease, along with the advantages of doing so. Next he teaches the means to heal the mind. To this end, he says: "The very objects themselves are pure" and so forth. As for "objects" here, when resting the intellect at ease, thoughts about other objects do not arise. "Not be attended to" means [objects] are not summoned hither and put at ease again. For those who then wonder how to take them, he says: "You should take them as empty only." Wherever objects are mentally fabricated, they are empty on their own. Therefore it is not necessary to summon them hither. This is the intent. To give an example, he says: "It is like a crow that has flown away from a ship" and so forth. When a crow that was put on a ship cannot be restrained, it flies away. You may let it go, for it will return from wherever it may fly since it will not find land; it will [always] alight again on the [ship]. The mind reaching out to the objects is like that. Wherever it reaches, it does not move out of the nature [of mind]. Not attached to being focused on a single object, consciousness stays relaxed.

It is as in the case of a poisonous snake that is [but] a black rope—
merely seeing [objects] frightens [those clinging to duality].

Friends, [even] good people
are fettered by this fault of dualistic objects.[101] 85

Do not create bondage by clinging to objects!
Hey, you fools! [This is what] Saraha says.
It is like the fish, the moth, the elephant,
the bee, and the deer[102]—look at [what happens to them]! 86
(DK_A 69)

To teach the danger of being attached to a single object, [Saraha] teaches the verse starting "[Do not create bondage] by clinging to objects!" This is easy to understand. These lines teach the fault of the yogin clinging to the objects of sensual pleasure.

Whatever spreads from the mind
has the nature of the world protector.
Are waves and water different?
Cyclic existence and calmness[103] [share] the nature of being like
space. 87 (DK_A 70)

Moreover, to teach the means to heal the mind through knowing that [everything] arises from the coemergent itself, [Saraha] teaches [the verse] starting "Whatever [spreads] from the mind." "Whatever" refers to thoughts, "spreads from the mind" to all arisen thoughts, and "has the nature of the world protector" to fundamental luminosity rising as thoughts; it is like, for example, water and waves. As for "Cyclic existence and calmness [share] the nature of being like space," the meaning is that cyclic existence is the thoughts of saṃsāra and calmness is nirvāṇa, fundamental luminosity. "[Share] the nature of being like space" means that both are without arising.

What is taught and what you hear—
if you correctly carry out what is intended,
[saṃsāra] dissolves into the mind,
it being removed like the dangerous dust of a tunnel. 88 (DK_A 71)

101. Verse 85 is not commented upon.

102. According to Advayavajra's commentary, the elephant finds its end through tangible objects in a trap, a bee by smell, and a deer by sound, a moth by sight (of fire), and a fish by taste.

103. According to DK_{AT}, which has *zhi ba* for Apa. *sama* (i.e., Skt. *śama*). Tib. *mnyam nyid* corresponds to Skt. *samatā*.

To show the advantage of teaching such knowledge, [Saraha] teaches [the verse] starting "What is taught." "What is taught" refers to any pith instruction given by the guru, "what you hear" to what is heard by the disciple. "What is intended" you fulfill. "Correctly carry out" means brought to completion. "Danger[ous]" are the defilements. The tunnel is the fundamental mind. "Removed like the ... dust" means purified from the root. Into what is it purified? It dissolves into the heart [of the miner]—that is, the indestructible drop.

> As long as you pour [only] water into water,
> its taste remains the same.
> Pondering faults and qualities,
> protector, no one identifies them.[104]
> O fool, this [pondering] is not an antidote.[105] 89 (DK_A 72)

How do the [defilements] dissolve into the [heart]? Saraha teaches [this] in [the lines] "As long as you pour [only] water into water, its taste remains the same." Just as when pouring water into water, its taste remains the same, likewise [the defilements] dissolve into the fundamental mind. Or rather, he teaches them as not being dual—that is, of equal taste. As for the water, it is empti[ness], and the poured water [stands for] compassion. "Its taste remains the same" must be taken as [emptiness and compassion] not being dual. To teach that they have always been of the same taste, [Saraha] teaches [the lines] starting "[Pondering] faults and." "Faults" refers to the fundamental consciousness (*ālayavijñāna*), which is not [yet] destroyed, and "qualities" to the luminous nature of mind. "No one identifies them" means that they are not realized by anyone without means. The rest is easy to understand.

> Like the tongue of fire feeding on the forest,
> turn all appearances that come before you
> into the root of mind,
> the coemergent within emptiness! 90

Now, because the coemergent is of equal taste in you throughout beginningless time, it [can] be experienced, whatever the course of your life, whatever

104. This line is missing in the Apabhraṃśa and DK_T.

105. This is the oldest attested verse, quoted in Bhavabhaṭṭa's (mid-10th-cent.) *Catuṣpīṭhanibandha* on *Catuṣpīṭhatantra* III.4.11 (MS Kaiser Library 134 [pc], fol. $39b_2$). Thus, if we accept that Saraha knew the *Hevajratantra* (ca. 900 CE), we can place him at the beginning of the 10th century.

you encounter. [Saraha] teaches this [in the verse] starting "Like the tongue of fire feeding on the forest." This is easy to understand.

> In case you think, "Is this not pleasing to the mind?"
> and you hold it in your heart as something dear,[106]
> even the mere husk of a sesame seed
> becomes a thorn and inevitably gives rise to painful experience. 91
> (DK$_A$ 73)

To teach the faults of not realizing the coemergent, [Saraha] teaches [the lines] starting "In case [you think, 'Is this not] pleasing.'" "Pleasing" here refers to something acceptable to the mind. As for "you think," if a mind of equal taste with empti[ness] has not arisen, the attachment to entities gives rise to painful experience. The meaning of the words is easy to understand.

> Friends, look at the pig and the elephant![107]
> [You may think the pig] is like that [elephant], but (*para*) this is not the case.[108]
> It is like the activity of a wish-fulfilling jewel.
> The paṇḍita who [claims] to destroy confusion is strange.
> The self-awareness in yourself is the mental imprint[109] of great bliss [or the] reflection [of emptiness]. 92b–e (DK$_A$ 74)

Some may wonder what [these reflections of] empti[ness] are like, so that they do not get bound through adherence to them. For them [Saraha] says: "Friends, look at the pig and the elephant! [You may think the pig] is like that [elephant], but (*para*) this is not the case." From whatever perspective [you look] at the pig and the elephant, the pig is not the elephant. Likewise, although similar to the [reflections of] empti[ness], empti[ness] determined in other vehicles (*yāna*) is not the path. How is confusion abandoned through these [reflections of] empti[ness]? He teaches [the lines] starting "It is like the activity of a wish-fulfilling jewel." Determining that a mad person's body is pre-

106. The first two lines differ in the Apabhraṃśa and DK$_T$ 75ab: "Do not become attached to empti[ness]! Friends! Think of this or that [appearance] as equal!"

107. This line is missing in B.

108. D and P have the extra line: "Friends, look at the pig and the elephant!" but only after the following line ("[You may think] they are like that...").

109. It should be noted that the Apabhraṃśa reads *bhāsia* instead of *vāsia*. So we get: "It is taught that great bliss has to be experienced by oneself."

cious, [your] confused [perception] of the mad [person's body] gets destroyed. Likewise, the confusion you have about entities gets destroyed through the concept of empti[ness]. To teach that these [reflections of] empti[ness] are the basis for bliss, he teaches [the line] starting "The self-awareness." The self-awareness in yourself, which is permeated by great bliss, is the cause for bliss. Again, when this [great bliss] is not purified, it is a mental imprint called ignorance. When purified, it is a reflection, the reflection of empti[ness].

> Everything will be made space-like at that time.
> Is it not acceptable to call it *kālakūṭa* poison?[110]
> The mental consciousness grasps its space-like nature.[111]
> When this mind has been made into no-mind,
> [its] nature is as beautiful as the supreme coemergent.[112] 93
> (DK$_A$ 75)

What comes from its realization? [Saraha] teaches "Everything" and so forth. "Everything" refers to the outside and inside, "at that time" to the time of realizing these [reflections of] empti[ness], and "will be made space-like" to it being seen as space. This experience of the reflection of empti[ness] cannot be expressed in words. To teach that, he says "*kālakūṭa*" and so forth. *Kālakūṭa* is an experiential term. "It is not acceptable to call it" means that words cannot express it. Well then, by what is it expressed? "Its space[-like] nature," i.e., the [reflections of] empti[ness], free from concepts. "The mental consciousness grasps" means it experiences. Well then, does mental consciousness exist? He says: "[When] this mind is made into no-mind, [its] nature is as beautiful as the supreme coemergent." "This mind" stands for the impure mental consciousness, "has been made into no-mind" for the pure mental consciousness.[113] What is pure mental consciousness? [Its] nature is beautiful in being the supreme coemergent, the reflection of empti[ness].

> In every house, they talk about it.
> [Yet] the place of great bliss is not properly known.

110. This line is missing in the Apabhraṃśa and DK$_T$ 77.

111. Apabhraṃśa and DK$_T$ 77b: "And in this space-like nature, the mental consciousness should be placed."

112. Apa.: "That supreme [being] shines forth within coemergent nature."

113. Mokṣākaragupta's (corrupted?) text has it the other way around, but the pure mind or mental consciousness does get transformed into impure no-mind. No-mind is so called in view of becoming nonconceptual—i.e., pure.

Saraha says: "Everybody bears his mental burden."
[Great bliss] is no-mind. No one realizes it. 94 (DK_A 76)

To teach that this is difficult to realize, [Saraha] says: "In every house, they talk about it" and so forth. The one dwelling in a house is the housewife. She is not somebody dwelling in the forest. What they talk about is the [reflections of] empti[ness]. These are the cause for the place of great bliss. Thanks to them, bliss arises. Therefore, not knowing that [the cause of bliss] is [the reflections of] empti[ness], all beings are confused. Confused, they cling to entities. "[Great bliss] is no-mind. No one realizes it": without instructions, this coemergent no-mind is not realized by anybody.

Hey, yogins are well acquainted with meditation.
Having left [fixation on the] head, heart, navel, secret place, and bodily parts behind, I [can] see.
It is through contemplation that I identify objects.
Through the contemplation of something else, the winds get blocked. 95

For those who wonder how yogins see [the reflection of] empti[ness] when the world does not see it, [Saraha] teaches [the line] starting "Hey." "Having left [fixation on the] head, heart, navel, secret place, and bodily parts behind, I [can] see" refers to [seeing] the formless form. This is as taught [in *Nāmasaṃgīti* VIII.3ab]: "[The *kāya*s are] the formless one, the one of beautiful shape,[114] the foremost one, the multi-formed one, and the one made of mind."[115] For those who wonder by which means these [reflections of] empti[ness] are seen, [Saraha] says: "It is through contemplation that I identify the objects." Through contemplation—that is, nonconceptual meditation—I identify objects. What appears as objects, I identify as reflections of empti[ness]. For those who wonder how these reflections of empti[ness] are seen through the power of nonconceptuality, he says: "Through the contemplation of something else, the winds get blocked." "Something else" is the nonconceptual. "Contemplation" means to rest the intellect in it. "The winds get blocked" means that winds enter the central [channel]. This teaches the fol-

114. To support his commentary, Mokṣākaragupta must have understood "formless beautiful shape."

115. *Nāmasaṃgīti* 86_{9-10}: *arūpo rūpavān agryo nānārūpo manomayaḥ* |. Standing for the *dharmakāya*, *saṃbhogakāya*, *svābhāvikakāya*, *nirmāṇakāya*, and *vipākakāya*. See Wayman 2006, 86.

lowing: Because the winds are the root of saṃsāra, they are purified by entering the central [channel]. Then the object-subject relationship is severed, and the reflections of empti[ness] are seen.

When mind comes to identify mind,
the winds and mental consciousness remain unmoving and stable.
Just as salt dissolves into water,
so does mind dissolve into its nature.
At this time, self and other are seen to be equal.
What is the use then of effort and the practice of meditation? 96

To elucidate the means for blocking the winds, [Saraha] teaches [the lines] starting "When mind." The nonconceptual mind coming to identify the empty mind means that with this seeing [functioning as] the cause, the winds and the mental consciousness become stable and unmoving; they dissolve into [mind's] nature. Giving an example for the thoughts from the mental consciousness dissolving into your uncontrived nature, he teaches [the lines] starting "Just as salt [dissolving] in water." This is easy to understand.

The one divinity is seen in many textual traditions.
It clearly manifests in accordance with our own preference. 97
(DK$_A$ 77)

For those who wonder why the Buddha taught many types of meditation when they are not needed, [Saraha] teaches [the verse] starting "The one divinity is seen in many textual traditions." "The one divinity" here means the one true reality. "Is seen in many textual traditions" implies that this true reality is taught with a lot of terminology. As for "It clearly manifests in accordance with our own preference," take, for example, something like the so-called mustard seed at the tip of the nose: those who like concepts see it through meditating on a drop at the upper and lower end of the nose. Those who trust in true reality see it as the wind, which is bodhicitta.

The self (*ātman*) alone is the lord, and others are the contrary.
This [Śaiva] tenet is common in every house.

One eats, and all others are sated.[116]
Having gone outside, she looks for the landlord.[117] 98 (DK_A 78)

Therefore it (i.e., the self) is ultimately not the way it is seen. The [true] lord is the coemergent, and therefore it accords with Saraha['s teaching] alone, but the others, who are conceptual, are the contrary. For those who wonder whether everybody, opposed as they are to the true meaning, is wrong, he says: "[in every] house." The tenets in mere accordance with people's respective capacities are not wrong. Whatever the Buddha taught comes down to true reality but not to conceptual meditation. Giving an example now for realizing all phenomena, since this is good for realizing the mind, [Saraha] teaches: "One eats and all others are sated." Here "one" stands for consciousness, "eats" for the taste of bliss transforming [it]; "all others" are like the [remaining] skandhas, and "sated" means satiated with the taste of bliss. There is also [the reading] "all others digest the food." Fire, for example, digests wood. It spreads as it feeds, digesting the rest of the forest [as well]. Teaching that when the coemergent is not recognized, one does not find it when searching for it, [Saraha] says: "Having gone outside" and so forth. "Having gone outside" means that she has not recognized him inside. The landlord is the coemergent. "She looks" means she searches and does not find [him]."

He is not seen to come or go,
nor is he perceived to abide.
The unfluctuating supreme lord
becomes [her] untroubled meditation.[118]
Leave the water alone to be clear and the lamp alone to shine.[119]
99 (DK_A 79)

Explaining this, [Saraha] teaches [the lines] starting "[He is not seen] to come." This is easy to understand. Wondering how he is found, [Saraha] teaches "the unfluctuating" and so forth. "Unfluctuating" means nonconceptual. Con-

116. According to the Apabhraṃśa and Advayavajra's commentary the line is pointing out the absurd consequence that God (Śiva) would destroy the world and the souls digest it.

Going by Rig pa'i ral gri, who explains that "by consuming only consciousness with luminescence, all the other aggregates are burned with its fire," one has to translate: "[Yet,] because one is eaten, everything else is burned" (see Schaeffer 2005, 162).

117. I.e., not finding the coemergent within herself.

118. DK_A: "She runs after the unwavering and unstained supreme lord."

119. This line is missing in the Apabhraṃśa.

cepts are the troubled [waters] of suffering. The meditation free from that [suffering] is nonconceptual. To give an example for this meditation, he teaches: "[Leave the] water [alone to be] clear" and so forth. Leave [your mind] alone, unaffected by thoughts, like the water becoming clear and the lamp shining.

> Coming or going—I neither take nor abandon.[120]
> Meeting[121] the extraordinary woman—[122] 100 (DK_A 80)

> The dreaming mind is based on nothing at all.
> Do not see [her] as separate from your own reflections.[123]
> Thus you hold the Buddha in the palm of your hand.[124]
> When body, speech, and mind are not separate
> the coemergent nature shines. 101 (DK_A 81)

As for "Coming or going—I neither take nor abandon," whatever the course of life is at this point, nothing should be stopped. This is as taught in the *Hevajratantra* [II.iii.42cd]: "Neither forsake sleep nor restrain the senses!" Now, to illustrate these reflections of empti[ness], [Saraha] teaches "[Meeting] the extraordinary woman" and so forth. Let us say a man dreams of lying with a maiden. She would be nothing but his own mind alone appearing in such a way. Likewise, this illusory body is just one's own mind appearing in such a way. Again, the bliss of attending to the maiden in the dream is inseparable from the maiden; they are of one taste.

In a like manner is one's own mind, the subjective form of bliss, the illusory body. "Do not see [her] as separate!" means perform the equality of bliss and emptiness! As taught in the [*Param*]*ādibuddha*: "In the magical image, the maiden sees a form[125] not yet seen before," and in the [*Vairocanābhisam*]-*bodhitantra*[*piṇḍārtha*]: "It is obtained by meditating on this rainbow-like

120. DK_A (Apa.): "He comes and goes, not [being able] to abandon [his own wife]."

121. DK_A (Apa.): "How will he win..."

122. This clearly is the end of verse in the Apabhraṃśa, as the meter changes from dohā to *pādākulaka*.

123. According to D and P. B has *sems* instead of *gzugs*. The corresponding first part of the *pādākulaka* verse in the Apabhraṃśa reads: "When the bodhicitta is set at the forehead it shines. Do not see it as separate from your own body."

124. This line is missing in the Apabhraṃśa.

125. In *Sekoddeśa* 32ab we have "thief and so forth" instead of "form." See Orofino 1994a, 64–65. For the Sanskrit see Orofino 1994a, 134: *adṛṣṭaṃ pratisenāyāṃ kumārī caurādi paśyati.*

body."[126] [In his *Pañcakrama* V.26bc,] Nāgārjuna, too, says: "This [vajra-like samādhi] is the completion stage, the illusion-like samādhi."[127] It is your own mind, which is meant by "from [your own] reflections." As for "[When] the three vajras[128] are not separate," they are the reflections of empti[ness], as it is said in the *Hevajratantra* [I.i.4b]: "The hero-being is the unity of the three existences [i.e., body, speech, and mind]."[129] Moreover, through this, bliss is taught. When the concepts on the level of body, speech, and mind are stopped, there is coemergent joy.

> Once the husband has eaten, the mistress of the house enjoys
> [the rest].
> Whatever she sees is hers to consume.
> I have played the game (i.e., given the teaching),
> and the disciples[130] are tired.[131]
> Without a mother, a son is not born.[132]
> The conduct of the yoginīs[133] is beyond compare.[134] 102 (DK$_A$ 82)

Through realizing emptiness, all appearances of objects, whichever you may encounter, are seen as empty. [Saraha] teaches this [in the line] starting "[Once] the husband." Just as, for example, the householder and his wife enjoy each other without fear, all object appearances should be enjoyed without the necessity of analyzing them as empty. Moreover, an example is given for enjoy-

126. Not identified, but the same two lines are quoted and attested in the *Kālacakragarbhālaṃkārasādhana* (D 1365, fol. 192b) to be from the *Mngon par byang chub pa'i rgyud* (which is probably only short for the *piṇḍārtha*).

127. *Pañcakrama* 53_{3-4}: *vajropamasamādhis tu niṣpannakrama eva ca | māyopamasamādhiś cāpi...*

128. The root text has "body, speech, and mind" instead of "three vajras."

129. *Hevajratantra* 6_5: *sattvaṃ tribhavasyaikatā*. Ratnākaraśānti explains: "In terms of the division into body, speech, and mind, these three are the three existences (*Hevajratantra* 6_{12}: *kāyavākcittabhedena | traya eva bhavās tribhavam...*).

130. Lit.: "fools."

131. These two lines are missing in the Apabhraṃśa and DK$_{AT}$.

132. B has three extra lines: "The fire burns, [consuming] its own fuel. Hey, otherwise it does not exist. Or else, is it based on something else?"

The lines "And the disciples are tired. The fire burns [consuming] its own fuel." are from the extensive Commentary (D 2257, lines 594–95).

133. Taking *rnal 'byor ma* instead of *rnal 'byor*.

134. The entire Apabhraṃśa verse is as follows: "In some places the mistress of the house eats the husband unbeknown, and when she has killed him, whom else will she honor? [No one]. The conduct of the *yoginīs* is at odds [with worldly convention]."

ing objects in a nonconceptual way. Now, although this has been taught above, it is not understood by others. [Saraha] thus teaches [the lines] starting "I." As for "I have played the game," it means that I have said it in stupid words. "And the disciples are tired" means they are not realized. "The fire has burned the tinder only"[135] means that I alone have realized it. Alternatively, "I have played the game, and the disciples are tired" means I have played the game of the coemergent and led the fools who have not realized my specific expression [around] in saṃsāra. "The fire has burned the tinder only" [also] means that the fire from the tinder of the experts who realized [my teaching] burns as wisdom.

Having taught bondage in such a way, [Saraha] now teaches retention of bodhicitta for the following reason: If bodhicitta is not retained, there will be no lasting bliss. Without it, awakening will not happen, so lasting bliss must be accomplished. [Saraha thus] teaches [the lines] starting "E ma."[136] As for "It does not exist somewhere else,"[137] it means that it is something else or oneself. Well then, if you say it is somewhere else, does it exist somewhere else? Then it exists permanently. As a reply he says: "The conduct of the yogin[īs] is beyond compare." This means that [the yoginī] is free from mental elaborations such as "exists" or "does not exist."

> The husband is eaten, and [his] nature shines.
> This mind, which is filled with objects of desire—
> perform passion and dispassion and place it in its natural state![138]
> As the [desirous] mind is dissipating, I see the yoginī. 103
> (DK_A 83)

In case you ask from what it arises and what its nature is like, [Saraha] teaches: "The husband is eaten, and [his] nature shines." "The husband is eaten" means [consumed by] the wisdom wind; "and [his] nature shines" means illusory appearances are beautiful. If you ask what this is for, he teaches: "This mind, which is filled with objects of desire." "Of desire" refers to contaminated bliss, "filled with objects" to the longing for the beautiful, and "this mind" to conceptual mind, the [ordinary] bliss, which is abandoned. If you ask how it is abandoned, he says: "Perform passion and dispassion and place it in its natu-

135. This line is not found in the root text.

136. Not found in the root text.

137. Not found in the root text.

138. I.e., a state of relaxation after union, in which passion is only remembered ("passion"), while its intense form has ceased ("dispassion").

ral state!" Here, "passion" refers to the abiding [of the drop] at the forehead, "dispassion" to releasing the drop into space, and "perform" to the emission on the path of descent. They are of equal taste. Placing it in your natural state means that from this [practice], the coemergent on the level of fruition occurs. If you ask by which means the illusory yoginī is seen, he says: "As the [desirous] mind is dissipating, I see the yoginī." When the mind is dissipating and the thoughts related to perceived objects and the perceiving subject have stopped, "I see the yoginī" with her illusory nature.

> She eats and drinks without conceptualizing.
> This [female] friend [does] whatever comes to mind.
> [Things] are thought to be external, but I understand that they cannot be fathomed.[139]
> Hey, the illusory yoginī is way beyond compare! 104 (DK_A 84)

As for "She eats and drinks without conceptualizing," apart from these two concerns, all others have been abandoned. The idea is that [this is how] one should meditate. For those who wonder how, at this time, one should look at appearances in the mind, [Saraha] teaches [the line] starting "This [female] friend." It means that if you think there is an external [reality] separate from the appearances in your mind, suffering will seize you. "Hey, the illusory yoginī is way beyond compare!" This means that what appears to the mind is regarded as mind, an illusory appearance. As for "She has been thinking only of this activity (i.e., eating and drinking) alone,"[140] it means that the activity of appearances is simply illusory. "Her intellect is indifferent toward any effort"[141] means that because nothing needs to be done, she has abandoned all effort and rests at ease.

> [Her] stainless [intellect] does not abide, nor does it arise in the threefold world.
> The fire burns, [consuming] its fuel,[142]
> and the dripping moon is a powerless jewel.[143]

139. The variant *sdug bsngal* in B against *mtshon med* in D and P must go back to *dukkha* (non-metrical) instead of *dullakkha*. DK_{AT} 86c reads: "When one [is busy with objects] outside the mind, suffering increases."

140. This line is not found in the standard Tibetan root text.

141. This line, too, is not found in the standard Tibetan root text.

142. In B this line is already found in verse 102 and is missing here.

143. The idea these metaphors convey is that the *caṇḍālī* fire at the lower entrance of the *avadhūtī*

She rules the entire kingdom by this means.
The yoginī who accomplished the true reality of the nature of
mind
should be known as the binding of the coemergent. 105 (DK_A 85)

"[Her] stainless [intellect does not abide, nor does it arise] in the threefold world" signifies that she has purified the three [aspects of] body, speech, and mind. Having thus taught emptiness as the means to bind bodhicitta, [Saraha] gives an example of how it is bound; therefore he taught [the line] starting with "and the dripping moon." As for "the dripping moon is a powerless jewel," when moonlight falls on a moon gem, it drips beyond control. "She rules the entire kingdom by this means" [indicates] with this example that lasting bliss [spreads] through the entire kingdom by the means of empti[ness]. "She rules" means that she independently does whatever she likes. "The yoginī who accomplished the true reality of the nature of mind" refers to *prajñā* [and] empti[ness]. The means of [binding] the coemergent is bliss. "Should be known as the binding [of the coemergent]" [*prajñā* and emptiness] means that one should know that the binding of these two is in terms of their having the same taste.

The whole world is [obsessed with][144] words;
there is nobody without words.[145]
Once you get past words,
words are thoroughly understood[146] [for what they truly are].[147]
106 (DK_A 86)

Now to teach the defining characteristic of indestructible bliss, [Saraha] teaches [the verse] starting "[The whole world is obsessed with] words." Here "words" stands for conventions, symbols, or characteristic signs. "The whole world" is "all sentient beings." "There is nobody without words" means there is not any sentient being that [operates] without characteristic signs. "Once you get past words" [points to] when the thoughts of characteristic signs are stopped. "Words are thoroughly understood" means that

makes the moon at the crest hopelessly drip, thus causing great bliss.

144. Provided from the Apabhraṃśa.

145. Going by the Apabhraṃśa, the second line reads: "there is no one who is not illiterate," i.e., "everybody is illiterate."

146. Tib.: *rab shes pa*. Apa. *gholiā* is not clear. Is it related to Skt. *ghūrṇitākṣara*?

147. The last two lines are in reverse order in DK_A.

when [the thoughts of] characteristic signs are stopped, all conventions are thoroughly understood. "Past words is the letter [*a*],"[148] means that words are symbols, and without symbols [we still get] the letter *a*, which is known [to stand for] the reflections of empti[ness]. Or else "words (*akṣara*) are thoroughly understood" means to know indestructible (*akṣara*) bliss, because "word/letter"[149] also means "indestructible." If you ask which letter, he said: "Past words is the letter [*a*]." Words are conceptual, and this [letter *a*] is not. The "letter [*a*]" is nonconceptual bliss.[150] This is said in the [*Param*]-*ādibuddha*: "The bliss that arises from the indestructible (*akṣara*)[151] is the fruit."[152]

> You are fond of ink yet not of reading.[153]
> Meaningless recitations of the Vedas ruined them.
> Good people, think! If you do not know the other (i.e., the reflections of emptiness),
> from where do you arise and into what do you disappear? 107

To stop attachment to the words in the external world, [Saraha] says: "Meaningless recitations of the Vedas ruined them." This [meaningless recitation] ruins the recitation of ultimate *oṃ* and turns it into suffering in saṃsāra. Although words/letters are [meaning]less in this way, they naturally abide [as vibrations] in your body. Therefore, to teach that they can be realized, he teaches the line "Good people, think!" and so forth. "Good people, think! If you do not know the other," which here means the reflections of empti[ness]: "do not know" means if you do not realize [them], you do not even know from where thoughts arise, abide, and disappear.

148. This line is missing in the root text.

149. Tib. *yi ge* can mean both.

150. This is similar to Maitrīpāda's *Amanasikārādhāra*, where the privative *a* in *amanasikāra* also stands for luminous emptiness (see Mathes 2015, 247).

151. Skt. *akṣara* also means "the letter *a*."

152. This line corresponds to a part of *Sekoddeśa* 146b. The entire verse (Sferra 2006, 197_{3-4}) reads as follows: "The reflections, which emerge from emptiness, are the cause, and bliss, which arises from the unchangeable, is the fruit. The cause is sealed by the fruit, and the fruit is sealed by the cause." (*bimbaṃ śūnyodbhavaṃ hetuḥ phalam akṣarajaṃ sukham | phalena mudrito hetur hetunā mudritaṃ phalam*). The reflections of emptiness and bliss thus stand in the causal relation that resembles the one between the support and the supported. Oral information from Dge bshes Blo bzang chos 'phel in 'Dzam thang in Sept. 2019.

153. This line is not commented upon.

As it is outside, so it is within.
[The masters of yoga] abide on the fourteenth level continuously.
The bodiless is hidden in the body.
Whoever realizes it is liberated. 108 (DK_A 87)

Once this is known, [everything is] the reflections of empti[ness]: "As it is outside, so it is within." "Abide on the fourteenth level continuously" means that they abide in the center at the heart.[154] This is [meant by] "The bodiless is hidden in the body." The person who realizes it is liberated. Or, if related to bliss, the other (the reflections of emptiness)[155] is bliss. "As it is outside, so it is within" means [then] that externally this semen is the moon—that is, the waxing moon from the first night until the fifteenth, the full moon, and the waning moon from its first day until the new moon. Likewise, [internally] this semen is at the forehead on the first night of the waxing moon and inside the jewel on the full moon. Then, having abided in the jewel, it rises [from the] jewel in the first night of the sixteen black phases (of the waning moon) [until it reaches] the crown of the head on the consummated new moon. "Abide on the fourteenth level continuously"[156] then refers to the true nature [of mind]. What is opposed is carried along the path.[157]

To abandon the habit of releasing the semen, one gazes upward and then at the six cakras and the six parts in between, twelve [spots all together]. Together with the nonconceptual cakra of the precious jewel and the seed vessel (*varāṭaka*), there are fourteen spots along which [one's focus] gradually travels. This is as taught in the *Hevajratantra* [II.iv.26cd and 25cd]: "[Bodhicitta is the moon that has fifteen digits.] Taking the form of vowels, it is great bliss. The yoginīs are its portions (26). One should carefully avoid the [vowel] at the very end (*aḥ*)[158] because the sixteenth is not a moon digit (25cd)."[159] "The

154. In his commentary on this verse, Advayavajra compares the fourteenth level to the supreme phase of the moon, which is not visible at the end of the new moon, and thus to liberation.

155. This explanation relates back to DK_T 107c.

156. The context requires taking the fourteenth level as enlightenment at the end of the path.

157. This means that ordinary states of mind are dissolved in their coemergent nature.

158. The syllable *aḥ*, even though not exactly a vowel from the viewpoint of Western phonetics, is regarded as the sixteenth vowel. It is sometimes considered to correspond to emission.

159. *Hevajratantra* 177_{2-5} (in the order quoted by Mokṣākaragupta): [*bodhicittam bhavec candram pañcadaśakalātmakam* ||] *ālirūpaṃ mahāsaukhyam yoginyas tasya aṃśakāḥ* || (v. 26) *sarvaśeṣāṃ tyajed yatnāt ṣoḍaśī na kalā yataḥ* || (v. 25cd).

In his commentary on these lines (*Hevajrapañjikā-yogaratnamālā* 144_{4-6}), Kṛṣṇācarya explains: "Thus there are fifteen moon digits during the bright fortnight, which correspond to [fifteen] lunar days. When doing a job, one should consider, among other things, the increase

bodiless is hidden in the body," but it is not born through [the body's] power], because it is said in the *Hevajratantra* [I.i.12d]: "Although abiding in a body, it is not born from a body."[160] This refers to the wisdom of the one who has traversed the ten [bodhisattva] levels.

First, I [could] read the word for realization.
[Later,] I drank the essence [of its meaning], and [the rest] became pointless.
That through which I came to know the single unchangeable [bliss],
its name I do not know [anymore]. 109 (DK_A 88)

In case you wonder from where and how bliss arises, [Saraha] teaches [the verse] starting "First, I [could] read the word for realization." "First...the word for realization" refers to the reflections of empti[ness]; "read" means to be aware of. "[Later,] I drank the essence [of its meaning], and [the rest] became pointless" means that thanks to these [reflections of] empti[ness], I drank the essence. This means that having abandoned the [habit of] releasing [the semen], I forgot about it. Once thoughts[161] [about it] have stopped, there will be bliss. In case you ask what its nature is like, he says "That through which" and so forth. "I came to know the single unchangeable"—that is, unchangeable bliss or, rather, *a*, the reflections of empti[ness]. "Its name I do not know" means that characteristic signs or phenomena [arising from] discrimination have subsided.

In the three jungles, there is the single letter.
In the center of the three letters, there is the deity.
The one who has fallen off these three
is an outcast like those [upholding] the Vedas. 110

in the [moon's] brightness. But because the sixteenth [digit] is the cause of decline, one should make an effort to avoid it" (*tathā hi tithikrameṇa śuklapakṣe pañcadaśaiva candrakalāḥ | ālokādibhir vṛddhir lakṣaṇārtham arthakriyāṃ kurvan ṣoḍaśī sā tu kṣayahetur ato yatnāt tyajet tām |*).

In other words, the digit after full moon, the sixteenth digit, is the cause of deline, as it is the first night without initial moonlight. In terms of *binduyoga*, the full moon correponds to the drop having arrived at the tip of the jewel (male organ), the sixteenth to the decline of the drop's release.

160. *Hevajratantra* 14_2: *dehastho 'pi na dehajaḥ.*

161. Lit.: "The thoughts of the mind."

The three jungles are the three [of the] body, speech, and mind. The single letter is *a*, the indestructible. "In the center of the three letters, there is the deity" means that in the center of the three invincible letters *oṃ āḥ hūṃ*, which are the filling, summoning, and paralyzing winds, there is the deity, which is a reflection of empti[ness]. "The one who has fallen off these three" is the one attached to what arises from body, speech, and mind. Through the kindness of empti[ness], the four nonconceptual joys arise in "an outcast [like those upholding] the Vedas."

> Those who do not grasp the nature[162] [of *sahaja*] completely
> [try] to accomplish great bliss during the [four] moments of erotic bliss.[163]
> It is just like the thirsty deer that runs toward the water of a mirage
> and dies of thirst. [Where] could it find such water in the sky? 111 (DK_A 89)

To abandon contaminated bliss after having taught uncontaminated bliss in such a way, Saraha says: "Those who do not grasp the nature [of *sahaja*] completely." Not knowing the luminous nature, he [thinks] that great or uncontaminated bliss [comes] from the erotic bliss [of engaging with] a *karmamudrā*. "It is just like the thirsty deer that runs toward the water of a mirage and dies of thirst. [Where] could it find such water in the sky?" Although similar to [real] bliss, it is not so. Mistaking it for being similar, one dies of thirst. Seized by suffering, one will not find great bliss.

> The erotic bliss between lotus and penis,
> by which you [hope to] produce [great] bliss—
> since [great bliss] cannot be shown [in the process],
> how [can] expectations within the threefold world be fulfilled by it? 112 (DK_A 92)

Why is it not found? [Saraha] says: "[The erotic bliss] between lotus and penis."[164] "The erotic bliss by which you [hope to] produce [great] bliss" means that although the erotic bliss between the two partially accords with [great]

162. The Tibetan mistook Apa. *ruaṇeṃ* ("through ascertainment") as *rang bzhin* ("nature").

163. *Kunduru* with the meaning of erotic bliss is first attested in the *Hevajratantra*.

164. The commentary on this line is merely the addition in square brackets and thus not repeated.

bliss itself, "since it cannot be shown"—which means since it cannot actualize uncontaminated bliss—"how [can] expectations within the threefold world be fulfilled by it?" meaning how could the three of body, speech, and mind ever be purified [in this way]?

> The bliss of the means (i.e., the male practitioner) is momentary,[165]
> or rather, this [bliss] is differentiated.
> [The goal can be] further [marked] thanks to the kindness of the guru.
> Few are those who come to know [it in this way]. 113 (DK_A 93)

Well then, does this uncontaminated bliss arise even without the bliss of the lotus and the penis? It is said that it does not. What is this erotic bliss like? Is it not natural bliss? [Saraha] says: "The bliss of means is momentary." "[It] is momentary, or rather, it is differentiated" means that if the wisdom arisen from a *prajñā* is the *prajñā* wisdom, then the wisdom arisen from means is also the "means wisdom" [as in the case of the wisdom from a] *prajñā*. In "[The goal can be] further [marked] thanks to the kindness of the guru. Few are those who come to know [it in this way]," "further" means that although *prajñā* wisdom arises in all sentient beings, there are only a few who come to recognize the coemergent at the end of the third drop. Therefore "further" means here later—that is, at the end of the third drop.

> O friends, [the teaching] is both profound and vast.
> [These two attributes] are neither different nor identical.
> During coemergent bliss in the fourth [moment],
> [the goal] is known by experiencing it as one's natural state. 114 (DK_A 94)

Now, to reveal the inseparable union of bliss and emptiness, [Saraha] teaches [the verse] starting "O friends." "Friends" is a vocative; "profound" refers to bliss and "vast" to empti[ness]. These two are neither different nor separate; "nor identical" means that they are not one either. They are also not two. Alternatively, if one [explains it] in terms of emptiness only, "profound" means that it is difficult to realize, and "vast" means that if you realize [its] emptiness only, all phenomena are realized [to be so]. "Neither different" [applies] because of [its] self-awareness. "Nor identical" means that they are not identical in terms of realization. If [this inseparable union] does not arise in this way at this time,

165. DK_A (Apa.): "The moments are [only] a means of bliss."

he says: "During coemergent bliss in the fourth [moment]"[166] and so forth. It has the luminous nature at the fourth [moment] concerning the three appearances.[167] "It is known by experiencing it as one's natural state" refers to the ever-present coemergent.

> Just as the jewel of the moon
> shines forth in frightful darkness,[168]
> supreme great bliss takes away
> all wrongdoings in one moment. 115 (DK_A 95)

To teach the qualities of the rising [coemergent], [Saraha] teaches [the verse] starting "[Just as the jewel of the moon shines forth in frightful] darkness." For those engulfed by darkness, just as all darkness is overcome in one moment when the moon rises, so are all wrongdoings undone at the very moment great bliss rises.[169] All thoughts are destroyed.

> The sun of suffering sets,
> and the leader of stars (i.e., the moon) appears together with the planet [Venus].
> Abiding thus, he emanates the emanating [meditation].
> This is the genuine circle of the maṇḍala. 116 (DK_A 96)

The sun of suffering, the thoughts, has set. The lord of the stars stands for nonconceptual wisdom. "Appears together with the planet [Venus]" means that it appears at the same time together with the interior planet of the wisdom wind. What happened because of that? He says: "Abiding thus, he emanates the emanating [meditation]"—that is, the emanation arises. "This is the genuine circle of the maṇḍala"—that is, one's own uncontrived maṇḍala.

> Hey, you fools! When the mind realizes the mind,
> you get free from all wrong views.
> Through this supreme great bliss,
> when abiding in it, there will be genuine accomplishment. 117 (DK_A 97)

166. The repetition of this line in the commentary is not translated.

167. Explained as the cause of saṃsāric hindrances in verse 33 (see above).

168. Tib. "great darkness" translates Apa. *ghorāndhara* ("frightful darkness").

169. Either Mokṣākaragupta's root text read differently here, or this sentence is a paraphrase.

"Hey" is a general vocative. You are like what because of that? [The first] "mind" refers to your own mind. [The second] "mind," which is naturally non-conceptual, is nothing at all. "Realizes" means to rest the mind in this. "You get free from all wrong views" means that since they are not anything at all, you get free from all superimpositions. In "through the power of supreme great bliss," "supreme great bliss" means uncontaminated joy. "Through this" means "through the power of." "When abiding in it, there will be genuine accomplishment" means that you will attain the rank of a buddha.

> Let the elephant of the mind wander freely!
> Let it answer to itself!
> Let it drink the river water of the sky mountain,
> and let it rest on its banks according to its wish! 118 (DK_A 98)

Having taught the qualities of such inseparable bliss and emptiness, [Saraha] now teaches the means of resting the mind in empti[ness] and bliss. To do so, he teaches [the lines] starting "[Let] the elephant of the mind." "Let the elephant of the mind wander freely!" means not to pressure or stop it. Now "Let it answer to itself!" means to leave the mind in its own way. "Once this is realized, do not ask [anymore]!"[170] This means not to mentally engage with characteristic signs at this time. Then to teach the means to rest the mind in bliss, he teaches [the lines] starting "[Let it drink the water of the river of] the sky mountain." Here "sky" refers to the top of the head, and "mountain" to the body. "Let it drink the water" means to experience the bliss of the semen. "Rest on its banks" means to rest in the channel of one's own organ.[171] "According to its wish" means easily, freely.

> Seized by the huge elephant of sense objects [with] its trunk,
> he, it appears,[172] was going to be killed.
> It appears that he was going to be moved around,[173]

170. This line is missing in the root text.

171. I.e., a literal translation of Tib. *gnyug ma'i dbang po'i rtsa*. The precise meaning of this technical term remains unknown to us.

172. It is not clear how Tib. *rang dbang* modifies "it appears," and it is missing in DK_{AT} 99b and Mokṣākaragupta's paraphrase.

173. According to Mokṣākaragupta's commentary. DK_T 119b and DK_{AT} 99b have "...going to be killed."

but like an elephant keeper, the yogin
escapes from that [situation].[174] 119 (DK_A 99)

To those wondering how to rest, [Saraha] teaches [the verse] starting "[Seized by the huge] elephant of sense objects [with its trunk]." "Of sense objects" means that led by the trunk of the huge elephant[175] of external [objects], it appears that he was going to be moved around. It is as if he were deliberately moved around, but the yogin controls the elephant of the mind. "But like an elephant keeper, the yogin" means that he was not squeezed, not made over. "Escapes from that [situation]" means that he himself escapes.

What is cyclic existence is indeed nirvāṇa as well.
Do not take them to be separate!
They are without distinction in terms of having a single nature.
[This] stainless [nonduality] I have realized. 120 (DK_A 100)

To teach the means to rest in inseparable [saṃsāra and nirvāṇa], [Saraha] teaches [the verse] starting "What is cyclic existence." "What is cyclic existence is indeed nirvāṇa as well" means that saṃsāra itself is liberation. "Do not take them to be separate!" means not to look outside and distinguish the five [sense] objects. "In terms of having a single nature" [refers to] not being separate in terms of object and subject. "They are without distinction" means without distinction into separate things. "Stainless" means without clinging to duality.

The reality of the mental consciousness is an object focus.
Emptiness is without an object focus.
Both of them have fault.
The yogin does not meditate with either one. 121

To teach the justification for [saṃsāra and nirvāṇa] being inseparable, [Saraha] teaches [the verses] starting "The reality of the mental consciousness." "Object focus" [involves] compassion, "without an object focus" empti[ness]. "Both of them have fault" when they are not combined.

[Whether] the meditation is with object focus or not,
meditation, non-meditation, or unconventional,

174. DK_A (Apa.): "[But] the yogin, who is taking little bits [of the sense objects], somehow escapes from it."

175. I.e., taking Tib. *glang po che rgyal po* as a translation of Sanskrit *gajendra*.

[all] have aspects of bliss as their nature.
It is supreme unsurpassed [bliss] arising naturally.
You know it by practicing [the instructions] of the master's
lineage.[176] 122

"Bliss as their nature" refers to their equal taste. "It is supreme unsurpassed [bliss] arising naturally" means that it arises without [having to] make contact with anything. The rest is easy to understand.

Neither go into the forest nor remain at home!
Wherever you are, when you know the mental consciousness
entirely,[177]
it is entirely and continuously grounded in the realization of
enlightenment.
Where [then] is saṃsāra and where is nirvāṇa? 123 (DK_A 101)

To teach now that the so-called abiding in nonduality [requires] being without a fixed place, [Saraha] teaches [the verse] starting "[Neither] go into the forest." "Wherever you are" means that whether in the forest or at home, consciousness [must rest] in equanimity. "It is entirely and continuously grounded in the realization of enlightenment" refers to your uncontrived nature. The rest is easy to understand.

When the stains of the mental consciousness are purified, the
coemergent [manifests].
Then you no longer enter what is opposed to it.
It is like the sea foam that is water
dissolving into the ocean when it gets clear. 124

To teach the qualities based on this [enlightenment], [Saraha] says: "Then you no longer enter what is opposed to it" and so forth.

Enlightenment depends on neither house nor forest;
you must understand distinctions [being made figuratively] with
such [words].

176. See *Hevajratantra* I.viii.34.

177. Tib. *yid kyis* is difficult to construe and should be *yid la*. In any case Apa. *maṇa pariāṇa* can be analyzed this way. In the original Tibetan translation there must have been something like *yid kyi yongs su shes pa*.

It is suitable that in terms of the stainless nature of mind
everything is based on nonconceptuality. 125 (DK_A 102)

"Nonconceptuality" [is taught] because one should not engage in conceptual reasoning. "You must understand distinctions [being made figuratively] with such [words]" refers equally to good and bad.

This is the self, and this the other. Meditation and meditator—
it is like when discerning something seen [reflected] in the ocean.
One needs to break loose from the bondage of [such] distinctions.
So[178] you must save yourself! 126 (DK_A 103)

"Needs to break loose from the bondage of [such] distinctions" means that dualistic discriminations are abandoned. Why then do they appear as separate? He says: "It is like when discerning something seen in the ocean" or like the reflection of a shape appearing in clear water.

Do not confusedly make self and other [two different things]!
Everybody has always been a buddha;
the mind being naturally pure,
this is the supreme stainless level. 127 (DK_A 104)

"Do not confusedly make self and other [two different things]!" means do not confuse one with two! After having thus taught four types of the coemergent in terms of means,[179] Saraha now teaches in detail the coemergent of the fruit [in the lines starting with] "Everybody has always been a buddha." "The mind being naturally pure" means that it is so throughout beginningless time.

Now, to teach in detail the coemergent of the fruit:

The supreme tree of nondual mind
pervades the entire threefold world!
It bears the flower of compassion and the fruit of benefitting
others.
This is what is called supreme benefit to others. 128 (DK_A 105)

"Nondual" means to be of equal taste. "[It] pervades the entire [threefold

178. Tib *'on kyang* corresponds to Apa. *kiu* in the sense of Skt. *kim u*.

179. I.e., coemergent joy embedded in the sequence of the four joys?

world]!" for the sake of sentient beings. "This is what is called supreme benefit to others" means that in reality there is no self or other.

> The supreme tree of emptiness[180] has blossomed
> in many kinds and shapes of compassion.
> It brings fruit in the future[181] without effort.
> This [ordinary] bliss [here] is not the supreme[182] mind. 129
> (DK$_A$ 106)

"Many kinds and shapes" refers to manifold activity. "[Is] without effort" means not to search for [anything]. "Fruit in the future" [is] for everybody. "This [ordinary] bliss [here] is not the supreme mind"—it is not the uncontaminated one.

> The tree of emptiness, which is not genuine compassion,
> will have no roots, flowers, or leaves.
> If someone turns [emptiness] into an object (i.e., tries to climb an empty tree),
> he will fall from it[183] and break his limbs. 130 (DK$_A$ 107)

Now to teach the opposite, [Saraha] says: "The tree of emptiness, which is [not] genuine," and so forth. This means that without the tree of emptiness, there will be no branches and leaves of compassion. Now, to teach the fault of clinging to an observed object, he says: "If someone turns [emptiness] into an object" and so forth. "Turned into an object" means to conceptually cling to the nondual in terms of characteristic signs. "He will fall from it" because of adhering to characteristic signs. "Break his limbs" means becoming defiled in saṃsāra.

> Two trees [come] from the same seed;
> therefore they bear the same [type of] fruit.
> Whoever considers their inseparability
> is liberated from [both] saṃsāra and nirvāṇa. 131 (DK$_A$ 108)

To teach the qualities of realizing that [they are] without defining character-

180. Lit.: "empty tree."

181. The Apabhraṃśa and and its Tibetan translation have "to others" instead of "in the future."

182. Apa. *paru* (Skt. *param*) means here "supreme" and not "other."

183. Lit.: "on it."

istics, [Saraha] teaches [the verse] starting "[Two trees come] from the [same] seed." "The same seed" is the natural mind. The "two trees" are the two of bliss and emptiness. "Therefore they bear the same [type of] fruit" means that they are of equal taste. "Their inseparability" means that they are unitary. "Whoever considers" or meditates "is liberated from [both] saṃsāra and nirvāṇa," which refers to the attainment of nonabiding nirvāṇa.

> If a beggar comes
> and leaves, there [should] be no hope.[184]
> It is better to take the broken[185] bowl that is cast out the door
> and thus [say:] "You'd better remain without a household." 132 (DK_A 109)

Beggars are in search of such [generous] persons.[186] "If a beggar comes and leaves, there [should] be no hope" means that [one should] give to whomever without any hope of reward. Teaching that one cannot [easily] achieve selfless benefit of others, [Saraha] says: "[It is better to take] the broken bowl" and so forth.

> You do not help others
> and do not give to the needy.
> What fruit do you [expect] in this saṃsāra?
> Therefore you had better abandon this [cherished] self. 133 (DK_A 110)

"Just as the beggar [comes" and so forth][187] means that you do not work for others, that you are not of any help to others. "Do not give to the needy" means that you do not give alms. "What fruit do you [expect] in this saṃsāra?" indicates that birth in saṃsāra does not serve any purpose. "Therefore you had better abandon this [cherished] self" means that you had better abandon seeking your own benefit and work for others. Or [from another perspective], [Saraha] teaches that if you are not attached when working for the benefit of yourself

184. Translated in the light of Mokṣākaragupta's commentary. DK_T and DK_{AT} read: "and leaves without having [his] hopes [fulfilled]."

185. Tib. *dum bu* is missing in the standard Tibetan root text but found in DK_{AT}.

186. I.e., persons who would prefer being beggars themselves to being stingy.

187. This and the following quotation differ from the standard Tibetan root text but are similar to what is found in the previous verse. In other words, this last portion of commenary is on verses 132 and 133 together.

and others, you are not tainted by the shortcomings of saṃsāra. "You do not work for the benefit of others"[188] means that you do not form the concept of helping others. "And do not give to the needy" means that you are not attached to giving. "What fruit do you [expect] in this saṃsāra?" means that you are [better] not tainted by saṃsāra. "Therefore you had better abandon this [cherished] self" signifies that [you had better] abandon attachment to an "I." "[It is better to take] the broken bowl"[189] and so forth means, for example, that you must see things as in the case of not expecting a reward for giving to beggars.

Thanks to the kindness of the guru,
I have explained the essential meaning only a little.
May all beings realize it
through the merit I have accumulated.

The *Dohākoṣapañjikā* by the learned master Mokṣākaragupta is ended. Translated by the Indian scholar Bhavideva and Rgya Lo tsā ba.

188. Similar to DK_T 133a.

189. Oddly, this is referring to the previous verse and seems out of place here.

Appendix: Concordance

Advayavajra	Tokyo	Göttingen	Sāṅkṛtyāyana	Tibetan
ø	ø	ø	— (= lacuna)	1 dug sprul
1 bahmaṇĕhiṃ	1 bahmaṇĕhiṃ	1 bahmaṇĕhiṃ	—	2 de nyid
2 maṭṭī	2 māṭṭī	2 maṭṭhī	—	3 sa chu
3 daṇḍi	3 dāṇḍi	3 daṇḍi	—	4 dbyu gu
4 aïriehiṃ	4 aïriehiṃ	4 aïriĕhi	—	5 e ra'i
5 akkhi	5 akkhi	5 akkhi	—	6 skyil krung
6 dīhaṇa-	6 dīhaṇa-	6 dīhaṇa-	—	7 sen mo
7 jaï	7 jaï	7 jaï	—	8 gcer bu
8 picchī-	8 piñchī-	8 picchī-	—	9 mjug spu
9 Saraha	9 Saraha	9 Saraha	8cd–9ab	10 mda'
10 cellū	10 cellu	10 cellu	9cd–10ab	11 dge tshul
11 aṇṇatahiṃ	11 aṇṇataṃhi	11 aṇṇatahiṃ	10cd–11ab	12 kha cig
ø	ø	ø	ø	13 la la
12 sahaja	12 sahaja	12 sahaja	11cd	14 lhan cig
13 jo jasu	15 jo jasu	13 jo jasu	12ab	15 gang zhig
14 kin taha	16 kin taha	14 kiṃ taha	12cd–13ab	16 mar me
ø	ø	15 karuṇarahia	16cd–17ab	17 snying rje
ø	ø	16 jo uṇa	17cd	18 gang yang
15 cchaḍḍahu	17 chaḍḍahu	17 chaḍḍaü	13cd–14ab	19 kye lags
16 sovi	18 so bi	18 so bi	14cd–15ab	20 klog pa
17 jaï	19 jaï	19 jaï	15cd–16ab	21 bla mas
18 jhāṇahīṇa	20 jhāṇahīṇa	20 jhāṇadīṇa	18	22 bsam gtan
19 jaï	21 jaï	21 jaï	19	23 gal te
20 jallaï	22 jallaï	22 jallaï	20	24 gang zhig
21 jhāṇarahia	23 jhāṇarahia	23 jhāṇarahia	42	25 bsam gtan
22 manta	24 tānta	24 manta	43	26 rgyud med

23 khāanteṃ	25 khānte	25 khāanteṃ	48	27 za zhing
24 jahi	26 jahi	26 jahi	49	28 gang du
25 ekku	27 eka	27 ekka	50	29 gnyis su
ø	28 āi	28 āi	51	30 der ni
ø	29 ageeṃ	29 aggeṃ	52	31 mdun
ø	30 indī	30 indī	29	32 dbang po
29 jahi	31 jahi	31 jahi	30	33 yid ni
30 saa-	32 saĕṃ-	32 saï-	88cd–89ab	34 kye ho
31 jhāṇeṃ	—	33 jhāṇeṃ	89cd–90ab	35 bsam gtan
32 paḍhameṃ	—	34 paḍhameṃ	33	36 gdod nas
33 ahimaṇa-	—	35 ahimaṇa-	34	37 skye bo
34 cittaha	—	36 cittaha	27	38 sems kyi
35 mūlarahia	—	37 mūlarahia	28ab & ?	39 rtsa ba
36 ṇiasahāva	—	38 ṇiasahāba	90cd–91ab	40 gnyug
37 ṇiamaṇa	—	39 ṇiamaṇa	36	41 gnyug
38 bajjhaï	—	40 bajjaï	24	42 'gro rnams
39 cittekka	—	41 cieka	23	43 sems nyid
40 citteṃ	—	42 citteṃ	91cd–92ab	44 sems
ø	—	ø	155cd–156ab	45 sems ni
ø	—	ø	~156cd–157ab	46 mkha'
ø	—	ø	ø	47 rlung dang
ø	—	ø	ø	48 khyim
ø	—	ø	ø	49 srog chags
ø	—	ø	ø	50 kha sang
ø	—	ø	ø	51 bya ba
ø	—	ø	ø	52 'jur bus
41 baddho	—	43 baddho	92cd–93ab	53 bcings
ø	—	ø	ø	54 kye lags
42 pavaṇa-	43(?) ... rajjaü	44 pabaṇa-	93cd–94ab	55 rlung
43 ehu	44 ehu	45 ehu	~94cd	56 'di la
44 javveṃ	45 jebe	46 jabbeṃ	95	57 gang tshe
45 etthu	46 ethu	47 etthu	96 (!)	58 'di ni
46 kkhettu	47 khetta	48 khetta	97	59 zhing kun
47 saṇḍa	48 sara-	49 saṇḍa-	98	60 'dab ldan
48 kā manta-	49 kammā	50 kāmantha	99	61 gang tshe

49 are putto	50 are putta	51 are putta	56	62 kye ho
50 are putto	51 are puta	52 are putta	104abc & ?	63 kye ho
51 buddhi	52 buddhi	53 buddhi	61	64 blo ni
52 bhāvarahia	53 bhaba	54 bhabahiṃ	62	65 dngos por
53 dekkhahu	54 dekkhaü	55 dekkhaha	63	66 mthong
54 guru-	55 guru-	56 guru-	44	67 gang zhig
ø	ø	ø	77	68 bla mas
ø	ø	ø	112	69 tshad mar
ø	ø	ø	ø?	70 gang tshe
55 cittācitta	56 cittācitta	57 cintācinta	64	71 nad gzhan
56 akkhara-	57 akṣara-	58 akkhara	65	72 kha dog
ø	ø	59 ṇa ttam	77	ø
57 bhāvā-	58 bhābā-	60 bhābā-	66	73 dngos
58 jāva	59 jāba	61 jāba	67	74 gang tshe
59 ṇaü	60 aṇu	62 ṇaü	68	75 rdul min
60 ghare	61 ghareṃ	63 meheṃ	69	76 khyim na
61 jaï	62 jaïṃ	64 jaï	70	77 gang tshe
62 visaa	63 bisaa	65 bisaa	71	78 yul rnams
63 deva	64 deba	66 deba	72	79 lha la
64 aṇimisa-	End of the text	67 aṇimisa-	ø	80 mig ni
65 jāu		68 jāu	ø	81 ji srid
66 paṇḍia		69 paṇḍia	75	82 mkhas pa
67 jīvantaha		70 jībantaha	ø	83 gson pa
68 visaa-		71 bisaa-	ø	84 yul nyid
ø		ø	ø	85 thag pa
69 visaāsatti		72 bisaāsatta	ø	86 yul la
70 jatta		73 jatta	76	87 gang zhig
71 kāsu		74 kāsu	ø	88 gang zhig
72 jatta		75 jattaï	78	89 ji ltar
ø		ø	ø	90 nags la
73 suṇṇahiṃ		76 suṇṇahi	ø	91 gal te
74 aïseṃ		77 aïso	ø	92 de ltar
75 savvarūa		78 sabba rūba	~155cd–156a & ?	93 thams cad
76 ghareṃ		79 ghare	128	94 khyim

ø		ø	ø	95 bde gsang
ø		ø	129ab & 46	96 gal te
77 ekku		80 ekku	121ab	97 lha cig
78 appaṇu		81 appaṇu	121cd & ?	98 mgon po
79 āvanta		82 ābanta	ø	99 'ongs
80 āvaï		83 ābai	ø	100 'gro 'ong
81 sohaï		84 sohaï	ø	101 nyal ba'i
ø		85 aïsa upa-	ø	ø
82 gharavaï		86 gharabaï	ø	102 khyim
83 gharavaï		87 gharabaï	ø	103 bdag po
84 khajjaï		88 khājjaï	ø	104 za zhing
85 ia diva-		89 aïa dari-	ø	105 sa gsum
86 akkhara-		90 akkhara	25	106 yi ge
ø		ø	~41	107 snag tsha
87 jima		91 jima	ø	108 ji ltar
88 siddhir		92 siddhir-	ø	109 nga yis
ø		ø	ø	110 nags
89 ruaṇeṃ		93 ruaṇa	ø	111 ma lus
90 kandha-		ø	ø	ø
91 paṇḍia-		ø	ø	ø
92 kamala-		94 kamala	ø	112 rdo rje
93 khaṇa-		95 ṇaba-	ø	113 yang na
94 gambhīraï		96 gaṃbhīraï	ø	114 grogs
95 ghorā-		97 ghora-	ø	115 mun nag
96 dukkha-		98 dukkha-	ø	116 sdug
97 cittahiṃ		99 cittehiṃ	ø	117 kye ho
98 mukkaü		100 mukkaü	ø	118 sems kyi
99 visaa-		101 biaga-	ø	119 yul gyi
100 jo		102 jo	ø	120 gang
ø		ø	ø	121 yid kyi
ø		ø	ø	122 sgom pa
101 gharahi		103 gharahi	ø	123 nags su
ø		ø	~76	124 yid kyi
102 ṇaü		104 ṇaü	ø	125 nags
103 ehu		105 ehu	ø	126 de ni

104 para		106 para	ø	127 bdag
105 addaa-		107 advaa-	ø	128 gnyis
106 suṇṇa-		108 suṇṇa-	ø	129 stong
107 suṇṇa-		109 suṇṇa-	ø	130 stong
108 ekkeṃ		110 ekkaṃ	ø	131 sa bon
109 jo		111 jo	ø	132 gang
110 para-		112 para-	ø	133 gzhan

Abbreviations

ø   Missing verse

~   Approximately

..   One *akṣara* missing

||| Two or more *akṣaras* missing

A   A single folio of the *Dohākoṣapañjikā* misplaced in the *Sahajāmnāyapañjikā* (NGMPP reel no. A 49/18, exposures 82–83)

ac   Ante correctionem

ĀM   *Ālokamālā*

Apa.   Apabhraṃśa

B   Dpal spungs edition of *Indian Mahāmudrā Works* (*Phyag chen rgya gzhung*). *See* Phun tshogs rgyal mtshan

BCA   *Bodhicaryāvatāra*

D   Dergé edition of the Tibetan Buddhist canon

DK$_{A}$ *Dohākoṣa* verses in Advayavajra's *Dohākoṣapañjikā*

DK$_{AT}$ Tibetan translation of DK$_{A}$ in DKP$_{A}$

DK$_{T}$ *Dohākoṣa*, the standard Tibetan root text

DKP$_{A}$ *Dohākoṣapañjikā* by Advayavajra

DKP$_{M}$ *Dohākoṣapañjikā* by Mokṣākaragupta

DP   D and P

E$_{B}$ *Dohākoṣapañjikā* by Advayavajra, Sanskrit ed. Bagchi 1938

E$_{Sh}$ *Dohākoṣapañjikā* by Advayavajra, Sanskrit ed. Śāstrī 1959

E$_{ShM}$ *Dohākoṣapañjikā* by Advayavajra, manuscript reading recorded by Śāstrī 1959

G   Ms Niedersächsische Staats- und Universitätsbibliothek Göttingen Xc 14/16. Praemittit : [1b$_{1}$] [*siddham*] namaḥ sarvajñāya ||

GT   G and T

HT   *Hevajratantra*

N   NGMPP reel no. A 932/4, 17b3–102b5. The Nepalese manuscript of Hemraj Sharma (now at the National Archives, Kathmandu).

NGMPP   Nepal-German Manuscript Preservation Project

om.	Omittit/omittant
pc	Post correctionem
P	Peking edition of the Tibetan Buddhist canon
PV	*Pramāṇavārttika*
RGV	*Ratnagotravibhāga Mahāyānottaratantraśāstra*
Skt.	Sanskrit
T	Ms Tokyo University Library no. 517. *Praemittit*: [16b$_4$] [*siddham*] namo vajraḍākāya ||.
TBRC	Buddhist Digital Resource Center (bdrc.io)
Tib.	Tibetan
Tōh.	Tōhōku
YṢ	*Yuktiṣaṣṭikā*

Bibliography

Primary Sources (Indian)

Amṛtakaṇikoddyotanibandha. In Āryamañjuśrīnāmasaṃgīti *with* Amṛtakaṇikāṭippaṇī *by Bhikṣu Raviśrījñāna and* Amṛtakaṇikodyota-nibhandha [sic] *of Vibhūticandra*, edited by Banarsi Lal. Bibliotheca Indo-Tibetica 30. Sarnath, Varanasi: Central Institute of Higher Tibetan Studies, 1994.

Ālokamālā. Edited by Christian Lindtner. See Lindtner 2003.

Āmnāyamañjarī. Draft edition courtesy of Tōru Tomabechi.

Bodhicaryāvatāra. Edited by Vidhushekhara Bhattacharya. Kalkota: Asiatic Society Calcutta, 1960.

Cakrasaṃvaratantra. See *Cakrasaṃvaratantravivṛti*.

Cakrasaṃvaratantravivṛti. Edited by Janardan Shastri Pandey. Rare Buddhist Sanskrit Texts 26. Sarnath: Central Institute of Higher Tibetan Studies, 2002.

Caturmudrānvaya. See Mathes 2015, 389–402.

Catuṣpīṭhanibandha. Ms Kaiser Library, call number 134.

Dharmadharmatāvibhāgavṛtti. Edited by Klaus-Dieter Mathes. See Mathes 1996, 69–98.

Dohākoṣa (the standard Tibetan root text).
B: *Phyag chen rgya gzhung*, vol. *oṃ*, 142b2–151a4.
D: Tōh. no. 2224, *rgyud 'grel*, vol. *wi*, 70b5–77a3.
P: No. 3068, *rgyud 'grel*, vol. *mi*, 74b6–81b8.

Dohākoṣapañjikā by Advayavajra (Sanskrit and Tibetan).
B: *Phyag chen rgya gzhung*, vol. *āḥ*, fols. 121a4–161a5 (see Phun tshogs rgyal mtshan).
D: Tōh. no. 2256, *rgyud 'grel*, vol. *wi*, fols. 180b3–207a7.
E_B: Edited by Prabodh Chandra Bagchi. See Bagchi 1938, 72–148.
E_{Sh}: Edited by Śāstrī. See Śāstrī 1959.
N: NGMPP reel no. A 932/4.
P: No. 3101, *rgyud 'grel*, vol. *mi*, 199a7–231a5.

Dohākoṣapañjikā by Mokṣākaragupta (Tibetan translation only).
B: *Phyag chen rgya gzhung*, vol. *āḥ*, 161a5–189b1.
D: Tōh. no. 2258, *rgyud 'grel*, vol. *wi*, 265a2–283b1.
P: No. 3103, *rgyud 'grel*, vol. *mi*, 295b1–317b8.

Guṇabharaṇī (*Ṣaḍaṅgayogaḥ Guṇabharaṇīnāmaṣaḍaṅgayogaṭippaṇyā sahitaḥ*). See Sferra 2000, 73–145.

Guṇavatī (= Ratnākaraśānti, *Guṇavatī nāma Mahāmāyāṭīkā*). Edited by Samdhong Rinpoche and Vrajavallabh Dwivedi. Rare Buddhist Texts 10. Sarnath: Central Institute of Higher Tibetan Studies, 1992 (Sanskrit and Tibetan).

Guhyasamājatantra. Edited by Benoytosh Bhattacharya, Gaekwad's Oriental Series 53. Baroda: University of Baroda Press, 1967.
Hevajrapañjikā-Yogaratnamālā. Edited by Ram Shankar Tripathi and Thakur Sain Negi. Bibliotheca Indo-Tibetica 65. Sarnath: Central Institute of Higher Tibetan Studies, 2006.
Hevajratantra. Edited (together with the *Hevajrapañjikā Muktāvalī*) by Ram Shankar Tripathi and Thakur Sain Negi. Bibliotheca Indo-Tibetica 48. Sarnath: Central Institute of Higher Tibetan Studies, 2001.
Kriyāsaṃgrahapañjikā. Preliminary edition courtesy of Ryugen Tanemura.
Laghukālacakratantra. See *Vimalaprabhā*.
Laṅkāvatārasūtra. Edited by Bunyiu Nanjio. Bibliotheca Otaniensis 1. Kyoto: Otani University Press, 1923.
Madhyāntavibhāgabhāṣya. Edited by Gadjin M. Nagao. Tokyo: Suzuki Research Foundation, 1964.
Nāmasaṃgīti. Edited by Alex Wayman. See Wayman 2006.
Pañcakrama. Edited by Katsumi Mimaki and Tōru Tomabechi. Bibliotheca Codicum Asiaticorum 8. Tokyo: The Centre for East Asian Cultural Studies for Unesco, 1994.
Pramāṇavārttika. Edited by Yūsho Miyasaka (Sanskrit and Tibetan), in *Acta Indologica* 2 (1972): 2–206.
Ratnagotravibhāga Mahāyānottaratantraśāstra. Edited by Edward H. Johnston. Patna: The Bihar Research Society, 1950. (Includes the *Ratnagotravibhāgavyākhyā*.)
Ratnagotravibhāgavyākhyā. See above.
Vol. 2 (chapters 3–4), edited by Vrajavallabh Dwivedi and S. S. Bahulkar. Rare Buddhist Texts 12. Sarnath: Central Institute of Higher Tibetan Studies, 1994.
Saṃdhinirmocanasūtra (Tibetan translation from the Kangyur). Ed. by Étienne Lamotte. Louvain (Belgium): Bureaux du Recueil, 1935.
Sarvabuddhasamāyogaḍākinījālaśamvara. Ms Collége de France IÉI Lévi no. 48 (Verse numeration is from my draft edition.)
Sekoddeśa. See Sferra 2006. We also consulted Orofino 1994a, 54–122.
Sekoddeśaṭīkā. Edited by Francesco Sferra. Serie Orientale Roma 99. Rome: Istituto italiano per il Medio ed Estremo Oriente, 2006.
Subhāṣitasaṃgraha. See Bendall 1903–4.
Svādhiṣṭhānakramaprabheda. Pandey, Janardan, ed. "Durlabh granth paricay." *Dhīḥ* 10 (1990): 3–24.
Vijñaptimātratāsiddhi. Edited by Sylvain Lévi. Bibliothèque de l'École des Hautes Études, Sciences historiques et philologiques 245. Paris, 1925.
Vimalaprabhā. Vol. 1 (chapters 1–2), edited by Jagannatha Upadhyaya. Biblioteca Indo-Tibetica 11. Sarnath: Central Institute of Higher Tibetan Studies, 1986.
Viṃśikā. See *Vijñaptimātratāsiddhi*.
Vyaktabhāvānugatatattvasiddhi. In *Guhyādi-Aṣṭasiddhi-saṅgraha*, edited by Samdhong Rinpoche and Vrajvallabh Dwivedi, 169–79. Rare Buddhist Texts 1. Sarnath: Central Institute of Higher Tibetan Studies, 1987.
Yogakuṇḍali-Upaniṣad. See Sastri 1968, 307–36.
Yogaśikhā-Upaniṣad. See Sastri 1968, 390–463.
Yuktiṣaṣṭikā. See *Yuktiṣaṣṭikākārikā*.
Yuktiṣaṣṭikākārikā. Edited by Xuezhu Li and Shaoyong Ye. Shanghai: Zhong xi shu ju, 2013.

Primary Sources (Tibetan)

Bcom ldan Rig pa'i ral gri. *Do ha rgyan gyi me tog*. CPN 007316(4) (according to Schaeffer 2005, 212).

'Bri gung bka' brgyud chos mdzod. See Kun dga' rin chen.

Bu ston Rin chen 'grub. "Bu ston gsan yig": "Bla ma dam pa rnams kyis rjes su gzung ba'i tshul bka' drin rjes su dran par byed pa zhes byar bzhugs so," *Bu ston thams cad mkhyen pa'i bka' 'bum*, vol. *la*, 1–142. Sata-Piṭaka Series 66. New Delhi: International Academy of Indian Culture, 1971.

Dpa' bo Gtsug lag phreng ba. *Chos byung mkhas pa'i dga' ston*. 2 vols. Beijing: Mi rigs dpe skrun khang, 1986.

Khro phu Lo tsā ba Byams pa dpal. *Paṇ grub gsum gyi rnam thar dpag bsam 'khri shing*. Printed version in *Sa skya pa'i bla ma kha shas kyi rnam thar dang sa skya pa min pa'i bla ma kha shas kyi rnam thar*, edited by Shar pa rdo rje 'od zer, vol. *ga*, 85–255. Kathmandu: Sa skya rgyal yongs gsung rab slob gnyer khang, 2008 (TBRC W1KG4275).

Kong sprul Blo gros mtha' yas. *Shes bya kun khyab mdzod*. 3 vols. Beijing: Mi rigs dpe skrun khang, 1982.

Kun dga' rin chen (?), ed. *Grub pa sde bdun dang snying po skor gsum yid la mi byed pa'i chos skor bzhugs so* (*'Bri gung bka' brgyud chos mdzod*, vol. *ka*). N.p., n.d.

———. *'Phags yul bka' brgyud grub chen gong ma'i do ha'i skor bzhugs so* (*'Bri gung bka' brgyud chos mdzod*, vol. *kha*). N.p., n.d.

Padma dkar po. *Phyag chen rgyal ba'i gan mdzod*. Sarnath: Vajra Vidya Institute Library, 2005.

Phun tshogs rgyal mtshan, ed. *Phyag rgya chen po'i rgya gzhung*. 3 vols (*oṃ*, *āḥ*, *hūṃ*). Dpal spungs block print. N.d. See also Zhva dmar pa Mi pham chos kyi blo gros.

Zhwa dmar pa Mi pham chos kyi blo gros, ed. "Rgya gzhung": "Phyag rgya chen po'i rgya gzhung." In *Nges don phyag rgya chen po'i khrid mdzod*, vols. *oṃ*, *āḥ*, and *hūṃ* (TBRC W23447).

Secondary Sources

Bagchi, Prabodh Chandra. 1935. "Dohākoṣa with Notes and Translations." *Journal of the Department of Letters* 28: 1–180.

———. 1938. "Dohākoṣa." *Journal of the Department of Letters*. Calcutta Sanskrit Series 25c. Calcutta University Press.

Bandurski, Frank. 1994. "Übersicht über die Göttinger Sammlungen der von Rāhula Sāṅkṛtyāyana in Tibet aufgefunden buddhistischen Sanskrit-Texte (Funde buddhistischer Sanskrit-Handschriften, III)." In *Untersuchungen zur buddhistischen Literatur*, edited by Frank Bandurski et al., 9–126. Göttingen: Vandenhoeck & Ruprecht.

Bendall, Cecil. 1903–4. "Subhāṣita-saṃgraha. An anthology of extracts from Buddhist works, compiled by an unknown author, to illustrate the doctrines of scholastic and of mystic (tāntrik) Buddhism." *Le Muséon* IV (part I: 375–402) and V (part II: 1–46, 245–74).

Bhayani, H. C. 1997. *Dohāgītikośa of Saraha-pāda (A Treasure of Songs in the Dohā Mātre and Caryāgītikośa (A Treasure of the Cārya Songs of Various Siddhas)*. Restored Text, Sanskrit Chāyā and Translation. Prakrit Text Series 32. Ahmedabad: Prakrit Text Society.

Bosma, Natasja. 2018. *Dakṣiṇa Kosala: A Rich Centre of Early Śaivism*. PhD diss., Leiden, 2018.

Cabezón, José, and Lobsang Dargyay. 2006. *Freedom from Extremes: Gorampa's "Distinguishing the Views" and the Polemics of Emptiness*. Boston: Wisdom Publications.

Dalton, Catherine, and Péter-Dániel Szántó. 2019. "Jñānapāda." In *Brill's Encyclopedia of Buddhism. Volume II: Lives*, edited by Jonathan A. Silk et al., 264–68. Boston/Leiden: Brill.

Damron, Ryan C. 2014. "The Great Illusion: A Preliminary Study of the *Mahāmāyā Tantra* and Its Corpus." MA thesis, University of California, Berkeley.

Dasgupta, Surendranath. 1988. *A History of Indian Philosophy*, vol. 1. Delhi: Motilal Banarsidass.

Eimer, Helmut, ed. 1978. *Bodhipathapradīpa: Ein Lehrgedicht des Atiśa (Dīpaṃkaraśrījñāna) in der tibetischen Überlieferung*. Wiesbaden: Otto Harrassowitz.

Forgues, Gregory (as Buddhavacana Translation Group). 2020. *Unraveling the Intent: Saṃdhinirmocana (Toh 106)*. 84000: Translating the Words of the Buddha. https://read.84000.co/translation/toh106.html.

Griffiths, Arlo, and Péter-Dániel Szántó. 2015. "Sarvabuddhasamāyogaḍākinījālaśaṃvara." In *Brill's Encyclopedia of Buddhism. Volume I: Literature and Languages*, edited by Jonathan A. Silk et al., 367–72. Boston/Leiden: Brill.

Gray, David B. 2012. *The Cakrasamvara Tantra (The Discourse of Śrī Heruka): Editions of the Sanskrit and Tibetan Texts.* New York: The American Institute of Buddhist Studies.

Grönbold, Günther. 1969. *Ṣaḍaṅgayoga: Raviśrījñāna's Guṇabharaṇī nāma Ṣaḍaṅgayogaṭippaṇī* mit Text, Übersetzung und literaturhistorischem Hintergrund. Munich.

Guenther, Herbert. 1993. *Ecstatic Spontaneity: Saraha's Three Cycles of Dohā*. Berkeley: Asian Humanities Press.

Halhed, Nathaniel Brassey. 1778. *A Grammar of the Bengal Language*. Hoogly.

Isaacson, Harunaga. 2009. "A Collection of Hevajrasādhanas and Related Works in Sanskrit." In *Sanskrit Manuscripts in China: Proceedings of a Panel at the 2008 Beijing Seminar on Tibetan Studies, October 13 to 17*, edited by Ernst Steinkellner, Duan Qing, and Helmut Krasser, 89–136. Beijing/Vienna: China Tibetology Publishing House / Austrian Academy of Sciences.

Isaacson, Harunaga, and Francesco Sferra, eds. 2014. *The* Sekanirdeśa *of Maitreyanātha (Advayavajra) with the* Sekanirdeśapañjikā *of Rāmapāla: Critical Edition of the Sanskrit and Tibetan Texts with English Translation and Reproductions of the MSS.* Manuscripta Buddhica 2. Naples: Università degli Studi Napoli "L'Orientale."

Jackson, Roger R. 2004. *Tantric Treasures: Three Collections of Mystical Verse from Buddhist India*. Oxford: Oxford University Press.

Kemp, Casey A. 2019. "The Definitive Meaning of *Mahāmudrā* according to the Kālacakra Tradition of Yu mo Mi bsykod rdo rje's *Phyag chen gsal sgron*. In *Mahāmudrā in India and Tibet*, edited by Roger R. Jackson and Klaus-Dieter Mathes, 185–203. Leiden/Boston: Brill.

Kvaerne, Per. 1977. *An Anthology of Buddhist Tantric Songs*. Oslo: Universitetsforlaget.

Lindtner, Christian. 2003. *A Garland of Light: Kambala's Ālokamālā*. Fremont, CA: Asian Humanities Press.

Luo, Hong. 2010. *Abhayākaragupta's Abhayapaddhati Chapters 9 to 14*. Critically edited and translated by Luo Hong with a preface by Harunaga Isaacson and Alexis Sanderson.

Sanskrit Texts from the Tibetan Autonomous Region 14. Beijing-Hamburg: China Tibetology Publishing House.

Mathes, Klaus-Dieter. 1996. *Unterscheidung der Gegebenheiten von ihrem wahren Wesen (*Dharmadharmatāvibhāga*)*. Indica et Tibetica 26. Swisttal-Odendorf: Indica et Tibetica Verlag.

———. 2006. "Blending the Sūtras with the Tantras: The Influence of Maitrīpa and His Circle on the Formation of *Sūtra Mahāmudrā* in the Kagyu Schools." In *Tibetan Buddhist Literature and Praxis: Studies in Its Formative Period 900–1400*, edited by Ronald M. Davidson and Christian K. Wedemeyer, 201–27. Proceedings of the Tenth Seminar of the IATS, Oxford 2003, vol. 10/4. Leiden: Brill.

———. 2008. *A Direct Path to the Buddha Within: Gö Lotsāwa's Mahāmudrā Interpretation of the Ratnagotravibhāga*. Boston: Wisdom Publications.

———. 2009. "The 'Succession of the Four Seals' (*Caturmudrānvaya*) Together with Selected Passages from Karopa's Commentary." In *Tantric Studies*, 1:89–130. Hamburg: Centre for Tantric Studies, University of Hamburg.

———. 2011. "The Collection of 'Indian Mahāmudrā Works' (*phyag chen rgya gzhung*) Compiled by the Seventh Karma pa Chos grags rgya mtsho." In *Mahāmudrā and the Bka'-brgyud Tradition*, edited by Roger R. Jackson and Matthew T. Kapstein, 89–130. PIATS 2006: Proceedings of the Eleventh Seminar of the International Association for Tibetan Studies, Königswinter 2006. Zentralasienforschung 25. Andiast: International Institute for Tibetan and Buddhist Studies.

———. 2014. "A Summary and Topical Outline of the *Sekanirdeśapañjikā* by 'Bum la 'bar." In The *Sekanirdeśa of Maitreyanātha (Advayavajra) with the Sekanirdeśapañjikā of Rāmapāla: Critical Edition of the Sanskrit and Tibetan Texts with English Translation and Reproductions of the MSS*, 367–84. Manuscripta Buddhica 2. Naples: Università degli Studi Napoli "L'Orientale."

———. 2015. *A Fine Blend of Mahāmudrā and Madhyamaka: Maitrīpa's Collection of Texts on Non-Conceptual Realization (*Amanasikāra*)*. Vienna: Österreichische Akademie der Wissenschaften.

———. 2015a. "Mind and Its Co-emergent (*Sahaja*) Nature in Advayavajra's Commentary on Saraha's *Dohākoṣa*." In *Zentralasiatische Studien* 44: 17–34.

———. 2016. "bKa' brgyud Mahāmudrā: 'Chinese rDzogs chen' or the Teachings of the Siddhas?" In *Zentralasiatische Studien* 45: 309–40.

———. 2019. "*Sahajavajra's Integration of Tantra into Mainstream Buddhism: An Analysis of his **Tattvadaśakaṭīkā* and **Sthitisamāsa*." In *Tantric Communities in Context*, edited by Nina Mirnig, Marion Rastelli, and Vincent Eltschinger, 137–69. Vienna: Austrian Academy of Sciences Press.

———. 2019a. "Maitrīpa's *Amanasikāra*-Based Mahāmudrā in the Works of the Eighth Karma pa Mi bskyod rdo rje." In *Mahāmudrā in India and Tibet*, edited by Roger R. Jackson and Klaus-Dieter Mathes, 269–301. Leiden/Boston: Brill.

———. 2021. *Maitrīpa: India's Yogi of Nondual Bliss*. Lives of the Masters. Boulder: Shambhala Publications.

McGregor, R. S. 1993. *The Oxford Hindi-English Dictionary*. Oxford: Oxford University Press.

Nakamura, Hajime. 1989. *Indian Buddhism: A Survey with Bibliographical Notes*. Buddhist Translation Series 1. Delhi: Motilal Banarsidass. First published 1980.

Matsunami, Seiren. 1965. *A Catalogue of the Sanskrit Manuscripts in the Tokyo University Library*. Tokyo: Suzuki Research Foundation.

Ōmi, Jishō. 2009a. "Ratnākaraśānti and Alaṃkāraśrī's Interpretations of the Mahāmāyātantra, chapter 1, passage 3, to chapter 1, passage 5." [In Japanese.] *Bulletin of the Research Institute of Esoteric Buddhist Culture/Mikkyō Bunka Kenkyūsho* 22: 179–208.

———. 2009b. "Ratnākaraśānti's and Alaṃkāraśrī's Interpretations of the Mahāmāyātantra, chap. 1, verse 18, and chap. 1, verse 23, to chap. 2, verse 5: Focused on the Critical Edition of the Sanskrit-Tibetan Text of the Mahāmāyānāmapañjikā with Commentaries." [In Japanese.] *Journal of Esoteric Buddhism / Mikkyō Bunka* 222: 27–65.

Orofino, Giacomella. 1994. "Mirror Divination: Observations on a Simile Found in the Kālacakra Literature." In *Proceedings of the 6th Seminar of the International Association for Tibetan Studies, Fagernes, 1992*, 2:612–28. Oslo: Institute for Comparative Research in Human Culture.

———. 1994a. *Sekoddeśa: A Critical Edition of the Tibetan Translations.* Serie Orientale Roma 72. Rome: IsMEO

———. 1996. "On the Saḍaṅgayoga and the Realisation of Ultimate Gnosis in the Kālacakratantra." *East and West* 46: 127–45.

Ray, Pranabesh Sinha. 2007. *The Mystic Songs of Kanha and Saraha (The Doha-kosa and the Carya)*. Kalkota: The Asiatic Society.

Rhys Davids, Caroline A. F. 1933. "Buddho or suddho?" *Journal of the Royal Asiatic Society* 65.4: 910–11.

Roberts, Peter Alan. 2014. *The Mind of Mahāmudrā: Advice from the Kagyü Masters.* Tibetan Classics. Boston: Wisdom Publications.

Roerich, George N. 1949–53. *The Blue Annals*. 2 vols. Monograph Series 7. Kalkota: Royal Asiatic Society of Bengal.

Sanderson, Alexis. 2009. "The Śaiva Age. The Rise and Dominance of Śaivism during the Early Medieval Period." In *Genesis and Development of Tantrism*, edited by Shingo Einoo, 41–349. Tokyo: Institute of Oriental Culture, University of Tokyo.

Sāṅkṛityāyana, Rāhula. 1937. "Second Search of Sanskrit Palm-leaf MSS. in Tibet." *Journal of the Bihar and Orissa Research Society* 23, part 1: 1–57.

———. 1957. *Dohā-koś [Hindī-chāyānuvād-sahit]*. Paṭnā: Bihār-Rāṣṭrabhāṣā-Pariṣad.

———. 1994 [1998]. *Merī Jīvan Yātrā*. Edited by Kamalā Sāṅkṛtyāyana et al. *Rāhul Vāṅmaya* Part I: vol. 2. Delhi: Rādhākṛṣṇa Prakāśan.

Sastri, A. Mahadeva. 1968. *The Yoga Upaniṣad-s with the Commentary of Śrīupaniṣadbrahmayogin*. Madras: Adyar Library and Research Centre. First published 1920.

Śāstrī, Haraprasād. 1959. "Saroja-Vajrer Bāṅgālā Dohākoṣa, Advaya-Vajrer Saṃskṛta Ṭīkā Saha." In *Hājār Bacharer Purāṇa Bāṅgālā Bhāṣāy Bauddha Gān o Dohā*, 84–118. Kalkota: Vaṅgīya Sāhitya Pariṣat. First published 1916.

Schaeffer, Kurtis R. 2005. *Dreaming the Great Brahmin: Tibetan Traditions of the Buddhist Poet-Saint Saraha*. Oxford: Oxford University Press.

Schmithausen, Lambert. 1969. *Der Nirvāṇa-Abschnitt in der Viniścayasaṃgrahaṇī der Yogācārabhūmiḥ*. Veröffentlichungen der Kommission für Sprachen und Kulturen Süd- und Ostasiens 8, philosophisch-historische Klasse, Sitzungsberichte, 264, vol. 2, Abhandlung. Vienna: Österreichische Akademie der Wissenschaften.

Seyfort Ruegg, David. 1981. *The Literature of the Madhyamaka School of Philosophy in India.* A History of Indian Literature 7, fasc. 1. Wiesbaden: Franz Steiner Verlag.

Seton, Gregory Max. 2019. "Ratnākaraśānti." In *Brill's Encyclopedia of Buddhism. Volume II: Lives*, edited by Jonathan A. Silk et al., 366–70. Boston/Leiden: Brill.

Sferra, Francesco. 2000. *The* Ṣaḍaṅgayoga *by Anupamarakṣita: With Raviśrījñāna's* Guṇabharaṇīnāmaṣaḍaṅgayogaṭippaṇī; *Text and annotated translation*. Serie Orientale Roma 85. Rome: Istituto Italiano per l'Africa e l'Oriente.

———. 2006. *The* Sekoddeśaṭīkā *by Nāropā (*Paramārthasaṃgraha*): Critical Edition of the Sanskrit Text by Francesco Sferra; Critical Edition of the Tibetan Translation by Stefania Merzagora*. Serie Orientale Roma 99. Rome: Istituto Italiano per l'Africa e l'Oriente.

———. 2008. *Sanskrit Texts from the Giuseppe Tucci Collection*. Manuscripta Buddhica 1. Serie Orientale Roma 104. Rome: Istituto Italiano per l'Africa e l'Oriente.

———. 2017. 'A Fragment of the Vajrāmṛtatantra: A Critical Edition of the Leaves Contained in Cambridge University Library Or.158.1.' In *Indic Manuscript Cultures Through the Ages: Material, Textual, and Historical Perspectives*, edited by V. Vergiani, D. Cuneo, and C. A. Formigatti, 409–48. Berlin/Boston: DeGruyter.

———. 2020. "Excerpts from the *Amṛtadhārā* by Śrībhāṇu: An Unpublished Commentary on the *Vajrāmṛtatantra* Kept in the TAR." In *Sanskrit Manuscripts in China III: Proceedings of a Panel at the 2016 Beijing International Seminar on Tibetan Studies, August 1 to 4*, edited by Birgit Kellner, Xuezhu Li, Jowita Kramer, 373–423. Beijing: China Tibetology Publishing House.

Shahidullah, Muhammad. 1928. *Les chants mystiques de Kāṇha et de Saraha: Les Dohākoṣa (en apabhraṃśa, avec les versions tibétaines) et les Caryā (en vieux-bengali)*. Paris: Adrien-Maisonneuve.

Snellgrove, David L. 1954. "Saraha's Treasury of Songs." In *Buddhist Texts Through the Ages, Newly Translated from the Original Pali, Sanskrit, Chinese, Tibetan, Japanese and Apabhramsa in collaboration with I. B. Horner, D. Snellgrove, A. Waley*, edited by Edward Conze, 13–14 (introduction to the text signed by "the editors") and 224–39 (translation). Oxford: Bruno Cassirer.

Steinkellner, Ernst. 1977. *Verse-Index of Dharmakīrti's Works (Tibetan Version)*. Wiener Studien zur Tibetologie und Buddhismuskunde 1. Vienna: Arbeitskreis für tibetische und buddhistische Studien.

Szántó, Péter-Dániel. 2012. "Selected Chapters from the Catuṣpīṭhatantra." 2 vols. Unpublished DPhil dissertation, University of Oxford.

———. 2015a. "Catuṣpīṭha." In *Brill's Encyclopedia of Buddhism. Volume I: Literature and Languages*, edited by Jonathan Silk et al., 320–25. Boston/Leiden: Brill.

———. 2015b. "Tantric Prakaraṇas." In *Brill's Encyclopedia of Buddhism. Volume I: Literature and Languages*, edited by Jonathan Silk et al., 755–61. Boston/Leiden: Brill.

———. 2019. "Siddhas." In *Brill's Encyclopedia of Buddhism. Volume II: Lives*, edited by Jonathan Silk et al., 433–51. Boston/Leiden: Brill.

———. 2019a. "Minor Vajrayāna Texts V: The *Gaṇacakravidhi* Attributed to Ratnākaraśānti." In *Tantric Communities in Context*, edited by Nina Mirnig, Marion Rastelli, and Vincent Eltschinger, 275–314. Vienna: Austrian Academy of Sciences Press.

———. 2020. "On Vāgīśvarakīrti's Influence in Kashmir and Among the Khmer." In *Śaivism and the Tantric Traditions: Essays in Honour of Alexis G.J.S. Sanderson*, edited by Dominic Goodall, Shaman Hatley, Harunaga Isaacson, and Srilata Raman, 170–93. Leiden/Boston: Brill.

———. *Forthcoming a*. "Minor Vajrayāna Texts VI: A Sanskrit Fragment of the *Anāvilatantra*."

———. *Forthcoming b*. "Digests of Dharmakīrti: Two Notes."

Takakusu, J. 1896. *A Record of the Buddhist Religion as Practised in India and the Malay Archipelago (A.D. 671–95) by I-Tsing*. Oxford: Clarendon Press.

Tanaka, Kimiaki. 2010. インドにおける曼荼羅の成立と発展 (Genesis and Development of the Maṇḍala in India). Tokyo: Shunjusha.

Tatz, Mark. 1994. "Philosophic Systems According to Advayavajra and Vajrapāṇi." *Journal of Buddhist and Tibetan Studies* 1: 65–120.

Templeman, David. 1989. *Tāranātha's Life of Kṛṣṇācārya/Kāṇha*. Dharamsala: Library of Tibetan Works and Archives.

Tomabechi, Tōru. 2006. "Étude du Pañcakrama: Introduction et traduction annotée." PhD diss., University of Lausanne.

Tucci, Giuseppe. 1954. "Ratnākaraśānti on Āśraya-parāvṛtti." In *Asiatica: Festschrift Friedrich Weller, Zum 65. Geburtstag gewidmet von seinen Freunden, Kollegen und Schülern*, edited by Johannes Schubert and Ulrich Schneider, 765–67. Leipzig: Otto Harrassowitz, 765–67.

Upādhyāy, Jagannāth. 1983. "Ācāryaratnākaraśāntiviracitā Khasamā-nāmaṭīkā." In *Saṅkāya Patrikā, Śramaṇavidyā (vol. 1)*, edited by Gokul Chandra Jain, 225–55. Varanasi: Sampurnanand Sanskrit Vishvavidyalay.

Verardi, Giovanni. 2011. *Hardships and Downfall of Buddhism in India*. Delhi: Manohar Publishers.

Vienna Buddhist Translation Studies Group under the supervision of Klaus-Dieter Mathes. 2020. *Summary of Empowerment: Sekoddeśa (Toh 361)*. 84000: Translating the Words of the Buddha. https://read.84000.co/translation/toh361.html.

Wayman, Alex. 2006. *Chanting the Names of Mañjuśrī: The Mañjuśrī-Nāma-Saṃgīti; Sanskrit and Tibetan Texts*. Buddhist Tradition Series 38. Delhi: Motilal Banarsidass.

Wedemeyer, Christian. 2007. *Āryadeva's Lamp That Integrates the Practices (Caryāmelāpakapradīpa): The Gradual Path of Vajrayāna Buddhism According to the Esoteric Community Noble Tradition*. American Institute of Buddhist Studies at Columbia University. New York: Columbia University Press.

Index

About the Authors

KLAUS-DIETER MATHES holds the Yuen Hang Professorship at the Centre of Buddhist Studies at the University of Hong Kong. His current research deals with exclusivism, inclusivism, and tolerance in Mahāyāna Buddhism. He obtained his PhD from Marburg University and completed his habilitation at Hamburg University, and he was previously the head of the Department of South Asian, Tibetan and Buddhist Studies at the University of Vienna. His major publications include a study of the Yogācāra text *Dharmadharmatāvibhāga* (published in 1996 in the Indica et Tibetica series), *A Direct Path to the Buddha Within: Gö Lotsāwa's Mahāmudrā Interpretation of the Ratnagotravibhāga* (2008), and *Maitrīpa: India's Yogi of Nondual Bliss* (2021).

PÉTER-DÁNIEL SZÁNTÓ started his higher education at ELTE, in Budapest, with degrees in Tibetan studies (2004) and Indology (2006). He wrote and defended his thesis at Oxford University (2012), where he was a research fellow at Merton College (2010–13) and All Souls College (2014–19). From 2019 to 2022, he worked at Leiden University for the Open Philology project. He is currently associate professor and head of department at ELTE, where his research focuses on the literature of Indian Buddhism with special emphasis on tantric texts. He is coauthor (with James Mallinson) of *The Amṛtasiddhi and the Amṛtasiddhimūla: The Earliest Texts of the Haṭhayoga Tradition* (2021) and has published more than fifty papers.

Studies in Indian and Tibetan Buddhism
Titles Previously Published

Among Tibetan Texts
History and Literature of the Himalayan Plateau
E. Gene Smith

Approaching the Great Perfection
Simultaneous and Gradual Methods of Dzogchen Practice in the Longchen Nyingtig
Sam van Schaik

Authorized Lives
Biography and the Early Formation of Geluk Identity
Elijah S. Ary

The Buddha's Single Intention
Drigung Kyobpa Jikten Sumgön's Vajra Statements of the Early Kagyü Tradition
Jan-Ulrich Sobisch

Buddhism Between Tibet and China
Edited by Matthew T. Kapstein

The Buddhist Philosophy of the Middle
Essays on Indian and Tibetan Madhyamaka
David Seyfort Ruegg

Buddhist Teaching in India
Johannes Bronkhorst

A Direct Path to the Buddha Within
Gö Lotsāwa's Mahāmudrā Interpretation of the Ratnagotravibhāga
Klaus-Dieter Mathes

The Essence of the Ocean of Attainments
The Creation Stage of the Guhyasamāja Tantra according to Panchen Losang Chökyi Gyaltsen
Yael Bentor and Penpa Dorjee

Foundations of Dharmakīrti's Philosophy
John D. Dunne

Freedom from Extremes
Gorampa's "Distinguishing the Views" and the Polemics of Emptiness
José Ignacio Cabezón and Geshe Lobsang Dargyay

Himalayan Passages
Tibetan and Newar Studies in Honor of Hubert Decleer
Benjamin Bogin and Andrew Quintman

Histories of Tibet
Essays in Honor of Leonard W. J. van der Kuijp
Edited by Kurtis Schaeffer, Jue Liang, and William McGrath

How Do Mādhyamikas Think?
And Other Essays on the Buddhist Philosophy of the Middle
Tom J. F. Tillemans

Jewels of the Middle Way
The Madhyamaka Legacy of Atiśa and His Early Tibetan Followers
James B. Apple

Living Treasure
Buddhist and Tibetan Studies in Honor of Janet Gyatso
Edited by Holly Gayley and Andrew Quintman

Luminous Lives
The Story of the Early Masters of the Lam 'bras Tradition in Tibet
Cyrus Stearns

Mind Seeing Mind
Mahāmudrā and the Geluk Tradition of Tibetan Buddhism
Roger R. Jackson

Mipham's Beacon of Certainty
Illuminating the View of Dzogchen, the Great Perfection
John Whitney Pettit

Ocean of Attainments
The Creation Stage of Guhyasamāja Tantra According to Khedrup Jé
Yael Bentor and Penpa Dorjee

Omniscience and the Rhetoric of Reason
Śāntarakṣita and Kamalaśīla on Rationality, Argumentation, and Religious Authority
Sara L. McClintock

Reasons and Lives in Buddhist Traditions
Studies in Honor of Matthew Kapstein
Edited by Dan Arnold, Cécile Ducher, and Pierre-Julien Harter

Reason's Traces
Identity and Interpretation in Indian and Tibetan Buddhist Thought
Matthew T. Kapstein

Remembering the Lotus-Born
Padmasambhava in the History of Tibet's Golden Age
Daniel A. Hirshberg

Resurrecting Candrakīrti
Disputes in the Tibetan Creation of Prāsaṅgika
Kevin A. Vose

Scripture, Logic, Language
Essays on Dharmakīrti and His Tibetan Successors
Tom J. F. Tillemans

Sexuality in Classical South Asian Buddhism
José I. Cabezón

The Svātantrika-Prāsaṅgika Distinction
What Difference Does a Difference Make?
Edited by Georges B. J. Dreyfus and Sara L. McClintock

Vajrayoginī
Her Visualizations, Rituals, and Forms
Elizabeth English

About Wisdom Publications

Wisdom Publications is the leading publisher of classic and contemporary Buddhist books and practical works on mindfulness. To learn more about us or to explore our other books, please visit our website at wisdomexperience.org or contact us at the address below.

Wisdom Publications
132 Perry Street
New York, NY 10014 USA

We are a 501(c)(3) organization, and donations in support of our mission are tax deductible.

Wisdom Publications is affiliated with the Foundation for the Preservation of the Mahayana Tradition (FPMT).